The ISS Directory of Overseas Schools

1993–94 Edition

Published by

**International Schools Services
Princeton, New Jersey, U.S.A.**

Fees and other data are accurate as reported to ISS by the individual schools as of July 15, 1993. Readers are advised to obtain updated information from the individual schools. Maps are representational and intended for general orientation only.

Published in 1981

Thirteenth edition in August 1993

ISBN 0-913663-10-7 paperback

Distributed by Peterson's, PO Box 2123, Princeton, New Jersey 08543-2123; telephone (800)338-3282, (609)243-9111.
Cost: $34.95 plus postage and handling charge of $6.75 domestic and $11.00 international.

Cover: Tina Kinney of T. C. inK Graphic Design, Princeton, NJ

International Schools Services, Inc.
PO Box 5910, Princeton, New Jersey 08543, U.S.A.
Telephone: (609) 452-0990
Facsimile: (609) 452-2690
Telex: 843 308 SCHOLSERV PRIN
Cable: SCHOOLSERV PRINCETON

CONTENTS

PREFACE ———————————————————

As struggles for territorial dominance alter the borders in country after country and send topographers into a constant state of uncertainty, the production of other works of a global nature are also affected—in this case, the *ISS Directory*.

In the 1993–94 edition, the International School in Zagreb is listed under the newly recognized country Croatia. The International School of Belgrade, which is in Serbia, remains under the auspices of the still-recognized but scaled-down country Yugoslavia. We are happy to report that both schools, as of the deadline for this book, intend to fulfill their roles as educational institutions for the upcoming school year.

We are also fortunate to have additional countries represented in this edition. Schools from Benin, Macau, Iraq, and Namibia have full-length entries. We hope to continue this trend by having additional countries represented each year.

Keeping up with the geographical changes is barely half the battle; tracking down the information for each school is actually more challenging. In our efforts to provide the most in-depth and accurate information, we've expanded the entries to include heads of computer services, heads of libraries, and school membership in regional organizations. As you turn the pages of the Directory, you may note that many schools took advantage of the opportunity to include this pertinent information.

The *ISS Directory* has been an indispensable resource for anyone interested in the international education community. It includes schools of all sizes—from the smallest, the Shenyang American Academy, with an enrollment of five, to the largest, the International School of Geneva, with 2,678 students.

We'd like to thank the administrators who take time out of their hectic schedules each year to update their listings. Thanks also to the ISS staff members for their support and encouragement. My appreciation to the publications staff is immeasurable; being a new editor, they allowed me time to learn and had patience when I changed my mind. And finally, my gratitude to my husband and family is immense; their faith in me is, and always has been, unfaltering.

Gina M. Parziale, editor
July 15, 1993

INTRODUCTION _____

For 38 years, International Schools Services has been an integral part of the international education community, providing a broad range of services to schools throughout the world. Founded in 1955 as a not-for-profit educational organization, it provides stateside support services to the growing number of American and international schools overseas. Over the years, hundreds of overseas schools, as well as many American corporations with overseas operations, have sought the services of ISS. In turn, ISS has expanded and changed according to the needs of the schools and the international communities overseas.

Among the ISS services sought by U.S. corporations are the establishment and operation of schools for their expatriate American/international communities and the consultation ISS provides regarding the educational needs of the dependents of overseas employees.

American and international schools throughout the world solicit the services of ISS to:

❏ recruit the best possible administrative and teaching staff
❏ procure quality school supplies at the best rates possible
❏ plan and implement school facilities
❏ plan and implement personnel, accounting, and benefit programs
❏ keep abreast of the most recent developments in U.S. education
❏ research and implement new programs
❏ consult on day-to-day operations, curriculum, and long-range planning
❏ operate U.S. foundations established by overseas schools

A range of services

Many people know ISS through one or another of its services, but few know the full extent of its activities. What follows is a description of the eight different departments that operate under the International Schools Services banner.

School Management and Consulting

When American corporations set up operations abroad, an employee community often follows. If an American or international school is nearby, most of the expatriate children enroll there. When the company is located in a remote area, however, it must establish its own educational facility. At this point, the company often calls upon ISS to establish and operate a company school in accordance with the highest professional standards of the best U.S. institutions. In such situations, ISS handles staffing, personnel management, curriculum, community relations, supplies, and all other aspects of the operation.

At present, ISS operates such schools for companies in Asia, Africa, Europe, the Caribbean, and the Middle East.

Administrator Search Services

The Administrator Search Services department works with governing boards in their searches for chief school officers and with heads of schools in their searches for principals. These services exist to expedite the recruiting process of administrators and to ensure that outstanding candidates are considered. Drawing on its experience of more than 35 years working with overseas administrators and schools, ISS is able to work closely with the schools, administrators, and candidates to provide the best possible match.

Educational Staffing

Since 1955, ISS has placed over 10,000 qualified teachers and administrators in overseas positions. The success of ISS in this field is due to its international network of contacts, its large pool of qualified candidates, and its personalized screening approach. In addition to continuous year-round recruitment, ISS hosts three International Recruitment Centers (IRCs) in the United States each year. Heavily attended by overseas school administrators as well as by candidates, the IRCs provide an opportunity for recruiting administrators of schools to interview and hire experienced, well-qualified teaching and administrative candidates.

School Supply

The School Supply Program provides a total procurement system for overseas schools. Offering 20 years' experience and utilizing a state-of-the-art computer program specifically designed by ISS, our purchasing program delivers efficient, cost-effective, and reliable service. The service has grown rapidly in the last few years and presently purchases for over 120 schools throughout the world. Any commodity that a school might need, be it a pencil or a computer system, a textbook or a complete library, can be procured and shipped according to a school's specific needs.

Facility Planning and Equipment Supply

ISS has brought together a team of consultants to provide overseas schools with a comprehensive and economical facility-planning service. This team can help with any of the steps of planning or implementation within a project or can deliver a completely planned, built, and supplied facility. Major services available include the development of a master plan, detailed educational specifications, architectural and interior designs, and procurement and installation of equipment.

Human Resources

Human Resources offers programs of critical importance including personnel services and the establishment and management of school support foundations. It assists with the design of comprehensive benefit packages for overseas schools. These services function both as recruiting tools and as incentives for valued employees to remain in place and can be linked to a school's stateside foundation and to fund-raising activites.

Business Affairs and Accounting
The ISS accounting department, using a computerized system specifically designed to meet the needs of overseas schools, offers business and accounting consulting services to overseas schools. This unique service includes customized payroll processing, processing payroll benefits and reports, bookkeeping, cash management, ledger maintenance, and preparation of quarterly financial statements.

Publications
In addition to the *ISS Directory of Overseas Schools*, an annual publication that describes in detail overseas schools appropriate for American and international students in expatriate communities, ISS publishes a newspaper, *NewsLinks*, which is distributed five times a year, free of charge, to schools, administrators, and companies interested in overseas education.

USER'S GUIDE ⸻

The *Directory* is arranged alphabetically, first by country, then city or town, and finally by school name. Isolated schools in rural areas are listed under the town nearest them. Schools in the suburbs of large cities are usually listed under the name of the city rather than that of the suburb. At the end of each country, there may be short entries for certain schools. These schools did not supply enough information to warrant a full-length entry. These "one-liners," as they are termed, are in alphabetical order by city after the full-length entries in each country.

School addresses: Street addresses often differ from mailing addresses. When they are specifically given, use the mailing address for correspondence. This will save you time and money, particularly when mail originates within the United States and the mailing address is also within the United States, as in the case of the U.S. Department of State, APO, and FPO addresses.

APO and FPO are U.S. military mail services with strict regulations. No personal name may appear in an APO or FPO address. Instead, use the title of the chief school officer, followed by the address. U.S. Department of State addresses may include personal names.

Telephone numbers: Schools that can be dialed directly from the United States are listed with the country and city codes in parentheses (or only the country code if that is all that is needed), followed by the telephone number. If you are using the AT&T long-distance phone system, dial the international access code 011 before dialing any overseas number, except for Caribbean/Atlantic islands with an 809 area code. For these, dial 1, followed by the area code and phone number as you would for any call within the United States. "No direct dial" means you need operator assistance to reach the number. To call from countries other than the United States, follow local procedures. To call the United States from abroad, use the local international access code followed by 1 (the U.S. country code), then the area code, and finally the phone number.

Multiple numbers are listed for schools that report them. Dissimilar numbers are indicated by a slash (444789/444802) and consecutive numbers by a dash (444789–91). For information on rates, codes, and time differences, call AT&T International Information Service, toll-free: 1-800-874-4000.

Facsimile, telex, and cable: Facsimile numbers are listed with the country and then city code, followed by the school's number. Telex numbers are listed with the appropriate 3-digit area code, then the school's number, followed by the answerback. Cables can be sent to a school's name and address if no cable code is listed. For assistance with telexes and cables, call Western Union toll-free at 1-800-325-6000.

Chief school officer: The name and title of the head of the school is listed first, followed by the names of academic division heads and other administrative staff as reported to us.

Head of computer services, head of library: Heads of these departments are listed here. These two categories are new to the 1993–94 edition.

Teaching staff: The number of both full- and part-time staff members are listed.

Staff and student nationalities: Both staff and students are defined by four nationality groups: United States, United Kingdom, host country, and other nationalities.

Grade levels: Grades are listed in terms used by the schools themselves, usually as "grades," sometimes as English "forms," and occasionally as "ages." Forms 1 through 6 normally correspond to grades 7 through 12. The following abbreviations are used: N for nursery (usually 3- to 4-year-olds); preK for prekindergarten; K for kindergarten (usually 5- to 6-year-olds); and preP for preprimary.

Enrollment and capacity: In most cases, grade-level enrollments are given, followed by a total enrollment figure. Capacity figures are arranged in the same way.

Teacher/student ratio: To find this ratio, the total student enrollment is divided by the number of full-time staff plus half the number of part-time staff, with decimals of .5 or more rounded up to 1. For example, for a school with 187 students, 12 full-time, and 3 part-time teachers, the equation is 187 divided by 14 equals 13.36, giving a teacher/student ration of 1/13.

Boarding facilities: Schools which offer boarding services are identified within their entries and in an appendix at the end of the *Directory*.

Tuition: Most tuition figures are given in U.S. dollars, indicated by a dollar sign. When a school reports its tuition in the currency of the host country, the first figure is marked with a double asterisk and the unit of currency noted at the bottom of the entry. Succeeding tuition figures are also reported in the host currency.

Other fees: School charges other than tuition are listed. As above, host-country currency is noted with a double asterisk.

School year: Most schools in the Northern Hemisphere are in session from September to June, in the Southern Hemisphere from March to December.

Year founded: The oldest school listed is Hvitfeldtska Gymnasiet in Goteborg, Sweden, founded in 1647; and the youngest school is the International

Community School, Thailand, starting in the fall of 1993.

Type of school: Individual schools have identified themselves as falling within the following categories: coeducational, boys only, girls only, boarding, day, company-sponsored, church-related, proprietary, private nonprofit.

School government: Most overseas schools are governed by a board of directors or the host country's equivalent, a company, religious organization, or individual proprietor. Sponsors or operators are listed when reported.

Accredited by: Accreditation is not mandatory, but many overseas schools elect to go through the voluntary process of evaluation and accreditation by private accrediting associations and may report this in the *ISS Directory* as either a completed activity or one still in process. Other schools may list the host-national ministry of education or another official body as the accrediting agency. U.S. private accrediting associations are listed in an appendix.

Regional organization(s): Many schools are members of regional organizations. Schools that reported membership will have the names of these organizations listed here. Information about the regional organizations is listed in an appendix of this book. This category is new to the 1993–94 edition.

Curriculum: Each school in the *ISS Directory* has an English-language curriculum, either alone or in combination with a host-national curriculum. Some offer the International Baccalaureate program (IB), a two-year course of study recognized by many colleges and universities throughout the world. Further explanation and a list of the schools offering the IB program are found in an appendix of this volume.

Languages of instruction: This is included only if the language of instruction is English in combination with one or more other languages. No listing within this category means that instruction is in English only.

Languages offered: This lists the languages offered within the curriculum.

Staff specialists, special programs, special curricular, and extracurricular activities: This category lists specialists and offerings outside the main academic curriculum.

Tests: A key to the tests given by American and British international schools is included in an appendix at the back of the *ISS Directory*.

Percentage of graduates attending college and the colleges they attend: Secondary schools were asked to list five colleges or universities recently attended by their graduates.

Location, campus, library, and facilities: These brief descriptions are intended to convey the physical resources of a school.

Statistical information on each country is taken from *The World Almanac and Book of Facts, 1993* (New York: Pharos Books, 1992).

ADVERTISERS ─────────────

Addison–Wesley Publishing Company, *197*
Baker & Taylor International Ltd., *35*
California State University, Northridge, *86*
The Educational Register, Vincent/Curtis, *87*
European Council of International Schools (ECIS), *130*
Flaghouse, Inc., *14*
J. L. Hammett Company, International Division, *161*
Harcourt Brace & Company International, *inside back cover*
International Schools Services (ISS), *48, 69, 103, 150, 151, 162, 176, 197, 461*
Living Abroad Publishing, Inc., *104*
Macmillan/McGraw–Hill International, *inside front cover*
MECC, *112*
National Audio–Visual Supply Company, *212*
Paramount Publishing, International School Division, *back cover*
Rand McNally, Educational Publishing Division, *15*
School Specialty Supply, Inc., *14*
ScottForesman, *69*
Social Studies School Service, *150*
Steck–Vaughn International, *62*
Winnebago Software Company, *63*

LIST OF SCHOOLS _____

Algeria
American School of Algiers, 1

Argentina
Asociacion Escuelas Lincoln (American Community School), 2
St. George's College, 3
St. John's School, 4
Colegio San Marcos, 4
St. Andrew's Scots School, 4
St. Catherine's School, 5
International School, 5

Aruba
International School of Aruba, 5

Austria
Innsbruck International High School, 6
Salzburg International Preparatory School, 7
American International School, 8
Vienna International School, 9

Bahrain
Bahrain Bayan School, 10
Bahrain School, 11
Ibn Khuldoon National School, 12

Bangladesh
American International School/Dhaka, 13

Belgium
Antwerp International School, 16
EEC International School, 17
The British School of Brussels, 18
Brussels' English Primary School S.P.R.L., 19
EEC International School, Brussels, 20
The International School of Brussels, 20
B.E.P.S. 2 – Limal International School, 21
St. John's International School, 22
Scandinavian School of Brussels–Ecole Reine Astrid, 23

Benin
Brilliant Stars International School, 23

Bermuda
The Bermuda High School for Girls, 24

The
Overseas
Schools

ALGERIA _____

Region: Africa
Size: 918,497 square miles
Population: 26,022,000
Capital: Algiers

Telephone code: 213
Currency: dinar
Languages: Arabic, Berber

ALGIERS

AMERICAN SCHOOL OF ALGIERS

Street address: 5 Chemin Cheikh Bachir Brahimi (ex-Beaurepaire), El Biar, Algiers, Algeria
Phone: (213)(2)603772   **Facsimile:** (213)(2)603979
   Telex: 93666047 AMCO DZ   **Cable:** AMEREMB ALGIERS
Mail: BP 549, 16000 Alger Gare, Algiers, Algeria
U.S. mail: c/o Algiers – Department of State, Washington, D.C. 20521-6030
Director: Elizabeth Amirouche
Staff: full-time, 13; part-time, 4
Nationalities of staff: U.S., 7; host, 3; other, 7
Grade levels: preK – 8
Enrollment: preK, 10; K, 11; 1 – 6, 60; 7 – 8, 19; total, 100
Nationalities of student body: U.S., 29; host, 2; other, 69
Capacity: preK, 20; K, 15; 1 – 6, 120; 7 – 8, 60; total, 215
Teacher/student ratio: 1/7
Tuition (annual): preK, $2,500; K – 8, $6,500
Other fees: registration*, $800
School year: September to June

Year founded: 1964. **Type of school:** coed, day, private nonprofit. **Governed by:** appointed and elected board of trustees. **Sponsored by:** U.S. Embassy. **Accredited by:** New England.

Curriculum/physical plant

Type: U.S. **Languages taught:** French. **Special programs:** ESL. **Special curricular:** computers, yearbook, newspaper, literary magazine, excursions/ expeditions.   **Tests:** Stanford. **Location:** in El Biar, 1 mile from downtown Algiers. **Campus:** 3 acres. **Library:** 8,000 volumes. **Facilities:** 8 buildings, 14 classrooms, 2 playing fields, science lab, computer lab.

*Once only fee

ARGENTINA _____

Region: South America
Size: 1,065,189 square miles
Population: 32,663,000
Capital: Buenos Aires

Telephone code: 54
Currency: peso
Languages: Spanish, Italian

BUENOS AIRES

Asociacion Escuelas Lincoln (American Community School)

Street address: Andres Ferreyra 4073, 1636 La Lucila, Buenos Aires, Argentina
Phone: (54)(1)7995100/7995151   **Facsimile:** (54)(1)7902117
Superintendent: Robert Ater
Assistant superintendent/secondary principal: Randall Howes
Elementary principal: Dalbert Warkentin
Directora, Spanish section: Elfrida Kelly
Business manager: Demetrio Anagnostopulos
Staff: full-time, 78
Nationalities of staff: U.S., 30; host, 45; other, 3
Grade levels: Early Childhood Education – 12
Enrollment: ECE, 36; K, 42; 1 – 6, 255; 7 – 8, 95; 9 – 12, 191; total, 619
Nationalities of student body: U.S., 247; U.K., 12; host, 123; other, 237
Capacity: ECE, 30; K, 60; 1 – 6, 375; 7 – 9, 200; 10 – 12, 250; total, 915
Teacher/student ratio: 1/8
Tuition (annual): ECE, $2,200; K, $6,050; 1 – 8, $10,900; 9 – 12, $11,750
Other fees (annual): registration*, $2,350; busing, $1300; lunch, $600; capital fund*, $2,000
School year: August to June

Year founded: 1936. **Type of school:** coed, day, proprietary, private nonprofit. **Governed by:** appointed board of governors. **Accredited by:** Southern, Argentine Provincial Ministry of Education.

Curriculum

Type: U.S., Argentine. **Languages of instruction:** English, Spanish. **Languages taught:** French, Spanish, German. **Staff specialists:** reading, computer, counselor, nurse. **Special programs:** ESL, advanced placement, honors sections. **Special curricular:** art, chorus, band, physical education, computer instruction. **Extracurricular:** drama, gymnastics, yearbook, newspaper, literary magazine, photography, excursions/expeditions, field trips. **Sports:** basketball, soccer, softball, swimming, tennis, volleyball, track and field. **Clubs:** drama, National Junior Honor Society, student council, chorus, band, Lettermen's Club (boys), girls' athletic association, student lounge, computer. **Tests:** SSAT, PSAT, SAT, ACT, AP, Iowa. **Graduates attending college:** 95%. **Graduates have attended:** Lafayette, Boston U., U. of Michigan, Yale, Dartmouth.

Physical plant
Location: in northern suburbs, 6 miles from downtown Buenos Aires. **Campus:** 6 acres. **Library:** 29,000 volumes. **Facilities:** 4 buildings, auditorium, cafeteria, infirmary, covered play area, 2 tennis courts, gymnasium, playing field, 2 science labs, computer lab, swimming pool, 39 classrooms, most of which are air-conditioned.

*Once only fee

ST. GEORGE'S COLLEGE
Street address: Guido 800, 1878 Quilmes, Buenos Aires, Argentina
Phone/facsimile: (54)(1)2530914/2538422/2573472–4
    Telex: 39023645 CAMAB AR
Mail: Casilla de Correo No. 2, 1878 Quilmes, Buenos Aires, Argentina
Director: Mr. N. P. O. Green
Staff: full-time, 39; part-time, 25
Nationalities of staff: U.S., 1; U.K., 9; host, 54
Grade levels: K; prep school (ages 6 – 12); secondary (ages 13 – 18)
Enrollment: K, 50; prep, 171; secondary, 233; total, 454
Teacher/student ratio: 1/9
Boarders: boys, 123; girls, 43   **Program:** planned 5- and 7-day
Tuition (6 months): prep, $4,332 – $6,168; secondary, $6,708 – $6,864
Tuition and board (6 months): $6,600 (for overseas students only)
School year: March to December

Year founded: 1898. **Type of school:** coed, day, boarding, private nonprofit. **Governed by:** elected board of governors. **Accredited by:** Headmaster's Conference (H.M.C.), IB.

Curriculum
Type U.K., Argentine, IB. **Languages of instruction:** English, Spanish. **Languages taught:** French. **Staff specialists:** math, counselor, learning disabilities, nurse. **Special programs:** ESL. **Special curricular:** art, physical education, computer instruction, vocational, music. **Extracurricular:** drama, gymnastics, dance, computers, yearbook, literary magazine, excursions/expeditions, field trips, sports. **Tests:** PSAT, SAT, ACT, TOEFL, IB, IGCSE. **Graduates attending college:** 95%. **Graduates have attended:** Dartmouth, Princeton, Middlebury, Bryn Mawr, Columbia.

Physical plant
Location: in suburban area, 20 kilometers south of Buenos Aires center. **Campus:** 54 acres. **Library:** 9,000 volumes. **Facilities:** 15 buildings, 23 classrooms, cafeteria, infirmary, 11 playing fields, 4 science labs, 2 swimming pools, all-weather surface for basketball, tennis, hockey, soccer, volleyball.

St. John's School

Street address: Pueyrredon 1499, 1640 Martinez, Buenos Aires, Argentina
Phone: (54)(1)7923944/7764   **Facsimile:** (54)(1)7908575
Headmaster: John Harrison
Business manager: Hector Brown
Staff: full-time, 50; part-time, 75
Nationalities of staff U.K., 6; host, 119
Grade levels: N – 12
Enrollment: N – preK, 80; K, 40; 1 – 6, 360; 7 – 9, 180; 10 – 12, 130; total, 790
Nationalities of student body: U.K., 8; host, 750; other, 32
Capacity: N – preK, 80; K, 40; 1 – 6, 360; 7 – 9, 180; 10 – 12, 180; total, 840
Teacher/student ratio: 1/9
Tuition (annual): N – preK, $2,200; K – 6, $4,800; 7 – 12, $6,000
School year: February to December

Year founded: 1950. **Type of school:** boys, girls, private nonprofit.
Governed by: appointed and elected board.

Curriculum/physical plant

Type: U.K., IB. **Languages of instruction:** English, Spanish. **Staff specialists:** reading, math, computer, speech/hearing, counselor, psychologist, nurse. **Special programs:** independent study. **Special curricular:** art, physical education, computer instruction, vocational. **Extracurricular:** gymnastics, dance, choral music, yearbook, newspaper, photography, excursions/expeditions, field trips. **Sports:** rugby, hockey, soccer, athletics. **Tests:** IB, A-level GCE, GCSE. **Graduates attending college:** 95%. **Graduates have attended:** Harvard, U. of San Andres, U. of Buenos Aires, Technological U. of Buenos Aires, Catholic U. of Buenos Aires. **Location:** in suburban area of Buenos Aires. **Campuses (3):** 25 acres. **Facilities:** library, cafeteria, infirmary, tennis court, playing field, science lab, computer lab.

BUENOS AIRES

Colegio San Marcos

Address: Jorges Miles 153, 1842 Monte Grande,
Buenos Aires, Argentina
Phone: (54)(1)2964215/2901261   **Facsimile:** (54)(1)2965135
General headmistress: Susana R. Raffo

St. Andrew's Scots School

Address: Nogoya 550, Olivos, Buenos Aires, Argentina
Phone: (54)(1)7908032 – 3   **Facsimile:** (54)(1)7998318
Headmaster: Kevan Prior

St. Catherine's School
Address: Carbajal 3250, 1426 Buenos Aires, Argentina
Phone: (54)(1)5522973   **Facsimile:** (54)(1)5544113
Principal: Mabel Mazzini

LA PAZ
International School
Address: CC107, 5870 Villa Dolores, La Paz, Cordoba, Argentina

ARUBA ————————————————————

Region: Dutch Caribbean
Size: 75 square miles
Population: 64,418
Capital: Oranjestad

Telephone code: 297
Currency: florin
Languages: Papiamento, Dutch, English, Spanish

SAN NICOLAS

INTERNATIONAL SCHOOL OF ARUBA
Phone: (297)(8)45365   **Facsimile:** (297)(8)47341
Mail: Seroe Colorado, Aruba, Dutch Caribbean
Headmaster: James Swetz
Guidance counselor: Johnny Johnson
Staff: total, 18
Grade levels: preK – 12
Enrollment: preK – K, 17; 1 – 4, 48; 5 – 8, 49; 9 – 12, 27; total, 141
Capacity: total, 250
Teacher/student ratio: 1/8
Tuition (annual): preK (full day), $4,543; K, $5,685; 1– 5, $6,829; 6 – 8, $7,900; 9 – 12, $8,543
Other fees (annual): registration, $571; new student enrollment*, $571
School year: August to June

Year founded: 1985. **Type of school:** coed, day, private nonprofit. **Governed by:** self-perpetuating board of trustees. **Accredited by:** New England, ECIS.

Curriculum/physical plant
Type: U.S., International. **Languages taught:** Dutch (5 – 12), Spanish (K – 12). **Staff specialists:** reading, computer, guidance counselor. **Special programs:** Discover program, IBM Writing-to-Read. **Special curricular:** art, physical education, computer instruction, journalism. **Extracurricular:** drama,

computers, yearbook, newspaper, excursions/expeditions, field trips. **Sports:** basketball, soccer, softball, tennis, track, volleyball. **Tests:** PSAT, Iowa, TAP. **Location:** in suburban area, 5 minutes from the nearest town. **Campus:** 20 acres. **Library:** 12,995 volumes. **Facilities:** 3 buildings, 19 classrooms, 2 playing fields, 3 science labs, computer lab, multi-purpose room, AV equipment, air conditioning.

*Once only fee

AUSTRIA _____

Region: Europe
Size: 32,374 square miles
Population: 7,665,000
Capital: Vienna

Telephone code: 43
Currency: schilling
Language: German

INNSBRUCK

INNSBRUCK INTERNATIONAL HIGH SCHOOL

Phone: (43)(5225)4201　　**Facsimile:** (43)(5225)4202
Mail: A-6141 Schoenberg No. 26, Austria
Headmaster: Gunther Wenko
Academic director: Edward Scruggs
Staff: full-time, 6; part-time, 2
Nationalities of staff: U.S., 5; host, 2; other, 1
Grade levels: 8 – 12, postgraduate
Enrollment: 8 – 9, 9; 10 – 12, 31; total, 40
Nationalities of student body: U.S., 25; host, 6; other, 9
Teacher/student ratio: 1/6
Boarders: boys, 24; girls, 13　　**Grades:** 8 – 12, postgraduate
　　Program: planned 7-day
Tuition, room and board (annual): 208,000**
Other fees (annual): registration*, $25; insurance, $25; books, $75;
　　building fee*, $600
School year: September to May

Year founded: 1986. **Type of school:** coed, day, boarding, private nonprofit. **Governed by:** elected board of directors. **Accredited by:** Austrian Board of Education, Tyrolean Board of Education.

Curriculum
　　Type: U.S., Austrian. **Languages taught:** French, German, Italian. **Special programs:** ESL, advanced placement, Austrian Matura. **Special curricular:** ski-racing, competitive tennis, competitive snow-boarding, technical programs. **Extracurricular:** instrumental music, photography, excursions/expeditions, field trips, physical education, journalism, student council. **Sports:** basketball, skiing, soccer, swimming, tennis, volleyball, ski-racing, self-defense, sailing, wind surfing, weight lifting, snow-boarding,

dance. **Tests:** PSAT, SAT, TOEFL, AP, Achievements. **Graduates attending college:** 95%. **Graduates have attended:** Georgetown, Sweet Briar, Southern Texas, Northern Colorado, Lewis and Clark.

Physical plant

Location: 10 kilometers south of Innsbruck. **Campus:** 2,500 square meters. **Library:** 3,000 volumes. **Facilities:** 2 buildings, 10 classrooms, auditorium, 2 infirmaries, tennis court, gymnasium, 2 playing fields, science lab, computer lab, dining hall, music room, shop room, photography lab, language lab; 2 dormitory buildings, double and single occupancy.

*Once only fee   **Austrian schilling

SALZBURG

SALZBURG INTERNATIONAL PREPARATORY SCHOOL

Street address: Moosstrasse 106, A-5020 Salzburg, Austria
Phone: (43)(662)824617 – 8   **Facsimile:** (43)(662)824555
Headmaster: David A. Hintzsche
Staff: full-time, 14; part-time, 16
Nationalities of staff: U.S., 22; host, 6; Australia, 2
Grade levels: 7 – 12, postgraduate
Enrollment: total, 140
Nationalities of student body: U.S., 70; other, 70
Capacity: total, 170
Teacher/student ratio: 1/6
Boarders: boys, 65; girls, 65   **Grades:** 7 – 12, postgraduate
     Program: planned 7-day
Tuition and fees (annual): 200,000**
Other fees: registration, 450**
School year: September to May

Year founded: 1976. **Type of school:** coed, day, boarding, private nonprofit. **Governed by:** board of directors. **Sponsored by:** Salzburg International School Association. **Accredited by:** Middle States, Austrian Ministry of Education.

Curriculum

Type: IB, American college preparatory. **Languages taught:** French, German. **Special programs:** ESL, advanced placement, honors sections, independent study, international curriculum. **Special curricular:** art, chorus, physical education, computer instruction. **Extracurricular:** drama, dance, choral music, instrumental music, computers, yearbook, newspaper, photography, excursions/expeditions, field trips. **Sports:** aerobics, basketball, bowling, cheerleading, dance, ice hockey, skiing, soccer, swimming, tennis, volleyball, squash, horseback riding, body-building. **Clubs:** Model UN, student council, debate, chess, language. **Tests:** PSAT, SAT, ACT, TOEFL, AP, IB. **Graduates attending college:** 95%. **Graduates have attended:** Princeton, Dartmouth, Stanford, UCLA, Harvard.

Physical plant
Location: in residential suburb of Salzburg. **Campus:** 6 acres. **Library:** 10,000 volumes. **Facilities:** 9 buildings, 16 classrooms, auditorium, cafeteria, science lab, computer lab, lounge, language lab, photo lab, music room, art room, separate fully supervised dormitory facilities for boys and girls, physical-education facilities (off campus).

**Austrian schilling

VIENNA

AMERICAN INTERNATIONAL SCHOOL
Street address: Salmanndorferstrasse 47, A-1190 Vienna, Austria
Phone: (43)(1)442763   **Facsimile:** (43)(1)443769
Director: Anthony Fruhauf
Upper school principal: Peter Dawson
Middle school principal: Joan F. Cammett
Lower school principal: Herman Glass
Business manager: Dietrich Probst
Staff: full-time, 77; part-time, 19
Nationalities of staff: U.S., 63; U.K., 6; host, 13; other, 14
Grade levels: N – 12
Enrollment: N – preK, 16; K, 36; 1 – 6, 300; 7 – 9, 212; 10 – 12, 215; 13, 6; total, 785
Nationalities of student body: U.S., 251; U.K., 19; host, 129; other, 386
Capacity: N – preK, 16; K, 40; 1 – 6, 345; 7 – 9, 210; 10 – 12, 225; 13, 5; total, 841
Teacher/student ratio: 1/9
Tuition (annual): N – preK, 56,150**; K, 93,500; 1 – 5, 104,150; 6 – 11, 116,100; 12, 117,850
Other fees (annual): registration*, 2,000**; busing, 5,700 – 6,300; lunch, 5,400; matriculation*, 4,000
School year: August to June

Year founded: 1959. **Type of school:** coed, day, private nonprofit, college preparatory. **Governed by:** elected executive board. **Accredited by:** Middle States.

Curriculum
Type: U.S., IB, Austrian Matura. **Languages taught:** French, German. **Staff specialists:** reading, math, computer, counselor, learning disabilities, nurse. **Special programs:** ESL, advanced placement. **Special curricular:** art,

physical education, computer instruction, choral and instrumental music. **Extracurricular:** drama, gymnastics, dance, computers, yearbook, newspaper, literary magazine, photography, excursions/expeditions, field trips. **Sports:** aerobics, baseball, basketball, soccer, softball, swimming, tennis, volleyball, dodgeball, kickball, track and field. **Clubs:** speech and debate, National Honor Society. **Tests:** PSAT, SAT, TOEFL, IB, AP, Iowa. **Graduates attending college:** 85%. **Graduates have attended:** U. of Vienna, Stanford, Georgetown, Harvard, Brown.

Physical plant
Location: on edge of Vienna Woods. **Campus:** 15 acres. **Library:** 20,000 volumes. **Facilities:** building complex, 63 classrooms, auditorium, cafeteria, 2 tennis courts, 2 gymnasiums, playing field, 5 science labs, 3 computer labs.

*Once only fee   **Austrian schilling

VIENNA INTERNATIONAL SCHOOL
Street address: Strasse der Menschenrechte 1, A-1220 Vienna, Austria
Phone: (43)(1)235595   **Facsimile:** (43)(1)230366
Acting director: Dr. W. K. Kirk
Head, secondary school: John Young
Head, primary school: Kevin Bartlett
Staff: full-time, 130; part-time, 13
Nationalities of staff: U.S., 19; U.K., 66; host, 22; other, 36
Grade levels: K – 13
Enrollment: K, 93; 1 – 6, 597; 7 – 9, 295; 10 – 12, 305; 13, 101; total, 1,391
Nationalities of student body: U.S., 87; U.K., 150; host, 314; other, 840
Capacity: K, 96; 1 – 6, 600; 7 – 9, 300; 10 – 12, 304; 13, 104; total, 1,404
Teacher/student ratio: 1/10
Tuition (annual, 1992–93 rates): preK (half day), $2,910; K, $5,030; 1 – 6, $6,580; 7 – 9, $8,025; 10 – 13, $8,800
Other fees (annual, 1992–93 rates): registration*, $530; busing, $802; lunch, $760; refundable security deposit, $352
School year: August to June

Year founded: 1978 (English School 1955). **Type of school:** coed, day, private nonprofit. **Governed by:** elected board of governors. **Accredited by:** Austrian Ministry of Education, ECIS.

Curriculum
Type: IB, International Schools Association curriculum for middle school, International Primary Program, 3 – 11 years. **Languages taught:** French, German, Latin, Arabic (mother tongue). **Staff specialists:** math, computer, speech/hearing, counselor, psychologist, learning disabilities, nurse. **Special

programs: ESL, special educational needs. **Special curricular:** art, chorus, band, physical education, computer instruction. **Extracurricular:** drama, gymnastics, dance, choral music, instrumental music, computers, yearbook, newspaper, photography, excursions/expeditions, field trips, tap-dancing. **Sports:** basketball, field hockey, swimming, tennis, volleyball, association football, athletics (field and track), gymnastics, skiing, skating, cricket, softball, rugby, table tennis. **Clubs:** scouts, chess, Scrabble, knitting, martial arts, fencing, collecting. **Tests:** PSAT, SAT, TOEFL, IB, O-level GCE, GCSE (Latin). **Graduates attending college:** 90%. **Graduates have attended:** Cambridge U., London U., Princeton, Harvard, Oxford U.

Physical plant

Location: in suburban setting, 15 minutes by underground from city center. **Campus:** 10.5 acres. **Facilities:** 1 building, 77 classrooms, auditorium, cafeteria, 2 tennis courts, 5 gymnasiums, 2 playing fields, 7 science labs, 2 computer labs, library, areas for art and music, outdoor amphitheatre, ecology area.

*Once only fee

BAHRAIN _____

Region: Middle East
Size: 268 square miles
Population: 536,000
Capital: Manama

Telephone code: 973
Currency: dinar
Languages: Arabic, Farsi, Urdu

ISA TOWN

BAHRAIN BAYAN SCHOOL

Phone: (973)682227   **Facsimile:** (973)780019
Mail: PO Box 32411, Isa Town, Bahrain
Director: Dr. Ameen Rihani
Secondary principal: Mr. Omer Troyer
Elementary principal: Mrs. Anna Kizirian
Business manager: Mrs. Samar Nabhan
Registrar: Mrs. Maha Tadros
Staff: full-time, 78; part-time, 6
Nationalities of staff: U.S., 19; U.K., 11; host, 26; other, 28
Grade levels: N – 11
Enrollment: N – preK, 98; K, 72; 1 – 5, 306; 6 – 11, 147; total, 623
Nationalities of student body: host, 582; other, 41
Capacity: N – preK, 60; K, 60; 1 – 5, 330; 6 – 9, 264; 10 – 11, 198; total, 912
Teacher/student ratio: 1/8

Tuition (annual): N, $2,515; K/1, $3,175; K/2 – 5, $3,835;
     6 – 11, $4,312
Other fees (annual): books, $132 – 159
School year: September through June

Year founded: 1982. **Type of school:** coed, day, private nonprofit.
Governed by: board of governers.

Curriculum/physical plant
     Type: U.S., Arabic. **Languages of instruction:** English, Arabic. **Languages taught:** French. **Staff specialists:** reading, math, computer, learning disabilities, nurse. **Special programs:** remedial. **Special curricular:** art, physical education, computer instruction, music. **Extracurricular:** drama, gymnastics, instrumental music, computers, newspaper, excursions/expeditions, various sports. **Location:** in suburban area. **Campus:** 10 acres. **Library:** 12,000 volumes. **Facilities:** 6 buildings, 46 classrooms, infirmary, covered play area, tennis court, gymnasium, 2 playing fields, 3 science labs, computer lab.

MANAMA

Bahrain School
     Phone: (973)727828   **Facsimile:** (973)725714   **Telex:** 9553622
     Mail: PO Box 934, Juffair, State of Bahrain, Arabian Gulf
     U.S. mail: (no personal name) Bahrain School, PSC 451,
          FPO AE 09834-5200
     Principal: Gilbert M. Fernandes, Ph.D.
     Deputy principal: Kathleen Cummings
     Assistant principal: Geoffrey Darlison
     Staff: full-time, 71; part-time,8
     Nationalities of staff: U.S., 68; U.K., 2; host, 1; other, 8
     Grade levels: K – 12
     Enrollment: K, 32; 1 – 6, 285; 7 – 9, 213; 10 – 12, 296; forms II – V,
          54; total, 880
     Nationalities of student body: U.S., 286; U.K., 68; host, 174;
          other, 352
     Capacity: total, 1,200
     Teacher/student ratio: 1/12
     Boarders: total, 112
     Tuition (annual): K, $3,662; 1 – 6, $7,322; 7 – 8, $7,676;
          9 – 12, $8,030
     Other fees (annual): building levy, 380**; boarding, $7,733
     School year: September to June

Year founded: 1968. **Type of school:** coed, day, boarding. **Governed by:** U.S. Department of Defense Dependents Schools. **Sponsored by:** U.S. government. **Accredited by:** North Central.

Curriculum

Type: U.S., U.K., IB. Languages taught: French, Arabic, Spanish. Staff specialists: reading, computer, counselor, learning disabilities, nurse, music, enrichment. Special programs: ESL, learning disabilities, enrichment. Special curricular: art, chorus, band, physical education, computer instruction, vocational. Extracurricular: drama, yearbook, excursions/expeditions, field trips, sports, choral and instrumental music. Clubs: National Honor Society, junior and senior senate, science, service, chess, computers. Tests: PSAT, SAT, ACT, IB, GCSE, CTBS, GCE, AP. Graduates attending college: 90%. Graduates have attended: Tufts, Princeton, U. of Rochester, Baylor, Georgetown.

Physical plant

Location: 5 minutes from downtown Manama. Campus: 25 acres. Library: 26,000 volumes. Facilities: 15 buildings, 60 classrooms, auditorium, cafeteria, 4 tennis courts, 4 playing fields, 7 science labs, computer lab, swimming pool, AV equipment, 2 squash courts, track, sports hall, home economics room, technology center, air conditioning.

**Bahraini dinar

IBN KHULDOON NATIONAL SCHOOL

Phone: (973)682451/780661   Facsimile: (973)689028
Mail: PO Box 20511, Manama, Bahrain
President: Mr. Samir J. Chammaa
Principal elementary: Miss Ghada Bou Zeineddine
Principal secondary: Mr. Leo LaMontagne
Business manager: Mr. Hassan Radhi
Staff: full-time, 87
Nationalities of staff: U.S., 24; Canada, 16; U.K., 1; host, 15; other, 31
Grade levels: K – 12
Enrollment: K, 150; 1 – 6, 520; 7 – 9, 230; 10 – 12, 150; total, 1,050
Nationalities of student body: host, 990; other, 60
Capacity: K, 150; 1 – 6, 520; 7 – 9, 240; 10 – 12, 160; total, 1,070
Teacher/student ratio: 1/12
Tuition (annual): K, 1,200**; 1 – 6, 1,450; 7 – 9, 1,650; 10 – 12, 2,100
Other fees (annual): registration*, 100**; lunch, 60 (K – 6)
School year: September through June

Year founded: 1983. Type of school: coed, day, private nonprofit. Governed by: elected board of trustees. Accredited by: Middle States (in process).

Curriculum/physical plant

Type: U.S., IB, national syllabi in Arabic, Islamic, and social studies. Languages of instruction: English, Arabic. Languages taught: English, French, Arabic. Staff specialists: reading, computer, nurse. Special programs: ESL. Special curricular: art, physical education, computer instruction. **Extracurricular:** drama, gymnastics, computers, yearbook, newspaper, literary magazine, photography, excursions/expeditions, field trips, choral music, band. **Sports:** basketball, soccer, tennis, volleyball, badminton. **Clubs:** chess, painting, social service, science and technology, photography. **Tests:** PSAT, SAT, IB. **Location:** in suburban area, 2 kilometers from Isa Town. **Campus:** 6 acres. **Library:** 18,000 volumes. **Facilities:** 6 buildings, 78 classrooms, infirmary, 3 covered play areas, 2 tennis courts, 2 gymnasiums, 3 playing fields, 4 science labs, 2 computer labs, 3 art rooms, 3 music rooms.

*Once only fee **Bahraini dinar

BANGLADESH

Region: South Asia
Size: 55,813 square miles
Population: 116,601,000
Capital: Dhaka

Telephone code: 880
Currency: taka
Languages: Bengali, Chakma, Magh

DHAKA

AMERICAN INTERNATIONAL SCHOOL/DHAKA

Street address: United Nations Road, Baridhara, Dhaka, Bangladesh
Phone: (880)(2)882452/882860/882414   **Facsimile:** (880)(2)883175
　　Telex: 642338 AIS D BJ
U.S. mail: American Embassy (AIS/D), Dhaka, Bangladesh, Department of State, Washington, D.C. 20521-6120
Superintendent: Frances J. Rhodes, Ph.D.
Middle and high school principal: Steven Richard Camp
Elementary principal: David Cramer, Ed.D.
Head of library: Claire Vickery
Head of computers: Alice Barr
Admissions: Sara Ann Lockwood
Business manager: Raquibul Husain
Staff: full-time, 45; part-time, 12
Nationalities of staff: U.S., 37; U.K., 9; host, 3; other, 8
Grade levels: preK – 12
Enrollment: preK, 18; K, 42; 1 – 6, 272; 7 – 9, 108; 10 – 12, 74; total, 514
Nationalities of student body: U.S., 140; host, 70; other, 304
Teacher/student ratio: 1/10
Tuition (annual): preK, $2,650; K, $4,450; 1 – 3, $6,570; 4 – 5, $7,100; 6, $8,200; 7, $8,150; 8, $8,580; 9, $8,630; 10, $9,130; 11, $8,730; 12, $9,130
Other fees: application*, $600; lunch, 30**/each; ESL surcharge; capital fee*, K – 6, $3,500, 7 – 12, $4,500
School year: August to June

Year founded: 1972. **Type of school:** coed, day, private nonprofit. **Governed by:** elected board from parent community. **Accredited by:** Middle States. **Regional organizations:** NE/SA, SAISA.

Curriculum/physical plant
Type: U.S. **Languages taught:** French, Spanish. **Staff specialists:** computer, nurse, remedial center, ESL, elementary guidance, secondary guidance. **Special programs:** ESL. **Special curricular:** art, chorus, band, physical education, computer instruction. **Extracurricular:** drama, gymnastics, yearbook, excursions/expeditions, field trips, computers, sports, choral music. **Tests:** SSAT, PSAT, CTP. **Location:** in residential area of Dhaka. **Campus:** 4.5 acres. **Library:** 25,000 volumes. **Facilities:** 2 buildings, 50 classrooms, auditorium, cafeteria, infirmary, gymnasium, playing field, science lab, computer lab, swimming pool, air conditioning.

*Once only fee   **Bangladesh taka

BELGIUM_____

Region: Europe
Size: 11,799 square miles
Population: 9,921,000
Capital: Brussels

Telephone code: 32
Currency: franc
Languages: Flemish (Dutch),
French, German, Italian

ANTWERP

ANTWERP INTERNATIONAL SCHOOL

Street address: Veltwijcklaan 180, 2180 Ekeren/Antwerp, Belgium
Phone: (32)(3)5416047   **Facsimile:** (32)(3)5418201
Headmaster: Robert F. Schaecher
Secondary school principal: Rene De Mol
Elementary school principal: Brian Schiller
Assistant elementary principal: Keith Boniface
Business manager: Theo Van Limbergen
Staff: full-time, 45; part-time, 6
Nationalities of staff: U.S., 27; U.K., 12; host, 9; other, 3
Grade levels: preschool – 12
Enrollment: preschool/preK, 60; K, 40; 1 – 6, 250; 7 – 9, 150;
10 – 12, 90; total, 590
Nationalities of student body: U.S., 150; U.K., 113; host, 25;
other, 302
Capacity: preschool/preK, 65; K, 50; 1 – 6, 288; 7 – 9, 120;
10 – 12, 120; total, 643
Teacher/student ratio: 1/12
Tuition (annual): preschool, 96,000**; preK, 133,000; K, 371,000;
1 – 5, 408,000; 6, 419,000; 7 – 8, 459,000; 9 – 12, 487,000
Other fees (annual): application*, 25,000**/family; busing, 37,000 –
47,000
School year: August to June

Year founded: 1967. **Type of school:** coed, day, private nonprofit.
Governed by: elected board of directors. **Accredited by:** New England, ECIS.

Curriculum/physical plant
Type: U.S., IB, IGCSE. **Languages taught:** French, German, Dutch. **Staff
specialists:** computer. **Special programs:** ESL, remedial, EFL. **Special
curricular:** art, music, computer, study skills, life skills, Theory of Knowledge,
physical education. **Extracurricular:** computers, yearbook, art, choir, orchestra, typing, word processing, newspaper, Model UN, environmental
concerns, sports, creative writing, business education, field week. **Sports:**
basketball, soccer, swimming, tennis, volleyball, track and field, racquet
sports. **Clubs:** Model NATO, student council, speech and debate, scouts,
music lessons. **Tests:** PSAT, SAT, ACT, TOEFL, IB, AP, GCSE, CTP - II.
Graduates attending college: 95%. **Graduates have attended:** Stanford,

Princeton, Villanova, Radford, Harvard. **Location:** in suburban area, 10 kilometers from Antwerp. **Campus:** 4 – 5 acres. **Library:** 15,000 volumes. **Facilities:** 5 buildings, 35 classrooms, cafeteria, infirmary, gymnasium, playing field, 3 science labs, 2 computer labs, early childhood center, fine arts center.

*Once only fee   **Belgian franc

EEC INTERNATIONAL SCHOOL

Street address: Jacob Jordaensstraat, 77, 2018 Antwerp, Belgium
Phone: (32)(3)2188182   **Facsimile:** (32)(3)2185868
President: Dr. X. Nieberding
Staff: full-time, 21; part-time, 8
Nationalities of staff: U.S., 1; U.K., 9; host, 9; other, 10
Grade levels: preK – 12
Enrollment: preK, 10; K, 10; 1 – 6, 62; 7 – 9, 51; 10 – 12, 95;
   total, 228
Nationalities of student body: U.S., 12; U.K., 33; host, 46; other, 137
Capacity: preK, 20; K, 20; 1 – 6, 70; 7 – 9, 70; 10 – 12, 100; total, 280
Teacher/student ratio: 1/9
Boarders: boys, 12; girls, 18   **Grades:** 4 – 12
   Program: planned 5-day
Tuition (annual): preK – K, 90,000**; 1 – 2, 150,000; 3 – 4, 170,000;
   5 – 6, 200,000; 7 – 8, 260,000; 9, 275,000; 10 – 12, 280,000;
   IGCSE O-levels, 290,000; GCE A-levels, 330,000
Other fees (annual): boarding, 240,000**; books, approximately
   5,000; application*, 10,000
School year: September to June

Year founded: 1979. **Type of school:** coed, day, boarding, proprietary. **Governed by:** appointed board of governors. **Sponsored by:** American European Educational Association.

Curriculum

Type: U.S., U.K. **Languages taught:** French, Spanish, German, Dutch. **Staff specialists:** reading, math, computer, speech/hearing, counselor, psychologist, learning disabilities. **Special programs:** ESL, remedial. **Special curricular:** art, physical education, computer instruction. **Extracurricular:** drama, gymnastics, dance, computers, yearbook, literary magazine, excursions/expeditions, field trips, choral and instrumental music. **Sports:** baseball, basketball, hockey, soccer, volleyball, gymnastics, handball, netball, squash, racquetball, badminton, korfball, physical fitness, jazz, aerobics, ping-pong. **Tests:** PSAT, SAT, TOEFL, A-level GCE, IGCSE. **Graduates attending college:** 97%. **Graduates have attended:** American College in Paris, Tufts, State U. of Leuven, U. of London.

Physical plant

Location: in Antwerp, on a quiet street near park. **Campus:** 2.5 acres. **Library:** 12,000 volumes. **Facilities:** 3 buildings, 25 classrooms, cafeteria, 2 covered play areas, gymnasium, 2 science labs, 3 computer labs, library, AV equipment, fitness center, boarding facilities.

*Once only fee   **Belgian franc

BRUSSELS

THE BRITISH SCHOOL OF BRUSSELS

Street address: Leuvensesteenweg 19, 3080 Tervuren, Belgium
Phone: (32)(2)7674700   **Facsimile:** (32)(2)7678070
Principal/acting head of upper school: Jennifer Bray
Head of middle school: Peter Saunders
Head of lower school: Carol Walker
Staff: full-time, 82; part-time, 17
Nationalities of staff: U.K., 87; host, 5; other, 7
Grade levels: K – 13
Enrollment: K, 36; reception, 36; 1 – 6, 425; 7 – 9, 227; 10 – 12, 226; 13, 70; total, 1,020
Nationalities of student body: U.S., 23; U.K., 772; host, 11; other, 214
Capacity: K, 40; reception, 60; 1 – 6, 475; 7 – 9, 240; 10 – 12, 240; 13, 80; total, 1,135
Teacher/student ratio: 1/11
Boarders: boys, 3   **Grades:** 8 – 13   **Program:** planned 5- and 7-day (host-family scheme)
Tuition (annual): K, 95,000**; reception, 175,000; 1 – 6, 419,000; 7, 436,000; 8 – 11, 488,000; 12 – 13, 527,000
Other fees (annual): registration*, 15,000**; boarding, 160,000 – 230,000; busing, 53,000
School year: September to July

Year founded: 1970. **Type of school:** coed, day, boarding. **Governed by:** appointed and elected board of trustees.

Curriculum

Type: U.K. **Languages taught:** French, German. **Staff specialists:** reading, math, speech/hearing, counselor, psychologist, learning disabilities, nurse. **Special programs:** ESL, advanced placement, remedial, honors sections. **Special curricular:** art, chorus, band, computer instruction, vocational. **Extracurricular:** drama, gymnastics, dance, excursions/expeditions, field trips, choral and instrumental music. **Sports:** basketball, football, hockey, rugby, swimming, tennis, squash, athletics, badminton. **Tests:** A-level GCE, GCSE. **Graduates have attended:** Oxford, Cambridge, London, Manchester, Sussex.

Physical plant

Location: 15 kilometers from center of Brussels. **Campus:** 50,000 square meters. **Library:** 40,000 volumes. **Facilities:** auditorium, cafeteria, infirmary, 5 gymnasiums, 4 playing fields, 9 science labs, 2 computer labs, 6 tennis courts (2 covered).

*Once only fee   **Belgian franc

BRUSSELS' ENGLISH PRIMARY SCHOOL S.P.R.L.

Street address: 23 Avenue Franklin Roosevelt, Brussels 1050,
  Belgium
Phone: (32)(2)6484311   **Facsimile:** (32)(2)6872968
Director: Charles A. Gellar
Headmistress: Beryl Green
Staff: full-time, 18; part-time, 6
Nationalities of staff: U.S., 1; U.K., 14; host, 6; other, 3
Grade levels: N – 6
Enrollment: N – preK, 24; K, 24; 1 – 6, 201; total, 249
Nationalities of student body: U.S., 14; U.K., 71; host, 23; other, 141
Capacity: N – preK, 24; K, 24; 1 – 6, 226; 7, 10; total, 274
Teacher/student ratio: 1/12
Tuition (annual): N (1/2 day), 104,000**; K/reception, 180,000;
  1 – 4, 240,000; 5 – 6, 254,000
Other fees: busing, 72,000** (optional); lunch, 1,000; refundable
  deposit, 20,000
School year: September through June

Year founded: 1972. **Type of school:** coed, day, proprietary. **Governed by:** director elected by company shareholders.

Curriculum/physical plant

Type: U.K., international. **Languages taught:** French. **Staff specialists:** computer. **Special programs:** ESL, remedial. **Special curricular:** computer instruction, swimming, woodwork. **Extracurricular:** instrumental music, computers, literary magazine, excursions/expeditions, field trips. **Sports:** football, swimming, jogging. **Tests:** Common Entrance Exam (U.K.). **Location:** 5 kilometers from center of Brussels, opposite large park and University of Brussels. **Campus:** 2,000 square meters. **Library:** 6,000 volumes. **Facilities:** 2 buildings, 15 classrooms, playing field, science lab, nearby tennis courts and swimming pool.

**Belgian franc

EEC International School, Brussels

Street address: Boulevard Louis Schmidt 103, Brussels 1040,
   Belgium
Phone: (32)(2)7344413   **Facsimile:** (32)(2)7333233
President: Dr. X. Nieberding
Headmaster: Mr. P. Van Landeghem
Headteacher: Mrs. G. Aston
Staff: full-time, 17; part-time, 14
Nationalities of staff: U.K., 18; host, 5; other, 8
Grade levels: preK – 12
Enrollment: K – 6, 95; 7 – 12, 73; total, 168
Teacher/student ratio: 1/7
Tuition (annual): preK – K, 180,000**; reception – 3, 220,000;
   primary 4 – 6, 240,000; sections 1 – 7, 340,000 – 400,000;
   A-level, 440,000
Other fees: registration, 15,000**
School year: September to June

Year founded: 1985. **Type of school:** coed, day, proprietary. **Governed by:** appointed board of governors. **Sponsored by:** American European Educational Association.

**Belgian franc

The International School of Brussels

Street address: 19 Kattenberg, Brussels 1170, Belgium
Phone: (32)(2)6722788   **Facsimile:** (32)(2)6751178
   Cable: INTERSCHOOL
Director: Richard P. Hall
High school headmaster: Walther Hetzer
Middle school headmaster: Malcolm Cromarty
Elementary school headmistress: Edna Murphy
Director of admissions: Raetta L. Mirgain
Business manager: Mario Renard
Staff: full-time, 118; part-time, 24
Nationalities of staff: U.S., 56; U.K., 33; host, 26; other, 27
Grade levels: N – 12
Enrollment: N – preK, 56; K, 55; 1 – 6, 455; 7 – 9, 323; 10 – 12, 388;
   special education, 7; total, 1,284
Nationalities of student body: U.S., 506; U.K., 103; host, 48;
   other, 627
Capacity: N – preK, 68; K, 54; 1 – 6, 464; 7 – 9, 330; 10 – 12, 400;
   total, 1,316
Teacher/student ratio: 1/10
Tuition (annual): N (mornings), 145,000**; full N – preK, 251,000; K, 457,000;
   1 – 2, 500,000; 3 – 6, 512,000; 7 – 9, 578,000; 10 – 12, 595,000
Other fees (annual): application*, N – preK, 10,000**, K – 12, 35,000;

busing, 60,000; capital building surcharge, 28,000; lunch (optional), 150/each
School year: September through June

Year founded: 1951. **Type of school:** coed, day. **Governed by:** appointed board of trustees. **Accredited by:** Middle States, ECIS.

Curriculum
Type: U.S., IB. **Languages taught:** French, Spanish, German; IB Language A in Japanese, Swedish, English, French. **Staff specialists:** computer, speech/hearing, counselor, psychologist, learning disabilities, nurse. **Special programs:** ESL, advanced placement, remedial, IB, special education. **Special curricular:** art, chorus, band, physical education, computer instruction, drama, chamber choir. **Extracurricular:** drama, gymnastics, computers, yearbook, newspaper, literary magazine, excursions/expeditions, field trips, choral and instrumental music, National Honor Society, forensics and debate, Model UN, film literature, technical theater. **Sports:** baseball, basketball, field hockey, football, rugby, soccer, softball, swimming, tennis, volleyball, cross-country, wrestling, track and field. **Tests:** SSAT, PSAT, SAT, ACT, TOEFL, IB, AP, Iowa. **Graduates attending college:** 93%. **Graduates have attended:** Princeton, Bryn Mawr, MIT, Stanford, Brown.

Physical plant
Location: beautiful wooded campus in residential area of southeast Brussels, approximately 7 kilometers from center city. **Campus:** 40 acres. **Libraries:** 65,000 volumes. **Facilities:** 7 buildings, 87 classrooms, 3 cafeterias, infirmary, 2 tennis courts, 2 gymnasiums, 3 playing fields, 11 science labs, 3 computer labs, theater, AV equipment.

*Once only fee   **Belgian franc

LIMAL

B.E.P.S. 2 – LIMAL INTERNATIONAL SCHOOL†
Street address: 13–15 Rue Leon Deladriere, 1300 Limal, Belgium
Phone: (32)(10)417227   **Facsimile:** (32)(2)6872968
Director: Charles A. Gellar
Head teacher: Diane Perry
Staff: full-time, 5; part-time, 3
Nationalities of staff: U.S., 1; U.K., 5; host, 2
Grade levels: N – 6
Enrollment: N – K, 13; 1 – 3, 13; 4 – 6, 15; total, 41
Nationalities of student body: U.S., 7; U.K., 18; host, 4; other, 12
Capacity: N – K, 32; 1 – 3, 24; 4 – 6, 34; total, 90
Teacher/student ratio: 1/6
Tuition (annual): N (half-day), 128,000**; K/reception, 214,000; 1 – 4, 272,000; 5 – 6, 288,000

Other fees (annual): busing, 72,000** (optional); lunch, 1,000; refundable deposit, 20,000
School year: September through June

Year founded: 1992. **Type of school:** coed, day, proprietary. **Governed
by:** director elected by company shareholders.

Curriculum/physical plant
Type: international. **Languages taught:** French. **Staff specialists:** arts,
crafts, music. **Extracurricular:** instrumental music, computers, literary
magazine, excursions/expeditions, field trips. **Sports:** swimming. **Tests:**
Common Entrance Exam (U.K.). **Location:** 25 kilometers from center of
Brussels, in a superb "green world" setting. **Campus:** 37,000 square meters.
Library: 1,000 volumes. **Facilities:** 2 buildings, 7 classrooms, tennis court,
science lab, theater, pet animals, museum for children.

**Belgian franc   †Brussels English Primary School second campus

WATERLOO

St. John's International School
Street address: Drève Richelle 146, 1410 Waterloo, Belgium
Phone: (32)(2)3541138   **Facsimile:** (32)(2)3530495
Superintendent: Sr. Barbara Hughes, F.C.J.
High school principal: Dennis McCann
Middle school principal: John Lepetit
Elementary school principal: Sr. Beatrice Molyneux, F.C.J.
Business manager: Richard Katherman
Staff: full-time, 83; part-time, 23
Nationalities of staff: U.S., 34; U.K., 33; host, 23; other, 16
Grade levels: N – 13
Enrollment: N – preK, 65; K, 55; 1 – 5, 320; 6 – 8, 185; 9 – 12, 220;
13, 5; total, 850
Nationalities of student body: U.S., 300; U.K., 170; host, 20; other, 360
Capacity: N – preK, 80; K, 60; 1 – 5, 348; 6 – 8, 198; 9 – 12, 240;
total, 926
Teacher/student ratio: 1/9
Tuition: (figures not available at time of publication)
Other fees (annual): registration*, 35,000**; capital levy, 20,000
School year: September to June

Year founded: 1964. **Type of school:** coed, day, private nonprofit.
Governed by: Conseil d'administration (nonprofit organization) and advisory
board. **Sponsored by:** Faithful Companions of Jesus. **Accredited by:** Middle
States, ECIS.

Curriculum

Type: U.S., U.K., IB. **Languages taught:** French (all students, K – 12); Spanish, German (optional); Dutch, Swedish (IB). **Staff specialists:** computer, counselor, psychologist, learning disabilities, nurse. **Special programs:** ESL, advanced placement, honors sections, remedial. **Special curricular:** art, chorus, band, physical education, computer instruction, drama, religion, swimming (K – 7). **Extracurricular:** drama, gymnastics, choral music, instrumental music, yearbook, newspaper, literary magazine, excursions/expeditions, field trips. **Sports:** baseball, basketball, soccer, softball, swimming, tennis, track and field, volleyball, cross-country. **Clubs:** Model UN, Model NATO, debating, International Schools Theater Association. **Tests:** SSAT, PSAT, SAT, TOEFL, IB, AP, O-level GCE, Iowa. **Graduates attending college:** 95%. **Graduates have attended:** Duke, MIT, Harvard, Tufts, Oxbridge (U.K.).

Physical plant

Location: pleasant residential suburb with good shopping facilities, 15 miles from Brussels. **Libraries (2):** 18,000 volumes. **Facilities:** 5 buildings, 38 classrooms, auditorium, 2 cafeterias, infirmary, 3 tennis courts, 2 gymnasiums, playing field, 4 science labs, 2 computer labs, local swimming pool, 3 art studios, 2 music rooms, boarding with local families as required.

*Once only fee   **Belgian franc

BRUSSELS

Scandinavian School of Brussels – Ecole Reine Astrid

Address: Chaussée de Waterloo 280, B-1640 Rhode-St-Genèse, Belgium
Phone: (32)(2)3583276   **Facsimile:** (32)(2)3581420

BENIN _____

Region: West Africa
Size: 43,483 square miles
Population: 4,831,000
Capitals: Porto-Novo (official),
     Cotonou (de facto)

Telephone code: 229
Currency: CFA franc
Language: French

COTONOU

Brilliant Stars International School

Street address: Lot 123 Residence-Ouest, Cotonou, Benin
Phone: (229)300539   **Facsimile:** (229)3137
Mail: BP 04-919, Cotonou, Benin
Director: Christina Hinshaw
Staff: full-time, 6; part-time, 3

Nationalities of staff: U.S., 2; U.K., 1; host, 1; other, 5
Grade levels: N – 8
Enrollment: N – preK, 24; K, 6; 1 – 6, 30; 7 – 8, 3; total, 63
Nationalities of student body: U.S., 6; U.K., 2; host, 10; other, 45
Capacity: N – preK, 30; K, 15; 1 – 6, 60; 7 – 8, 30; total, 135
Teacher/student ratio: 1/8
Tuition (annual): N – K, 450,000**; 1 – 8, 675,000
Other fees: registration, 75,000**
School year: September to June

Year founded: 1986. **Type of school:** coed, day, private nonprofit.
Regional organizations: AISA.

Curriculum/physical plant
Type: U.S. **Languages taught:** French, ESL. **Staff specialists:** learning disabilities. **Special programs:** ESL, independent study. **Special curricular:** physical education. **Location:** in residential green oasis, 200 meters from U.S. Embassy in Cotonou. **Library:** 2,500 volumes. **Facilities:** 2 buildings, 9 classrooms, 2 tennis courts, shaded garden with jungle gym and swings.

**CFA franc

BERMUDA _____

Region: Western Atlantic
Size: 20.6 square miles
Population: 59,800
Capital: Hamilton

Telephone code: 809
Currency: Bermudian dollar
Language: English

HAMILTON

THE BERMUDA HIGH SCHOOL FOR GIRLS
Street address: 27 Richmond Road, Pembroke HM08, Bermuda
Phone: (1)(809)2956153   **Facsimile:** (1)(809)2952754
Principal: John H. Wright, Jr.
Secondary department director of studies: Teresa Sousa
Dean of students: Brenda Brown
Head, primary department: Lorna Andersen
Registrar: Diane Gordon
Financial controller: William Ingham
Staff: full-time, 45; part-time, 8
Grade levels: 1 – 12 (British)
Enrollment: total, 535

Saltus Grammar School

Phone: (1)(809)2926177   **Facsimile:** (1)(809)2954977
Mail: PO Box HM 2224, Pembroke HM JX, Hamilton, Bermuda
Headmaster: J. K. McPhee
Staff: full-time, 50; part-time, 2
Nationalities of staff: U.K., 36; host, 15; other, 1
Grade levels: K – 12
Enrollment: K, 69; 1 – 6, 394; 7 – 9, 170; 10 – 12, 142; total, 775
Capacity: K, 75; 1 – 6, 450; 7 – 9, 225; 10 – 12, 200; total, 950
Teacher/student ratio: 1/15
Tuition (annual): K – 12, $5,600
Other fees (annual): books, $100; refundable deposit, $600
School year: September through June

Year founded: 1888. **Type of school:** coed, day. **Governed by:** appointed trustees.

Curriculum/physical plant

Type: U.K., U.S. in grade 12. **Languages taught:** French, Spanish. **Staff specialists:** reading, counselor. **Special curricular:** art, physical education, computer instruction, vocational, choir. **Extracurricular:** drama, gymnastics, dance, instrumental music, computers, yearbook, newspaper, photography. **Sports:** basketball, rugby, soccer, swimming, tennis, volleyball, cricket, squash, sailing, running, cycling, hockey, netball. **Tests:** PSAT, SAT, ACT, AP, GCSE. **Graduates have attended:** Queens, Yale, Princeton, Brown, MIT. **Location:** 5 minutes from city center. **Facilities:** 9 buildings, 40 classrooms, auditorium, cafeteria, covered play area, gymnasium, playing field, science labs, swimming pool, computer center, darkroom, administration center, music center, arts and crafts center.

BOLIVIA ————————————————————

Region: South America
Size: 424,165 square miles
Population: 6,730,000
Capitals: Sucre, La Paz

Telephone code: 591
Currency: boliviano
Languages: Spanish, Quechua, Aymara

COCHABAMBA

American International School of Bolivia

Street address: Avenida Cerveceria Taquina to Malteria Linde turn-off
Phone: (591)(14)94300   **Facsimile:** (591)(42)32879
Mail: Casilla 5309, Cochabamba, Bolivia
U.S. mail: Superintendent, AIS/B, U.S. Embassy, La Paz, Bolivia, APO Miami 34032, U.S.A.
Superintendent: Dennis Smith

Staff: full-time, 17
Nationalities of staff: U.S., 12; host, 2; other, 3
Capacity: 200
Tuition (annual): preK, $550; K, $1,100; 1 – 4, $3,300; 5 – 8, $3,575;
    9 – 12, $3,850
Other fees (annual): registration, $50 – $350; busing, $250; member-
    ship, $200; entry share, $2,000
School year: mid-August through early June

Year founded: 1993. **Type of school:** coed, day, boarding, private
nonprofit. **Governed by:** permanently-vested board of directors. **Sponsored
by:** private donations. **Accredited by:** Southern, Bolivian Ministry of Education.

Curriculum/physical plant

Type: U.S., IB, national. **Languages taught:** French, Spanish, German,
Italian, Portuguese. **Staff specialists:** library, counselor, resource,learning
disabilities. **Special curricular:** IB, Model UN, creative expression, studio art,
home economics, computer programming. **Special programs:** ESL, IB,
independent study, learning disabilities. **Extracurricular:** karate, driver's
education, trekking, publications, National Honor Society, student council,
classrooms without walls. **Sports:** soccer, softball, swimming, tennis, volleyball, basketball.

COCHABAMBA COOPERATIVE SCHOOL

Street address: Avenida Circunvalacion, Cochabamba, Bolivia
Phone: (591)(42)32643   **Facsimile:** (591)(42)32906
Mail: Casilla 1395, Cochabamba, Bolivia
U.S. mail: (no personal name) Cochabamba Cooperative School,
    U.S. Embassy, La Paz, APO AA 34032
Director: Mark Higgins
Staff: full-time, 23
Nationalities of staff: U.S., 11; host, 10; other, 2
Grade levels: preK – 12
Enrollment: total, 190
Nationalities of student body: U.S., 20; host, 145; other, 25
Capacity: total, 350
Teacher/student ratio: 1/8
Tuition (annual): preK, $1,050; K – 6, $2,600; 7 – 12, $2,700
Other fees (annual): registration, $105 – 270; insurance, $15; busing,
    $160; building fund*, $625; entrance fee*, $625
School year: August to June

Year founded: 1958. **Type of school:** coed, day, private nonprofit.
Governed by: elected board of directors. **Sponsored by:** parents. **Accredited
by:** Southern, Bolivian Ministry of Education.

Curriculum/physical plant

Type: U.S., Bolivian. **Languages taught:** French, Spanish, German.

Staff specialists: librarian, counselor, resource. **Special programs:** ESL, advanced placement, independent study. **Special curricular:** art, chorus, physical education, computer instruction. **Extracurricular:** choral music, computers, yearbook, newspaper, literary magazine, excursions/expeditions, student council, National Honor Society. **Sports:** basketball, soccer, track, volleyball. **Tests:** PSAT, SAT, ACT, TOEFL, Iowa. **Graduates attending college:** 80%. **Graduates have attended:** Penn State, Texas A&M, MIT, Harvard, U. of California at Berkeley. **Location:** in suburb, 1 mile east of city. **Campus:** 11 acres. **Library:** 13,000 volumes. **Facilities:** 6 buildings, 30 classrooms, cafeteria, 2 playing fields, science lab, computer lab, AV equipment, playground.

*Once only fee

LA PAZ

AMERICAN COOPERATIVE SCHOOL

Street address: Calle Las Kantutas y Calle 10, Calacoto, La Paz, Bolivia
Phone: (591)(2)792302/794750   **Facsimile:** (591)(2)797218
Mail: c/o U.S. Embassy, La Paz, Bolivia
U.S. mail: (no personal name) American Cooperative School, U.S. Embassy – La Paz, APO AA 34032
Superintendent: Herm Penland
Secondary school principal: Mike Donohue
Elementary school principal: Dennis Sheehan, Ph.D.
Staff: full-time, 50; part-time, 5
Nationalities of staff: U.S., 46; host, 7; other, 2
Grade levels: preK – 12
Enrollment: preK, 18; K, 32; 1 – 6, 294; 7 – 9, 141; 10 – 12, 143; total, 628
Nationalities of student body: U.S., 196; host, 311; other, 121
Capacity: preK, 22; K, 54; 1 – 6, 250; 7 – 9, 140; 10 – 12, 150; total, 616
Teacher/student ratio: 1/12
Tuition (annual): preK – K, $2,865; 1 – 5, $4,255; 6 – 12, $4,435
Other fees (annual): capital levy*, $1,000; busing, $400
School year: August to May

Year founded: 1955. **Type of school:** coed, day, private nonprofit. **Governed by:** elected board of directors. **Accredited by:** Southern.

Curriculum/physical plant
Type: U.S. **Languages taught:** French, Spanish. **Staff specialists:** reading, computer, counselor, learning disabilities, nurse. **Special programs:** ESL, advanced placement, independent study, correspondence, remedial. **Special curricular:** art, chorus, band, physical education, computer instruction. **Extracurricular:** drama, gymnastics, instrumental music, yearbook,

literary magazine, photography, excursions/expeditions, field trips. **Sports:** basketball, soccer, swimming, track, volleyball. **Clubs:** computer, service organizations. **Tests:** SSAT, PSAT, SAT, ACT, AP, Iowa. **Graduates attending college:** 95%. **Graduates have attended:** Notre Dame, Dartmouth, UCLA, U. of Miami, U. of Illinois. **Location:** in residential area, 4 miles from La Paz. **Campus:** 7 acres. **Library:** 12,000 volumes. **Facilities:** 9 buildings, auditorium, cafeteria, infirmary, 2 covered play areas, 2 tennis courts, gymnasium, playing field, 2 science labs, computer lab, swimming pool, 2 racquetball courts, sauna, weightroom.

*Once only fee

SANTA CRUZ

SANTA CRUZ CHRISTIAN LEARNING CENTER

Street address: Km. 6-1/2 Carretera a Cochabamba, Santa Cruz, Bolivia
Phone: (591)(3)526666   **Facsimile:** (591)(3)526667
Mail: Cajon 4049, Santa Cruz, Bolivia
Director: Thomas Hilgeman
High school principal: Virginia Swartzendruber
Elementary principal: Billie Sue Dunn
Business manager: Elwood Webb
Staff: full-time, 24; part-time, 16
Nationalities of staff: U.S., 26; host, 12; other, 2
Grade levels: preK – 12
Enrollment: preK, 8; K, 10; 1 – 6, 108; 7 – 9, 34; 10 – 12, 19; total, 179
Nationalities of student body: U.S., 70; U.K., 6; host, 57; other, 46
Capacity: preK, 12; K, 18; 1 – 6, 120; 7 – 9, 60; 10 – 12, 40; total, 250
Teacher/student ratio: 1/5
Tuition (annual): preK – K, $825; 1 – 6, $1,650; 7 – 12, $1,815 (2nd and 3rd child discount available)
Other fees (annual): registration, $225; busing, $25/month; lab, $25; capital*, $500/family
School year: August to May

Year founded: 1977. **Type of school:** coed, day, church-related. **Governed and sponsored by:** Gospel Missionary Union, South America Mission, World Gospel Mission. **Accredited by:** Bolivian government, ACSI (in process).

Curriculum/physical plant
Type: U.S. **Languages taught:** English, Spanish. **Staff specialists:** speech/hearing, nurse, special education/learning disabilities. **Special programs:** honors sections. **Special curricular:** art, physical education, computer instruction, yearbook, newspaper. **Extracurricular:** drama, gymnas-

tics, field trips, art/science fair, field day, spelling/math competitions, interschool competitions, student social organization. **Sports:** basketball, soccer, volleyball. **Tests:** PSAT, SAT, ACT, Stanford, GRE (testing center). **Graduates attending college:** 98%. **Graduates have attended:** American U., Boston State U., Kansas State U., George Mason U., Grace Bible College. **Location:** in suburb, 7 kilometers from center of Santa Cruz. **Campus:** 2.5 hectares. **Library:** 10,000 volumes. **Facilities:** 8 buildings, 20 classrooms, 2 playing fields, 2 science labs, computer lab, gymnasium/multipurpose building, kitchen, partial air conditioning, nearby boarding facilities operated by World Gospel Mission.

*Once only fee

SANTA CRUZ COOPERATIVE SCHOOL

Street address: Calle Barcelona No. 1, Santa Cruz, Bolivia
Phone: (591)(3)520729/523122
  Facsimile: (591)(3)526993 (late afternoon/evening)
Mail: Casilla 753, Santa Cruz, Bolivia
U.S. mail: Director, Santa Cruz Cooperative School, U.S. Embassy –
  Bolivia, APO AA 34032
Director: David Deuel
Assistant secondary principal: Bryn Gabriel
Elementary principal: Louis Yannotta
Head of library: Kathy Hemmat
Staff: full-time, 40; part-time, 3
Nationalities of staff: U.S., 28; host, 12; other, 3
Grade levels: preK – 12
Enrollment: preK, 52; K, 51; 1 – 6, 280; 7 – 9, 118; 10 – 12, 89;
  total, 590
Nationalities of student body: U.S., 66; host, 442; other, 82
Capacity: preK, 50; K, 50; 1 – 6, 300; 7 – 9, 150; 10 – 12, 150;
  total, 700
Teacher/student ratio: 1/14
Tuition (annual): preK, $1,599; K, $2,439; 1 – 6, $2,701;
  7 – 12, $3,122
Other fees (annual): registration, $130; capital levy, $3,000/family
School year: August to June

Year founded: 1959. **Type of school:** coed, day, parent cooperative. **Governed by:** elected board of directors. **Accredited by:** Bolivian Ministry of Education, Southern. **Regional organization:** AASSA.

Curriculum

Type: U.S. **Languages taught:** French, Spanish. **Staff specialists:** counselor, librarian, computer coordinator. **Special programs:** ESL, advanced placement, correspondence, independent study, highly capable students' program. **Special curricular:** art, chorus, physical education, computer instruction, debating, drama, economics, ecology, dance, photography. **Extracurricular:** drama, computers, yearbook, newspaper, literary magazine, photography, field trips, choral music, cheerleading. **Sports:** basketball, soccer, track and field, volleyball. **Tests:** PSAT, SAT, ACT, TOEFL, AP, Iowa. **Graduates attending college:** 98%. **Graduates have attended:** Georgetown, Texas A&M, Harvard, William and Mary, MIT.

Physical plant
Location: 2 miles from center city. **Campus:** 10 acres. **Library:** 9,000 volumes. **Facilities:** 5 buildings, 36 classrooms, cafeteria, covered play area, 2 tennis courts, 2 playing fields, 2 science labs, computer labs, gymnasium/ auditorium, AV area, teachers' workroom/lounge.

COCHABAMBA
Instituto Cochabamba
  Address: Casilla Correo 175, Cochabamba, Bolivia

BOTSWANA ————————————————

Region: Southern Africa
Size: 231,804 square miles
Population: 1,300,000
Capital: Gaborone

Telephone code: 267
Currency: pula
Languages: English, Tswana, Shona

GABORONE

MARU A PULA SCHOOL
  Street address: Maru a Pula Way, Gaborone, Botswana
  Phone: (267)312953   **Facsimile:** (267)373338
  Mail: Private Bag 0045, Gaborone, Botswana
  Principal: Malcolm H. McKenzie
  Deputy principals: John O'Brien, Alan Wilson, Chris Madeley
  Directors of studies: Guy Walker, Sheila Case
  Bursar: Greta Steele
  Staff: full-time, 36; part-time, 7
  Nationalities of staff: U.S., 4; U.K., 6; host, 7; other, 26
  Grade levels: 8 – A-level
  Enrollment: 8 – 9, 192; 10 – 12, 250; A-level, 70; total, 512
  Capacity: 8 – 9, 192; 10 – 12, 250; A-level, 70; total, 512
  Teacher/student ratio: 1/13
  Boarders: boys, 78; girls, 72   **Grades:** 8 – A-level
    Program: planned 7-day

Tuition (annual): 8 – 12, 8,400**
Other fees (annual): registration*, 20**; boarding, 5,700;
lunch, 200/term
School year: January to December

Year founded: 1972. **Type of school:** coed, day, boarding, private
nonprofit. **Governed by:** elected Council of Maru a Pula. **Accredited by:**
Botswana Ministry of Education.

Curriculum/physical plant
Type: U.K. **Languages taught:** French, Setswana. **Staff specialists:**
computer, nurse, guidance counselor. **Special programs:** advanced placement, honors sections. **Special curricular:** art, computer instruction. **Extracurricular:** drama, dance, instrumental music, computers, yearbook. **Sports:**
basketball, soccer, softball, swimming, tennis, volleyball, netball, athletics.
Clubs: debating, chess, bridge, sewing, cooking, library, social service, service
projects within the school. **Tests:** A-level GCE, O-level GCE. **Graduates
attending college:** 85%. **Graduates have attended:** U. of Pennsylvania,
Middlebury, Stanford, Oxford, Cambridge. **Location:** in suburbs. **Campus:**
50 acres. **Library:** 15,000 volumes. **Facilities:** 35 buildings, 23 classrooms,
auditorium, cafeteria, infirmary, 2 tennis courts, 2 playing fields, 6 science
labs, computer lab, AV center, boarding in shared cubicles, 30 faculty houses.

*Once only fee   **Botswana pula

NORTHSIDE PRIMARY SCHOOL
Street address: Tshekedi Road, Gaborone, Botswana
Phone: (267)352440   **Facsimile:** (267)353573
Mail: PO Box 897, Gaborone, Botswana
Headmistress: Margaret Dixon-Warren, Ed.D.
Deputy head: Mandy Watson
Staff: full-time, 27; part-time, 1
Nationalities of staff: U.K., 19; host, 1; other, 8
Grade levels: K – 7
Enrollment: K, 66; 1 – 6, 324; 7, 43; total, 433
Nationalities of student body: U.S., 12; U.K., 78; host, 116; other, 227
Capacity: K, 64; 1 – 6, 312; 7, 52; total, 428
Teacher/student ratio: 1/16
Tuition (annual): K – 7, $2,747
Other fees: registration*, $21
School year: January through December

Year founded: 1934. **Type of school:** coed, day, private nonprofit.
Governed by: elected school council. **Sponsored by:** Botswana government.
Accredited by: ECIS.

Curriculum/physical plant
Type: U.K., Botswanian. **Languages taught:** French, Setswana. **Staff**

specialists: reading, math, computer, counselor, learning disabilities, music, physical education, science. **Special programs**: remedial. **Special curricular:** art, chorus, band, physical education, computer instruction. **Extracurricular:** drama, gymnastics, dance, choral music, computers, yearbook, excursions/expeditions, field trips. **Sports**: basketball, softball, swimming, tennis, volleyball, netball, soccer, table tennis, badminton, cricket, traditional dancing. **Clubs:** Brownies, Cub Scouts, philately, Girl Guides, pottery. **Location:** in attractive suburb. **Campus**: 7 acres. **Library:** 10,000 volumes. **Facilities:** 16 classrooms, auditorium, 2 tennis courts, gymnasium, playing field, science lab, computer lab, swimming pool, language rooms, music/visual arts room, partial air conditioning.

*Once only fee

Westwood Primary School

Phone: (267)306736   **Facsimile:** (267)306734
Mail: PO Box 2446, Gaborone, Botswana
U.S. mail: c/o Administrative Officer – American Embassy Gaborone, U.S. State Department, Washington, D.C. 20521
Principal: Bob Sylvester
Deputy principal: Rhiain Jackson
Staff: full-time, 30; part-time, 3
Nationalities of staff: U.S., 5; U.K., 9; host, 1; other, 18
Grade levels: K – 7
Enrollment: K, 56; 1 – 6, 352; 7, 48; total, 456
Nationalities of student body: U.S., 38; U.K., 69; host, 135; other, 214
Capacity: K, 50; 1 – 6, 375; 7, 50; total, 475
Teacher/student ratio: 1/14
Tuition (annual): $3,900
School year: January to December

Year founded: 1988. **Type of school:** coed, day. **Governed by:** appointed and elected private school board. **Sponsored by:** diplomatic/corporate.

Curriculum/physical plant

Type: U.S., U.K. **Languages taught:** French, Setswana. **Staff specialists:** reading, math, counselor, learning disabilities, nurse. **Special programs:** ESL, independent study, remedial. **Special curricular:** art, physical education, computer instruction, vocational. **Extracurricular:** drama, gymnastics, choral music, computers, literary magazine, excursions/expeditions, field trips. **Sports:** basketball, soccer, softball, swimming, volleyball, cricket. **Clubs:** Sunbeams, history, chess. **Tests:** Iowa. **Location:** in Gaborone. **Campus:** 12 acres. **Library:** 6,000 volumes. **Facilities:** 12 buildings, 24 classrooms, auditorium, infirmary, tennis court, 5 playing fields, science lab, computer lab, swimming pool, air conditioning.

BRAZIL _____

Region: South America
Size: 3,286,470 square miles
Population: 148,000,000
Capital: Brasilia

Telephone code: 55
Currency: cruzeiro
Languages: Portuguese, English
German, Italian

BELEM

Amazon Valley Academy

Phone: (55)(91)2352166   **Facsimile:** (55)(91)2413293 (voice, then fax)   **Cable:** MICEBRA
Mail: Caixa Postal 3030, Agencia Independencia, 66.040-970 Belem, Para, Brazil
Principal: Albert F. Roth
Vice-principals: Ellen Johnson, Markus Bosshart
Staff: full-time, 17; part-time, 9
Nationalities of staff: U.S., 13; U.K., 4; host, 1; other, 8
Grade levels: K – 12
Enrollment: K – 6, 45; 7 – 9, 27; 10 – 12, 13; total, 85
Nationalities of student body: U.S., 40; other, 45
Capacity: total, 160
Teacher/student ratio: 1/4
Tuition (annual): K, $2,140; 1 – 9, $3,560; 10 – 12, $4,440
Other fees: typing, yearbook, computer
School year: August to June

Year founded: 1957. **Type of school:** coed, day. **Governed by:** elected local mission board. **Sponsored by:** UFM International. **Accredited by:** Southern.

Curriculum/physical plant

Type: U.S., U.K., German/Swiss (grades 1 – 9). **Languages of instruction:** English, German. **Languages taught:** German, Portuguese. **Special curricular:** chorus, physical education, computer instruction. **Extracurricular:** drama, yearbook, photography, field trips, stamp club. **Sports:** basketball, soccer, swimming, volleyball. **Tests:** PSAT, SAT, ACT, AP, GCSE, Stanford. **Graduates attending college:** 95%. **Graduates have attended:** Wheaton, Biola, Hardin-Simmons, Georgia Tech, Aberdeen (Scotland). **Location:** 3 kilometers outside city. **Campus:** 22 acres. **Libraries (English and German):** 15,000 volumes. **Facilities:** auditorium, tennis court, gymnasium, 2 playing fields, science lab, computer lab, swimming pool, air conditioning.

BELO HORIZONTE

Associacao Internacional de Educacao

Street address: Av. Dom Joao VI, 3002-Buritis, Belo Horizonte,
Minas Gerais, Brazil
Phone: (55)(31)3122711 **Facsimile:** (55)(31)3122918
Mail: Caixa Postal 2.501, 30.161 Belo Horizonte, Minas Gerais, Brazil
U.S. mail: (no personal name) American School/Belo Horizonte,
U.S.I.S. Unit 3505, APO AA 34030
Director: Sid R. Stewart
Assistant director/IB coordinator: Padric Piper
Staff: full-time, 12; part-time, 2
Nationalities of staff: U.S., 10; host, 4
Grade levels: preK – 12
Enrollment: preK, 4; K, 4; 1 – 6, 40; 7 – 9, 25; 10 – 12, 28; total, 101
Nationalities of student body: U.S., 38; U.K., 4; host, 34; other, 25
Capacity: preK, 5; K, 5; 1 – 6, 60; 7 – 9, 45; 10 – 12, 45; total, 160
Teacher/student ratio: 1/8
Tuition (annual): preK, $4,670; K – 6, $6,838; 7 – 12, $8,354
Other fees (annual): registration*, $420; capital levy*, $1,300; busing,
$1,000; books, $500; cap fund, $900
School year: August to June

Year founded: 1956. **Type of school:** coed, day, private nonprofit.
Governed by: elected board of governors. **Sponsored by:** association of
parents. **Accredited by:** Southern.

Curriculum/physical plant
Type: U.S., IB. **Languages taught:** French, Portuguese. **Staff specialist:**
counselor. **Special curricular:** physical education, computer instruction.
Extracurricular: drama, computers, yearbook. **Sports:** basketball, soccer,
volleyball. **Tests:** PSAT, SAT, ACT, IB, Iowa. **Graduates attending college:**
90%. **Graduates have attended:** Stanford, Keio U. (Tokyo), U. of Southern
California, Stetson U., U. of Florida. **Location:** in suburban area, 20
kilometers from city center. **Campus:** 26,000 square meters. **Library:** 14,000
volumes. **Facilities:** 5 buildings, 10 classrooms, cafeteria, infirmary, gymnasium, 2 playing fields, science lab, computer lab, AV equipment.

*Once only fee

BRASILIA

AMERICAN SCHOOL OF BRASILIA

Street address: Avenida L-2 Sul, SGAS Q-605-E, Brasilia, D.F., Brazil
Phone: (55)(61)2433237   **Facsimile:** (55)(61)2444303
U.S. mail: Headmaster, American School of Brasilia, American
  Embassy/Brasilia, Unit 3500, APO AA 34030
Headmaster: Paul Greben, Ph.D.
Secondary school principal: Terry Waters, Ph.D.
Elementary school principal: G. Michael Anthony
Director of guidance: David A. Topham
Staff: full-time, 60
Nationalities of staff: U.S., 35; host, 20; other, 5
Grade levels: preK – 12
Enrollment: preK – 6, 375; 7 – 12, 245; total, 620
Nationalities of student body: U.S., 124; host, 370; other, 126
Teacher/student ratio: 1/10
Tuition (annual): preK – 6, $5,587; 7 – 12, $6,988
Other fees (annual): registration*, $2,500
School year: August to June

Year founded: 1964. **Type of school:** coed, day. **Governed by:** elected board of directors. **Accredited by:** Southern.

Curriculum/physical plant

Type: U.S. **Languages of instruction:** English, Portuguese. **Languages taught:** English, French, Portuguese. **Staff specialists:** reading, counselor, learning disabilities, nurse, gifted. **Special programs:** ESL, advanced placement. **Special curricular:** art, chorus, physical education, computer instruction. **Extracurricular:** drama, computers, yearbook, photography, field trips. **Sports:** basketball, soccer, softball, girls' volleyball, Brazilian salao. **Organizations**: National Junior Honor Society, student council, National Honor Society. **Tests:** SSAT, PSAT, SAT, ACT, AP, Iowa, DAT. **Graduates attending college:** 90%. **Graduates have attended:** U. of Lowell, Lafayette, U. of Pennsylvania, Brown, Harvard. **Location:** 5 minutes from downtown area. **Campus:** 7 acres. **Library:** 16,300 volumes. **Facilities:** 5 buildings, 39 classrooms, cafeteria, infirmary, tennis court, gymnasium, playing field, 3 science labs, computer lab, partial air conditioning.

*Once only fee

CAMPINAS

ESCOLA AMERICANA DE CAMPINAS

Street address: Rua Cajamar 35, Chacara de Barra, Campinas,
Sao Paulo, Brazil
Phone: (55)(192)517377   **Facsimile:** (55)(192)532321
Mail: Caixa Postal 1183, 13.001-970 Campinas, SP, Brazil
Superintendent: David E. Cardenas
Principal: Judith Buonamano
Staff: full-time, 30; part-time, 8
Nationalities of staff: U.S., 13; host, 25
Grade levels: preK – 12
Enrollment: preK, 44; K, 23; 1 – 6, 148; 7 – 9, 54; 10 – 12, 42;
total, 311
Nationalities of student body: U.S., 97; host, 151; other, 63
Capacity: preK, 44; K, 22; 1 – 6, 158; 7 – 9, 81; 10 – 12, 81; total, 386
Teacher/student ratio: 1/9
Tuition (annual): preK – K, $2,850; 1 – 6, $4,000; 7 – 12, $4,500
Other fees (annual): registration*, $2,000; busing, $800
School year: August to June

Year founded: 1957. **Type of school:** coed, day, private nonprofit.
Governed by: elected board of directors. **Accredited by:** Southern.

Curriculum/physical plant

Type: U.S., Brazilian, IB. **Languages of instruction:** English, Portuguese. **Languages taught:** French, Portuguese. **Staff specialists:** computer, counselor, psychologist, learning disabilities, gifted. **Special programs:** advanced placement, honors sections, independent study, remedial, gifted. **Special curricular:** art, physical education, computer instruction, music. **Extracurricular:** computers, yearbook, newspaper, literary magazine, field trips. **Sports:** basketball, softball, volleyball, indoor soccer, outdoor soccer, golf, track. **Tests:** PSAT, SAT, ACT, IB, AP, Iowa. **Graduates attending college:** 100%. **Graduates have attended:** Yale, MIT, Smith, Cornell, Princeton. **Location:** 10 minutes from center of Campinas. **Campus:** 14 acres. **Library:** 15,000 volumes. **Facilities:** 7 buildings, 35 classrooms, auditorium, tennis court, gymnasium, 2 playing fields, 2 science labs, 2 computer labs.

*Once only fee

CURITIBA

INTERNATIONAL SCHOOL OF CURITIBA

Street address: Av. Desembargador Hugo Simas, 1800, Bom Retiro, Curitiba, Parana, Brazil 80520-250
Phone: (55)(41)3386611   **Facsimile:** (55)(41)3386782
Mail: PO Box 7004, Curitiba, Brazil, 80230-150
Director: Ronald James McCluskey
Business manager: Jaime Figueiredo de Souza
Staff: full-time, 16; part-time, 6
Nationalities of staff: U.S., 10; host, 10; other, 2
Grade levels: preK – 12
Enrollment: preK, 14; K, 10; 1 – 6, 66; 7 – 9, 44; total, 134
Nationalities of student body: U.S., 16; host, 74; other, 44
Capacity: preK, 20; K, 20; 1 – 6, 60; 7 – 9, 40; 10 – 12, 40; total, 180
Teacher/student ratio: 1/7
Tuition (annual): preK – 6, $4,800; 7 – 12, $6,000
Other fees: enrollment: K – 12, $3,000
School year: August to June

Year founded: 1959. **Type of school:** coed, day, private nonprofit. **Governed by:** elected association of families via board of directors. **Sponsored by:** association of parents. **Accredited by:** Southern.

Curriculum/physical plant

Type: U.S. **Languages of instruction:** English, Portuguese. **Languages taught:** Spanish, Swedish. **Staff specialists:** reading, computer, counselor. **Special programs:** ESL, independent study, remedial, college-prep seminar. **Special curricular:** art, physical education, computer instruction, music. **Extracurricular:** computers, yearbook, excursions/expeditions, field trips, judo. **Sports:** basketball, volleyball, full-field soccer. **Tests:** PSAT, SAT, Iowa. **Graduates attending college:** 95%. **Graduates have attended:** Kansas State, U. of Arizona, Bradley U., Duquesne. **Location:** in Curitiba. **Campus:** 7,000 square meters. **Facilities:** 3 buildings, 15 classrooms, library, cafeteria, gymnasium, 2 courts, soccer field, math lab, science lab, computer lab, video room, all-purpose room.

PORTO ALEGRE

PAN AMERICAN SCHOOL OF PORTO ALEGRE

Street address: Rua João Paetzel 440, Porto Alegre, Rio Grande do Sul, Brazil
Phone/facsimile (55)(51)3345866
Mail: Rua João Paetzel 440, Três Figueiras, Porto Alegre, RS, Brazil 91.330

Director: Jennifer Sughrue
Business manager: Sérgio Nunes
Staff: full-time, 10; part-time, 5
Nationalities of staff: U.S., 6; host, 9
Grade levels: preK – 9
Enrollment: preK, 11; K, 9; 1 – 6, 47; 7 – 9, 10; total, 77
Nationalities of student body: U.S., 14; host, 43; other, 20
Capacity: preK, 15; K, 15; 1 – 6, 50; 7 – 8, 20; total, 100
Teacher/student ratio: 1/6
Tuition (annual): preK, $4,680; K – 9, $6,090
Other fees (annual): registration, $900; development fee, $240
School year: August to June

Year founded: 1966. **Type of school:** coed, day, private nonprofit.
Governed by: elected board of directors. **Sponsored by:** Association of P.A.S.
Accredited by: MEC, Southern.

Curriculum/physical plant
Type: U.S. **Languages of instruction:** English, Portuguese. **Languages taught:** Portuguese. **Staff specialists:** computer, counselor. **Special programs:** ESL. **Special curricular:** physical education, computer instruction. **Extracurricular:** computers, newspaper, field trips, soccer. **Tests:** PSAT, SAT, Iowa. **Location:** in city of Porto Alegre. **Library:** 5,000 volumes. **Facilities:** 1 building, 12 classrooms, cafeteria, science lab, basketball court.

RECIFE

AMERICAN SCHOOL OF RECIFE

Street address: Rua Sa e Souza, 408, Boa Viagem, Recife,
  Pernambuco, Brazil 51030–060
Phone: (55)(81)3414716   Facsimile: (55)(81)3410142
U.S. mail: (no personal name) Superintendent, American School of
  Recife, c/o U.S. Consulate – Recife, APO AA, Unit 3503, 34030
Superintendent: Helen Ruth VanDerVeer Gueiros
Principal: Norman E. Kuhne
Portuguese coordinator: Helma Barbosa
Business manager: Fernanda Teodoro
Staff: full-time, 28; part-time, 12
Nationalities of staff: U.S., 14; host, 20; other, 6
Grade levels: preK – 12
Enrollment: preK, 20; K, 22; 1 – 5, 115; 6 – 8, 50; 9 – 12, 59;
  total, 266
Nationalities of student body: U.S., 29; host, 185; other, 52
Capacity: preK, 32; K, 32; 1 – 5, 150; 6 – 8, 66; 9 – 12, 70; total, 350
Teacher/student ratio: 1/8
Tuition (annual): preK – K, $2,700; 1 – 6, $3,700; 7 – 12, $4,300
Other fees: registration*, $90; re-registration, $45; capital levy*, $1,000

School year: August to June

Year founded: 1966. **Type of school:** coed, day, private nonprofit. **Governed by:** elected board of directors. **Accredited by:** Southern.

Curriculum/physical plant

Type: U.S., Brazilian university requirements. **Languages taught:** French, German, Portuguese. **Staff specialists:** math, computer, nurse, guidance counselor. **Special programs:** ESL, independent study, remedial. **Special curricular:** art, chorus, physical education, computer instruction, Model UN. **Extracurricular:** drama, Math Counts, Odyssey of the Mind, stamp club, calligraphy, woodcraft. **Sports:** basketball, soccer, softball, volleyball. **Tests:** PSAT, SAT, ACT, TOEFL, Iowa, SLEP, ESL, reading. **Graduates attending college:** 100%. **Graduates have attended:** Texas A&M, Georgetown, Purdue, Indiana U., Boston U. **Location:** in suburban area adjacent to city. **Campus:** 8.5 acres. **Library:** 9,000 volumes. **Facilities:** 8 buildings, 23 classrooms, covered play area, science lab, AV room, canteen, partial air conditioning.

*Once only fee

RIO DE JANEIRO

ESCOLA AMERICANA DO RIO DE JANEIRO

Street address: 132 Estrada da Gávea, 22451 Rio de Janeiro, RJ-Brazil
Phone: (55)(21)3220825   **Facsimile:** (55)(21)3220050/3221293
   Telex: 3912123972 EARJ BR
Headmaster: Dennis Klumpp
High school principal: Lee Fertig
Middle school principal: Ken Parker
Elementary school principal: Robert Woods
Early childhood coordinator: Suely Pecanha
Staff: full-time, 102; part-time, 12
Nationalities of staff: U.S., 30; U.K., 3; host, 60; other, 21
Grade levels: preK – 12
Enrollment: preK, 145; K, 55; 1 – 5, 320; 6 – 8, 200; 9 – 12, 185; total, 905
Nationalities of student body: U.S., 225; U.K., 10; host, 570; other, 100
Capacity: preK, 150; K, 60; 1 – 5, 410; 6 – 8, 240; 9 – 12, 255; total, 1,115
Teacher/student ratio: 1/8
Tuition (annual): preK – 5, $6,400; 6 – 8, $7,175; 9 – 12, $7,540
Other fees: capital levy*, $3,000
School year: August through June

Year founded: 1937. **Type of school:** coed, day, private nonprofit. **Governed by:** appointed board of directors. **Sponsored by:** community. **Accredited by:** Southern. **Regional organizations:** AASB, AASSA, AAIE.

Curriculum

Type: U.S., IB. **Languages taught:** French, German, Portuguese. **Staff specialists:** computer, counselor, psychologist, learning disabilities, nurse, high capacity/high potential. **Special programs:** ESL. **Special curricular:** art, band, physical education, computer instruction. **Extracurricular:** drama, dance, instrumental music, computers, yearbook, newspaper, excursions/expeditions, field trips, National Honor Society. **Sports:** basketball, soccer, softball, track, volleyball, handball. **Tests:** PSAT, SAT, ACT, IB, AP, Iowa. **Graduates attending college:** 100%. **Graduates have attended:** Brandeis, Carleton, Stanford, Duke, Tufts.

Physical plant

Location: in suburban area, 8 kilometers west of city. **Campus:** 16.5 acres. **Library:** 30,000 volumes. **Facilities:** 9 buildings, 60 classrooms, auditorium, cafeteria, infirmary, 3 covered play areas, gymnasium, playing field, 6 science labs, 3 computer labs, swimming pool.

*Once only fee

SALVADOR

PAN AMERICAN SCHOOL OF BAHIA

Street address: Loteamento Patamares s/n, Salvador, Bahia, Brazil
Phone: (55)(71)2499099   **Facsimile:** (55)(71)2499090
Mail: Caixa Postal 231, 40.000 Salvador, Bahia, Brazil
U.S. mail: (no personal name) American Consular Agency PAS, Salvador, Brazil, APO Miami 34030
High school principal: Linda Lee Parcel
Preschool and elementary school principal: Dr. Mary Jo Heatherington
Staff: full-time, 35
Nationalities of staff: U.S., 21; host, 12; other, 2
Grade levels: preK – 12
Enrollment: preK, 53; K, 40; 1 – 6, 157; 7 – 9, 52; 10 – 12, 24; total, 326
Capacity: preK, 80; K, 40; 1 – 6, 250; 7 – 9, 100; 10 – 12, 60; total, 530
Teacher/student ratio: 1/9
Tuition (annual): preK – K, $3,168; 1 – 6, $4,332; 7 – 12, $4,908
Other fees (annual): registration*, $1,500; capital levy*, $6,000; busing, $1,100; ESL, $1,380
School year: August through June

Year founded: 1960. **Type of school:** coed, day, private nonprofit. **Governed by:** elected board of directors. **Accredited by:** Southern.

Curriculum/physical plant

Type: U.S., Brazilian college entrance. **Languages of instruction:** English, Portuguese. **Languages taught:** Portuguese. **Staff specialists:** computer, counselor, learning disabilities, nurse. **Special programs:** ESL. **Special curricular:** art, physical education, computer instruction. **Extracurricular:** computers, yearbook, field trips, National Honor Society. **Sports:** basketball, soccer, volleyball. **Tests:** SSAT, PSAT, SAT, Iowa. **Graduates attending college:** 100%. **Graduates have attended:** Bennington College, St. Olaf College, Jacksonville College. **Location:** near beach, 15 minutes from downtown Salvador. **Library:** 35,000 volumes. **Facilities:** 2 buildings, 29 classrooms, cafeteria, infirmary, covered play area, 2 gymnasiums, 2 playing fields, 2 science labs, computer lab.

*Once only fee

SAO PAULO

Associacao Escola Graduada de Sao Paulo

Street address: Av. Presidente Giovanni Gronchi, 4710, Sao Paulo, SP, Brazil
Phone: (55)(11)8422499   **Facsimile:** (55)(11)8429358
   Cable: AMERSCOL
Mail: Caixa Postal 7432; 01051 Sao Paulo, SP, Brazil
Superintendent: Günther Brandt, Ph.D.
Dean, secondary school: Fred F. Wesson
Dean, elementary school: Clifford Paulson
Dean, pre-primary school: (to be announced)
Dean, Brazilian studies: Angelina Fregonesi
Business manager: Rodolpho Lichy
Staff: full-time, 98; part-time, 7
Nationalities of staff: U.S., 54; host, 45; other, 6
Grade levels: N – 12
Enrollment: N – preK, 93; K, 81; 1 – 6, 442; 7 – 9, 205; 10 – 12, 187; total, 1,008
Nationalities of student body: U.S., 302; U.K., 15; host, 437; other, 254
Teacher/student ratio: 1/10
Tuition (annual): (estimated) N – preK, $7,500; K – 4, $9,000; 5 – 8, $10,000; 9 – 12, $11,000
Other fees (annual): registration*, $200; busing, $1,200; entrance*, $4,000
School year: August to June

Year founded: 1920. **Type of school:** coed, day, private nonprofit. **Governed by:** appointed board of directors. **Sponsored by:** American Chamber of Commerce. **Accredited by:** Southern.

Curriculum

Type: U.S., IB. **Languages taught:** French, Portuguese. **Staff specialists:** computer, counselor, learning disabilities, nurse, art, music. **Special programs:** ESL, advanced placement, IB. **Special curricular:** art, physical education, computer instruction, journalism, photography. **Extracurricular:** drama, yearbook, literary magazine, excursions/expeditions, field trips. **Sports:** basketball, soccer, softball, tennis, volleyball. **Clubs:** Brownies, Cub Scouts, National Honor Society, student council, thespian, chess. **Tests:** SSAT, PSAT, SAT, ACT, IB, AP, Iowa. **Graduates attending college:** 98%. **Graduates have attended:** Clark, Smith, U. of Pennsylvania, Colgate, Brown.

Physical plant

Location: mainly residential, fast-developing suburban area within city limits of Sao Paulo. **Campus:** 16 acres. **Library:** 36,500 volumes. **Facilities:** 12 buildings, 68 classrooms, auditorium, cafeteria, infirmary, covered play area, 6 tennis courts, gymnasium, 2 playing fields, 6 science labs, 3 computer labs, graphics department, AV center.

*Once only fee

ESCOLA MARIA IMACULADA

Street address: Rua Vigário João de Pontes, 537, Sao Paulo, Brazil
Phone: (55)(11)2477455/2477007   **Facsimile:** (55)(11)5217763
Mail: Caixa Postal 21293, Brooklin 04698 Sao Paulo-SP, Brazil
Superintendent: Gerald C. Gates
High school principal: Mary Ellen Dahl
Lower school principal: John Ciallelo
Brazilian program director: Silvia P. Barreto
Business manager: Peter F. Curran
Staff: full-time, 68; part-time, 7
Nationalities of staff: U.S., 30; U.K., 3; host, 35; other, 7
Grade levels: N – 12
Enrollment: N – preK, 73; K, 53; 1 – 6, 293; 7 – 9, 166; 10 – 12, 153; total, 738
Nationalities of student body: U.S., 132; host, 295; other, 311
Teacher/student ratio: 1/10
Tuition (annual): N – preK, $2,100; K – 6, $3,600; 7 – 12, $4,500
Other fees (annual): registration, $400; books, $200
School year: August to June

Year founded: 1947. **Type of school:** coed, day, church-related, private nonprofit. **Governed by:** appointed advisory council. **Sponsored by:** Oblates of Mary Immaculate. **Accredited by:** Southern.

Curriculum/physical plant

Type: U.S., Brazilian, IB. **Languages of instruction:** English, Portuguese. **Languages taught:** French, Spanish. **Staff specialists:** reading, computer, counselor, nurse. **Special programs:** ESL, honors sections, independent study, remedial, IB. **Special curricular:** art, physical education, computer instruction. **Extracurricular:** drama, gymnastics, computers, yearbook, newspaper, literary magazine, excursions/expeditions, field trips. **Sports:** basketball, soccer, tennis, track, volleyball, handball, indoor soccer, Olympic gym. **Clubs:** art, arts and crafts, computer, National Honor Society, scouts, student council, retreats, first aid, CPR. **Tests:** PSAT, SAT, ACT, TOEFL, IB, AP, Stanford, MAT, Otis-Lennon, DAT. **Graduates attending college:** 82%. **Graduates have attended:** Brown, Boston U., MIT, Cornell, Tufts. **Location:** in residential suburb of Sao Paulo. **Campus:** 4 acres. **Libraries:** 21,000 volumes. **Facilities:** 3 buildings, 45 classrooms, auditorium, cafeteria, infirmary, covered play area, 2 tennis courts, gymnasium, playing field, 2 science labs, computer lab, AV room, playgrounds.

PAN AMERICAN CHRISTIAN ACADEMY

Street address: Rua Cassio de Campo Nogueira, 393, Sao Paulo, Brazil
Phone/facsimile: (55)(11)5209655
Mail: Caixa Postal 12.491, 04798-970 Sao Paulo, SP, Brazil
Director: Eugene Berends, Ph.D.
Guidance counselor: Sharon Staples
High school coordinator: Robert Brennan
Head of library: Phyllis Cook
Staff: full-time, 28; part-time, 4
Nationalities of staff: U.S., 22; host, 9; other, 1
Grade levels: K – 12
Enrollment: K, 20; 1 – 6, 140; 7 – 9, 69; 10 – 12, 57; total, 286
Nationalities of student body: U.S., 120; host, 115; other, 51
Capacity: K, 25; 1 – 6, 170; 7 – 9, 75; 10 – 12, 80; total, 350
Teacher/student ratio: 1/9
Tuition (annual): K – 5, $2,220; 6 – 8, $2,520; 9 – 12, $3,480
Other fees: registration*, $400; books, $150; academic development, K – 8, $10; 9 – 12, $20
School year: August to June

Year founded: 1960. **Type of school:** coed, day, interdenominational, private nonprofit. **Governed by:** appointed board of directors. **Accredited by:** Southern, Ministry of Education and Culture. **Regional organizations:** AASSA, AASB.

Curriculum/physical plant

Type: U.S., Brazilian. **Languages of instruction:** English, Portuguese. **Staff specialists:** counselor, learning disabilities. **Special curricular:** art, chorus, physical education, computer instruction. **Extracurricular:** drama, choral music, instrumental music, computers, excursions/expeditions. **Sports:** basketball, cheerleading, soccer, softball, swimming, volleyball, track and field, futebol de salao. **Clubs:** National Honor Society, pep club. **Tests:** PSAT, SAT, ACT, TOEFL, Iowa, COGAT. **Graduates attending college:** 95%. **Graduates have attended:** Wheaton College, Cedarville College, U. of California at Berkeley, Johns Hopkins, U. of Texas. **Location:** near lake in southwestern part of city. **Campus:** 7.5 acres. **Library:** 10,000 volumes. **Facilities:** 5 buildings, 19 classrooms, cafeteria, 2 tennis courts, gymnasium, playing field, science lab, computer lab, swimming pool, AV equipment.

*Once only fee

ST. PAUL'S SCHOOL
ESCOLA BRITANICA DE SAO PAULO

Street address: Rua Juquia 166, Jardim Paulistano, CEP 01440, Sao Paulo, SP, Brazil
Phone: (55)(11)8533399   **Facsimile:** (55)(11)8533708
Mail: Caixa Postal 3472, CEP 01051, Sao Paulo, SP, Brazil
Headmaster: M. T. M. Casey McCann
Staff: full-time, 70
Nationalities of staff: U.K., 26; host, 44
Grade levels: age 3 – IGCSE, IB
Enrollment: ages 3 – 7, 250; ages 7 – 11, 250; ages 11 – 18, 280; total, 780
Nationalities of student body: U.K., 283; host, 276; other, 221
Capacity: pre-prep (ages 3 – 7), 210; preparatory (ages 7 – 11), 210; senior school (ages 11 – 18), 280; total, 700
Teacher/student ratio: 1/11
Tuition (annual): ages 3 – 4, $6,072; ages 4 – 11, $7,550; ages 11 – 18, $9,794
School year: August to June

Year founded: 1926. **Type of school:** coed, day, private nonprofit. **Governed by:** board of governors.

Curriculum/physical plant

Type: U.K., IGCSE, IB. **Languages taught:** English, French, Spanish, Portuguese. **Special programs:** ESL. **Special curricular:** art, physical education, computer instruction, choir, orchestra. **Extracurricular:** drama, instrumental music, computers, excursions/expeditions, field trips. **Tests:** IB, Portuguese 'A' level, IGCSE. **Graduates attending college:** 80%. **Graduates have attended:** British, Brazilian, North American, and other Latin American universities. **Location:** in city, 5 minutes' walk to shopping, banking, and center. **Campus:** 17,000 square meters. **Library:** 6,000 volumes. **Facilities:** 3 buildings, 50 classrooms, auditorium, cafeteria, infirmary, 2 tennis courts, gymnasium, playing field, 6 science labs, computer lab, swimming pool, AV department.

SANTOS

Escola Americana de Santos

Address: Rua Lucinda de Matos, 293-Nova Cintra, 11080-Santos, SP, Brazil   **Mail:** Caixa Postal 810, Santos, SP, Brazil

DEPENDABILITY
QUALITY
EXPERIENCE

Chief School Administrator Search Program

International Schools Services offers assistance in the selection of the chief school administrator. We utilize worldwide screening, in-depth evaluation, personalized service, board/community consultation, and the experience gained from conducting over one hundred searches to ensure that qualified candidates are presented, that all deadlines are met, and that all issues are resolved in a professional manner.

International Schools Services

15 Roszel Road, PO Box 5910
Princeton, New Jersey 08543
Telephone: 609-452-0990
Facsimile: 609-452-2690

BULGARIA

Region: Europe
Size: 44,365 square miles
Population: 8,910,000
Capital: Sofia

Telephone code: 359
Currency: leva
Languages: Bulgarian, Turkish

SOFIA

AMERICAN COLLEGE OF SOFIA

Street address: Floyd Black Lane, Sofia 1799, Bulgaria
Phone: (359)(2)763041   **Facsimile:** (359)(2)803943
    U.S. phone: (1)(212)3192453
Mail: PO Box 873, Sofia 1000, Bulgaria
U.S. mail: Director, American College of Sofia, 850 Third Avenue, 18th
    floor, New York, NY 10022, U.S.A.
Director: Roger Whitaker, Ph.D.
Administrative coordinator: Rositsa Bateson
Business manager: Dr. Vladimir Zlatev
Staff: full-time, 9; part-time, 11
Nationalities of staff: U.S., 10; host, 10
Grade levels: prep ESL and 9, adding one grade each year, to grade
    12 by 1997
Enrollment: total, 200
Nationalities of student body: host, 200
Capacity: total, 200
Teacher/student ratio: 1/14
Tuition (annual): 10,000**
Other fees: registration, $12
School year: September to June

Year founded: 1860's, closed 1942 and reopened 1992. **Type of school:**
coed, private nonprofit. **Governed by:** elected board of trustees. **Sponsored
by:** Sofia-American Schools, Inc.

Curriculum/physical plant

Type: U.S., Bulgarian. **Languages taught:** French, German, Bulgarian.
Staff specialists: math, computer, nurse. **Special programs:** ESL. **Special
curricular:** art, chorus, physical education, computer instruction. **Extracurricular:** drama, gymnastics, dance, choral music, instrumental music, computers, newspaper, field trips, sports. **Clubs:** art, dance, student newspaper,
music, tennis, language and culture. **Location:** at base of 6,000 foot mountain on outskirts of capital city. **Campus:** 50 acres. **Facilities:** 6 academic and
6 residential buildings, auditorium, library, cafeteria, infirmary, tennis court,
playing field, science lab, computer lab.

**Bulgarian leva

ANGLO-AMERICAN SCHOOL

Street address: 8, Studen Kladenets, 1619 Sofia, Bulgaria
Phone: (359)(2)570267 **Facsimile:** (359)(2)570161
 Telex: 86522690 AM EMB **Cable:** AM EMB Sofia
U.S. mail: c/o American Embassy, Sofia, Department of State,
 Washington, D.C. 20521-5740
Director: Frank Sawyer
Curriculum coordinator: Glenda Gay Scott
Staff: full-time, 14; part-time, 2
Nationalities of staff: U.S., 7; U.K., 6; host, 3
Grade levels: preK – 8
Enrollment: preK, 15; K, 15; 1 – 8, 100; total, 130
Nationalities of student body: U.S., 32; U.K., 20; host, 10; other, 68
Capacity: preK, 15; K, 15; 1 – 6, 112; 7 – 8, 36; total, 178
Teacher/student ratio: 1/9
Tuition (annual): preK, $2,000; K – 8, $7,000
Other fees: registration*, $250; capital levy*, $1,250 (new students),
 $250 (returning students); busing, $545
School year: August to June

Year founded: 1967. **Type of school:** coed, day. **Governed by:** board appointed by U.S. and British ambassadors, plus representative of PTO. **Accredited by:** New England, ECIS.

Curriculum/physical plant

 Type: U.S. **Languages taught:** French. **Staff specialists:** reading, computer, art, ESL, library, music, physical education. **Extracurricular:** choral music, computers, newspaper, excursions/expeditions, field trips. **Sports:** skiing, swimming, volleyball, skating. **Tests:** SAT. **Location:** in suburb, Knjazhevo. **Library:** 7,000 volumes. **Facilities:** 7 buildings, 14 classrooms, small playground.

1992-93 listing

*Once only fee

BURKINA FASO

Region: West Africa
Size: 105,869 square miles
Population: 9,359,000
Capital: Ouagadougou

Telephone code: 226
Currency: CFA franc
Languages: French, Sudanic tribal
languages

OUAGADOUGOU

INTERNATIONAL SCHOOL OF OUAGADOUGOU

Phone: (226)362143   **Facsimile:** (226)308903   **Telex:** 9855290 BF
   Cable: AMEMB OUAGA
Mail: BP 35, Ouagadougou 01, Burkina Faso
U.S. mail: Administrative Officer (ISO), Ouagadougou, Department of
   State, Washington, D.C. 20521-2440
Director: Bernard Holler, Ph.D.
Staff: full-time, 6; part-time, 5
Nationalities of staff: U.S., 7; other, 4
Grade levels: preK – 8 (9 – 12 tutorial correspondence)
Enrollment: preK, 21; K, 11; 1 – 6, 40; 7 – 9, 14; total, 86
Nationalities of student body: U.S., 23; other, 63
Capacity: preK, 15; K, 15; 1 – 6, 120; 7 – 9, 20; total, 170
Teacher/student ratio: 1/10
Tuition (annual): preK, $2,850; K, $7,220; 1 – 2, $8,500;
   3 – 4, $9,125; 5 – 8, $9,450; 9 – 12, $9,800
Other fees: capital levy*, $3,000
School year: September to June

Year founded: 1977. **Type of school:** coed, day, private nonprofit.
Governed by: elected school board. **Accredited by:** Middle States.

Curriculum/physical plant
   Type: U.S. **Languages taught:** French. **Staff specialists:** computer,
librarian. **Special curricular:** art, chorus, physical education, computer
instruction, environmental education. **Extracurricular:** drama, dance, choral music, computers, yearbook, excursions/expeditions, field trips. **Sports:**
soccer, softball, swimming, tennis, karate. **Tests:** SSAT, Iowa. **Location:** in
residential area outside Ouagadougou. **Campus:** 5 acres. **Library:** over 8,000
volumes. **Facilities:** 7 buildings, 12 classrooms, infirmary, science lab,
computer lab, softball/soccer field, access to swimming pool, air conditioning,
tennis court, recreation, snack bar.

*Once only fee

CAMBODIA _____

Region: South Asia
Size: 70,238 square miles
Population: 7,146,000
Capital: Phnom Penh

Telephone code: 855
Currency: riel
Languages: Khmer, French

PHNOM PENH

INTERNATIONAL SCHOOL OF PHNOM PENH – CAMBODIA

Phone: (855)(23)26057   **Facsimile:** (855)(23)26209
Mail: PO Box 2420, Bangkok, 10501, Thailand
Principal: Ann Greve
Business manager: Helga Smith
Staff: full-time, 6; part-time, 8
Nationalities of staff: U.S., 5; host, 8; other, 1
Grade levels: preK – 9
Enrollment: preK, 20; K, 20; 1 – 6, 80; 7 – 9, 10; total, 130
Nationalities of student body: U.S., 20; U.K., 10; other, 100
Teacher/student ratio: 1/13
Tuition: preK, $2,000; K, $3,200; 1 – 9, $3,900
Other fees: registration, $500; enrollment*, $1,500
School year: August to June

Year founded: 1989. **Type of school:** coed, day, private nonprofit. **Governed by:** elected board of directors.

Curriculum/physical plant

Type: U.S., international. **Languages taught:** French, Khmer. **Staff specialists:** reading, math. **Special programs:** ESL. **Special curricular:** art, chorus, physical education. **Extracurricular:** excursions/expeditions, field trips. **Location:** in Phnom Penh. **Facilities:** 2 buildings, 7 classrooms, library, outdoor cafeteria, art room, access to sports stadium.

*Once only fee

CAMEROON

Region: West Africa
Size: 179,714 square miles
Population: 11,390,000
Capital: Yaounde

Telephone code: 237
Currency: CFA franc
Languages: English, French,
24 African groups

DOUALA

AMERICAN SCHOOL OF DOUALA

Street address: 39 Rue de Palmier, Douala, Cameroon
Phone: (237)421437   **Facsimile:** (237)427790
Mail: BP 1909, Douala, Cameroon, West Africa
U.S. mail: Administrative Officer (ASD), Department of State—Douala,
Washington, DC 20521-2530
Administrator: June C. Burrow
Staff: full-time, 6; part-time, 2
Nationalities of staff: U.S., 3; other, 5
Grade levels: preK – 8
Enrollment: preK, 14; K, 7; 1 – 6, 28; 7 – 8, 3; total, 52
Nationalities of student body: U.S., 14; U.K., 3; host, 5; other, 30
Capacity: preK, 20; K, 10; 1 – 6, 60; 7 – 8, 20; total, 110
Teacher/student ratio: 1/7
Tuition: preK, 840,000**; K, 1,260,000; 1 – 8, 1,890,000
Other fees: registration*, 100,000**; annual entry fee, 45,000
School year: September to June

Year founded: 1978. **Type of school:** coed, day, private nonprofit.
Governed by: elected school board. **Regional organizations:** ECIS, AISA.

Curriculum/physical plant
Type: U.S. **Languages taught:** French. **Staff specialists:** speech therapist. **Special programs:** ESL. **Special curricular:** art, physical education,
computer instruction, music, Cameroonian culture. **Extracurricular:** musical drama, modern dance, African dance, needlework, sewing, crafts, swimming. **Clubs:** computer, game, video. **Tests:** Iowa, COGAT. **Location:** in
residential area of Douala. **Campus:** 1.5 acres. **Library:** 6,000 volumes.
Facilities: 1 building (4 portables), 13 classrooms, 2 playing fields, science
lab, air conditioning.

*Once only fee   **CFA franc

YAOUNDE

AMERICAN SCHOOL OF YAOUNDE

Phone: (237)230421   **Facsimile:** (237)236011
   Telex: 9788223 KN (c/o U.S. Embassy)
Mail: B.P. 7475, Yaounde, Cameroon
U.S. mail: (no personal name) Department of State – Yaounde
   Washington, D.C. 20521-2520
Director: Kathryn S. Edwards, Ph.D.
Administrative assistant: Valerie Ngolle
Head of library: Caroline Peck
Head of computer services: Carol McCammon
Staff: full-time, 19; part-time, 9
Nationalities of staff: U.S., 16; U.K., 1; host, 3; other, 8
Grade levels: preK – 10
Dschang branch campus: K – 8 (temporarily closed)
Enrollment: preK, 45; K, 15; 1 – 5, 80; 6 – 10, 60; total, 200
Nationalities of student body: U.S., 75; U.K., 2; host, 16; other, 107
Capacity: preK, 54; K, 18; 1 – 5, 100; 6 – 10, 90; total, 262
Teacher/student ratio: 1/9
Tuition (annual): preK, $1,666; K, $5,500; 1 – 5, $7,050;
   6 – 8, $7,450; 9 – 10, $7,600
Other fees (annual): registration*, $50; busing, $1,000; ESL, $850
School year: September to June

Year founded: 1964. **Type of school:** coed, day, private nonprofit.
Governed by: elected board of directors. **Accredited by:** Middle States, ECIS
(associate member). **Regional organization:** AISA.

Curriculum/physical plant
   Type: U.S. **Languages taught:** French. **Staff specialists:** computer,
music, physical education. **Special programs:** ESL, limited remedial. **Special
curricular:** art, physical education, computer instruction, swimming, music.
Extracurricular: drama, dance, choral music, instrumental music, computers, yearbook, excursions/expeditions, field trips. **Sports:** basketball, soccer,
softball, swimming, tennis, volleyball, karate, mountain climbing. **Clubs:** arts
and crafts, French, student council, knowledge bowl, Girl Scouts, Boy Scouts,
National Junior Honor Society. **Tests:** SSAT, PSAT, TOEFL, Iowa, COGAT.
Location: in city. **Campus:** 5 acres; separate half-acre for early childhood
center. **Library:** 14,000 volumes. **Facilities:** 6 buildings, 19 classrooms, 4
tennis courts, playing field, science lab, computer lab, swimming pool, shared
facilities with adjacent American club.

*Once only fee

CANADA _____

Region: North America
Size: 3,849,000 square miles
Population: 26,835,500
Capital: Ottawa

Telephone code: 1
Currency: Canadian dollar
Languages: English, French

VICTORIA, BRITISH COLUMBIA

LESTER B. PEARSON COLLEGE OF THE PACIFIC

Street address: Pearson College Drive, Victoria, British Columbia,
Canada
Phone: (1)(604)4785591   **Facsimile:** (1)(604)4786421
   Telex: 3890497488 UWC CANADA
Mail: RR #1, Victoria, British Columbia, Canada, V9B 5T7
Director: James McLellan
Director of studies: Jean Godin
IB coordinator: Eileen Dombrowski
Staff: full-time, 20; part-time, 4
Nationalities of staff: host, 20; other, 4
Grade levels: IB (grades 12 – 13)
Enrollment: 12 – 13, 204
Nationalities of student body: U.S., 6; host, 57; other, 141
Capacity: total, 200
Teacher/student ratio: 1/9
Boarders: boys, 100; girls, 104   **Grades:** 12 – 13
   Program: planned 7-day
Tuition and fees: all attend on scholarships
School year: September to May

Year founded: 1974. **Type of school:** coed, boarding, nonprofit. **Governed by:** elected board of trustees.

Curriculum
   Type: IB. **Languages of instruction:** English, French, Spanish. **Languages taught:** French, Spanish, German, Japanese, Chinese. **Staff specialists:** counselor, nurse. **Special programs:** ESL, international affairs. **Special curricular:** art, computer instruction, choir. **Extracurricular:** drama, dance, instrumental music, computers, yearbook, newspaper, photography, excursions/expeditions, field trips, ham radio club. **Service organizations:** land search and rescue, sea, forestry, humanitarian, firefighting. **Tests:** SAT, ACT, TOEFL, IB. **Graduates attending college:** 98%.

Physical plant
   Location: on forested seafront, 18 miles west of the city of Victoria. **Campus:** 80 acres. **Library:** 13,500 volumes. **Facilities:** 20 buildings, 15 classrooms, auditorium, cafeteria, infirmary, 2 tennis courts, playing field, 4 science labs, computer lab, swimming pool, 5 residence buildings.

CHAD ────────────────────────────────

Region: Africa
Size: 495,755 square miles
Population: 5,122,000
Capital: N'Djamena

Telephone code: 235
Currency: CFA franc
Languages: French, Arabic

N'DJAMENA

AMERICAN INTERNATIONAL SCHOOL OF N'DJAMENA

Phone: (235)512103   **Facsimile:** (235)515002/513372
   Telex: 9845203 KD
Mail: BP 413, N'Djamena, Chad
U.S. mail: Administrator, American International School of
   N'Djamena, U.S. Embassy (N'Djamena, Chad), Department of
   State, Washington, D.C. 20521-2410
Administrator: Richard Ashley
Staff: full-time, 6; part-time, 2
Nationalities of staff: U.S., 5; other, 3
Grade levels: K – 7
Enrollment: K – 1, 9; 2 – 3, 10; 4 – 5, 10; 6 – 7, 7; total, 36
Nationalities of student body: U.S., 25; other, 11
Capacity: K – 1, 10; 2 – 3, 10; 4 – 5, 10; 6 – 7, 10; total, 40
Teacher/student ratio: 1/5
Tuition (annual): K – 7, $11,500
School year: September to June

Year founded: 1985. **Type of school:** coed, day. **Governed by:** board of directors.

Curriculum/physical plant
Type: U.S. **Languages taught:** French. **Special curricular:** art, physical education, computer instruction, music, library. **Extracurricular:** newspaper, field trips. **Sports:** soccer, softball, swimming, volleyball. **Tests:** PSAT, Iowa. **Location:** within city limits. **Campus:** .5 acre. **Library:** 2,500 volumes. **Facilities:** 4 classrooms, playing field, 8 computers, AV room, offices, air conditioning.

CHILE

Region: South America
Size: 292,257 square miles
Population: 13,286,000
Capital: Santiago

Telephone code: 56
Currency: peso
Language: Spanish

CONCEPCION

St. John's School

Street address: Pedro de Valdivia 1711, Concepcion, Chile
Phone: (56)(41)331044   **Facsimile:** (56)(41)340809
Mail: Casilla 284, Concepcion, Chile
Headmaster: Alun Cooper
Other academic head: Patricia Artigues
Business manager: Victor Pino
Staff: full-time, 72; part-time, 12
Nationalities of staff: U.K., 4; host, 80
Grade levels: preK – 12
Enrollment: preK, 90; K, 90; 1 – 6, 500; 7 – 9, 78; 10 – 12, 268; total, 1,026
Nationalities of student body: U.S., 10; U.K., 24; other, 992
Capacity: preK, 90; K, 90; 1 – 6, 540; 7 – 9, 270; 10 – 12, 270; total, 1,260
Teacher/student ratio: 1/13
Tuition (annual): preK – 12, 384,000**
Other fees (annual): registration, 50,000**; busing, 60,000
School year: March to December

Year founded: 1942. **Type of school:** coed, day, private nonprofit. **Governed by:** elected board of governors.

Curriculum/physical plant

Type: Chilean, IB. **Languages of instruction:** English, Spanish. **Languages taught:** English, Spanish. **Staff specialists:** reading, math, computer, counselor, learning disabilities, nurse. **Special programs:** remedial. **Special curricular:** art, chorus, physical education, computer instruction, vocational. **Extracurricular:** drama, gymnastics, dance, choral music, instrumental music, computers, yearbook, literary magazine, photography, excursions/expeditions. **Sports:** basketball, football, hockey, rugby, volleyball, athletics. **Tests:** IB, GCSE. **Graduates attending college:** 95%. **Graduates have attended:** U. de Concepcion, U. de Chile, U. de Santiago. **Location:** in suburban area, 3 kilometers from Concepcion. **Facilities:** 8 buildings, 45 classrooms, cafeteria, tennis court, gymnasium, playing fields, science labs, computer labs.

**Chilean peso

SANTIAGO

THE GRANGE SCHOOL S.A.

Street address: Principe de Gales 6154, Santiago, Chile
Phone: (56)(2)2771181   **Facsimile:** (56)(2)2770946
Mail: Casilla 218, Correo 12, Santiago, Chile
Headmaster: James Cowan
Deputy head: John MacKenzie
Head, senior school: Donald MacAulay
Business manager: Ronald G. Brown
Staff: full-time, 115; part-time, 10
Nationalities of staff: U.K., 10; host, 115
Grade levels: preK – 12
Enrollment: preK, 120; K, 120; 1 – 6, 730; 7 – 9, 375; 10 – 12, 375;
   total, 1,720
Teacher/student ratio: 1/14
Tuition (annual): preK – K, $1,594; 1 – 12, $2,114
Other fees (annual): registration, $30; insurance, $44; lunch, $400;
   4 shares/bonds, $390 (saleable on market)
School year: March to December

Year founded: 1928. **Type of school:** coed, day, private nonprofit.
Governed by: elected limited liability company. **Accredited by:** Chilean
Ministry of Education.

Curriculum/physical plant

Type: Chilean, IB. **Languages of instruction:** English, Spanish. **Languages taught:** French. **Staff specialists:** reading, math, computer, counselor, psychologist, learning disabilities, nurse. **Special programs:** ESL, remedial. **Special curricular:** art, chorus, band, physical education, computer instruction, vocational. **Extracurricular:** drama, gymnastics, dance, choral music, instrumental music, computers, yearbook, literary magazine, photography, excursions/expeditions. **Sports:** basketball, football, hockey, rugby, tennis, volleyball, table tennis, karate. **Clubs:** arts and crafts, computer, philately, social service, chess, journalism, outdoor pursuits, technical drawing. **Tests:** IB, Chilean universities' entrance exams, O-levels Cambridge.
Graduates attending college: 80%. **Graduates have attended:** Texas A&M, Utah State, U. of California at Berkeley, Cambridge, Vassar. **Location:** 6 kilometers from city center. **Campus:** 8 hectares. **Library:** 14,500 volumes.
Facilities: 16 buildings, 94 classrooms, auditorium, cafeteria, infirmary, 2 gymnasiums, playing field, 4 science labs, 2 computer labs, creative arts building.

THE INTERNATIONAL PREPARATORY SCHOOL

Phone: (56)(2)2151094/2153783   **Facsimile:** (56)(2)2153848
Mail: Pastor Fernandez 16001, Lo Barnechea, Santiago, Chile
Headmistress: Lesley Easton Allen
Curriculum coordinator: Pamela Thomson
Financial administrator: Carlos Willson
Staff: full-time, 15; part-time, 8
Nationalities of staff: U.S., 3; U.K., 5; host, 4; other, 11
Grade levels: playgroup – 12
Enrollment: PG – K2, 49; 1 – 6, 68; 7 – 9, 13; 10 – 12, 12; total, 142
Nationalities of student body: U.S., 30; U.K., 28; host, 12; other, 72
Teacher/student ratio: 1/7
Tuition (annual): preK, $1,490; K, $4,660; 1 – 4, $5,200;
     5 – 6, $5,320; 7 – 12, $5,590
Other fees (annual): registration*, $3,500; book rental and materials,
     $350; matriculation, $130
School year: March to December

Year founded: 1976. **Type of school:** coed, day. **Governed by:** private
governing body. **Accredited by:** ECIS.

Curriculum
Type: British/U.S. **Languages taught:** French, Spanish. **Staff special-ists:** reading, math, speech/hearing, counselor, psychologist, learning dis-abilities, resource. **Special programs:** ESL, advanced placement, indepen-dent study, correspondence, remedial. **Special curricular:** art, physical education, computer instruction. **Extracurricular:** drama, gymnastics, dance, instrumental music, newspaper, scouts, horseback riding. **Sports:** baseball, football, tennis, athletics. **Clubs:** ecology, table tennis, chess, animal, back-gammon, book. **Tests:** Chilean Ministry of Education examinations, Common Entrance examinations to independent and public schools, Bristol Achieve-ment Tests, IGCSE-recognized center, U. of Cambridge. **Graduates have attended:** U. of Cambridge, British public schools Bedales, Wellington, Sherbourne, Perdue.

Physical plant
Location: El Arrayan, at foot of mountain. **Campus:** 20,000 square meters. **Library:** 12,000 volumes. **Facilities:** auditorium, 3 covered play areas, science lab, computer lab, 3 tennis courts, extensive multipurpose sports and football field, use of swimming pool.

*Once only fee

THE INTERNATIONAL SCHOOL NIDO DE AGUILAS

Street address: Camino Nido de Aguilas 14515, Lo Barnechea, Los
     Condes, Santiago, Chile
Phone: (56)(2)2166842   **Facsimile:** (56)(2)2167603
Mail: Casilla 16211 — Correo 9, Santiago, Chile

Headmaster: Clifford H. Strommen, Ed.D.
High school principal: Pat Raimondo
Chilean director: Renan Munoz
Middle school principal: Rick McBee
Elementary school principal: Dale Eineder
Staff: full-time, 85; part-time, 5
Nationalities of staff: U.S., 29; U.K., 2; host, 54; other, 5
Grade levels: preK – 12
Enrollment: preK, 84; K, 58; 1 – 6, 356; 7 – 12, 337; total, 835
Nationalities of student body: U.S., 228; U.K., 5; host, 278; other, 324
Teacher/student ratio: 1/10
Tuition (annual): preK, $1,311; K, $5,197; 1 – 6, $5,731;
    7 – 12, $5,925
Other fees (annual): registration, $315; capital levy*, $4,000; busing,
    $370; lunch, $150
School year: August to December, March to July

Year founded: 1934. **Type of school:** coed, day. **Governed by:** board of
directors. **Accredited by:** Southern, Chilean Ministry.

Curriculum
Type: U.S., Chilean, IB. **Languages taught:** French, Spanish. **Staff
specialists:** reading, counselor, psychologist, learning disabilities, nurse,
ESL. **Special programs:** ESL, learning disabilities, reading, summer school,
Suzuki strings. **Special curricular:** art, chorus, band, physical education,
computer instruction, orchestra. **Extracurricular:** drama, choral music,
instrumental music, yearbook, literary magazine, sports, outdoor, handicrafts, student interest groups. **Sports:** basketball, soccer, softball, tennis,
volleyball, track and field. **Tests:** SSAT, PSAT, SAT, ACT, TOEFL, IB, Iowa, PAA
(Chile). **Graduates attending college:** 97%. **Graduates have attended:**
Brown, MIT, William and Mary, Purdue, U. of Chile.

Physical plant
Location: in rural Santiago suburb at the foot of the Andes mountains.
Library: 16,000 volumes. **Facilities:** 8 buildings, 65 classrooms, cafeteria,
infirmary, 4 tennis courts, 4 playing fields, 6 science labs, 3 computer labs,
gymnasium/auditorium, 2 art labs, band room, music room.

*Once only fee

LINCOLN INTERNATIONAL ACADEMY
Street address: Camino San Antonio 55, Las Condes, Santiago, Chile
Phone: (56)(2)2171907/2424128   **Facsimile:** (56)(2)2151080
Mail: Casilla 20.000, Correo 20, Santiago, Chile
Director/principal of primary levels: Verónica Caroca
Principal of upper levels: Guacolda Espinace
Principal of elementary levels: Verónica Roa
Business manager: Paz Suarez
Staff: full-time, 48; part-time, 8

Nationalities of staff: U.S., 4; host, 51; other, 1
Grade levels: preK – 12
Enrollment: preK, 38; K, 41; 1 – 6, 240; 7 – 9, 78; 10 – 12, 47; total, 444
Capacity: preK, 50; K, 50; 1 – 6, 300; 7 – 9, 100; 10 – 12, 100; total, 600
Teacher/student ratio: 1/9
Tuition (annual): preK – 12, $2,300
Other fees (annual): registration, $72; capital levy*, $963; insurance, $25
School year: March to December

Year founded: 1976. **Type of school:** coed, day, proprietary. **Governed by:** appointed board. **Accredited by:** Chilean Ministry of Education, Southern (in process).

Curriculum/physical plant

Type: U.S., Chilean. **Languages of instruction:** English, Spanish. **Languages taught:** French, grades 5 – 8. **Staff specialists:** math, computer, counselor, psychologist, nurse. **Special curricular:** art, chorus, physical education, computer instruction. **Extracurricular:** drama, gymnastics, dance, choral music, computers, yearbook, excursions/expeditions, field trips, Suzuki strings. **Sports:** basketball, soccer, track, volleyball, handball. **Graduates attending college:** 99%. **Graduates have attended:** U. of Chile, Catholic U. (Chile), U. of Santiago, U. of Texas, U. of Oxford. **Location:** northeast edge of city, near Andes mountains. **Campus:** 2.5 acres. **Library:** over 7,000 volumes. **Facilities:** 11 buildings, 26 classrooms, infirmary, covered play area, tennis court, playing field, 2 science labs, computer lab.

*Once only fee

SANTIAGO COLLEGE

Street address: Los Leones 584, Santiago, Chile
Phone: (56)(2)2321813   **Facsimile:** (56)(2)2320755
Mail: Casilla 130-D, Santiago 9, Chile
Headmistress: Elisabeth Fox
Dean of studies: Cristina Rodriguez
Upper school principal: Walter Calinger
Middle school principal: Annabella Farba
Lower school principal: Lorna Prado
Staff: full-time, 78; part-time, 78
Nationalities of staff: U.S., 7; host, 143; other, 6
Grade levels: preK – 12
Enrollment: preK, 129; K, 130; 1 – 6, 764; 7 – 9, 385; 10 – 12, 433; total, 1,841
Nationalities of student body: U.S., 44; host, 1,687; other, 110
Teacher/student ratio: 1/16
Tuition (annual): preK – 12, $2,322
Other fees (annual): registration, $24; insurance, $40; lunch, $1.80/each; books, $42; initial registration*, $1,125
School year: March to December

Year founded: 1880. **Type of school:** coed, day. **Governed by:** appointed board of trustees, New York. **Sponsored by:** local board, Santiago, Chile. **Accredited by:** Southern.

Curriculum

Type: North American, Chilean, IB. **Languages of instruction:** English (preK – 9), Spanish (10 – 12). **Languages taught:** English, French. **Staff specialists:** reading, counselor, psychologist, librarian. **Special curricular:** art, chorus, band, physical education, computer instruction. **Extracurricular:** computers, field trips, chess, chorus, ceramics, science club, cooking, musical group, drama (English and Spanish), French, journalism, piano, glass painting, violin, social service. **Sports:** basketball, hockey, rugby, soccer, volleyball, handball, athletics. **Tests:** PSAT, IB, Iowa. **Graduates attending college:** 90%. **Graduates have attended:** U. de Chile, Catholic U., U. de Santiago, Catholic U. of Valparaiso, American universities.

Physical plant

Location: in Santiago. **Campuses (2):** 147,710 square meters. **Library:** 34,281 volumes. **Facilities:** 10 buildings, 80 classrooms, 3 auditoriums, cafeteria, infirmary, covered play area, 3 gymnasiums, 4 playing fields, 6 science labs, 3 computer labs.

*Once only fee

More reasons to choose Winnebago Software

In a nationwide survey on library automation, library professionals said that Winnebago Software Company™ delivers what it promises, is easy to use, and is extremely dependable.

They also said that Winnebago:

- is highly responsive
- provides excellent customer support
- has high ethical standards and integrity
- stands behind its products

If you'd like to know why your colleagues recommend Winnebago for your library, call 1-800-533-5430, ext. 23. We'll send you information on the complete line of Winnebago programs and services, plus the **FREE** booklet, *Guide to Library Automation: A Step-by-Step Introduction.* All at no charge and with no obligation. Call today!

1-800-533-5430, ext. 23
Winnebago Software Company™

457 East South Street, Caledonia MN 55921

CHINA, People's Republic of _____

Region: Asia
Size: 3,696,100 square miles
Population: 1,151,486,000
Capital: Beijing

Telephone code: 86
Currency: yuan
Languages: Mandarin, Chinese, Yue, Wu Hakka, Min, Xiang, Gan, Zhuang, Hui, Yi

BEIJING

THE INTERNATIONAL SCHOOL OF BEIJING

Street address: Jiang Tai Road, Dong Zhi Men Wai, Beijing 100004, People's Republic of China
Phone: (86)(1)4377119   **Facsimile:** (86)(1)4376989
    Telex: 71622701 AMEMB CN   **Cable:** AMEMBASSY BEIJING
Mail: ISB American Embassy Beijing, PSC 461, Box 50, FPO AP 96521-0002
Director: David Eaton
Upper school principal: Stephen Asp-Schussheim
Middle school coordinator: Colin Huwes
Elementary principal: Kenneth Parker
Business manager: Patty Davis
Staff: full-time, 55; part-time, 13
Nationalities of staff: U.S., 25; U.K., 8; other, 35
Grade levels: preK – 12
Enrollment: preK, 30; K, 36; 1 – 6, 286; 7 – 9, 111; 10 – 12, 45; total, 508
Nationalities of student body: U.S., 95; other, 413
Capacity: preK, 30; K, 36; 1 – 6, 344; 7 – 9, 120; 10 – 12, 100; total, 630
Teacher/student ratio: 1/8
Tuition (annual): preK, $6,655; K – 6, $8,100; 7 – 9, $8,600; 10 – 12, $8,800; ESL prep school, $9,000
School year: August to June

   Year founded: 1980. **Type of school:** coed, day. **Governed by:** appointed and elected board of directors. **Sponsored by:** the embassies of the U.S., Australia, New Zealand, Canada, and Great Britain. **Accredited by:** Western.

Curriculum/physical plant
   Type: U.S.-based, IB. **Languages taught:** French, Chinese. **Staff specialists:** computer, nurse, art, ESL, music, resource. **Special programs:** China studies. **Special curricular:** art, physical education, computer instruction, drama, journalism. **Extracurricular:** gymnastics, dance, instrumental music, computers, yearbook, excursions/expeditions, field trips. **Sports:** basketball, soccer, swimming, volleyball. **Clubs:** scouting, student council. **Tests:** SSAT, Iowa, TAP, IB. **Location:** adjacent to Holiday Inn Lido complex,

5 kilometers from downtown Beijing; 14 kilometers from the airport. **Campus:** 2.5 acres. **Library:** 14,000 volumes. **Facilities:** 2 buildings, 40 classrooms, gymnasium, infirmary, playing field, 3 science labs, 2 computer labs, cafeteria/auditorium, 2 music rooms, 2 art rooms, air conditioning.

GUANGZHOU

AMERICAN SCHOOL OF GUANGZHOU

Street address: Garden Hotel Office Tower, Podium Level,
    368 Huanshi Dong Lu, Guangzhou, People's Republic of China
Phone: (86)(20)3338999 ext. 7433
    Facsimile: (86)(20)3350706 (Attn: Principal of American School)
    Telex: 71644788 GDHTL CN (c/o Garden Hotel)
    Cable: c/o American Consulate, Guangzhou
U.S. mail: (no personal name) American School of Guangzhou,
    PSC 461, Box 100, FPO AP 96521-0002
Principal: Robert S. Livingston
Staff: full-time, 6; part-time, 13
Nationalities of staff: U.S., 12; other, 7
Grade levels: K – 8
Enrollment: K, 14; 1 – 6, 55; 7 – 8, 4; total, 73
Nationalities of student body: U.S., 31; other, 42
Capacity: K, 15; 1 – 6, 90; 7 – 8, 15; total, 120
Teacher/student ratio: 1/6
Tuition (annual): K – 8, $10,500
Other fees: registration, $500 (deducted from tuition); ESL, $1,400
School year: September through June

Year founded: 1981. **Type of school:** coed, day. **Governed by:** elected board. **Sponsored by:** American Consulate. **Accredited by:** Western.

Curriculum/physical plant
Type: U.S. **Languages taught:** English, Mandarin. **Special programs:** ESL. **Special curricular:** art, physical education, music, Chinese culture. **Extracurricular:** computers, excursions/expeditions, field trips, various afters-chool activities. **Sports:** swimming, tennis. **Tests:** Iowa, Gates-MacGinitie. **Location:** in Guangzhou. **Campus:** school occupies 5,000 square feet of open space in hotel complex; interior approximates typical school setting. **Library:** 5,000 volumes. **Facilities:** 6 classrooms, tennis court, swimming pool, AV equipment, air conditioning.

SHANGHAI

SHANGHAI AMERICAN SCHOOL

Street address: 155 Jiang Su Lu, Shanghai, People's Republic of
China
Phone: (86)(21)4336880   **Facsimile:** (86)(21)4334122
Telex: 71633383 USCGCN
U.S. mail: (no personal name) Shanghai American School, PSC 461,
Box 200, FPO AP 96521-0002
Administrator: Ronald I. Montgomery
Staff: full-time, 29; part-time, 4
Nationalities of staff: U.S., 23; host, 3; other, 7
Grade levels: preK – 9
Enrollment: preK, 34; K, 30; 1 – 5, 162; 6 – 9, 72; total, 298
Nationalities of student body: U.S., 60; other, 238
Capacity: total, 350
Teacher/student ratio: 1/10
Tuition (annual): preK, $4,333; K – 8, $9,750
Other fees: registration*, $250
School year: September to June

Year founded: 1980. **Type of school:** coed, day, private nonprofit.
Governed by: elected board of management. **Sponsored by:** American
Consulate General. **Accredited by:** Western.

Curriculum/physical plant

Type: U.S. **Languages taught:** French, Spanish, Chinese. **Special curricular:** art, physical education, computer instruction, drama, choral music,
Chinese language and culture classes, yearbook, newspaper, field trips.
Tests: Iowa. **Location:** on grounds of the #3 Girls' Middle School. **Campus:**
3 acres. **Library:** 10,000 volumes. **Facilities:** 3 newly renovated buildings
with 29 classrooms, track and field, air conditioning.

*Once only fee

SHEKOU

SHEKOU INTERNATIONAL SCHOOL

Phone: (86)(755)6693669   **Facsimile:** (86)(755)6693849
Telex: 71644658 AOPSK CN
Mail: c/o Amoco Orient Petroleum Company, 7th floor SKIZ Building,
Shekou Industrial Zone, Shenzhen, People's Republic of China
U.S. mail: c/o Amoco Orient — China, PO Box 4381, Houston, TX 77210,
U.S.A.
Principal: Allen Hansen

Staff: full-time, 5
Nationalities of staff: U.S., 5
Grade levels: K – 8
Enrollment: K, 12; 1 – 6, 36; 7 – 8, 7; total, 55
Nationalities of student body: U.S., 40; other, 15
Capacity: K, 15; 1 – 8, 45; total, 60
Teacher/student ratio: 1/11
School year: August to June

Year founded: 1988. **Type of school:** coed, day, company sponsored. **Sponsored by:** international oil companies. **Operated by:** International Schools Services, Princeton, New Jersey.

Curriculum/physical plant
Type: U.S. **Languages taught:** Mandarin. **Special curricular:** physical education, computer instruction, Chinese language and culture. **Extracurricular:** field trips, soccer, swimming, crafts. **Tests:** Stanford. **Location:** in Shekou, 1 hour from Hong Kong by Hovercraft. **Library:** 2,000 volumes. **Facilities:** 5 classrooms, computer lab, playing fields, swimming pool, air conditioning.

SHENYANG

SHENYANG AMERICAN ACADEMY
Street address: No. 52, 14 Wei Road, Heping District, Shenyang, Liaoning, People's Republic of China
Phone/facsimile: (86)(24)220012/220074
U.S. mail: (no personal name) Shenyang American Academy, PSC 461, Box 45, FPO AP 96521-0002
Principal: Janis Sotherden, Ed.D.
Staff: full-time, 1; part-time, 2
Nationalities of staff: U.S., 2; other, 1
Grade levels: K – 8
Enrollment: K, 1; 1 – 6, 4; total, 5
Nationalities of student body: U.S., 4; other, 1
Capacity: K – 6, 20; 7 – 8, 20; total, 40
Teacher/student ratio: 1/2
Tuition (annual): K – 8, $12,000
School year: September to June

Year founded: 1985. **Type of school:** coed, day. **Governed by:** appointed board of education. **Sponsored by:** American Consulate General.

Curriculum/physical plant
Type: U.S. **Languages taught:** Chinese. **Special curricular:** art, physical education, computer instruction, music. **Extracurricular:** drama, instru-

mental music, field trips, cooking, swimming, arts and crafts, sports. **Tests:** Iowa. **Location:** on American Consulate compound. **Campus:** .25 acre. **Library:** 4,000 volumes. **Facilities:** 1 building, 5 classrooms, tennis court, playing field, computer lab, air conditioning.

TIANJIN

TIANJIN MTI INTERNATIONAL SCHOOL

Street address: 804 ITC Building, 23 Youyi Road, HeXi District, Tianjin 300201, People's Republic of China
Phone: (86)(22)359115, ext. 804   **Facsimile:** (86)(22)359391
Principal: Gregg A. Vossler
Staff: full-time, 8; part-time, 4
Nationalities of staff: U.S., 10; other, 2
Grade levels: K – 12
Enrollment: preK, 12; K, 5; 1 – 6, 20; 7 – 9, 14; 10 – 12, 5; total, 56
Nationalities of student body: U.S., 19; U.K., 5; other, 32
Capacity: preK, 12; K, 8; 1 – 6, 40; 7 – 9, 25; 10 – 12, 25; total, 110
Teacher/student ratio: 1/6
Tuition (annual): preK, $1,500; K, $4,800; 1 – 12, $7,550
Other fees (annual): registration, $150; capital levy, $500
School year: September to June

Year founded: 1986. **Type of school:** coed, day, private nonprofit. **Governed by:** appointed school committee. **Sponsored by:** MTI. **Accredited by:** Western.

Curriculum/physical plant
Type: U.S. **Languages taught:** Chinese. **Staff specialists:** computer, counselor, nurse. **Special programs:** ESL. **Special curricular:** art, chorus, physical education, computer instruction. **Extracurricular:** drama, choral music, computers, yearbook, excursions/expeditions. **Sports:** basketball, volleyball. **Tests:** PSAT, SAT, Iowa. **Graduates attending college:** 98%. **Graduates have attended:** Trinity College, U. of North Carolina, Baylor, Bethel College, Wheaton College. **Location:** in city. **Library:** 5,000 volumes. **Facilities:** 1 building, 12 classrooms, auditorium, tennis court, playing field, 2 science labs, computer lab, air conditioning.

COLOMBIA _____

Region: South America
Size: 439,735 square miles
Population: 33,777,000
Capital: Bogota

Telephone code: 57
Currency: peso
Language: Spanish

BARRANQUILLA

COLEGIO ALBANIA

Location: Albania, Guajira, Colombia
Phone: (57)(58)562131 ext. 5804
   Facsimile: (57)(58)562131 ext. 5697
Mail: Apartado Aereo 52-499, Barranquilla, Colombia
U.S. mail: c/o Intercor, PO Box 02-5573, Miami, FL 33102-5573, U.S.A.
Director: Jorge Leyva
Staff: full-time, 80
Nationalities of staff: U.S., 20; host, 60
Grade levels: preK – 11
Enrollment: preK, 78; K, 69; 1 – 5, 359; 6 – 8, 203; 9 – 11, 127; total, 836
Nationalities of student body: U.S., 9; host, 812; other, 15
Capacity: preK, 75; K, 75; 1 – 6, 648; 7 – 9, 270; 10 – 11, 108; total, 1,176
Teacher/student ratio: 1/10
School year: August to June

Year founded: 1983. **Type of school:** coed, day, company sponsored.
Governed by: elected school advisory board. **Sponsored by:** Intercor-FECEN.
Accredited by: Southern, Colombian Ministry of Education.

Curriculum
Type: U.S., Colombian. **Languages of instruction:** English, Spanish.
Languages taught: English, Spanish. **Staff specialists:** computer, learning
disabilities, nurse, gifted & talented, 3 counselors. **Special programs:** ESL,
computer, learning disabilities, talented & gifted. **Special curricular:** art,
physical education, computer instruction, vocational, yearbook. **Extracurricular:** drama, dance, computers, newspaper, excursions/expeditions, field
trips. **Sports:** baseball, basketball, bowling, soccer, swimming, tennis, volleyball, racquetball, cycling. **Tests:** TOEFL, Iowa.

Physical plant
Location: at coal-mining camp, 1-hour company-plane flight from
Barranquilla, 1.5 hours by highway to state capital. **Campus:** 10 acres.
Libraries: 11,000 volumes. **Facilities:** auditorium, infirmary, 4 playing fields,
3 science labs, 2 computer labs, 2 swimming pools, air conditioning.

Colegio Karl C. Parrish

Street address: Kilometro 2 Carretera Antigua a Puerto Colombia,
Barranquilla, Colombia
Phone: (57)(58)568789/568972   **Facsimile:** (57)(58)568828
   Cable: COLPARRISH
Mail: Apartado Aereo 52962, Barranquilla, Colombia, S.A.
Director: Michael Farr, Ph.D.
High school principal: Conrad Pholar
Elementary school principal: Hectalina Donado
Staff: full-time, 66; part-time, 7
Nationalities of staff: U.S., 18; host, 47; other, 8
Grade levels: N – 12
Enrollment: N – preK, 60; K, 54; 1 – 6, 348; 7 – 9, 140; 10 – 12, 125;
   total, 727
Nationalities of student body: U.S., 23; host, 663; other, 41
Capacity: preK, 56; K, 60; 1 – 6, 360; 7 – 9, 180; 10 – 12, 180; total, 836
Teacher/student ratio: 1/10
Tuition (annual): preK – K, $1,380; 1 – 5, $1,638; 6 – 8, $1,842;
   9 – 11, $1,926; 12, $1,998
Other fees: registration*: preK – 5, $1,000; 6 – 12, $1,500
School year: August to June

Year founded: 1938. **Type of school:** coed, day, private nonprofit.
Governed by: board of directors appointed by board of trustees. **Accredited by:** Southern, Colombian Ministry of Education.

Curriculum/physical plant

Type: U.S., Colombian. **Languages of instruction:** English, Spanish.
Languages taught: English, Spanish. **Staff specialists:** reading, computer, counselor, psychologist. **Special programs:** ESL, remedial reading, learning disabilities. **Special curricular:** art, band, physical education, computer instruction, vocational. **Extracurricular:** gymnastics, instrumental music, computers, yearbook, newspaper, photography, field trips. **Sports:** baseball, soccer. **Organizations:** National Honor Society, student council. **Tests:** SSAT, PSAT, SAT, ACT, TOEFL, Iowa. **Graduates attending college:** 100%.
Graduates have attended: Brown, Georgia Institute of Technology, U. of Pennsylvania, Worcester Polytechnic Institute, U. of Texas. **Location:** in suburban area, 2 kilometers from Barranquilla. **Campus:** 18.78 acres.
Library: 25,000 volumes. **Facilities:** 8 buildings, 35 classrooms, 2 tennis courts, gymnasium, 2 playing fields, 2 science labs, 2 computer labs, partial air conditioning.

*Once only fee

Marymount

Street address: Carrera 59B #84-52, Barranquilla, Colombia
Phone: (57)(58)342249/580763   **Facsimile:** (57)(58)459667
Mail: Apartado Aereo No. 51766, Barranquilla, Colombia

Director: Kathleen Cunniffe, Ph.D.
Secondary school principal: Lissy García de Buendia
Elementary school principal: Patricia Olarte de Gómez
Staff: full-time, 125; part-time, 15
Nationalities of staff: U.S., 14; host, 119; other, 7
Grade levels: N – 12
Enrollment: N – K, 400; 1 – 6, 500; 7 – 9, 200; 10 – 12, 400;
    total, 1,500
Nationalities of student body: U.S., 15; host, 1,470; other, 15
Teacher/student ratio: 1/11
Tuition (annual): N – K, $500; 1 – 9, $1,100; 10 – 12, $1,300
Other fees (annual): registration*, $750; insurance, $80; books, $50
School year: August through June

Year founded: 1953. **Type of school:** coed, day. **Governed by:** appointed board of trustees. **Accredited by:** Colombian Ministry of Education.

Curriculum/physical plant

Type: U.S., Colombian. **Languages taught:** English, Spanish. **Staff specialists:** computer, counselor, psychologist, fine arts, remedial. **Special programs:** business education, community service. **Extracurricular:** drama, choir, dance, computers, yearbook, cooking, arts and crafts, study skills, math club, leadership training. **Sports:** basketball, soccer, softball, baseball, swimming, volleyball, aerobics, dance, track and field. **Tests:** PSAT, SAT, TOEFL, Colombian ICFES, U. of Michigan English Proficiency. **Graduates have attended:** Columbia U., Boston U., Boston College, Javeriana and U. del Norte in Colombia. **Location:** in residential section, north of city. **Campus:** 4 hectares in residential section, plus recreational campus of 44 hectares at city's perimeter. **Library:** 17,000 volumes. **Facilities:** 10 buildings, 80 classrooms, auditorium, gymnasium, playing fields, 3 science labs, 2 art labs, swimming pool, AV room, chapel, all-purpose room, computer room, typing room, dance room, family center.

*Once only fee

BOGOTA

COLEGIO NUEVA GRANADA

Street address: K 2 Este #70-20, Bogota, Colombia
Phone: (57)(1)2355350   **Facsimile:** (57)(1)2113720
Mail: Carrera 2a-E, no. 70-20, A.A. 51339, Bogota, Colombia
U.S. mail: 6964 NW 50th Street, Suite 8258, Miami, FL
    33166-5632, U.S.A.
Director: Steven T. Holbrook, Ph.D.
High school principal: Eric Habeggar
Middle school principal: Linda Leonard, Ed.D.
Elementary school principal: Joe Nagy
Primary school principal: Connie Turner

Head of library: Lisa Habeggar
Head of computer services: Gustavo Vega
Head of pupil services: Annie Acevedo
Business manager: German Torres
Staff: full-time, 124; part-time, 1
Nationalities of staff: U.S., 45; U.K., 2; host, 68; other, 10
Grade levels: preK – 12
Enrollment: preK, 80; K, 97; 1 – 6, 663; 7 – 9, 325; 10 – 12, 283;
    total, 1,448
Capacity: preK, 80; K, 105; 1 – 6, 655; 7 – 9, 330; 10 – 12, 330; total, 1,500
Teacher/student ratio: 1/12
Tuition (annual): preK – 6, $2,400; 7 – 8, $2,700; 9 – 10, $2,800;
    11 – 12, $2,900
Other fees: registration*: preK – K, $3,000; 1 – 5, $3,500; 6 – 11,
    $4,000; 12, $2,000
School year: late August through June

Year founded: 1938. **Type of school:** coed, day, private nonprofit.
Governed by: elected board of directors. **Accredited by:** Southern, Colombian Ministry of Education.

Curriculum/physical plant
Type: U.S., Colombian. **Languages of instruction:** English, Spanish.
Languages taught: English, French, Spanish. **Staff specialists:** computer, counselor, psychologist, learning disabilities, nurse, ESL. **Special programs:** ESL, advanced placement, honors sections, independent study, remedial, gifted. **Special curricular:** art, chorus, band, physical education, computer instruction, debating, drama, speech. **Extracurricular:** drama, gymnastics, choral music, instrumental music, computers, yearbook, newspaper, photography, excursions/expeditions, field trips. **Sports:** baseball, basketball, soccer, track, volleyball. **Tests:** PSAT, SAT, ACT, AP, Iowa, DAT. **Graduates attending college:** 95%. **Graduates have attended:** Tufts, Georgetown, Pennsylvania, Texas, Stanford. **Location:** on wooded hillside overlooking Bogota. **Campus:** 18 acres. **Library:** 28,000 volumes. **Facilities:** 12 buildings, 74 classrooms, cafeteria, infirmary, covered play area, 2 gymnasiums, 12 playing fields, 7 science labs, 2 computer labs, theater.

*Once only fee

BUCARAMANGA

COLEGIO PANAMERICANO
Street address: Calle 34 #8-73 Canaveral Alto, Bucaramanga,
    Santander, Colombia
Phone: (57)(73)387336/386213   **Facsimile:** (57)(76)337628
Mail: Apartado Aereo 522, Bucaramanga, Colombia
Director: Laura Wheatley Garcia
Secondary school principal: Nancy Chaparro

Primary school principal: Lisa Perskie Rodriguez
Staff: full-time, 24; part-time, 9
Nationalities of staff: U.S., 9; other, 24
Grade levels: preK – 12
Enrollment: preK, 29; K, 27; 1 – 6, 153; 7 – 9, 61; 10 – 12, 48; total, 318
Nationalities of student body: U.S., 19; host, 290; other, 9
Capacity: preK, 40; K, 30; 1 – 6, 150; 7 – 9, 75; 10 – 12, 75; total, 370
Teacher/student ratio: 1/11
Tuition (annual): K, $950; 1 – 6, $2,300; 7 – 9, $2,500; 10 – 12, $2,700
Other fees: registration*, $547; insurance, $50; busing, $340;
    lunch, $399
School year: February to November

Year founded: 1963. **Type of school:** coed. **Governed by:** elected board of directors. **Accredited by:** Colombian Ministerio.

Curriculum/physical plant
    Type: U.S., Colombian. **Languages of instruction:** English, Spanish. **Languages taught:** English, French, Spanish. **Staff specialists:** counselor. **Special programs:** ESL. **Extracurricular:** drama, dance, computers, newspaper, photography, excursions/expeditions, field trips, scouting. **Sports:** basketball, soccer, volleyball. **Tests:** PSAT, SAT. **Graduates attending college:** 90%. **Graduates have attended:** U. of Florida, U. of Alabama, Florida State. **Location:** 5 miles south of Bucaramanga. **Facilities:** cafeteria, covered play area, playing field, science lab, computer lab, new library.

*Once only fee

CALI

COLEGIO BOLIVAR

Street address: Calle 5 #122-21, Cali, Valle, Colombia
Phone: (57)(23)552039   **Facsimile:** (57)(23)552041
Mail: Apartado Aereo 26300, Cali, Colombia
Director: Martin Felton, Ph.D.
Secondary school principal: James Fellabaum, Ph.D.
Middle school coordinator: Inge Koele
Primary coordinator: Peggy Pastor, Ph.D.
Pre-primary coordinator: Rosemary Palencin
Staff: full-time, 98; part-time, 4
Nationalities of staff: U.S., 45; host, 50; other, 7
Grade levels: preK – 12
Enrollment: pre-primary, 300; primary, 300; middle, 250; secondary,
    250; total, 1,100
Teacher/student ratio: 1/11
Tuition (annual): pre-primary, $2,600; primary, $2,900; middle,
    $3,300; secondary, $3,600

Other fees (annual): registration, $160; busing, $350; entrance donation*, $2,000
School year: September to June

Year founded: 1948. **Type of school:** coed, day. **Governed by:** bondholding companies, appointed board of directors. **Accredited by:** Southern, Colombian Ministry of Education.

Curriculum
Type: U.S., Colombian. **Languages of instruction:** English, Spanish. **Languages taught:** Spanish. **Staff specialists:** reading, counselor, learning disabilities, nurse. **Special programs:** ESL, advanced placement, honors sections. **Special curricular:** art, chorus, physical education, computer instruction, vocational. **Extracurricular:** drama, gymnastics, dance, choral music, instrumental music, computers, yearbook, newspaper, literary magazine, photography, excursions/expeditions, field trips, sports, Boy Scouts, Girl Scouts. **Tests:** PSAT, SAT, ACT, Stanford, Iowa, Otis-Lennon, Strong-Campbell. **Graduates attending college:** 95%. **Graduates have attended:** Brandeis, Boston U., Harvard, Brown, Georgetown.

Physical plant
Location: in rural area, 10 miles from city center. **Campus:** 21 acres. **Library:** 20,000 volumes. **Facilities:** 10 buildings, 60 classrooms, auditorium, cafeteria, infirmary, covered play area, gymnasium, 3 playing fields, 9 science labs, computer lab, swimming pool, AV equipment.

*Once only fee

CARTAGENA

COLEGIO JORGE WASHINGTON
Street address: Carrera 1ª, No. 12-120, Bocagrande, Cartagena, Colombia
Phone: (57)(53)653136/654035   **Facsimile:** (57)(53)656447
Mail: Apartado Aereo 2899, Cartagena, Colombia, South America
Director: Stephen Field
High school principal: David Nelson
Elementary school principal: Barbara Field
Head of library: Norah Porto
Head of computer services: Eduardo Vera
Staff: full-time, 45; part-time, 7
Nationalities of staff: U.S., 16; U.K., 1; host, 28; other, 7
Grade levels: preK – 12
Enrollment: preK, 40; K, 43; 1 – 6, 243; 7 – 9, 97; 10 – 12, 86; total, 509
Nationalities of student body: U.S., 23; U.K., 1; host, 466; other, 19
Capacity: preK, 40; K, 40; 1 – 6, 264; 7 – 9, 132; 10 – 12, 132; total, 608
Teacher/student ratio: 1/10

Tuition (annual): preK – 12, $1,600
Other fees (annual): registration, $125; entrance*, $2,200
School year: August to June

Year founded: 1952. **Type of school:** coed, day, private nonprofit. **Governed by:** elected board of directors. **Accredited by:** Southern. **Regional organization:** AASSA, ACCAS.

Curriculum/physical plant
Type: U.S., Colombian. **Languages of instruction:** English, Spanish. **Languages taught:** English, Spanish. **Staff specialists:** math, computer, psychologist. **Special programs:** remedial. **Special curricular:** physical education, computer instruction. **Extracurricular:** drama, computers, yearbook, newspaper, excursions/expeditions. **Tests:** PSAT, SAT, TOEFL, Iowa. **Graduates attending college:** 100%. **Graduates have attended:** Georgia Tech, Duke, Boston U., Georgetown. **Location:** on oceanfront within Cartagena city limits. **Campus:** 2 acres. **Library:** 10,000 volumes. **Facilities:** 4 buildings, 20 classrooms, cafeteria, tennis court, playing field, science lab, computer lab, air conditioning.

*Once only fee

MANIZALES

COLEGIO GRANADINO
Phone: (57)(68)745884/746065   **Facsimile:** (57)(68)844955/746066
Mail: Apartado Aereo 2138, Manizales, Colombia
Director: Gonzalo Arango
Secondary school principal: Silvia L. Spaggiari G.
Elementary school principal: Catherine A. Riess
Head of library: Constanza Maria González
Staff: full-time, 48; part-time, 4
Nationalities of staff: U.S., 5; U.K., 1; host, 44; other, 2
Grade levels: preK – 12
Enrollment: preK, 40; K, 40; 1 – 5, 220; 6 – 12, 140; total, 440
Nationalities of student body: U.S., 10; host, 420; other, 10
Capacity: preK, 48; K, 48; 1 – 5, 240; 6 – 8, 111; 9 – 12, 192; total, 639
Teacher/student ratio: 1/9
Tuition (annual): preK – K, $890; 1 – 5, $955; 6 – 12, $1,140
Other fees (annual): registration*, $1,630; busing, $210; lunch, $280; books, $135
School year: late August through June

Year founded: 1980. **Type of school:** coed, day, private nonprofit, parent-owned. **Governed by:** appointed board of directors, school director. **Accredited by:** Colombian Ministry, Southern (in process). **Regional organization:** ACCAS.

Curriculum/physical plant

Type: U.S., Colombian. **Languages of instruction:** English, Spanish. **Staff specialists:** math, computer, speech/hearing, counselor, psychologist, instrumental music. **Special programs:** ESL, advanced placement, SSL, resource center. **Special curricular:** art, chorus, physical education, computer instruction, vocational, music, seminars, advanced placement. **Extracurricular:** drama, scouts, reading club, painting, cooking, judo, skating, sports teams, ceramics. **Sports:** basketball, soccer, softball, track, volleyball. **Tests:** PSAT, SAT, TOEFL, Iowa, ICFES. **Location:** 5 miles from Manizales. **Campus:** 12.5 acres. **Library:** 6,000 volumes. **Facilities:** 7 buildings, 28 classrooms, auditorium, cafeteria, infirmary, 5 playing fields, 2 science labs, 2 computer labs.

*Once only fee

MEDELLIN

THE COLUMBUS SCHOOL

Street address: Calle 78B #72A-220, Medellin, Colombia
Phone: (57)(4)4415151   **Facsimile:** (57)(4)2577531
Mail: Apartado Aereo 5225, Medellin, Colombia
Superintendent: John K. Schober, Ph.D.
High school principal: Mike Cooper
Elementary school principal: Susan Jaramillo
Staff: full-time, 80; part-time, 4
Nationalities of staff: U.S., 43; host, 34; other, 7
Grade levels: N – 12
Enrollment: N – preK, 86; K, 84; 1 – 6, 460; 7 – 9, 200; 10 – 12, 190; total, 1,020
Capacity: N – preK, 88; K, 89; 1 – 6, 530; 7 – 9, 220; 10 – 12, 200; total, 1,127
Teacher/student ratio: 1/12
Tuition (annual): N – K, $1,800; 1 – 6, $1,850; 7 – 9, $1,900; 10 – 12, $2,000
Other fees (annual): registration, $125; capital levy*, $1,500; busing, $300; books, $60
School year: August to June

Year founded: 1947. **Type of school:** coed, day, private nonprofit. **Governed by:** elected board of directors. **Accredited by:** Southern.

Curriculum/physical plant

Type: binational (U.S./Colombian). **Languages of instruction:** English, Spanish. **Languages taught:** French. **Staff specialists:** reading, math, counselor, learning disabilities. **Special programs:** ESL, honors sections. **Special curricular:** physical education, computer instruction. **Extracurricu-**

lar: drama, gymnastics, choral music, computers, yearbook, newspaper. **Sports:** basketball, soccer, volleyball. **Tests:** PSAT, SAT, ACT, TOEFL, Iowa. **Graduates attending college:** 95%. **Graduates have attended:** Stanford, Johns Hopkins, Emory, Loyola, U. of Miami. **Location:** on mountainside, 3 miles northwest of center city. **Campus:** 10 acres. **Library:** 15,000 volumes. **Facilities:** 7 buildings, 48 classrooms, cafeteria, gymnasium, computer lab, playing fields, science labs.

*Once only fee

COSTA RICA ⎯⎯⎯⎯⎯⎯⎯⎯⎯⎯⎯⎯

Region: Central America
Size: 19,575 square miles
Population: 3,111,000
Capital: San José

Telephone code: 506
Currency: colone
Language: Spanish

SAN JOSÉ

ANGLO AMERICAN SCHOOL

Street address: Calle 37, Av. Central, San José, Costa Rica
Phone: (506)251723/251729
Mail: Apartado 3188, 1000 San Jose, Costa Rica
Principal: Marianne de Villalobos
Head of library: Lucia Jiménez
Head of computer services: Lorena Coto
Staff: full-time, 40; part-time, 7
Nationalities of staff: host, 47
Grade levels: N – 6
Enrollment: N, 70; preK, 90; K, 90; 1 – 6, 550; total, 800
Capacity: total, 800
Teacher/student ratio: 1/18
Tuition (annual): preK – 6, $1,080
Other fees: registration, $50/year; busing, $25/month; entrance*, $60; book rental, $12/month
School year: February to December
Year founded: 1949. **Type of school:** coed, day, proprietary.

Curriculum/physical plant
Type: U.S., Costa Rican. **Languages of instruction:** English, Spanish. **Languages taught:** English. **Special curricular:** art, band, physical education, music, religion. **Extracurricular:** yearbook, excursions/expeditions.

Clubs: chorus, football, soccer, basketball, cheerleaders, volleyball, painting, computer. **Location:** in San José. **Campus:** 1 acre. **Library:** 1,500 volumes. **Facilities:** 1 building, 30 classrooms (2 with computers), 3 playing fields, auditorium/gymnasium, multiple-use room, preschool yard.

*Once only fee

COSTA RICA ACADEMY

Street address: Bosques De Dona Rosa, Ciudad Cariari, San José,
   Costa Rica
Phone: (506)390376/391300   **Facsimile:** (506)390625
Mail: Apartado 4941, San Jose 1000, Costa Rica
Headmaster: William D. Rose
Assistant headmaster: Larue Goldfinch
Staff: full-time, 37
Grade levels: preK – 12
Enrollment: preK, 11; K, 10; 1 – 6, 98; 7 – 9, 84; 10 – 12, 85; total, 288
Nationalities of student body: U.S., 96; host, 45; other, 147
Capacity: K, 36; 1 – 6, 150; 7 – 9, 75; 10 – 12, 75; total, 336
Teacher/student ratio: 1/8
Tuition (annual): K – 12, $4,000
Other fees (annual): registration*, $50; busing, $500; matriculation
   fee*, $1,000; building fund, $600 for 3 years; PTA, $10
School year: August to June

Year founded: 1970. **Type of school:** coed, day, private nonprofit. **Governed by:** elected board of directors. **Accredited by:** Southern.

Curriculum/physical plant
Type: U.S. **Languages of instruction:** English, Spanish (one lesson daily). **Languages taught:** English, French, Spanish. **Staff specialists:** math, computer, counselor, nurse, AV. **Special programs:** ESL, advanced placement, independent study, remedial, tutoring, learning disabilities (K – 12), enrichment. **Special curricular:** art, physical education, computer instruction, introduction to music. **Extracurricular:** drama, gymnastics, computers, yearbook, newspaper, photography, excursions/expeditions, field trips. **Tests:** SSAT, PSAT, SAT, ACT, AP, Iowa, MAT. **Graduates attending college:** 90%. **Location:** adjacent to Cariari Country Club, 10 miles from San José. **Library:** 19,000 volumes. **Facilities:** 28 classrooms, cafeteria, infirmary, covered play area, gymnasium, 2 playing fields, science lab, 2 computer labs.

*Once only fee

THE COUNTRY DAY SCHOOL

Phone: (506)280873/281187/280385   **Facsimile:** (506)282798
Mail: Apartado 1139, 1250 Escazú, Costa Rica/Apartado 8-6170,
   1000 San José, Costa Rica
U.S. mail: Acct. 191, PO Box 025216, Miami, FL 33102-5216, U.S.A.
Director general: Sonya Vargas-Brown
Secondary school principal: Maria Battle
Elementary school principal: William Large
Business director: Woodson C. Brown
Staff: full-time, 67; part-time, 13
Nationalities of staff: U.S., 32; host, 42; other, 6
Grade levels: preK – 12
Enrollment: preK, 37; K – 3, 253; 4 – 5, 95; 6 – 8, 126; 9 – 12, 144;
   total, 655
Nationalities of student body: U.S., 195; host, 176; other, 284
Capacity: preK, 40; K – prep, 120; 1 – 6, 280; 7 – 9, 180; 10 – 12, 200;
   total, 820
Teacher/student ratio: 1/9
Tuition (annual): K – prep (half day), $1,995; K – prep (full day),
   $2,975; 1 – 12, $4,100
Other fees (annual): matriculation, $350
School year: August to June

Year founded: 1963. **Type of school:** coed, day, proprietary. **Accredited by:** Costa Rican Ministry of Education, Southern.

Curriculum

Type: U.S. **Languages taught:** French, Spanish. **Staff specialists:** computer, psychologist, learning disabilities, nurse. **Special programs:** ESL, advanced placement, honor courses, remedial assistance. **Special curricular:** art, chorus, band, physical education, computer instruction, violin, orchestra. **Extracurricular:** drama, dance, choral music, instrumental music, computers, yearbook, newspaper, photography, excursions/expeditions, field trips. **Sports:** basketball, cheerleading, soccer, swimming, volleyball. **Clubs:** international, chess, anthropology, social service, European seminar, drama. **Tests:** PSAT, SAT, ACT, TOEFL, AP, Iowa, Achievement Tests. **Graduates attending college:** 95%. **Graduates have attended:** Brown, Dartmouth, Yale, Columbia, Trinity College Dublin.

Physical plant

Location: in town of Escazú, 10 minutes from San José. **Campus:** 8 acres. **Library:** 12,000 volumes. **Facilities:** 9 buildings, 52 classrooms, 2 infirmaries, covered play area, gymnasium, 2 playing fields, 2 science labs, 3 computer labs, swimming pool, 2 art rooms, photography lab, band room, cafeteria/auditorium.

LINCOLN SCHOOL

Phone: (506)357733   **Facsimile:** (506)361706
Mail: PO Box 1919, San José, Costa Rica
U.S. mail: PO Box 025216, Miami, FL 33102-5216, U.S.A.
Director: Jack Delman
High school principal: Dr. Carlos Lepiz
Elementary school principal: Iris Prada-Mora
Staff: full-time, 92
Nationalities of staff: U.S., 25; host, 67
Grade levels: preK – 12
Enrollment: preK, 100; K, 100; preparatory, 100; 1 – 6, 620;
    7 – 9, 375; 10 – 12, 335; total, 1,630
Capacity: total, 1,600
Teacher/student ratio: 1/18
Tuition (annual): preK – K, $700; prep – 3, $1,000; 4 – 6, $1,150;
    7 – 12, $1,250
Other fees (annual): registration, $41; insurance, $11.50; busing,
    $200; enrollment*, $452/family; various fees, $50
School year: February to December

Year founded: 1945. **Type of school:** coed, day, private nonprofit.
Accredited by: Southern, Costa Rica Ministry of Education.

Curriculum/physical plant

Type: U.S., Costa Rican. **Languages of instruction:** English, Spanish.
Languages taught: English, French, Spanish. **Staff specialists:** reading,
math, computer, counselor, psychologist, learning disabilities, nurse. **Special programs:** honors sections, independent study, honors thesis. **Special curricular:** art, chorus, band, physical education, computer instruction.
Extracurricular: drama, gymnastics, choral music, instrumental music,
yearbook, newspaper, excursions/expeditions, field trips. **Sports:** basketball,
soccer, softball, volleyball, flag football, cheerleaders. **Clubs:** community
service, French, National Honor Society, square dance, Tae Kwon Do, chess,
Junior National Honor Society. **Tests:** PSAT, SAT, ACT, TOEFL, Iowa,
Slingerland Screening. **Graduates attending college:** 98%. **Graduates have
attended:** Auburn, Boston College, Cornell, Harvard, McGill. **Location:** in
suburb, Moravia. **Campus:** 9 acres. **Facilities:** 25 buildings, 77 classrooms,
cafeteria, infirmary, gymnasium, 2 playing fields, 2 science labs, 3 computer
labs, 2 libraries.

*Once only fee

MARIAN BAKER SCHOOL

Phone/facsimile: (506)344609
Mail: Apartado 4269, San José 1000, Costa Rica
Director: Gloria J. Doll
Elementary principal: Sofia Solis
Business manager: Bonnie Heigold
Staff: full-time, 29; part-time, 5
Nationalities of staff: U.S., 16; host, 16; other, 2

Grade levels: prep – 12
Enrollment: prep, 20; 1 – 6, 99; 7 – 9, 58; 10 – 12, 37; total, 214
Nationalities of student body: U.S., 75; host, 75; other, 64
Capacity: total, 250
Teacher/student ratio: 1/7
Tuition (annual): prep – 6, $3,100; 7 – 9, $3,300; 10 – 12, $3,600
Other fees (annual): registration*, $300; busing, $380; insurance, books, and class photo included in tuition
School year: August to June

Year founded: 1984. **Type of school:** coed, day, proprietary, private nonprofit. **Governed by:** school owners and appointed board of directors. **Accredited by:** Costa Rican Ministry, Southern (in process).

Curriculum/physical plant

Type: U.S. **Languages taught:** French, Spanish. **Staff specialists:** reading, computers, counselor, psychologist, learning disabilities. **Special programs:** ESL, advanced placement. **Special curricular:** art, band, physical education, computer instruction. **Extracurricular:** drama, instrumental music, yearbook, science club, excursions/expeditions, field trips. **Sports:** basketball, soccer, softball, volleyball, ultimate frisbee. **Tests:** PSAT, SAT, TOEFL, AP, Iowa. **Graduates attending college:** 90%. **Graduates have attended:** Emory, U. of San Diego, U. of Costa Rica, William and Mary, Pomona. **Location:** beautiful, wooded area in hills northeast of San José, 4 kilometers from San Pedro. **Campus:** 4 acres. **Library:** 4,000 volumes. **Facilities:** 3 buildings, 29 classrooms, auditorium, cafeteria, gymnasium, playing field, science lab, computer lab.

*Once only fee

COTE D'IVOIRE ⎯⎯⎯⎯⎯⎯⎯⎯⎯⎯

Region: West Africa
Size: 124,503 square miles
Population: 12,977,000
Capital: Abidjan

Telephone code: 225
Currency: CFA franc
Languages: French, tribal languages

ABIDJAN

INTERNATIONAL COMMUNITY SCHOOL OF ABIDJAN

Phone: (225)431152   **Facsimile:** (225)431996
Mail: 06 BP 544, Abidjan 06, Cote d'Ivoire, West Africa
U.S. mail: Administrative Officer (ICSA), Abidjan, Department of State, Washington, D.C. 20521-2010
Director: Larry Jones
Upper school principal: Barbara A. Ainsworth, Ph.D.
Lower school principal: Robert Walbridge
Staff: full-time, 39; part-time, 3

Nationalities of staff: U.S., 25; U.K., 1; other, 6
Grade levels: K – 12
Enrollment: K, 24; 1 – 6, 194; 7 – 9, 73; 10 – 12, 50; total, 341
Nationalities of student body: U.S., 100; U.K., 3; other, 228
Capacity: K, 30; 1 – 6, 272; 7 – 9, 90; 10 – 12, 75; total, 467
Teacher/student ratio: 1/8
Tuition (annual): K, $7,140; 1 – 6, $7,490; 7 – 9, $8,930; 10 – 12, $9,140
Other fees (annual): registration, $540** ($180 credited toward tuition); capital development, $1,620; special services, $719
School year: September to June

Year founded: 1972. **Type of school:** coed, day, private nonprofit. **Governed by:** elected board of directors. **Sponsored by:** U.S. Embassy. **Accredited by:** Middle States (preK – 12), ECIS (7 – 12).

Curriculum/physical plant

Type: U.S. **Languages taught:** French. **Staff specialists:** counselor, nurse. **Special programs:** ESOL, reception. **Special curricular:** art, physical education, computer instruction, music, health. **Extracurricular:** drama, computers, yearbook, field trips, student government, other clubs. **Sports:** basketball, soccer, volleyball, intramurals. **Tests:** SSAT, PSAT, SAT, TOEFL, Iowa, Test of Achievement and Proficiency. **Graduates attending college:** 98%. **Graduates have attended:** Lafayette, Hamilton, Oberlin, Ohio Wesleyan U., U. of Massachusetts at Amherst. **Location:** Riviera III, a residential area on the outskirts of Abidjan. **Campus:** 13 acres. **Library:** 10,000 volumes. **Facilities:** new purpose-built facilities, 17 single-story buildings, infirmary, 2 science labs, computer center, language and special services rooms, music room, art room, regulation-sized soccer/football pitch, 400-meter track, softball field, air conditioning.

**CFA franc

CROATIA _____

Region: Europe
Size: 35,139 square miles
Population: 4,760,344
Capital: Zagreb

Telephone code: 38
Currency: dinar
Language: Croatian

ZAGREB

THE AMERICAN SCHOOL OF ZAGREB

Street address: 45 1/B Zelengaj, 41000 Zagreb, Croatia
Phone/facsimile: (38)(41)275541
U.S. mail: c/o Department of State, Washington, D.C. 20520-5080
Director: Gary Eubank
Staff: full-time, 8
Nationalities of staff: U.S., 4; other, 4

Grade levels: K – 8
Enrollment: K, 10; 1 – 6, 40; 7 – 8, 10; total, 60
Nationalities of student body: U.S., 10; U.K., 5; other, 45
Capacity: K, 10; 1 – 6, 40; 7 – 8, 10; total, 60
Tuition (annual): K – 8, $8,000
School year: August to June

Year founded: 1966. **Type of school:** coed, day, private nonprofit. **Governed by:** elected school board. **Accredited by:** Middle States.

Curriculum/physical plant

Type: U.S. **Special curricular:** art, physical education, computer instruction. **Extracurricular:** drama, gymnastics, newspaper, field trips, video club, sports. **Tests:** SSAT, SAT, ACT, TOEFL, Iowa, GRE, GMAT. **Location:** in suburban area. **Library:** 4,300 volumes. **Facilities:** 6 classrooms, computer lab, rented gymnasium, public playing field.

CUBA

Region: Western Atlantic
Size: 44,218 square miles
Population: 10,732,000
Capital: Havana

Telephone code: no direct dial
Currency: peso
Language: Spanish

HAVANA

INTERNATIONAL SCHOOL OF HAVANA

Street address: #315 18th Street & 5th Avenue, Miramar, Havana, Cuba
Phone: (no direct dial) 332540/332818/332960
U.S. mail: International School c/o USINT (Havana), U.S. Department of State, Washington, D.C. 20521-3200
U.K. mail: International School of Havana c/o FCO (Havana), King Charles Street, London SW1A 2AH, England
Principal: Judith A. Ford
Staff: full-time, 6; part-time, 9
Nationalities of staff: U.K., 2; host, 13
Grade levels: N – 12
Enrollment: N, 6; preK – 5, 53; 6 – 8, 19; 9 – 12, 26; total, 104
Nationalities of student body: U.S., 7; U.K., 3; other, 94
Capacity: N, 20; preK – 5, 84; 6 – 8, 48; 9 – 12, 30; total, 182
Teacher/student ratio: 1/9
Tuition (annual): N, $1,000 (half day), preK – 5, $3,400; 6 – 8, $3,750; 9 – 12, $4,500
Other fees (annual): registration*, $60; busing, $360
School year: September to June

Year founded: 1974. **Type of school:** coed, day, private nonprofit. **Governed by:** patronage (board of governors) of 12 ambassadors.

Curriculum/physical plant

Type: U.S., U.K. (9 – 12 correspondence courses, U. of Nebraska-Lincoln), IGCSE (from 1994). **Languages taught:** French, Spanish. **Special programs:** ESL. **Extracurricular:** field trips, interschool sports. **Clubs:** student council, debating, yearbook, handicrafts, computers, drama, basketball, football. **Tests:** SAT, TOEFL, Iowa. **Location:** in residential suburb, 2 blocks from sea. **Library:** 3,000 volumes. **Facilities:** 2 buildings, 13 classrooms, science lab, computer lab, playground.

*Once only fee

CURAÇAO†

Region: West Indies
Size: 171 square miles
Population: 191,000
Capital: Willemstad

Telephone code: 599
Currency: guilder
Language: Dutch, Papiamento, English, Spanish

WILLEMSTAD

INTERNATIONAL SCHOOL OF CURAÇAO

Street address: Koninginnelaan, Emmastad, Netherlands Antilles
Phone: (599)(9)373633   **Facsimile:** (599)(9)373142
Mail: PO Box 3090, Curaçao, Netherlands Antilles
Director: David Buck
Elementary principal: Lory Thiessen
Guidance counselor: Norm Flach
Business manager: Emma Van Delden
Staff: full-time, 25; part-time, 11
Nationalities of staff: U.S., 21; host, 8; other, 7
Grade levels: preK – 12
Enrollment: preK, 20; K, 25; 1 – 5, 130; 6 – 9, 95; 10 – 12, 50; total, 320
Nationalities of student body: U.S., 34; U.K., 17; host, 105; other, 164
Capacity: preK, 24; K, 24; 1 – 5, 135; 6 – 8, 72; 9 – 12, 96; total, 351
Teacher/student ratio: 1/11
Tuition (annual): preK – K, $2,730; 1 – 5, $4,520; 6 – 9, $5,070; 10 – 12, $5,800
Other fees (annual): registration, $835; capital levy*, $420
School year: August to June

Year founded: 1971. **Type of school:** coed, day, private nonprofit. **Governed by:** board of directors. **Accredited by:** Southern.

Curriculum/physical plant

Type: U.S. **Languages taught:** Spanish. **Staff specialists:** computer, counselor, college placement officer. **Special programs:** ESL, advanced placement, learning resource. **Special curricular:** art, physical education, computer instruction, music, journalism, Model UN. **Extracurricular:** dance, computers, newspaper, field trips, chorus, pottery, young astronauts, cooking, bowling, general outdoor games. **Sports:** basketball, soccer, softball, tennis, volleyball, badminton. **Organizations**: National Honor Society, National Junior Honor Society. **Tests:** PSAT, SAT, ACT, AP, Iowa. **Graduates attending college:** 85%. **Location:** in suburban area, 5 kilometers from Willemstad. **Campus:** 2 acres. **Library:** 9,000 volumes. **Facilities:** 6 buildings, 17 classrooms, playing field, science lab, computer lab, media resource room, 3 playgrounds, air conditioning.

*Once only fee   †Curaçao is actually part of Netherlands Antilles

CYPRUS _____

Region: Middle East
Size: 3,572 square miles
Population: 708,000
Capital: Nicosia

Telephone code: 357
Currency: pound
Languages: Greek, Turkish, English

LARNACA

AMERICAN ACADEMY LARNACA, CYPRUS

Street address: Gregory Afxentiou Avenue, Larnaca, Cyprus
Phone: (357)(46)52046/57206   **Facsimile:** (357)(46)51046
Mail: PO Box 112, Larnaca, Cyprus
Principal: Graham Watson
Assistant principals: Mr. E. Nittis, Miss M. Pambou, Mr. A. Ellinas,
   Mr. D. Koumandaris
Staff: full-time, 62; part-time, 9
Nationalities of staff: U.K., 8; host, 59; other, 4
Grade levels: 1 – 13
Enrollment: 1 – 6, 240; 7 – 9, 430; 10 – 12, 417; 13, 110; total, 1,197
Capacity: 1 – 6, 300; 7 – 9, 440; 10 – 12, 420; 13, 120; total, 1,280
Teacher/student ratio: 1/18
Tuition (annual): 1 – 6, $770; 7 – 9, $1,850; 10 – 12, $2,080; 13,
   $2,140
Other fees (annual): books, $300 average
School year: September to June

Year founded: 1908. **Type of school:** coed, day, private nonprofit.
Governed by: elected body of governors from the alumni of the school.

Curriculum/physical plant
   Type: U.S., U.K. **Languages taught:** English, French, Greek. **Staff specialists:** counselor. **Special curricular:** art, physical education, computer instruction. **Extracurricular:** drama, dance, computers, yearbook, newspaper, excursions/expeditions, field trips. **Sports:** basketball, football, hockey, softball, tennis, volleyball. **Clubs:** debating, French, science, folklore, folkdancing, economics and current affairs, literary, cultural. **Tests:** SAT, Achievement Tests, TOEFL, O- and A-level GCE, GCSE. **Graduates attending college:** 40%. **Graduates have attended:** Manchester, Sheffield, Yale, Kalamazoo, Trenton State College. **Location:** in center city. **Campus:** 8 acres. **Library:** 3,700 volumes. **Facilities:** 3 buildings, 50 classrooms, auditorium, 6 science labs, computer lab, medical room, tennis, basketball and volleyball courts, football pitch, typing room.

LIMASSOL

Logos School of English Education

Street address: 27 Yialousa Street, Limassol, Cyprus
Phone: (357)(5)336061   **Facsimile:** (357)(5)335578
Mail: PO Box 1075, Limassol, Cyprus
Principal: Levon Yergatian
Deputy principal: Peter Ross
Assistant principal: John Ross
Staff: full-time, 16; part-time, 2
Nationalities of staff: U.K., 8; host, 7; other, 3
Grade levels: 1 – 13
Enrollment: total, 180
Teacher/student ratio: 1/11
Boarders: boys, 13; girls, 5
Tuition (annual): 1 – 6, $1,653; 7 – 9, $2,020; 10 – 12, $2,204; 13, $2,388
Other fees (annual): registration, $48 (day), $96 (boarding); boarding,
$2,885

Year founded: 1973. **Type of school:** coed, day, boarding. **Governed by:**
appointed board of directors.

Curriculum/physical plant

Type: U.K., Cambridge U. approved IGCSE. **Languages taught:** French,
Arabic, Greek. **Special curricular:** physical education, biology, chemistry,
physics, history, geography. **Extracurricular:** drama, computers, Duke of
Edinburgh's Award activities. **Tests:** IGCSE, O- and A-level GCE. **Location:**
in city. **Campus:** 3 acres. **Facilities:** auditorium, cafeteria, covered play area,
playing field, science labs, library, computer lab.

NICOSIA

The American Academy Nicosia

Street address: 3A Michael Paridis, Nicosia, Cyprus
Phone: (357)(2)462886   **Facsimile:** (357)(2)466290
Mail: PO Box 1967, Nicosia, Cyprus
Principal: Christo Psiloinis
Assistant principals: Mary Psiloinis, Derrick Lewis, Jon Pomeroy
Staff: full-time, 56; part-time, 10
Nationalities of staff: U.S., 5; U.K., 10; host, 39; other, 12
Grade levels: 1 – 13
Enrollment: 1 – 6, 180; 7 – 9, 298; 10 – 12, 301; 13, 96; total, 875
Nationalities of student body: U.S., 7; U.K., 46; host, 680; other, 142

Capacity: total, 900
Teacher/student ratio: 1/14
Tuition (annual): 1 – 6, 770**; 7 – 9, 790; 10 – 13, 1,090
Other fees (annual): registration*, 50**; insurance, 2.50; books, 100;
   uniform, 100
School year: September through June

Year founded: 1922. **Type of school:** coed, day, private nonprofit.
Governed by: elected board of directors. **Accredited by:** Ministry of Education, Cyprus.

Curriculum/physical plant

Type: U.S., U.K. **Languages taught:** French, Greek. **Staff specialists:**
reading, math, computer, speech/hearing, counselor, nurse. **Special programs:** advanced placement, remedial, special language. **Special curricular:**
art, chorus, band, physical education, computer instruction, photography,
orchestra, guitar, UNESCO, cultural. **Extracurricular:** drama, gymnastics,
dance, choral music, instrumental music, computers, yearbook. **Sports:**
basketball, football, volleyball, badminton, olympic gym, scouts, St. John
ambulance. **Tests:** SSAT, TOEFL, A- and O-level GCE. **Graduates attending
college:** 10%. **Graduates have attended:** Oxford, London U. **Location:** in
city. **Library:** 20,000 volumes. **Facilities:** 44 classrooms, 2 auditoriums,
cafeteria, infirmary, covered play area, 2 playing fields, 4 science labs,
computer lab.

*Once only fee   **Cypriot pound

AMERICAN INTERNATIONAL SCHOOL OF CYPRUS

Street address: 11 Kassos Street, Nicosia, Cyprus
Phone: (357)(2)316345   **Facsimile:** (357)(2)316549
Mail: PO Box 3847, Nicosia, Cyprus
U.S. mail: (no personal name) Superintendent, American International
   School of Cyprus, PSC 815, FPO AE 09836
Superintendent: Walid Abushakra
Deputy superintendent: Larry May, Ed.D.
Boarding directors: Jeff and Lisa Squires
Activities director: Paul Maurer
Counselor/college placement officer: Joanna Ramos
Staff: full-time, 28; part-time, 2
Nationalities of staff: U.S., 17; U.K., 4; host, 8; other, 1
Grade levels: preK – 12
Enrollment: K3, 7; K4,12; K5, 13; 1 – 5, 82; 6 – 8, 60; 9 – 12, 82;
   total, 256
Nationalities of student body: U.S., 69; U.K., 12; host, 10; other, 165
Capacity: preK, 18; K, 18; 1 – 5, 108; 6 – 8, 60; 9 – 12, 100; total, 304
Boarders: boys, 20; girls, 10   **Grades:** 8 – 12   **Program:** planned 5-
   and 7-day in a separate dorm facility
Teacher/student ratio: 1/9

Tuition (annual): K3, 1,045**; K4, 1,365; K5 – 5, 2,471; 6 – 8, 2,516; 9 – 12, 3,312

Other fees (annual): registration, 50**; boarding, 6,900 (inclusive of day school fees); busing, 210 (optional); building surcharge (new students only), 500; ESL, 200

School year: September to June

Year founded: 1987. **Type of school:** coed, day, boarding, private.

Curriculum/physical plant

Type: U.S. **Languages taught:** French, Spanish, Modern Greek. **Staff specialists:** reading, math, computer, counselor, learning disabilities, nurse. **Special programs:** ESL, advanced placement, independent study, resource room, outdoor education. **Special curricular:** art, physical education, computer instruction, music. **Extracurricular:** drama, gymnastics, computers, yearbook, newspaper, literary magazine, photography. **Sports:** basketball, soccer, swimming, badminton, track and field, various intramural activities. **Tests:** PSAT, SAT, ACT, TOEFL, AP, Iowa, Gates-MacGinitie. **Location:** overlooking Nicosia. **Campus:** 4 acres. **Library:** 10,000 volumes. **Facilities:** 3 buildings, 25 classrooms, auditorium, 2 cafeterias, infirmary, covered play area, 2 tennis courts, playing field, 2 science labs, 3 computer labs, swimming pool, AV equipment, recreation room, video rooms, playground, air conditioning.

**Cypriot pound

THE GRAMMAR SCHOOL

Phone: (357)(2)621744   **Facsimile:** (357)(2)623044
Mail: Anthoupolis Highway, Nicosia, Cyprus
U.S. mail: PO Box 2262, Nicosia, Cyprus
Director general: Akis Gregoriou
Headmaster: Vassos Hajiyerou
Headmistress: Marina Koni
Staff: full-time, 43
Nationalities of staff: host, 43
Grade levels: first class (ages 12 – 13) – seventh class (ages 18 – 19)
Enrollment: total, 800
Nationalities of student body: U.S., 25; U.K., 100; host, 650; other, 25
Capacity: total, 1,000
Teacher/student ratio: 1/19

Year founded: 1963. **Type of school:** coed, day, proprietary. **Governed by:** board of directors. **Accredited by:** Cyprus government.

Curriculum

Type: U.S., U.K. **Languages of instruction:** English, Greek. **Languages taught:** English, French, Greek. **Staff specialists:** reading, math, computer, counselor, psychologist, nurse. **Special programs:** advanced placement. **Special curricular:** art, chorus, physical education, computer instruction.

Extracurricular: drama, gymnastics, dance, choral music, computers, yearbook, newspaper, photography, excursions/expeditions, field trips, sports. **Clubs:** debate, science, environment, flower arrangement, chess, radio, drama, music. **Tests:** SAT, TOEFL, A-level GCE, GCSE, LCCI. **Graduates attending college:** 75%. **Graduates have attended:** Rutgers, William and Mary, Iowa, London, Kent.

Physical plant
Location: in suburban area. **Library:** 10,000 volumes. **Facilities:** 7 buildings, 40 classrooms, auditorium, tennis court, gymnasium, playing field, science lab, computer lab, central heating.

PAPHOS

THE INTERNATIONAL SCHOOL OF PAPHOS
Street address: 22-26 Hellas Avenue, Paphos, Cyprus
Phone: (357)(6)232236   **Facsimile:** (357)(6)242541
Mail: PO Box 2018, Paphos, Cyprus
Administrator/business manager: Nic Nicolaides
Acting headmaster: Keith Smith
Staff: full-time, 16; part-time, 6
Nationalities of staff: U.K., 9; host, 8; other, 5
Grade levels: K – 12
Enrollment: total, 210
Capacity: preK, 20; K, 25; 1 – 6, 148; 7 – 9, 80; 10 – 12, 86; total, 359
Teacher/student ratio: 1/11
Tuition (annual): K, $678; reception, $1,038; infants, $1,242; junior 1 & 2, $1,485; junior 3 & prep, $1,530; forms 1 & 2, $1,680; form 3, $1,770; forms 4 & 5, $1,845; form 6, $1,905
Other fees (annual): boarding, $3,056 (ages 11 – 18); enrollment*, $300
School year: September to July

Year founded: 1980. **Type of school:** coed, day, boarding, private nonprofit. **Governed by:** elected board of governors. **Accredited by:** government of Cyprus.

Curriculum
Type: U.K., GCSE in general science. **Languages of instruction:** English, Greek. **Languages taught:** English, French, German, Greek. **Staff specialists:** reading, counselor. **Special programs:** advanced placement. **Special curricular:** art, chorus, physical education, computer instruction. **Extracurricular:** drama, gymnastics, dance, choral music, computers, yearbook, newspaper, excursions/expeditions, field trips. **Sports:** basketball, hockey, swimming, tennis, volleyball, diving, sailing, football (U.K.). **Clubs:** drama, Girl Guides, scouts, computer, orienteering. **Tests:** PSAT, SAT, TOEFL, AP, A-level GCE, GCSE. **Graduates attending college:** 100%. **Graduates have**

attended: Penn State, Skidmore, Johns Hopkins, U. of Massachusetts, Florida Institute of Technology.

Physical plant
    Location: just outside main town in residential/rural area. **Campus:** 6 acres. **Library:** 3,200 volumes. **Facilities:** 3 buildings, 21 classrooms, 2 auditoriums, covered play area, tennis court, gymnasium, playing field, 2 science labs, computer lab, AV facilities, hobbies room.

*Once only fee

CZECH REPUBLIC ──────────

Region: Europe
Size: 49,365 square miles
Population: 15,724,000
Capital: Prague

Telephone code: 42
Currency: koruna
Languages: Czech, Slovak
                    Hungarian, Romany

PRAGUE

INTERNATIONAL SCHOOL OF PRAGUE

Street address: Mylnerovka 2, Prague 6, Czech Republic
Phone: (42)(2)3112044   **Facsimile:** (42)(2)3118578
Mail: c/o U.S. Embassy, Trziste 15, 125 48 Prague 1, Czech Republic
U.S. mail: c/o U.S. Embassy, Department of State, Washington, D.C. 20521-5630
Director: Alan Conkey
Deputy director/high school principal: Richard Gillogly
Middle school principal/admissions: Ken Vogel
Lower school principal: Anne Ross
Business manager: Alena Svobodova
Staff: full-time, 36; part-time, 8
Nationalities of staff: U.S., 35; host, 3; other, 6
Grade levels: preK – 11
Enrollment: preK, 30; K, 30; 1 – 6, 225; 7 – 11, 125; total, 410
Capacity: preK, 30; K, 30; 1 – 6, 220; 7 – 11, 130; total, 410
Teacher/student ratio: 1/10
Tuition (annual): preK, $2,500 (half-day); K – 2, $7,300;
    3 – 6, $7,700; 7 – 8, $8,300; 9 – 11, $8,700
Other fees (annual): registration*, $100; building levy, $1,500
School year: August to June

    Year founded: 1948. **Type of school:** coed, day. **Governed by:** appointed/elected school board. **Accredited by:** Middle States.

Curriculum/physical plant

Type: U.S. **Languages taught:** French, German, Czech. **Staff specialists:** computer, art, ESL, music, physical education. **Extracurricular:** drama, dance, computers, yearbook, newspaper, literary magazine, music, volleyball, student council, choir. **Tests:** ITBS. **Location:** 3 campuses, all in residential area of Prague 6. **Library:** 12,000 volumes. **Facilities:** 3 buildings, 34 classrooms, playing fields, gyms (rented from nearby sports clubs).

*Once only fee

DENMARK _____

Region: Europe
Size: 16,633 square miles
Population: 5,134,000
Capital: Copenhagen

Telephone code: 45
Currency: krone
Language: Danish

COPENHAGEN

COPENHAGEN INTERNATIONAL SCHOOL†

Street address: Hellerupvej 26, 2900 Hellerup, Denmark
Phone: (45)(31)612230
Director: Leif Berntsen
Senior school principal: James Keson
Primary and middle school principal: Susan R. Stengel, Ed.D.
Business manager: Ronald A. Spinner
Staff: full-time, 32; part-time, 16
Nationalities of staff: U.S., 17; U.K., 15; host, 8; other, 8
Grade levels: preK – 13
Enrollment: preK, 15; K, 16; 1 – 6, 151; 7 – 9, 88; 10 – 13, 122;
    total, 392
Nationalities of student body: U.S., 45; U.K., 33; host, 60; other, 254
Capacity: preK, 20; K, 20; 1 – 6, 240; 7 – 9, 120; 10 – 13, 150;
    total, 550
Teacher/student ratio: 1/10
Tuition (annual): preK – 6, 24,740**; 7 – 9, 28,680; 10 – 11, 65,290;
    12 – 13, 69,950
Other fees (annual): registration*, 500**; busing, 11,000 – 15,000;
    application*, 500; ESL*, 4,200 – 9,600
School year: August to June

Year founded: 1963. **Type of school:** self-owning, independent. **Governed by:** eleven-member board. **Accredited by:** New England, ECIS.

Curriculum/physical plant

Type: IB, international. **Languages taught:** French, German, Danish.

Staff specialists: high school counselor, 2 librarians. **Special programs:** ESL. **Special curricular:** writing in all subjects, house system. **Extracurricular:** drama, computers, yearbook, charity, ballet, journalism, art, sports, music, Model UN, math club. **Graduates attending college:** 95%. **Graduates have attended:** MIT, Columbia, Stanford, London School of Economics, Cambridge. **Location:** suburban Copenhagen, 15 minutes from center city, with easy access to greater Copenhagen by train. **Facilities:** 2 gymnasiums, science labs, 2 computer labs, 2 libraries, outdoor play areas.

*Once only fee   **Danish krone   †new school is merger of Copenhagen International School and Copenhagen International Junior School

DOMINICAN REPUBLIC ⎯⎯⎯⎯

Region: Caribbean
Size: 18,704 square miles
Population: 7,384,000
Capital: Santo Domingo

Telephone code: 809
Currency: peso
Language: Spanish

JARABACOA

Escuela Caribe
Caribe – Vista School

Street address: Pinar Quemado, Jarabacoa, Dominican Republic
Phone: (1)(809)5742760   **Facsimile:** (1)(809)5742917
   U.S. facsimile: (1)(800)3334009
U.S. mail: c/o New Horizons Ministries, Roads 100 South at 350 East, Marion, IN 46953, U.S.A.
Program director: Phil Redwine
Director of education: Dee Lal
Director of home life: Michael Harmon
Business manager: Mercedes Abreu
Staff: full-time, 33; part-time, 2
Nationalities of staff: U.S., 33; other, 2
Grade levels: 8 – 12
Enrollment: 8 – 9, 14; 10 – 12, 26; total, 40
Nationalities of student body: U.S., 40
Capacity: total, 40
Boarders: boys, 18; girls, 19   **Grades:** 8 – 12   **Program:** planned 7-day
Tuition: $1,240 – 2,640 per month, based on income
School year: January to December

Year founded: 1971. **Type of school:** coed, boarding, evangelical, private nonprofit, therapeutic education. **Governed by:** elected board of directors. **Sponsored by:** New Horizons Ministries.

Curriculum/physical plant

Type: U.S. **Languages taught:** Spanish. **Staff specialists:** counselor, psychologist, special education teacher. **Special programs:** independent study, correspondence, remedial. **Special curricular:** chorus, physical education, computer instruction, instruments. **Extracurricular:** choral music, instrumental music, computers, yearbook, excursions/expeditions, field trips, student achievement club, student committee, community service projects. **Tests:** ACT, Stanford, DATA. **Graduates attending college:** 30%. **Graduates have attended:** Westmont, Indiana Wesleyan, Pensacola Christian, Taylor College, Azusa Pacific. **Location:** in the beautiful highlands near Jarabacoa. **Campus:** 25 acres. **Library:** 3,000 volumes. **Facilities:** 10 buildings, 5 classrooms, 2 playing fields, computer lab, basketball court, AV equipment, vocational shop, 4 student boarding houses.

LA ROMANA

ABRAHAM LINCOLN SCHOOL

Phone: (1)(809)6877787 ext. 1284   **Facsimile:** (1)(809)6879740
   Telex: ITT 3460511   **Cable:** CENTROMANA Dominican Republic
Mail: Central Romana Corporation, La Romana, Dominican Republic
U.S. mail: c/o Americas Export Corporation, 626 North Dixie Highway, West Palm Beach, FL 33401, U.S.A.
Headmaster: Harry Magee
Deputy head teacher: Alan Wood
Head of primary school: Teresa Dodkin
Staff: full-time, 34; part-time, 2
Nationalities of staff: U.K., 24; host, 12
Grade levels: preK – 12
Enrollment: preK, 36; K, 36; 1 – 6, 210; 7 – 9, 78; 10 – 12, 68; total, 428
Capacity: preK, 36; K, 36; 1 – 6, 216; 7 – 9, 90; 10 – 12, 90; total, 468
Teacher/student ratio: 1/12
Tuition (annual): preK – 12, 60,000**
School year: September to June

Year founded: 1917. **Type of school:** coed, day, company sponsored. **Governed by:** board of governors. **Sponsored by:** Central Romana Corporation. **Accredited by:** Department of Education of Dominican Republic.

Curriculum/physical plant

Type: U.K., Dominican. **Languages of instruction:** English, Spanish. **Languages taught:** French. **Special programs:** remedial. **Special curricular:** art, chorus, physical education, computer instruction. **Extracurricular:** drama, dance, choral music, computers, literary magazine, photography, field trips. **Sports:** basketball, soccer, softball, volleyball, golf. **Clubs:** natural history, photography, ceramics, chess, gymnastics. **Tests:** SAT, TOEFL. **Graduates attending college:** 90%. **Graduates have attended:** Wisconsin, Louisiana State U., Columbia, Notre Dame, York (U.K.). **Location:** 1 mile from

city of La Romana, overlooking Caribbean Sea. **Library:** 10,000 volumes.
Facilities: 7 buildings, 28 classrooms, auditorium, 3 science labs, computer
lab, softball field, soccer field, volleyball/basketball court, air conditioning.

**Dominican peso

SANTO DOMINGO

THE CAROL MORGAN SCHOOL OF SANTO DOMINGO

Street address: Ave. Sarasota esq. Nunez de Caceres, Santo Domingo,
   Dominican Republic
Phone: (1)(809)5378080   **Facsimile:** (1)(809)5339222
   Cable: CARMORGAN
Mail: Apartado 1169, Santo Domingo, Dominican Republic
U.S. mail: (no personal name) The Carol Morgan School of Santo
   Domingo, EPS-P-2379, PO Box 02-5261, Miami, FL 33102-5261,
   U.S.A.
Headmaster: J. Edward Mandrell, Ed.D.
Secondary school principal: Mark Klimesh
Assistant principal: Thomas Eisenhower
Elementary school principal: Peggy McLeod
Assistant principal: Helen Faber
Head of computer services: Quirico Perez
Business manager: Rebeca Paiewonsky
Staff: full-time, 90
Nationalities of staff: U.S., 62; host, 18; other, 10
Grade levels: preK – 12
Enrollment: preK, 25; K, 45; 1 – 6, 320; 7 – 9, 205; 10 – 12, 205;
   total, 800
Nationalities of student body: U.S., 150; host, 540; other, 110
Capacity: total, 1,000
Teacher/student ratio: 1/9
Tuition (annual): preK, $3,120; K – 3, $4,880; 4 – 6, $5,280; 7 – 8,
   $5,600; 9 – 12, $5,760
Other fees (annual): registration, $80; capital levy, $80; entrance*:
   preK – K $1,600; 1 – 6, $2,400; 7 – 12, $2,800
School year: August to June

Year founded: 1933. **Type of school:** coed, day. **Governed by:** elected
board of directors. **Accredited by:** Southern.

Curriculum/physical plant
   Type: U.S. **Languages taught:** French, Spanish. **Staff specialists:**
reading, computer, counselor, psychologist, learning disabilities, nurse.
Special programs: ESL, advanced placement, remedial. **Special curricular:**
art, chorus, band, physical education, computer instruction, drama, creative

writing. **Extracurricular:** drama, yearbook, newspaper, literary magazine, interscholastic and intramural athletics, various clubs. **Tests:** SSAT, PSAT, SAT, ACT, AP, Iowa, MAT, ACH. **Graduates attending college:** 95%. **Graduates have attended:** Stanford, U. of Pennsylvania, Smith, U. of Texas, MIT. **Location:** in city. **Campus:** 12 acres. **Library:** 18,000 volumes. **Facilities:** 8 buildings, 49 classrooms, cafeteria, infirmary, gymnasium, 5 playing fields, 2 computer labs, science building with 6 laboratories.

*Once only fee

ECUADOR

Region: South America
Size: 109,483 square miles
Population: 10,751,000
Capital: Quito

Telephone code: 593
Currency: sucre
Languages: Spanish, Quechuan, Jivaroan

GUAYAQUIL

COLEGIO AMERICANO DE GUAYAQUIL

Street address: Ave. Juan Tanca Marengo, Km. 6-1/2 via a Daule, Guayaquil, Ecuador
Phone: (593)(4)255509/255496   **Facsimile:** (593)(4)250453
Mail: PO Box 3304, Guayaquil, Ecuador
U.S. mail: Air Center 1452, PO Box 522970, Miami, FL 33152-2970, U.S.A.
Director general: S. James Whitman, Jr.
High school principal: Patricia Ayala
Elementary school principal: Nancy Rohde
Preschool director: Maria Elena Pin
Staff: full-time, 140; part-time, 10
Nationalities of staff: U.S., 25; host, 123; other, 2
Grade levels: N – 12
Enrollment: N – K, 300; 1 – 6, 900; 7 – 12, 600; total, 1,800
Nationalities of student body: U.S., 90; host, 1,590; other, 120
Teacher/student ratio: 1/12
Tuition (annual): N – 6, $1,000; 7 – 12, $1,190
Other fees (annual): registration, $130; busing, $15/month; books, $100
School year: May to January

Year founded: 1942. **Type of school:** coed, day, private nonprofit. **Governed by:** elected board of directors. **Sponsored by:** school board. **Accredited by:** Southern.

Curriculum/physical plant

Type: U.S., Ecuadorean, IB. **Languages of instruction:** English, Spanish. **Languages taught:** French. **Staff specialists:** counselor, nurse, IB coordinator-English. **Special programs:** ESL. **Special curricular:** art, physical education, computer instruction. **Extracurricular:** drama, gymnastics, computers, newspaper, soccer, baseball, softball, volleyball, chorus, music instruction. **Tests:** PSAT, TOEFL, IB, CTBS. **Graduates attending college:** 80%. **Graduates have attended:** Brown, Laica U., Catholic U., Polytechnical U., Oklahoma U. **Location:** on outskirts of city. **Campus:** 30 acres. **Library:** 15,000 volumes. **Facilities:** 18 buildings, 66 classrooms, auditorium, cafeteria, infirmary, gymnasium, 2 playing fields, 2 science labs, 2 computer labs.

INTER-AMERICAN ACADEMY

Street address: Km. 10-1/2 via a la Costa, Guayaquil, Ecuador
Phone: (593)(4)871790   **Facsimile:** (593)(4)873358
Mail: PO Box 09-06-209-U, Guayaquil, Ecuador
U.S. mail: (no personal name) Inter-American Academy, AMCONGEN
     Guayaquil, APO Miami 34039
Executive director: Brent Hudson, Ed.D.
Assistant director: Myriam Rodriguez
Lower school coordinator: Beth Hudson
Business manager: William Sanchez
Staff: full-time, 35
Nationalities of staff: U.S., 16; host, 9; other, 10
Grade levels: preK – 12
Enrollment: preK, 19; K, 22; 1 – 6, 171; 7 – 9, 80; 10 – 12, 55; total, 347
Nationalities of student body: U.S., 113; host, 88; other, 146
Teacher/student ratio: 1/10
Tuition (annual): preK – K, $2,475; 1 – 8, $3,690; 9 – 12, $4,140
Other fees (annual): registration, $300; books, $75; entrance*, $1,500
School year: August to May

Year founded: 1979. **Type of school:** coed, day. **Governed by:** elected board of directors. **Accredited by:** Southern, Ecuadorean Ministry of Education.

Curriculum/physical plant

Type: U.S., IB. **Languages taught:** French, Spanish. **Staff specialists:** counselor. **Special programs:** ESL. **Special curricular:** art, physical education, computer instruction, music. **Extracurricular:** drama, gymnastics, computers, yearbook, newspaper, literary magazine, photography, excursions/expeditions, National Honor Society, student council. **Tests:** SSAT, PSAT, SAT, ACT, TOEFL, IB, Stanford, MAT. **Graduates attending college:** 99%. **Graduates have attended:** Brown, Cornell, Carleton, St. John's (Minnesota), U. of Virginia. **Location:** in Puerto Azul, a suburb of Guayaquil. **Campus:** 20,000 square meters. **Facilities:** 8 buildings, 28 classrooms, cafeteria, tennis court, 2 playing fields, science lab, computer labs, video room, air conditioning.

*Once only fee

QUITO

ALLIANCE ACADEMY

Street address: Villalengua 187, Quito, Ecuador
Phone: (593)(2)240142   **Facsimile:** (593)(2)440350
Mail: Casilla 17-11-06186, Quito, Ecuador
Director: Bennett J. Schepens, Ph.D.
Secondary school principal: Daniel Egeler
Elementary school principal: Timothy Sheppard
Staff: full-time, 66; part-time, 22
Nationalities of staff: U.S., 66; other, 22
Grade levels: preK – 12
Enrollment: preK, 23; K, 26; 1 – 6, 215; 7 – 8, 89; 9 – 12, 154; total, 507
Nationalities of student body: U.S., 338; host, 25; other, 144
Capacity: preK, 24; K, 40; 1 – 6, 240; 7 – 8, 120; 9 – 12, 240; total, 664
Teacher/student ratio: 1/7
Boarders: boys, 31; girls, 30   **Grades:** 1 – 12   **Program:** planned 7-day
Tuition (annual): K, $1,200; 1 – 6, $4,250; 7 – 8, $4,450; 9 – 12, $4,850
Other fees (annual): insurance, $7; activities, $8.50; yearbook, $35
School year: August to June

Year founded: 1929. **Type of school:** coed, day, boarding, church-related. **Governed by:** elected and appointed school board. **Sponsored by:** Christian and Missionary Alliance. **Accredited by:** Southern.

Curriculum

Type: U.S. **Languages taught:** French, Spanish. **Staff specialists:** reading, computer, learning disabilities, nurse, counselors. **Special programs:** ESL, advanced placement. **Special curricular:** art, chorus, band, physical education, computer instruction, home economics, woodshop, photography, journalism, pre-vocational education. **Extracurricular:** drama, gymnastics, choral music, instrumental music, computers, yearbook, newspaper, photography, field trips. **Sports:** basketball, soccer, track, volleyball, intramural sports. **Clubs:** art, National Honor Society, student council, music ensemble, Christian Service Organization, mountain-climbing, garden, video. **Tests:** PSAT, SAT, ACT, TOEFL, AP, Stanford. **Graduates attending college:** 95%. **Graduates have attended:** Wheaton College, U. of Pennsylvania, Flagler College, Bryn Mawr, Bethel College.

Physical plant

Location: in northern section of Quito. **Campus:** 5 acres. **Library:** 32,000 volumes. **Facilities:** 8 buildings, 50 classrooms, auditorium, infirmary, covered play area, tennis court, gymnasium, 2 playing fields, 3 science labs, 3 computer labs, 5 dormitories.

AMERICAN SCHOOL OF QUITO

Street address: Carcelén, Quito, Ecuador
Phone: (593)(2)472974 – 5   **Facsimile:** (593)(2)472972
   Telex: 39321029 FTONIA ED
Mail: PO Box 1701157, Quito, Ecuador
U.S. mail: Director (ASQ), c/o U.S. Embassy Quito,
   Unit #5372-Box 004, AA Miami 34039-3420
Director: Ms. Pilar de Ponce
High school rector: Mercedes de Merino
Elementary principal: Susane Hervas
International coordinator: Pilar Ponce
Secondary English coordinator: Susan Davalos
Elementary English coordinator: Susan Barba
Manager: Gonzalo Lune
Staff: full-time, 230; part-time, 30
Nationalities of staff: U.S., 54; host, 185; other, 21
Grade levels: preK – 12
Enrollment: preK, 195; 1 – 6, 1,071; 7 – 12, 1,170; total, 2,436
Capacity: K, 200; 1 – 6, 1,200; 7 – 12, 1,200; total, 2,600
Teacher/student ratio: 1/10
Tuition (annual): international section: K, $1,800; 1 – 6, $3,900;
   7 – 12, $4,500; national section: K, $795; 1 – 6, $682; 7 – 12,
   $733
Other fees (annual): registration, $200; capital levy*, $150; insurance,
   $15; busing, $150; books and materials, $200
School year: late September to July

Year founded: 1939. **Type of school:** coed, day, private nonprofit,
bilingual. **Governed by:** elected board of administration. **Accredited by:**
Ecuadorean Ministry of Education, Southern.

Curriculum/physical plant

Type: U.S., Ecuadorean, IB. **Languages taught:** English, Spanish. **Staff
specialists:** nurse, counselors, psychologists, medical doctor. **Special programs:** ESL, honors sections. **Extracurricular:** computers, newspaper, literary magazine, field trips, book club, mathematics, physics, English. **Sports:**
baseball, basketball, soccer, volleyball, track and field, ping-pong, Olympic
gymnastics. **Clubs:** ecology, Girl Scouts, Model UN, journalism, get-to-know
Ecuador, ceramics, flower and garden, video, theater and drama. **Tests:**
PSAT, SAT, TOEFL, IB, Iowa. **Graduates attending college:** 92%. **Graduates
have attended:** Cornell, Notre Dame, Brown, Drexel, Harvard. **Location:** in
suburban area, 17 kilometers north of city. **Campus:** 22 acres. **Libraries:**
25,000 volumes. **Facilities:** 14 buildings, 109 classrooms, auditorium,
infirmary, gymnasium, 7 playing fields, 7 science labs, 5 computer labs, 2
snack bars, 3 audio-visual rooms, language lab, track and stadium.

*Once only fee

Cotopaxi Academy

American International School

Street address: De las Higuerillas y Alondras (Monteserrin), Quito, Ecuador

Phone: (593)(2)433602/434976   **Facsimile:** (593)(2)445195
   Telex: 39322298 ECUAME   **Cable:** PAX

Mail: PO Box 17-01-199, Quito, Ecuador

U.S. mail: (no personal name) Cotopaxi Academy, c/o U.S. Embassy Quito, APO Miami 34039

Superintendent: Arthur Pontes

High school principal: Arthur Charles, Ph.D.

Elementary school principal: Terry Factor

Staff: full-time, 76; part-time, 10

Nationalities of staff: U.S., 56; U.K., 2; host, 18; other, 10

Grade levels: preK – 12

Enrollment: preK, 69; K, 60; 1 – 5, 239; 6 – 9, 216; 10 – 12, 126; total, 710

Teacher/student ratio: 1/9

Tuition (annual): preK, $1,554; K, $2,244; 1 – 2, $4,302; 3 – 5, $4,554; 6 – 8, $5,364; 9 – 12, $5,730

Other fees (annual): registration*, $100; capital levy*, $750; insurance, $10; busing, $150

School year: August to June

Year founded: 1959. **Type of school:** coed, day, private nonprofit. **Governed by:** elected board of directors. **Accredited by:** Southern.

Curriculum/physical plant

Type: U.S., IB. **Languages taught:** French, Spanish. **Staff specialists:** reading, math, computer, psychologist, learning disabilities, nurse, counselors. **Special programs:** ESL, honors sections, remedial, IB. **Special curricular:** art, band, physical education, orchestra, glee club, computer instruction. **Extracurricular:** drama, dance, choral music, instrumental music, computers, yearbook, newspaper, photography, excursions/expeditions, field trips, Model UN. **Sports:** basketball, fencing, soccer, softball, volleyball. **Clubs:** cheerleaders, honor society, student council, outing clubs, social action. **Tests:** PSAT, SAT, ACT, TOEFL, IB, MAT, Otis-Lennon. **Graduates attending college:** 85%. **Graduates have attended:** Harvard, Brown, Virginia Tech, U. of Pennsylvania, Cornell. **Location:** in city. **Campus:** 7 hectares. **Libraries:** 30,000 volumes. **Facilities:** 70 classrooms, auditorium, 2 cafeterias, infirmary, gymnasium, 2 playing fields, swimming pool, music complex, 3 art rooms.

*Once only fee

International Schools Services

presents the

1994
INTERNATIONAL
RECRUITMENT CENTERS

- **BOSTON, MA**
3–6 February 1994

- **SAN FRANCISCO, CA**
17–20 February 1994

- **PHILADELPHIA, PA**
24–26 June 1994

Call or write for details
INTERNATIONAL SCHOOLS SERVICES
Educational Staffing Department
PO Box 5910, Princeton, NJ 08543
Phone: 609-452-0990; Fax: 609-452-2690

EGYPT

Region: Africa
Size: 386,650 square miles
Population: 54,451,000
Capital: Cairo

Telephone code: 20
Currency: pound
Languages: Arabic, English

ALEXANDRIA

SCHUTZ AMERICAN SCHOOL

Street address: 51 Schutz Street, Alexandria, Egypt
Phone: (20)(3)5701435/5712205   **Facsimile:** (20)(3)5710229
Mail: PO Box 1000, Alexandria, Egypt
Headmaster: Dr. Lawrence Pattee
Assistant headmaster: Ronald Walters
Staff: full-time, 26; part-time, 2
Nationalities of staff: U.S., 17; U.K., 1; host, 3; other, 7
Grade levels: N – 12
Enrollment: N – preK, 10; K, 8; 1 – 6, 83; 7 – 9, 43; 10 – 12, 31; total, 175
Nationalities of student body: U.S., 65; host, 35; other, 75
Capacity: N – preK, 15; K, 15; 1 – 6, 100; 7 – 9, 60; 10 – 12, 60; total, 250
Teacher/student ratio: 1/6
Tuition (annual): N, $3,150; K, $5,880; 1 – 4, $6,930; 5 – 8, $7,140; 9 – 12, $7,560
Other fees: registration*, $890
School year: September to June

Year founded: 1924. **Type of school:** coed, day, private nonprofit. **Governed by:** local board. **Accredited by:** ECIS, New England.

Curriculum/physical plant

Type: U.S. **Languages taught:** French, Arabic. **Staff specialists:** computer, nurse, EFL. **Special programs:** advanced placement, honors sections, EFL. **Special curricular:** art, computer instruction, music, woodshop. **Extracurricular:** drama, dance, computers, yearbook, newspaper, athletics. **Tests:** PSAT, SAT, ACT, TOEFL, AP, Iowa. **Graduates attending college:** 95%. **Location:** in residential area of Alexandria. **Campuses (2):** 3 acres. **Libraries:** 20,000 volumes. **Facilities:** 7 buildings, 20 classrooms, auditorium, cafeteria, 2 infirmaries, tennis court, playing field, 2 science labs, computer lab, swimming pool, snack bar.

*Once only fee

CAIRO

THE AMERICAN INTERNATIONAL SCHOOL IN EGYPT

Street address: Tiba 2000 Centre-Al Nasr Street, Nasr City, Cairo, Egypt
Phone: (20)(2)2623147/2635699   **Facsimile:** (20)(2)2628641
Mail: PO Box 8090 Masaken, Nasr City 11371, Cairo, Egypt
Chairman/superintendent: Walid Abushakra
High school principal: Lee Webb, Ed.D.
Elementary school principal: Jo An Horton, Ed.D.
Counselor, high school: Nancy Foster
Business manager: Mamdouh Mazhar
Staff: full-time, 65; part-time, 3
Nationalities of staff: U.S., 57; host, 11
Grade levels: preK – 12
Enrollment: preK, 20; K, 40; 1 – 6, 240; 7 – 9, 160; 10 – 12, 145; total, 605
Nationalities of student body: U.S., 75; U.K., 15; host, 300; other, 215
Capacity: preK, 20; K, 40; 1 – 6, 240; 7 – 9, 160; 10 – 12, 200; total, 660
Teacher/student ratio: 1/9
Tuition (annual): preK – K, $3,500; 1 – 4, $4,500; 5 – 12, $5,500
Other fees (anual): busing, $500; building fund*, $1,000
School year: September to June

Year founded: 1990. **Type of school:** coed, day. **Accredited by:** Middle States.

Curriculum

Type: U.S., IB. **Languages taught:** English, French, Arabic. **Staff specialists:** computer, counselor, nurse. **Special programs:** ESL, honors sections. **Special curricular:** art, chorus, band, physical education, computer instruction, Model UN. **Extracurricular:** drama, choral music, instrumental music, computers, yearbook, newspaper, excursions/expeditions, field trips. **Sports:** basketball, soccer, tennis, track and field, volleyball, intramurals. **Clubs:** chess, computer, drama, science, French, intramurals, backgammon, running, aerobics. **Tests:** PSAT, SAT, TOEFL, IB, Iowa. **Graduates attending college:** 100%.

Physical plant

Location: in the modern Nasr City section of Cairo. **Campus:** 3 acres. **Library:** 15,000 volumes. **Facilities:** 1 building, 40 classrooms, cafeteria, infirmary, 2 playing fields, 3 science labs, computer lab, commons.

*Once only fee

BRITISH INTERNATIONAL SCHOOL CAIRO

Street address: Imara el Yemani Street, Zamalek, Cairo, Egypt
Phone: (20)(2)3406674/3415959   **Facsimile:** (20)(2)3414168
Mail: PO Box 137, Gezira, Cairo, Egypt

Principal: Cameron Cochrane
Head of seniors: Geoffery Fisher
Head of primary: Barry McCormick
Staff: full-time, 38; part-time, 5
Nationalities of staff: U.K., 33; other, 10
Grade levels: primary (ages 4 – 11); seniors (ages 11 – 18)
Enrollment: primary, 288; seniors, 190; total, 478
Nationalities of student body: U.S., 32; U.K., 145; host, 88; other, 213
Capacity: primary, 320; seniors, 200; total, 520
Teacher/student ratio: 1/12
Tuition (annual): primary, 3,540**; seniors, 4,200; IB, 4,575
Other fees: registration*, 50**; admission*: primary, 1,180; seniors, 1,400; IB, 1,525; supply fund*, 550
School year: September to June

Year founded: 1976. **Type of school:** coed, day, private nonprofit. **Governed by:** board of directors.

Curriculum/physical plant

Type: U.K., IB, GCSE. **Languages taught:** French, Spanish, German, Arabic. **Staff specialists:** reading, computer, counselor, nurse, librarian. **Special curricular:** art, chorus, physical education, computer instruction. **Extracurricular:** drama, gymnastics, dance, computers, yearbook, field trips. **Sports:** basketball, dance, soccer, tennis, volleyball, netball, badminton, table tennis, Tae Kwon Do, gymnastics, athletics. **Clubs:** Brownies, Guides, chess, Bookworms, Cubs. **Tests:** IB, GCSE. **Graduates attending college:** 80%. **Graduates have attended:** Oxford U., London U., London School of Economics, Sorbonne. **Location:** in Zamalek, a residential, multinational area on an island in Cairo. **Libraries:** 10,000 volumes. **Facilities:** 1 building, 30 classrooms, auditorium, infirmary, 2 covered play areas, 2 gymnasiums, 3 playing fields, 3 science labs, computer lab, AV-aids room.

*Once only fee   **Pound sterling

CAIRO AMERICAN COLLEGE

Street address: 1 Midan Digla, Maadi, Cairo, Egypt 11431
Phone: (20)(2)3529244   **Facsimile:** (20)(2)3523057
Mail: PO Box 39, Maadi, Cairo, Egypt 11431
U.S. mail: Superintendent, Cairo American College, c/o American Embassy, Unit 64900, Box 21, APO AE 09839-4900
Superintendent: David J. Chojnacki
High school principal: Michael Levinson
Middle school principal: Douglas Joy
Elementary school principal: Ronald Dowty
Assistant superintendent for fiscal affairs: Wahib Girgis
Staff: full-time, 147; part-time, 19
Nationalities of staff: U.S., 138; U.K., 3; host, 14; other, 11

Grade levels: K – 12
Enrollment: K, 73; 1 – 5, 499; 6 – 8, 359; 9 – 12, 476; total, 1,407
Nationalities of student body: U.S., 829; U.K., 32; host, 201;
   other, 345
Capacity: K, 75; 1 – 5, 533; 6 – 8, 360; 9 – 12, 480; total, 1,448
Teacher/student ratio: 1/9
Tuition (annual): K, $6,070; 1 – 12, $7,950
Other fees (annual): registration*, $2,250; busing, $1,130; assess-
   ment fee, $850; ESL $2,300; building and construction fee, $200;
   AP and IB tests
School year: August to June

Year founded: 1945. **Type of school:** coed, day, private nonprofit.
Governed by: appointed board of directors. **Accredited by:** Middle States.
Regional organizations: NE/SA, AISA.

Curriculum

Type: U.S., IB. **Languages taught:** French, Spanish, Arabic. **Staff
specialists:** reading, computer, counselor, psychologist, nurse, speech/
language, learning resource. **Special programs:** ESL, advanced placement,
honors sections, remedial. **Special curricular:** chorus, band, physical education, computer instruction, fine and applied arts, business education. **Co-
curricular:** drama, choral music, instrumental music, computers, literary
magazine, Model UN, Close Up, math, speech and debate, student council,
National Honor Society, Arabic, French, Spanish, World Rights, International,
Quill and Scroll, Future Business Leaders, middle school intramural program, elementary after-school activities program. **Sports:** baseball, basketball, cheerleading, soccer, softball, swimming, tennis, track, volleyball, cross-
country, wrestling. **Tests:** SSAT, PSAT, SAT, ACT, TOEFL, AP, Iowa. **Graduates attending college:** 95%. **Graduates have attended:** American U. in
Cairo, Hamilton, Oberlin, Stanford, Swarthmore.

Physical plant

Location: in Maadi, a residential suburb near River Nile about 6 miles
south of Cairo. **Campus:** 11 acres. **Library:** 52,000 volumes; 15,000 AV
materials. **Facilities:** 16 buildings, over 100 classrooms, auditorium, health
clinic, gymnasium, 2 playing fields, 7 science labs, 5 computer labs, swimming pool, tennis courts, media center, industrial arts building, 400-meter
all-weather track, air conditioning.

*Once only fee

EL SALVADOR

Region: Central America
Size: 8,124 square miles
Population: 5,418,000
Capital: San Salvador

Telephone code: 503
Currency: colon
Languages: Spanish

SAN SALVADOR

COLEGIO INTERNACIONAL DE SAN SALVADOR

Street address: Calle La Reforma, Colonia San Benito, San Salvador, El Salvador
Phone: (503)241330/237335   **Facsimile:** (503)711248
Mail: Apartado 05-15, San Salvador, El Salvador
U.S. mail: Box 02-5324, SPE SAL 0071, Miami, FL 33102, U.S.A.
Principal: Chester Stemp
Staff: full-time, 17; part-time, 13
Nationalities of staff: U.S., 11; host, 18; other, 1
Grade levels: preK – 12
Enrollment: preK, 22; K, 27; 1 – 6, 145; 7 – 9, 75; 10 – 12, 60; total, 329
Nationalities of student body: U.S., 77; U.K., 2; host, 198; other, 52
Capacity: preK, 24; K, 24; 1 – 6, 144; 7 – 9, 72; 10 – 12, 72;   total, 336
Teacher/student ratio: 1/14
Tuition (annual): preK – K, $852; 1 – 9, $1,000; 10 – 12, $1,120
Other fees (annual): registration*, $350; books, $50 – 100
School year: August to June

Year founded: 1979. **Type of school:** coed, day, proprietary. **Governed by:** appointed board of owners (Stemp family). **Accredited by:** Ministry of Education.

Curriculum/physical plant

Type: U.S., equivalency to local program. **Languages of instruction:** English, Spanish for some electives. **Languages taught:** English, Spanish. **Staff specialists:** nurse, counselor. **Special programs:** ESL, correspondence. **Special curricular:** physical education. **Extracurricular:** drama, gymnastics, dance, yearbook, newspaper, excursions/expeditions. **Sports:** basketball, soccer, volleyball, swimming, gymnastics, intramurals. **Clubs:** student council, newspaper, yearbook, first-aid, French. **Tests:** SAT, PSAT, ACT, TOEFL, Iowa. **Graduates attending college:** 100%. **Graduates have attended:** Oberlin, Goucher, San José State, Liberty, Florida International. **Location:** in Upper-income residential area. **Campus:** 1 acre. **Library:** 3,000 volumes. **Facilities:** 2 buildings, 17 classrooms, gymnasium, science lab, swimming pool.

*Once only fee

ESCUELA AMERICANA

Street address: Final Calle La Mascota #3, Colonia La Mascota,
San Salvador, El Salvador
Phone: (503)234353   **Facsimile:** (503)790337   **Cable:** AMSCHOOL
Mail: PO Box 01-35, San Salvador, El Salvador
Superintendent: William Scotti, Ed.D.
Secondary school principal: John R. Hooper
Elementary school principal: Barbara Lopez
Staff: full-time, 124; part-time, 2
Nationalities of staff: U.S., 58; host, 60; other, 8
Grade levels: preK – 12
Enrollment: preK, 88; K, 109; 1 – 6, 544; 6 – 8, 375; 9 – 12, 446;
total, 1,562
Nationalities of student body: U.S., 175; host, 1,297; other, 90
Capacity: preK, 110; K, 125; 1 – 6, 800; 7 – 9, 375; 10 – 12, 300;
total, 1,710
Teacher/student ratio: 1/12
Tuition (annual): preK – K, $3,300; 1 – 12, $3,800
Other fees (annual): registration*, $2,500; activity, $25
School year: August to June

Year founded: 1946. **Type of school:** coed, day. **Governed by:** elected board of directors. **Accredited by:** Southern, Salvadorean Ministry of Education.

Curriculum/physical plant

Type: U.S. **Languages taught:** French, Spanish. **Staff specialists:** reading, math, computer, counselor, learning disabilities, nurse. **Special programs:** honors sections, remedial, AP courses. **Special curricular:** art, chorus, physical education, computer instruction. **Extracurricular:** drama, dance, choral music, computers, yearbook, newspaper, photography, field trips. **Sports:** basketball, soccer, softball, volleyball, intramurals. **Clubs:** social service, chess, math, computer. **Tests:** SSAT, PSAT, SAT, ACT, TOEFL, Stanford, Iowa. **Graduates attending college:** 99%. **Graduates have attended:** U. of Texas, Texas A&M, Purdue, Harvard, Emory. **Location:** in pleasant residential area, 10 minutes from San Salvador. **Campus:** 40 acres. **Libraries:** 35,000 volumes. **Facilities:** 19 buildings, auditorium, 2 cafeterias, 3 playing fields, 4 science labs, 3 computer labs, 2 health rooms.

*Once only fee

SANTA TECLA

Academia Britanica Cuscatleca

Address: Apartado Postal 121, Santa Tecla, El Salvador
Phone: (503)282011   **Facsimile:** (503)282956

ETHIOPIA

Region: East Africa
Size: 471,776 square miles
Population: 53,131,000
Capital: Addis Ababa

Telephone code: 251
Currency: birr
Languages: Amharic, Tigre, Galla

ADDIS ABABA

BINGHAM ACADEMY

Phone: (251)(1)792080/791401/791791   **Facsimile:** (251)(1)511242
Mail: Box 4937, Addis Ababa, Ethiopia
U.S. mail: c/o SIM, PO Box 7900, Charlotte, NC 28241, U.S.A.
Principal: Judy Neil
Staff: full-time, 18; part-time, 1
Nationalities of staff: U.S., 10; U.K., 1; other, 8
Grade levels: K – 8
Enrollment: K, 18; 1 – 6, 125; 7 – 8, 32; total, 175
Nationalities of student body: U.S., 44; U.K., 10; host, 20; other, 101
Capacity: K, 15; 1 – 6, 132; 7 – 8, 22; total, 169
Teacher/student ratio: 1/9
Boarders: girls, 5   **Grades:** 1 – 8   **Program:** planned 5-day
Tuition (annual): K, 5,320**; 1 – 8, 8,220
Other fees: testing, 10 – 15**
School year: September to June

Year founded: 1946. **Type of school:** coed, day, boarding, church-related, private nonprofit. **Governed by:** SIM International.

Curriculum/physical plant

Type: international. **Languages taught:** French. **Staff specialists:** computer, nurse, music. **Special curricular:** art, physical education, computer instruction, vocational. **Sports:** soccer, track. **Tests:** MAT. **Graduates attending college:** 95%. **Graduates have attended:** John Brown U., Wheaton College. **Location:** secluded, wooded setting in Addis Ababa. **Campus:** 8 acres. **Library:** 12,000 volumes. **Facilities:** 9 buildings, 12 classrooms, auditorium, covered play area, tennis court, playing field, science lab, computer lab, small family-style boarding facilities.

**Ethiopian birr

INTERNATIONAL COMMUNITY SCHOOL/ADDIS ABABA

Phone: (251)(1)711695/710870/711062   **Facsimile:** (251)(1)710722
Telex: 97621282 AMEMB ET
Mail: PO Box 70282, Addis Ababa, Ethiopia
Director: Gordon Quigley, Ph.D.

High school principal: Earl Harris
Elementary school principal: Cynthia Stults
Business manager: Neamin Ogbatensae
Staff: full-time, 50
Grade levels: preK – 12
Enrollment: preK, 37; K, 30; 1 – 6, 226; 7 – 9, 95; 10 – 12, 127; total, 515
Nationalities of student body: U.S., 43; host, 233; other, 239
Capacity: preK, 60; K, 50; 1 – 6, 280; 7 – 9, 120; 10 – 12, 120; total, 630
Teacher/student ratio: 1/10
Tuition (annual): preK, $2,215; K – 6, $4,772; 7 – 8, $5,215; 9 – 12, $5,454
Other fees: registration: $100 (new student), $50 (returning student); capital levy*, $580; IB
School year: August to June

Year founded: 1964. **Type of school:** coed, day. **Governed by:** elected board of governors. **Accredited by:** Middle States.

Curriculum

Type: U.S., IB, Ethiopian Ministry requirements for Ethiopian students. **Languages taught:** French, Spanish, Amharic. **Staff specialists:** computer, counselor, resource. **Special programs:** ESL, independent study, remedial. **Special curricular:** art, band, physical education, computer instruction. **Extracurricular:** instrumental music, yearbook, newspaper, excursions/ expeditions, magazine, student council. **Sports:** basketball, soccer, softball, swimming, tennis, track, volleyball, house intramurals. **Tests:** SSAT, SAT, IB, Iowa. **Graduates attending college:** 80%. **Graduates have attended:** Harvard, Swarthmore, Dartmouth, Ohio Wesleyan, Catholic U.

Physical plant

Location: on sloping, terraced land at base of mountains on edge of Addis Ababa. **Campus:** 15 acres. **Library:** 12,000 volumes. **Facilities:** 11 buildings, gymnasium, 2 playing fields, 3 science labs, 2 computer labs, 3 outdoor tennis courts, outdoor amphitheater.

*Once only fee

FIJI

Region: South Pacific
Size: 7,056 square miles
Population: 744,000
Capital: Suva

Telephone code: 679
Currency: Fiji dollar
Languages: English, Fijian, Hindi

SUVA

INTERNATIONAL SCHOOL, SUVA

Street address: Siga Road, Laucala Beach Estate, Suva, Fiji
Phone: (679)393300   **Facsimile:** (679)340017
Mail: PO Box 2393, Government Buildings, Suva, Fiji
Director: T. Blair Forster
Staff: full-time, 47
Nationalities of staff: U.K., 5; host, 29; other, 13
Grade levels: K – 12
Enrollment: K – 6, 420; 7 – 9, 150; 10 – 12, 80; total, 650
Capacity: K – 6, 400; 7 – 9, 150; 10 – 12, 150; total, 700
Teacher/student ratio: 1/14
Tuition (annual): K – 6, 900 – 1,500**; 7 – 9, 1,500 – 2,500; 10 – 12, 2,500
Other fees (annual): registration, 500 – 1,650**; capital levy, 350;
    busing, optional
School year: January to December

Year founded: primary, 1973; secondary, 1979. **Type of school:** coed,
day, private nonprofit. **Governed by:** elected board of governors. **Accredited
by:** IBO; U.K., Fiji, and Australia ministries of education.

Curriculum/physical plant

Type: U.K., New Zealand, Fiji, IB. **Languages taught:** French, Japanese,
Fijian, Hindi. **Staff specialists:** reading, computer, counselor, nurse. **Special
programs:** ESL, remedial. **Special curricular:** art, chorus, physical education, computer instruction, vocational, drama. **Extracurricular:** drama,
gymnastics, dance, choral music, yearbook, photography, excursions/expe-
ditions, field trips. **Sports:** basketball, field hockey, rugby, swimming, tennis,
rowing, cricket, netball, squash, athletics. **Tests:** SSAT, PSAT, TOEFL, IB,
IGCSE, PAT (New Zealand aptitude tests), Fiji Form 7. **Graduates attending
college:** 75%. **Location:** in suburban area, 9 kilometers from city center.
Campus: 10 acres. **Library:** 12,000 volumes. **Facilities:** 2 buildings, 30
classrooms, 3 science labs, computer lab, woodwork room, home economics
room, music room, art/craft room.

**Fiji dollar

FINLAND

Region: Europe
Size: 130,119 square miles
Population: 4,991,000
Capital: Helsinki

Telephone code: 358
Currency: markka
Languages: Finnish, Swedish

HELSINKI

THE ENGLISH SCHOOL

Street address: Mantytie 14, 00270 Helsinki, Finland
Phone: (358)(0)904771123
Principal: Biruta Meirans, Ph.D.
Assistant principal: Liisa Kaskinen
Head of library: Marjatta Kurtén
Head of computer services: Heikki Naakka
Staff: full-time, 22; part-time, 6
Nationalities of staff: U.S., 6; U.K., 1; host, 18; other, 3
Grade levels: preK – 9
Enrollment: preK, 49; K, 47; 1 – 6, 205; 7 – 9, 99; total, 400
Capacity: preK, 51; K, 51; 1 – 6, 206; 7 – 9, 105; total, 413
Teacher/student ratio: 1/16
Tuition (annual): K, 6,000**; 1 – 3, 19,300; 4 – 9, 21,500
Other fees: registration*, 200**
School year: mid-August to June

Year founded: 1945. **Type of school:** coed, day, private nonprofit.
Governed by: appointed board of directors. **Accredited by:** Finnish Ministry
of Education.

Curriculum/physical plant

Type: U.S., Finnish. **Languages of instruction:** English, Finnish. **Languages taught:** French, German, Swedish. **Staff specialists:** reading, math,
computer, nurse. **Special curricular:** art, chorus, physical education, computer instruction, vocational. **Extracurricular:** drama, choral music, computers, yearbook, photography, excursions/expeditions, field trips, magazine, service, weaving. **Sports:** skiing, track, skating. **Parent associations:**
English School Friends, Alumni-Senior Association. **Graduates attending
college:** 96%. **Location:** in Helsinki. **Library:** 9,680 volumes. **Facilities:** 16
classrooms, auditorium, cafeteria, gymnasium, science lab, computer lab.

*Once only fee   **Finnmark

INTERNATIONAL SCHOOL OF HELSINKI

Street address: Stahlberginkuja 1, 00570 Helsinki, Finland
Phone: (358)(0)6848166   Facsimile: (358)(0)6849859
Headmaster: Eugene Vincent
Staff: full-time, 18; part-time, 5
Nationalities of staff: U.S., 10; U.K., 8; host, 3; other, 2
Grade levels: K – 12
Enrollment: K, 15; 1 – 6, 105; 7 – 12, 60; total, 180
Nationalities of student body: U.S., 30; U.K., 15; host, 45; other, 90
Capacity: K, 30; 1 – 6, 108; 7 – 12, 72; total, 210
Teacher/student ratio: 1/9
Tuition (annual): K – 6, 36,000**; 7 – 12, 38,000
Other fees (annual): registration*, 1,000**; busing, 11,000; lunch,
approximately 13/day
School year: August to June

Year founded: 1963. **Type of school:** coed, day, private nonprofit.
Governed by: elected board of governors. **Accredited by:** New England, ECIS.

Curriculum/physical plant

Type: U.S., U.K. **Languages taught:** French, Finnish. **Staff specialists:**
computer, learning disabilities, nurse, librarian, music, physical education.
Special programs: ESL, remedial, IB. **Special curricular:** art, chorus,
physical education, computer instruction, skiing/skating during winter.
Extracurricular: chorus, field trips, afterschool club. **Tests:** Iowa, Richmond.
Location: in Helsinki, in rented half of a Finnish private school. **Library:**
5,000 volumes. **Facilities (shared):** 13 classrooms, auditorium, cafeteria, 2
gymnasiums, playing field, computer lab, AV room, local swimming pool.

*Once only fee   **Finnmark

FRANCE _____

Region: Europe
Size: 220,668 square miles
Population: 56,595,000
Capital: Paris

Telephone code: 33
Currency: franc
Language: French

BORDEAUX

BORDEAUX INTERNATIONAL SCHOOL

Street address: 53 Rue de Laseppe, 33000 Bordeaux, France
Phone: (33)(56)442795
Director: Marion Strudwick
Co-director: Christine Cussac
Head, primary school: Judith Huguenin
Staff: full-time, 6; part-time, 6
Nationalities of staff: U.S., 1; U.K., 5; host, 5; other, 1
Grade levels: K – 13
Enrollment: K, 4; 1 – 6, 16; 7 – 9, 20; 10 – 12, 20; 13, 7; total, 67
Nationalities of student body: U.S., 10; U.K., 30; host, 12; other, 15
Capacity: K, 6; 1 – 6, 20; 7 – 9, 20; 10 – 12, 25; 13, 10; total, 81
Teacher/student ratio: 1/7
Boarders: boys, 6; girls, 7   **Grades:** 5 – 13
Tuition (annual): 1 – 9, 20,000**; 10 – 13, 42,000
Other fees (annual): capital levy*, 2,500**; lunch, 25/day (10 – 13,
    lunch included in tuition)
School year: September through June

Year founded: 1988. **Type of school:** coed, day, boarding, private
nonprofit. **Governed by:** Association Linguistique Culturelle Internationale.
Regional organization: ECIS.

Curriculum/physical plant

Type: U.S., U.K., French in primary. **Languages of instruction:** English,
French. **Languages taught:** English, French, Spanish. **Special programs:**
ESL. **Special curricular:** art, chorus, band, computer instruction. **Extracurricular:** drama, dance, choral music, instrumental music, newspaper, excursions/expeditions, field trips. **Clubs:** debating, drama. **Tests:** SAT, ACT, A-level GCE, GCSE. **Graduates attending college:** 90%. **Graduates have attended:** London U.–Kings, Royal Holloway, Cardiff U., Cambridge – Fitzwilliam
College. **Location:** 5 minutes from city center. **Facilities:** 10 classrooms,
cafeteria, covered play area, 2 science labs, computer lab, neighborhood
sports facilities, boarding in 2 apartments run by teachers and with French
families.

*Once only fee   **French franc

LE CHAMBON-SUR-LIGNON

COLLEGE LYCEE CEVENOL INTERNATIONAL

Phone: (33)(71)597252   **Facsimile:** (33)(71)658738
  Cable: COLCEV
Mail: 43400 Le Chambon-sur-Lignon, France
Head: Jean-Louis Gavat
Grade levels: 9 – 13
Enrollment: total, 500
Nationalities of student body: U.S., 10; host, 390; other, 100
Capacity: total, 500
Boarders: boys, 150; girls, 150   **Grades:** 9 – 13
  Program: planned 7-day
Tuition (annual, for foreign students): 9 – 13 (with special French),
  7,650**; 11 – 13 (IB), 22,110; 9 – 13 (state education), 2,070
Other fees (annual, for foreign students): registration, 1,960**;
  boarding, 30,060; medical insurance, 700
School year: September to June

Year founded: 1938. **Type of school:** coed, day, boarding, private
nonprofit with state contract. **Governed by:** elected board of directors.
Accredited by: French government.

Curriculum/physical plant
  Type: French lycee, IB. **Languages of instruction:** English, French.
Languages taught: English, French, Spanish, German, Italian, Latin, Greek.
Special programs: IB, International Option of French Baccalaureate. **Special
curricular:** art, band, physical education, computer instruction. **Extracurricular:** drama, gymnastics, dance, choral music, instrumental music, computers, yearbook. **Sports:** basketball, soccer, tennis, handball, horseback
riding. **Tests:** PSAT, SAT, ACT, IB. **Location:** in the Cevenne mountains,
southwest of Lyon. **Campus:** 40 acres. **Facilities:** 15 buildings, 4 tennis
courts, gymnasium, computer lab.

**French franc

LILLE

ECOLE INTERNATIONAL DE LILLE METROPOLE†

Street address: 418 bis rue Albert Bailly, Marq-en-Barocul 59700,
  France
Phone: (33)(20)981124   **Facsimile:** (33)(20)980641
Headmistress: Madame Lux
Grade levels: 6 – 12
Enrollment: total, 350
Nationalities of student body: host, 280; other, 70

Boarding capacity: 150
Tuition (annual): bilingual classes, 8,850**; international classes, 14,100
Other fees: registration, 600**; boarding, 41,652; lunch, 6,028

Year founded: 1992. **Type of school:** coed, day, boarding, proprietary. **Governed by:** appointed board of directors. **Sponsored by:** French Ministry of Education. **Accredited by:** French Ministry of Education, IB, ECIS.

Curriculum/physical plant

Type: French, IB, French Baccalaureate International Option. **Languages of instruction:** English, French. **Languages taught:** English, French, Spanish, German, Italian, Latin. **Special programs:** IB, French International Option. **Extracurricular:** yearbook, newspaper, games, ecology, excursions, field trips, Red Cross, third-world awareness. **Sports:** basketball, football, swimming, tennis, volleyball, gymnastics, athletics. **Tests:** PSAT, SAT, IB, Cambridge certificates. **Facilities:** assembly room, cafeteria, infirmary, covered play area, 3 science labs, computer lab, AV equipment, library, access to playing fields and swimming pools.

**French franc   †Ecole Active Bilingue Jeannine Manuel in Paris is parent school.

LYON

Cite Scolaire Internationale de Lyon Gerland–Section Anglophone

Street address: 22, Avenue Torry Garnier, 69007 Lyon, France
Phone: (33)(78)696006   **Facsimile:** (33)(78)696011
Headmaster: Ivan Delbarre
Assistant headmaster: Mme. C. Lebourgeois
Assistant principal: Mr. M. Charleux
Directress: Mme. S. Burlet-Bebuze
Director, Anglophone section: Dr. J. F. Larner
Staff: full-time, 8; part-time, 1
Nationalities of staff: U.S., 4; U.K., 4; other, 1
Grade levels: 1 – 12
Enrollment: 1 – 5, 120; 6 – 9, 212; 10 – 12, 66; total, 398
Nationalities of student body: U.S., 20; U.K., 20; host, 279; other, 79
Tuition (annual): 7,210**
Other fees (annual): busing, 400**; lunch, 21.50/each
School year: September to July

Year founded: 1987. **Type of school:** coed, day, public. **Governed by:** elected parental board. **Sponsored by:** parents. **Accredited by:** French Ministry of Education.

Curriculum/physical plant

Type: French International Option. **Languages of instruction:** English, French (80%). **Languages taught:** Spanish, German, Italian. **Staff specialists:** math, nurse, French foreign language. **Extracurricular:** drama, yearbook, newspaper, excursions/expeditions, field trips, Model UN. **Tests:** PSAT, SAT, TOEFL, IGCSE, French International Option of Baccalaureat, Cambridge language exams. **Graduates attending college:** 100%. **Graduates have attended:** Georgetown, U. of Southern California, Edinburgh, Cardiff, French universities. **Location:** in Lyon on riverfront parkland. **Facilities:** 1 building, auditorium, 3 cafeterias, infirmary, 2 gymnasiums, 4 science labs, 3 computer labs, library.

**French franc

MOUGINS

MOUGINS SCHOOL†

Street address: 615, avenue Maurice Donat, 06250 Mougins, France
Phone: (33)(93)901547   **Facsimile:** (33)(93)753140
Mail: BP 101, 06251 Mougins Cedex, France
Principal: John Jackson, Ph.D.
Deputy: Brian Hickmore
Head of primary: Sue Filer
Staff: full-time, 16; part-time, 10
Nationalities of staff: U.S., 1; U.K., 19; host, 4; other, 2
Grade levels: preK – 12, postgraduate
Enrollment: preK – K, 19; 1 – 6, 103; 7 – 9, 58; 10 – 12, 57; total, 237
Nationalities of student body: U.S., 25; U.K., 84; host, 47; other, 81
Capacity: preK – K, 32; 1 – 6, 132; 7 – 9, 66; 10 – 12, 66; total, 296
Teacher/student ratio: 1/11
Tuition (annual): preK, 45,000**; K – 5, 51,000; 6 – 8, 54,000;
    9 – 10, 62,400; 11 – 12, 63,500
Other fees: registration*, 1,000**
School year: September through June

Year founded: 1982. **Type of school:** coed, day, private nonprofit. **Governed by:** elected board of directors.

Curriculum

Type: U.K. **Languages taught:** English, French, German. **Staff specialists:** reading, math, computer, counselor, learning disabilities, nurse. **Special programs:** ESL, remedial, enrichment, advanced GCSE. **Special curricular:** art, physical education, computer instruction, local studies. **Extracurricular:** drama, gymnastics, dance, computers, yearbook, excursions/expeditions, field trips. **Sports:** baseball, basketball, skiing, soccer, tennis, volleyball, athletics, gymnastics, cross country, orienteering. **Clubs:** orienteering, Brownies, student council, science, chess, drama, Rainbows. **Tests:** PSAT, SAT, GCSE, AS and A-level GCE. **Graduates attending college:**

80%. **Graduates have attended:** Bath U., King's College, U. of Massachusetts, Ecole Nationale Supérieure, Toulouse.

Physical plant

Location: Sophia Antipolis multinational high-tech park on the French Riviera, 10 kilometers from Cannes. **Campus:** 5 acres. **Library:** 6,000 volumes. **Facilities:** 7 buildings, 22 classrooms, infirmary, gymnasium, 2 science labs, 2 play areas, access to pool, playing fields, skiing.

*Once only fee   **French franc
†formerly the Anglo-American School, Mougins

NEUILLY-SUR-SEINE

MARYMOUNT SCHOOL

Street address: 72, boulevard de la Saussaye, 92200 Neuilly-sur-Seine, France
Phone: (33)(1)46241051   **Facsimile:** (33)(1)46370750
Headmistress: Sr. Maureen Vellon, RSHM
Staff: full-time, 41; part-time, 10
Nationalities of staff: U.S., 13; U.K., 13; host, 7; other, 18
Grade levels: preK – 8
Enrollment: preK – K, 60; 1 – 6, 240; 7 – 8, 52; individual learning center, 5; total, 357
Nationalities of student body: U.S., 196; U.K., 22; host, 36; other, 103
Capacity: preK – K, 60; 1 – 6, 240; 7 – 8, 52; individual learning center, 5; total, 357
Teacher/student ratio: 1/8
Tuition (annual): preK – K, 53,000**; 1 – 3, 59,000; 4 – 5, 60,000; 6 – 8, 64,700
Other fees: registration*, 2,000**
School year: September to June

Year founded: 1923. **Type of school:** coed, day, church-related. **Governed by:** Religious of the Sacred Heart of Mary. **Accredited by:** Middle States.

Curriculum/physical plant

Type: U.S. **Languages taught:** French. **Staff specialists:** reading, math, speech/hearing, learning disabilities, nurse, resource. **Special programs:** ESL, remedial, self-contained special education class. **Special curricular:** art, chorus, physical education, computer instruction. **Extracurricular:** drama, gymnastics, dance, choral music, instrumental music, computers, excursions/expeditions, field trips, French theater. **Sports:** basketball, soccer, swimming, tennis, judo, karate. **Tests:** Iowa. **Location:** in western suburb of Paris. **Campus:** 5,115 square meters. **Library:** 9,000 volumes. **Facilities:** 5 buildings, 32 classrooms, auditorium, cafeteria, infirmary, gymnasium, 2 playing fields, science lab, computer lab.

*Once only fee   **French franc

NICE/MONACO

American International School
on the Cote d'Azur

Street address: 15, rue Claude Debussy, 06200 Nice, France
   Monaco Primary Section: Stade Louis II, Fontvieille, MC 98000 Monaco
Phone: (33)(93)210400   **Facsimile:** (33)(93)216911
Headmaster/director: Marc Greenside
Assistant headmaster: David Russell
IB coordinator: Katherine Gandolfo
Middle school head: Patricia McCann
Elementary school head: Pauline Clarke
Staff: full-time, 32; part-time, 4
Nationalities of staff: U.S., 11; U.K., 10; host, 8; other, 7
Grade levels: K – 12 (Nice), K – 4 (Monaco)
Enrollment: K, 12; 1 – 5, 85; 6 – 8, 58; 9 – 12, 115; Monaco, 40; total, 310
Nationalities of student body: U.S., 75; U.K., 42; host, 31; other, 162
Capacity: K, 15; 1 – 5, 110; 6 – 8, 80; 9 – 12, 140; Monaco, 40; total, 385
Teacher/student ratio: 1/9
Tuition (annual): K – 5 and Monaco, 48,650**; 6 – 8, 52,650; 9 – 12, 61,200
Other fees (annual): busing, 7,000** (average); lunch, 4,000; capital assessment, 4,000
School year: September to June

Year founded: 1977. **Type of school:** coed, day, private nonprofit. **Governed by:** appointed and elected board of directors. **Accredited by:** Middle States, ECIS.

Curriculum
Type: U.S., U.K., IB. **Languages taught:** French, others available by arrangement. **Staff specialists:** computer, counselor, learning specialist. **Special programs:** advanced placement, honors sections, IB, ESOL, IGCSE. **Special curricular:** physical education, computer instruction, art. **Extracurricular:** drama, gymnastics, dance, computers, yearbook, newspaper, photography, excursions/expeditions, field trips. **Sports:** basketball, skiing, soccer, softball, swimming, tennis, volleyball, floor hockey, badminton, cross-country, athletics. **Tests:** SSAT, PSAT, SAT, ACT, TOEFL, AP, IB, IGCSE, CAT. **Graduates attending college:** 91%. **Graduates have attended:** Yale, Carnegie-Mellon, Princeton, London School of Economics, McGill.

Physical plant
   Location: in suburban area, 5 minutes from Nice airport. **Campus:** 3 acres. **Library:** 5,000 volumes. **Facilities:** 1 building, 24 classrooms, auditorium, cafeteria, infirmary, covered play area, gymnasium, playing field, 2 science labs, computer lab, boarding with local families in certain circumstances.

**French franc

PARIS

AMERICAN SCHOOL OF PARIS

   Street address: 41, rue Pasteur, 92210 Saint Cloud, France
   Phone: (33)(1)46025443   **Facsimile:** (33)(1)46022390
   Headmaster: James Moriarty
   Upper school director: John Guse, Ph.D.
   Middle school director: Ms. Pat Schapira
   Lower school director: Stanley Brown
   Staff: full-time, 79; part-time, 21
   Nationalities of staff: U.S., 58; U.K., 22; host, 20
   Grade levels: preK – 12
   Enrollment: preK, 16; K, 24; 1 – 5, 250; 6 – 8, 185; 9 – 12, 369; total, 844
   Nationalities of student body: U.S., 500; host, 41; other, 302
   Teacher/student ratio: 1/9
   Tuition (annual): preK, 32,000**; K – 5, 58,500; 6 – 8, 64,000; 9 – 11, 69,800; 12, 70,800
   Other fees (annual): registration*, 2,000**; capital levy*, 7,500; busing, 7,200
   School year: September to June

   Type of school: coed, day, private nonprofit. **Governed by:** appointed and elected board. **Accredited by:** Middle States.

Curriculum
   Type: U.S., IB. **Languages taught:** French, Spanish, German, Swedish. **Staff specialists:** computer, counselor, learning disabilities, nurse, resource. **Special programs:** ESL, advanced placement, honors sections, independent study, remedial. **Special curricular:** art, chorus, band, physical education, computer instruction. **Extracurricular:** drama, choral music, instrumental music, computers, yearbook, newspaper, literary magazine, photography, excursions/expeditions, field trips, sports. **Tests:** SSAT, PSAT, SAT, ACT, TOEFL, IB, AP, ERB. **Graduates attending college:** 98%.

Physical plant

Location: in suburban area. **Campus:** 12 acres. **Libraries:** 28,000 volumes. **Facilities:** cafeteria, infirmary, covered play area, playing field, performing arts center, tennis courts, gymnasiums, science labs, computer labs.

*Once only fee   **French franc

ECOLE ACTIVE BILINGUE JEANNINE MANUEL†

Street address: 70, rue du Théâtre, 75015 Paris, France
Phone: (33)(1)45756298   **Facsimile:** (33)(1)45790666
Mail: 70, rue du Théâtre, 75739 Paris Cedex 15, France
Headmistress: Madame Roubinet
Headmistress business management: Madame Zeboulon
Staff: full-time, 156; part-time, 45
Nationalities of staff: U.S., 2; U.K., 20; host, 173; other, 6
Grade levels: preK – Baccalaureate (International and French)
Enrollment: preK, 84; K, 177; 1 – 6, 703; 6 – 9, 671; 10 – 12, 516; total, 2,151
Nationalities of student body: U.S., 142; U.K., 70; host, 1,629; other, 310
Capacity: total 2,400
Teacher/student ratio: 1/12
Tuition (annual): preK, 9,510**; K, 12,357; 1 – 5, 13,635 – 16,980; 6 – 13, 13,050 – 22,710
Other fees (annual): registration*, 525**; lunch, 6,990
School year: September through June

Year founded: 1954. **Type of school:** coed, day, proprietary. **Governed by:** appointed board of direction. **Sponsored by:** French Ministry of Education. **Accredited by:** French Ministry of Education, IBO, ECIS.

Curriculum/physical plant

Type: French, IB, French Baccalaureate International Option. **Languages of instruction:** English, French. **Languages taught:** French, Spanish, German, Italian, Arabic, Lebanese, Hebrew, Farsi. **Staff specialists:** math, computer, counselor, nurse. **Special programs:** ESL, IB, honors sections. **Special curricular:** art, physical education, computer instruction. **Extracurricular:** drama, gymnastics, dance, computers, yearbook, newspaper, photography, excursions/expeditions, field trips, music. **Sports:** football, swimming, tennis, athletics. **Clubs:** chess, theater. **Tests:** PSAT, SAT, TOEFL, IB. **Graduates attending college:** 98%. **Graduates have attended:** Princeton, Yale, Harvard, Vassar, Oxford. **Location:** in heart of city, near Eiffel Tower. **Library:** 9,000 volumes. **Facilities:** auditorium, cafeteria, infirmary, covered play area, gymnasium, playing field, 7 science labs, computer lab, AV equipment, 2 outdoor swimming pools.

*Once only fee   **French franc
†Parent school of Ecole Internationale de Lille Metropole

International School of Paris

Street addresses: primary school: 96 bis rue du Ranelagh, 75016 Paris, France; middle/high schools: 6, rue Beethoven, 75016 Paris, France

Phones: primary school: (33)(1)42244340; high school: (33)(1)42240954

Facsimile: (33)(1)45271593

Headmaster: Nigel Prentki

Principal (primary school): Jonathan Daitch

Director of admissions: Brenda King

Staff: full-time, 45; part-time, 11

Grade levels: preK – 12

Enrollment: preK, 10; K, 40; 1 – 5, 86; 6 – 8, 54; 9 – 12, 160; total, 350

Nationalities of student body: U.S., 50; U.K., 30; host, 29; other, 241

Capacity: preK, 20; K, 20; 1 – 6, 175; 7 – 9, 80; 10 – 12, 140; total, 435

Teacher/student ratio: 1/7

Tuition (annual): preK, 15,000** (half day); K1, 32,000 (full day); K2 – grade 1, 60,000; 2 – 5, 64,000; 6 – 8, 66,000; 9 – 12, 75,000

Other fees (annual): insurance, 60**; busing, 8,500; entry*, 7,000

School year: September to June

Year founded: 1964. **Type of school:** coed, day, private nonprofit. **Governed by:** appointed and elected board of trustees. **Accredited by:** New England, ECIS.

Curriculum/physical plant

Type: U.S., U.K., IB, IGCSE. **Languages taught:** English, French, German; Spanish, Dutch, Japanese, Swedish to native speakers of these languages. **Staff specialists:** reading, math, computer, counselor, learning disabilities (primary and middle schools). **Special programs:** ESL. **Special curricular:** art, chorus, physical education, computer instruction. **Extracurricular:** drama, gymnastics, computers, yearbook, photography, excursions/expeditions, field trips. **Sports:** basketball, soccer, swimming, volleyball, karate, judo, table tennis. **Clubs:** chess, computer, Model UN. **Tests:** PSAT, SAT, ACT, TOEFL, IB, AP, ICGSE. **Graduates attending college:** 95%. **Graduates have attended:** Tufts, Harvard, Columbia, Northeastern, Cambridge. **Location:** in Paris. **Libraries:** 12,000 volumes. **Facilities:** 2 campuses, 3 buildings, 40 classrooms, 2 gymnasiums, 2 science labs, 2 computer labs, access to tennis courts, kinder playground.

*Once only fee   **French franc

United Nations Nursery School Association, Paris

Street address: 40, rue Pierre Guerin, 75016 Paris, France

Phone: (33)(1)45272024

Directrice: Brigitte Weill

Grade levels: K

Enrollment: K, 70

Nationalities of student body: U.S., 25; U.K., 4; host, 30; other, 11
Capacity: total, 70
Tuition: 7,600** per term
Other fees (annual): registration*, 800**; lunch, 960; membership, 110
School year: September to June

Year founded: 1951. **Type of school:** coed, day, private nonprofit.
Governed by: elected board. **Accredited by:** French ministries of health and
education.

Curriculum/physical plant
Type: U.S., French. **Languages of instruction:** English, French. **Languages taught:** English, French. **Special programs:** English lessons (ages 6–10); summer school (July). **Extracurricular:** excursions/expeditions. **Location:** in Paris, on cul-de-sac. **Campus:** 350 square meters. **Library:** 500
volumes. **Facilities:** 1 building, 4 classrooms, large garden with animals.

*Once only fee   **French franc

ST. GERMAIN-EN-LAYE

LYCEE INTERNATIONAL, AMERICAN SECTION†
Phone: (33)(1)34517485   **Facsimile:** (33)(1)39109404
Mail: BP 230, rue du Fer A Cheval, St. Germain-en-Laye 78104 Cedex,
    France
Director: Michael Veitch
Headmaster, Lycée International: Jean-Pierre Maillard
Staff: full-time, 8; part-time, 2
Nationalities of staff: U.S., 9; other, 1
Grade levels: K – 12
Enrollment: K, 18; 1 – 5, 170; 6 – 9, 100; 10 – 12, 108; total, 396
Nationalities of student body: U.S., 190; U.K., 11; host, 156;
    other, 39
Tuition (annual): K – 12, 17,500**, with family reductions available
Other fees (annual): registration, 500**; insurance, 60; busing, 500;
    lunch, 2,500; application, 500
School year: September to early July

Year founded: 1952. **Type of school:** coed, day. **Governed by:** elected
parents board. **Accredited by:** French Ministry of Education.

Curriculum
Type: U.S., French. **Languages of instruction:** English, French. **Languages taught:** English, Spanish, German, Italian, Russian, Latin, Portuguese. **Staff specialists:** nurse. **Special programs:** advanced placement,
French Baccalaureate with American International Option, IB certificates.
Special curricular: computer instruction. **Extracurricular:** drama, year-

book, literary magazine, excursions/expeditions, field trips, Model UN, European Youth Parliament. **Sports:** basketball, soccer, tennis, volleyball, judo, horseback riding. **Clubs:** computer, photo, bioethics. **Tests:** PSAT, SAT, AP, Iowa, French Baccalaureate (International Option), CTP III (ERB), IB (certificates only). **Graduates attending college:** 100%. **Graduates have attended:** Harvard, Yale, Princeton, Stanford, French universities.

Physical plant
Location: in suburban area, 20 kilometers from Paris. **Library:** 100,000 volumes. **Facilities:** 5 buildings, auditorium, cafeteria, infirmary, tennis court, gymnasium, playing field, science lab, computer lab.

**French franc   †Associated schools: Lycee Marcel Roby, College Pierre and Marie Curie, Ecole Henri Dunant

VALBONNE

CENTRE INTERNATIONAL DE VALBONNE: INTERNATIONAL SCHOOL OF SOPHIA ANTIPOLIS
Phone: (33)(93)653334 ext. 446   **Facsimile:** (33)(93)652215
   Telex: 842970849 F
Mail: CIV-BP 097, 06902 Sophia Antipolis Cedex, France
Headmaster: Ian Hill
IB coordinator: Carole Labrousse
College counselor: Judith Guérard
Staff: full-time, 13; part-time, 27
Nationalities of staff: U.S., 8; U.K., 6; host, 22; other, 4
Grade levels: 4 – 12
Enrollment: 4 – 5, 40; 6 – 9, 370; 10 – 12, 170; total, 580
Nationalities of student body: U.S., 42; U.K., 98; host, 310; other, 130
Capacity: 4 – 5, 40; 6 – 9, 370; 10 – 12, 170; total, 580
Teacher/student ratio: 1/22
Boarders: boys, 35; girls, 50
Tuition (annual): 4 – 5, 8,000**; 6 – 9, 8,000 – 18,000;
   10 – 12, 20,000 – 35,500
Other fees: boarding, 39,900**/year; busing, 1,300/trimester; lunch,
   1,200/trimester; books, 500 (refundable); activities and sports
   card, 900/trimester
School year: September to June

Year founded: 1979. **Type of school:** coed, day, boarding, bilingual. **Governed by:** elected board of governors. **Accredited by:** French Ministry of Education.

Curriculum
Type: French, Cambridge IGCSE, IB. **Languages of instruction:** English, French. **Languages taught:** Spanish, German, Italian, Russian, Arabic.

Special programs: ESL, intensive French. **Special curricular:** art, physical education, computer instruction. **Extracurricular:** drama, gymnastics, dance, computers, yearbook, photography, excursions/expeditions, field trips, Model UN, theater and film festival visits, chess club. **Sports:** basketball, rugby, skiing, soccer, tennis, volleyball, track and field, judo, squash, sailing. **Tests:** PSAT, SAT, TOEFL, IB, French Baccalaureate International Option, IGCSE, GMAT, Brevet du College. **Graduates attending college:** 95%. **Graduates have attended:** Cornell, Oxford, Brown, MIT, H.E.C. Lausanne.

Physical plant
Location: on the Riviera between Nice (20 km) and Cannes (15 km) in Europe's largest science park (technopolis). **Campus:** 40 acres. **Library:** over 10,000 volumes. **Facilities:** 14 buildings, 70 classrooms, 2 cafeterias, infirmary, covered play area, 8 tennis courts, gymnasium, 4 playing fields, 6 science labs, computer lab, AV center, theater, cinema, 8 boarding pavilions.

**French franc

GABON

Region: Central Africa
Size: 103,346 square miles
Population: 1,079,000
Capital: Libreville

Telephone code: 241
Currency: CFA franc
Languages: French, Bantu dialects

LIBREVILLE

AMERICAN INTERNATIONAL SCHOOL OF LIBREVILLE

Phone: (241)731449   **Facsimile:** (241)745507 (c/o Am. Embassy)
    or (241)732728 (direct)
Mail: BP 4000, Libreville, Gabon
U.S. mail: c/o Department of State – Libreville, Washington, D.C.
    20521-2270
Director: Don O. Hill
Staff: full-time, 8; part-time, 1
Nationalities of staff: U.S., 5; U.K., 1; other, 3
Grade levels: N – 8 (9 – 12, correspondence)
Enrollment: N, 8; K, 5; 1 – 6, 32; 7 – 8, 5; total, 50
Nationalities of student body: U.S., 11; U.K., 2; host, 1; other, 36
Capacity: N, 10; K, 10; 1 – 6, 50; 7 – 8, 10; total, 80
Teacher/student ratio: 1/6
Tuition (annual): K, $7,778; 1 – 8, $12,850
Other fees (annual): registration, $370
School year: September to June

Year founded: 1975. **Type of school:** coed, day, private nonprofit. **Governed by:** appointed and elected board of directors. **Accredited by:** Middle States. **Regional organizations:** AAIE, AISA.

Curriculum/physical plant

Type: U.S. **Languages taught:** French. **Staff specialists:** ESL. **Special programs:** ESL. **Special curricular:** art, physical education, computer instruction, music, supervised U. of Nebraska correspondence class (9 – 12). **Extracurricular:** drama, chorus, yearbook, field trips, sports day. **Tests:** SSAT, Iowa, Brigance, GCE. **Location:** in detached bungalow situated on own grounds, Quartier Hauts de Gue Gue. **Campus:** 2 acres. **Library:** 5,000 volumes. **Facilities:** 3 buildings, 10 classrooms, playing field, computer lab, air conditioning.

THE GAMBIA _____

Region: Western Africa
Size: 4,127 square miles
Population: 874,000
Capital: Banjul

Telephone code: 220
Currency: dalasi
Languages: English, Malinke, Wolof

BANJUL

Banjul American Embassy School

Phone: (220)495920   **Facsimile:** (220)492475
Mail: P.M.B. #19, GPO Banjul, The Gambia
U.S. mail: BANJUL-EMBSCHOOL, Washington, D.C. 20521-2070
Director: Stephen E. Plisinski
Staff: full-time, 10; part-time, 10
Nationalities of staff: U.S., 6; U.K., 4; other, 10
Grade levels: preK – 8
Enrollment: preK, 15; K, 10; 1 – 6, 70; 7 – 8, 10; total, 105
Nationalities of student body: U.S., 13; U.K., 17; other, 75
Capacity: preK, 15; K, 15; 1 – 6, 120; 7 – 8, 30; total, 180
Teacher/student ratio: 1/7
Tuition (annual): preK, $2,000; K – 6, $5,720; 7 – 8, $6,820
Other fees: application, $50; ESL/special needs, $1,000; school
    development (upon enrollment)*, $850; extended day (preK and K),
    $750
School year: September to June

Year founded: 1984. **Type of school:** coed, day, private nonprofit. **Governed by:** board of directors. **Sponsored by:** parent association.

Curriculum/physical plant

Type: U.S. **Languages taught:** French. **Staff specialists:** computer, art, physical education, music. **Special programs:** ESL/special needs. **Special curricular:** school house competitions. **Extracurricular:** field trips, interscholastic sports, sports tournament, yearbook, student council, field trips.

Tests: Iowa. **Location:** in tourist/residential suburb on Atlantic Ocean, 15 kilometers from Banjul. **Campus:** 3 acres. **Library:** 4,500 volumes. **Facilities:** 3 buildings, 12 classrooms, 2 playing fields, science lab, computer lab, art room, surfaced play area.

*Once only fee

Marina International Primary School

Phone: (220)96109   **Facsimile:** (220)92866
Mail: PO Box 717, Banjul, The Gambia
Headmaster: C. W. Cole
Staff: full-time, 30
Nationalities of staff: U.K., 5; host, 13; other, 12
Grade levels: preK – 9
Enrollment: preK, 88; K, 92; 1 – 9, 243; total, 423
Nationalities of student body: U.S., 2; U.K., 7; host, 332; other, 82
Capacity: preK, 88; K, 96; 1 – 6, 234; total, 418
Teacher/student ratio: 1/14
Tuition (annual): preK – 9, 3,300**
Other fees (annual): expatriate, 6,000**; fully reimbursed, 720 pound
    sterling
School year: September to July

Year founded: 1972. **Type of school:** coed, day, private nonprofit. **Governed by:** elected Parent/Teacher Association executive committee.

Curriculum/physical plant

Type: U.K., Gambian. **Staff specialists:** reading, learning disabilities. **Sports:** football, swimming, rounders. **Tests:** Richmond. **Location:** on outskirts of Banjul. **Library:** 5,000 volumes. **Facilities:** 7 buildings, 22 classrooms, 2 playing fields, AV equipment.

**Gambian dalasi

EUROPEAN COUNCIL OF INTERNATIONAL SCHOOLS

Publications for 1993/94 include:

THE INTERNATIONAL SCHOOLS JOURNAL

96 pp, twice-yearly, US$26

The "ISJ" is a forum for views, ideas and research of international schools' educators. *The Journal* is unique in its field, reflecting that education in a multi-cultural, multi-lingual setting is recognized as an important goal in national and international education systems. Articles have included research reviews on bi-lingualism and cognitive development; learning disabilities of the bi- or multi-lingual; culture and language shock; the International Baccalaureate; Japanese education; and culture-fair testing. Authors have included Jacques Barzun, Neil Postman, HRH Prince Philip, and Sir Asa Briggs.

THE INTERNATIONAL SCHOOLS DIRECTORY

490 pp, published annually, US$35

The ECIS Directory of International Schools is the most complete volume of its kind; included are one-page descriptions of more than 300 schools worldwide affiliated with The Council; there are in total some 750 international schools and each is listed in tabular form, giving the enrolment, fees, language of instruction and curriculum, in addition to basic name and address information.

ECIS HIGHER EDUCATION DIRECTORY

Institutions in Membership of The European Council of International Schools

Fourth edition available September 1993, US$30

Described in this new publication are the 270+ universities and colleges, in Europe and the USA, all of which are actively encouraging enrolment by overseas students. In addition to one-page descriptions of each of the institutions, it contains a listing of some 80 major fields of study showing which university or college offers each field. Introductory articles written by university admissions personnel give helpful advice to those applying for admission to university from overseas.

THE ECIS POLICY PLANNER

250 pp, second, fully revised edition, US$100

The ECIS Policy Planner (first published in 1978) has been completely revised by its original editor, Johanna Crighton. It is a practical, step-by-step, do-it-yourself guide for those developing a coherent set of policies and procedures in an international school. Sample policies included.

ECIS is a non-profit association of schools throughout the world that provide education for children (mainly but not exclusively expatriate) in a multi-cultural, multi-ethnic environment. The Council's services include teacher recruitment, in-service training, a school accreditation program and the publication of specialist magazines and handbooks.

To obtain copies of any of the above publications, orders with full payment should be sent to:
Publications Office (1), European Council of International Schools
21B Lavant Street, Petersfield, Hampshire, GU32 3EL, England.

GERMANY, Federal Republic of __

Region: Europe
Size: 137,838 square miles
Population: 79,548,000
Capital: Berlin

Telephone code: 49
Currency: mark
Language: German

BERLIN

JOHN F. KENNEDY SCHOOL

Street address: Teltower Damm 87-93, 14167 Berlin, Federal Republic of Germany
Phone: (49)(30)8072713/8072701   **Facsimile:** (49)(30)8073377
Managing principal: Charles C. Hanna
American high school principal: Darryl E. Hersant, Ph.D.
German high school principal: Hans Karl Behrend, Ph.D.
German elementary principal: Gudula Lennert
Staff: full-time, 121; part-time, 15
Nationalities of staff: U.S., 59; U.K., 2; host, 75
Grade levels: K – 13
Enrollment: K, 105; 1 – 6, 604; 7 – 9, 373; 10 – 12, 229; 13, 43; total, 1,354
Nationalities of student body: U.S., 638; host, 695; other, 21
Capacity: K, 112; 1 – 6, 600; 7 – 9, 300; 10 – 12, 336; 13, 64; total, 1,412
Teacher/student ratio: 1/10
School year: August to July

Year founded: 1960. **Type of school:** coed, day, public. **Governed by:** State of Berlin. **Accredited by:** New England.

Curriculum/physical plant

Type: U.S., German Arbitur. **Languages of instruction:** English, German. **Languages taught:** French, Spanish, Latin. **Staff specialists:** reading. **Special programs:** advanced placement. **Special curricular:** art, chorus, band, physical education, computer instruction. **Extracurricular:** drama, choral music, instrumental music, computers, yearbook, newspaper, literary magazine, excursions/expeditions, field trips. **Sports:** basketball, rugby, soccer, swimming, volleyball, rowing, wrestling, track. **Tests:** PSAT, SAT, AP. **Graduates attending college:** 90%. **Graduates have attended:** Georgetown, Tufts, U. of Michigan, Princeton, Stanford. **Location:** in suburban area, 20 minutes from downtown Berlin. **Campus:** 10 acres. **Libraries:** 24,000 volumes. **Facilities:** 6 buildings, 2 auditoriums, cafeteria, 2 gymnasiums, 3 playing fields, 7 science labs, 3 computer labs.

BONN

BONN AMERICAN HIGH SCHOOL

Street address: Martin Luther King Strasse 14, 5300 Bonn 2, Federal
Republic of Germany
Phone: (49)(228)379234   **Facsimile:** (49)(228)379357
Telex: 841885452
U.S. mail: (no personal name) Bonn American High School, American
Embassy Bonn, Unit 21701, Box 390, APO AE 09080-0005
Principal: Lavonne K. Tawney
Assistant principal: William F. Ryall
Guidance counselor: Michael S. Butterbaugh
Staff: full-time, 31; part-time, 4
Nationalities of staff: U.S., 34; U.K., 1
Grade levels: 6 – 12
Enrollment: total, 305
Nationalities of student body: U.S., 170; other, 135
Teacher/student ratio: 1/9
Tuition (annual): 6 – 12, $7,850
School year: August to June

Year founded: 1971. **Type of school:** coed, day. **Accredited by:** North
Central.

Curriculum

Type: U.S., IB. **Languages taught:** French, Spanish, German. **Staff
specialists:** reading, counselor, learning disabilities, nurse. **Special programs:** ESL, advanced placement, independent study. **Special curricular:**
art, chorus, band, physical education, computer instruction, vocational.
Extracurricular: drama, choral music, instrumental music, computers,
yearbook, newspaper, literary magazine, photography, excursions/expedi-
tions, field trips. **Sports:** basketball, football, soccer, swimming, tennis,
volleyball, cross-country, wrestling, track and field. **Clubs:** National Honor
Society, stamp, swimming, drama, photography, teen, Math-Counts, National Junior Honor Society, business. **Tests:** PSAT, SAT, ACT, IB, AP.
Graduates attending college: 90%. **Graduates have attended:** Northwestern, Brown, U. of Michigan, Franklin and Marshall, Georgia Institute of
Technology.

Physical plant

Location: in Bonn, along the Rhine River, a few minutes' drive to the
Parliament. **Campus:** 2 acres. **Library:** 6,730 volumes. **Facilities:** 25 classrooms, tennis court, gymnasium, playing field, 3 science labs, computer lab,
swimming pool, technology center, industrial arts lab, business lab, humanities center, TV studio, AV equipment.

BRITISH EMBASSY PREPARATORY SCHOOL E.V.

Street address: Tulpenbaumweg 42, 5300 Bonn 2, Federal Republic
of Germany
Phone: (49)(228)323166   **Facsimile:** (49)(228)323958
Headmaster: Mr. P. A. Ward
Staff: full-time, 15; part-time, 5
Nationalities of staff: U.K., 17; host, 3
Grade levels: preK – 7
Enrollment: preK – K, 53; 1 – 6, 150; 7, 22; total, 225
Nationalities of student body: U.S., 7; U.K., 86; host, 7; other, 125
Capacity: preK – K, 48; 1 – 6, 180; 7, 24; total, 252
Teacher/student ratio: 1/13
Tuition: 1 – 7, 3,850**/term (3 terms per year)
Other fees: registration*, 600**
School year: September to July

Year founded: 1963. **Type of school:** coed, day, private nonprofit.
Governed by: appointed and elected governing body.

Curriculum/physical plant

Type: U.K. **Languages taught:** French, German. **Staff specialists:** math,
learning disabilities, music, science, English. **Special programs:** ESL, remedial. **Special curricular:** physical education, computer instruction. **Extracurricular:** drama, gymnastics, dance, choral music, instrumental music,
computers, photography, excursions/expeditions, field trips, bowling. **Sports:**
hockey, volleyball, football (association), athletics, handball. **Tests:** GCSE
(German only), Common Entrance, Richmond. **Location:** on the Heiderhof, a
southern area of Bad Godesberg, 15 minutes from Bonn center. **Campus:** 1
acre. **Library:** 3,500 volumes. **Facilities:** 4 buildings, 24 classrooms, gymnasium, science lab, home economics center.

*Once only fee   **Deutsche mark

DUESSELDORF

INTERNATIONAL SCHOOL OF DUESSELDORF E.V.

Street address: Leuchtenberger Kirchweg 2, 40489 Duesseldorf,
Federal Republic of Germany
Phone: (49)(211)407056 – 7   **Facsimile:** (49)(211)4080774
Director: George Hoffmeier
High school principal: Richard Long
Middle school principal: Beverly Von Zielonka
Elementary school principal: Conal Atkins
Business manager: Dieter Kapteina
Staff: full-time, 71; part-time, 10
Nationalities of staff: U.S., 39; U.K., 15; host, 14; other, 13

Grade levels: preK – 13
Enrollment: preK, 20; K, 36; 1 – 5, 159; 6 – 8, 126; 9 – 13, 249;
total, 590
Capacity: preK, 20; K, 40; 1 – 5, 200; 6 – 8, 126; 9 – 13, 270; total,
656
Teacher/student ratio: 1/8
Tuition: preK, 11,250**; K, 17,750; 1 – 5, 20,350; 6 – 8, 22,000; 9 –
10, 23,500; 11 – 13, 26,250 (35% tax refundable)
Other fees: registration*, 7,500**
School year: August to June

Year founded: 1968. **Type of school:** coed, day, private nonprofit.
Governed by: elected board of trustees. **Accredited by:** New England, ECIS.

Curriculum/physical plant

Type: U.S., IB. **Languages taught:** French, Spanish, German, Japanese.
Staff specialists: computer, counselor, learning disabilities. **Special programs:** ESL, IB, learning disabilities. **Special curricular:** art, physical
education, computer instruction, choral music, instrumental music. **Extracurricular:** drama, gymnastics, music, yearbook, newspaper, literary magazine, adventure club, French club. **Sports:** basketball, soccer, softball,
volleyball, track and field. **Tests:** SSAT, PSAT, SAT, TOEFL, IB. **Graduates
attending college:** 95%. **Graduates have attended:** Duke, Oxford, Tokyo,
Stanford, Yale.   **Location:** in affluent suburb, 10 kilometers north of
Duesseldorf. **Campus:** 7 acres. **Library:** 12,000 volumes. **Facilities:** 9
buildings, 48 classrooms, auditorium, cafeteria, gymnasium, playing field, 5
science labs, 2 computer labs.

*Once only fee   **Deutsche mark

FRANKFURT

THE FRANKFURT INTERNATIONAL SCHOOL E.V.

Street address: An der Waldlust 15, 61440 Oberursel 1, Federal
Republic of Germany
Phone: (49)(6171)2020   **Facsimile:** (49)(6171)202384
Headmaster: James E. Buckheit
High school principal: David B. Hawley
Middle school principal: Moyra Hadley
Elementary school principal: Dennison MacKinnon
Business manager: Detlev Siebrecht
Staff: full-time, 129
Nationalities of staff: U.S., 64; U.K., 46; host, 11; other, 8
Grade levels: preP – 12
Enrollment: preP – P, 107; 1 – 5, 470; 6 – 8, 284; 9 – 12, 421;
total, 1,282

Nationalities of student body: U.S., 432; U.K., 161; host, 121; other, 568

Capacity: preP – P, 108; 1 – 5, 550; 6 – 8, 330; 9 – 12, 440; total, 1,428

Teacher/student ratio: 1/10

Tuition (annual): preP (half day), 8,530**; preP (full day) – 4, 17,060; 5, 17,360; 6 – 8, 19,270; 9 – 10, 19,860; 11, 20,260; 12, 20,660

Other fees (annual): registration*, 1,000**; busing, 1,350 – 2,170; capital contribution: year 1, 4,000; years 2 – 5, 1,500; activities: grade 5, 300; grades 6 – 12, 500

School year: August to June

Year founded: 1961. **Type of school:** coed, day. **Governed by:** elected board of directors. **Accredited by:** ECIS, Middle States.

Curriculum

Type: U.S., U.K., IB. **Languages taught:** French, German. **Staff specialists:** librarians, counselors, learning disabilities teachers, nurses. **Special programs:** ESL. **Special curricular:** art, band, physical education, computer instruction, drama, choir, music appreciation, word processing. **Extracurricular:** yearbook, newspaper, literary magazine, field trips, orchestra, band, choir. **Sports:** basketball, skiing, soccer, tennis, volleyball, track and field, cross-country. **Tests:** PSAT, SAT, ACT, TOEFL, IB, GCE. **Graduates attending college:** 75%. **Graduates have attended:** McGill U., Michigan State U., Bath U., Kent at Canterbury, Waseda U., Japan.

Physical plant

Location: at foot of Taunus Mountains, 23 kilometers from Frankfurt/Main. **Main campus:** 48 hectares. **Libraries:** 23,000 volumes. **Facilities:** 93 classrooms, auditorium, 2 cafeterias, infirmary, covered play area, 2 tennis courts, 2 gymnasiums, 2 playing fields, 8 science labs, 3 computer labs, playground, 2 A/V rooms, A/V center, career center, band and practice rooms, choir room, 2 faculty lounges, central administration building. **Primary campus:** 1 kilometer from main campus; 4 hectares. **Library:** 4,000 volumes. **Facilities:** 15 classrooms, PE room, indoor play area, cafeteria, playground.

*Once only fee   **Deutsche mark

HALLBERGMOOS

Bavarian International School e.V.

Street address: Schwaig Hallbergmooser Str. 5, 85445 Oberding, Federal Republic of Germany

Phone: (49)(811)8985   **Facsimile:** (49)(811)93229

Principal: Don Vinge

Program coordinator: Kelvin Sparks

Business manager: Knut Mohring
Staff: full-time, 19; part-time, 2
Grade levels: reception (ages 4 – 5) – 9
Enrollment: total, 169
Nationalities of student body: U.S., 43; U.K., 51; host, 22; other, 40
Teacher/student ratio: 1/8
Tuition (annual): reception – 5, 13,380**; 6 – 8, 15,680; 9, 16,930
Other fees: entrance*, 6,000** (first year), 1,500/child (2nd and 3rd
    years); busing, 700 – 2,400
School year: August to June

Year founded: 1991. **Type of school:** coed, day, private nonprofit.
Governed by: board of directors. **Sponsored by:** Association of Bavarian
International School.

Curriculum/physical plant
Type: U.S., U.K. (including IGCSE), German IB (starting in 1995). **Languages taught:** English, French, German. **Special program:** ESL. **Special curricular:** art, physical education, computer instruction. **Extracurricular:** sports, fine arts, global education. **Location:** in Schwaig, near Franz-Josef Strauss Airport, 35 kilometers north of Munich City center, 100 kilometers from Bavarian Alps. **Facilities:** 14 classrooms, science lab, library, art room, music rooms, computer in every classroom.

*Once only fee   **Deutsche mark

HAMBURG

International School Hamburg

Street address: Holmbrook 20, 2000 Hamburg 52, Federal Republic of
    Germany
Phone: (49)(40)8830010   **Facsimile:** (49)(40)8811405
U.S. mail: (no personal name) International School Hamburg, c/o U.S.
    Consulate Hamburg, APO New York 09215
Headmaster: Geoffrey Clark
Secondary school principal: Dieter Hachmann
Junior school principal: James L. Liebzeit, Ph.D.
Staff: full-time, 64; part-time, 16
Nationalities of staff: U.S., 15; U.K., 35; host, 11; other, 19
Grade levels: preK – 12
Enrollment: preK, 27; K, 35; 1 – 6, 245; 7 – 9, 120; 10 – 12, 115; total, 542
Nationalities of student body: U.S., 87; U.K., 66; host, 78; other, 311
Capacity: preK, 36; K, 40; 1 – 6, 300; 7 – 9, 180; 10 – 12, 180; total, 736
Teacher/student ratio: 1/8
Tuition (annual): preK, 9,000**; K – 2, 13,800; 3 – 5, 14,400; 6 – 8,
    16,200; 9 – 10, 17,000; 11 –12, 18,000

Other fees (annual): registration*, 500**; capital levy*, 4,000; busing, 1,000
School year: August to June

Year founded: 1957. **Type of school:** coed, day. **Governed by:** elected board of trustees. **Accredited by:** ECIS, New England.

Curriculum/physical plant
Type: U.S., U.K., IB. **Languages taught:** French, German, Japanese. **Staff specialists:** reading, math. **Special programs:** ESL, remedial. **Special curricular:** art, chorus, physical education, computer instruction. **Extracurricular:** drama, gymnastics, choral music, instrumental music, computers, yearbook, photography, excursions/expeditions, field trips, Cub Scouts, Brownies. **Sports:** basketball, soccer, volleyball, track and field. **Tests:** PSAT, SAT, TOEFL, IB, Stanford, IGCSE. **Graduates attending college:** 90%. **Graduates have attended:** Brown, Cornell, Princeton, Oxford, Cambridge. **Location:** in western suburbs of Hamburg. **Campus:** 3 acres. **Library:** 25,000 volumes. **Facilities:** 2 buildings, 33 classrooms, auditorium, 3 gymnasiums, 4 science labs, 2 computer labs, AV equipment.

*Once only fee   **Deutsche mark

MUNICH

MUNICH INTERNATIONAL SCHOOL
Street address: Schloss Buchhof, Percha, 8130 Starnberg, Federal Republic of Germany
Phone: (49)(8151)26060   **Facsimile:** (49)(8151)260649
Headmaster: Lister Hannah
Senior school principal: Michael Webster
Senior school associate principal: Anna Wietrzychowska
Middle school principal: Eifion Phillips
Junior school principal: Carol Maoz
Counselor (6–12): Bill York
Business manager: Wilfried Schnoor
Staff: full-time, 65; part-time, 16
Nationalities of staff: U.S., 25; U.K., 25; host, 7; other, 24
Grade levels: K – 12
Enrollment: K, 40; 1 – 6, 365; 7 – 9, 204; 10 – 12, 186; total, 795
Nationalities of student body: U.S., 211; U.K., 151; host, 161; other, 272
Capacity: K, 50; 1 – 6, 365; 7 – 9, 200; 10 – 12, 185; total, 800
Teacher/student ratio: 1/11
Tuition (annual): K – 5, 13,380**; 6 – 8, 15,680; 9 – 12, 16,930
Other fees (annual): capital levy*, 6,000**, plus 1,500 (2nd and 3rd years); busing, 814 – 2,642
School year: September through June

Year founded: 1966. **Type of school:** coed, day, private nonprofit. **Governed by:** elected board of directors. **Sponsored by:** Association of MIS. **Accredited by:** New England, ECIS.

Curriculum

Type: U.S., U.K., IB. **Languages taught:** English, French, German. **Staff specialists:** math, computer, counselor, nurse, art, ESL, music, drama. **Special programs:** ESL, remedial. **Special curricular:** art, chorus, physical education, computer instruction, drama. **Extracurricular:** drama, gymnastics, dance, choral music, instrumental music, computers, yearbook, newspaper, photography, excursions/expeditions, field trips, speech/debate. **Sports:** basketball, skiing, soccer, swimming, tennis, volleyball, track and field, gymnastics, squash, badminton, canoeing. **Clubs:** sports, environmental, drama, chess. **Tests:** SSAT, PSAT, SAT, TOEFL, IB, A-level GCE, IGCSE. **Graduates attending college:** 87%. **Graduates have attended:** London School of Economics, Cambridge, Yale, MIT, Princeton.

Physical plant

Location: on wooded grounds of Schloss Buchhof, near Lake Starnberg, 20 kilometers south of Munich, 60 kilometers from Alps. **Campus:** 12 acres. **Libraries:** 15,000 volumes. **Facilities:** 4 buildings, 46 classrooms, 2 auditoriums, cafeteria, infirmary, 2 tennis courts, 3 playing fields, 4 science labs, 2 computer labs, double gymnasium.

*Once only fee   **Deutsche mark

POTSDAM

Internationale Schule Berlin/Potsdam

Street address: Seestrasse 33, 14467 Potsdam, Federal Republic of Germany
Phone/facsimile: (49)(331)22738
Headmaster: Matthias Trüper
Staff: full-time, 6; part-time, 4
Nationalities of staff: U.S., 3; U.K., 2; host, 4; other, 1
Grade levels: K – 6
Enrollment: K, 12; 1 – 6, 48; total, 60
Nationalities of student body: U.S., 2; host, 20; other, 38
Capacity: K, 14; 1 – 6, 64; total, 78
Teacher/student ratio: 1/8
Tuition (annual): K, 9,450**; 1 – 6, 13,650 – 14,437 (reduction for siblings)

Other fees: registration*, 1,000** (deducted from tuition); capital levy*,
    5,000; busing, approximately 950
School year: September through June/July

Year founded: 1991. **Type of school:** coed, day, private nonprofit.
Governed by: elected nonprofit association. **Sponsored by:** national and
foreign companies. **Accredited by:** State of Brandenburg.

Curriculum/physical plant
    Type: IB. **Languages taught:** English, French, German. **Staff special-
ists:** reading, math, computer, counselor, learning disabilities, music, swimming. **Special programs:** ESL. **Special curricular:** art, computer instruction,
student theater, pottery. **Extracurricular:** computers, field trips. **Sports:**
physical education, ski trip, swimming. **Location:** villa, bordering a lake, in
residential area. **Campus:** 3,000 square meters. **Library:** approximately
5,000 volumes. **Facilities:** 1 building, 12 classrooms, computer lab, wood
workshop, pottery.

*Once only fee   **Deutsche mark

STUTTGART

INTERNATIONAL SCHOOL OF STUTTGART E.V.
    Street address: Vaihinger Strasse 28, 70567 Stuttgart 80, Federal
        Republic of Germany
    Phone: (49)(711)7189161   **Facsimile:** (49)(711)7189485
    Headmaster: Mr. N. J. Ronai
    Staff: full-time, 12; part-time, 3
    Nationalities of staff: U.S., 7; U.K., 2; host, 4; other, 2
    Grade levels: K – 8
    Enrollment: K, 11; 1 – 6, 66; 7 – 8, 24; total, 101
    Nationalities of student body: U.S., 59; U.K., 14; other, 28
    Capacity: K, 18; 1 – 6, 77; 7 – 8, 25; total, 120
    Teacher/student ratio: 1/7
    Tuition (annual): K – 4, 13,500**; 5 – 8, 13,800
    Other fees (annual): registration, 500**; capital levy*, 2,500;
        busing, 3,900
    School year: August to June

Year founded: 1985. **Type of school:** coed, day, private nonprofit.
Governed by: elected board of directors.

Curriculum/physical plant
    Type: U.S., U.K. **Languages taught:** German. **Staff specialists:** reading,
math, computer, music, physical education, German. **Special programs:**
ESL. **Special curricular:** art, physical education, computer instruction.

Extracurricular: excursions/expeditions, field trips, recorder groups. **Tests:** CTBS 4. **Location:** in suburban area close to airport, 10 kilometers south of Stuttgart. **Campus:** 1 acre. **Library:** 5,000 volumes. **Facilities:** 7 classrooms, auditorium, gymnasium.

*Once only fee   **Deutsche mark

FRANKFURT
Goethe Gymnasium
>**Address:** Friedrich-Ebert-Anlage 24, 6000 Frankfurt am Main, Federal Republic of Germany
>**Phone:** (49)(69)21233525   **Facsimile:** (49)(69)21230717

GHANA

Region: Western Africa
Size: 92,098 square miles
Population: 15,616,000
Capital: Accra

Telephone code: 233
Currency: cedi
Languages: English, tribal languages

ACCRA

GHANA INTERNATIONAL SCHOOL
>**Street address:** Second Circular Road, Cantonments, Accra, Ghana
>**Phone:** (233)(21)777163/773299   **Facsimile:** (233)(21)777098
>   **Telex:** 9743047 BTH 24 GH
>**Mail:** PO Box 2856, Accra, Ghana
>**Principal:** Judith S. Sawyerr
>**Deputy principal:** David Kodwo Arku
>**Principal, junior mistress:** Diana Nyatepe-Coo
>**Principal, infant mistress:** Agnes Asante-Abedi
>**Staff:** full-time, 87; part-time, 6
>**Nationalities of staff:** U.S., 7; U.K., 9; host, 63; other, 14
>**Grade levels:** N – A-level
>**Enrollment:** N – K, 65; 1 – 6, 515; secondary, 465; total, 1,045
>**Nationalities of student body:** U.S., 49; U.K., 75; host, 528; other, 393
>**Capacity:** N – K, 65; 1 – 6, 515; secondary, 465; total, 1,045
>**Teacher/student ratio:** 1/12
>**Tuition (annual):** N – K, $2,079; 1 – 7, $2,904; secondary, $4,158
>**Other fees:** admission, $2,200 – 2,800
>**School year:** September to June

Year founded: 1955. **Type of school:** coed, day, private nonprofit. **Governed by:** appointed board of governors. **Accredited by:** Ghana Ministry of Education; International Schools Association, Geneva; Association of International Schools in Africa.

Curriculum/physical plant

Type: U.K. **Languages taught:** French. **Staff specialists:** reading, math, computer, art, ESL, music, physical education, French, science. **Special programs:** ESL. **Special curricular:** art, physical education, vocational, music, computer studies. **Extracurricular:** drama, choral music, literary magazine, art. **Sports:** basketball, hockey, soccer, swimming, tennis, volleyball, handball, international sports exchanges. **Clubs:** wildlife, music, current affairs, Scrabble, chess, Boy Scouts, Girl Guides. **Tests:** SSAT, SAT, ACT, A- and O-level GCE. **Graduates attending college:** 90%. **Graduates have attended:** U. of Pennsylvania, Swarthmore, Columbia, Leeds U., Warwick U. **Location:** in pleasant suburban setting, 15 minutes from center city. **Campuses (2):** 10.5 acres. **Libraries:** 15,000 volumes. **Facilities:** 18 buildings, 40 classrooms, 3 covered play areas, 2 tennis courts, 3 playing fields, 3 science labs, computer lab, basketball courts, film room, language lab.

LINCOLN COMMUNITY SCHOOL

Street address: No. 196/21, Antebo Road, Abelenkpe, Accra, Ghana
Phone: (233)(21)774018
Mail: c/o U.S. Embassy, PO Box 194, Accra, Ghana
U.S. mail: c/o Department of State – Accra, Washington, D.C. 20521-2020
Superintendent : Richard T. Eng
Office manager: Gytha Sabeh
Staff: full-time, 15; part-time, 3
Nationalities of staff: U.S., 10; U.K., 2; host, 5; other, 1
Grade levels: preK – 9
Enrollment: preK, 32; K, 19; 1 – 6, 67; 7 – 9, 15; total, 133
Nationalities of student body: U.S., 35; U.K., 20; host, 21; other, 57
Capacity: preK, 40; K, 20; 1 – 6, 120; 7 – 9, 60; total, 240
Teacher/student ratio: 1/8
Tuition (annual): preK, $2,240; K, $2,640; 1 – 9, $5,445
Other fees: registration*, $1,000; capital development fund, 10% of annual tuition
School year: September to June

Year founded: 1968. **Type of school:** coed, day, private nonprofit. **Governed by:** elected board of directors. **Accredited by:** government of Ghana, Middle States (in process).

Curriculum/physical plant

Type: U.S. **Languages taught:** French. **Staff specialists:** computer, speech/hearing, learning disabilities. **Special programs:** ESL, gifted. **Special curricular:** art, physical education, computer instruction. **Extracurricular:**

yearbook, newspaper, field trips, Tae Kwon Do, ballet, tennis, swimming. **Tests:** Iowa. **Location:** in suburban area. **Campus:** 5 acres. **Library:** 6,000 volumes. **Facilities:** 2 buildings, 7 classrooms, covered play area, 2 playing fields, science lab, computer lab, art room, new classroom building and administrative office, air conditioning.

*Once only fee

ACCRA
Christ the King International School
Address: PO Box 4263, Accra, Ghana

Ridge Church School
Address: PO Box 2316, Accra, Ghana

GREECE

Region: Europe
Size: 51,146 square miles
Population: 10,066,000
Capital: Athens

Telephone code: 30
Currency: drachma
Language: Greek

ATHENS

THE AMERICAN COLLEGE OF GREECE (PIERCE COLLEGE)
Street address: 6 Gravias Street, 153 42 Aghia Paraskevi, Athens, Greece
Phone: (30)(1)6009800 – 9   **Facsimile:** (30)(1)6009819
Telex: 863222011 ACG GR
President: John S. Bailey, Ed.D., L.L.D.
Assistant principal/chairman of English department/dean of afternoon program: Olga E. Julius
Lykeiarchis: George Kalyvas
Gymnasiarchis: Mary Styliara
Dean of library resources: Maria Stergiou
Dean, school of business administration: Theodore Lyras
Vice president for financial affairs/dean of administration: Anastasia Alexopoulou

Vice president for administrative affairs: Vassilis Protopsaltis
Staff: full-time, 120; part-time, 3
Nationalities of staff: U.S., 12; host, 102; other, 9
Grade levels: 7 – 12
Enrollment: 7 – 9, 618; 10 – 12, 603; total, 1,221
Nationalities of student body: U.S., 27; U.K., 19; host, 1,142; other, 33
Capacity: 7 – 9, 630; 10 – 12, 630; total, 1,260
Teacher/student ratio: 1/10
Tuition (annual): 7 – 12, $3,587
Other fees (annual): registration, $83; busing, $344 – 527
School year: September to June

Year founded: 1875. **Type of school:** coed, day, private nonprofit.
Governed by: elected board of trustees. **Accredited by:** Greek Ministry of
Education.

Curriculum
Type: Greek. **Languages of instruction:** English, Greek. **Staff specialists:** computer, nurse, vocational counselor. **Special programs:** ESL, advanced placement, remedial. **Special curricular:** art, chorus, band, physical
education, computer instruction, vocational, orchestra. **Extracurricular:**
drama, gymnastics, dance, choral music, instrumental music, computers,
yearbook, newspaper, literary magazine, photography, excursions/expeditions, field trips, journalism. **Sports:** basketball, soccer, tennis, track, volleyball, handball, ping-pong, olympic gymnastics. **Tests:** TOEFL. **Graduates
attending college:** 80%. **Graduates have attended:** Princeton, Yale, Brown,
U. of Massachusetts at Amherst, Swarthmore.

Physical plant
Location: on side of Mount Hymettus in northern suburb of Athens.
Campus: 9,958 square meters. **Libraries:** 21,000 volumes. **Facilities:** 10
buildings, 51 classrooms, auditorium, cafeteria, infirmary, covered play area,
8 tennis courts, gymnasium, playing field, 4 science labs, computer lab, media
center, AV equipment, amphitheater, language lab, home economics lab.

AMERICAN COMMUNITY SCHOOLS OF ATHENS
Street address: 129 Aghias Paraskevis Street, 152 34 Halandri,
    Athens, Greece
Phone: (30)(1)6393200   **Facsimile:** (30)(1)6390051
    Telex: 863223355 ACS GR   **Cable:** AMSCHATH – Athens
Superintendent: John Dorbis, Ph.D.
Assistant to the superintendent: Anthony Powell
High school principal: Steven O'Brien, Ph.D.
Middle school principal: Michael Norelli
Elementary school principal: Mark Fox
Business manager: Leonidas Fenekos
Staff: full-time, 95; part-time, 20
Nationalities of staff: U.S., 94; host, 14; other, 7

Grade levels: preK – 12
Enrollment: preK, 14; K, 37; 1 – 5, 299; 6 – 8, 312; 9 – 12, 620; total, 1,282
Nationalities of student body: U.S., 588; host, 207; other, 487
Capacity: preK, 40; K, 60; 1 – 5, 420; 6 – 8, 430; 9 – 12, 850; total, 1,800
Teacher/student ratio: 1/12
Boarders: boys, 11; girls, 17   **Grades:** 9 – 12   **Program:** planned 5-day
Tuition (annual): preK – K, 826,400**; 1 – 5, 1,174,000;
     6 – 8, 1,297,000; 9 – 12, 1,397,200
Other fees (annual): registration*, 201,700**; boarding (1992–93
     rate), $18,500; busing, 148,000 – 174,000
School year: September to June

Year founded: 1945. **Type of school:** coed, day, boarding, private nonprofit. **Governed by:** elected board of education. **Accredited by:** Middle States.

Curriculum

Type: U.S., IB, AP. **Languages taught:** French, Spanish, German, Arabic, Greek. **Staff specialists:** reading, math, computer, counselors, psychologist, nurse, business education, resource center. **Special programs:** ESL, advanced placement, honors sections, remedial. **Special curricular:** art, chorus, band, physical education, computer instruction, vocational. **Extracurricular:** drama, gymnastics, dance, choral music, instrumental music, computers, yearbook, newspaper, literary magazines, photography, excursions/expeditions, field trips. **Sports:** basketball, soccer, softball, tennis, volleyball, wrestling, track and field, cross-country, gymnastics. **Clubs:** computer, French, Model UN, Spanish, forensics, German, Greek, Arabic, science, photo, booster, drama. **Tests:** SSAT, PSAT, SAT, ACT, TOEFL, IB, AP, CTBS. **Graduates attending college:** 80%. **Graduates have attended:** Harvard, Boston U., U. of California, Cornell, McGill.

Physical plant

Location: 7 miles northeast of downtown Athens. **Campus:** 27,200 square meters. **Library:** 26,800 volumes. **Facilities:** 7 buildings, auditorium, cafeteria, infirmary, 3 tennis courts, gymnasium, 3 playing fields, 8 science labs, 4 computer labs, boarding single/double rooms with private bathrooms, dining room, lounges, family atmosphere.

*Once only fee   **Greek drachma

GREEN HILL INTERNATIONAL SCHOOL

Street address: 31, Afroditis Street, Hellenikon 167.77, Greece
Phone: (30)(1)9640006/9646866   **Facsimile:** (30)(1)9612732
Mail: PO Box 73817, Hellenikon 167.10, Greece
Director: M. A. Sbeiti
Principal: Tatiana Bouri
Business manager: W. Charari
Staff: full-time, 17; part-time, 8
Nationalities of staff: U.S., 15; host, 5; other, 5

Grade levels: preK – 12
Enrollment: preK, 12; K, 15; 1 – 6, 74; 7 – 9, 31; 10 – 12, 29; total, 161
Nationalities of student body: U.S., 46; host, 38; other, 77
Capacity: preK, 16; K, 18; 1 – 6, 120; 7 – 9, 54; 10 – 12, 54; total, 262
Teacher/student ratio: 1/8
Boarders: boys, 3; girls, 2   **Program:** planned 7-day
Tuition (annual): preK, $3,300; K, $3,700; 1 – 6, $4,100; 7 – 9,
    $4,500; 10 – 12, $4,900
Other fees (annual): registration*, $300; boarding, $16,000; busing,
    $950
School year: September to June

Year founded: 1987. **Type of school:** coed, day, boarding, proprietary.
Governed by: elected board of trustees. **Accredited by:** Greek Ministry of
Education. **Regional organizations:** NE/SA.

Curriculum/physical plant
Type: U.S. **Languages taught:** French, German, Arabic, Greek. **Staff
specialists:** computer, speech/hearing, learning disabilties, nurse. **Special
curricular:** art, physical education, computer instruction, music. **Extracurricular:** drama, gymnastics, instrumental music, computers, yearbook, newspaper, photography, excursions/expeditions, field trips. **Sports:** basketball,
soccer, swimming, tennis, volleyball. **Clubs:** languages, sports, environmental, yearbook. **Tests:** SAT, ACT, TOEFL. **Graduates attending college:** 90%.
Graduates have attended: U. of Laverne, Deree College, U. of California at
San Diego, Stanford. **Location:** in suburb area 15 miles from Athens.
Campuses (2): 1 acre. **Library:** 3,000 volumes. **Facilities:** 1 building, 16
classrooms, covered play area, 3 playing fields, boarding facilities in a beach-
front hotel.

*Once only fee

TASIS HELLENIC International School
in Athens
Street address: Artemodos and Xenias Streets, Kefalari-Kifissia,
    Athens, Greece
Phone: (30)(1)8081426   **Facsimile:** (30)(1)8018421
Mail: PO Box 51025, GR-145 10, Kifissia, Greece
U.S. mail: 326 East 69 Street, New York, NY 10021, U.S.A.
Director/headmaster: George B. Salimbene
Elementary school principal: Patrice Yassoglou
Academic dean: Chris Tragas
Business manager: Fanis Malakondas
Staff: full-time, 58; part-time, 3
Nationalities of staff: U.S., 25; U.K., 18; host, 8; other, 10
Grade levels: preK – 12, postgraduate year
Enrollment: preK – 6, 100; 7 – 9, 120; 10 – 12, 200; 13, 2; total, 422

Nationalities of student body: U.S., 116; host, 108; other, 198
Capacity: preK – 6, 150; 7 – 9, 180; 10 – 12, 220; total, 550
Teacher/student ratio: 1/7
Tuition (annual): preK – K, 700,000**; 1 – 6, 840,000; 7 – 8, 920,000; 9 – 12, 952,000
Other fees (annual): registration*, 70,000**; boarding, $15,200; busing, 150,000 – 200,000
School year: September to June

Year founded: 1971. **Type of school:** coed, day, boarding, proprietary.
Governed by: appointed governing board. **Accredited by:** Middle States.

Curriculum

Type: U.S., U.K. **Languages taught:** French, Spanish, Modern Greek.
Staff specialists: computer, college counselor, learning disabilities (elementary only). **Special programs:** ESL, advanced placement, honors sections, independent study, remedial (elementary only). **Special curricular:** art, chorus, band, physical education, computer instruction, drama, field trips.
Extracurricular: drama, dance, choral music, instrumental music, computers, yearbook, newspaper, literary magazine, photography, excursions/expeditions. **Sports:** basketball, soccer, softball, tennis, volleyball, track and field, handball, netball. **Clubs:** National Honor Society, musical society, chess/games, Girl/Boy Scouts, journalism, student council, prefecture. **Tests:** PSAT, SAT, TOEFL, AP, A-level GCE, Iowa, ACH, TAP, IGCSE, Gates-MacGinitie. **Graduates attending college:** 90%. **Graduates have attended:** Princeton, Georgetown, Hamilton, U. of Newcastle, U. of California.

Physical plant

Location: in wooded residential suburb, 10 miles north of Athens; elementary school 3 miles from high school. **Libraries:** 15,000 volumes.
Facilities: 4 buildings, 40 classrooms, 2 auditoriums, tennis court, gymnasium, 2 playing fields, 4 science labs, computer lab, snack bar, art studio, darkroom, music room, typing room, 4 changing rooms. **Boarding facilities:** Self-contained family-style hotel facilities nearby include double rooms with private bathrooms, dining room, terrace, lounges.

*Once only fee   **Greek drachma

THESSALONIKI

ANATOLIA COLLEGE

Location: Pylea, Thessaloniki, Greece
Phone: (30)(31)301071 – 7   **Facsimile:** (30)(31)301076
    Telex: 863410452
Mail: PO Box 21021, 55510 Pylea, Thessaloniki, Greece
U.S. mail: 130 Bowdoin Street, Suite 1009, Boston, MA 02108, U.S.A.
President: William W. McGrew, Ph.D.

Vice-president: Peter Nanos, Ed.D.
Principal: John P. Gateley
Director of public services: Rea Samara
Business manager: Byron Alexiades
Staff: full-time, 95; part-time, 32
Nationalities of staff: U.S., 21; U.K., 6; host, 92; other, 8
Grade levels: 7 – 15
Enrollment: 7 – 9, 610; 10 – 12, 580; 13 – 15, 350; total, 1,540
Nationalities of student body: U.S., 15; host, 1,515; other, 10
Teacher/student ratio: 1/14
Boarders: boys, 28; girls, 26   **Grades:** 7 – 15
   Program: planned 7-day
Tuition (annual): 7 – 12, $3,000; 13 – 15, $3,200
Boarding fees: 7 – 12, $4,300; 13 – 15, $4,800
School year: September to June

Year founded: 1886. **Type of school:** coed, day, boarding, private nonprofit. **Governed and sponsored by:** Trustees of Anatolia College. **Accredited by:** Greek Ministry of Education.

Curriculum/physical plant

Type: U.S., Greek. **Languages of instruction:** English, Greek. **Staff specialists:** computer, counselor, nurse. **Special programs:** ESL. **Special curricular:** art, chorus, band, physical education, computer instruction. **Extracurricular:** drama, gymnastics, dance, choral music, instrumental music, computers, yearbook, newspaper, literary magazine, excursions/expeditions, forensics, many clubs. **Sports:** basketball, soccer, track, volleyball, handball. **Tests:** PSAT, SAT, TOEFL, ACH, Michigan, Cambridge, GRE, GMAT. **Graduates attending college:** 70%. **Graduates have attended:** Harvard, Princeton, MIT, Yale, Dartmouth. **Location:** in suburban area, 30 minutes from Thessaloniki. **Campuses (2):** 45 acres. **Library:** 22,000 volumes. **Facilities:** 22 buildings, 72 classrooms, infirmary, covered play area, gymnasium, computer lab, auditoriums, tennis courts, playing fields, science labs, 1 boys' dormitory, 1 girls' dormitory.

PINEWOOD SCHOOLS OF THESSALONIKI, GREECE

Street address: Panorama Highway, Thessaloniki, Greece
Phone: (30)(31)301221   **Facsimile:** (30)(31)311439
   Telex: 863412634 PHAR GR
Mail: PO Box 21001, 555 10 Pilea, Thessaloniki, Greece
U.S. mail: (no personal name) Pinewood Schools of Thessaloniki,
   c/o American Consulate General, PSC 108 Box 37, APO AE 09842
Director: Peter B. Baiter
Business manager: Despina Douptsiou
Staff: full-time, 16; part-time, 6
Nationalities of staff: U.S., 9; U.K., 4; host, 6; other, 3
Grade levels: K – 12
Enrollment: K, 9; 1 – 6, 49; 7 – 9, 46; 10 – 12, 46; total, 150
Nationalities of student body: U.S., 67; U.K., 10; host, 2; other, 71

Teacher/student ratio: 1/8
Boarders: girls, 5   **Grades:** 9 – 12   **Program:** planned 5-day
Tuition (annual, 1992–93 rates): K, $2,696; 1 – 12, $4,710
Other fees (annual, 1992–93 rates): boarding, $5,000; capital levy*,
    $363; busing, $789; yearbook, $48
School year: September to June

Year founded: 1950. **Type of school:** coed, day, boarding†, private
nonprofit. **Governed by:** elected Pinewood School Board. **Accredited by:**
Middle States.

Curriculum/physical plant
Type: U.S. **Languages taught:** French, Modern Greek (required). **Special
programs:** ESL, correspondence. **Special curricular:** physical education,
computer instruction. **Extracurricular:** computers, yearbook, excursions/
expeditions, field trips. **Sports:** basketball, soccer, softball, tennis, volleyball.
Clubs: Girl Scouts, National Honor Society, forensics. **Tests:** PSAT, SAT,
TOEFL, ERB, CTP-II. **Graduates attending college:** 75%. **Graduates have
attended:** Clark, Loyola of Chicago, Boston College, Cornell, Princeton.
Location: in suburb overlooking city, 15 – 20 minutes from center of
Thessaloniki. **Campus:** 4 acres. **Library:** 18,000 volumes. **Facilities:** 1
building, 16 classrooms, auditorium, 2 tennis courts, gymnasium, 2 playing
fields, science lab, media center, computer/science lab.

*Once only fee
†Boarding at neighboring Anatolia College, a coed Greek secondary school

ATHENS
Athens College
    Address: PO Box 65005, 154 10 Psychico, Athens, Greece
    Phone: (30)(1)6712771   **U.S. facsimile:** (1)(212)9662981
    U.S. mail: 75 Varick Street, 2nd Floor, New York, NY 10013, U.S.A.

GRENADA

Region: East Caribbean
Size: 133 square miles
Population: 84,000
Capital: St. George's

Telephone code: 809
Currency: East Caribbean dollar
Languages: English, French-
    African patois

ST. GEORGE'S

INTERNATIONAL SCHOOL OF GRENADA
    Phone: (1)(809)4444785   **Facsimile:** (1)(809)4442802
    Mail: PO Box 744, St. George's, Grenada, West Indies
    U.S. mail: c/o Administrative Officer, American Embassy Grenada,
        Washington, DC 20502

Principal: (to be announced)
Staff: full-time, 3; part-time, 7
Nationalities of staff: U.S., 5; U.K., 1; host, 2; other, 2
Grade levels: preK – 7
Enrollment: preK, 11; K, 11; 1 – 7, 18; total, 40
Teacher/student ratio: 1/6
Tuition (annual): preK (3 days), $1,010, (5 days), $1,346; K, $3,030;
   1 – 7, $3,366
Other fees (annual): registration, $100; captial assessment, $180
School year: August to June

Year founded: 1984. **Type of school:** coed, day, private nonprofit.
Governed by: appointed and elected board of directors.

Curriculum/physical plant
Type: U.S. **Languages taught:** French. **Special curricular:** art, physical education, music. **Extracurricular:** field trips, sports, earth club, card making. **Tests:** Iowa. **Location:** 2 miles from Lance aux Epines, in True Blue. **Library:** over 1,000 volumes. **Facilities:** 5 classrooms, playing field.

GUAM

Region: West Pacific
Size: 209 square miles
Population: 133,152
Capital: Agana

Telephone code: 671
Currency: dollar
Languages: English, Chamorro

TUMON BAY

ST. JOHN'S SCHOOL
Street address: 911 Marine Drive, Tumon Bay, Guam 96911
Phone: (671)6465644/5626/8080   **Facsimile:** (671)6491055
Headmaster: A. Ronald Tooman
Head, upper school: Dale Jenkins, Ed.D.
Head, lower school: Imelda Santos
Staff: full-time, 62; part-time, 3
Grade levels: preK – 12
Enrollment: preK, 48; K, 60; 1 – 6, 332; 7 – 9, 173; 10 – 12, 97;
   total, 704
Teacher/student ratio: 1/12
Tuition (annual): preK – K, $5,240; 1 – 2, $5,622; 3 – 4, $5,693;
   5 – 6, $5,762; 7 – 8, $6,374; 9 – 12, $7,299
Other fees (annual): registration, $250; books, $140; capital levy*;
   tuition insurance*, $300 – 500
School year: August to June

Year founded: 1962. **Type of school:** coed, day, church-related, private nonprofit. **Governed by:** board of trustees. **Sponsored by:** Episcopal Church. **Accredited by:** Western.

Curriculum/physical plant

Type: U.S., IB. **Languages taught:** French, Spanish, Japanese. **Staff specialists:** reading, math, computer, counselor, nurse. **Special programs:** honors sections. **Special curricular:** art, physical education, computer instruction. **Extracurricular:** drama, computers, yearbook, newspaper, field trips, sports. **Clubs:** National Honor Society, Lettermen. **Tests:** SSAT, PSAT, SAT, IB. **Graduates have attended:** U. of California at Berkeley, Vassar, Harvard, Brown. **Location:** on tropical island. **Campus:** 7.5 acres. **Library:** 25,000 volumes. **Facilities:** 3 science labs, 2 computer labs, air conditioning.

*Once only fee

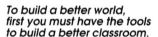

GUATEMALA _____

Region: Central America
Size: 42,042 square miles
Population: 9,266,000
Capital: Guatemala City

Telephone code: 502
Currency: quetzal
Languages: Spanish, Mayan languages

GUATEMALA CITY

THE AMERICAN SCHOOL OF GUATEMALA

Street address: 11 Calle 15-79, zon 15, V.H. III, Guatemala City, Guatemala
Phone: (502)(2)690791 – 95 ext. 124; (502)(2)380336 – 40 ext. 124
     Facsimile: (502)(2)380212   **Cable:** AMSCHOOL
Mail: Apartado Postal No. 83, 01901, Guatemala, C.A.
U.S. mail: (no personal name) The American School of Guatemala, c/o U.S. Embassy Guatemala, Unit 3325, APO AA 34024
Director: George G. Miller
Secondary school principal: Barbara Barillas
Elementary school principal: María Regina de Cordón
Staff: full-time, 130; part-time, 29
Nationalities of staff: U.S., 33; host, 121; other, 5
Grade levels: K – 12
Enrollment: K, 120; transition, 120; 1 – 6, 704; 7 – 10, 324; 11 – 12, 313; total, 1,581
Nationalities of student body: U.S., 172; host, 1,334; other, 75
Capacity: K, 120; 1 – 6, 700; 7 – 9, 350; 10 – 12, 315; total, 1,485
Teacher/student ratio: 1/11
Tuition (annual): K – transition, 4,750**; 1 – 3, 5,625; 4 – 6, 6,050; 7 – 10, 6,900; 11 – 12, 7,050
Other fees (annual): registration*, 25**; capital levy*, 400; insurance*, 40; busing, 500; books, 360 – 420; matriculation, 700
School year: January to October

Year founded: 1945. **Type of school:** coed, day, private nonprofit. **Governed by:** appointed board of directors. **Sponsored by:** Foundation of the University of the Valley of Guatemala. **Accredited by:** Southern.

Curriculum
Type: U.S., Guatemalan. **Languages of instruction:** English, Spanish. **Languages taught:** French, Spanish, German. **Staff specialists:** reading, counselor, psychologist, learning disabilities. **Special programs:** ESL, advanced placement, remedial. **Special curricular:** art, chorus, band, physical education, computer instruction, vocational. **Extracurricular:** drama, gymnastics, dance, choral music, instrumental music, computers, yearbook, newspaper, literary magazine, field trips. **Sports:** baseball, basketball, soccer,

softball, swimming, track and field, water polo, flag football, volleyball. **Tests:** PSAT, SAT, ACT, TOEFL, Stanford (elementary only), NMSQT. **Graduates attending college:** 92%. **Graduates have attended:** Pennsylvania, Texas A&M, Duke, Wellesly, Purdue.

Physical plant

Location: in new residential area on outskirts of Guatemala City, surrounded by gardens and sports fields. **Campus:** 52 acres. **Library:** 27 ,394 volumes. **Facilities:** 18 buildings, 42 classrooms, auditorium, cafeteria, covered play area, gymnasium, 10 playing fields, science lab, 2 computer labs, swimming pool.

*Once only fee   **Guatemalan quetzal

COLEGIO MAYA, THE AMERICAN INTERNATIONAL SCHOOL

Street address: Km. 12-1/2 Carretera a El Salvador, Guatemala City, Guatemala
Phone: (502)(9)341209/340649   **Facsimile:** (502)(9)340077
Mail: Apartado Postal 2-C, Guatemala City, Guatemala
U.S. mail: Colegio Maya, Unit 3326 – APO: AA Miami 34024
Director: (to be announced)
Principal: Nancy Medis
Staff: full-time, 38
Nationalities of staff: U.S., 28; host, 7; other, 3
Grade levels: preK – 12
Enrollment: preK – 5, 164; 6 – 8, 84; 9 – 12, 107; total, 355
Teacher/student ratio: 1/9
Tuition (annual): preK, $2,285; K – 12, $4,200
Other fees (annual): registration*, $1,000; busing, $350; other*, $2,000
School year: August to June

Year founded: 1957. **Type of school:** coed, day, private nonprofit. **Governed by:** elected board of directors. **Accredited by:** Southern.

Curriculum/physical plant

Type: U.S. **Languages taught:** Spanish. **Staff specialists:** computer, counselor, learning disabilities, nurse. **Special programs:** ESL, independent study. **Special curricular:** art, physical education, computer instruction, music. **Extracurricular:** computers, yearbook, newspaper, field trips, sports. **Clubs:** student council, honor society. **Tests:** PSAT, SAT, ACT, TOEFL, AP. **Graduates attending college:** 95%. **Graduates have attended:** U. of Pennsylvania, MIT, Notre Dame, U. of Florida, Georgetown. **Location:** on rural mountainside, 6 miles from city center. **Campus:** 12 acres. **Library:** 10,000 volumes. **Facilities:** 7 buildings, 25 classrooms, infirmary, playing field, science lab, computer lab, cafeteria/all-purpose room.

*Once only fee

GUINEA —————————————————————————

Region: West Africa
Size: 94,964 square miles
Population: 7,455,000
Capital: Conakry

Telephone code: 224
Currency: franc
Languages: French, Peul, Mande

CONAKRY

THE INTERNATIONAL SCHOOL OF CONAKRY

Facsimile: c/o U.S. Embassy (224)441522
All mail: c/o Department of State—Conakry, Washington, D.C. 20521-2110
Director: Edward Pisani, Ed.D.
Staff: full-time, 9; part-time, 1
Nationalities of staff: U.S., 5; other, 5
Grade levels: N – 8
Enrollment: N – preK, 5; K, 6; 1 – 6, 32; 7 – 8, 7; total, 50
Capacity: preK, 10; K, 10; 1 – 6, 40; 7 – 8, 10; total, 70
Teacher/student ratio: 1/5
Tuition (annual): N – preK, $3,500; K, $7,500; 1 – 8, $9,500
Other fees (annual): registration, $500; building fund* (students of new Association members), $1,500
School year: late August to mid-June

Year founded: 1963. **Type of school:** coed, day. **Governed by:** elected school board. **Sponsored by:** school association.

Curriculum/physical plant
Type: U.S. **Languages taught:** English, French. **Staff specialists:** reading, math, librarian. **Special programs:** ESL. **Special curricular:** art, music. **Extracurricular:** newspaper, field trips, black history month activities, choir, drumming class. **Tests:** Iowa. **Location:** district of Matam, Conakry. **Facilities:** 1 building, 6 classrooms, shaded play area, oceanfront site, air conditioning.

*Once only fee

GUYANA ⸻

Region: South America
Size: 83,000 square miles
Population: 748,000
Capital: Georgetown

Telephone code: 592
Currency: dollar
Languages: English, Amerindian dialects

GEORGETOWN

GEORGETOWN AMERICAN SCHOOL

Street address: 9/10 Delhi Street, Georgetown, Guyana
Phone: (592)(2)61595
U.S. mail: c/o Department of State, Washington, D.C. 20520
Principal: Thurston Riehl
Staff: full-time, 7; part-time, 5
Nationalities of staff: U.S., 4; U.K., 1; host, 4; other, 3
Grade levels: N – 11
Enrollment: N, 4; K, 10; 1 – 6, 45; 7 – 11, 15; total, 74
Nationalities of student body: U.S., 18; U.K., 11; host, 2; other, 43
Teacher/student ratio: 1/8
Tuition (annual): N – K, $2,300; 1 – 11, $4,600
School year: September to June

Year founded: 1971. **Type of school:** coed, day, private nonprofit.
Governed by: elected board of directors.

Curriculum/physical plant

Type: U.S. **Languages taught:** French. **Special programs:** independent study, correspondence. **Special curricular:** art, chorus, physical education, computer instruction, music. **Extracurricular:** choral music, computers, yearbook, field trips. **Tests:** Iowa. **Location:** in suburban Georgetown. **Campus:** 1 acre. **Facilities:** 2 buildings, 8 classrooms, auditorium, science lab, air conditioning.

HAITI _____

Region: Caribbean
Size: 10,579 square miles
Population: 6,286,000
Capital: Port-au-Prince

Telephone code: 509
Currency: gourde
Languages: French, Creole

DESCHAPELLES

ECOLE FLAMBOYANT

Mail: c/o Hopital Albert Schweitzer, PO Box 1744, Port-au-Prince, Haiti
Headmistress: (to be announced)
Principal: Tim Dutton
Staff: full-time, 3
Nationalities of staff: U.S., 2; host, 1
Grade levels: preK – 8
Enrollment: preK – K, 12; 1 – 5, 5; 6 – 8, 5; total, 22
Nationalities of student body: U.S., 9; other, 13
Capacity: total, 30
Teacher/student ratio: 1/7
School year: September to May

Type of school: day, church-related, private nonprofit. **Governed by:** Hopital Albert Schweitzer/Grant Foundation. **Sponsored by:** Hopital Albert Schweitzer/missionary families.

Curriculum/physical plant
Type: U.S., Haitian. **Languages of instruction:** English, French (Haitian). **Languages taught:** English, French. **Special programs:** ESL. **Special curricular:** art, physical education, music. **Extracurricular:** excursions/expeditions, field trips. **Tests:** SAT. **Location:** in Deschapelles, 2.5 hours by car from Port-au-Prince. **Library:** 1,500 volumes. **Facilities:** 2 buildings on the H.A.S. compound, 3 classrooms, tennis court, playing field, swimming pool.

PETIONVILLE

THE CARIBBEAN-AMERICAN SCHOOL

Street address: 56 rue Lambert, Petionville, Haiti, West Indies
Phone: (509)577961   **U.S. phone:** (609)2758730
Director: Ernestine Rochelle Robinson
Executive director: Antoinette Presley Sanon

High school principal/math department head: Florence Benjamin
Elementary head: Connie Deroneth
Staff: full-time, 10
Nationalities of staff: U.S., 5; host, 5
Grade levels: preK – 12
Enrollment: total, 200
Capacity: total, 300
Teacher/student ratio: 1/20
Tuition (annual): preK – 8, $2,000; 9 – 11, $2,250; 12, $2,500
Other fees: entrance*, $700/family; registration, $175; lunch, $3.50/
    day; books, $150; busing: preK – K, $200/month, 1 – 8, $225/month,
    9 – 12, $250/month
School year: September to May

   Year founded: 1980. **Type of school:** coed, day, private nonprofit.
Governed by: board of directors.

Curriculum/physical plant
   Type: U.S. **Languages taught:** French, Spanish. **Staff specialists:**
reading, math, computer. **Special programs:** ESL, advanced placement,
honors sections, independent study. **Special curricular:** art, physical education, computer instruction, music. **Extracurricular:** gymnastics, dance,
computers, excursions/expeditions, field trips. **Sports:** aerobics, swimming,
tennis, weight lifting. **Tests:** SSAT, PSAT, TOEFL, Iowa, CAT. **Graduates
attending college:** 100%. **Graduates have attended:** U. of Florida, Miami-
Dade Community College, Pratt Institute, New York U., Howard. **Location:**
in suburban area of Port-au-Prince. **Campus:** .5 acre. **Facilities:** 2 buildings,
12 classrooms, music and art rooms, cafeteria, playing field, computer lab,
library (under construction); new building scheduled for completion 1992–93;
boarding available in Petionville, with transportation provided.

*Once only fee

PORT-AU-PRINCE

UNION SCHOOL
   Phone: (509)570206/577434   **Facsimile:** (509)573131
   Mail: PO Box 1175, Port-au-Prince, Haiti
   U.S. mail: Lynx Air/UNSCH, PO Box 407139, Fort Lauderdale, FL 33340,
       U.S.A.
   Director: Rita Maselli-Boucicaut
   Staff: full-time, 40
   Nationalities of staff: U.S., 22; host, 8; other, 10
   Grade levels: preK – 12
   Enrollment: preK, 9; K, 13; 1 – 6, 133; 7 – 9, 76; 10 – 12, 85; total, 316
   Nationalities of student body: U.S., 119; host, 119; other, 78
   Capacity: preK, 20; K, 25; 1 – 6, 175; 7 – 9, 80; 10 – 12, 80; total, 380

Teacher/student ratio: 1/8
Tuition (annual): preK – K, $3,212; 1 – 6, $3,662; 7 – 12, $4,000
Other fees (annual): registration, $250 (new student), $100 (returning student) ; family entrance*, $750; student activities, $75
School year: August to June

Year founded: 1919. **Type of school:** coed, day, private nonprofit.
Governed by: elected board of trustees. **Accredited by:** Southern.

Curriculum/physical plant
Type: U.S. **Languages taught:** English, French, Spanish. **Staff specialists:** computer, counselor, learning disabilities, nurse. **Special programs:** ESL, advanced placement, honors sections. **Special curricular:** art, physical education, computer instruction. **Extracurricular:** choral music, computers, yearbook, field trips, student council. **Sports:** basketball, soccer, volleyball. **Clubs:** National Honor Society, service (affiliated with Rotary International), chess, Spanish, French. **Tests:** SSAT, PSAT, SAT, ACT, TOEFL, AP, Iowa. **Graduates attending college:** 90%. **Graduates have attended:** American U., Duke, Tulane, Georgetown U., Princeton. **Location:** on wooded hillside overlooking the bay of Port-au-Prince. **Campus:** 4 acres. **Library:** 11,000 volumes. **Facilities:** 2 buildings, infirmary, playing field, computer lab, learning resource center.

*Once only fee

HONDURAS ⸺

Region: Central America
Size: 43,277 square miles
Population: 4,949,000
Capital: Tegucigalpa

Telephone code: 504
Currency: lempira
Languages: Spanish, Indian dialects

LA CEIBA

Mazapan School
Phone: (504)432716   **Facsimile:** (504)422995
Telex: 3118806   **Cable:** STANFRUCO
Mail: (first class) 6964 NW 50th Street, Suite H0-202, Miami, FL, 33166-5632, U.S.A.; (boxes) PO Box 1747, Gulfport, MS 39502, U.S.A.
Superintendent: Frederick L. Thompson, Ph.D.
Principal: Ron Renna
Staff: full-time, 21; part-time, 4
Nationalities of staff: U.S., 16; host, 9
Grade levels: 1 – 12

Enrollment: 1 – 6, 172; 7 – 9, 87; 10 – 12, 88; total, 347
Capacity: 1 – 6, 150; 7 – 9, 75; 10 – 12, 75; total, 300
Teacher/student ratio: 1/15
Tuition (annual): 1 – 6, $1,133; 7 – 9, $1,149; 10 – 12, $1,272
Other fees (annual): registration, $50
School year: August to June

Year founded: 1928. **Type of school:** coed, day, company sponsored. **Governed by:** Standard Fruit Company. **Accredited by:** Southern, Honduran Ministry of Education.

Curriculum/physical plant

Type: U.S. **Languages taught:** Spanish, Portuguese. **Staff specialists:** math, computer, counselor, art, librarian, music, physical education, science. **Special programs:** correspondence. **Special curricular:** art, chorus, band, physical education, computer instruction. **Extracurricular:** drama, instrumental music, computers, yearbook, excursions/expeditions, island survival. **Sports:** basketball, soccer, softball, volleyball. **Tests:** PSAT, SAT, ACT, TOEFL, Stanford. **Graduates attending college:** 90%. **Graduates have attended:** U.S. Coast Guard Academy, U.S. Air Force Academy, U. of Houston, Louisiana State U., Auburn. **Location:** park-like setting in city. **Campus:** 4 acres. **Library:** 8,000 volumes. **Facilities:** 7 buildings, 16 classrooms, 2 playing fields, science lab, computer lab.

SAN PEDRO SULA

Escuela Internacional Sampedrana

Street address: Colonia Gracias a Dios, San Pedro Sula,
    Cortes, Honduras
Phone: (504)575722   **Facsimile:** (504)531458
    Cable: ESCUELAINT
Mail: Apt. #565, San Pedro Sula, Honduras, C.A.
Superintendent: Gregory E. Werner
Principals: Martha Thompson, Craig Hoogendoom, Maria T. Peña
Business manager: Angela Bavaea
Staff: full-time, 85; part-time, 10
Grade levels: N – 12
Enrollment: N – preK, 119; K, 95; 1 – 6, 613; 7 – 9, 233; 10 – 12, 188;
    total, 1,248
Capacity: N – preK, 131; K, 153; 1 – 6, 453; 7 – 9, 593; 10 – 12, 116; 13,
    54; total, 1,500
Teacher/student ratio: 1/14
Tuition (annual): N – K, $535; 1 – 6, $680; 7 – 9, $777;
    10 – 12, $890
Other fees (annual): registration, $40; books, $225; gym, $150; land/
    construction, $500 per family; locker (7 – 12), $15; lab (9 – 12), $100
School year: August to June

Year founded: 1953. **Type of school:** coed, day, private nonprofit. **Governed by:** elected board of directors. **Sponsored by:** Sociedad Educacional Internacional Sampedrana. **Accredited by:** Southern, Honduran Ministry of Education.

Curriculum/physical plant

Type: U.S., Honduran. **Languages of instruction:** English, Spanish. **Languages taught:** Spanish. **Staff specialists:** reading, math, computer, speech/hearing, counselor, psychologist, learning disabilities, nurse. **Special programs:** ESL, honors sections, remedial. **Special curricular:** art, band, physical education, computer instruction. **Extracurricular:** drama, instrumental music, computers, yearbook, newspaper, literary magazine, excursions/expeditions, field trips. **Sports:** basketball, soccer, volleyball. **Clubs:** National Honor Society, film society, drama. **Tests:** PSAT, SAT, ACT, TOEFL, Iowa. **Graduates attending college:** 95%. **Graduates have attended:** Citadel, Tufts, Auburn, U. of Pennsylvania, U. of Miami. **Location:** in San Pedro Sula. **Library:** 15,000 volumes. **Facilities:** 2 campuses, 10 buildings, 40 classrooms, gymnasium, 2 playing fields, 2 science labs, 2 computer labs.

TEGUCIGALPA

THE AMERICAN SCHOOL OF TEGUCIGALPA

Street address: Las Lomas del Guijarro, Tegucigalpa, Honduras
Phone: (504)324696   **Facsimile:** (504)322380
Mail: c/o U.S. Embassy, Tegucigalpa, Honduras
Superintendent: James Shepherd, Ed.D.
Director: Linda Duron
High school principal: James Di Sebastian
Elementary principal: Tom Mosseau
Staff: full-time, 63
Nationalities of staff: U.S., 29; U.K., 1; host, 30; other, 3
Grade levels: N – 12
Enrollment: N – K, 210; 1 – 6, 420; 7 – 12, 475; total, 1,105
Nationalities of student body: U.S., 168; U.K., 7; host, 744; other, 186
Capacity: N, 66; K, 66; 1 – 6, 486; 7 – 9, 243; 10 – 12, 243; total, 1,104
Teacher/student ratio: 1/18
Tuition (annual): preK – K, $1,600; 1 – 6, $1,750; 7 – 12, $2,100
Other fees (annual): busing, $275; initial enrollment*, $2,500
School year: August to June

Year founded: 1946. **Type of school:** coed, day, private nonprofit. **Governed by:** elected board of directors, Sociedad Educacional Interamericana de Tegucigalpa. **Accredited by:** Southern.

Curriculum/physical plant

Type: U.S., Honduran. **Languages of instruction:** English, Spanish (1 hour daily). **Languages taught:** English, Spanish. **Staff specialists:** computer, counselor, learning disabilities, nurse. **Special curricular:** chorus, band, physical education, computer instruction. **Extracurricular:** drama, yearbook, newspaper, literary magazine, photography, field trips. **Clubs:** National Honor Society, senior community service. **Tests:** SSAT, PSAT, SAT, ACT, Iowa. **Graduates attending college:** 95%. **Graduates have attended:** Northwestern, Stanford, Duke, William and Mary, U. of Pennsylvania. **Location:** on hilltop overlooking city. **Campus:** 12 acres. **Library:** 12,818 volumes. **Facilities:** 6 buildings, 45 classrooms, auditorium, cafeteria, infirmary, 2 playing fields, 4 science labs, 2 computer labs.

*Once only fee

HONG KONG

Region: East Asia
Size: 409 square miles
Population: 5,700,000
Capital: Hong Kong

Telephone code: 852
Currency: dollar
Languages: Chinese, English

HONG KONG

CALIFORNIA INTERNATIONAL (U.S.A.) SCHOOL

Street address: 125 Waterloo Road, Kowloon Tong, Hong Kong
Phone: (852)3363812   **Facsimile:** (852)3365276
Mail: 123, 125 & 143 Waterloo Road, Kowloon Tong, Hong Kong
Principal: Rose Ng
Section head, high school: Linda O'Donnell
Section head, elementary school: Kathy Pang
Staff: full-time, 28
Grade levels: 1 – 12
Enrollment: 1 – 6, 140; 7 – 9, 118; 10 – 12, 129; total, 387
Capacity: total, 500
Teacher/student ratio: 1/14
Tuition (annual): 1 – 3, 48,000**; 3 – 6, 50,400; 7 – 9, 55,200; 10 – 12, 60,000
Other fees (annual): busing, 500 – 850**; lunch, 13; books, 1,500 – 2,500; sport and activities, 200; PSAT, 100; application*, 1,000
School year: August to June

Year founded: 1986. **Type of school:** coed, day. **Governed by:** appointed board of directors. **Accredited by:** Western.

Curriculum/physical plant
Type: U.S. **Staff specialists:** reading, math, computer, counselor. **Special programs:** ESL, advanced placement. **Special curricular:** art, physical education, computer instruction. **Extracurricular:** drama, instrumental music, computers, yearbook, newspaper, field trips, Earth Club. **Sports:** hockey, soccer, swimming, tennis, volleyball, badminton. **Tests:** PSAT, SAT, TOEFL, AP. **Graduages attending college:** 64%. **Graduates have attended:** U. of Michigan, U. of Rochester, New York U., Kanagawa U., Ritsumeikan U. **Location:** in city. **Facilities:** 3 buildings, 21 classrooms, 3 auditoriums, playing field, 2 science labs, computer lab, swimming pool, multi-purpose hall, air conditioning.

*Once only fee   **Hong Kong dollar

CHINESE INTERNATIONAL SCHOOL

Street address: 1 Hau Yuen Path, Braemar Hill, Hong Kong
Phone: (852)5107288   **Facsimile:** (852)5107488
Headmaster: Christopher Berrisford

Head, senior division: Catherine Fleming
Head, junior division: John Oates
Head, infant division: Ann Leddy
Head of library: Marilyn McMahon
Head of computer services: Anthony Bernardo
Business administration manager: Paul Cabrelli
Staff: full-time, 80; part-time, 4
Nationalities of staff: U.S., 10; U.K., 36; host, 24; other, 14
Grade levels: preK – 12
Enrollment: preK – 1, 225; 2 – 5, 300; 6 – 8, 293; 9 – 12, 135; total, 953
Capacity: preK – 1, 225; 2 – 5, 300; 6 – 8, 295; 9 – 12, 230; total, 1,050
Teacher/student ratio: 1/12
Tuition (annual): preK, 30,000**; K – 5, 40,000; 6 – 11, 48,000
Other fees (annual): capital levy*, 6,000**; debenture at 75,000 and
    200,000; books, 1,500 – 2,500; transport (optional), 3,000 – 8,000
School year: September to June

Year founded: 1983. **Type of school:** coed, day, private nonprofit.
Governed by: Chinese International School Foundation Ltd.

Curriculum/physical plant

Type: U.K., IB, bilingual. **Languages of instruction:** English, Mandarin.
Languages taught: French, Mandarin. **Staff specialists:** computer, art,
music, physical education, economics, craft, design and technology, science,
drama, librarians. **Special programs:** ESL, CSL. **Special curricular:** art,
physical education, computer instruction. **Extracurricular:** gymnastics,
dance, computers, literary magazine, excursions/expeditions, field trips,
ballet, choral and instrumental music, Mandarin. **Sports:** basketball, hockey,
rugby, soccer, swimming, tennis, netball, table tennis. **Tests:** SAT, TOEFL, IB,
IGCSE. **Location:** on Hong Kong Island. **Campus:** 2.5 acres. **Library:** 20,000
volumes. **Facilities:** 1 building, 59 classrooms, auditorium, cafeteria, 2
gymnasiums, 5 science labs, 2 computer labs, swimming pool, CDT workshop, language laboratory, dance studio, air conditioning.

*Once only fee   **Hong Kong dollar

HONG KONG INTERNATIONAL SCHOOL

Street address: 6 & 23 South Bay Close, Repulse Bay, Hong Kong
Phone: (852)8122305   **Facsimile:** (852)8127037
    Cable: HKISCHOOL
Headmaster: David F. Rittmann
High school principal: James A. Handrich
Middle school principal: Phillip S. Woodall
Elementary school principal: Mary Hoff
Business manager: Gary H. Rasmussen
Staff: full-time, 166; part-time, 25; paraprofessionals, 20
Nationalities of staff: U.S., 167; U.K./host, 28; other, 16

Grade levels: preP – 12
Enrollment: preP – 5, 1,000; 6 – 8, 475; 9 – 12, 620; total, 2,095
Nationalities of student body: U.S., 1,185; other, 910
Capacity: total, 2,100
Teacher/student ratio: 1/12
Tuition (annual): preP, 39,200**; K – 5, 78,450; 6 – 8, 82,250; 9 – 12, 89,950
Other fees (annual): registration*, 15,000**; busing, 10,000
School year: August to June

Year founded: 1966. **Type of school:** coed, day, church-related. **Governed by:** appointed board of managers for Lutheran Church – Missouri Synod. **Accredited by:** Western.

Curriculum

Type: U.S. **Languages taught:** French, Spanish, Mandarin. **Staff specialists:** reading, counselor, psychologist, nurse, resource. **Special programs:** advanced placement, independent study. **Special curricular:** art, chorus, band, physical education, computer instruction. **Extracurricular:** drama, gymnastics, dance, computers, yearbook, newspaper, choral and instrumental music. **Sports:** basketball, field hockey, rugby, soccer, swimming, track, volleyball, water polo, crew, squash. **Tests:** PSAT, SAT, ACT, TOEFL. **Graduates attending college:** 90%. **Graduates have attended:** Cornell, Brown, Rice, Princeton, Stanford.

Physical plant

Location: high-school building on Tai Tam Road, 5 miles from elementary and middle-school campuses, in residential areas on south side of Hong Kong Island (Repulse Bay). **Campuses (3):** 10 acres. **Libraries:** 60,000 volumes. **Facilities:** 3 buildings, auditorium, 2 cafeterias, covered play area, 3 gymnasiums, playing field, 2 swimming pools, tennis courts, science labs, computer labs, nurse infirmary, 2 squash courts, full facilities for the arts, air conditioning.

*Once only fee   **Hong Kong dollar

INTERNATIONAL CHRISTIAN SCHOOL

Street address: 45 Grampiagn Road, Kowloon City, Hong Kong
Phone: (852)3389606   **Facsimile:** (852)3389517
Mail: PO Box 89009, Kowloon City, Hong Kong
Principal: Frank Martens, Ed.D.
Staff: full-time, 13; part-time, 4
Nationalities of staff: U.S., 15; host, 1; other, 1
Grade levels: K – 12
Enrollment: K, 20; 1 – 6, 124; 7 – 9, 68; 10 – 12, 30; total, 242
Nationalities of student body: U.S., 140; U.K., 6; host, 36; other, 60
Capacity: K, 24; 1 – 6, 144; 7 – 9, 72; 10 – 12, 72; total, 312
Teacher/student ratio: 1/16
Tuition (annual): K – 5, 27,000**; 6 – 12, 47,000

Other fees (annual): registration, 1,000**; books, 1,500
School year: September to mid-June

Year founded: 1992. **Type of school:** private nonprofit. **Governed by:** International Christian Schools, Ltd.

Curriculum/physical plant

Type: U.S. **Languages taught:** Mandarin, Cantonese. **Special programs:** ESL, correspondence, remedial. **Special curricular:** art, chorus, band, physical education, computer instruction. **Extracurricular:** drama, choral and instrumental music, computers, yearbook, newpaper, field trips. **Tests:** PSAT, SAT. **Location:** in city. **Campus:** 2 acres. **Library:** 3,000 volumes. **Facilities:** 5 buildings, 14 classrooms, gymnasiums, science lab, computer lab.

**Hong Kong dollar

ISLAND SCHOOL

Street address: 20 Borrett Road, Hong Kong
Phone: (852)5247135   **Facsimile:** (852)8401673
Academic head: Mr. D. J. James
Staff: full-time, 70; part-time, 22
Grade levels: 7 – 13
Enrollment: 7 – 9, 584; 10 – 13, 616; total, 1,200
Capacity: 7 – 9, 600; 10 – 13, 610; total, 1,210
Teacher/student ratio: 1/15
Tuition (annual): 7 – 13, 46,700**
Other fees (annual): busing, 900**; books, 420 – 480
School year: September through June

Year founded: 1967. **Type of school:** coed, nonprofit, community. **Governed by:** appointed and elected school council, English Schools Foundation. **Accredited by:** London University Schools Examination Board; Southern Regions Examination Board, United Kingdom; UCCA.

Curriculum/physical plant

Type: U.K. **Special curricular:** art. **Extracurricular:** drama, yearbook, newspaper, literary magazine, all major games, orchestra, debating, Model UN, choirs, brass group, string group, theater club, zoo. **Tests:** SSAT, PSAT, SAT, ACT, TOEFL, A-level, AS-level, GCSE. **Graduates have attended:** Oxford, Cambridge, Stanford, MIT, Berkeley. **Location:** on mountainside, overlooking Victoria Harbor, above heart of central district. **Library:** 26,000 volumes. **Facilities:** swimming pool, science labs, language lab, darkroom, Arthur Samy Studio Theater, computer centers, private study areas, careers center, 3 playgrounds, bookshop, first-aid room, pottery workshop.

**Hong Kong dollar

KING GEORGE V SCHOOL

Street address: 2 Tin Kwong Road, Kowloon, Hong Kong
Phone: (852)7113028 – 9   **Facsimile:** (852)7607116
Principal: Michael J. Behennah
Staff: full-time, 78; part-time, 11
Grade levels: 7 – 13
Enrollment: 7 – 9, 700; 10 – 13, 500; total, 1,200
Capacity: 7 – 9, 700; 10 – 13, 500; total, 1,200
Teacher/student ratio: 1/14
Tuition (annual): $5,897
Other fees (annual): busing, $350; books, $200
School year: September through June

Year founded: 1900. **Type of school:** coed, nonprofit, community. **Governed by:** appointed and elected school council, English Schools Foundation. **Accredited by:** London University Schools Examination Board, Southern Regions Examination Board – United Kingdom, U.C.C.A., P.C.A.S., C.R.C.H.

Curriculum/physical plant

Type: U.K. **Special curricular:** art, drama. **Extracurricular:** yearbook, newspaper, literary magazine, orchestra, choirs, pop group, theater club, Times network, sports club. **Tests:** PSAT, SAT, ACT, TOEFL, AP, GCSE, A-level, A/S level, Pitmans, RSA. **Graduates have attended:** Oxford, Cambridge, Princeton, Sydney, London. **Location:** on spacious 10-acre site close to Kai Tak International Airport. **Facilities:** language labs, computer center, private study areas, student information center for U.K. and U.S. university placement, 10 science labs, medical room with qualified nurse, pottery workshop, tennis courts, swimming pool, playing field for football and rugby, athletics track. Resource center including educational video library, conference rooms, 3 computer suites, teachers' in-service training center.

LI PO CHUN UNITED WORLD COLLEGE
OF HONG KONG

Street address: Lok Wo Sha Lane, Sha Tin, Hong Kong
Phone: (852)6400441   **Facsimile:** (852)6434088
Principal: David Wilkinson, Ph.D.
Director of studies: Sadru Damji, Ph.D.
Business manager: Y. C. Lee
Staff: full-time, 21; part-time, 2
Nationalities of staff: U.S., 1; U.K., 8; host, 7; other, 7
Grade levels: 11 – 12
Enrollment: total, 240
Capacity: total, 250
Teacher/student ratio: 1/11
Boarders: boys, 120; girls, 120   **Program:** planned 7-day
Tuition and board (annual): $16,000
School year: September to June

Year founded: 1991. **Type of school:** coed, boarding, private nonprofit. **Governed by:** board of directors.

Curriculum/physical plant
Type: IB. **Extracurricular:** drama, dance, choral music, computers, yearbook, newspaper, photography, excursions/expeditions. **Tests:** IB. **Location:** purpose-built campus on seashore location, 10 kilometers from Sha Tin. **Campus:** 6.5 hectares. **Library:** 5,000 volumes. **Facilities:** 7 buildings, cafeteria, infirmary, 4 science labs, computer lab, swimming pool, air conditioning, full boarding facilities.

HUGARY ———————————————

Region: Europe
Size: 35,919 square miles
Population: 10,588,000
Capital: Budapest

Telephone code: 36
Currency: forint
Language: Hungarian

BUDAPEST

AMERICAN INTERNATIONAL SCHOOL OF BUDAPEST
Street address: Kakukk U. 1 – 3, Budapest XII, 1121 Hungary
Phone: (36)(1)1758685   **Facsimile:** (36)(1)1758993
Mail: PO Box 53, 1525 Budapest, Hungary
U.S. mail: (no personal name) American International School of Budapest, AMCONGEN (BUD), APO New York 09213-5270
Director: John K. Johnson
Upper school principal: Brett Engisch
Lower school principal: Bret Anderson
Director of student services: Faith Wassersug
Staff: full-time, 48; part-time, 10
Nationalities of staff: U.S., 38; U.K., 5; host, 3; other, 12
Grade levels: K – 12
Enrollment: K, 36; 1 – 6, 238; 7 – 12, 166; total, 440
Nationalities of student body: U.S., 131; U.K., 25; host, 28; other, 256
Teacher/student ratio: 1/8
Tuition (annual): K – 5, $7,500; 6 – 8, $8,000; 9 – 12, $8,300
Other fees (annual): registration*, $250; building fee, $1,700
School year: August to June

Year founded: 1973. **Type of school:** coed, day. **Governed by:** appointed board of directors. **Accredited by:** Middle States, ECIS.

Curriculum

Type: U.S. **Languages taught:** French, German. **Staff specialists:** computer, art, music, physical education. **Special programs:** ESL. **Special curricular:** art, chorus, physical education, computer instruction, Hungarian studies. **Extracurricular:** drama, gymnastics, choral music, computers, excursions/expeditions, stamp collecting, board games. **Sports:** basketball, soccer, swimming. **Clubs:** computer, cooking, dance, judo, drama, film, stamp collecting, choir, art, swimming, sports. **Tests:** PSAT, SAT, Iowa.

Physical plant

Upper School (6–12): rented facilities in quaint old building situated in forest, 5 kilometers from lower school. **Library:** 4,000 volumes. **Facilities:** 2 buildings, 12 classrooms, outside sports facilities. **Lower School (K–5):** in residential area in Buda hills, 5 kilometers from Budapest. **Campus:** 3 acres. **Library:** 5,000 volumes. **Facilities:** 1 building, 18 classrooms, auditorium, cafeteria, tennis court, gymnasium, science lab, computer lab, swimming pool.

*Once only fee

INTERNATIONAL KINDERGARTEN & SCHOOL OF BUDAPEST

Street address: 19b Konkoly Ut., Budapest, Hungary
Phone: (36)(60)16766
Director: Peter Jones
Principal: Lesley Snowball
Staff: full-time, 12; part-time, 3
Nationalities of staff: U.S., 2; U.K., 1; host, 2; other, 10
Grade levels: preK – 2
Enrollment: preK, 45; K, 25; 1 – 2, 12; total, 82
Teacher/student ratio: 1/6
Tuition (annual): preK, $5,200; K, $5,900; 1 – 2, $6,500
Other fees: registration*, $200
School year: September to mid-June

Year founded: 1992. **Type of school:** coed, day, private nonprofit.

Curriculum/physical plant

Type: international based on U.S./U.K. **Languages taught:** Hungarian. **Staff specialists:** computer, learning disabilities, nurse. **Special programs:** ESL. **Special curricular:** art, physical education, computer instruction. **Extracurricular:** dance. **Sports:** aerobics, skiing, swimming. **Location:** peaceful tree-studded area surrounded by forest, 15 kilometers from Budapest. **Campus:** 2 acres. **Facilities:** 1 building, 6 classrooms, covered play area, gymnasium, playing field, swimming pool.

*Once only fee

ICELAND ───────────────────────

Region: North Atlantic
Size: 39,769 square miles
Population: 259,000
Capital: Reykjavik

Telephone code: 354
Currency: kronur
Language: Icelandic

REYKJAVIK

AMERICAN EMBASSY SCHOOL

Phone: (354)(1)18209/42037
Mail: c/o American Embassy, Reykjavik, Iceland
U.S. mail: (no personal name) American Embassy School, c/o American
   Embassy, PSC 1003, Box 40, FPO AE 09728-0340
Head teacher: Barbara Sigurbjornsson
Staff: full-time, 1; part-time, 4
Nationalities of staff: U.S., 4; other, 1
Grade levels: K – 6
Enrollment: K, 5; 1 – 6, 18; total, 23
Capacity: K, 10; 1 – 6, 18; total, 28
Teacher/student ratio: 1/8
Tuition (annual): K, $3,050 – 3,550; 1 – 6, $4,290 – 5,000
School year: September through May

Year founded: 1959. **Type of school:** coed, day. **Governed by:** appointed school board. **Sponsored by:** American Embassy.

Curriculum/physical plant
Type: U.S. **Languages taught:** Icelandic. **Special curricular:** art, chorus, computer instruction, swimming. **Extracurricular:** literary magazine, field trips. **Tests:** Stanford. **Location:** in city, near American, British, and Norwegian embassies. **Library:** 2,500 volumes. **Facilities:** 2 classrooms, use of local swimming pool, playground, park.

INDIA

Region: South Asia
Size: 1,266,595 square miles
Population: 866,000,000
Capital: New Delhi

Telephone code: 91
Currency: rupee
Languages: Hindi, English, others

BOMBAY

AMERICAN SCHOOL OF BOMBAY

Street address: 75 B. Desai Road, Bombay 400-026, India
Phone: (91)(22)3630026   **Facsimile:** (91)(22)8220350/3630026
    Telex: 95301175425 ACON IN   **Cable:** CONGEN, Bombay India
U.S. mail: c/o American Consulate General, Bombay, Department of State, Washington, DC 20520-6240
Director: Hal Strom (1993 – 94)
Staff: full-time, 14; part-time, 14
Nationalities of staff: U.S., 15; U.K., 5; host, 3; other, 5
Grade levels: N – 12
Enrollment: N – preK, 21; K, 8; 1 – 6, 76; 7 – 9, 13; total, 118
Nationalities of student body: U.S., 24; U.K., 14; other, 80
Capacity: N – preK, 24; K, 20; 1 – 6, 78; 7 – 12, 28; total, 150
Teacher/student ratio: 1/6
Tuition (annual): N – preK, $2,500; K – 12, $5,250
Other fees (annual): registration, $2,500
School year: August to May

Year founded: 1981. **Type of school:** coed, day, private nonprofit. **Governed by:** elected board of governors. **Accredited by:** Middle States (in process).

Curriculum/physical plant

Type: U.S. **Languages taught:** French, (grades 3 – 9). **Staff specialists:** computer. **Special programs:** ESL, remedial. **Special curricular:** art, chorus, physical education, computer instruction. **Extracurricular:** gymnastics, dance, instrumental music, yearbook, excursions/expeditions, field trips. **Sports:** soccer, swimming, tennis, karate, gymnastics. **Clubs:** arts and crafts, art, dance, cooking, oragami, jazz. **Tests:** Iowa. **Location:** in metropolitan Bombay. **Library:** 8,000 volumes. **Facilities:** 2 campuses, 2 buildings, 12 classrooms, tennis court, playing field, science lab, 2 computer labs, swimming pool, AV equipment, air conditioning.

1992-93 listing

HYDERABAD

INTERNATIONAL SCHOOL OF HYDERABAD

Phone: (91)(842)221110   **Cable:** CRISAT, HYDERABAD
Mail: c/o ICRISAT, Patancheru PO, Andhra Pradesh 502 324, India
Principal: Peter Reavey
Staff: full-time, 5; part-time, 4
Nationalities of staff: U.K., 1; host, 8
Grade levels: N – 7
Enrollment: N – preK, 2; K, 7; 1 – 6, 22; 7, 1; total, 32
Nationalities of student body: U.S., 8; U.K., 7; other, 17
Capacity: N – K, 10; 1 – 6, 24; total, 34
Teacher/student ratio: 1/5
Tuition (annual): N – 7, $1,200
Other fees: registration*, 200**
School year: July to March

Year founded: 1972. **Type of school:** coeducational, day, company-sponsored. **Governed by:** partially elected board. **Sponsored by:** International Crops Research Institute for the Semi-Arid Tropics.

Curriculum/physical plant
Type: U.S., U.K. **Special program:** ESL. **Special curricular:** art, physical education, computer instruction. **Extracurricular:** drama, literary magazine, field trips. **Sports:** basketball, soccer, baseball, swimming. **Tests:** Richmond. **Location:** in suburban Hyderabad. **Campus:** .5 acre. **Library:** 1,800 volumes. **Facilities:** 1 building, 6 classrooms, auditorium, tennis court, computer lab, access to swimming pool.

*Once only fee   **Indian rupee

KODAIKANAL

KODAIKANAL INTERNATIONAL SCHOOL

Phone: (91)(4542)4282   **Facsimile:** (91)(4542)4369
    Telex: 95304412207 KIS IN   **Cable:** HIGHCLERC Kodaikanal
Mail: PO Box 25, Kodaikanal 624101, Tamilnadu, India
U.S. mail: c/o Mrs. Jane Cummings, 159 Ralph McGill Boulevard,
    Room 408, Atlanta, GA 30308, U.S.A.
U.S. phone/facsimile: (404)5240988
Principal: Paul Wiebe, Ph.D.
Vice-principal: Peter Lugg
Admissions officer: Peter Jenks
Business manager: D. E. Chandrasakaran
Staff: full-time, 90; part-time, 10

Nationalities of staff: U.S., 23; U.K., 6; host, 54; other, 17
Grade levels: preK – 12
Enrollment: preK, 15; K, 10; 1 – 5, 93; 6 – 8, 130; 9 – 12, 294; total, 542
Nationalities of student body: U.S., 50; U.K., 21; host, 327; other, 144
Capacity: preK, 15; K, 15; 1 – 5, 90; 6 – 8, 120; 9 – 12, 275; total, 515
Teacher/student ratio: 1/6
Boarders: boys, 220; girls, 150   **Grades:** 3 – 12   **Program:** planned 7-day
Annual consolidated fee: $6,000 (boarding included)
Other fees: registration*
School year: July to May

Year founded: 1901. **Type of school:** coed, day, boarding, church-related, private nonprofit. **Governed by:** elected board of management. **Accredited by:** Middle States.

Curriculum

Type: U.S., IB. **Languages taught:** French, Spanish, German, Bengali, Hindi, Tamil. **Staff specialists:** computer, counselor, nurse. **Special programs:** ESL. **Special curricular:** art, chorus, band, physical education, computer instruction. **Extracurricular:** drama, gymnastics, dance, computers, yearbook, newspaper, photography, excursions/expeditions, field trips, choral and instrumental music. **Sports:** basketball, field hockey, soccer, softball, tennis, track, volleyball, badminton, racquetball, golf, cricket. **Clubs:** National Honor Society, stamp, chess, literary, photography, sports, computer, student government. **Tests:** PSAT, SAT, ACT, TOEFL, IB, ACH. **Graduates attending college:** 95%. **Graduates have attended:** Princeton, Haverford, Oxford, Reed, U. of Pennsylvania.

Physical plant

Location: in rural area, 120 kilometers northwest of Madurai (airport), 500 kilometers southwest of Madras (international airport). **Campuses (2):** 20 acres. **Library:** 40,000 volumes. **Facilities:** 30 buildings, 40 classrooms, auditorium, cafeteria, infirmary, covered play area, 10 tennis courts, gymnasium, 2 playing fields, 5 science labs, 2 computer labs, AV facilities, 2 typing/business education labs, 12 dormitories.

*Once only fee

MUSSOORIE

WOODSTOCK SCHOOL

Phone: (91)(1362)2547   **Telex:** 953595238 PRES IN
Cable: WOODSTOCK, Mussoorie, India
Mail: Mussoorie, UP 248 179, India
Principal: R. Flaming
Vice-principal: K. Gingerich
Staff: full-time, 49; part-time, 7

Nationalities of staff: U.S., 15; U.K., 12; host, 23; other, 6
Grade levels: preK – 12
Enrollment: preK, 15; K, 5; 1 – 6, 126; 7 – 9, 133; 10 – 12, 191; total, 470
Nationalities of student body: U.S., 75; U.K., 26; host, 194; other, 175
Capacity: preK, 14; K, 10; 1 – 6, 130; 7 – 9, 135; 10 – 12, 195; total, 484
Teacher/student ratio: 1/9
Boarders: boys, 189; girls, 181   **Grades:** 1 – 12   **Program:** planned 7-day
Tuition (annual): preK, $100; K – 12, $4,000 – 5,500
Other fees (annual): registration*, $35; boarding, $1,000
School year: July to June

Year founded: 1854. **Type of school:** coed, day, boarding, church-related, private nonprofit. **Governed by:** elected board of directors. **Sponsored by:** various mission groups. **Accredited by:** Middle States.

Curriculum

Type: U.S., U.K. **Languages taught:** French, German, Hindi. **Staff specialists:** math, computer, counselor, nurse. **Special programs:** ESL, advanced placement, honors sections, independent study. **Special curricular:** art, chorus, band, physical education, computer instruction. **Extracurricular:** drama, gymnastics, choral music, instrumental music, computers, yearbook, newspaper, literary magazine, photography, excursions/expeditions, field trips. **Sports:** basketball, field hockey, soccer, track, volleyball, cricket, badminton. **Clubs:** philately, hiking. **Tests:** PSAT, SAT, ACT, AP, A-level GCE, O-level GCE, PLAN. **Graduates attending college:** 95%. **Graduates have attended:** Amherst, Smith, Oberlin, Bard, Beloit.

Physical plant

Location: on outskirts of Mussoorie, in the Himalayan foothills (altitude of 6,000 feet). **Campus:** 300 acres. **Library:** 56,000 volumes. **Facilities:** 28 classrooms, 2 auditoriums, 2 cafeterias, 2 covered play areas, 2 tennis courts, 2 gymnasiums, 3 playing fields, 4 science labs, computer lab, swimming pool, health center, 4 residential dormitories.

*Once only fee

NEW DELHI

AMERICAN EMBASSY SCHOOL

Street address: Chandragupta Marg, Chanakyapuri,
    New Delhi 110021, India
Phone: (91)(11)605949   **Facsimile:** (91)(11)6873320
    Telex: 9533172344 AESA IN
U.S. mail: AES-New Delhi, Department of State, Washington, D.C.
    20521-9000
Director: Stephen M. Kapner
High school principal: Michael Stagg

Middle school principal: Roger Bicksler
Elementary school principal: Harvey Alvy, Ed.D.
Staff: full-time, 67; part-time, 22
Nationalities of staff: U.S., 58; U.K., 8; host, 16; other, 7
Grade levels: Early Childhood Education – 12
Enrollment: ECEC, 46; K, 44; 1 – 5, 239; 6 – 8, 146; 9 – 12, 171; total, 646
Nationalities of student body: U.S., 222; U.K., 57; other, 367
Capacity: ECEC, 45; K, 80; 1 – 6, 400; 7 – 9, 180; 10 – 12, 180; total, 885
Teacher/student ratio: 1/8
Tuition (annual, 1992–93 rates): ECEC, $2,000; K – 4, $7,500; 5, $7,600; 6 – 8, $7,800; 9 – 11, $8,570; 12, $8,640
Other fees (annual 1992–93 rates): application*, $60; registration*, $1,700; busing, $145 – 290
School year: August through May

Year founded: 1952. **Type of school:** coed, day, private nonprofit. **Governed by:** elected board of governors. **Accredited by:** Middle States.

Curriculum
Type: U.S., IB. **Languages taught:** French, Spanish, Hindi. **Staff specialists:** counselor, psychologist, learning disabilities, nurse, curriculum. **Special programs:** ESL, advanced placement, independent study, correspondence, IB, mild learning disabilities. **Special curricular:** art, chorus, band, physical education, computer instruction, swimming, photography. **Extracurricular:** drama, choral music, instrumental music, yearbook, newspaper, literary magazine, photography, many clubs. **Sports:** basketball, field hockey, soccer, softball, swimming, tennis, track, volleyball, badminton, water polo. **Tests:** SSAT, PSAT, SAT, ACT, IB, AP, Iowa, Cognitive Abilities Test. **Graduates attending college:** 94%. **Graduates have attended:** Harvard, Princeton, Stanford, George Mason College, Carnegie-Mellon.

Physical plant
Location: in the heart of diplomatic section of New Delhi. **Campus:** 12 acres. **Library:** 20,000 volumes. **Facilities:** 8 buildings, 56 classrooms, auditorium, cafeteria, infirmary, tennis courts, gymnasium, playing fields, science labs, computer labs, swimming pool.

*Once only fee

BANGALORE
Bangalore International School
Address: No. 14, Benson Cross Road, Benson Town, Bangalore 560 046, India   **Phone:** (91)(812)574007   **Principal:** Mrs. Meera Menon

INDONESIA

Region: Southeast Asia
Size: 735,268 square miles
Population: 193,000,000
Capital: Jakarta

Telephone code: 62
Currency: rupiah
Languages: Bahasa Indonesian,
Javanese, other
Austronesian
languages

BALI

Bali International School

> **Street address:** Banjar Taman Sari, Sanur, Bali, Indonesia
> **Phone:** (62)(361)88467   **Facsimile:** (62)(361)88770
> **Mail:** PO Box 259, Denpasar, Bali, Indonesia
> **Acting principal:** Diane Lutman
> **Staff:** full-time, 12; part-time, 2
> **Nationalities of staff:** U.S., 2; U.K., 1; host, 4; other, 7
> **Grade levels:** preK – 7 (correspondence 8 – 12)
> **Enrollment:** preK, 15; K, 15; 1 – 7, 90; correspondence, 5; total, 125
> **Nationalities of student body:** U.S., 17; Australia, 40; other, 68
> **Capacity:** preK, 20; K, 18; 1 – 8, 125; total, 163
> **Teacher/student ratio:** 1/10
> **Tuition (annual):** preK, $2,500; K, $3,400; 1 – 8, $4,500
> **Other fees (annual):** capital levy, $500; busing, $450; ESL, $300
> **School year:** August to June

Year founded: 1986. **Type of school:** coed, day. **Governed by:** elected seven-member school board.

Curriculum/physical plant

Type: U.S., Australian. **Languages taught:** English, Indonesian. **Staff specialists:** computer, art, music, physical education. **Special programs:** ESL, correspondence. **Extracurricular:** dance, newspaper, hobbies. **Sports:** soccer, softball, volleyball. **Location:** in beachside resort town, 10 kilometers from Denpasar. **Campus:** 2.5 acres. **Library:** 2,500 volumes. **Facilities:** 7 buildings, 10 classrooms, 2 playing fields, computers in each classroom, air conditioning.

BALIKPAPAN

Pasir Ridge International School

> **Location:** Balikpapan, East Kalimantan, Indonesia
> **Phone:** (62)(542)34000 ext. 3474   **Facsimile:** (62)(21)7204499
>   **Telex:** 79637174 UNOCAL IA
> **Mail:** c/o UNOCAL, Locked Bag No. 3, Tampines South Post Office, Singapore 9152, R.O.S.

Principal: Joseph Cuthbertson, Ph.D.
Staff: full-time, 11; part-time, 1
Nationalities of staff: U.S., 6; U.K., 2; Australia, 3; host, 1
Grade levels: preK – 8
Enrollment: total, 90
Nationalities of student body: U.S., 36; Australia, 27; other, 27
Teacher/student ratio: 1/8
Tuition (annual): preK, $2,250; K, $8,000; 1 – 8, $12,000
School year: September to June

Year founded: 1972. **Type of school:** coed, day, company sponsored.
Sponsored by: Unocal Ltd. **Operated by:** International Schools Services,
Princeton, New Jersey. **Accredited by:** Western.

Curriculum/physical plant

Type: U.S. **Languages taught:** French (6 – 8), Indonesian (all grades).
Special programs: remedial, limited ESL. **Special curricular:** art, physical
education, computer instruction, music. **Extracurricular:** drama, computers, yearbook, photography, excursions/expeditions, field trips, rain forest:
care of orangutans. **Sports:** softball, swimming, tennis, volleyball, floor
hockey, squash. **Tests:** Iowa. **Location:** company camp overlooking Balikpapan.
Library: 10,000 volumes. **Facilities:** 12 classrooms, auditorium, tennis
court, playing field, science lab, swimming pool, computer room, preschool
annex, aviary, air conditioning.

BANDUNG

BANDUNG ALLIANCE SCHOOL

Street address: Jalan Gunung Agung 14, Bandung 40142, Java,
  Indonesia
Phone: (62)(22)81844   **Facsimile:** (62)(22)441048
  Cable: PAROUSIA BANDUNG
Principal: Wayne Thompson
Staff: full-time, 5; part-time, 2
Nationalities of staff: U.S., 2; host, 2; other, 3
Grade levels: 1 – 6
Enrollment: total, 35
Nationalities of student body: U.S., 24; other, 11
Capacity: total, 85
Teacher/student ratio: 1/6
Boarding grades: 1 – 6   **Program:** planned 7-day
Tuition (annual): 1 – 6, $3,850
Other fees (annual): registration*, $1,000; boarding, $225/month;
  books, $500
School year: August to June

Year founded: 1956. **Type of school:** coed, day, boarding, church-related. **Governed by:** elected mission executive. **Sponsored by:** The Christian and Missionary Alliance.

Curriculum/physical plant

Type: U.S. **Staff specialists:** special education. **Special programs:** remedial. **Special curricular:** art, chorus, physical education, computer instruction. **Extracurricular:** field trips. **Sports:** basketball, soccer, softball, volleyball. **Tests:** Iowa. **Graduates attending college:** 95%. **Graduates have attended:** Canadian Bible College, Wheaton College, Westmount, Nyack Bible College. **Location:** in city. **Campus:** .25 acre. **Library:** 5,000 volumes. **Facilities:** 3 buildings, 5 classrooms, 2 playing fields, computer lab, all purpose room, dormitory, air-conditioned library.

*Once only fee

BANDUNG INTERNATIONAL SCHOOL

Street address: Jl. Drg. Suria Sumantri, Bandung, West Java, Indonesia
Phone: (62)(22)212688/214995   **Facsimile:** (62)(22)212688
Mail: PO Box 1167, Bandung, Indonesia
Principal: Gaynor Day
Staff: full-time, 16; part-time, 9
Nationalities of staff: U.S., 6; U.K., 5; other, 14
Grade levels: preK – 9 (adding 10 in 1994–95)
Enrollment: preK, 51; K – 6, 120; 6 – 8, 38; correspondence, 8; total, 217
Nationalities of student body: U.S., 30; U.K., 41; other, 146
Capacity: preK, 54; K – 5, 130; 6 – 8, 60; correspondence, 15; total, 259
Teacher/student ratio: 1/10
Tuition (annual): preK, $1,550; K – 8, $5,000
Other fees: capital levy*, $2,750
School year: September to July

Year founded: 1972. **Type of school:** coed, day. **Governed by:** elected board of parents.

Curriculum/physical plant

Type: U.S., U.K., Australia/New Zealand. **Languages taught:** French, Dutch, Indonesian. **Staff specialists:** math, computer, art, ESL, music, science, English. **Special programs:** ESL. **Special curricular:** art, physical education, computer instruction, drama, music. **Extracurricular:** drama, gymnastics, literary magazine, field trips. **Sports:** hockey, rugby, soccer, softball, swimming, volleyball, cricket, badminton. **Clubs:** cooking, Girl Scouts, stamp, gymnastics. **Location:** in city. **Library:** 11,000 volumes. **Facilities:** 20 classrooms, 2 playing fields, science lab, computer lab, auditorium/gymnasium, AV equipment.

*Once only fee

BOGOR

BOGOR EXPATRIATE SCHOOL

Street address: Jalan Papandayan 7, Bogor, West Java, Indonesia
Phone: (62)(251)324360   **Facsimile:** (62)(251)328512
Mail: PO Box 258, Bogor, 16001 Indonesia
Principal: Paul Walsh
Staff: full-time, 4; part-time, 5
Nationalities of staff: U.S., 1; host, 4; other, 4
Grade levels: preK – 6
Enrollment: preK, 25; K – 6, 52; total, 77
Capacity: preK, 30; K – 6, 55; total, 85
Teacher/student ratio: 1/11
Tuition (annual): K – 6, $5,775
Other fees: capital levy*, $3,000
School year: August to June

Year founded: 1974. **Type of school:** coed, day, private nonprofit. **Governed by:** elected board of directors.

Curriculum/physical plant

Type: U.S., U.K., Australia. **Staff specialists:** computer, art, EFL, drama. **Special curricular:** art, physical education, computer instruction, music. **Extracurricular:** dance, instrumental music, excursions/expeditions, field trips, swimming, football. **Sports:** soccer, swimming, tennis, cricket. **Clubs:** stamp, swimming. **Tests:** placement, diagnostic, and performance as required. **Location:** in university city of Bogor, 65 kilometers south of Jakarta. **Campus:** 10,000 square meters. **Library:** 5,000 volumes. **Facilities:** 2 buildings, 7 classrooms, covered play area, 2 playing fields, AV equipment, computers, art/craft room, nearby swimming pool.

*Once only fee

BONTANG

BONTANG INTERNATIONAL SCHOOL

Location: Bontang, Kalimantan, Indonesia
Phone: (62)(541)42100 ext. 1176 or dial direct (62)(548)551176
    Facsimile: (62)(541)43100/42548   **Telex:** 79661417 BDKLNG IA
Mail: c/o VICO, 9 Penang Road, 07-08 Park Mall, Singapore 0923, R.O.S.
Principal: Barry Benger
Staff: full-time, 4
Nationalities of staff: Canada, 2; U.S., 1; other, 1
Grade levels: preK – 8
Enrollment: total, 18

Nationalities of student body: U.S., 7; Canada, 4; U.K., 2; other, 5
Capacity: total, 100
Teacher/student ratio: 1/5
School year: September to June

Year founded: 1975. **Type of school:** coed, day, company sponsored.
Sponsored by: PT Badak NGL. **Operated by:** International Schools Services,
Princeton, New Jersey. **Accredited by:** Western.

Curriculum/physical plant

Type: U.S. **Languages taught:** Indonesian. **Special curricular:** art,
physical education, computer instruction. **Extracurricular:** Bali dance,
drama, computers, newspaper, field trips, cooking. **Sports:** swimming, sailing, racquetball, golf, water skiing, bowling, Bali dance. **Tests:** SSAT, Iowa.
Location: in company camp, 30-minute flight from Balikpapan. **Library:**
5,500 volumes. **Facilities:** covered play area, tennis court, playing field,
science lab, computer lab, swimming pool, ceramics room, air conditioning.

JAKARTA

BRITISH INTERNATIONAL SCHOOL

Street address: Kebon Nanas II, Kebayoran Lama, Jakarta, Indonesia
Phone: (62)(21)5484376/5480858   **Facsimile:** (62)(21)5494899
Mail: PO Box 4120, Jakarta 12041, Indonesia
Academic head: Ronald Stones
Staff: full-time, 60; part-time, 6
Nationalities of staff: U.K., 57; host, 1; other, 8
Grade levels: preK – 9
Enrollment: preK, 70; K, 70; 1 – 6, 450; 7 – 9, 170; total, 760
Capacity: preK, 70; K, 70; 1 – 6, 450; 7 – 9, 170; total, 760
Teacher/student ratio: 1/12
Tuition (annual): preK – 9, $7,500
School year: September to July

Year founded: 1976. **Type of school:** coed, day, private nonprofit.
Governed by: appointed and elected board of governors.

Curriculum/physical plant

Type: U.K./GCSE. **Languages taught:** French, Bahasa Indonesian. **Staff
specialists:** reading. **Special curricular:** art, physical education, computer
instruction. **Extracurricular:** drama, gymnastics, computers. **Location:** in
western suburbs. **Library:** 15,000 volumes. **Facilities:** 25 classrooms,
gymnasium, playing field, science lab, computer lab, swimming pool, air
conditioning.

JAKARTA INTERNATIONAL SCHOOL

Street address: J1. Terogong Raya 33, Jakarta 12430, Indonesia
Phone: (62)(21)7692555   **Facsimile:** business office, (62)(21)7697852;
   headmaster office, (62)(21)7503644   **Telex:** 76947494 INTSCH IA
Mail: PO Box 1078 JKS, Jakarta 12010, Indonesia
Headmaster: Niall C. W. Nelson, Ed.D.
Deputy headmaster: Richard H. Carignan, Ph.D.
High school principal: Monica Greeley
Middle school principal: Bruce Leiper
Elementary school principals: Robert Youel, M. Katherine Stewart, Ph.D.
Business manager: William K. Roney
Staff: full-time, 263; part-time, 22
Nationalities of staff: U.S., 164; U.K., 22; host, 12; other, 87
Grade levels: K – 12
Enrollment: K, 171; 1 – 5, 894; 6 – 8, 658; 9 – 12, 961; total, 2,684
Nationalities of student body: U.S./Canada, 1,189; other, 1,495
Teacher/student ratio: 1/10
Tuition (annual): K, $5,400; 1 – 5, $7,500; 6 – 8, $8,400; 9 – 12, $8,500
Other fees (annual): busing, $1,000; chaperone fee, $135 (K – 5 only)
School year: August to June

Year founded: 1951. **Type of school:** coed, day, private nonprofit.
Governed by: elected school council. **Accredited by:** Western, ECIS.

Curriculum

Type: U.S., IB. **Languages taught:** French, Spanish, German, Dutch, Indonesian, Japanese, Korean. **Staff specialists:** math/science, speech/hearing, counselors, psychologist, learning disabilities, nurse, resource teachers, college adviser. **Special programs:** ESL, advanced placement, independent study, IB, work study. **Special curricular:** art, chorus, band, physical education, computer instruction, vocational. **Co-curricular:** dance, choral music, instrumental music, computers, yearbook, newspaper, photography, excursions/expeditions, field trips. **Sports:** basketball, soccer, softball, swimming, tennis, track, volleyball, intramurals. **Organizations**: National Honor Society, Model UN, jazz band, Joint Sound, Thespians, student government, chess, forensics, Tolong Anak-Anak, amelan, stained glass, yoga, Tae Kwon Do, cricket, outdoor, peer helpers, help and information club. **Tests:** SSAT, PSAT, SAT, ACT, TOEFL, IB, AP, Iowa, ACH. **Graduates attending college:** 96%. **Graduates have attended:** major universities in the U.K., Australia, the Philippines, Japan, Korea, and the U.S. (approximately 50%).

Physical plant

Location: on three sites in suburban setting of South Jakarta. **Campuses (3):** 46 acres. **Libraries (4):** 100,000 volumes. **Facilities:** 206 classrooms, 4 auditoriums, 3 cafeterias, 3 tennis courts, 4 gymnasiums, 5 playing fields, 19 science labs, 7 computer labs, 2 swimming pools, AV equipment, fine arts building, wood shop, auto shop, photography lab, air-conditioned classrooms.

North Jakarta International School

Street address: Jl. Raya Kelapa Nias, Kelapa Gading Permai, North Jakarta 14067, Indonesia
Phone: (62)(21)4500683   **Facsimile:** (62)(21)4500682
Mail: PO Box 6759-JKUKP, Jakarta 14067, Indonesia
Head: Michael S. Dougherty
Staff: full-time, 32
Nationalities of staff: U.S., 18; U.K., 2; host, 2; other: 10
Grade levels: preK – 8
Enrollment: total, 320
Capacity: total, 400
Teacher/student ratio: 1/10
Tuition (annual): preK, $2,200; K, $5,400; 1 – 5, $7,500; 6 – 8, $7,900
Other fees: capital levy, $8,000 for a four-year certificate; busing, $985
School year: August to June

Year founded: 1990. **Type of school:** coed, day, private nonprofit. **Governed by:** appointed board of governors. **Accredited by:** Western (in process). **Regional organizations:** EARCOS

Curriculum/physical plant

Type: U.S. **Languages taught:** French, Spanish, Bahasa Indonesian, Mandarin. **Staff specialists:** computer, nurse, librarian. **Special programs:** ESL. **Special curricular:** art, band, physical education, computer instruction, music. **Extracurricular:** field trips. **Location:** in self-contained suburban village, 2 miles from central Jakarta. **Campus:** 2 hectares. **Facilities:** 7 buildings, 32 classrooms, infirmary, covered play area, gymnasium, playing field, computer lab, swimming pool, air conditioning.

LHOKSEUMAWE

International School of Lhokseumawe

Phone: (62)(645)43444 ext. 5209   **Facsimile:** (62)(645)43922/43422
  Telex: 79651696 PTASLM IA
Mail: c/o PT Arun NGL Co., Tromol Pos 22, Lhokseumawe, Aceh Utara, Sumatra, Indonesia
Principal: Bruce Werber
Staff: full-time, 9
Nationalities of staff: U.S., 8; host, 1
Grade levels: preK – 8
Enrollment: total, 32
Capacity: total, 100
Teacher/student ratio: 1/4
School year: August to May

Year founded: 1972. **Type of school:** coed, day, company sponsored. **Sponsored by:** PT Arun NGL Company. **Operated by:** International Schools Services, Princeton, New Jersey.

Curriculum/physical plant

Type: U.S. **Languages taught:** Bahasa Indonesian. **Special curricular:** art, physical education, Macintosh computer lab, music. **Extracurricular:** drama, yearbook, newspaper, swimming, science club, computer club, sports clubs. **Library:** 6,000 volumes. **Tests:** Iowa. **Facilities:** 8 classrooms, covered play area, playing fields, tennis courts, swimming pool, air conditioning.

MALANG

WESLEY INTERNATIONAL SCHOOL

Street address: J1. Telaga Bodas 1, Badut Permai, Malang, East Java, Indonesia
Phone: (62)(341)66580
Mail: Kotak Pos 88, Malang 65101, East Java, Indonesia
Principal: Deborah Wittig
Business manager: Mr. Wasito
Staff: full-time, 4; part-time, 2
Nationalities of staff: U.S., 4; other, 2
Grade levels: K – 8
Enrollment: K, 5; 1 – 7, 32; total, 37
Nationalities of student body: U.S., 2; other, 35
Capacity: K, 12; 1 – 6, 60; 7 – 8, 8; total, 80
Teacher/student ratio: 1/7
Tuition (annual): K, $1,650; 1 – 8, $2,200
Other fees: registration, $50; capital fund*, $2,500
School year: August through May

Year founded: 1971. **Type of school:** coed, day, Christian. **Sponsored by:** OMS International and WEC International.

Curriculum/physical plant

Type: U.S. **Languages taught:** Indonesian. **Special programs:** correspondence. **Special curricular:** art, physical education, computer instruction, music. **Extracurricular:** yearbook. **Tests:** CAT. **Campus:** 4,000 square meters. **Library:** over 6,000 volumes. **Facilities:** 7 classrooms, covered play area, playing field.

*Once only fee

MEDAN

Medan International School

Phone: (62)(61)532894   **Facsimile:** (62)(61)532894/616750
Mail: PO Box 191, Medan, Sumatra, Indonesia
Principal: John McBryde
Staff: full-time, 7; part-time, 1
Nationalities of staff: Australian, New Zealand, U.K., U.S., Indonesian
Grade levels: preK – 8
Enrollment: preK, 5; K, 12; 1 – 6, 49; 7 – 8, 5; total, 71
Nationalities of student body: U.S., 4; other, 67
Capacity: preK, 10; K, 15; 1 – 6, 90; 7 – 8, 45; total, 160
Teacher/student ratio: 1/9
Tuition (annual): preK, $3,600; K – 8, $6,000
Other fees: registration*, $500
School year: August through June

Year founded: 1969. **Type of school:** coed, day, private nonprofit. **Governed by:** board of governors. **Accredited by:** Western. **Regional organizations:** EARCOS.

Curriculum/physical plant
Type: U.S. **Languages taught:** Indonesian. **Special programs:** ESOL. **Special curricular:** physical education, computer instruction, gamelan music. **Extracurricular:** instrumental music, tennis, art, karate, swim club, cooking, gymnastics, athletics, sports clubs, stamp club, computer club, yearbook. **Location:** in suburban area, 10 kilometers north of Medan. **Library:** 6,000 volumes. **Facilities:** 7 buildings, 8 classrooms, auditorium, tennis court, gymnasium, playing field, science lab, computer lab, swimming pool, air conditioning.

*Once only fee

PEKANBARU

Caltex American School

Location: PT Caltex Pacific Indonesia, Rumbai and Duri, Pekanbaru,
    Sumatra, Riau, Indonesia
Phone: (62)(761)33377 ext. 44466   **Facsimile:** (65)7340587
    Telex: 79656112 CALRUM IA/78621349 AMOSEAS RS
    Cable: CALPACEM, Pekanbaru, Indonesia
Mail: c/o American Overseas Petroleum, PO Box 237, Orchard Post
    Office, Singapore 9123, Republic of Singapore
Superintendent: Joe Fleming, Ed.D.
Principal: Tom Jenkins (Duri Campus)

Staff: full-time, 21; part-time, 8
Nationalities of staff: U.S., 24; host, 2; other, 3
Grade levels: preK – 8
Enrollment: preK, 32; K, 22; 1 – 6, 130; 7 – 8, 21; total, 205
Nationalities of student body: U.S., 190; U.K., 5; other, 10
Capacity: preK, 30; K, 30; 1 – 6, 120; 7 – 8, 40; total, 220
Teacher/student ratio: 1/8
School year: August to June

Year founded: 1953. **Type of school:** coed, day, company sponsored. **Sponsored by:** PT Caltex Pacific Indonesia. **Accredited by:** Western. **Operated by:** International Schools Services, Princeton, New Jersey.

Curriculum

Type: U.S. **Languages taught:** Bahasa Indonesian. **Staff specialists:** math, computer, art, music, physical education. **Special curricular:** art, physical education, computer instruction, music, cooking. **Extracurricular:** drama, dance, yearbook, newspaper, literary magazine. **Sports:** basketball, bowling, soccer, swimming, tennis, gymnastics, softball/T-ball, golf, roller skating. **Clubs:** Brownies, Cub Scouts, Girl Scouts, Boy Scouts, ecology. **Tests:** SSAT, ITBS.

Physical plant

Location: central Sumatra in rural jungle/oilfield setting. **Campuses (3):** Rumbai, 10 kms from Pekanbaru; Duri, 120 kms from Pekanbaru; Minas, 17 kms from Rumbai. Each campus, 5 acres. **Library (each campus):** 6,000 volumes. **Facilities (each campus):** 2 buildings, 9 classrooms, tennis courts, gymnasium, playing field, computer lab, swimming pool, golf course, bowling alley, squash courts, softball field, air conditioning.

SALATIGA

CENTRAL JAVA INTERMISSION SCHOOL

Street address: Cabean RT 5 RK I Mangunsari, Salatiga, Jateng, Indonesia
Phone/facsimile: (62)(298)21609
Mail: PO Box 42, Salatiga 50701, Jateng, Indonesia
Headmaster: Mr. O. L. Liles
Dormitory director: Elaine Cox
Staff: full-time, 14; part-time, 4
Nationalities of staff: U.S., 12; host, 3; other, 3
Grade levels: K – 12
Enrollment: K – 6, 60; 7 – 9, 35; 10 – 12, 25; total, 120
Nationalities of student body: U.S., 42; other, 78
Capacity: 1 – 6, 80; 7 – 9, 40; 10 – 12, 40; total, 160
Teacher/student ratio: 1/7
Boarders: boys, 23; girls, 20   **Grades:** 3 – 12
    Program: planned 5- and 7-day

Tuition (annual): 1 – 12, $3,500 (mission reduction available)
Other fees: capital levy*, $2,000; boarding: 5-day, $192/month, 7-day
  $300/month
School year: August through May

Year founded: 1981. **Type of school:** coed, day, boarding, church-
related, private nonprofit. **Governed by:** elected school board. **Sponsored by:**
founding missions, Bethany Fellowship, Christian churches in Indonesia,
Overseas Crusades, Southern Baptist, Assemblies of God, Nazarene.

Curriculum/physical plant

Type: U.S. **Languages taught:** Spanish, Indonesian. **Staff specialists:**
math, computer, nurse, chemistry, English drama. **Special programs:** remedial. **Special curricular:** art, chorus, band, physical education, computer
instruction, English hand bells. **Extracurricular:** computers, yearbook,
photography, excursions/expeditions, field trips, choral and instrumental
music, sports. **Tests:** PSAT, SAT, ACT, Stanford. **Graduates attending
college:** 100%. **Location:** 1 kilometer from Salatiga. **Campuses (2):** .5
hectare. **Library:** 6,300 volumes. **Facilities:** 6 buildings, 14 classrooms,
auditorium, playing field, science lab, computer lab, 3 dorms.

*Once only fee

SEMARANG

SEMARANG INTERNATIONAL SCHOOL

Street address: Jl. Argopuro 14, Candi, Semarang 50231, Indonesia
Phone: (62)(24)315391
Head teacher: Jacqueline Dias-Jayasinha
Board chairman: Valerie Nieuwenhuys
Staff: full-time, 7
Nationalities of staff: U.K., 3; host, 3; other, 1
Grade levels: N – 7
Enrollment: N – preK, 12; K, 9; 1 – 7, 21; total, 42
Capacity: N – preK, 15; K, 15; 1 – 7, 45; total, 75
Teacher/student ratio: 1/6
Tuition (annual): N – preK, $1,050; K, $2,500; 1 – 7, $4,050 (reduction
  possible)
School year: September to mid-July

Year founded: 1982. **Type of school:** coed, day, private nonprofit.
Governed by: elected school board. **Accredited by:** Indonesian Ministry of
Education.

Curriculum/physical plant

Type: U.S./U.K./Australia/international. **Languages taught:** Indonesian. **Special programs:** ESL. **Special curricular:** art, physical education,

computer instruction, instrumental music, field trips. **Extracurricular:** choral, sports, handicrafts. **Tests:** English-based assessment. **Location:** in expatriate suburb of Candi, 1 kilometer from Semarang. **Campus:** 2 acres. **Library:** 2,500 volumes. **Facilities:** 2 buildings, gardens, air conditioning.

SENTANI

SENTANI INTERNATIONAL SCHOOL

Street address: Jalan Pos 7, Sentani 99352, Irian Jaya, Indonesia
Phone: (62)(967)91064/91207   **Facsimile:** (62)(967)31536
Mail: PO Box 239, Sentani 99352, Irian Jaya, Indonesia
Principal: Alex Valley
Staff: full-time, 10; part-time, 5
Nationalities of staff: U.S., 10; other, 5
Grade levels: K – 8
Enrollment: total, 100
Nationalities of student body: U.S., 68; other, 32
Capacity: K – 6, 120; 7 – 8, 40; total, 160
Teacher/student ratio: 1/8
Boarders: boys, 10; girls, 14   **Grades:** 1 – 8
    Program: planned 5- and 7-day
Tuition (annual): K, $1,000 (mission), $1,500 (non-mission); 1 – 8, $2,600 (mission), $4,000 (non-mission)
School year: August to May

Year founded: 1958. **Type of school:** coed, day, boarding, church-related. **Governed and sponsored by:** Intermission School Board. **Accredited by:** Indonesian government, Western.

Curriculum/physical plant
Type: U.S., international in development. **Languages taught:** English, Indonesian. **Staff specialists:** math, computer, physical education, science, special education, Indonesian. **Special curricular:** art, physical education, computer instruction, special education, vocal music, instrumental music when staff is available. **Extracurricular:** intramural sports, gymnastics for boys and girls. **Tests:** Iowa, Otis-Lennon. **Graduates attending college:** 90%. **Location:** in Sentani, up the hill from the Irian Jaya airport, about 32 kilometers from Jayapura, capital of the province. **Campus:** 10 acres. **Library:** 5,500 volumes. **Facilities:** 6 buildings, 8 classrooms, lunch room, video library, gymnasium, playing field, science lab, computer lab, swimming pool available, 3 hostels operated by individual missions.

SERUKAM

BAMBOO RIVER INTERNATIONAL SCHOOL

Location: Serukam, Samalantan, Kalimantan Barat, Indonesia
Cable: CONBAPMIS
Mail: Kotak Pos 20, Singkawang 79101, Kalimantan Barat, Indonesia
Principal: Barbara J. Pio
Staff: full-time, 4 (two teachers, two dorm parents); part-time, 2
Nationalities of staff: U.S., 5; host, 1
Grade levels: K – 8
Enrollment: K, 1; 1 – 6, 8; 7 – 8, 1; total, 10
Nationalities of student body: U.S., 8; other, 2
Capacity: K, 5; 1 – 6, 36; 7 – 8, 12; total, 53
Boarders: boys, 4; girls, 6   **Program:** planned 7-day
Tuition (annual): K, $375; 1 – 8, $775
Other fees (annual): registration*, $25; boarding, $1,250; administration, $25
School year: August to May

Year founded: 1968. **Type of school:** coed, day, boarding, church-related. **Governed by:** appointed board of directors. **Sponsored by:** Conservative Baptist Foreign Mission Society.

Curriculum/physical plant

Type: U.S. **Languages taught:** Indonesian. **Special curricular:** art, chorus, physical education, computer instruction. **Extracurricular:** instrumental music, field trips. **Tests:** Stanford, Iowa, Monroe. **Location:** 30 miles from nearest city, in rural mission station, among hills thick with jungle. **Campus:** 2 acres. **Library:** 5,000 volumes. **Facilities:** 2 buildings, 5 classrooms, covered play area, playing field, science lab, computer lab, swimming pool, assembly hall, basketball court, 6 double boarding rooms, lounge, recreation room, laundry, kitchen, dining room, reception area.

1992-93 listing

*Once only fee

SURABAYA

SURABAYA INTERNATIONAL SCHOOL

Street address: Jl. Kupang Indah IX/17, Surabaya, East Java, Indonesia
Phone: (62)(31)714583   **Facsimile:** (62)(31)712544
Mail: Tromol Pos 2/SBDK, Surabaya 60225, East Java, Indonesia
U.S. mail: Superintendent, Surabaya International School, U.S. Embassy, (Surabaya, Indonesia), APO AP 96520

Superintendent: James A. Mains
Head of library: Cora Nunez
Head of computer services: Jim Dehner
Business manager: Retno Budirahardjo
Staff: full-time, 36; part-time, 8
Nationalities of staff: U.S., 24; host, 5; other, 15
Grade levels: N – 12
Enrollment: N – preK, 15; K, 30; 1 – 5, 170; 6 – 8, 90; 9 – 12, 55; total, 360
Nationalities of student body: U.S., 28; U.K., 16; other, 316
Capacity: N – preK, 15; K, 40; 1 – 5, 200; 6 – 8, 120; 9 – 12, 80; total, 455
Teacher/student ratio: 1/9
Tuition (annual): N – preK, $3,250; K, $4,900; 1 – 5, $6,400; 6 – 8, $6,500; 9 – 12, $6,700
Other fees: registration*, $500; building fund*, $5,000
School year: August to June

Year founded: 1972. **Type of school:** coed, day, private nonprofit. **Governed by:** school board. **Accredited by:** Western. **Regional organizations:** SEATCCO, EARCOS.

Curriculum/physical plant

Type: U.S. **Languages taught:** French, Spanish, Bahasa Indonesia. **Staff specialists:** computer, nurse, art, music. **Special programs:** ESL. **Special curricular:** art, physical education, computer instruction, music, drama, photography. **Extracurricular:** drama, dance, computers, yearbook, newspaper, literary magazine, field trips. **Sports:** basketball, soccer, volleyball, swim team. **Tests:** Iowa. **Location:** in suburb. **Campus:** 3 acres. **Library:** 8,000 volumes. **Facilities:** 10 buildings, 31 classrooms, infirmary, gymnasium, playing field, science lab, 2 computer labs, swimming pool, air conditioning.

*Once only fee

TEMBAGAPURA

ISS School at Tembagapura

Location: Tembagapura, Irian Jaya, Indonesia
Phone: (62)(21)979540 ext. 7641   **Facsimile:** (1)(504)5821639
    Telex: 79646703 FIITPR IA
Mail: c/o Freeport Indonesia, Inc., PO Box 616, Cairns, Queensland 4870, Australia
Principal: Bruce Goforth
Staff: full-time, 12; part-time, 2
Nationalities of staff: U.S., 11; other, 3
Grade levels: preK – 8
Enrollment: preK, 17; K, 10; 1 – 6, 77; 7 – 8, 16; total, 120

Nationalities of student body: U.S., 89; other, 31
Capacity: K, 15; 1 – 6, 90; 7 – 8, 30; total, 135
Teacher/student ratio: 1/9
School year: September to June

⸀ ear founded: 1972. **Type of school:** coed, day, company sponsored.
Sponsored by: Freeport Indonesia, Inc. **Operated by:** International Schools
Services, Princeton, New Jersey.

Curriculum/physical plant
Type: U.S. **Languages taught:** Indonesian. **Staff specialists:** computer,
art. **Special curricular:** art, physical education, computer instruction, music.
Extracurricular: drama, instrumental music, computers, yearbook, photography, excursions/expeditions, baseball, soccer, tennis, basketball, student
council. **Tests:** Stanford, Iowa, SSAT. **Location:** in small company town in
remote area. **Library:** 4,000 volumes. **Facilities:** 12 classrooms, covered play
area, 2 tennis courts, 3 gymnasiums, playing field, science lab, computer lab,
photography lab.

UJUNG PANDANG

Makassar International School
Street address: Jl. Andi Mappanyukki No. 15, Ujung Pandang, Sulawesi
   Selatan, Indonesia
Phone: (62)(411)82591/83035   **Facsimile:** (62)(411)27008
Mail: PO Box 1327, Ujung Pandang, Indonesia
Principal: Ms. C. Thiem
Business manager: Sumanto Musa
Staff: full-time, 5; part-time, 8
Nationalities of staff: U.S., 1; host, 5; other, 7
Grade levels: preschool – 8
Enrollment: preK, 4; K, 8; 1 – 6, 31; 7 – 8, 4; total, 47
Nationalities of student body: U.S., 8; other, 39
Capacity: preK, 12; K, 15; 1 – 6, 40; 7 – 8, 15; total, 82
Teacher/student ratio: 1/5
Tuition (annual): preK, $2,750; K, $4,126; 1 – 8, $5,500
Other fees (annual): registration*, $250; ESL, $170
School year: September through June

Year founded: 1981; registered international school, 1991. **Type of
school:** coed, private nonprofit. **Governed by:** elected board of governors.
Regional organizations: EARCOS.

Curriculum/physical plant
Type: U.S., U.K., Australia. **Languages taught:** Indonesian. **Staff specialists:** reading, math, science. **Special programs:** ESL. **Special curricular:**
art, physical education, computer instruction, music, swimming, Indonesian
studies. **Extracurricular:** yearbook, newspaper, excursions/expeditions,

field trips. **Organizations:** Friends of Makassar International School. **Location:** on a tree-lined street within city. **Facilities:** 1 building, 5 classrooms, infirmary, science lab, library, garden, badminton court, 2 small covered play areas, nearby gymnasium, close to sports stadium and Olympic-size pool with 2 smaller pools, air conditioning.

*Once only fee

IRAQ

Region: Middle East
Size: 167,924 square miles
Population: 19,524,000
Capital: Baghdad

Telephone code: 964
Currency: dinar
Languages: Arabic, Kurdish

BAGHDAD

BAGHDAD INTERNATIONAL SCHOOL

Phone: (964)(1)5563603   **Facsimile:** (964)(1)5569852
Mail: PO Box 571, Baghdad, Iraq
Director: Helen Al-Soudi
Principal, high school: Awatif Rubayi
Principal, elementary school: Nisreen Awqati
Business manager: Elizabeth Saghagian
Grade levels: K – 12
Enrollment: preK, 10; K, 20; 1 – 6, 121; 7 – 9, 85; 10 – 12, 58; total, 294
Nationalities of student body: host, 82; other, 212
School year: September to June

Year founded: 1967. **Type of school:** coed, private nonprofit. **Governed by:** board of trustees. **Accredited by:** Middle States.

Curriculum/physical plant
Type: combined U.S./U.K. **Languages taught:** French, Arabic. **Staff specialists:** nurse. **Special programs:** ESL, advanced placement. **Special curricular:** art, physical education, computer instruction. **Extracurricular:** dance, computers, yearbook, newspaper, literary magazine, excursions/expeditions. **Tests:** A-level GCE, GCSE. **Graduates attending college:** 98%. **Graduates have attended:** McGill U. (Canada); Amherst, U. of Connecticut; Keel U. (U.K.). **Location:** 20 kilometers outside of Baghdad on the way to the airport. **Library:** 25,000 volumes. **Facilities:** 2 buildings, 2 auditoriums, 2 cafeterias, infirmary, 3 tennis courts, 2 gymnasiums, playing field, 4 science labs, 2 computer labs, 2 language labs, air conditioning.

IRELAND _____

Region: Europe
Size: 27,137 square miles
Population: 3,489,000
Capital: Dublin

Telephone code: 353
Currency: pound
Languages: English, Irish (Gaelic)

DUBLIN

St. Andrew's College

Street address: Booterstown Avenue, Blackrock, Dublin, Ireland
Phone: (353)(1)2882785   **Facsimile:** (353)(1)2831627
Headmaster: Arthur Godsil
Elementary school principal: William Mansfield
Vice-principal: Ian Keegan
Director of studies: J. R. Hay
Staff: full-time, 43; part-time, 12
Nationalities of staff: U.S., 1; U.K., 3; host, 51
Grade levels: 1 – 12
Enrollment: preparatory, 253; secondary, 752; total, 1,005
Nationalities of student body: U.S., 65; U.K., 36; host, 814; other, 90
Teacher/student ratio: 1/20
Tuition (annual): preparatory, $2,300; secondary, $1,980
Other fees (annual): boarding, $4,500
School year: September to June

Year founded: 1894. **Type of school:** coed, day, boys' boarding. **Governed by:** appointed board of governors. **Accredited by:** New England, ECIS.

Curriculum

Type: U.S., Irish Leaving Certificate, IB. **Languages taught:** French, Spanish, German, Irish. **Staff specialists:** math, counselor, psychologist, learning disabilities, nurse, resource. **Special programs:** ESL, honors sections. **Special curricular:** art, chorus, physical education, computer instruction. **Extracurricular:** drama, dance, choral music, computers, newspaper, excursions/expeditions, field trips. **Sports:** basketball, field hockey, rugby, soccer, swimming, tennis, cricket, athletics, badminton. **Clubs:** computer, Boy Scouts, drama, debating society. **Tests:** PSAT, SAT, ACT, TOEFL, IB, achievement tests. **Graduates attending college:** 65%. **Graduates have attended:** Harvard, Yale, Princeton, Middlebury, U. of California at Berkeley.

Physical plant

Location: in suburban area, 5 miles south of Dublin's city center. **Campus:** 10.5 acres. **Library:** 5,000 volumes. **Facilities:** 2 buildings, 52 classrooms, auditorium, cafeteria, infirmary, tennis court, gymnasium, 3 playing fields, 3 science labs, computer lab, AV equipment, 5 dormitories.

DUBLIN
Newman College
    Address: 82, 83 Merrion Square, Dublin 2, Ireland
    Phone: (353)(1)6766792   **Facsimile:** (353)(1)6761798
    Telex: 85290918 NWMN
    Director: John McDermott

ISRAEL _____

Region: Middle East
Size: 7,847 square miles
Population: 4,477,000
Capital: Jerusalem

Telephone code: 972
Currency: shekel
Languages: Hebrew, Arabic

JERUSALEM

ANGLICAN SCHOOL, JERUSALEM
    Street address: 82 Rehov Haneviim, Jerusalem, Israel 91001
    Phone: (972)(2)385220 – 1   **Facsimile:** (972)(2)384874
    Mail: PO Box 191, Jerusalem 91001, Israel
    Headmaster: D. Jeffery
    Business manager: Mohammed RasRas
    Staff: full-time, 29; part-time, 7
    Nationalities of staff: U.S., 6; U.K., 14; host, 15; other, 1
    Grade levels: N – 12
    Enrollment: N, 11; K, 44; 1 – 6, 129; 7 – 9, 57; 10 – 12, 63; total, 304
    Nationalities of student body: U.S., 68; U.K., 24; host, 55; other, 157
    Capacity: N, 12; K, 36; 1 – 6, 152; 7 – 9, 78; 10 – 12, 80; total, 358
    Teacher/student ratio: 1/9
    Tuition (annual): K, $2,000; 1 – 6, $4,500; 7 – 12, $5,250
    Other fees: registration*, $50; building, $250
    School year: September to June

    Year founded: 1948. **Type of school:** coed, day, church-related. **Governed by:** appointed school board. **Sponsored by:** Israel Trust of the Anglican Church. **Accredited by:** Middle States.

Curriculum/physical plant
    Type: U.S., U.K. **Languages taught:** French, Arabic, Hebrew. **Staff specialists:** reading, math, computer, counselor, music, physical education, art and ceramics, religious studies, economics, languages, physical sciences, biology, history, geography, English. **Special programs:** ESL, advanced placement, remedial, Jerusalem studies, music, first language schools in German, Korean, and Swedish. **Special curricular:** art, chorus, band, physical education, computer instruction. **Extracurricular:** drama, choral music, instrumental music, computers, yearbook, photography, excursions/expeditions, field trips. **Sports:** basketball, soccer, softball, swimming, tennis,

street hockey, physical fitness, table tennis. **Clubs:** Brownies, Girl Scouts, student council, yearbook, Boys Club, gymnastics, orchestra, stamp, choir, Christian fellowship, chess, storybook. **Tests:** PSAT, SAT, ACT, TOEFL, AP, A-level GCE, GCSE, Iowa, IGCSE. **Graduates attending college:** 75%. **Graduates have attended:** Hebrew U., Boston, Davis, Calvin, Wheaton. **Location:** in center city in historic buildings. **Campus:** 3 acres. **Library:** 10,000 volumes. **Facilities:** 12 buildings, 22 classrooms, tennis court, playing field, 2 science labs, computer lab.

*Once only fee

RAMALLAH

RAMALLAH FRIENDS SCHOOL

Phone: (972)(2)956230   **Facsimile:** (972)(2)956231
Mail: PO Box 66, Ramallah, West Bank, via Israel
U.S. mail: 864 Weisgarber Road, N.W., Knoxville, TN 37909, U.S.A.
U.S. phone: (1)(615)5843131
Director: Mr. Khalil Mahshi
Principal: Mrs. Abla Nasser
Business manager: Mr. Hanna Ghanayem
Staff: full-time, 56; part-time, 12
Nationalities of staff: U.S., 13; U.K., 1; host, 54
Grade levels: K – 12
Enrollment: K, 50; 1 – 6, 360; 7 – 9, 210; 10 – 12, 190; total, 810
Nationalities of student body: U.S., 40; host, 770
Capacity: K, 100; 1 – 6, 480; 7 – 9, 260; 10 – 12, 260; 13, 100; total, 1,200
Teacher/student ratio: 1/13
Tuition (annual): K, $600; 1 – 6, $700; 7 – 9, $800; 10 – 12, $900
School year: September to June

Year founded: 1889. **Type of school:** coed, day, private nonprofit. **Governed by:** elected board of trustees. **Sponsored by:** Friends United Meeting. **Accredited by:** Jordanian Ministry of Education.

Curriculum/physical plant
Type: U.S., U.K., national. **Languages of instruction:** English, Arabic. **Languages taught:** English, Arabic. **Staff specialists:** reading, math, computer, counselor. **Special curricular:** art, physical education, computer instruction, vocational. **Extracurricular:** gymnastics, dance, computers, yearbook, photography, excursions/expeditions, field trips, choir, student council. **Sports:** basketball, soccer, tennis. **Tests:** SAT, TOEFL, A-level GCE, Tawjihi (General Secondary Education Certificate–Jordan). **Graduates attending college:** 85%. **Graduates have attended:** Earlham, U. of California, Guilford, Bir Zeit, Jordan U. **Location:** close to center of Ramallah/El-Bireh commercial area. **Campuses (2):** 4 acres. **Library:** 2,500 volumes. **Facilities:** 7 buildings, 20 classrooms, auditorium, tennis court, playing field, science lab, computer lab.

TEL AVIV

THE WALWORTH BARBOUR AMERICAN INTERNATIONAL SCHOOL IN ISRAEL

Street address: Hazorea Street, Kfar Shmaryahu, Israel
Phone: (972)(52)584225/582603   **Facsimile:** (972)(52)582881
Mail: PO Box 9005 Kfar Shmaryahu, 46910 Israel
U.S. mail: (no personal name) American Embassy (AIS), PSC 98 Box 100, APO AE 09830
Superintendent: Richard M. Detwiler
High school principal: Edwin Ladd
Elementary school principal: Elaine Levy
Business manager: Sammy Azuelos
Staff: full-time, 44; part-time, 23
Nationalities of staff: U.S., 39; U.K., 6; host, 13; other, 9
Grade levels: preK – 12
Enrollment: preK, 10; K, 40; 1 – 6, 220; 7 – 9, 115; 10 – 12, 125; total, 510
Nationalities of student body: U.S., 130; U.K., 5; host, 60; other, 315
Capacity: preK, 20; K, 42; 1 – 6, 246; 7 – 9, 130; 10 – 12, 150; total, 588
Teacher/student ratio: 1/9
Tuition (annual): preK, $4,200; K, $7,300; 1 – 5, $8,085; 6 – 8, $8,430; 9 – 12, $9,020
Other fees (annual): busing, $1,000 – 2,500; building levy, additional 5 percent
School year: September to June

Year founded: 1958. **Type of school:** coed, day, private nonprofit. **Governed by:** elected corporation. **Accredited by:** Middle States.

Curriculum/physical plant

Type: U.S. **Languages taught:** French, Spanish, Hebrew. **Staff specialists:** counselor, psychologist, learning disabilities, nurse. **Special programs:** ESL, Advanced Placement, learning disabilities. **Special curricular:** art, physical education, computer instruction. **Extracurricular:** drama, computers, yearbook, newspaper, literary magazine, photography, excursions/expeditions, field trips, chorus, extensive after-school activities program. **Sports:** basketball, field hockey, soccer, softball, cross-country. **Tests:** PSAT, SAT, ACT, TOEFL, AP. **Graduates attending college:** 75%. **Graduates have attended:** Harvard/Radcliffe, Brown, Johns Hopkins, Middlebury. **Location:** in pleasant residential suburb, 10 miles north of Tel Aviv. **Campus:** 6 acres. **Library:** 22,000 volumes. **Facilities:** 35 classrooms, gymnasium, 2 playing fields, 3 science labs, 2 computer labs, 2 art rooms, fitness center, 2 viewing rooms, air conditioning.

ITALY_____

Region: Europe
Size: 116,303 square miles
Population: 57,772,000
Capital: Rome

Telephone code: 39
Currency: lira
Language: Italian

AVEZZANO

AVEZZANO INTERNATIONAL SCHOOL

Street address: Via Meucci, 4, 67051 Avezzano, (AQ) Italy
Phone: (39)(863)509292   **Facsimile:** (39)(863)509255
Co-directors: Virginia Simpson, Claudio De Santis-Chisholm
Staff: full-time, 3
Grade levels: K – 8 (9 – 12, U. of Nebraska correspondence courses)
Enrollment: total, 15
Capacity: total, 25
Teacher/student ratio: 1/5
Tuition (annual): 1 – 8, $12,000
Other fees (annual): capital levy*, $1,150; enrollment and books, $350
School year: September to June

Year founded: 1990. **Type of school:** coed, day, boarding, grades 9 – 12 (in private homes), company sponsored. **Sponsored by:** Texas Instruments, Inc. (open to other company children also).

Curriculum/physical plant

Type: U.S. **Special programs:** correspondence, U. of Nebraska for high school, special education consultant available. **Special curricular:** art, physical education, computer instruction, Italian, music, special courses off-campus in Italian facilities. **Extracurricular:** drama, field trips, sports. **Tests:** Iowa, DAB, HESI-W, Q-SAT, TORC, HESI-M. **Location:** industrial zone. **Campus:** 2,000 square meters. **Facilities:** new building, computer lab, library, playground, AV equipment.

*Once only fee

FLORENCE

AMERICAN INTERNATIONAL SCHOOL OF FLORENCE

Street address: Via del Carota 23/25, 50012 Bagno a Ripoli,
    Florence, Italy
Phone: (39)(55)640033   **Facsimile:** (39)(55)644226
U.S. mail: AmConGen Florence, APO AE 09613
Headmaster: Francisco J. Grijalva, Ed.D.

Staff: full-time, 17; part-time, 8
Nationalities of staff: U.S., 16; U.K., 2; host, 4; other, 3
Grade levels: preK – 12
Enrollment: preK – K, 20; 1 – 5, 64; 6 – 8, 30; 9 – 12, 57; total, 171
Nationalities of student body: U.S., 59; host, 57; other, 55
Capacity: preK – K, 35; 1 – 5, 65; 6 – 8, 45; 9 – 12, 70; total, 215
Teacher/student ratio: 1/8
Tuition (annual): preK, 7,900,000**; K, 8,500,000; 1 – 5, 10,200,000; 6 – 8, 11,200,000; 9 – 12, 12,300,000 (rates are estimated)
Other fees (annual): registration*, 1,000,000**; capital levy*, 1,000,000 (5% reduction after first child); application, 75,000; IB, 1,500,000; senior fee, 250,000; EFL, 1,500,000; Italian program: elementary, 1,500,000, middle, 2,000,000
School year: September to June

Year founded: 1952. **Type of school:** coed, day, private nonprofit. **Governed by:** board of advisers. **Accredited by:** Middle States, ECIS.

Curriculum/physical plant

Type: U.S., IB. **Languages taught:** English, French, Italian. **Staff specialists:** computer, art, music, physical education. **Special programs:** EFL, preparation for Italian national exams. **Special curricular:** art, chorus, physical education, computer instruction. **Extracurricular:** yearbook, newspaper, field trips, student council. **Tests:** SSAT, PSAT, SAT, ACT, TOEFL, IB. **Graduates attending college:** 95%. **Location:** in Renaissance villa on hilltop in countryside, 12 kilometers from Florence. **Campus:** 18 acres. **Library:** 14,000 volumes. **Facilities:** 1 building, 18 classrooms, 3 playing fields, science lab, lunch room, MacIntosh computer lab.

*Once only fee   **Italian lira

GENOA

AMERICAN INTERNATIONAL SCHOOL IN GENOA

Street address: Via Quarto 13/C, 16148 Genoa, Italy
Phone: (39)(10)386528   **Facsimile:** (39)(10)398700
Director: Louis J. Perske
Staff: full-time, 16; part-time, 6
Nationalities of staff: U.S., 15; U.K., 1; host, 4; other, 2
Grade levels: preK – 8
Enrollment: total, 137
Capacity: preK, 30; K, 30; 1 – 6, 80; 7 – 8, 20; total, 160
Teacher/student ratio: 1/7
Tuition (annual): preK, 6,675,000**; K, 7,300,000; 1 – 4, 10,420,000; 5 – 8, 11,040,000
Other fees (annual): registration, 1,250,000**; family inscription, 500,000
School year: September to June

Year founded: 1966. **Type of school:** coed, day, private nonprofit. **Governed by:** elected board of directors. **Accredited by:** New England, ECIS.

Curriculum/physical plant

Type: U.S. **Languages taught:** French, Italian. **Staff specialists:** math, computer, art, library, physical education. **Special programs:** ESL. **Special curricular:** art, physical education, computer instruction. **Extracurricular:** drama, gymnastics, computers, excursions/expeditions, field trips, 4-week summer school program. **Sports:** basketball, soccer, volleyball. **Tests:** TOEFL. **Location:** 20 minutes from center city by train or bus, 100 meters from sea. **Campus:** 1 acre. **Library:** 4,000 volumes. **Facilities:** 3 buildings, 12 classrooms, cafeteria, gymnasium, playing field, computer lab.

**Italian lira

GROTTAFERRATA

CASTELLI INTERNATIONAL BILINGUAL SCHOOL

Street address: Via degli Scozzesi 13, 00046 Grottaferrata 00046, Italy
Phone/facsimile: (39)(6)94315779
Director of studies: Marianne Palladino
Staff: full-time, 5; part-time, 6
Nationalities of staff: U.S., 3; U.K., 5; host, 3
Grade levels: 1 – 8
Enrollment: 1 – 5, 60; 6 – 8, 30; total, 90
Nationalities of student body: U.S., 20; U.K., 15; host, 28; other, 27
Capacity: 1 – 5, 60; 6 – 8, 30; total, 90
Teacher/student ratio: 1/11
Tuition (annual): 1 – 5, 7,100,000**; 6 – 8, 8,000,000
Other fees (annual): registration, 250,000**; capital levy, 500,000; busing, 1,750,000; lunch, 1,350,000
School year: September to June

Year founded: 1977. **Type of school:** coed, day, private nonprofit. **Governed by:** elected board of trustees. **Accredited by:** Italian Ministry of Education.

Curriculum/physical plant

Type: U.S., U.K., Italian. **Languages of instruction:** English, Italian. **Languages taught:** French, German, Russian, Latin. **Staff specialists:** reading, math, learning disabilities, nurse. **Special programs:** ESL, independent study, remedial, IFL. **Special curricular:** art, chorus, physical education, computer instruction. **Extracurricular:** drama, gymnastics, yearbook, field trips. **Sports:** baseball, soccer, volleyball, badminton, ping-pong. **Tests:** SSAT, PSAT. **Graduates attending college:** 80%. **Graduates have attended:**

Middlebury, Bennington, Sarah Lawrence, U. of Rome, Boston U. **Location:** nestled amidst vineyards and olive groves, 3 kilometers from Grottaferrata. **Campus:** 13 acres. **Library:** 5,000 volumes. **Facilities:** 4 buildings, 8 classrooms, cafeteria, gymnasium, 3 playing fields, computer lab, AV equipment.

**Italian lira

MILAN

AMERICAN SCHOOL OF MILAN

Street address: 20090 Noverasco di Opera, Milan, Italy
Phone: (39)(2)57601546 – 9   **Facsimile:** (39)(2)57606274
Director: David Ottaviano
Business manager: Luisa G. Linzani
Staff: full-time, 44; part-time, 11
Nationalities of staff: U.S., 38; U.K., 5; host, 7; other, 5
Grade levels: N – 13
Enrollment: N – preK, 13; K, 31; 1 – 6, 172; 7 – 10, 152; 11 – 13, 74; total, 442
Nationalities of student body: U.S., 149; host, 154; other, 139
Capacity: N – preK, 30; K, 40; 1 – 6, 240; 7 – 9, 120; 10 – 13, 120; total, 550
Teacher/student ratio: 1/9
Tuition (annual): N, 8,740,000**; K, 9,215,000; 1 – 2, 11,015,000; 3 – 5, 12,500,000; 6 – 10, 14,065,000; 11 – 13, 14,400,000
Other fees (annual): registration, 831,000**; new student admission*, 2,140,000; senior*, 593,000; transportation (optional), 2,280,000 – 3,720,000
School year: September through June

Year founded: 1962. **Type of school:** coed, day, private nonprofit. **Governed by:** elected board of trustees. **Accredited by:** Middle States.

Curriculum/physical plant
Type: U.S., IB. **Languages taught:** French, Italian. **Staff specialists:** computer, counselor, learning disabilities, nurse. **Special programs:** ESL, advanced placement, honors sections, IB. **Special curricular:** art, chorus, physical education, computer instruction. **Extracurricular:** drama, gymnastics, choral music, computers, photography, excursions/expeditions, field trips, sports. **Tests:** SSAT, PSAT, SAT, ACT, TOEFL, IB, AP, Iowa, Italian national exams. **Graduates attending college:** 100%. **Graduates have attended:** U. of Pennsylvania, MIT, Yale, Georgetown, Carnegie-Mellon. **Location:** in suburban area of Milan. **Campus:** 8 acres. **Library:** 20,000 volumes. **Facilities:** 3 buildings, auditorium, cafeteria, infirmary, 3 tennis courts, gymnasium, 3 playing fields, 2 science labs, 2 computer labs, early elementary center.

*Once only fee   **Italian lira

International School of Milan

Street address: Via Bezzola 6, 20153 Milano, Italy
Phone: (39)(2)40910067 – 8   **Facsimile:** (39)(2)48703644
Head, high/middle schools: Terence F. Haywood
Head, lower schools: Elizabeth Sloane
Business manager: Franco Formiga
Staff: full-time, 61; part-time, 9
Nationalities of staff: U.S., 2; U.K., 59; host, 5; other, 4
Grade levels: K – 13
Enrollment: preK, 150; K, 45; 1 – 6, 280; 7 – 9, 130; 10 – 12, 130; 13, 30; total, 765
Capacity: preK, 180; K, 50; 1 – 6, 300; 7 – 9, 150; 10 – 12, 150; 13, 40; total, 870
Teacher/student ratio: 1/12
Tuition (annual): preK – K, 6,250,000**; 1, 7,500,000; 2 – 5, 9,400,000; 6, 9,600,000; 7 – 9, 10,000,000; 10 – 11, 10,600,000; 12 – 13, 11,250,000
Other fees (annual): registration*, 750,000**; capital levy, 600,000; busing, 2,000,000 (optional); lunch, 900,000 (optional); books, 150,000 (approximate)
School year: September to June

Year founded: 1958. **Type of school:** coed, day, proprietary. **Governed by:** headteachers, sponsor, elected parents' group. **Sponsored by:** Oxford Institutes Italiani. **Accredited by:** Italian Ministry of Public Instruction.

Curriculum

Type: U.K., IB. **Languages taught:** French, Italian. **Staff specialists:** reading, math, computer, counselor, nurse. **Special programs:** ESL, advanced placement, remedial. **Special curricular:** art, chorus, physical education, computer instruction, drama, dance. **Extracurricular:** drama, gymnastics, dance, choral music, instrumental music, computers, yearbook, photography, excursions/expeditions, field trips, Model UN. **Sports:** basketball, hockey, rugby, soccer, swimming, tennis, volleyball, athletics. **Clubs:** art, chess. **Tests:** PSAT, IB, A-level GCE, GCSE. **Graduates attending college:** 95%. **Graduates have attended:** London-Imperial College, London-University College, Oxford, Brown, Carnegie-Mellon.

Physical plant

Location: 4 main centers in city (kindergarten and elementary, middle, high schools) with 5 satellite kindergartens. **Libraries:** 18,000 volumes. **Facilities:** 2 auditoriums, 3 cafeterias, 3 infirmaries, covered play area, 3 gymnasiums, 3 playing fields, 4 science labs, 2 computer labs, 2 art studios, darkroom.

*Once only fee   **Italian lira

NAPLES

THE INTERNATIONAL SCHOOL OF NAPLES

Street address: HQ AFSOUTH Post, Building "D," Bagnoli, Naples 80125, Italy
Phone: (39)(81)7212037   **Facsimile:** (39)(81)7628429
Principal: Josephine Sessa
Staff: full-time, 16; part-time, 8
Nationalities of staff: U.S., 11; U.K., 1; host, 11; other, 1
Grade levels: N – 12
Enrollment: N, 35; 1 – 6, 48; 7 – 9, 47; 10 – 12, 34; total, 164
Nationalities of student body: U.S., 26; U.K., 14; host, 33; other, 91
Capacity: total, 300
Teacher/student ratio: 1/8
Tuition (annual): N, 2,500,000**; K – 3, 4,025,000; 4 – 6, 4,990,000; 7 – 12, 5,955,000
Other fees (annual): registration, 300,000**; capital levy*, 500,000; busing, 1,000,000; lunch, 400,000
School year: September to June

Year founded: 1979. **Type of school:** coed, day, private nonprofit. **Governed by:** school board.

Curriculum/physical plant

Type: U.S. **Languages taught:** French, Italian. **Staff specialists:** math, educational and learning disabilities. **Special programs:** ESL, independent study, remedial. **Special curricular:** physical education. **Extracurricular:** drama, gymnastics, computers, yearbook, newspaper, photography, excursions/expeditions, field trips. **Sports:** basketball, soccer, volleyball. **Tests:** PSAT, SAT, ACT, ERB, SRA. **Graduates attending college:** 90%. **Graduates have attended:** U. of Maryland, Stonybrook, St. Francis College, U. of California at Los Angeles. **Location:** in Naples, on NATO base. **Facilities:** 1 building, auditorium, cafeteria, gymnasium, 3 playing fields, science lab, library, computer equipment, AV equipment.

*Once only fee   **Italian lira

PESCARA

PANTERRA AMERICAN SCHOOL

Street address: Via Piane, 13, Francavilla (CH) 65100, Italy
Phone: (39)(85)4910958   **Facsimile:** (39)(863)509293
Mail: Via Ventre D'Oca, 41, Fontanelle (Pescara) 65131, Italy
Co-directors: Virginia Simpson, Claudio De Santis-Chisholm
Staff: full-time, 2; part-time, 2

Nationalities of staff: U.S., 3; other, 1
Grade levels: K – 8 (9 – 12, U. of Nebraska correspondence courses)
Enrollment: K, 2; 1 – 6, 13; 7 – 12, 1; total, 16
Nationalities of student body: U.S., 3; U.K., 5; other, 8
Capacity: total, 25
Teacher/student ratio: 1/5
Tuition (annual): $12,000
Other fees (annual): capital levy*, $1,000; enrollment and book fee, $200; busing; sports (in Italian facilities)
School year: September to June

Year founded: 1980. **Type of school:** coed, day, proprietary. **Accredited by:** Italian Ministry of Public Instruction.

Curriculum/physical plant

Type: U.S. **Languages taught:** Italian. **Special programs:** ESL, remedial, University of Nebraska correspondence courses, special education consultants available. **Special curricular:** art, physical education, computer instruction. **Extracurricular:** drama, computers, field trips, sports. **Tests:** Iowa, Q-SAT, DAB, TORC, HESI-M, HESI-W. **Location:** Francavilla, near sports stadium. **Campus:** 1,500 square meters. **Library:** 2,000 volumes. **Facilities:** 1 building, playing field, computer lab, AV equipment.

*Once only fee

ROME

AMERICAN OVERSEAS SCHOOL OF ROME

Street address: Via Cassia 811, Rome, Italy 00189
Phone: (39)(6)33264841   **Facsimile:** (39)(6)33268531
U.S. mail: (no personal name) Headmaster, American Overseas School of Rome, APO AE 09624
Headmaster: Robert M. Silvetz, M.D.
Dean of faculty: Edward Tatko
Business manager: Salvatore M. Quattrone
Staff: full-time, 34; part-time, 3
Nationalities of staff: U.S., 25; U.K., 4; host, 5; other, 3
Grade levels: preK – 13
Enrollment: preK, 14; K, 20; 1 – 6, 155; 7 – 9, 90; 10 – 13, 100; total, 379
Nationalities of student body: U.S., 140; U.K., 4; host, 70; other, 165
Capacity: preK, 14; K, 20; 1 – 6, 250; 7 – 9, 120; 10 – 13, 150; total, 554
Teacher/student ratio: 1/10
Tuition (annual): preK, 7,400,000**; K, 9,600,000; 1 – 2, 12,700,000; 3–5, 13,700,000; 6, 15,180,000; 7–8, 15,900,000; 9–11, 17,000,000; 12 – 13, 17,200,000
Other fees (annual): registration, 400,000**; capital levy*, 1,000,000; busing, 2,000,000; lunch, 900,000
School year: September to June

Year founded: 1947. **Type of school:** coed, day, private nonprofit. **Governed by:** elected board of trustees. **Accredited by:** Middle States.

Curriculum/physical plant
Type: U.S., IB. **Languages taught:** French, Italian. **Staff specialists:** reading, computer, counselor, learning disabilities, nurse. **Special programs:** ESL, advanced placement, honors sections, remedial, IB. **Special curricular:** art, chorus, physical education, computer instruction, music. **Extracurricular:** drama, choral music, computers, yearbook, newspaper, excursions/ expeditions, field trips. **Sports:** basketball, fencing, soccer, swimming, tennis, track, volleyball, wrestling. **Clubs:** student council, computer, chess, drama. **Tests:** PSAT, SAT, ACT, IB, AP, Iowa. **Graduates attending college:** 90%. **Graduates have attended:** Stanford, Oxford, Smith, Wellesley, Tufts. **Location:** in residential section, with easy access to center of Rome. **Campus:** 6 acres. **Libraries:** 22,000 volumes. **Facilities:** 5 buildings, 43 classrooms, cafeteria, infirmary, 2 tennis courts, gymnasium, playing field, 4 science labs, computer lab.

*Once only fee   **Italian lira

GREENWOOD GARDEN SCHOOL
Street address: Via Vito Sinisi, 5, Rome 00189, Italy
Phone: (39)(6)33266703
Directress: Donna Seibert Ricci
Staff: full-time, 3; part-time, 1
Nationalities of staff: U.S., 1; U.K., 1; host, 1; other, 1
Grade levels: playgroup – K (ages 2 – 6)
Enrollment: N – preK, 15; K, 15; total, 30
Nationalities of student body: U.S., 3; U.K., 3; host, 14; other, 10
Capacity: N – preK, 17; K, 18; total, 35
Teacher/student ratio: 1/8
Tuition (annual): 5,200,000 – 6,000,000**
Other fees (annual): registration, 250,000**; busing, 1,900,000; deposit, 500,000
School year: September to June†

Year founded: 1974. **Type of school:** coed, day, proprietary. **Accredited by:** Italian Ministry of Education, Rome International Schools Association.

Curriculum/physical plant
Type: U.S. **Languages of instruction:** English, Italian. **Staff specialists:** early childhood. **Special programs:** ESL. **Special curricular:** art, physical education, drama, music, tumbletots, cooking, mime. **Location:** 1 kilometer from Rome. **Facilities:** apartment with 700-square-meter garden/playground, 4 classrooms, cafeteria, AV equipment, piano, library.

**Italian lira   †Summer school in July

THE INTERNATIONAL ACADEMY

Street address: Via di Grottarossa 295, 00189 Rome, Italy
Phone: (39)(6)33266071 – 2   **Facsimile:** (39)(6)33266071
Headmistress: Joan Bafaloukas Bulgarini
Staff: full-time, 10; part-time, 8
Nationalities of staff: U.S., 6; U.K., 5; host, 6; other, 1
Grade levels: preK – 8
Enrollment: preK, 35; K, 18; 1 – 5, 45; 6 – 8, 20; total, 118
Nationalities of student body: U.S., 11; U.K., 5; host, 40; other, 62
Capacity: preK, 40; K, 25; 1 – 5, 135; 6 – 8, 50; total, 250
Teacher/student ratio: 1/8
Tuition (annual): preK – K, $5,000; elementary, $6,500; middle school, $8,500
Other fees (annual): registration*, $300; boarding, $12,000; busing, $1,500; food services, $1,500
School year: September to mid-June

Year founded: 1974. **Type of school:** coed, day, boarding, private nonprofit. **Governed by:** group of professional teachers. **Accredited by:** Italian Ministry of Public Education.

Curriculum/physical plant

Type: U.S., U.K. **Languages taught:** English, French, Italian. **Staff specialists:** reading, math, speech/hearing, counselor, psychologist, learning disabilities, nurse, ESL. **Special programs:** ESL, remedial. **Special curricular:** art, chorus, computer instruction, AT&T network summer camp. **Extracurricular:** gymnastics, dance, choral music, instrumental music, computers, newspaper, literary magazine, excursions/expeditions, field trips. **Sports:** basketball, soccer, volleyball. **Location:** renovated 18th-century farmstead in suburban Rome. **Campus:** 10 acres. **Library:** 3,500 volumes. **Facilities:** 3 buildings, 10 classrooms, auditorium, cafeteria, infirmary, covered play area, gymnasium, 2 playing fields, science lab, swimming pool, computer and AV equipment, boarding facilities in private homes.

*Once only fee

KENDALE PRIMARY INTERNATIONAL SCHOOL

Street address: Via Gradoli, 86, 00189 Rome , Italy
Phone: (39)(6)33267608   **Facsimile:** (39)(6)33267608
Directress: Gloria Hughes Fabriani
Staff: full-time, 8; part-time, 5
Nationalities of staff: U.S., 3; U.K., 5; host, 2; other, 3
Grade levels: preK – 5
Enrollment: preK, 12; K, 12; 1 – 5, 60; total, 84
Nationalities of student body: U.S., 15; U.K., 10; host, 42; other, 17
Capacity: preK, 17; K, 17; 1 – 5, 60; total, 94
Teacher/student ratio: 1/8
Tuition (annual): preK, 6,750,000**; K, 7,800,000; 1 – 5, 9,300,000

Other fees (annual): registration, 300,000**; busing, 2,000,000; books, 300,000
School year: September to June

Year founded: 1972. **Type of school:** coed, day, private nonprofit.

Curriculum/physical plant
Type: U.K. **Languages taught:** French, Italian. **Staff specialists:** reading, learning disabilities, mother-tongue Italian and French. **Special programs:** ESL. **Special curricular:** art, physical education, music. **Extracurricular:** newspaper. **Tests:** Iowa. **Location:** in city. **Library:** 3,100 volumes. **Facilities:** 1 building, 7 classrooms, music room, playing field, computer lab, AV equipment.

** Italian lira

Marymount International School
Street address: Via di Villa Lauchli 180, Via Cassia Antica 7 km, 00191 Rome, Italy
Phone: (39)(6)3312770   **Facsimile:** (39)(6)3312712
Headmistress: Sr. Anne Marie Hill, RSHM
Business manager: Mrs. Solveig Belanga
Staff: full-time, 49; part-time, 9
Nationalities of staff: U.S., 25; U.K., 18; host, 8; other, 7
Grade levels: early childhood – 13
Enrollment: early childhood – K, 92; 1 – 6, 231; 7 – 9, 93; 10 – 12, 148; total, 564
Nationalities of student body: U.S., 150; host, 234; other, 180
Capacity: early childhood – K, 96; 1 – 5, 187; 6 – 8, 88; 9 – 13, 194; total, 565
Teacher/student ratio: 1/10
Boarders: girls, 36   **Grades:** 7 – 12   **Program:** planned 7-day
Tuition (annual): early childhood, 7,000,000**; K, 8,000,000; 1 – 2, 12,200,000; 3 – 5, 13,400,000; 6 – 8, 14,500,000; 9 – 10, 15,800, 000; 11 – 13, 16,300,000
Other fees (annual): application*, 200,000**; capital levy*, 1,000,000; lunch, 1,050,000
Boarding/tuition: $18,000; application, $200; capital assessment, $800
School year: September to June

Year founded: 1946. **Type of school:** coed, church-related, girls' boarding. **Governed by:** Sisters of the Sacred Heart of Mary. **Accredited by:** Middle States, ECIS.

Curriculum/physical plant
Type: U.S., IB. **Languages taught:** French, Spanish, Italian. **Staff specialists:** counselor, psychologist, learning disabilities, nurse. **Special programs:** ESL, IB. **Special curricular:** art, chorus, physical education, computer instruction. **Extracurricular:** drama, gymnastics, dance, choral

music, instrumental music, yearbook, photography, excursions/expeditions, field trips, sports. **Clubs:** aerobics, Model UN, student council, boarders' council, intercultural, National Honor Society, National Junior Honor Society, Search (religious retreat). **Tests:** PSAT, SAT, ACT, TOEFL, IB, AP, ERB. **Graduates attending college:** 85%. **Graduates have attended:** U. of Pennsylvania, Oxford, London School of Economics, William and Mary, Tufts. **Location:** 7 kilometers from Rome. **Campus:** 7 acres. **Library:** 4,000 volumes. **Facilities:** 4 buildings, auditorium, cafeteria, infirmary, 2 tennis courts, gymnasium, playing field, 2 science labs, computer lab, swimming pool, weight room.

*Once only fee   **Italian lira

St. George's English School, Rome

Street address: Via Cassia, Km. 16, 00123 Rome, Italy
Phone: (39)(6)3790141–3   **Facsimile:** (39)(6)3792490
Acting principal: Robert Guthrie, Ph.D.
Head of primary school: Clive Birch
Bursar: Malcolm Graham
Staff: full-time, 64; part-time, 6
Nationalities of staff: U.S., 62; other, 8
Grade levels: K – 13
Enrollment: K – 6, 321; 7 – 13, 445; total, 766
Capacity: total, 900
Teacher/student ratio: 1/11
Tuition (annual): K (half-day), 5,300,000**; K (full day), 7,000,000; reception, 7,500,000; 1, 9,000,000; 2, 11,100,000; 3, 12,850,000; 4, 14,050,000; 5, 14,650,000; 6, 15,500,000; 7, 16,000,000; 8 – 9, 16,400,000; 10 – 11, 16,800,000; 12 – 13, 17,300,000
Other fees (annual): registration*: K – reception, 650,000**; 1 – 13, 1,000,000; busing, 2,150,000 (optional)
School year: September to June

Year founded: 1958. **Type of school:** coed, day, private nonprofit. **Governed by:** appointed and elected board of governors.

Curriculum/physical plant

Type: U.K. **Languages taught:** French, German, Italian, Spanish, Latin. **Staff specialists:** reading, learning disabilities, physician. **Special programs:** ESL, advanced placement, remedial. **Special curricular:** art, chorus, band, physical education, computer instruction, vocational, orchestra. **Extracurricular:** drama, gymnastics, dance, choral music, instrumental music, computers, photography, excursions/expeditions, field trips. **Sports:** basketball, field hockey, soccer, swimming, tennis, volleyball, athletics, netball, badminton. **Clubs:** expeditions, computers. **Tests:** PSAT, SAT, TOEFL, A-level GCE, GCSE. **Graduates attending college:** 95%. **Graduates have attended:** Oxford, Cambridge, Princeton, MIT, Stanford. **Location:** in rural area, 16 kilometers from center Rome. **Campus:** 27 acres. **Library:** 20,000 volumes.

Facilities: 3 buildings, 47 classrooms, cafeteria, infirmary, covered play area, 2 tennis courts, gymnasium, playing field, 8 science labs, 3 computer labs, 2 swimming pools.

*Once only fee **Italian lira

St. Stephen's School, Rome

Street address: Via Aventina 3, 00153 Rome, Italy
Phone: (39)(6)5750605 **Facsimile:** (39)(6)5741941
U.S. mail: 15 Gramercy Park So., New York, NY 10003, U.S.A.
Headmaster: Philip H. Allen
Director of studies: Angela Raymond
Staff: full-time, 18; part-time, 11
Nationalities of staff: U.S., 13; U.K., 4; host, 8; other, 4
Grade levels: 9 – 12, postgraduate year
Enrollment: 9 – 12, 123; PG, 7; total, 130
Nationalities of student body: U.S., 50; other, 80
Capacity: total, 150
Teacher/student ratio: 1/5
Boarding capacity: boys, 25; girls, 25   **Grades:** 9 – 12, postgraduate
    Program: planned 7-day
Tuition (annual): 17,650,000**
Other fees (annual): boarding, 9,000,000**; application*, 200,000; capital levy: new student, 800,000, returning student, 425,000
School year: September to June

Year founded: 1965. **Type of school:** coed, day, boarding, private nonprofit, college preparatory, nondenominational. **Governed by:** elected board of trustees. **Accredited by:** New England, ECIS.

Curriculum

Type: U.S., IB. **Languages taught:** French, Italian, Latin, Greek; Russian, Spanish, German, Japanese, Dutch, and Arabic by tutorial. **Staff specialists:** counselor, librarian. **Special curricular:** chorus, computer instruction, drama, studio art, sculpture, music appreciation, dance. **Extracurricular:** yearbook, newspaper, photography, trip program, community service, Italian cinema and theater, debating, gardening, junior and senior math teams. **Sports:** basketball, soccer, tennis, track, volleyball. **Clubs:** computer, cooking, hiking, Classics-Rome. **Tests:** SSAT, PSAT, IB, AP. **Graduates attending college:** 93%. **Graduates have attended:** Princeton, Georgetown, Dartmouth, Brown, Bryn Mawr.

Physical plant

Location: in historic center of Rome. **Campus:** 2.5 acres. **Library:** 14,000 volumes. **Facilities:** 1 building, 13 classrooms, auditorium, cafeteria, infirmary, tennis court, gymnasium, 3 science labs, computer lab, basketball court, 2 art studios, AV room, 36 double and triple boarding rooms.

*Once only fee **Italian lira

TRIESTE

INTERNATIONAL SCHOOL OF TRIESTE

Street address: Villaggio del Fanciullo, Via Conconello 16 (Opicina), 34100 Trieste, Italy
Phone: (39)(40)211452   **Facsimile:** (39)(40)213122
Director: Peter Metzger
Staff: full-time, 20; part-time, 7
Nationalities of staff: U.S., 10; U.K., 7; host, 6; other, 4
Grade levels: N – 8
Enrollment: N – preK, 55; K, 25; 1 – 6, 79; 7 – 8, 28; total, 187
Nationalities of student body: U.S., 5; U.K., 4; host, 140; other, 38
Capacity: N – preK, 60; K, 25; 1 – 6, 120; 7 – 8, 40; total, 245
Teacher/student ratio: 1/8
Tuition (annual): N – preK, 5,500,000**; K, 6,500,000; 1 – 5, 7,100,000; 6 – 8, 7,700,000
Other fees (annual): registration*, 650,000**; busing, 800,000
School year: September to June

Year founded: 1964. **Type of school:** coed, day, private nonprofit. **Governed by:** appointed and elected board of directors. **Accredited by:** Middle States.

Curriculum/physical plant

Type: U.S. **Languages taught:** French, German, Italian, Latin. **Staff specialists:** computer, physical education, art. **Special programs:** ESL. **Special curricular:** art, physical education, computer instruction. **Extracurricular:** computers, yearbook, excursions/expeditions, field trips. **Sports:** basketball, soccer, volleyball. **Tests:** 3R. **Location:** in suburban area, 2 kilometers from Trieste. **Campus:** 4 acres. **Library:** 4,000 volumes. **Facilities:** 2 buildings, 18 classrooms, auditorium, cafeteria, infirmary, gymnasium, playing field, science lab, computer lab.

*Once only fee   **Italian lira

TURIN

INTERNATIONAL SCHOOL OF TURIN (ACAT)

Street address: Vicolo Tiziano 10, 10024 Moncalieri, Torino, Italy
Phone: (39)(11)645967/6407810   **Facsimile:** (39)(11)643298
Headmaster: Tomm Elliott
Elementary principal: Diana Travis
IB coordinator: Sylvia Lymbury
Business manager: Milena Chiarle
Staff: full-time, 25; part-time, 7

Nationalities of staff: U.S., 12; U.K., 10; host, 6; other, 4
Grade levels: N (3 years old) – 12
Enrollment: N – preK, 20; K, 16; 1 – 6, 95; 7 – 9, 47; 10 – 12, 47;
  total, 225
Nationalities of student body: U.S., 31; U.K., 28; host, 121; other, 45
Capacity: N – preK, 30; K, 20; 1 – 6, 120; 7 – 9, 60; 10 – 12, 60; total, 290
Teacher/student ratio: 1/8
Tuition (annual): N – preK, 6,900,000**; K, 7,500,000; 1, 8,200,000; 2, 9,000,000;
  3 – 5, 9,300,000; 6 – 8, 10,500,000; 9, 11,200,000; 10 – 12, 12,500,000
Other fees (annual): registration, 1,000,000** (new student), 650,000
  (returning student); busing, 14,000,000; lunch, 5,500/each;
  IB, 600,000 – 800,000
School year: September to June

Year founded: 1974. **Type of school:** coed, day. **Governed by:** elected
board of directors. **Accredited by:** New England, ECIS.

Curriculum/physical plant
Type: U.S., Italian, IB. **Languages of instruction:** English, Italian.
Languages taught: French, Italian, Latin. **Staff specialists:** learning-needs
teacher. **Special curricular:** art, physical education, computer instruction,
music. **Extracurricular:** yearbook, excursions/expeditions, field trips, student
council, Model UN. **Sports:** basketball, soccer, swimming, tennis, volleyball. **Tests:** PSAT, SAT, TOEFL, IB. **Graduates attending college:** 100%.
Location: in suburb adjacent to Turin. **Library:** 15,000 volumes. **Facilities:**
cafeteria, playing field, science lab, computer lab, audio/video room.

**Italian lira

VICENZA

Vicenza International School

Street address: Via de Gasperi 6, 36030 Villaverla (VI) Italy
Phone: (39)(445)855344   **Facsimile:** (39)(445)855072
Director/business manager: Dr. Antonio Baldo
IB coordinator: Antonietta Spiller
Staff: part-time, 18
Nationalities of staff: U.S., 1; U.K., 1; host, 1; other, 15
Grade levels: 11 – 12
Enrollment: total, 25
Nationalities of student body: U.S., 1; host, 9; other, 15
Capacity: total, 60
Teacher/student ratio: 1/3
Tuition (annual): 700,000**
Other fees (annual): books, 500,000**
School year: September to June

Year founded: 1987. **Type of school:** coed, private nonprofit. **Governed by:** elected board of directors.

Curriculum/physical plant

Type: IB. **Languages taught:** French, Italian, English, Russian. **Extracurricular:** computers, excursions/expeditions. **Tests:** IB. **Graduates attending college:** 100%. **Graduates have attended:** Italian universities. **Location:** in suburban area, 15 kilometers from Vicenza. **Facilities:** 6 classrooms, science lab, computer lab.

**Italian lira

LUCCA
Liceo Linguistico
Address: "G. G. Byron" Via Del Seminario 577 – Villa Sardi, Localita Tre Cancelli – Monte San Quirico, Lucca, Italy
Phone: (39)(583)330160   **Facsimile:** (39)(583)419212
Director: Aldo Casali

TRIESTE
United World College of the Adriatic
Address: Via Trieste 29, 34013 Duino (Trieste), Italy
Phone: (39)(40)3739111   **Facsimile:** (39)(40)3739225

JAMAICA _____

Region: West Indies
Size: 4,232 square miles
Population: 2,489,000
Capital: Kingston

Telephone code: 809
Currency: Jamaican dollar
Languages: English, Jamaican Creole

KINGSTON

THE PRIORY SCHOOL

Street address: 32 Hope Road, Kingston 10, Jamaica, West Indies
Phone: (1)(809)9266636   **Facsimile:** (1)(809)9267583
Director: Jean Bertram
High school principal: Claudette Carter
Junior school principal: Marguerite Narinesingh
Accountant: Joan Wauchope
Staff: full-time, 50; part-time, 10
Nationalities of staff: U.S., 5; host, 48; other, 7
Grade levels: preK – 13
Enrollment: preK – 6, 250; 7 – 12, 170; total, 420
Nationalities of student body: U.S., 50; host, 220; other, 150
Capacity: preK, 40; K, 40; 1 – 6, 300; 7 – 9, 150; 10 – 12, 200; 13, 20; total, 750
Teacher/student ratio: 1/8
Tuition (annual): preK – K, $720; 1 – 6, $984; 7 – 9, $1,247; 10 – 13, $1,425
Other fees: registration*, $15; entrance*, $175 per family; PTA, $2.25/ year; school photo/yearbook, $15
School year: September through June

Year founded: 1944. **Type of school:** coed, day, private nonprofit. **Governed by:** Priory School Trust Society, Ltd. **Accredited by:** Southern. **Recognized by:** Jamaican Ministry of Education.

Curriculum

Type: U.S., U.K. **Languages taught:** French, Spanish. **Staff specialists:** reading, counselor, learning disabilities, nurse, enrichment/gifted. **Special programs:** ESL. **Special curricular:** art, physical education, music, computer, home economics, vocational (woodwork). **Extracurricular:** drama, gymnastics, yearbook, newspaper, excursions/expeditions, field trips, sewing, cooking. **Sports:** basketball, football, soccer, swimming, tennis, volleyball, Tae Kwon Do, netball, dance, track and field, badminton. **Clubs:** photography, chess, Red Cross, student council, prefect group. **Tests:** SSAT, PSAT, ACT, Iowa, A- and O-level GCE. **Graduates attending college:** 45%. **Graduates have attended:** Georgia Tech, Radford, Princeton, Georgetown, U. of the West Indies.

Physical plant

Location: in suburb, St. Andrew. **Campus:** 15 acres. **Library:** over 12,000 volumes. **Facilities:** 20 buildings, 35 classrooms, auditorium, cafeteria, infirmary, 2 tennis courts, 2 playing fields, 3 science labs, music room, art room, AV room, home economics room, woodshop.

*Once only fee

MANDEVILLE

BELAIR SCHOOL

Street address: 43 DeCarteret Road, Mandeville, Jamaica
Phone: (1)(809)9623396/9622168/9620216   **Cable:** Belair, Mandeville
Mail: PO Box 156, Mandeville, Jamaica
Director: Burnett St. C. Burton
Elementary school principal: Sylvan Shields
Guidance counselor: Sarah Brown
Staff: full-time, 56; part-time, 3
Nationalities of staff: host, 54; other, 5
Grade levels: K – 12 and 6th form
Enrollment: K, 79; 1 – 6, 231; 7 – 9, 99; 10 – 12, 113; 6th form, 34; total, 556
Capacity: K, 75; 1 – 6, 250; 7 – 9, 90; 10 – 12, 110; 6th form, 30; total, 555
Teacher/student ratio: 1/10
Boarders: girls, 30   **Grades:** 7 – 13   **Program:** planned 7-day
Tuition (annual): K, 12,813**; 1 – 6, 21,117; 7 – 12, 29,550; 6th form, 32,784
Other fees: registration*, 100**; boarding, 2,000/month; insurance, 3.50; busing, 200/month; teaching materials: K – 6, 1,032 – 1,152/term; 7 – 12, 504/term
School year: September to August

Year founded: 1967. **Type of school:** coed, day, boarding. **Governed by:** elected board of governors. **Accredited by:** Southern.

Curriculum/physical plant

Type: U.S., U.K., Jamaican. **Languages taught:** English, French, Spanish. **Staff specialists:** reading, math, computer, counselor, nurse. **Special programs:** honors sections, correspondence, remedial. **Special curricular:** art, physical education, computer instruction. **Extracurricular:** drama, computers, yearbook, newspaper, excursions/expeditions, field trips. **Sports:** football, hockey, softball, swimming, netball. **Clubs:** Cub Scouts, Girl Guides, Brownies, ISCF. **Tests:** PSAT, SAT, ACT, TOEFL, A-level GCE, O-level GCE, Caribbean Examinations Council. **Graduates attending college:** 40%. **Loca-**

tion: in rural area. **Campus:** 13 acres. **Library:** 25,300 volumes. **Facilities:** 1 building, 31 classrooms, auditorium, cafeteria, infirmary, 2 tennis courts, 2 playing fields, 3 science labs, computer lab.

*Once only fee   **Jamaican dollar

JAPAN _____

Region: East Asia
Size: 145,856 square miles
Population: 124,017,000
Capital: Tokyo

Telephone code: 81
Currency: yen
Language: Japanese

FUKUOKA

FUKUOKA INTERNATIONAL SCHOOL

Street address: Momochi 3-chome 18-50, Sawara-ku, Fukuoka-shi 814, Japan
Phone: (81)(92)8417601   **Facsimile:** (81)(92)8417602
Principal: Dennis Clark
Staff: full-time, 10; part-time, 11
Nationalities of staff: U.S., 10; U.K., 1; host, 8; other, 2
Grade levels: K – 12
Enrollment: K, 10; 1 – 5, 45; 6 – 8, 28; 9 – 12, 33; total, 116
Nationalities of student body: U.S., 25; U.K., 4; host, 30; other, 57
Capacity: K, 20; 1 – 5, 90; 6 – 12, 90; total, 200
Teacher/student ratio: 1/7
Tuition (annual): K – 5, 830,000**; 6 – 8, 918,000; 9 – 12, 930,000
Other fees (annual): registration*, 100,000**; application*, 20,000; building and grounds, 30,000 per family; PTA dues, 2,000; athletic fee, 4,000 – 6,000
School year: September to June

Year founded: 1972. **Type of school:** coed, day, private nonprofit. **Governed by:** elected operating committee, board of directors, board of trustees. **Accredited by:** Western, Japanese Board of Education.

Curriculum/physical plant

Type: U.S. **Languages taught:** French, Japanese. **Special programs:** ESL, advanced placement and remedial individualized in each classroom. **Special curricular:** art, band, physical education, computer instruction, music, yearbook/newspaper. **Extracurricular:** excursions/expeditions, field trips. **Clubs:** Brownies, Bible, sports. **Tests:** PSAT, SAT, College Board ATP, Wechsler (available). **Graduates attending college:** 100%. **Graduates have**

attended: Sophia, Kent, U. of California at Berkeley, Harvard, MIT. **Location:** in western part of the city near Fujisaki Eki and Seinan Gakuin U. **Library:** 6,000 volumes. **Facilities:** 2-story building,11 classrooms, gymnasium, science lab, computer/language lab, art room, dispensary, kitchen, music/ band room, dining area. New building with dormitory is scheduled to be completed by the end of 1994.

*Once only fee   **Japanese yen

HIROSHIMA

HIROSHIMA INTERNATIONAL SCHOOL

>**Street address:** 3-49-1 Kurakake, Asa Kita-ku, Hiroshima 739-17,
>   Japan
>**Phone/facsimile:** (81)(82)8434111
>**Head:** Terry Donaldson
>**Staff:** full-time, 6; part-time, 5
>**Nationalities of staff:** U.S., 2; host, 2; other, 7
>**Grade levels:** K – 8†
>**Enrollment:** K, 5; 1 – 6, 36; 7 – 8, 5; total, 46
>**Capacity:** total, 150
>**Teacher/student ratio:** 1/5
>**Tuition (annual):** K – 8, $11,000
>**Other fees (annual):** busing, $400 – 1,700; application*, $1,200

Year founded: 1962. **Type of school:** coed, day. **Governed by:** elected board of directors, board of trustees. **Sponsored by:** Hiroshima Prefecture Board of Education. **Accredited by:** Western.

Curriculum/physical plant
Type: U.S., U.K. **Languages taught:** Japanese. **Special programs:** independent study, correspondence, remedial. **Special curricular:** computer instruction, integrated topics, music, craft, photography, Japanese culture. **Extracurricular:** drama, dance, instrumental music, computers, newspaper, literary magazine, photography, excursions/expeditions, field trips. **Sports:** basketball, volleyball. **Clubs:** tennis, sports, aerobics, photography, pottery, woodwork, drama, science. **Location:** suburban/rural setting in new area of Hiroshima. **Campus:** 2 acres. **Library:** 25,000 volumes. **Facilities:** 1 building, 9 classrooms, infirmary, gymnasium, 2 playing fields, science lab, computer lab, craft room, dark room, 4 ESL classrooms, air conditioning.

*Once only fee   †ESL/culture programs (grades 3 – adult)

KITAKYUSHU

INTERNATIONAL SCHOOL KITAKYUSHU

Street address: Yahata Higashi-ku Takami 2-chome Shinnittetsu Shijo
Kaikan, Kitakyushu, Japan
Phone: (81)(93)6520682   **Facsimile:** (81)(93)6511257
Principal/director: Ann Ratnayake
Head teacher: Mark Allingham
Staff: full-time, 9; part-time, 5
Nationalities of staff: U.S., 6; U.K., 3; other, 5
Grade levels: preK – junior high
Enrollment: preK, 11; 1 – 6, 7; total, 18
Nationalities of student body: host, 16; other, 2
Capacity: total, 250
Teacher/student ratio: 1/2
Tuition (per month): preK – K, 40,000**; 1 – 6, 70,000; 7 – 12, 100,000
Other fees: registration, capital levy, insurance, busing, extras
School year: January to September

Year founded: 1990. **Type of school:** coed, day, proprietary.

Curriculum/physical plant
Type: U.S. **Languages taught:** English, Japanese. **Staff specialists:**
reading, math, computer, speech/hearing, psychologist, learning disabilities,
nurse. **Special programs:** independent study. **Special curricular:** art, band,
physical education. **Extracurricular:** gymnastics, instrumental music, field
trips, sports. **Location:** in spacious green area in Yahata.   **Facilities:** 3
classrooms, gymnasium, playing field, swimming pool.

**Japanese yen

KOBE

CANADIAN ACADEMY

Street address: 4-1 Koyo-cho Naka, Higashinada-ku, Kobe 658,
Japan
Phone: (81)(78)8570100   **Facsimile:** (81)(78)8573250
    Cable: CANADACADEMY   **Network:** Applelink: CANADEMY.GEJ
Headmaster: Stuart J. Young, Ph.D.
Middle/high school principal: Thomas Hall, Ed.D.
Elementary school principal: Leila Metcalf, Ed.D.
Director of admissions and new programs: Charles A. Kite, Ph.D.
Computer coordinator: David Burr
Business manager: Timothy Thornton
Staff: full-time, 64; part-time, 5
Nationalities of staff: U.S., 43; host, 9; other, 17

Grade levels: preK – 12, postgraduate
Enrollment: preK, 19; K, 42; 1 – 5, 244; 6 – 8, 169; 9 – 12, 226; total, 700
Nationalities of student body: U.S., 257; U.K., 39; host, 111; other, 293
Teacher/student ratio: 1/10
Boarders: boys, 19; girls, 22   **Grades:** 8 – 12
   Program: planned 7-day
Tuition (annual): preK, 907,000**; K – 5, 1,032,000;
   6 – 12, 1,240,000; 13, 907,000
Other fees (annual): registration*, 154,500**; boarding, 1,135,000
School year: late August to June

Year founded: 1913. **Type of school:** coed, day, boarding, private
nonprofit. **Governed by:** appointed board of trustees. **Accredited by:** Western. **Regional organizations:** EARCOS.

Curriculum/physical plant

   Type: U.S., IB. **Languages taught:** French, German, Japanese. **Staff
specialists:** counselor, learning disabilities, nurse. **Special programs:** honors sections, IB, ESOL. **Special curricular:** art, chorus, band, physical
education, computer instruction. **Extracurricular:** drama, yearbook, newspaper, field trips. **Sports:** baseball, basketball, soccer, volleyball. **Tests:**
PSAT, SAT, ACT, TOEFL, IB, AP, Iowa. **Graduates attending college:** 98%.
Graduates have attended: U. of California, U. of Pennsylvania, MIT, Princeton,
Vassar. **Location:** on Rokko Island, near Kobe. **Campus:** 9 acres. **Library:**
30,000 volumes. **Facilities:** 63 classrooms, auditorium, cafeteria, 2 tennis
courts, gymnasium, 2 playing fields, 5 science labs, 3 computer labs, AV
equipment, air conditioning, boarding facilities.

*Once only fee   **Japanese yen

MARIST BROTHERS INTERNATIONAL SCHOOL

Street address: 1-2-1, Chimori-cho, Suma-ku, Kobe 654, Japan
Phone: (81)(78)7326266   **Facsimile:** (81)(78)7326268
Headmaster: Br. George Fontana, FMS
Upper school principal: Br. Vincent Moriarty, FMS
Guidance: Br. Vincent Doughty, FMS
Business manager: Mr. M. Sasahara
Staff: full-time, 31
Nationalities of staff: U.S., 17; U.K., 1; host, 4; other, 9
Grade levels: preK – 12, ESL
Enrollment: preK, 17; K, 17; 1 – 6, 86; 7 – 9, 67; 10 – 12, 59; ESL, 10;
   total, 256
Capacity: preK, 20; K, 20; 1 – 6, 120; 7 – 9, 75; 10 – 12, 75; total, 310
Teacher/student ratio: 1/8
Tuition (annual): preK – K, 890,000**; 1 – 6, 995,000; 7 – 12,
   1,070,000; ESL, 1,070,000
Other fees: registration*, 150,000**; facility improvement, 50,000
School year: September to June

Year founded: 1951. **Type of school:** coed, day, church-related. **Governed by:** board of directors. **Sponsored by:** Marist Brothers. **Accredited by:** Western.

Curriculum/physical plant

Type: U.S. **Staff specialists:** computer, counselor. **Special programs:** ESL, advanced placement, honors sections, independent study, remedial, Values. **Special curricular:** art, chorus, band, physical education, computer instruction. **Extracurricular:** yearbook, newspaper, literary magazine, photography, excursions/expeditions, field trips, sports. **Tests:** PSAT, SAT, ACT, TOEFL, AP, Iowa. **Graduates attending college:** 75%. **Graduates have attended:** CalTech, U. of Pennsylvania, Lafayette College, U. of California, Georgetown. **Location:** in city. **Campus:** 2.5 acres. **Library:** 10,000 volumes. **Facilities:** 2 buildings, 17 classrooms, cafeteria, infirmary, gymnasium, playing field, science lab, chapel, IBM computer lab, Apple computer lab.

*Once only fee   **Japanese yen

St. Michael's International School

Street address: 17-2 Nakayamate-dori 3-chome, Chuo-ku, Kobe 650, Japan
Phone: (81)(78)2318885   **Facsimile:** (81)(78)2318899
Headmaster: George E. Gibbons
Staff: full-time, 10; part-time, 6
Nationalities of staff: U.S., 2; U.K., 7; host, 7
Grade levels: preK – 6
Enrollment: preK, 43; K, 30; 1 – 6, 73; total, 146
Capacity: preK, 56; K, 30; 1 – 6, 100; total, 186
Teacher/student ratio: 1/11
Tuition (annual): preK, 630,000**; K, 750,000;
    1 – 6, 750,000 – 780,000
Other fees (annual): registration*, 120,000**; insurance, 3,000;
    maintenance, 65,000/family
School year: September to June

Year founded: 1946. **Type of school:** coed, day, church-related. **Governed by:** elected school council. **Sponsored by:** Anglican Church. **Accredited by:** Hyogo Prefecture government.

Curriculum/physical plant

Type: U.K. **Languages taught:** Japanese. **Staff specialists:** reading, math. **Special curricular:** art, band, physical education, computer instruction, typing. **Extracurricular:** instrumental music, computers, field trips, soccer, typing. **Clubs:** art, Girl and Boy Scouts, cookery, handicraft. **Location:** in city. **Library:** 50,000 volumes. **Facilities:** auditorium, gymnasium, computer lab.

*Once only fee   **Japanese yen

KYOTO

KYOTO INTERNATIONAL SCHOOL

Street address: 29-1 Kami Miyanomae-cho, Shishigatani, Sakyo-ku,
   Kyoto 606, Japan
Phone: (81)(75)7714022   **Facsimile:** (81)(75)7521184
Principal: Cheryl Burghardt
Staff: full-time, 5; part-time, 4
Nationalities of staff: U.S., 4; host, 2; other, 3
Grade levels: preschool – 8
Enrollment: total, 75
Nationalities of student body: U.S., 30; U.K., 7; host, 15; other, 23
Teacher/student ratio: 1/11
Tuition (annual): preschool, 320,000**; preK – 8, 1,020,000
Other fees: registration*, 100,000**
School year: September to June

Year founded: 1957. **Type of school:** coed, day, private nonprofit.
Governed by: elected board of governors. **Accredited by:** Western.

Curriculum/physical plant
   Type: U.S., U.K. **Languages taught:** Japanese. **Extracurricular:** computers, excursions/expeditions, field trips, magazine, recorders. **Tests:** Iowa.
Location: in northeastern Kyoto, near the Silver Pavillion. **Library:** 5,000
volumes. **Facilities:** 7 classrooms, language room, air conditioning.

*Once only fee   **Japanese yen

NAGOYA

NAGOYA INTERNATIONAL SCHOOL

Street address: 2686 Minamihara, Nakashidami, Moriyama-ku,
   Nagoya 463, Japan
Phone: (81)(52)7362025   **Facsimile:** (81)(52)7363883
Executive director of planning and development: Gerald F. Craig
Interim head: Charles Barton
Business manager: Zenichi Yamada
Staff: full-time, 47
Nationalities of staff: U.S., 27; host, 16; other, 4
Grade levels: N – 12
Enrollment: N – preK, 74; K, 40; 1 – 6, 181; 7 – 9, 55; 10 – 12, 67;
   total, 417
Nationalities of student body: U.S., 115; U.K., 7; host, 245; other, 50
Teacher/student ratio: 1/9

Tuition (annual): N – preK, 340,000**; K, 900,000; 1 – 6, 1,010,000;
7 – 8, 1,090,000; 9 – 12, 1,140,000
Other fees (annual): registration*, 100,000**; busing, 180,000;
lunch, 300/meal
School year: August to June

Year founded: 1963. **Type of school:** coed, day, private nonprofit.
Governed by: elected board of directors. **Accredited by:** Western.

Curriculum/physical plant

Type: U.S. **Languages taught:** Japanese. **Staff specialists:** reading,
math, art, computer, physical education, special needs. **Special programs:**
ESL, advanced placement, independent study. **Special curricular:** art,
chorus, physical education, computer instruction. **Extracurricular:** drama,
dance, choral music, instrumental music, computers, yearbook, newspaper,
literary magazine, excursions/expeditions, field trips. **Sports:** basketball,
cheerleading, softball, tennis, volleyball, badminton. **Clubs:** cooking, English
grammar, flower arranging, study session, indoor/outdoor games for K – 2
students, TOEFL prep/English, typing, weight training. **Tests:** PSAT, SAT,
ACT, TOEFL, Iowa, TAP. **Graduates attending college:** 90%. **Graduates have
attended:** Tufts, Harvard, Michigan State U., U. of California, Auburn.
Location: 40 minutes from downtown Nagoya. **Campus:** 7 acres. **Library:**
15,000 volumes. **Facilities:** 3 buildings, 28 classrooms, cafeteria, tennis
court, gymnasium, playing field, 2 science labs, computer lab.

*Once only fee   **Japanese yen

OKINAWA

OKINAWA CHRISTIAN SCHOOL

Street address: 1300 Aza Makiminato, Urasoe, Okinawa, Japan
Phone: (81)(988)773661   **Facsimile:** (81)(988)762665;
(domestic facsimile) (098)8762665
Mail: PO Box 42, Urasoe, Okinawa, Japan 901-21
U.S. mail: PO Box 90031, Gainesville, FL 32607, U.S.A.
U.S. phone: (1)(904)3716012   **U.S. facsimile:** (1)(904)3733949
Superintendent: Paul A. Gieschen
High school principal: Janice Skillman
Elementary school principal: Donna Russell
U.S. administrator: Bob Greninger
Staff: full-time, 25; part-time, 10
Nationalities of staff: U.S., 27; U.K., 1; host, 6; other, 1
Grade levels: preK – 12†
Enrollment: preK – K, 66; 1 – 6, 107; 7 – 9, 41; 10 – 12, 83; ESL, 40;
total, 337
Nationalities of student body: U.S., 179; U.K., 7; host, 70; other, 81
Capacity: preK, 45; K, 30; 1 – 6, 145; 7 – 9, 75; 10 – 12, 75; total, 370

Teacher/student ratio: 1/11
Tuition (annual): preK, 161,500**; K – 6, 266,000; 7 – 12, 294,500
Other fees (annual): registration*, 10,000**; books, 4,500;
  family*, 10,000; camp fee, 7,000
School year: September to June

Year founded: 1957. **Type of school:** coed, day, private nonprofit.
Governed by: elected board of directors. **Sponsored by:** Okinawa Christian
School Association. **Accredited by:** Western.

Curriculum/physical plant

Type: U.S. **Languages taught:** Japanese. **Staff specialist:** counselor.
Special programs: ESL. **Special curricular:** art, physical education, computer instruction. **Extracurricular:** drama, computers, yearbook, photography, field trips, student council, National Honor Society. **Sports:** basketball,
soccer, volleyball. **Tests:** PSAT, Stanford. **Graduates attending college:** 60%.
Graduates have attended: Baylor U., Grand Canyon U., U. of Alabama,
DePauw, California Baptist. **Location:** in Urasoe city. **Campus:** 10,800
square meters. **Facilities:** 5 buildings, 22 classrooms, cafeteria, gymnasium,
playing field, science lab, computer lab, library.

*Once only fee   **Japanese yen   †ESL program, K – adult

OSAKA

OSAKA INTERNATIONAL SCHOOL

Street address: 4-16, Onohara-Nishi 4-chome, Mino City, Osaka 562,
  Japan
Phone: (81)(727)275050   **Facsimile:** (81)(727)275055
U.S. mail: c/o International Schools Services, PO Box 5910,
  Princeton, NJ 08543, U.S.A.
Headmaster: James L. Wiese
High/middle school principal: Dennis L. Calkins
Elementary school principal: Paul W. Johnson, Ed.D.
Business manager: Martin E. Tromburg
Staff: full-time, 43; part-time, 6
Grade levels: K – 12, postgraduate
Enrollment: total, 165
Capacity: K, 30; 1 – 6, 90; 7 – 9, 45; 10 – 12, 45; 13, 5; total, 215
Teacher/student ratio: 1/4
Tuition (annual): K – 5, 1,110,000**; 6 – 10, 1,225,000; 11 – 13,
  1,355,000
Other fees (annual): registration*, 60,000**; busing, 150,000 –
  260,000; lunch, 85,000; ESL, 320,000; ESL test*, 20,000
School year: September to June

Year founded: 1991. **Type of school:** coed, day, private nonprofit.
Governed by: elected board of governors. **Accredited by:** Western (candidate).

Curriculum/physical plant

Type: IB. **Languages of instruction:** English, Japanese. **Languages taught:** French, Spanish, ESL, Japanese. **Staff specialists:** computer, counselor, nurse, ESL. **Special programs:** ESL, independent study. **Special curricular:** art, chorus, band, physical education, computer instruction. **Extracurricular:** drama, dance, choral music, instrumental music, computers, yearbook, newspaper, photography, field trips. **Sports:** baseball, basketball, soccer, softball, swimming, tennis, volleyball, judo, kendo. **Tests:** SSAT, PSAT, SAT, ACT, IB, Iowa, CAT, PAP. **Location:** in new residential development, 30 minutes from central Osaka. **Facilities:** 1 building, 31 classrooms, auditorium, cafeteria, infirmary, 2 covered play areas, tennis court, 2 gymnasiums, playing field, 5 science labs, 2 computer labs, swimming pool, TV studio, 4 music practice rooms, athletic training room, bookstore, air conditioning.

*Once only fee   **Japanese yen

SAPPORO

HOKKAIDO INTERNATIONAL SCHOOL

Street address: 5-35, 3-jo, 2-chome Fukuzumi, Toyohira-ku, Sapporo 062, Japan
Phone: (81)(11)8511205   **Facsimile:** (81)(11)8551435
Headmaster: R. D. McClain, Ed.D.
Staff: full-time, 11; part-time, 2
Grade levels: preK – 12
Enrollment: preK – K, 22; 1 – 6, 42; 7 – 12, 30; total, 94
Nationalities of student body: U.S., 26; host, 20; other, 48
Teacher/student ratio: 1/8
Tuition (annual): preK, $3,000; 1 – 5, $4,500; 6 – 8, $4,650; 9 – 12, $4,800
Entrance fee*: preK, $800; K, $600; 1 – 8, $1,125; 9 – 12, $1,500
School year: September to June

Year founded: 1958. **Type of school:** coed, day, private nonprofit. **Accredited by:** Western. **Regional organizations:** EARCOS.

Curriculum/physical plant

Type: U.S. **Languages of instruction:** English, Japanese. **Special programs:** ESL. **Special curricular:** art, physical education, computer instruction, drama, music. **Extracurricular:** yearbook, newspaper, excursions/expeditions, field trips. **Sports:** basketball, skiing, soccer, softball, volleyball, wrestling. **Tests:** SAT, ACT, TOEFL, Iowa, GRE. **Graduates attending college:** 99%. **Location:** 8 kilometers from center of Sapporo. **Campus:** 4 acres. **Library:** 5,000 volumes. **Facilities:** 1 building, gymnasium, playing field, computer lab.

*Once only fee

SENDAI

Sᴇɴᴅᴀɪ Aᴍᴇʀɪᴄᴀɴ Sᴄʜᴏᴏʟ

Street address: 4-8-1 Komatsushima, Aoba-Ku, Sendai 981, Japan
Phone: (81)(22)2348567   **Facsimile:** (81)(22)2727161
Headmaster: Maynard Yutzy, Ed.D.
Staff: full-time, 3; part-time, 6
Nationalities of staff: U.S., 5; host, 3; other, 1
Grade levels: 1 – 9
Enrollment: 1 – 6, 12; 7 – 9, 12; total, 24
Nationalities of student body: U.S., 18; host, 2; other, 4
Capacity: 1 – 6, 25; 7 – 9, 25; total, 50
Teacher/student ratio: 1/4
Tuition (annual): 1 – 9, 600,000**
Other fees (annual): registration, 10,000**; insurance, 5,000; enroll-
    ment*, 30,000
School year: September through June

Year founded: 1989. **Type of school:** coed, day. **Governed by:** elected
board comprised of 3 Japanese and 3 international members. **Sponsored by:**
Tohoku-Koko.

Curriculum/physical plant
Type: U.S. **Languages taught:** Japanese. **Special programs:** ESL.
Special curricular: art, chorus, physical education, computer instruction.
Extracurricular: drama, dance, computers, yearbook, newspaper, photography. **Location:** in Sendai. **Campus:** .5 acre. **Library:** 2,500 volumes. **Facilities:** 1 building, 3 classrooms, cafeteria, playing field, computer lab, swimming pool.

*Once only fee   **Japanese yen

TOKYO

Tʜᴇ Aᴍᴇʀɪᴄᴀɴ Sᴄʜᴏᴏʟ ɪɴ Jᴀᴘᴀɴ

Street address: 1-1-1, Nomizu, Chofu-shi, Tokyo 182, Japan
Phone: (81)(422)345300   **Facsimile:** (81)(422)345308
    Cable: AMSCHOOL CHOFU
U.S. mail: c/o International Schools Services, PO Box 5910,
    Princeton, NJ 08543, U.S.A.
Headmaster: Peter R. Cooper
High school principal: Donald J. Benes

Middle school principal: Sue O. Hale
Elementary school principal: Daniel J. Bender
Nursery–kindergarten director: Douglas Rowe
Business manager: John D. Hale
Staff: full-time, 124; part-time, 11
Nationalities of staff: U.S., 112; host, 15; other, 8
Grade levels: N – 12, postgraduate
Enrollment: total, 1,390
Nationalities of student body: U.S., 968; U.K., 23; host, 229; other, 170
Capacity: N – preK, 75; K, 88; 1 – 5, 482; 6 – 8, 360; 9 – 13, 560; total, 1,565
Teacher/student ratio: 1/11
Tuition (annual): N – 12, 1,648,000**
Other fees (annual): registration*, 250,000**; busing, 280,000 (optional); building maintenance*, 250,000
School year: September to June

Year founded: 1902. **Type of school:** coed, day, private nonprofit. **Governed by:** elected board of directors. **Sponsored by:** board of trustees. **Accredited by:** Western.

Curriculum

Type: U.S. **Languages taught:** French, Spanish, Japanese. **Staff specialists:** reading, math, computer, counselor, nurse. **Special programs:** advanced placement, honors sections, independent study. **Special curricular:** art, chorus, physical education, computer instruction, Japanese studies, outdoor education, band and strings, television production. **Extracurricular:** drama, gymnastics, dance, choral music, instrumental music, computers, yearbook, newspaper, literary magazine, photography, excursions/expeditions, field trips. **Sports:** 42 teams, 16 varsity sports. **Tests:** PSAT, SAT, ACT, TOEFL, AP, Iowa, SRA. **Graduates attending college:** 95%. **Graduates have attended:** Bucknell, Cornell, Harvard, MIT, Princeton.

Physical plant

Location: N – K, downtown Tokyo; K – 13, 45 minutes from Tokyo, in suburban area adjacent to 150-acre public park. **Library:** 41,000 volumes. **Facilities:** 9 buildings, 87 classrooms, auditorium, cafeteria, infirmary, 4 tennis courts, 3 gymnasiums, 3 playing fields, 7 science labs, 6 computer labs, swimming pool, TV-radio studio, vivarium.

*Once only fee   **Japanese yen

AOBA INTERNATIONAL SCHOOL

Street address: 2-10-34 Aobadai, Meguro-ku, Tokyo, Japan 153
Phone: (81)(3)34611442   **Facsimile:** (81)(3)34639873
Headmistress/principal: Regina Doi
Deputy headmistress: Mineko Koshikawa
Head teacher: Elizabeth de Souza

Staff (each session): full-time, 21; part-time, 6
Nationalities of staff: U.S., 7; U.K., 3; host, 6; other, 11
Grade levels: N – preP
Enrollment: N, 50; K – preP, 170; total, 220
Nationalities of student body: U.S., 40; U.K., 10; host, 85; other, 65
Capacity: N, 50; K – preP, 170; total, 220
Teacher/student ratio: 1/9
Tuition (annual): N, 740,000**; K – pre-1, 825,000 (half-day session average); 1,525,000 (full-day session average)
Other fees: registration*, 200,000**
School year: September to June†

Year founded: 1976. **Type of school:** coed, day, private nonprofit. **Governed by:** board of directors. **Affiliated with:** Japan International School.

Curriculum/physical plant
Type: U.S., bilingual. **Languages taught:** English, Japanese. **Special programs:** ESL, JSL, swimming. **Extracurricular:** yearbook, field trips, graduation trip, ballet, seasonal festivities (Western and Japanese). **Location:** in Tokyo. **Facilities:** 2 buildings, 10 classrooms, play area, air conditioning.

*Once only fee   **Japanese yen
†Summer school, mid-June to mid-July

CHRISTIAN ACADEMY IN JAPAN

Street address: 1-2-14 Shinkawa-cho, Higashi Kurume Shi, Tokyo 203, Japan
Phone: (81)(424)710022   **Facsimile:** (81)(424)762200
Headmaster: Bruce Hekman, Ph.D.
High school principal: Jack Smith
Middle school principal: Judi Mollenkof
Elementary school principal: Grant Nelson
Business manager: Richard Owen
Staff: full-time, 45; part-time, 13
Nationalities of staff: U.S., 43; host, 7; other, 8
Grade levels: K – 12
Enrollment: K, 13; 1 – 5, 139; 6 – 8, 88; 9 – 12, 117; total, 357
Nationalities of student body: U.S., 217; U.K., 6; host, 97; other, 37
Capacity: K, 15; 1 – 5, 120; 6 – 8, 90; 9 – 12, 140; total, 365
Teacher/student ratio: 1/7
Tuition (annual): K, 735,000**; 1 – 5, 1,000,000; 6 – 8, 1,100,000; 9 – 12, 1,200,000
Other fees: registration, 45,000**; application*, 15,000; entrance*, 200,000; English test*, 10,000
School year: September to June

Year founded: 1950. **Type of school:** coed, day, church-related. **Governed by:** elected board of directors. **Sponsored by:** Christian Reformed,

Conservative Baptist, TEAM, Evangelical Covenant, SEND, OMS missions.

Curriculum/physical plant
Type: U.S. **Languages taught:** French, Spanish, Japanese. **Staff specialists:** reading, speech/hearing, counselor, nurse. **Special programs:** ESL, advanced placement, independent study, correspondence. **Special curricular:** art, chorus, band, physical education, computer instruction, vocational. **Extracurricular:** drama, choral music, instrumental music, computers, yearbook, newspaper, photography, excursions/expeditions, field trips. **Sports:** basketball, hockey, soccer, tennis, track, volleyball, cross-country, wrestling. **Tests:** PSAT, SAT, ACT, TOEFL, AP, Iowa, Lorge-Thorndike. **Graduates attending college:** 85%. **Graduates have attended:** Wheaton, Biola, Seattle Pacific, Gordon, Calvin. **Location:** in suburban area of Tokyo. **Campus:** 19,000 square meters. **Library:** 21,000 volumes. **Facilities:** 7 buildings, 20 classrooms, auditorium, cafeteria, infirmary, tennis court, gymnasium, playing field, science lab, computer lab.

*Once only fee   **Japanese yen

INTERNATIONAL SCHOOL OF THE SACRED HEART
Street address: 3-1, Hiroo 4-chome, Shibuya-ku, Tokyo 150, Japan
Phone: (81)(3)34003951   **Facsimile:** (81)(3)34003496
Headmistress: Sr. Ruth Sheehy
High school dean: Michael Scullion
Middle school dean: Dorothy Loveland
Kindergarten/junior school principal: Susan Sullivan
Business manager: Ryozo Naraoka
Staff: full-time, 77; part-time, 31
Nationalities of staff: U.S., 28; U.K., 30; host, 15; other, 35
Grade levels: preK – 12
Enrollment: preK, 10; K, 103; 1 – 6, 286; 7 – 9, 151; 10 – 12, 153; total, 703
Nationalities of student body: U.S., 212; U.K., 64; host, 95; other, 332
Capacity: preK, 8; K, 100; 1 – 6, 300; 7 – 9, 150; 10 – 12, 150; total, 708
Teacher/student ratio: 1/8
Tuition (annual): preK (3.5 years), 820,000**; K (full day), 1,340,000; 1 – 4, 1,430,000; 5 – 8, 1,450,000; 9 – 12, 1,470,000
Other fees (annual): registration, 200,000**
School year: late August to June

Year founded: 1908. **Type of school:** day, girls, coeducational kindergarten, church-related. **Governed by:** elected board of directors. **Sponsored by:** Catholic Society of the Sacred Heart. **Accredited by:** Western.

Curriculum
Type: U.S., U.K., IB. **Languages taught:** French, Japanese. **Staff specialists:** reading, math, computer, counselor, nurse. **Special programs:** ESL, honors sections, IB. **Special curricular:** art, chorus, band, physical education, computer instruction, vocational. **Extracurricular:** drama, dance, cho-

ral music, instrumental music, computers, yearbook, newspaper, literary magazine, photography, excursions/expeditions, field trips. **Sports:** basketball, swimming, tennis, track, volleyball, cross-country. **Tests:** PSAT, SAT, TOEFL, IB, Iowa, Achievement Test. **Graduates attending college:** 100%. **Graduates have attended:** Princeton, U. of Pennsylvania, Wellesley, Oxford, Cambridge.

Physical plant

Location: in heart of Tokyo. **Campus:** 5.7 acres. **Library:** 33,000 volumes. **Facilities:** 3 buildings, 49 classrooms, 4 auditoriums, cafeteria, infirmary, covered play area, 2 tennis courts, gymnasium, 2 playing fields, 4 science labs, 4 computer labs.

**Japanese yen

JAPAN INTERNATIONAL SCHOOL

Street address: 2-10-7 Miyamae, Suginami-ku, Tokyo 168, Japan
Phone: (81)(3)33356620   **Facsimile:** (81)(3)33326930
Headmistress: Regina Doi
Deputy headmaster: Steven Parr
Staff: full-time, 44; part-time, 12
Nationalities of staff: U.S., 13; U.K., 5; host, 20; other, 18
Grade levels: 1 – 9, postgraduate
Enrollment: total, 320
Nationalities of student body: U.S., 40; U.K., 10; host, 130; other, 140
Capacity: 1 – 6, 300; 7 – 9, 200; total, 500
Teacher/student ratio: 1/6
Tuition (annual): 1 – 9, 1,600,000** (average)
Other fees (annual): registration, 200,000**; busing available by request
School year: September to June

Year founded: 1980. **Type of school:** coed, day. **Governed by:** board of directors. **Affiliated with:** Aoba International School.

Curriculum/physical plant

Type: U.S., bilingual (all children learn Japanese). **Languages taught:** Japanese, others by request. **Staff specialists:** reading, math, resource. **Special programs:** ESL. **Special curricular:** art, chorus, physical education, computer instruction, abacus. **Extracurricular:** drama, dance, computers, newspaper, excursions/expeditions, field trips, Japanese arts and crafts, band. **Sports:** swimming, aikido, gym. **Clubs:** Japanese handicrafts, dance, model club, et al. **Tests:** Iowa. **Location:** Tokyo. **Library:** 5,000 volumes. **Facilities:** 1 building, 25 classrooms, infirmary, computer lab, AV equipment, playground, tennis court, air conditioning.

**Japanese yen

NISHIMACHI INTERNATIONAL SCHOOL

Street address: 2-14-7 Moto-Azabu, Minato-ku, Tokyo 106, Japan
Phone: (81)(3)34515520   **Facsimile:** (81)(3)34560197
Head: Hikojiro Katsuhisa
Principal: John L. Wilson
Director of administration: Ichiro Ueno
Administrative assistant: Zelia G. Lobo-Hagiwara
Staff: full-time, 44; part-time, 9
Nationalities of staff: U.S., 22; host, 21; other, 10
Grade levels: K – 9
Enrollment: K, 55; 1 – 6, 255; 7 – 9, 75; total, 385
Nationalities of student body: U.S., 185; U.K., 14; host, 106; other, 80
Capacity: K, 57; 1 – 6, 287; 7 – 9, 85; total, 429
Teacher/student ratio: 1/8
Tuition (annual): K, 1,494,000**; 1 – 3, 1,548,000; 4 – 6, 1,575,000;
    7 – 9, 1,596,000
Other fees (annual): registration, 200,000**; building, 50,000
School year: late August to June

Year founded: 1949. **Type of school:** coed, day, private nonprofit.
Governed by: elected board of trustees and board of directors. **Accredited by:**
Western.

Curriculum/physical plant

Type: U.S. **Languages of instruction:** English, Japanese. **Languages
taught:** French, Japanese. **Staff specialists:** reading, math, computer,
speech/hearing, counselor, nurse. **Special programs:** Japanese social studies. **Special curricular:** art, chorus, physical education, computer instruction. **Extracurricular:** drama, gymnastics, choral music, instrumental music, computers, yearbook, newspaper, photography, excursions/expeditions,
field trips. **Sports:** basketball, skiing, swimming, volleyball, sumo, aikido.
Clubs: Brownies, Cub Scouts, Girl Scouts, student council, Japanese drama,
Webelos. **Tests:** Iowa. **Graduates have attended:** Georgetown, U. of California at Berkeley, Wesleyan, U. of California at Davis, Dartmouth. **Location:**
in an upper-class residential and business center of Tokyo. **Campus:** 1 acre.
Library: 15,000 volumes. **Facilities:** 7 buildings, 36 classrooms, auditorium,
covered play area, gymnasium, 2 science labs, computer lab, camp site
(Kazuno) about 100 miles north of Tokyo, air conditioning.

**Japanese yen

ST. MARY'S INTERNATIONAL SCHOOL

Street address: 1-6-19, Seta, Setagaya-ku, Tokyo 158, Japan
Phone: (81)(3)37093411   **Facsimile:** (81)(3)37071950
    Cable: INTERSCHOOLTOK
Headmaster: Bro. Michel Jutras
High school principal: Harold Fleetham

Junior high principal: Saburo Kagei
Elementary school principal: Bro. Lawrence Guy Lambert
Business manager: Unryu Haku
Staff: full-time, 90; part-time, 22
Nationalities of staff: U.S., 58; U.K., 3; host, 18; other, 22
Grade levels: K – 12
Enrollment: K, 50; 1 – 6, 463; 7 – 9, 237; 10 – 12, 198; total, 948
Capacity: K, 50; 1 – 6, 520; 7 – 9, 260; 10 – 12, 220; total, 1,050
Teacher/student ratio: 1/9
Tuition (annual): K – 6, 1,510,000**, 7 – 12, 1,560,000
Other fees (annual): registration*, 200,000**; busing, 280,000; lunch, 121,000; milk, 15,000
School year: late August to June

Year founded: 1954. **Type of school:** boys, day, church-related. **Governed by:** appointed and elected board of directors. **Sponsored by:** Brothers of Christian Instruction of Ploërmel. **Accredited by:** Japanese government, Western.

Curriculum

Type: U.S., IB. **Languages taught:** French, Spanish, German, Korean, Latin, Japanese, Chinese, Finnish, Swedish. **Staff specialists:** counselor, nurse. **Special programs:** ESL, SAT review, interactive communications simulation. **Special curricular:** art, chorus, band, physical education, computer instruction, bell choir, mechanical drawing. **Extracurricular:** drama, choral music, instrumental music, computers, yearbook, newspaper, literary magazine, photography, excursions/expeditions, field trips, ski trips, musical, math contest, "artscape." **Sports:** baseball, basketball, hockey, soccer, swimming, tennis, track, ice hockey, wrestling, cross-country. **Clubs:** drama, boosters, chess, table tennis, aikido, scouts, cubs, speech, ice hockey, debate, brain bowl, yearbook, Leo Club, National Honor Society. **Tests:** SSAT, PSAT, SAT, TOEFL, IB, AP, Iowa, NMSQT. **Graduates attending college:** 98.5%. **Graduates have attended:** Princeton, Harvard, Stanford, Brown, MIT.

Physical plant

Location: in southwestern residential area of Setagaya-ku in Tokyo. **Campus:** 7 acres. **Library:** 40,000 volumes. **Facilities:** 3 buildings, 47 classrooms, auditorium, cafeteria, infirmary, covered play area, 4 tennis courts, gymnasium, 3 playing fields, 4 science labs, 2 computer labs, swimming pool, 3 art rooms, weight room, darkroom, 3 music rooms, typing room, mechanical drawing room, TV center, AV room, 2 ski lodges in Tsumagoi, Gunma Prefecture.

*Once only fee   **Japanese yen

Seisen International School

Street address: 12-15 Yoga 1-chome, Setagaya-ku, Tokyo 158, Japan
Phone: (81)(3)37042661   **Facsimile:** (81)(3)37011033
   Cable: SEISENINT
Headmistress: Sr. Asuncion Lecubarri
High school principal: Suzanne Kawasumi
Elementary school coordinator: Fiona McGrory
Kindergarten coordinator: Sheila O'Donoghue
Counselor: Cathy Williams
IB coordinator: Ulrich Nikolai
Staff: full-time, 53; part-time, 26
Nationalities of staff: U.S., 21; U.K., 13; host, 17; other, 28
Grade levels: K – 12
Enrollment: K, 171; elementary, 265; high school, 191; total, 627
Nationalities of student body: U.S., 176; U.K., 41; host, 75;
   other, 335
Capacity: K, 175; 1 – 6, 300; 7 – 12, 210; total, 685
Teacher/student ratio: 1/9
Tuition (annual): K, 825,000** (half day), 1,300,000 (full day); 1 – 6,
   1,440,000; 7 – 12, 1,490,000
Other fees (annual): registration*, 200,000**; busing, 280,000; lunch,
   120,000; graduation*, 21,000
School year: August to June

Year founded: 1962. **Type of school:** girls, day, church-related, coeducational kindergarten. **Governed by:** Seisen Jogakuin Educational Foundation. **Sponsored by:** Handmaids of the Sacred Heart of Jesus. **Accredited by:** Western, ECIS.

Curriculum

Type: U.S., IB. **Languages taught:** French, Spanish, and Japanese IB. Languages taught on tutorial basis according to demand. **Staff specialists:** counselor, nurse. **Special programs:** ESL. **Special curricular:** art, physical education, computer instruction, choir, bell choir. **Extracurricular:** drama, choral music, computers, yearbook, newspaper, photography, excursions/expeditions, field trips, math contest, "artscape," pottery. **Sports:** basketball, soccer, swimming, tennis, track, volleyball, cross-country. **Clubs:** Brownies, debating, National Honor Society, drama, boosters, brain bowl, Adventurers, ecology, speech, yearbook. **Tests:** SSAT, PSAT, SAT, TOEFL, IB, AP, Stanford, Iowa, NMSQT. **Graduates attending college:** 99%. **Graduates have attended:** Harvard, MIT, London School of Economics, Brown, Cambridge.

Physical plant

Location: 30 – 40 minutes from central Tokyo. **Campus:** 6,932.86 square meters. **Library:** 15,000 volumes. **Facilities:** 3 buildings, 36 classrooms, cafeteria, infirmary, 2 covered play areas, gymnasium, playing field, 2 science labs, 2 computer labs, tennis courts, AV room, music, art, and home economics rooms.

*Once only fee   **Japanese yen

YOKOHAMA

ST. JOSEPH INTERNATIONAL SCHOOL

Street address: 85 Yamate-cho, Naka-ku, Yokohama 231, Japan
Phone: (81)(45)6410065   **Facsimile:** (81)(45)6416572
Principal: Bro. DuWayne Brisendine
Assistant principal/admissions & development: Mr. James
   McAuliffe
Business manager: Bro. Luke Asayama
Staff: full-time, 32; part-time, 6
Nationalities of staff: U.S., 19; U.K., 2; host, 9; other, 8
Grade levels: preschool – 12
Enrollment: preschool, 8; K, 33; 1 – 6, 147; 7 – 9, 45; 10 – 12, 43; total,
   276
Nationalities of student body: U.S., 40; U.K., 7; host, 162; other, 67
Capacity: preschool – K, 50; 1 – 6, 240; 7 – 9, 120; 10 – 12, 120; total,
   530
Teacher/student ratio: 1/8
Tuition (annual): preschool – K, 952,400**; 1 – 5, 1,175,000; 6 – 8,
   1,352,000; 9 – 12, 1,415,000
Other fees (annual): matriculation*, 208,000**; entrance exam (when
   required), 10,000
School year: September to June

Year founded: 1901. **Type of school:** coed, day. **Governed by:** elected
board of directors. **Sponsored by:** Marianists of Japan. **Accredited by:**
Western.

Curriculum/physical plant

Type: U.S., international. **Languages taught:** Spanish, Japanese. **Staff
specialists:** reading, math, computer, ESL, drama, speech. **Special curricular:** art, physical education, computer instruction, choir. **Extracurricular:**
drama, computers, yearbook, photography, excursions/expeditions, brain
bowl, scouts. **Sports:** baseball, field hockey, soccer, tennis, volleyball, cross-
country. **Clubs:** computer, National Honor Society, sports, student council,
Interact, junior girls' club, photo, scouting, drama. **Tests:** PSAT, SAT, AP,
Iowa, Achievements. **Graduates attending college:** 93%. **Graduates have
attended:** Brown, Cornell, Dartmouth, Stanford, U. of Pennsylvania. **Location:** in city. **Campus:** 3.5 acres. **Library:** 16,500 volumes. **Facilities:** 4
buildings, 25 classrooms, auditorium, cafeteria, covered play area, tennis
court, gymnasium, playing field, 2 science labs, computer lab, AV equipment.

*Once only fee   **Japanese yen

SAINT MAUR INTERNATIONAL SCHOOL

Street address: 83 Yamate-cho, Naka-ku, Yokohama, Japan 231
Phone: (81)(45)6415751   **Facsimile:** (81)(45)6416688
   Cable: STMAURINT
Headmistress: Jeanette K. Thomas
Principal, K – 12: Richard B. Rucci
Director of development: Sr. Carmel O'Keeffe
Guidance counselor: Catherine O. Endo
Staff: full-time, 50; part-time, 14
Nationalities of staff: U.S., 26; U.K., 16; host, 9; other, 13
Grade levels: preK – 12
Enrollment: preK, 30; K, 83; 1 – 6, 187; 7 – 9, 72; 10 – 12, 71; total, 443
Nationalities of student body: U.S., 118; U.K., 65; host, 114; other, 146
Capacity: preK – K, 100; 1 – 6, 180; 7 – 9, 90; 10 – 12, 90; total, 460
Teacher/student ratio: 1/8
Tuition (annual): preK, 630,000**; K, 930,000; 1 – 5, 1,150,000;
   6 – 12, 1,270,000
Other fees (annual): registration*, 200,000**; books, 30,000 – 80,000
School year: September to June

Year founded: 1872. **Type of school:** coed, day, church-related. **Governed by:** appointed board of directors, administrative team. **Sponsored by:** Catholic Sisters of the Infant Jesus. **Accredited by:** Western, ECIS.

Curriculum

Type: U.S., IB. **Languages taught:** English, French, Spanish, Japanese, other languages as independent study. **Staff specialists:** computer, counselor, nurse, ESL. **Special programs:** ESL, advanced placement, honors sections, independent study, IB. **Special curricular:** art, physical education, computer instruction, drama, music, dressmaking/tailoring, home economics. **Extracurricular:** drama, choral music, yearbook, literary magazine, elementary newspaper, excursions/expeditions, field trips, junior high and high school student councils, Latin American dance, band. **Sports:** basketball, soccer, tennis, volleyball, badminton, floor hockey, karate, table tennis. **Clubs:** art, ballet, band, choir, computer, drama, dressmaking and tailoring, Friendship Volunteers, DJ, BBC, Green, golf, softball, aerobics/jazz dance, film, gymnastics, Japanese calligraphy. **Tests:** PSAT, SAT, IB, AP, Iowa, Otis-Lennon, Purdue. **Graduates attending college:** 90 – 100%. **Graduates have attended:** Bryn Mawr, Johns Hopkins, Stanford, Oxford, Yale.

Physical plant

Location: in residential area of Yokohama. **Campus:** 7,810 square meters. **Library:** 14,000 volumes. **Facilities:** 3 buildings, 25 classrooms, auditorium, cafeteria, infirmary, 2 covered play areas, tennis court, gymnasium, playing field, 2 science labs, computer lab, AV room, dressmaking/tailoring room, home economics room.

*Once only fee   **Japanese yen

YOKOHAMA INTERNATIONAL SCHOOL

Street address: 258 Yamate-cho, Naka-ku, Yokohama 241, Japan
Phone: (81)(45)6220084   **Facsimile:** (81)(45)6210379
Headmaster: Alan Derry
Staff: full-time, 37; part-time, 8
Nationalities of staff: U.S., 10; U.K., 21; host, 9; other, 5
Grade levels: preK – 13
Enrollment: preK, 35; K, 40; 1 – 6, 220; 7 – 9, 95; 10 – 12, 100; total, 490
Capacity: preK, 45; K, 50; 1 – 6, 230; 7 – 9, 120; 10 – 12, 100; total, 545
Teacher/student ratio: 1/12
Tuition (annual): K, 625,000** (half day), 945,000 (full day);
    1 – 6, 1,210,000; 7 – 12, 1,345,000
Other fees (annual): registration*, 130,000** (half day), 210,000 (full
    day); capital levy, 71,000; books, 4,000; field studies,
    55,000 – 75,000
School year: September to June

Year founded: 1924. **Type of school:** coed, day. **Governed by:** elected
school committee.

Curriculum/physical plant

Type: U.S., U.K., IB. **Languages taught:** French, German, Japanese,
Dutch. **Special programs:** ESL. **Special curricular:** art, chorus, band,
physical education, computer instruction. **Extracurricular:** drama, gymnas-
tics, dance, computers, yearbook, photography. **Sports:** basketball, field
hockey, soccer, track, volleyball, cross-country. **Tests:** PSAT, SAT, ACT,
TOEFL, IB, AP, Iowa, NEDT, GCE. **Graduates attending college:** 85%.
Graduates have attended: Harvard, Brown, Bucknell, Stanford, London.
Location: in residential area of Yokohama. **Campus:** 4,896 square meters.
Library: 20,000 volumes. **Facilities:** 4 buildings, 35 classrooms, auditorium,
gymnasium, science lab, AV center, use of playing field.

*Once only fee   **Japanese yen

JORDAN

Region: Middle East
Size: 37,737 square miles
Population: 3,412,000
Capital: Amman

Telephone code: 962
Currency: dinar
Language: Arabic

AMMAN

AMERICAN COMMUNITY SCHOOL

Phone: (962)(6)813944/813946   **Facsimile:** (962)(6)823357
   Telex: 92521510 USEMB JO
Mail: c/o U.S. Embassy, Amman, Jordan
Superintendent: Gary Duckett, Ed.D.
Principal: Brian Lahan
Business manager: Hamdi Hamdi
Staff: full-time, 32; part-time, 8
Nationalities of staff: U.S., 30; host, 4; other, 6
Grade levels: K – 12
Enrollment: K, 15; 1 – 5, 109; 6 – 8, 72; 9 – 12, 123; total, 319
Nationalities of student body: U.S., 127; host, 112; other, 80
Capacity: K, 25; 1 – 6, 150; 7 – 9, 120; 10 – 12, 130; total, 425
Teacher/student ratio: 1/9
Tuition (annual): K, $3,745; 1 – 5, $5,136; 6 – 8, $5,885; 9 – 12,
   $6,848
Other fees (annual): capital levy*, $3,000; busing, $680
School year: August to June

Year founded: 1957. **Type of school:** coed, day, private nonprofit.
Governed by: elected school board. **Accredited by:** Middle States.

Curriculum/physical plant
   Type: U.S. **Languages taught:** French, Spanish, Arabic. **Staff specialists:** reading, math, computer, counselor, nurse. **Special programs:** ESL,
advanced placement. **Special curricular:** art, chorus, band, physical education, computer instruction. **Extracurricular:** drama, gymnastics, choral
music, instrumental music, computers, yearbook, newspaper, literary magazine, photography. **Sports:** baseball, basketball, soccer, tennis, track, volleyball, cross-country. **Organizations:** National Honor Society, student council.
Tests: SSAT, PSAT, SAT, TOEFL, Iowa. **Graduates attending college:** 95%.
Graduates have attended: Georgetown, Bryn Mawr, U. of Southern California, U. of Michigan, Harvard. **Location:** in city. **Campus:** 5 acres. **Library:**
11,000 volumes. **Facilities:** 5 buildings, 26 classrooms, auditorium, tennis
court, gymnasium, playing field, science lab, computer lab.

*Once only fee

AMMAN BACCALAUREATE SCHOOL

Phone: (962)(6)845572   **Facsimile:** (962)(6)834603
Telex: 92524226 ABS JO
Mail: PO Box 441, Sweileh, Jordan
Principal: Samia Al Farra
Vice-principal: Dermot Keegan
Head of senior school: Mary Tadros
Head of middle school: Riham Kawar
Head of junior school: Nora Shrydeh
Head of kindergarten: Rima Sukkar
Staff: full-time, 97; part-time, 12
Nationalities of staff: U.S., 4; U.K., 10; host, 84; other, 11
Grade levels: K – 12
Enrollment: K, 100; 1 – 5, 233; 6 – 8, 275; 9 – 12, 375; total, 983
Nationalities of student body: U.S., 14; U.K., 19; host, 849;
    other, 101
Teacher/student ratio: 1/9
Tuition (annual): K, 750**; 1 – 3, 1,450 – 1,475; 4 – 5, 1,625 – 1,650;
    6, 1,725; 7 – 8, 2,075 – 2,100; 9 – 12, 2,125 – 3,375
Other fees (annual): registration*, 30**; busing, 300 (optional);
    lunch, 250 (optional); supplies: K, 30; 1 – 12, 50; non-refundable
    enrollment fee (grades 1 –12), 250
School year: August to June

Year founded: 1981. **Type of school:** coed, day, private nonprofit.
Governed by: appointed board of trustees. **Sponsored by:** Hashemite Society
for Education. **Accredited by:** Jordanian Ministry of Education.

Curriculum

Type: U.K., Jordanian, IB. **Languages of instruction:** English, Arabic.
Languages taught: English, French, Arabic. **Staff specialists:** math, computer, counselor, nurse, Arabic as a Second Language. **Special curricular:**
art, physical education, computer instruction, drama. **Extracurricular:**
drama, gymnastics, dance, choral music, instrumental music, computers,
yearbook, newspaper, literary magazine, photography, excursions/expeditions, field trips. **Sports:** basketball, fencing, soccer, swimming, volleyball,
table tennis, Tae Kwon Do, horseback riding. **Clubs:** community service,
cross-country, science, conservation, chess, Thursday club, Crown Prince's
Award program. **Tests:** SAT, ACT, TOEFL, IB, IGCSE, Jordanian Tawjihi
(GCSE). **Graduates attending college:** 100%. **Graduates have attended:** U.
of Jordan, McGill, Harvard, Cambridge, MIT.

Physical plant

Location: on outskirts of Amman, 30 minutes from city center. **Campus:**
5 acres. **Library:** 12,400 volumes. **Facilities:** 4 buildings, auditorium,
cafeteria, infirmary, gymnasium, 8 science labs, 2 computer labs, technology
lab, multipurpose hall, 2 music rooms, 2 junior libraries, workshops, technical drawing office, print room, 2 art rooms, ceramics room, AV facilities.

*Once only fee   **Jordanian dinar

KENYA

Region: East Africa
Size: 224,960 square miles
Population: 25,241,000
Capital: Nairobi

Telephone code: 254
Currency: shilling
Languages: Swahili, Kikuyu,
Luhya, Luo, Meru

KIJABE

Rift Valley Academy

Phone: (no direct dial) Kijabe 1   **Cable:** ACADEMY
Mail: Box 80, Kijabe, Kenya
Principal: Roy E. Entwistle
Vice-principal for instruction and discipline: Mark Buhler
Vice-principal for staff development: Dr. Norm Dixon
Business manager: Robert Christian
Staff: full-time, 100
Nationalities of staff: U.S., 87; other, 13
Grade levels: 1 – 12
Enrollment: 1 – 6, 110; 7 – 9, 130; 10 – 12, 235; total, 475
Nationalities of student body: U.S., 344; U.K., 10; host, 46; other, 75
Capacity: 1 – 6, 120; 7 – 9, 130; 10 – 12, 240; total, 490
Teacher/student ratio: 1/5
Boarders: boys, 210; girls, 196   **Grades:** 1 – 12
   Program: planned 7-day
Tuition (annual): Kenya citizens and mission children: 1 – 6, $1,240;
   7 – 12, $1,280; others, $3,800
Other fees (annual): boarding, $840; private lessons, $18
School year: September to July (3 trimesters)

Year founded: 1906. **Type of school:** coed, day, boarding, private nonprofit, mission sponsored. **Governed by:** elected school board. **Sponsored by:** Africa Inland Mission Int. **Accredited by:** Middle States.

Curriculum
   Type: U.S. **Languages taught:** French, Spanish, Swahili. **Staff specialists:** reading, math, computer, speech/hearing, counselor, psychologist, learning disabilities, nurse, art, drama, band, photography. **Special programs:** ESL, advanced placement, independent study, remedial, speech. **Special curricular:** art, chorus, band, physical education, computer instruction, vocational. **Extracurricular:** drama, choral music, instrumental music, computers, yearbook, photography, excursions/expeditions, field trips. **Sports, boys:** basketball, soccer, volleyball, rugby, track and field. **Sports, girls:** field hockey, basketball, track and field, volleyball. **Clubs:** Caring Community,

stamps, cooking, wrestling, barbershop quartet, etc. **Tests:** PSAT, SAT, ACT, AP, Iowa, GCSE. **Graduates attending college:** 95%. **Graduates have attended:** Wheaton, West Point, Cornell, Messiah, Rice.

Physical plant
Location: in rural area, 35 miles from Nairobi, within one degree of equator at 7,300-foot elevation. **Campus:** 88 acres. **Library:** 15,000 volumes. **Facilities:** 80 buildings, 30 classrooms, 2 auditoriums, cafeteria, infirmary, 3 tennis courts, gymnasium, 3 playing fields, 2 science labs, 2 computer labs, 19 dormitories, 2 student centers, 5 racquetball courts.

KISUMU

KISUMU INTERNATIONAL SCHOOL

Phone: (254)(35)40752
Mail: PO Box 1276, Kisumu, Kenya
Head teacher: Marguerite Leahy
Staff: full-time, 5; part-time, 1
Nationalities of staff: U.K., 1; host, 1; other, 4
Grade levels: K – 7
Enrollment: 1 – 6, 37; 7, 15; total, 52
Nationalities of student body: U.S., 4; U.K., 6; host, 39; other, 3
Capacity: K, 10; 1 – 6, 30; 7, 15; total, 55
Teacher/student ratio: 1/9
Tuition (annual): K – 7, 80,000**
Other fees (annual): capital levy, 10,000**
School year: September to July

Year founded: 1986. **Type of school:** day, private nonprofit. **Governed by:** board of directors.

Curriculum/physical plant
Type: U.S. **Languages taught:** French. **Staff specialists:** learning disabilities. **Special curricular:** art, computer instruction. **Extracurricular:** drama, dance, choral music, field trips. **Sports:** hockey, soccer. **Clubs:** wildlife, Red Cross, drama, sports. **Location:** in city. **Campus:** 1 acre. **Facilities:** 6 classrooms, computer lab, library.

**Kenyan shilling

NAIROBI

INTERNATIONAL SCHOOL OF KENYA, LTD.
Street address: Peponi Road, Nairobi, Kenya
Phone: (254)(2)582421 – 2/582556   **Facsimile:** (254)(2)582451
  Telex: 96322370 CALWANG (ISK/AISA)
  Cable: U.S. Embassy, Nairobi
Mail: PO Box 14103, Nairobi, Kenya
Superintendent: Daniel L. Scinto
High school principal: Thomas Taylor, Ed.D.
Middle school coordinator: Peter Ostrom
Elementary school principal: John Zito
Business manager: Kamal Rajani
Staff: full-time, 60; part-time, 5
Nationalities of staff: U.S., 48; U.K., 6; host, 11
Grade levels: preK – 13
Enrollment: preK, 13; K – 6, 257; 7– 8, 90; 9 – 13, 214; total, 574
Nationalities of student body: U.S., 227; host, 40; other, 307
Teacher/student ratio: 1/9
Tuition (annual): preK, $1,902; K, $6,937; 1 – 6, $7,037; 7 – 12, $8,362
Other fees (annual): registration, $1,300; busing, $650; yearbook*, $30; graduation*, $35
School year: August to June

Year founded: 1976. **Type of school:** coed, day, private nonprofit. **Governed by:** board of governors/board of directors. **Sponsored by:** Canadian High Commission, American Embassy. **Accredited by:** Middle States, ECIS.

Curriculum/physical plant
Type: U.S., IB. **Languages taught:** French, Spanish, German, Kiswahili. **Staff specialists:** computer, speech/hearing, counselor, psychologist, learning disabilities, nurse. **Special programs:** ESL, remedial. **Special curricular:** art, band, physical education, computer instruction, intercultural program. **Extracurricular:** drama, gymnastics, instrumental music, computers, yearbook, newspaper, literary magazine, excursions/expeditions, field trips. **Sports:** basketball, hockey, rugby, soccer, swimming, tennis, track, volleyball, netball. **Clubs:** National Honor Society, social service. **Tests:** PSAT, SAT, TOEFL, IB, Iowa, ACH. **Graduates attending college:** 75%. **Graduates have attended:** Harvard, Yale, MIT, Stanford, Williams. **Location:** surrounded by a coffee plantation, 8 kilometers from Nairobi. **Campus:** 49 acres. **Library:** 13,500 volumes. **Facilities:** 20 buildings, 43 classrooms, auditorium, infirmary, 3 tennis courts, gymnasium, 4 playing fields, 4 science labs, 2 computer labs, swimming pool, darkroom, student center with snackbar and video and periodical rooms.

*Once only fee

KENTON COLLEGE

Street address: Gichugu Road, Kilileshwa, Nairobi, Kenya
Phone: (254)(2)560260   **Facsimile:** (254)(2)882160/882723
Mail: PO Box 30017, Nairobi, Kenya
Acting head: Judy Arliss
Deputy head: N. Price
Director of studies: Janet Bass
Head of junior school: Lynn Savage
Staff: full-time, 20; part-time, 2
Nationalities of staff: U.K., 17; host, 1; other, 4
Grade levels: 1 – 7
Enrollment: 1 – 5, 104; 6 – 7, 68; total, 172
Nationalities of student body: U.S., 3; U.K., 9; host, 72; other, 88
Capacity: 1 – 5, 200; 6 – 7, 80; total, 280
Teacher/student ratio: 1/8
Boarders: boys, 60   **Grades:** 1 – 9   **Program:** planned 7-day
Tuition (annual): 1 – 9, 135,000**
Other fees (annual): registration*, 2,000**; boarding, 148,500;
    insurance, 200/term; extra activities
School year: September through August

Year founded: 1924. **Type of school:** coed, day, boarding, private nonprofit. **Governed by:** elected board of governors.

Curriculum/physical plant

Type: U.K. **Languages taught:** French, Latin. **Staff specialists:** nurse. **Extracurricular:** drama, dance, instrumental music, computers, yearbook, newspaper, literary magazine, excursions/expeditions, field trips. **Sports:** hockey, rugby, cricket, rounders, netball, others. **Clubs:** Cub Scouts, cookery, chess, riding, music, drama, others. **Tests:** Common Entrance Board. **Graduates have attended:** Rydall College, Strathallan College, Charter House, Bradfield, Stowe. **Location:** beautiful old building with outstanding grounds in suburban area of Nairobi. **Campus:** 35 acres. **Facilities:** 13 buildings, 14 classrooms, auditorium, infirmary, tennis court, playing field, science lab, swimming pool, library.

*Once only fee   **Kenyan shilling

ROSSLYN ACADEMY

Phone: (254)(2)520039/520702   **Facsimile:** (254)(2)521306
Mail: PO Box 14146, Nairobi, Kenya
Principal: Jim Richardson
Vice-principal: Jim Leaman
Staff: full-time, 35; part-time, 7
Nationalities of staff: U.S., 34; other, 8
Grade levels: K – 12
Enrollment: K, 17; 1 – 6, 155; 7 – 8, 59; 9 – 12, 118; total, 349
Nationalities of student body: U.S., 239; other, 110

Capacity: K, 15; 1 – 6, 160; 7 – 8, 56; 9 – 12, 125; total, 356
Teacher/student ratio: 1/9
Tuition (annual): mission rates: K, $805; 1 – 6, $1,570;
    9 – 12, $1,870; non-mission rates: K, $1,110; 1 – 6, $3,300;
    9 – 12, $4,295
Other fees (annual): capital levy, $300; busing, $216 – 360;
    lunch, $1/day
School year: September to June

Year founded: 1967. **Type of school:** coed, day, church-related. **Governed by:** appointed board of governors. **Sponsored by:** Baptist Mission, Assemblies of God, Mennonite Mission. **Accredited by:** Middle States, Association of Christian Schools International.

Curriculum/physical plant

Type: U.S. **Languages taught:** French, Spanish, Swahili. **Staff specialists:** computer, counselor, learning disabilities, speech. **Special curricular:** art, chorus, physical education, computer instruction, drama, industrial arts, photography, yearbook. **Extracurricular:** field trips. **Sports:** field hockey, rugby, soccer, track, volleyball, boys' and girls' basketball. **Tests:** PSAT, SAT, Iowa, PACT. **Location:** on a coffee plantation, 12 miles from Nairobi city center. **Campus:** 40 acres. **Library:** 20,000 volumes. **Facilities:** 13 buildings, 22 classrooms, 3 playing fields, 2 science labs, computer lab.

NAIROBI

St. Mary's School
Address: PO Box 40580, Nairobi, Kenya
Phone: (254)(2)751739/751740   **Facsimile:** (254)(2)751744

KOREA, Republic of ————————

Region: East Asia
Size: 38,025 square miles
Population: 43,919,000
Capital: Seoul

Telephone code: 82
Currency: won
Language: Korean

PUSAN

INTERNATIONAL SCHOOL OF PUSAN
Phone: (82)(51)4683331   **Facsimile:** (82)(51)4640349
Mail: PO Box 534, Pusan, Republic of Korea
Headmaster: Mark Gifford
Staff: full-time, 7
Nationalities of staff: U.S., 1; U.K., 5; host, 1
Grade levels: preK – 8

Enrollment: preK, 11; K, 9; 1 – 6, 25; 7 – 8, 5; total, 50
Capacity: preK, 15; K, 15; 1 – 6, 60; 7, 10; 8, 10; total, 110
Teacher/student ratio: 1/7
Tuition (annual): preK, 2,700,000**; K – 8, 5,800,000
Other fees: registration*, 50,000**; capital levy*, 4,000,000 (refundable less 10% per annum)
School year: September to June

Year founded: 1983. **Type of school:** coed, day, private nonprofit. **Governed by:** elected board of governors.

Curriculum/physical plant
Type: U.S., U.K. **Staff specialists:** computer. **Special programs:** ESL. **Special curricular:** physical education, computer instruction, French, Korean culture. **Extracurricular:** drama, dance, computers, yearbook, newspaper, excursions/expeditions, field trips, ball games. **Tests:** SAT. **Location:** downtown Pusan. **Campus:** 3 acres. **Library:** 7,000 volumes. **Facilities:** 7 classrooms, auditorium.

*Once only fee   **Korean won

SEOUL

INTERNATIONAL CHRISTIAN SCHOOLS
Street address: Main campus: Ga Neung 1 Dong, Uijongbu, Seoul, Korea
Phone: (82)(351)8723267   **Facsimile:** (82)(351)8721458
Mail: PO Box 23, Uijongbu, Seoul, Korea 480-600
U.S. mail: c/o Network of International Christian Schools (NICS), PO Box 18151, Memphis, TN 38181, U.S.A.
Chancellor: Rev. Joe Hale
Superintendent, Uijongbu campus: Dr. Sam Rodriguez
Principal, Seoul campus: Dr. George Cochran
Principal, Songtan campus: Jim Korver
Administrator, Tongduchon campus: Rev. Ed Utz
Staff: full-time, 33; part-time, 5
Nationalities of staff: U.S., 35; host, 3
Grade levels: preK – 12
Enrollment: preK, 18; K, 55; 1 – 6, 296; 7 – 9, 75; 10 – 12, 60; total, 504
Nationalities of student body: U.S., 327; other, 177
Capacity: preK, 25; K, 70; 1 – 6, 320; 7 – 9, 80; 10 – 12, 70; total, 565
Teacher/student ratio: 1/14
Tuition (monthly): Seoul campus: K, 130,000**; 1 – 6, 260,000. Uijongbu campus: K, 105,000; 1 – 5, 190,000; 6 – 12, 210,000. Songtan campus: K, 80,000; 1 – 6, 160,000. Tongduchon campus: $150

Other fees: registration, 50,000**; busing: 25,000 – 70,000/month; library*
School year: August to June

Year founded: 1983. **Type of school:** coed, day, church-related, private nonprofit. **Governed by:** elected school board. **Sponsored by:** Network of International Christian Schools. **Accredited by:** Western. **Regional organization:** EARCOS.

Curriculum

Type: U.S. **Languages taught:** Korean, German, Spanish. **Staff specialists:** math, computer. **Special programs:** ESL, independent study, video supplementary material. **Special curricular:** art, physical education, computer instruction. **Extracurricular:** drama, choral music, yearbook, newspaper, excursions/expeditions, field trips. **Sports:** basketball, soccer, cross-country. Girls: volleyball, cheerleading. Boys: tennis, wrestling. **Clubs:** science, drama, computer, math, Youth Quest, sports card. **Tests:** SAT, ACT, TOEFL, Stanford. **Graduates attending college:** 95%. **Graduates have attended:** U. of Hawaii, Southern Illinois U., Liberty U., James Madison U., U. of Maryland.

Physical plant

Location: buildings leased in urban districts. **Library:** 10,000 volumes. **Facilities:** 4 campuses, 6 buildings, 31 classrooms, 4 auditoriums, cafeteria, gymnasium, 4 playing fields, science lab, 2 computer labs.

*Once only fee   **Korean won

SEOUL ACADEMY INTERNATIONAL SCHOOL

Street address: 988-5 Dae chi Dong, Seoul, Republic of Korea
Phone: (82)(2)5541690   **Facsimile:** (82)(2)5620451
Mail: Young Dong, PO Box 85, Seoul, Republic of Korea
Director: Thomas P. O'Connor
Principal: Pat Jones
Staff: full-time, 23; part-time, 2
Grade levels: preK – 8
Enrollment: preK, 15; K, 31; 1 – 6, 199; total, 245
Capacity: total, 300
Teacher/student ratio: 1/10
Tuition (annual): K – 8, 5,200,000**
School year: August to June†

Year founded: 1983. **Type of school:** coed, day, private nonprofit.

Curriculum/physical plant

Type: U.S. **Languages taught:** Korean. **Staff specialists:** reading, computer, nurse, ESL. **Special programs:** ESL, remedial, special education. **Special curricular:** art, physical education, computer instruction. **Extracurricular:** drama, yearbook, excursions/expeditions, field trips. **Clubs:** Girl

Scouts, Boy Scouts. **Location:** in suburban area, 20 minutes from Seoul.
Library: 6,000 volumes. **Facilities:** 1 building, air conditioning.

**Korean won   †Summer school/ESL school, June – August

SEOUL FOREIGN SCHOOL

Street address: 55 Yonhi-Dong, Seoul, Republic of Korea
Phone: (82)(2)3355101 – 5   **Facsimile:** (82)(2)3351857
Mail: 55 Yonhi-Dong, Sudaemun-Ku, Seoul 120-113, Korea
Headmaster: Harlan E. Lyso, Ph.D.
High school principal: Paul S. Johnston
Middle school principal: Jonathan F. Borden
Elementary school principal: Ronald R. Richter, Ed.D.
British school headteacher: Timothy Gray
Business manager: William R. Rothman
Staff: full-time, 104; part-time, 9
Nationalities of staff: U.S., 86; U.K., 11; host, 6; other, 10
Grade levels: preK – 12
Enrollment: preK, 35; K, 69; 1 – 5, 349; 6 – 8, 236; 9 – 12, 349;
    total, 1,038
Nationalities of student body: U.S., 675; U.K., 166; other, 197
Capacity: preK, 60; K, 100; 1 – 5, 465; 6 – 8, 274; 9 – 12, 352;
    total, 1,251
Teacher/student ratio: 1/10
Tuition (annual): preK – K, 2,945,000** plus $1,500 (half-day);
    K – 5, 5,260,000 plus $3,000; 6 – 8, 5,810,000 plus $3,000;
    9 – 12, 6,360,000 plus $3,000; British school, 5,720,000 plus
    $3,000
Other fees (annual): registration*, 360,000**; busing, 1,120,000
School year: August to June

Year founded: 1912. **Type of school:** coed, day, private nonprofit,
Christian. **Governed by:** elected school board. **Sponsored by:** community,
five church groups. **Accredited by:** Western.

Curriculum

Type: U.S., U.K., IB. **Languages taught:** French, Spanish, Korean. **Staff
specialists:** reading, math, computer, counselor, nurse. **Special programs:**
ESL, advanced placement, remedial, IB. **Special curricular:** art, chorus,
band, physical education, computer instruction. **Extracurricular:** drama,
choral music, instrumental music, computers, yearbook, newspaper, literary
magazine, photography, excursions/expeditions, field trips. **Sports:** basketball, cheerleading, soccer, tennis, volleyball, cross-country. **Clubs:** National
Honor Society, student council, Fellowship of Christian Students, variety of
student interest clubs. **Tests:** SSAT, PSAT, SAT, ACT, TOEFL, IB, AP, Iowa,
CLEP. **Graduates attending college:** over 95%. **Graduates have attended:**
U. of California at Berkeley, Princeton, Brown, U. of Massachusetts – Amherst,
Smith.

Physical plant
    Location: in park-like environment within city. **Campus:** over 20 acres. **Libraries:** 47,000 volumes. **Facilities:** 6 educational buildings, 87 classrooms, 2 auditoriums, cafeteria, infirmary, 4 tennis courts, 2 gymnasiums, playing field, 4 science labs, 3 computer labs, 11 residential buildings (72 units), partial air conditioning.

*Once only fee   **Korean won

SEOUL INTERNATIONAL SCHOOL
    Street address: Bokjung-dong, Song Nam City, Republic of Korea
    Phone: (82)(2)2334551 – 2   **Facsimile:** (82)(342)7595133
    Mail: Kangdong PO Box 61, Seoul, Korea 134-600
    Headmaster: Edward B. Adams
    Deputy headmaster for academics: Robert Dunn, Ph.D.
    Deputy headmaster for business: Hyung Shik Kim
    Principal for elementary grades: Francelle Grisham
    Staff: full-time, 71
    Nationalities of staff: U.S., 40; other, 31
    Grade levels: preK – 12
    Enrollment: preK, 16; K, 35; 1 – 6, 257; 7 – 9, 168; 10 – 12, 163;
        Language Center, 67; total, 706
    Nationalities of student body: U.S., 502; other, 204
    Teacher/student ratio: 1/10
    Tuition (annual): preK, $3,900; K, $7,300; 1 – 5, $7,900; 6 – 8,
        $8,800; 9 – 12, $9,300
    Other fees (annual): registration*, $200 – 500; busing, $1,000; books,
        $60 – 140 deposit; testing*, $40; AP*, $100; senior*, $100
    School year: August to June

    Year founded: 1973. **Type of school:** coed, day, proprietary, private nonprofit. **Governed by:** Edward B. Adams, headmaster. **Accredited by:** Western.

Curriculum/physical plant
    Type: U.S. **Languages taught:** French, Spanish, Japanese, Korean. **Staff specialists:** reading, speech/hearing, counselor, nurse, resource. **Special programs:** ESL, advanced placement, remedial. **Special curricular:** art, chorus, band, physical education, computer instruction. **Extracurricular:** drama, choral music, instrumental music, computers, yearbook, newspaper, literary magazine, field trips. **Sports:** basketball, cheerleading, soccer, tennis, volleyball, cross-country. **Tests:** PSAT, SAT, AP, CTBS. **Graduates attending college:** over 90%. **Graduates have attended:** Duke, Mount Holyoke, U. of Pennsylvania, Smith, Stanford. **Location:** in suburban area, 40 minutes from Seoul. **Campus:** 8 acres. **Library:** 20,000 volumes. **Facilities:** 2 buildings, 62 classrooms, auditorium, cafeteria, infirmary, gymnasium, playing field, 3 science labs, 3 computer labs.

*Once only fee

TAEJON

TAEJON CHRISTIAN INTERNATIONAL SCHOOL†

Street address: 210-1 O Jung Dong, PO Box 310, Taejon,
 Republic of Korea 300-603
Phone: (82)(42)6333663 – 5   **Facsimile:** (82)(42)6315732
Headmaster: James L. Wootton, Ed.D.
Staff: full-time, 16; part-time, 12
Nationalities of staff: U.S., 20; host, 5; other, 3
Grade levels: K – 12
Enrollment: K, 11; 1   6, 34; 7 – 9, 30; 10 – 12, 28; total, 103
Nationalities of student body: U.S., 70; host, 5; other, 28
Capacity: K, 15; 1 – 6, 60; 7 – 9, 60; 10 – 12, 62; total, 197
Teacher/student ratio: 1/5
Boarders: boys, 15; girls, 14   **Grades:** 7 – 12
  Program: planned 7-day
Tuition (annual): K, $3,195; 1 – 6, $5,855; 7 – 12, $7,925
Other fees (annual): boarding, $6,100; registration*, $300
School year: August to June

Year founded: 1958. **Type of school:** coed, day, boarding, church-related. **Governed by:** appointed and elected board of trustees. **Sponsored by:** missions. **Accredited by:** Western.

Curriculum/physical plant

Type: U.S., college preparatory. **Languages taught:** French, Korean. **Staff specialists:** counselor, nurse. **Special programs:** ESL, honors sections, independent study. **Special curricular:** art, chorus, band, physical education, computer instruction. **Extracurricular:** drama, gymnastics, choral music, instrumental music, yearbook, newspaper, excursions/expeditions, field trips. **Clubs:** Girl Scouts, National Honor Society, Quill and Scroll, Boy Scouts, Youth for Christ, Tri M Music Honor Society. **Tests:** SSAT, PSAT, SAT, ACT, TOEFL, Stanford. **Graduates attending college:** 90%. **Graduates have attended:** Vanderbilt, Wheaton, U. of Illinois, Auburn, U., Oklahoma Baptist U. **Location:** on outskirts of Taejon. **Campus:** 9 acres. **Library:** 10,000 volumes. **Facilities:** 7 buildings, 20 classrooms, cafeteria, 4 tennis courts, gymnasium, playing field, science lab, computer lab, boys/girls dorm, small auditorium, limited busing system.

*Once only fee   †formerly Korea Christian Academy

YONGGWANG

THE YONGGWANG FOREIGN SCHOOL

Street address: c/o C-E International, Inc., Korea Branch, Yonggwang Nuclear Site, 517 Kyema-ri, Hongnong-up, Yonggwang-kun, Jeonnam, Republic of Korea 513-880

Mail: c/o CEII Site Office, Hongnong, PO Box 9, Yonggwang-Kun, Jeonnam, Republic of Korea 513-880

Phone/facsimile: (82)(686)3567647

Principal: Eleanor Jones

Staff: full-time, 2; part-time, 1

Nationalities of staff: U.S., 3

Grade levels: K – 8

Enrollment: K – 5, 8; 6 – 8, 7; total, 15

Nationalities of student body: U.S., 15

Teacher/student ratio: 1/5

Year founded: 1992. **Type of school:** coed, day, company sponsored. **Sponsored by:** C-E International Inc. **Operated by:** International Schools Services, Princeton, New Jersey.

Curriculum/physical plant

Type: U.S. **Languages taught:** Korean. **Special curricular:** art, physical education, computer instruction. **Extracurricular:** newspaper, excursions/ expeditions, field trips, sports. **Tests:** Iowa. **Location:** company camp near Yonggwang, Korea. **Library:** 1,200 volumes. **Facilities:** auditorium, tennis court, gymnasium, playing field, swimming pool.

KUWAIT

Region: Middle East
Size: 6,880 square miles
Population: 2,024,000
Capital: Kuwait

Telephone code: 965
Currency: dinar
Language: Arabic

AL-SURRA

THE AMERICAN INTERNATIONAL SCHOOL IN KUWAIT

Street address: Lot 570, Area 2, Al-Surra, Kuwait
Phone: (965)5318173 – 6   **Facsimile:** (965)5318166
Mail: PO Box 17464, Khaldiya 72455, Kuwait
Superintendent: Walid Abushakra
Deputy superintendent: Raja Abu Shakra
High school principal: Mike McQuin
Elementary principal: Arthur Hudson
Head of library: Gail Fike
Head of computer services: Betsy MacDonald
Business manager: Mrs. Wafa'a Amarah
Staff: full-time, 92
Grade levels: preK – 12; full IB program (grades 11 – 12)
Enrollment: preK, 75; K, 125; 1 – 6, 610; 7 – 9, 175; 10 – 12, 215; total, 1,200
Nationalities of student body: U.S., 71; U.K., 16; host, 610; other, 503
Capacity: preK, 150; K, 150; 1 – 6, 700; 7 – 9, 300; 10 – 12, 300; total, 1,600
Teacher/student ratio: 1/13
Tuition (annual): preK – K, $3,300; 1 – 4, $4,900; 5 – 8, $5,250;
    9 – 12, $5,950
Other fees (annual): busing, $800
School year: September to June

HAWALLI

THE AMERICAN SCHOOL OF KUWAIT

Phone: (965)5318120   **Facsimile:** (965)5318124
Mail: PO Box 6735, Hawalli 32042, Kuwait, Arabian Gulf
Superintendent: Donald C. Holt
High school principal: Douglas Wolf
Middle school principal: Barry Clough
Elementary school principal: Maxine Al-Refai
Business manager: Anwar Dhanani

Staff: full-time, 90
Nationalities of staff: U.S., 75; other, 15
Grade levels: preK – 12
Enrollment: K – 5, 439; 6 – 12, 485; total, 924
Nationalities of student body: U.S., 250; U.K., 15; host, 280; other, 379
Capacity: preK, 75; K, 75; 1 – 5, 375; 6 – 8, 225; 9 – 12, 300; total, 1,050
Teacher/student ratio: 1/10
Tuition (annual): K, 1,100**; 1 – 5, 1,800; 6 – 8, 1,950; 9 – 12, 2,150
School year: late August through May

Year founded: 1964. **Type of school:** coed, day, private nonprofit. **Governed by:** appointed and elected board of trustees. **Accredited by:** Middle States.

Curriculum

Type: U.S., Kuwait Ministry of Education (Arabic and Islamic studies). **Languages of instruction:** English, Arabic. **Languages taught:** English, French, Spanish, Arabic. **Staff specialists:** reading, computer, counselor, learning disabilities, nurse, ESL, science, instrumental music, vocal music, performing arts. **Special programs:** ESL, advanced placement, correspondence study, learning disabilities, basic/remedial. **Special curricular:** art, chorus, physical education, computer instruction, yearbook, instrumental music. **Extracurricular:** drama, computers, excursions/expeditions, field trips, choral music, forensics, Model UN. **Sports:** basketball, soccer, softball, swimming, tennis, track, volleyball, gymnastics, badminton, weight training. **Clubs:** National Honor Society, photography, computer, Spanish, student government. **Tests:** PSAT, SAT, ACT, TOEFL, AP, ITBS, TAP. **Graduates attending college:** 100%. **Graduates have attended:** Stanford, MIT, Kuwait U., U. of California at Berkeley, Cornell.

Physical plant

Location: 2 air-conditioned campuses, each located in suburban residential areas. **Surra campus (6 –12):** 1.5 acres. **Library:** 10,000 volumes. **Facilities:** 2 buildings, 40 classrooms, auditorium, infirmary, gymnasium, playing field, 4 science labs, 2 computer labs, swimming pool, 3 basketball courts, 3 volleyball courts, outdoor theater, fitness center. **Salwa campus (K – 5):** 2 buildings, 21 classrooms, library/media center with 5,500 volumes, large playground, labs for art, computer, ESL, learning disabilities, reading, and science, 2 music rooms.

**Kuwaiti dinar

SAFAT

AL-BAYAN SCHOOL

Phone: (965)5315125   **Facsimile:** (965)5332836
Mail: PO Box 24472, Safat, Kuwait 13105
Owner representative: May Al-Essa

Director: Eamonn Hogan
Assistant director: Khadija Awwad
Staff: full-time, 75; part-time, 2
Nationalities of staff: U.S., 18; U.K., 15; other, 44
Grade levels: N – 10
Enrollment: N – preK, 60; K, 200; 1 – 5, 345; 6 – 8, 120; 9 – 10, 57;
total, 782
Capacity: N – preK, 60; K, 200; 1 – 5, 375; 6 – 8, 150; 9 – 10, 75;
total, 860
Teacher/student ratio: 1/10
Tuition: N – K, 1,000**; 1 – 5, 1,600; 6 – 8, 1,700; 9 – 10, 1,800
School year: September to June

Year founded: 1977. **Type of school:** coed, day, private nonprofit.
Governed by: school board. **Accredited by:** ECIS, New England.

Curriculum/physical plant
Type: U.S., Kuwaiti. **Languages of instruction:** English, Arabic. **Languages taught:** English, Arabic. **Staff specialists:** reading, computer, counselor, nurse, music. **Special programs:** advanced placement, bilingual. **Special curricular:** physical education, computer instruction. **Extracurricular:** drama, choral music, computers, yearbook, newspaper, excursions/expeditions. **Sports:** basketball, football, volleyball, badminton. **Clubs:** science, pottery, cookery, painting, fabric printing. **Tests:** SAT, TOEFL, AP. **Location:** in suburb of Kuwait City. **Library:** 21,000 volumes. **Facilities:** 35 classrooms, auditorium, infirmary, gymnasium, computer lab, canteen, air conditioning.

**Kuwaiti dinar

SALWA

THE UNIVERSAL AMERICAN SCHOOL

Street address: Al Taween Street, Subdivision 387, Area 11, Salwa,
Kuwait
Phone: (965)5615857 – 8   **Facsimile:** (965)5625343
Mail: PO Box 17035, Code 72451, Khaldiya, Kuwait
Director: Dr. A. Latif Al Shamali
Principal: Dr. Dale R. Koch
Business manager: Mohammed Rashwan
Staff: full-time, 55
Grade levels: preK – 12
Enrollment: preK – K, 175; 1 – 6, 325; 7 – 9, 100; 10 – 12, 100;
total, 700
Teacher/student ratio: 1/13
Tuition (annual): preK – K, $3,800; 1 – 4, $4,800; 5 – 8, $5,400;
9 – 12, $6,000

Other fees (annual): registration, $175; busing, $840
School year: September to June
Accredited by: Middle States.

Curriculum/physical plant

Type: U.S. **Languages of instruction:** English, Arabic (required of all Arab students). **Staff specialists:** computer, art, music, physical education, French, Arabic. **Special programs:** advanced placement. **Location:** in Salwa, a suburb of Kuwait City. **Facilities:** 52 classrooms, science labs, computer labs, art room, music room, small gym, playground.

LEBANON _____

Region: Middle East
Size: 4,015 square miles
Population: 3,384,000
Capital: Beirut

Telephone code: 961
Currency: pound
Languages: Arabic, French

BEIRUT

AMERICAN COMMUNITY SCHOOL AT BEIRUT

Street address: Rue de Paris, Beirut, Lebanon
Phone: (961)(1)632283   **Facsimile:** (961)(1)632279
     Telex: 92320801 AMUNOB LE   **Cable:** AMERCOMS
Mail: PO Box 8129, Beirut, Lebanon
U.S. mail: c/o I.I.S., 850 Third Avenue, 18th Floor, New York, NY 10022, U.S.A.
U.S. phone: (1)(212)3192453   **U.S. facsimile:** (1)(212)7526971
Headmistress: Catherine C. Bashshur
High school director: Manahil B. Kobeisi
Elementary director: Ebba El Hage
Registrar: Najwa Zabad
Head of library: Haifa Hijazi
Head of computer services: Spiro Habash
Preschool coordinator: Maysa Boubess
Staff: full-time, 75; part-time, 28
Nationalities of staff: U.S., 8; host, 81; other, 14
Grade levels: N – 13
Enrollment: N – preK, 119; K, 73; 1 – 5, 342; 6 – 9, 208; 10 – 12, 102; total, 844
Nationalities of student body: U.S., 117; U.K., 23; host, 555; other, 149
Capacity: N – preK, 140; K, 75; 1 – 6, 400; 7 – 9, 250; 10 – 12, 250; 13, 20; total, 1,135
Teacher/student ratio: 1/9

Tuition (annual): N – preK, $2,800; K – 5, $3,200; 6 – 11, $3,400; 12, $3,800
Other fees (annual): registration, 750,000**; expansion*, $1,000
School year: September to June

Year founded: 1905. **Type of school:** coed, day, private nonprofit. **Governed by:** self-perpetuating board of trustees. **Sponsored by:** American U. of Beirut, Presbyterian Church USA. **Licensed by:** Lebanese government. **Chartered by:** Board of Regents of the University of the State of New York in 1955. **Accredited by:** Middle States.

Curriculum

Type: U.S., Lebanese, IB. **Languages taught:** French, Spanish, Arabic. **Staff specialists:** reading, computer, counselor. **Special programs:** ESL, advanced placement, correspondence, remedial. **Special curricular:** art, chorus, physical education, computer instruction. **Extracurricular:** drama, music, gymnastics, computers, yearbook, newspaper, excursions/expeditions, field trips. **Sports:** basketball, fencing, soccer, softball, tennis, volleyball, track and field, handball. **Clubs:** social service, aerobics, student activities. **Tests:** PSAT, SAT, ACT, TOEFL, AP. **Graduates attending college:** 100%. **Graduates have attended:** American U. of Beirut, American U., Boston U., Tufts, U. of North Carolina.

Physical plant

Location: in Beirut, next to American U. of Beirut, one block from the Mediterranean. **Campus:** 1,600 square meters. **Library:** 40,000 volumes. **Facilities:** 4 buildings, 62 classrooms, 2 auditoriums, cafeteria, infirmary, covered play area, 2 tennis courts, gymnasium, 3 playing fields, 3 science labs, computer lab.

*Once only fee   **Lebanese pound (lira)

INTERNATIONAL COLLEGE

Phone: (961)(1)867207   **Telex:** 92322223 SAMAK LE
    Cable: AMUNOB, Beirut
Mail: Ras Beirut, Bliss Street, PO Box 11-0236, Beirut, Lebanon
U.S. mail: c/o I.I.S., 850 Third Avenue, 18th Floor, New York, NY 10022, U.S.A.
U.S. phone: (1)(212)3192450   **U.S. facsimile:** (1)(212)7582327
President: Gerrit Keator
Deputy president: Edmond Tohme
Directors: Nabil Rahhal, Randa Khouri, Marie Christine Mojabbert, Gaby Charma'a
Staff: full-time, 228; part-time, 29
Nationalities of staff: host, 239; other, 18
Grade levels: preK – 12
Enrollment: preK – K, 449; 1 – 5, 773; 6 – 9, 768; 10 – 12, 610; total, 2,600
Teacher/student ratio: 1/11

Tuition (annual): preK – K, 2,370,000**; 1 – 9, 2,490,000;
10 – 12, 2,560,000
Other fees (annual): registration, 300,000** (deductible from fees);
busing, 760,000; development*, $1,000
School year: October to June

Year founded: 1891. **Type of school:** coed, day. **Governed by:** board of trustees. **Accredited by:** Commonwealth of Massachusetts.

Curriculum/physical plant

Type: U.S., Lebanese, French Baccalaureate. **Languages taught:** French, Arabic. **Staff specialists:** counselor, nurse. **Special programs:** remedial. **Special curricular:** art, physical education, computer instruction. **Extracurricular:** drama, gymnastics, computers, yearbook, photography. **Sports:** basketball, soccer, volleyball, varsity and junior varsity, scholastic and interscholastic. **Organizations:** social service, modeling, chess, backgammon, stamp, archery, woodwork, International College Alumni Association. **Tests:** SAT, TOEFL, Scientific Quantitative. **Graduates attending college:** 100%. **Graduates have attended:** American U. of Beirut, Georgia Tech, Yale, Stanford, MIT. **Location:** in city. **Campus:** 38,000 square meters. **Library:** 16,276 volumes. **Facilities:** 6 buildings, 108 classrooms, 2 infirmaries, covered play area, 2 playing fields, 2 science labs, computer lab, AV equipment.

*Once only fee   ** Lebanese pound (lira)

LESOTHO _____

Region: Africa
Size: 11,716 square miles
Population: 1,801,000
Capital: Maseru

Telephone code: 266
Currency: maloti
Languages: English, Sotho

MASERU

AMERICAN INTERNATIONAL SCHOOL OF LESOTHO

Street address: 14 Old Europa, Maseru 100, Lesotho
Phone: (266)322987   **Facsimile:** (266)310116
Mail: PO Box 333, Maseru 100, Lesotho
U.S. mail: Maseru, Department of State, Washington, D.C. 20521-2340
Director: Elaine Stainburn
Staff: full-time, 8; part-time, 3
Nationalities of staff: U.S., 4; host, 2; other, 5
Grade levels: K – 6
Enrollment: K, 15; 1 – 6, 30; total, 45
Nationalities of student body: U.S., 9; U.K., 6; host, 9; other, 21

Capacity: K, 15; 1 – 6, 45; total, 60
Teacher/student ratio: 1/5
Tuition (annual): K – 6, $7,623
Other fees: registration*, $65
School year: August to June

Year founded: 1991. **Type of school:** coed, day, private nonprofit. **Governed by:** appointed and elected 7-member school board.

Curriculum/physical plant
Type: U.S. **Staff specialists:** computer, art, music. **Special curricular:** art, physical education, computer instruction, music. **Extracurricular:** stamp club, arts & crafts club. **Location:** in residential neighborhood. **Campus:** 2 acres. **Facilities:** 3 buildings, 6 classrooms, computer lab, library, air conditioning.

*Once only fee

MACHABENG HIGH SCHOOL
Street address: Tonakholo Road, Maseru, Lesotho
Phone: (266)313224   **Facsimile:** (266)316109
Mail: PO Box 1570, Maseru 100, Lesotho
Headmaster: Neil Richards
Deputy headmistress: Denise Frost
Business manager: Mapulane Mahloka
Staff: full-time, 34; part-time, 7
Nationalities of staff: U.K., 15; host, 9; other, 17
Grade levels: 6 – 12
Enrollment: 6, 56; 7 – 9, 245; 10 – 12, 105; total, 406
Nationalities of student body: U.S., 15; U.K., 20; host, 253; other, 118
Capacity: 6, 80; 7 – 9, 240; 10 – 12, 170; total, 490
Teacher/student ratio: 1/11
Boarders: boys, 22; girls, 18   **Grades:** 6 – 12
    Program: planned 7-day
Tuition (annual): fully aided, 21,650**
Other fees (annual): registration*, 250**; boarding, 9,000; book deposit, 300
School year: September to July

Year founded: 1977. **Type of school:** coed, day, boarding. **Governed by:** appointed and elected board of governors. **Sponsored by:** Lesotho government. **Accredited by:** Middle States, ECIS.

Curriculum
Type: U.K., IB. **Languages taught:** English, French, Sesotho, (other languages/IB only). **Staff specialists:** math, computer, counselor, nurse, languages, history, geography, chemistry, physics, biology, home economics, English literature, physical education, art & design, performing arts. **Special curricular:** art, physical education, computer instruction. **Extracurricular:**

drama, gymnastics, dance, computers, yearbook, newspaper, photography, excursions/expeditions, field trips. **Sports:** basketball, football, softball, swimming, volleyball, netball, athletics, table tennis. **Clubs:** Tae Kwon Do, chess, bird-watching, library, scripture union. **Tests:** SAT, ACT, TOEFL, IB, IGCSE. **Graduates attending college:** 90%. **Graduates have attended:** Cornell, London School of Economics, Imperial College London, Rhodes U., Royal College Surgeons (Dublin).

Physical plant
Location: in Maseru. **Campus:** 3 hectares. **Library:** 6,500 volumes. **Facilities:** 6 buildings, 20 classrooms, auditorium, cafeteria, infirmary, gymnasium, playing field, 4 science labs, computer lab, boarding house with kitchen and dining facilities.

*Once only fee   **Lesotho maloti

MASERU ENGLISH MEDIUM PREPARATORY SCHOOL
Street address: Caldwell Road, Maseru West, Maseru, Lesotho
Phone: (266)312276   **Facsimile:** (266)310016
Mail: PO Box 34, Maseru 100, Lesotho
Principal: Dr. M. T. Coghlan
Staff: full-time, 30; part-time, 3
Nationalities of staff: U.S., 4; U.K., 6; host, 4; other, 19
Grade levels: 1 – 6
Enrollment: total, 398
Capacity: total, 450
Teacher/student ratio: 1/12
Tuition (annual): assisted fees, $2,850; unassisted, $986
Other fees: books*, $10
School year: August to June

Year founded: 1891. **Type of school:** coed, day, private nonprofit. **Governed by:** elected management committee.

Curriculum/physical plant
Type: U.S., U.K. **Languages taught:** English, French, Sesotho. **Staff specialists:** reading, computer, learning disabilities, art, music, physical education, French, Sesotho, science. **Special programs:** ESL, remedial. **Special curricular:** art, chorus, physical education. **Extracurricular:** drama, gymnastics, choral music, instrumental music, excursions/expeditions. **Sports:** football, softball, tennis, track and field, gymnastics. **Clubs:** chess, scripture union, macramé and needlework, drama, public speaking, choir, philately, math, science. **Location:** in suburban area, 2 kilometers from Maseru. **Campus:** 8 acres. **Library:** more than 2,000 volumes. **Facilities:** 34 buildings, 27 classrooms, auditorium, 2 tennis courts, gymnasium, playing field, science lab, computer lab.

*Once only fee

LIBYA _____

Region: North Africa
Size: 679,359 square miles
Population: 4,350,000
Capital: Tripoli

Telephone code: 218
Currency: dinar
Language: Arabic

TRIPOLI

THE MARTYRS SCHOOL

Phone: (218)(21)70094   **Facsimile:** (218)(21)74235
Telex: 051261443 CUSAM LY
Mail: PO Box 860, Tripoli, Libya
Superintendent: Ahmed S. Fitori, Ph.D.
Principal: Elsa Dickson
Financial manager: Mohammed Bin-Mulahum
Staff: full-time, 48
Nationalities of staff: U.S., 3; U.K., 3; host, 14; other, 28
Grade levels: preK – 11
Enrollment: total, 580
Capacity: total, 600
Teacher/student ratio: 1/12
Tuition (annual)†: preK – K, 950**; 1 – 11, 1,900
School year: September through June

Year founded: 1958. **Type of school:** coed, day, company sponsored.
Governed by: Ministry of Education. **Sponsored by:** Libyan oil companies.

Curriculum/physical plant
Type: U.S. **Languages taught:** French, Arabic. **Staff specialists:** computer, learning disabilities, nurse, resource. **Special programs:** ESL, remedial. **Special curricular:** art, band, physical education, computer instruction, vocational. **Extracurricular:** gymnastics, instrumental music, computers, yearbook, newspaper, photography, field trips. **Sports:** basketball, soccer, softball, tennis, volleyball, floor hockey. **Clubs:** recorders, chess, teen, stamp collecting. **Tests:** Iowa. **Location:** 3.5 kilometers from city center. **Campus:** 5 acres. **Library:** 14,000 volumes. **Facilities:** 11 buildings, 47 classrooms, auditorium, infirmary, 2 tennis courts, gymnasium, 2 playing fields, 2 science labs, computer lab.

**Libyan dinar   †25% of tuition must be paid in hard currency

LUXEMBOURG ────────────────

Region: Europe
Size: 998 square miles
Population: 388,000
Capital: Luxembourg

Telephone code: 352
Currency: franc
Languages: French, German,
Luxembourgish

LUXEMBOURG

AMERICAN INTERNATIONAL SCHOOL OF LUXEMBOURG

Street address: 188 ave. de la Faïencerie, L-1511 Luxembourg,
Luxembourg
Phone: (352)470020   **Facsimile:** (352)460924
Director: Harry C. Barteau, Ph.D.
Upper school principal: John D. Osbo
Lower school principal: Catherine P. Smart
Registrar: Jacqueline R. Bray
Staff: full-time, 49; part-time, 12
Nationalities of staff: U.S., 37; U.K., 7; host, 2; other, 15
Grade levels: K – 12
Enrollment: K, 70; 1 – 6, 256; 7 – 9, 82; 10 – 12, 60; total, 468
Nationalities of student body: U.S., 130; U.K., 49; host, 4;
other, 285
Capacity: K, 90; 1 – 6, 260; 7 – 9, 100; 10 – 12, 90; total, 540
Teacher/student ratio: 1/9
Tuition (annual): K – 6, 304,000**; 7 – 12, 382,000
Other fees: registration*, 40,000**
School year: September to June

Year founded: 1963. **Type of school:** coed, day, private nonprofit.
Governed by: appointed and elected board of directors. **Sponsored by:**
American International School Association. **Accredited by:** Middle States,
ECIS.

Curriculum/physical plant

Type: U.S. **Languages taught:** French, German. **Staff specialists:**
reading, computer, speech/hearing, counselor, physical education. **Special
programs:** ESL, advanced placement, honors sections, Swedish language and
culture. **Special curricular:** art, chorus, band, physical education, computer
instruction. **Extracurricular:** drama, choral music, instrumental music,
yearbook, excursions/expeditions, field trips. **Sports:** basketball, soccer,
swimming, track, volleyball. **Organizations**: National Honor Society, National

Junior Honor Society, student council. **Tests:** PSAT, SAT, TOEFL, AP, Nelson Reading Skills. **Graduates attending college:** 85%. **Graduates have attended:** Stanford, Dartmouth, Duke, New York U., Smith. **Location:** on outskirts of city. **Campus:** 10 acres. **Libraries:** 15,000 volumes. **Facilities:** 3 buildings, 32 classrooms, auditorium, gymnasium, playing field, 3 science labs, 2 computer labs, AV room, band room.

*Once only fee   **Luxembourg franc

MACAU

Region: East Asia	**Telephone code:** 853
Size: 6 square miles	**Currency:** Hong Kong dollar
Population: 399,000	**Languages:** Chinese, English,
Capital: Macau	Portuguese

MACAU

SCHOOL OF THE NATIONS, MACAU

Street address: Rua Luis G. Gomes, 136 Edificio Lei San, 4 Andar, Macau (via Hong Kong), Macau
Phone: (853)552859   **Facsimile:** (853)552924
School administrator: Mrs. Anula Samuel
Secondary level coordinator: Mr. Lloyd Brown
Upper primary level coordinator: Mr. Keith Barnes
Lower primary level coordinator: Mrs. Clare Nobbs
Staff: full-time, 30; part-time, 5
Nationalities of staff: U.S., 4; U.K., 4; other, 27
Grade levels: preK – 12
Enrollment: preK, 50; K, 100; 1 – 6, 200; 7 – 9, 100; total, 450
Capacity: preK, 50; K, 150; 1 – 6, 300; 7 – 9, 200; 10 – 12, 100; total, 800
Teacher/student ratio: 1/14
Tuition (annual): 1 – 6, 16,000**; 7 – 12, 20,000
School year: September to June

Year founded: 1988. **Type of school:** coed, day, private nonprofit. **Governed by:** Badi Foundation. **Accredited by:** government of Macau.

Curriculum
Type: IB. **Languages taught:** Chinese (Mandarin). **Special programs:** ESL, remedial. **Special curricular:** chorus. **Extracurricular:** drama, gymnastics, dance, instrumental music, newspaper, field trips. **Clubs:** stamp, chess. **Tests:** A-level GCE, GCSE.

**Hong Kong dollar

MADAGASCAR ─────────────

Region: Africa (Indian Ocean)
Size: 226,657 square miles
Population: 12,185,000
Capital: Antananarivo

Telephone code: 261
Currency: franc
Languages: Malagasy, French

ANTANANARIVO

AMERICAN SCHOOL OF ANTANANARIVO

Street address: Ivandry, Antananarivo 101, Madagascar
Phone: (261)(2)42039   **Facsimile:** (261)(2)34539   **Telex:** 98322202
Mail: BP 1717, Antananarivo 101, Madagascar
Director: Richard Sands
Staff: full-time, 6; part-time, 5
Nationalities of staff: U.S., 4; U.K., 1; host, 1; other, 5
Grade levels: preschool – 8
Enrollment: preschool, 5; preK, 6; K, 7; 1 – 6, 35; 7 – 8, 5; total, 58
Nationalities of student body: U.S., 30; U.K., 2; host, 5; other, 21
Capacity: preschool, 10; preK, 10; K, 10; 1 – 6, 42; 7 – 8, 16; total, 88
Teacher/student ratio: 1/7
Tuition (annual): preschool, $1,500; preK, $2,000; K, $5,750; 1 – 8, $6,300
Other fees (annual): registration, $250
School year: September to June

Year founded: 1969. **Type of school:** coed, day, private nonprofit. **Governed by:** elected board of directors. **Sponsored by:** U.S. Embassy. **Accredited by:** Middle States (in process). **Regional organizations:** AISA.

Curriculum/physical plant

Type: U.S. **Languages taught:** French. **Special programs:** ESL. **Special curricular:** art, physical education, computer instruction, music. **Extracurricular:** drama, choral music, computers, newspaper, field trips. **Sports:** baseball, basketball, swimming, track, volleyball. **Tests:** Iowa. **Location:** in pleasant suburban area, 5 miles from Antananarivo. **Library:** 3,250 volumes. **Facilities:** 9 buildings, 11 classrooms (7 portable), playing field, computer lab, air conditioning.

MALAWI _____

Region: Southeast Africa
Size: 45,747 square miles
Population: 9,438,000
Capital: Lilongwe

Telephone code: 265
Currency: kwacha
Languages: English, Chewa,
Lomwe, Yao

LILONGWE

BISHOP MACKENZIE SCHOOL

Phone: (265)744817/740412   **Facsimile:** (265)740179
Mail: PO Box 102, Lilongwe, Malawi
School head: Graham Burgess
Staff: full-time, 40; part-time, 10
Grade levels: preK – 10
Enrollment: total, 650
Nationalities of student body: U.S., 44; host, 199; other, 407
Teacher/student ratio: 1/14
Tuition (annual): preK – 6, $4,489; 7 – 10, $7,474
Other fees (annual): registration, $6
School year: September to July

Year founded: 1944. **Type of school:** coed, day, private nonprofit, non-religious. **Governed by:** appointed and elected board of governors. **Sponsored and accredited by:** Malawi government.

Curriculum/physical plant

Type: U.K., GCSE in upper school. **Staff specialists:** computer, art, music, physical education. **Special programs:** ESL. **Special curricular:** art, chorus, physical education, American history, swimming, excursions, field trips, Brownies, Scouts, Cubs. **Location:** in suburban area, 2 kilometers from Lilongwe city. **Campus:** 25 acres. **Facilities:** 20 buildings, 21 classrooms, 2 tennis courts, 3 playing fields, 2 science labs, 2 computer labs, swimming pool, home economics room.

MALAYSIA ——————————————

Region: Southeast Asia
Size: 127,316 square miles
Population: 17,981,000
Capital: Kuala Lumpur

Telephone code: 60
Currency: ringgit
Languages: Malay, English, Chinese,
Indian languages

KERTEH

Esso Expatriate School†

Street address: No. 165/166 Lorong 13, Kompleks Perumahan Petronas,
Fasa 2, 24300 Kerteh, Terengganu, Malaysia
Phone: (60)(9)861013   **Facsimile:** (60)(9)540133
Principal: Sharon A. Sperry
Staff: full-time, 3; part-time, 2
Nationalities of staff: U.S., 2; host, 2; other, 1
Grade levels: K – 6
Enrollment: K, 4; 1 – 6, 11; total, 15
Nationalities of student body: U.S., 11; other, 4
Capacity: K, 10; 1 – 6, 20; total, 30
Teacher/student ratio: 1/4
School year: August to June

Year founded: 1989. **Type of school:** day, company sponsored. **Sponsored by:** Esso Production Malaysia Inc. **Operated by:** International Schools Services, Princeton, New Jersey. **Accredited by:** Western.

Curriculum/physical plant
Type: U.S. **Languages taught:** Malay. **Staff specialists:** learning disabilities. **Special curricular:** art, physical education, computer instruction. **Extracurricular:** field trips. **Sports:** soccer, swimming, tennis. **Location:** in seaside fishing village (population 10,000); amenities available. **Campus:** 1 acre. **Library:** 2,000 volumes. **Facilities:** 2 buildings, 6 classrooms, tennis court, playing field, swimming pool, air conditioning.

†limited to Esso students

KUALA LUMPUR

Garden International School

Street address: No. 2A Jalan Selasih, Taman Cheras, 56100 Kuala
Lumpur, Selangor, Malaysia
Phone: (60)(3)9303000   **Facsimile:** (60)(3)9716402
Principal: Joseph Eales
Staff: full-time, 108
Nationalities of staff: U.K., 15; host, 89; other, 4

Grade levels: K3/K4, P1 – P6, S1 – S5
Enrollment: K, 250; P1 – P6, 690; S1 – S5, 500; total, 1,440
Teacher/student ratio: 1/13
Tuition (annual): K, $2,400; P1 – P6, $3,555 – 3,975; S1 – S5, $6,210 – 6,780
Other fees: busing, approximately $280 per term
School year: September to July

Year founded: 1951. **Type of school:** coed, proprietary.

Curriculum/physical plant

Type: U.K. **Languages taught:** French, Malay. **Staff specialists:** reading, math, computer, nurse. **Extracurricular:** drama, gymnastics, yearbook, newspaper, excursions/expeditions, field trips, sports. **Tests:** O-level GCE (5th form/grade 11). **Graduates attending college:** 85%. **Facilities:** auditorium, cafeteria, gymnasium, playing field, science lab, computer lab, air conditioning.

THE INTERNATIONAL SCHOOL OF KUALA LUMPUR

Street address: Jalan Kerja Ayer Lama, 68000 Ampang, Malaysia
Phone: (60)(3)4560522   **Facsimile:** (60)(3)4579044
   Cable: INTERSCHOL
Mail: PO Box 12645, 50784 Kuala Lumpur, Malaysia
Headmaster: Richard T. Krajczar, Ed.D.
High school principal: F. Joseph Stucker
Middle school principal: George H. Robinson
Elementary school principal: James R. Rogers, Ph.D.
Business manager: Dixie Wai
Staff: full-time, 129; part-time, 10
Nationalities of staff: U.S., 101; U.K., 8; host, 7; other, 23
Grade levels: preP – 12
Enrollment: preP, 28; K, 62; 1 – 5, 502; 6 – 8, 319; 9 – 12, 483; total,
   1,394
Nationalities of student body: U.S., 365; U.K., 39; host, 128;
   other, 862
Teacher/student ratio: 1/10
Tuition (annual): K – 5, $6,000; 6 – 8, $6,400; 9 – 12, $6,700
Other fees (annual): registration*, $3,922; busing, $253 – 455;
   reenrollment, $784
School year: August to June

Year founded: 1965. **Type of school:** coed, day, private nonprofit.
Governed by: elected board of directors. **Accredited by:** Western.

Curriculum

Type: U.S., IB. **Languages taught:** French, Spanish, Malay. **Staff specialists:** reading, computer, speech/hearing, counselor, psychologist, learning disabilities, nurse. **Special programs:** ESL, advanced placement. **Special curricular:** art, chorus, band, physical education, computer instruction. **Extracurricular:** drama, gymnastics, dance, choral music, instrumental music, computers, yearbook, photography, excursions/expeditions, field trips, debate, Model UN. **Sports:** basketball, soccer, softball, swimming, tennis, track, volleyball, water polo, badminton, judo, Tae Kwon Do, Little League. **Clubs:** Brownies, Cub Scouts, Girl Scouts, National Honor Society, thespian. **Tests:** PSAT, SAT, ACT, TOEFL, AP, Iowa, Gates-MacGinitie. **Graduates attending college:** 95%. **Graduates have attended:** Sophia U. Japan, Texas A&M, Stanford, Tufts, Harvard.

Physical plant

Campuses (2): elementary school at Melawati; middle and high schools at Ampang. **Library:** 16,000 volumes at Melawati; 18,000 volumes at Ampang. **Facilities:** air-conditioned, carpeted classrooms, canteens, gymnasiums, sports fields, swimming pools, art, music, and computer instruction rooms. Ampang also has 8 science labs, dance room, 2 tennis courts.

*Once only fee

PENANG

DALAT SCHOOL

Street address: Tanjung Bunga, 11200 Penang, Malaysia
Phone: (60)(4)801197   **Facsimile:** (60)(4)802141
Director: Dwight Carlblom
Principal: Steve Livingston
Staff: full-time, 24; part-time, 6
Nationalities of staff: U.S., 28; other, 2
Grade levels: 1 – 12
Enrollment: 1 – 6, 47; 7 – 9, 66; 10 – 12, 79; total, 192
Nationalities of student body: U.S., 150; host, 9; other, 33
Capacity: 1 – 6, 60; 7 – 9, 80; 10 – 12, 100; total, 240
Teacher/student ratio: 1/7
Boarders: boys, 48; girls, 67   **Grades:** 1 – 12
   Program: planned 7-day
Tuition (annual): 1 – 6, $4,288; 7 – 12, $4,417
Other fees (annual): registration, $10; boarding, $4,417; capital levy, $600; lunch, $250/semester
School year: August to June

Year founded: 1928. **Type of school:** coed, day, boarding, church-related. **Governed by:** appointed advisory committee of missionary field chairmen. **Sponsored by:** Christian and Missionary Alliance. **Accredited by:** Western.

Curriculum

Type: U.S., college preparatory. **Languages taught:** French, Spanish, Malay. **Staff specialists:** reading, computer, counselor, psychologist, learning disabilities, nurse, chaplain. **Special programs:** advanced placement, honors sections, correspondence, remedial, learning lab. **Special curricular:** art, chorus, band, physical education, computer instruction, vocational, piano, yearbook, newspaper. **Extracurricular:** drama, gymnastics, choral music, instrumental music, computers, yearbook, newspaper, photography, excursions/expeditions, field trips. **Sports:** basketball, soccer, tennis, track, volleyball. **Clubs:** National Honor Society, chess, drama, ensemble, tennis. **Tests:** PSAT, SAT, AP, Iowa. **Graduates attending college:** 90%. **Graduates have attended:** Northwestern U., Wheaton College, Stanford U., Pepperdine U., Houghton College.

Physical plant
    Location: 6 miles from center of Georgetown, on north shore of Penang Island. **Campus:** 8 acres. **Library:** 12,000 volumes. **Facilities:** 27 buildings, 16 classrooms, auditorium, cafeteria, infirmary, tennis court, gymnasium, 2 playing fields, science lab, 2 computer labs, 6 dormitories, AV equipment, chapel, student center, air conditioning.

MALI _____

Region: Africa
Size: 478,764 square miles
Population: 8,338,000
Capital: Bamako

Telephone code: 223
Currency: franc
Languages: French,
                Bambara, Senufo

BAMAKO

AMERICAN INTERNATIONAL SCHOOL OF BAMAKO
    Phone: (223)224738   **Facsimile:** (223)228059   **Telex:** 972448
    Mail: BP 34, Bamako, Mali
    U.S. mail: c/o Bamako, Department of State, Washington, D.C.
        20521-2050
    Director: William Vodarski
    Staff: full-time, 9; part-time, 2
    Nationalities of staff: U.S., 8; other, 3
    Grade levels: preK – 8
    Enrollment: preK, 15; K, 10; 1 – 8, 55; total, 80
    Nationalities of student body: U.S., 35; other, 45
    Capacity: preK, 20; K, 20; 1 – 8, 120; total, 160
    Teacher/student ratio: 1/8
    Tuition (annual): preK, $1,750; K, $5,750; 1 – 8, $7,450
    Other fees (annual): registration, $250; transport, $925; capital
        development*, $750
    School year: September to June

    Year founded: 1977. **Type of school:** coed, day, private nonprofit.
Governed by: elected board of directors. **Accredited by:** Middle States.

Curriculum/physical plant

Type: U.S. **Languages taught:** French. **Special curricular:** art, physical education, computer instruction, music. **Extracurricular:** drama, yearbook, newspaper, field trips, Boy Scouts, Girl Scouts, Brownie Scouts, Cub Scouts, art club, French club. **Sports:** baseball, basketball, soccer, volleyball. **Tests:** Iowa. **Location:** in city. **Campus:** 2 acres. **Library:** 8,000 volumes. **Facilities:** playing field, science lab, computer lab, air conditioning.

*Once only fee

MALTA ─────────────────────────────────

Region: Europe	**Telephone code:** 356
Size: 122 square miles	**Currency:** lera
Population: 354,000	**Languages:** Maltese, English
Capital: Valletta	

ST. ANDREWS

Verdala International School

Street address: Fort Pembroke, St. Andrews, Malta
Phone: (356)332361/374285   **Facsimile:** (356)372387
Headmaster: William F. Russell, Ph.D.
High school coordinator: Kevin Black
Middle school coordinator: Cathy Marchmont
Elementary school coordinator: (to be announced)
Staff: full-time, 23; part-time, 3
Nationalities of staff: U.S., 7; U.K., 7; host, 8; other, 4
Grade levels: preK – 12
Enrollment: preK – K, 15; 1 – 6, 60; 7 – 9, 45; 10 – 12, 60; total, 180
Nationalities of student body: U.S., 28; U.K., 47; host, 49; other, 56
Capacity: K, 12; 1 – 6, 90; 7 – 9, 90; 10 – 12, 90; total, 282
Teacher/student ratio: 1/7
Boarders: boys, 10; girls, 5   **Grades:** 7 – 12
    Program: planned 7-day
Tuition (annual): K – 5, 1,350**; 6 – 8, 1,550; 9 – 12, 1,750
Other fees (annual): registration*, 300**; boarding, 1,750; busing, 60
School year: September to June

Year founded: 1976. **Type of school:** coed, day, boarding, private nonprofit. **Governed by:** appointed and elected board of directors.

Curriculum/physical plant

Type: U.S., U.K. **Languages taught:** English, French, Spanish, Italian. **Special programs:** ESL, advanced placement, remedial. **Special curricular:** art, physical education, computer instruction. **Extracurricular:** yearbook, newspaper, excursions/expeditions, field trips. **Sports:** basketball, soccer, volleyball. **Tests:** PSAT, SAT, ACT, TOEFL, AP, Iowa, IGCSE. **Graduates attending college:** 75%. **Graduates have attended:** Regents College, Pennsylvania State, Simon Fraser, U. of Waterloo, Colorado State. **Location:** in ex-fort (with moat) in quiet residential area. **Campus:** 6 acres. **Library:** 5,000 volumes. **Facilities:** 9 buildings, 21 classrooms, auditorium, cafeteria, playing field, 3 science labs, computer lab, self-contained apartments with resident and daily supervisors, access to swimming pool, tennis courts, gymnasium.

*Once only fee   **Maltese (lera)

COTTONERA
St. Edward's College
>   **Address:** Cottonera, Malta
>   **Phone:** (356)825978   **Facsimile:** (356)681557
>   **Headmaster:** G. Briscoe

MARSHALL ISLANDS _____

Region: South Pacific
Size: 70 square miles
Population: 49,000
Capital: Majuro

Telephone code: 692
Currency: U.S. dollar
Languages: English, Japanese,
Marshallese

KWAJALEIN

KWAJALEIN SCHOOL SYSTEM

Phone: (1)(805)2387994 ext. 3761   **Facsimile:** (1)(805)2387994 ext.
1787 (Attention: Kwajalein School System)
U.S. facsimile: (205)7213769
U.S. mail: (no personal name), Kwajalein School System, Box 51,
APO AP 96555-2650
Superintendent: Ted R. Williams, Ph.D.
Junior/senior high principal: Mike Gaul
Elementary principal: Karen Amman
Head of library: Marie Overman
Head of computer services (high school): Vern Curtis
Head of computer services (elementary school): Carol Hockenberger
Staff: full-time, 58; part-time, 1
Nationalities of staff: U.S., 59
Grade levels: preK – 12
Enrollment: preK, 81; K, 54; 1 – 6, 276; 7 – 9, 108; 10 – 12, 91;
total, 610
Nationalities of student body: U.S., 570; host, 40
Teacher/student ratio: 1/10
Tuition (annual): K – 12, varies up to $5,200
School year: August to June

Year founded: 1950. **Type of school:** coed, day, company sponsored.
Governed by: U.S. government/Johnson Controls World Services, Inc.,
contractor. **Accredited by:** North Central (elementary and secondary).

Curriculum/physical plant
Type: U.S. **Languages taught:** French, Spanish. **Staff specialists:**
counselor. **Special curricular:** art, chorus, band, physical education, computer instruction, typing, accounting. **Extracurricular:** choral music, instrumental music, yearbook, newspaper, photography, student government.
Sports: basketball, soccer, softball, tennis, volleyball, water skiing, fishing,
water polo. **Tests:** PSAT, SAT, ACT, TOEFL, AP, Iowa, ERB, ASVAB. **Graduates have attended:** Stanford, Harvard, Brown, MIT, Baylor. **Location:** on
island, 2,100 miles southwest of Honolulu.   **Library:** 17,000 volumes.
Facilities: 8 buildings, 42 classrooms, auditorium, 2 tennis courts, gymnasium, 2 playing fields, 2 science labs, 2 computer labs, 2 swimming pools, air
conditioning.

MAJURO

MAJURO COOPERATIVE SCHOOL

Phone: (692)(9)6253144   **Facsimile:** (692)(9)6253719
Mail: PO Box 81, Majuro, Marshall Islands 96960
Principal: Frank Cabral
Staff: full-time, 12
Grade levels: preK – 8
Enrollment: total, 250
Teacher/student ratio: 1/21
Tuition: $100 per month
Other fees: registration, $50
School year: August to June

Year founded: 1975. **Type of school:** elementary, nonsectarian. **Governed by:** 7-member board composed of parents. **Accredited by:** Western (candidate).

Curriculum/physical plant
Type: U.S. **Languages taught:** Marshallese. **Tests:** SATB. **Graduates have attended:** schools in Guam, Hawaii, continental U.S. **Location:** Delap, Majuro, Marshall Islands. **Facilities:** computer lab, library, AV room, playing fields with limited sports/playground equipment.

MAURITANIA _____

Region: West Africa
Size: 397,954 square miles
Population: 1,995,000
Capital: Nouakchott

Telephone code: 222
Currency: ouguiya
Languages: French, Hassanya
                Arabic, Arabic

NOUAKCHOTT

AMERICAN INTERNATIONAL SCHOOL
OF NOUAKCHOTT

Phone: (222)252967   **Facsimile:** (222)251592   **Telex:** 93555 MTN
        Cable: c/o American Embassy Nouakchott
Mail: BP 222, Nouakchott, Mauritania
U.S. mail: c/o American Embassy Nouakchott, Department of State, Washington, D.C. 20521-2430
School administrator: Robert W. Harper
Business manager: Fimelita R. Celiz
Staff: full-time, 3; part-time, 3
Nationalities of staff: U.S., 3; other, 3

Grade levels: preK – 8
Enrollment: preK, 6; K – 8, 20; total, 26
Nationalities of student body: U.S., 3; other, 23
Capacity: preK, 15; K, 15; 1 – 6, 30; 7 – 8, 15; total, 75
Teacher/student ratio: 1/5
Tuition (annual): preK, $1,100; K – 8, $9,000
School year: September to June

Year founded: 1978. **Type of school:** coed, day. **Governed by:** elected board of directors. **Sponsored by:** AISN Association.

Curriculum/physical plant
Type: U.S. **Languages taught:** French. **Special programs:** ESL. **Special curricular:** art, physical education, computer instruction, music, video, Mauritania studies, hands-on learning. **Extracurricular:** field trips, community service. **Sports:** soccer, swimming, tennis, volleyball. **Clubs:** computer, cooking, drama. **Tests:** Iowa. **Location:** on U.S. Embassy compound. **Campus:** 1 acre. **Library:** 6,000 volumes. **Facilities:** 2 buildings, 7 classrooms, infirmary, covered play area, tennis court, science lab, swimming pool, children's museum, all-purpose room, kitchen and cooking facilities, air conditioning.

MAURITIUS _____

Region: Indian Ocean
Size: 790 square miles
Population: 1,081,900
Capital: Port Louis

Telephone code: 230
Currency: rupee
Languages: English, French, Creole, Bhojpuri

MOKA

LE BOCAGE HIGH SCHOOL
Street address: Montagne Ory, Moka, Mauritius
Phone/facsimile: (230)4334914
Headmaster: Ian J. Gulliford, Ph.D.
Staff: full-time, 26; part-time, 1
Nationalities of staff: U.S., 1; host, 22; other, 4
Grade levels: 7 – 11†
Enrollment: total, 360
Nationalities of student body: 20 nationalities including host
Capacity: total, 360
Teacher/student ratio: 1/13
Tuition (annual): 7 – 11, 51,600**
Other fees: busing, 350**/month; book deposit, 1,200; admission,
     1,000

School year: January through November

Year founded: 1990. **Type of school:** coed, day, private nonprofit. **Governed by:** board of directors. **Sponsored by:** Mauritian business sector.

Curriculum/physical plant
Type: U.K. **Languages taught:** French, Spanish. **Staff specialists:** reading, math, computer, learning disabilities, music, physical education, fine arts. **Special programs:** ESL, remedial. **Special curricular:** art, chorus, band, physical education, computer instruction. **Extracurricular:** drama, dance, choral music, instrumental music, computers, newspaper, literary magazine, photography, excursions/expeditions, field trips, sports. **Clubs:** photography, math, nature, video, cooking. **Tests:** Iowa, modified ITBS. **Location:** on rural mountainside, overlooking the sea. **Campus:** 8 acres. **Facilities:** 3 buildings, 17 classrooms, cafeteria, infirmary, covered play area, 2 playing fields, 2 science labs, 2 computer labs, library, home economics lab.

**Mauritian rupee   †increasing to grades 12 – 13 by 1995

MEXICO ————————————————

Region: North America
Size: 761,604 square miles
Population: 90,007,000
Capital: Mexico City

Telephone code: 52
Currency: peso
Language: Spanish, Ameridian
languages

DURANGO

Colegio Americano de Durango, A.C.
Street address: Francisco Sarabia No. 416 Pte., Durango, Mexico
Phone: (52)(181)33636   **Facsimile:** (52)(181)12839
Mail: Apartado Postal No. 495, Durango, Mexico 34000
Director: Patrick J. Sweeney
High school/junior high coordinator: Maria Elsa Mier
Elementary school coordinator: Nancy Gilmore
Business manager: Alberto Bustamante
Staff: full-time, 46; part-time, 8
Nationalities of staff: U.S., 12; host, 41; other, 1
Grade levels: preK – 12
Enrollment: K, 113; 1 – 6, 287; 7 – 9, 125; 10 – 12, 78; total, 603
Capacity: K, 120; 1 – 6, 300; 7 – 9, 150; 10 – 12, 80; total, 650
Teacher/student ratio: 1/12
Tuition (annual): K, $1,072; 1 – 6, $1,537; 7 – 9, $1,931;
10 – 12, $2,081
Other fees: family*, $312; registration, $154; insurance, busing,$375;
books, $80

School year: September to June

Year founded: 1954. **Type of school:** coed, day, private nonprofit. **Governed by:** appointed board of directors. **Accredited by:** Mexican state government, Southern (in process).

Curriculum/physical plant

Type: U.S., Mexican. **Languages of instruction:** English, Spanish. **Languages taught:** English, Spanish. **Staff specialists:** computer, counselor, psychologist, art. **Special programs:** ESL. **Special curricular:** art, chorus, band, physical education, computer instruction, vocational. **Extracurricular:** drama, gymnastics, dance, choral music, instrumental music, computers, yearbook, newspaper, photography, excursions/expeditions. **Sports:** basketball, soccer, track and field, volleyball. **Tests:** Iowa. **Graduates attending college:** 90%. **Graduates have attended:** Stanford, UCLA, Arizona State, Texas A&M, Technologico de Monterrey. **Location:** in the mountain-valley city of Durango. **Campus:** 2 acres. **Library:** 10,500 volumes. **Facilities:** 6 buildings, 27 classrooms, playing field, science lab, computer lab, soccer field, basketball/volleyball courts, vocational equipment. New campus under construction.

*Once only fee

GUADALAJARA

THE AMERICAN SCHOOL FOUNDATION
OF GUADALAJARA

Street address: Colomos 2100, Guadalajara, Jalisco, Mexico
Phone: (52)(3)6413300   **Facsimile:** (52)(3)6412954
Mail: Apartado 6-280, Guadalajara, Jalisco, Mexico
Director general: Charles E. Prince
High school principal: Soledad Avalos
Middle school principal: Stephen Herrera
Primary school principal: Melody Martin del Campo
Assistant principal: Sheree Nuncio
Staff: full-time, 114; part-time, 1
Nationalities of staff: U.S., 60; host, 47; other, 8
Grade levels: preK – 12
Enrollment: preK, 101; K, 100; 1 – 6, 731; 7 – 9, 265; 10 – 12, 180; total, 1,377
Nationalities of student body: U.S., 158; host, 1,180; other, 39
Capacity: preK, 90; K, 90; 1 – 6, 780; 7 – 9, 300; 10 – 12, 200; total, 1,460
Teacher/student ratio: 1/12
Tuition (annual): preK – K, $1,608; 1 – 6, $2,294; 7 – 9, $2,680; 10 – 12, $2,914
Other fees (annual): registration, $1,412; books, $98
School year: September to June

Year founded: 1956. **Type of school:** coed, day, private nonprofit. **Governed and sponsored by:** board of directors. **Accredited by:** Southern.

Curriculum

Type: U.S. **Languages taught:** English, French, Spanish. **Staff specialists:** reading, math, computer, counselor, psychologist, doctor. **Special programs:** ESL, advanced placement, honors sections, independent study, correspondence, remedial. **Special curricular:** art, chorus, band, physical education, computer instruction. **Extracurricular:** drama, choral music, instrumental music, computers, yearbook, newspaper, literary magazine, photography, excursions/expeditions, field trips. **Sports:** basketball, swimming, volleyball, track and field. **Clubs:** photography, chorus, drama, art, math, science, computers, yearbook, school paper, cheerleaders. **Tests:** PSAT, SAT, ACT, TOEFL. **Graduates attending college:** 97%. **Graduates have attended:** Wellesley, Trinity, Hofstra, Brown, Princeton.

Physical plant

Location: in city. **Campus:** 5 acres. **Library:** 28,000 volumes. **Facilities:** 70 classrooms, auditorium, infirmary, gymnasium, 2 playing fields, 3 science labs, 3 computer labs, swimming pool, weight room.

MEXICO CITY

AMERICAN SCHOOL FOUNDATION, A.C.

Street address: Bondojito 215, Mexico, DF 01120, Mexico
Phone: (52)(5)2274900   **Facsimile:** (52)(5)2734357
Superintendent: (to be announced)
High school principal: James Curlett
Middle school principal: Susan Mancera
Elementary principal: Janet Cruz
Kindergarten principal: Lucia Lukac
Head of computer services: Alfonso Wilson
Staff: full-time, 169
Nationalities of staff: U.S., 86; U.K., 1; host, 73; other, 9
Grade levels: K – 12
Enrollment: K – pre/1, 337; 1 – 5, 809; 6 – 8, 539; 9 – 12, 700;
    total, 2,385
Teacher/student ratio: 1/14
Tuition (annual): K – pre/1, $3,822; 1 – 5, $5,208; 6 – 12, $6,516
Other fees: registration (twice a year), one month's fees; busing, $920;
    admission*, twice first month's tuition
School year: September to June

Year founded: 1888. **Type of school:** coed, day, private nonprofit. **Governed by:** elected board of directors. **Accredited by:** Southern. **Regional organizations:** ASOMEX (Joint Association).

Curriculum

Type: U.S., Mexican. **Languages of instruction:** English, Spanish. **Languages taught:** French, Italian. **Staff specialists:** computer, counselor, psychologist, learning disabilities, nurse. **Special programs:** ESL, advanced placement, honors sections. **Special curricular:** art, chorus, band, physical education, computer instruction. **Extracurricular:** drama, dance, choral music, computers, yearbook, newspaper, literary magazine, photography, excursions/expeditions, field trips, writing conferences, American Legion oratorio, Art and Science Expositions, Art Festival, Foreign Language Week, Special Olympics. **Sports:** baseball, football, soccer, swimming, tennis, track. **Clubs:** cheerleaders, French, student council, Italian, Japanese, drama, Project Lead, Bear Boosters, Harvard UN, class officers, "Solidaridad Internacional Juvenil," honor society, presidential classroom. **Tests:** SSAT, PSAT, SAT, ACT, TOEFL. **Graduates attending college:** 95%. **Graduates have attended:** U. of Texas at Austin, Stanford, U. of Pennsylvania, Brigham Young U., U. of Southern California.

Physical plant

Location: in Mexico City, set on extensive lawn area. **Campus:** 17 acres. **Library:** 39,000 volumes. **Facilities:** 4 buildings, 124 classrooms, auditorium, infirmary, 4 tennis courts, gymnasium, 3 science labs, 6 computer labs, 2 snack bars, 2 multipurpose buildings, playing fields, covered swimming pool.

*Once only fee

COLEGIO PETERSON

Street addresses: Rocio 142, Colonia Pedregal de San Angel, Mexico City, D.F. Mexico (K – 6); Huizachitos 80, Colonia Vista Hermosa, Mexico City, D.F. Mexico (K – 12); Montes Himalaya 615, Colonia Lomas de Chap., Mexico City, D.F. Mexico (K)
Phone: (52)(5)5683139/5202213/8130114
   Facsimile: (52)(5)5404215
Mail: Apartado Postal 10-900, Mexico, DF 11000, Mexico
Superintendent: Marvin Peterson, Ph.D.
Assistant superintendents: Helen Peterson, Nancy Peterson
Business manager/assistant superintendent: Kenneth Peterson
Staff: full-time, 100; part-time, 20
Nationalities of staff: host, 90; other, 30
Grade levels: K – 12
Enrollment: K, 350; 1 – 6, 450; 7 – 9, 100; 10 – 12, 100; total, 1,000
Nationalities of student body: host, 750; other, 250
Capacity: K, 350; 1 – 6, 600; 7 – 9, 150; 10 – 12, 150; total, 1,250
Teacher/student ratio: 1/9
Tuition (annual): K, $2,000; 1 – 6, $3,000; 7 – 9, $3,800;
   10 – 12, $4,100
Other fees: capital levy*, $500
School year: September to June

Year founded: 1965. **Type of school:** coed, day, proprietary. **Accredited by:** Mexican government, Southern (in process).

Curriculum/physical plant

Type: U.S., Mexican. **Languages of instruction:** English, Spanish. **Languages taught:** French. **Staff specialists:** reading, math, computer, counselor, psychologist, physician. **Special programs:** ESL, advanced placement, independent study. **Special curricular:** art, physical education, computer instruction, vocational. **Extracurricular:** drama, computers, yearbook, newspaper, excursions/expeditions, field trips, honor society. **Sports:** basketball, soccer, track, volleyball, ping-pong, archery. **Tests:** PSAT, SAT, Stanford. **Graduates attending college:** over 95%. **Graduates have attended:** Instituto Tecnológico de Monterrey, Stanford, Rice, U. Ibero Americano. **Location:** on quiet street on west side of Mexico City, above the smog. **Campuses (3):** 5 acres. **Library:** 14,000 volumes. **Facilities:** 5 buildings, 70 classrooms, cafeteria, infirmary, tennis court, science lab, computer lab, playing fields.

1992 – 93 listing

*Once only fee

GREENGATES SCHOOL

Street address: Circumvalacion Poniente 102, Balcones de San Mateo, Naucalpan, Mexico
Phone: (52)(5)3730088/3730099   **Facsimile:** (52)(5)3604120
Mail: Apartado Postal 41-659, 11000 Mexico DF, Mexico
Principal: Susan Mayer
Head of primary school: Michael Ward
Staff: full-time, 70; part-time, 5
Nationalities of staff: U.S., 8; U.K., 44; host, 15; other, 8
Grade levels: K – 12
Enrollment: K – preP, 90; 1 – 6, 430; 7 – 9, 250; 10 – 12 200; total, 970
Nationalities of student body: U.S., 180; U.K., 90; host, 360; other, 340
Capacity: total, 970
Teacher/student ratio: 1/13
Tuition (annual): $4,000 – 6,000
Other fees (annual): busing, $130/month; books, $200
School year: September to June

Year founded: 1951. **Type of school:** coed, day, private nonprofit.

Curriculum/physical plant

Type: U.K., IB. **Languages taught:** French, Spanish. **Staff specialists:** reading, math, computer, counselor, psychologist, nurse. **Special curricular:** art, band, physical education, computer instruction. **Extracurricular:** drama, gymnastics, instrumental music, computers, yearbook, literary magazine, photography, excursions/expeditions, field trips. **Sports:** basketball, hockey, rugby, swimming, volleyball, badminton, athletics. **Tests:** PSAT, SAT, ACT, TOEFL, IB, GCSE. **Graduates attending college:** 100%. **Graduates have attended:** MIT, Yale, Brandeis. **Location:** on outskirts of Mexico City. **Library:** 10,000 volumes. **Facilities:** 6 buildings, 38 classrooms, auditorium, cafeteria, infirmary, gymnasium, playing field, 6 science labs, 3 computer labs, swimming pool.

MONTERREY

AMERICAN SCHOOL FOUNDATION OF MONTERREY, A.C.

Street address: Missouri 555 Ote., Col. del Valle, Garza García, Nuevo Leon, Mexico
Phone: (52)(83)353181/354850   **Facsimile:** (52)(83)782535
Mail: Apartado Postal 1762, Monterrey, NL 64000, Mexico
Superintendent: Donald Wise, Ph.D.
High school principal: D. Jeffrey Keller
Elementary school principal: Sonia Keller
Business manager: Arturo Anzaldua
Staff: full-time, 98; part-time, 23
Nationalities of staff: U.S., 41; host, 65; other, 15
Grade levels: N – 12
Enrollment: N – preK, 240; K, 120; 1 – 6, 740; 7 – 9, 360; 10 – 12, 49; total, 1,509
Nationalities of student body: U.S., 246; host, 1,208; other, 55
Capacity: total, 1,500
Teacher/student ratio: 1/14
Tuition (annual): N – K, $2,250; 1 – 2, $2,595; 3 – 4, $3,050; 5 – 6, $3,250; 7 – 9, $3,505; 10 – 12, $4,000; Bach I – II, $4,000
Other fees (annual): registration, $300; maintenance, $420 – 840; equipment, $310; contribution*, $3,500
School year: September to June

Year founded: 1928. **Type of school:** coed, day. **Governed by:** appointed board members. **Sponsored by:** 16 U.S. corporations. **Accredited by:** Southern, state educational authorities.

Curriculum
Type: U.S., Mexican. **Languages of instruction:** English, Spanish. **Languages taught:** Spanish. **Staff specialists:** reading, counselor, learning disabilities, nurse, psychometrist. **Special curricular:** art, chorus, physical education, computer instruction, drama. **Extracurricular:** computers, yearbook, newspaper. **Sports:** basketball, soccer, softball, track, volleyball. **Clubs:** National Honor Society, senior and junior student councils, Junior National Honor Society, drama, science, computer, German, environmental. **Tests:**

SSAT, PSAT, SAT, ACT, AP, Iowa, CTBS. **Graduates attending college:** 98%. **Graduates have attended:** U. de Nuevo León, Southern Methodist U., U. of Texas, Cornell, MIT.

Physical plant
    Location: in suburban Monterrey. **Campus:** 8.5 acres. **Library:** 20,000 volumes. **Facilities:** 3 buildings, 72 classrooms, auditorium, cafeteria, infirmary, 2 tennis courts, gymnasium, 4 playing fields, 4 science labs, 2 computer labs, partial air conditioning, AV equipment.

*Once only fee

Colegio Ingles

Street address: Real San Agustín #100 – San Agustín Campestre,
    Garza García, Nuevo León, Mexico
Phone: (52)(83)631117/631717/631202   **Facsimile:** (52)(83)631985
Mail: Apartado Postal 585, Col. del Valle, Garza García, N.L., Mexico
U.S. mail: 422 Rio Grande Drive, Mission, Texas 78572-7420, U.S.A.
Principal: Norma Guerra
Principal, elementary: Alejandra Tapia
Principal, preschool: Patricia Navarro
Business manager: Leticia Montemayor
Staff: full-time, 89; part-time, 6
Grade levels: K – 9
Enrollment: K, 359; 1 – 6, 683; 7 – 9, 235; total, 1,277
Teacher/student ratio: 1/14
Tuition (annual): K, 9,900**; 1 – 6, 12,000; 7 – 9, 14,940
Other fees (annual): registration*, 1,400**; books: preschool, 450,
    elementary, 650, junior high, 900, parents' association, 45;
    scholarship fund*
School year: September to June

Year founded: 1971. **Type of school:** coed, day, private nonprofit. **Accredited by:** National Secretariat of Education.

Curriculum/physical plant
    Type: Mexican, bilingual. **Languages of instruction:** English, Spanish. **Staff specialists:** psychologist, learning disabilities, nurse. **Special programs:** remedial. **Special curricular:** art, physical education. **Extracurricular:** gymnastics, computers, yearbook, excursions/expeditions, field trips. **Sports:** basketball, soccer, track and field. **Graduates attending college:** 100%. **Graduates have attended:** Instituto Technologico de Monterrey, U. de Monterrey. **Location:** near the foot of surrounding mountains in lush, green area, 8 kilometers from Monterrey. **Campus:** 7 acres. **Library:** 4,000 volumes. **Facilities:** 2 buildings, 49 classrooms, infirmary, 4 playing fields, 2 science labs, 2 computer labs,

*Once only fee   **Mexican peso

PAN AMERICAN SCHOOL

Street address: Hidalgo 656 Pte., Monterrey, N.L., Mexico 64000
Phone: (52)(83)420778   **Facsimile:** (52)(83)423624
Mail: Apartado Postal 474, Monterrey, N.L., Mexico 64000
Directors: L. H. Arpee, Laura Arpee
Assistant director: Robert L. Arpee
Academic supervisor: Leonor Fernandez
Secondary school principal: Hermelinda Coronado
Upper primary school principal: Delia Gonzalez
Lower primary school principal: Teresa Perez
Spanish supervisor: Vidimara Garza
Staff: full-time, 120
Nationalities of staff: U.S., 23; host, 97
Grade levels: preschool (3 years) – 9, 2-year commercial
Enrollment: total, 2,400
Capacity: preK, 832; 1 – 6, 1,323; 7 – 9, 467; commercial, 29;
    total, 2,651
Teacher/student ratio: 1/20
Tuition: (contact school for current rates)
School year: September to June

Year founded: 1952. **Type of school:** coed, day, private nonprofit.
Governed by: board of directors. **Accredited by:** federal government.

Curriculum/physical plant

Type: U.S., Mexican. **Languages taught:** English, Spanish. **Staff specialists:** math, counselor, psychologist, nurse. **Special curricular:** physical education, computer instruction. **Extracurricular:** gymnastics, choral music. **Graduates attending college:** 100%. **Graduates have attended:** U. of Texas, U. de Nuevo Leon, Instituto Tecnologico, U. de Monterrey, U. of Chicago. **Location:** on fringe of downtown Monterrey. **Facilities:** 5 buildings, covered play area, playing field, science lab, computer lab, air conditioning. **Future campus:** 10-acre campus under construction: 30 classrooms for preschool, 80 classrooms for primary and secondary, gymnasium-auditorium, library, cafeteria, infirmary, 2 multipurpose tennis courts, swimming pool, playing fields, 4 computer labs, 4 science labs, conference rooms, covered playground area, partial air conditioning.

PACHUCA

American School of Pachuca

Street address: Boulevard Valle de San Javier S/N, Pachuca, Hidalgo, Mexico
Phone: (52)(771)39608/31058   **Facsimile:** (52)(771)39608
Mail: Apartado Postal 131, Pachuca, Hgo. 42000 Mexico
General director: James H. Douglass
Principals: Martha Cipres, Esthela Olvera, Niceforo Ramírez
Business manager: Raul Padilla
Staff: full-time, 64; part-time, 11
Nationalities of staff: U.S., 9; host, 65; other, 1
Grade levels: preK – 9
Enrollment: preK, 13; K, 24; preP, 45; 1 – 6, 275; 7 – 9, 127; total, 484
Nationalities of student body: U.S., 3; host, 481
Capacity: preK, 50; K, 50; 1 – 6, 360; 7 – 9, 180; total, 640
Teacher/student ratio: 1/7
Tuition (annual): preK, 3,000**; 1 – 6, 3,480; 7 – 9, 5,400
Other fees: pre-registration*: preK, 250**; 1 – 6, 290; 7 – 9, 450
School year: September to June

Year founded: 1889. **Type of school:** coed, day. **Governed by:** elected board.

Curriculum/physical plant

Type: U.S., Mexican. **Languages of instruction:** English, Spanish. **Languages taught:** English, Spanish. **Staff specialists:** reading, computer. **Special curricular:** physical education, computer instruction. **Extracurricular:** computers, field trips. **Sports:** basketball, soccer, track, volleyball. **Location:** in Pachuca. **Campus:** 20,000 square meters. **Facilities:** 6 buildings, 24 classrooms, science lab, computer lab, library, playing fields.

*Once only fee   **Mexican peso

PUERTO VALLARTA

The American School of Puerto Vallarta

Street address: Km. 7.5 Carretera Aeropuerto, Puerto Vallarta, Jalisco, Mexico
Phone: (52)(322)11125
Mail: Apartado Postal 275-B, Puerto Vallarta, Jalisco, Mexico
Superintendent: Gerald Selitzer
Upper school coordinator: Deborah Brayton
Lower school coordinator: Guadalupe Gonzalez

Staff: full-time, 28; part-time, 2
Nationalities of staff: U.S., 12; host, 13; other, 5
Grade levels: preK – 12
Enrollment: preK, 15; K, 17; pre-1, 21; 1 – 6, 129; 7 – 9, 72;
 10 – 12, 43; total, 297
Nationalities of student body: U.S., 58; host, 222; other, 17
Capacity: preK, 18; K, 18; pre-1, 18; 1 – 6, 120; 7 – 9, 90; 10 – 12, 90;
 total, 354
Teacher/student ratio: 1/10
Tuition (annual): preK – K, $2,664; pre-1, $2,784; 1 – 6, $2,916;
 7 – 9, $3,072; 10 – 12, $3,144
Other fees (annual): registration: preK, $300; K, $400; pre-1 – 12,
 $900; capital levy*: pre-1 – 6, $375; junior high, $575; high
 school, $675
School year: September to June

Year founded: 1986. **Type of school:** coed, day, private nonprofit.
Governed by: appointed board. **Accredited by:** Southern, Mexican Ministry
of Education.

Curriculum/physical plant

Type: U.S. **Languages of instruction:** English, Spanish. **Languages
taught:** English, Spanish. **Special programs:** ESL, SSL. **Special curricular:**
art, computer instruction, music. **Extracurricular:** drama, computers, yearbook, excursions/expeditions, Interact club, student council, National Honor
Society. **Sports:** baseball, soccer, tennis, volleyball, scuba diving. **Tests:**
CTBS. **Graduates have attended:** Monterrey Tech, U. of New Mexico, Central
Washington U., Instituto de Estudios Superiores del Oriente, Savannah Art
and Design School. **Location:** in tropical beach resort, 2 kilometers from
Puerto Vallarta. **Campus:** 5 acres. **Facilities:** 3 buildings, science lab,
computer lab, media learning center.

*Once only fee

QUERÉTARO

JOHN F. KENNEDY SCHOOL, A.C.

Street address: Av. Sabinos 272, Jurica, Querétaro, Mexico
Phone: (52)(42)180075/180400   **Facsimile:** (52)(42)181784
Mail: Apartado Postal 93, Querétaro, Qro. 76000, Mexico
U.S. mail: c/o Cahm Star Forwarding Agency, 8535 San Gabriel Drive,
 Laredo, TX 78041, U.S.A.
Director: Dr. Francisco Galicia
High school director: Dr. Guadalupe Alvarez
Junior high school director: Marta Pinet
Primary director: Blanca Iglesias de Raymond
Kindergarten director: Cristina Franco

Director of staff: Jay Phelps
Accountant: Martha Ramírez
Staff: full-time, 47; part-time, 40
Nationalities of staff: U.S., 11; host, 73; other, 3
Grade levels: K – 12
Enrollment: K – 6, 644; 7 – 9, 169; 10 – 12, 67; total, 880
Nationalities of student body: U.S., 38; host, 825; other, 17
Teacher/student ratio: 1/13
Tuition (annual): K, $1,444; primary, $1,747; junior high school, $2,100; high school, $2,475
Other fees: registration: K, $241; primary, $291; junior high school, $350; high school, $412; admission*: K, $1,250; primary, $1,172; junior high school, $1,094; high school, $937
School year: September to June

Year founded: 1964. **Type of school:** coed, day, private nonprofit. **Governed by:** board of directors. **Accredited by:** Southern, Mexican Ministry of Education.

Curriculum/physical plant

Type: U.S., Mexican. **Languages of instruction:** English, Spanish. **Languages taught:** English, Spanish. **Staff specialists:** reading, computer, counselor, psychologist, nurse, photography, automotive mechanics. **Special programs:** ESL. **Special curricular:** art, physical education, computer instruction, music. **Sports:** basketball, soccer, volleyball, track and field. **Graduates have attended:** Instituto Tecnológico y de Estudios Superiores de Monterrey, U. Autónoma de Querétaro. **Location:** within a country residential area, 13 kilometers from Querétaro. **Campus:** 12 acres. **Library:** 12,000 volumes. **Facilities:** 14 buildings, 38 classrooms, cafeteria, 3 playing fields, science lab, 2 computer labs, reading lab, 2 AV rooms.

*Once only fee

TAMPICO

Escuela Americana de Tampico, A.C.

Street address: Hidalgo S/N, Col. Tancol, Tampico, Tamaulipas, Mexico
Phone: (52)(12)143230   **Facsimile:** (52)(12)126046
Mail: Apartado 407, Tampico, Tam., Mexico
Director: Jorge Correa
Principal: Emma Gutierrez
Director, secondary: Juana Campoy
Director, elementary: Elsa Paredes
Business manager: Sandra Treviño
Staff: full-time, 50; part-time, 2
Nationalities of staff: U.S., 2; host, 43; other, 7
Grade levels: preK – 11

Enrollment: preK, 84; K, 83; 1 – 6, 354; 7 – 9, 129; 10 – 11, 35; total, 685
Nationalities of student body: U.S., 6; host, 679
Capacity: preK, 84; K, 84; 1 – 6, 400; 7 – 9, 150; 10 – 11, 50; total, 768
Teacher/student ratio: 1/13
Tuition (annual): preK – K, $2,215; 1 – 6, $2,370; 7 – 9, $2,635; 10 – 11, $2,800
Other fees (annual): registration, $492; books, $100; admission*, $1,575
School year: September to June

Year founded: 1917. **Type of school:** coed, day, private nonprofit. **Governed by:** appointed board of directors. **Accredited by:** Southern (in process).

Curriculum/physical plant
Type: U.S. **Languages taught:** English, Spanish. **Staff specialists:** counselor, psychologist, nurse, librarian. **Special programs:** accelerated science. **Extracurricular:** gymnastics, yearbook, newspaper, literary magazine. **Sports:** baseball, basketball, soccer, volleyball. **Clubs:** student council, book club. **Tests:** SSAT, CTBS. **Location:** port with river, lagoons, beach, business, and agriculture; 15 kilometers from downtown Tampico. **Campus:** 25 acres. **Library:** 7,000 volumes. **Facilities:** 6 buildings, 34 classrooms, infirmary, 3 playing fields, science lab, computer lab, music room, air conditioning.

*Once only fee

TORREON

COLEGIO AMERICANO DE TORREON, A.C.
Street address: Ave. Mayran y Nogal, Col. Torreon Jardin 27200, Torreon, Coahuila, Mexico
Phone: (52)(17)135389   **Facsimile:** (52)(17)135389
Director general: John J. Ketterer
High school principal: Ralph Navarre
Assistant high school principal: Jeff C. Fraser
Elementary principal: Naomi Engstrom
Assistant elementary principal: Ma. del Socorro F. de Obregón
Curriculum coordinator: Richard A. Ramsey
Staff: full-time, 84
Nationalities of staff: U.S., 31; host, 51; other, 2
Grade levels: preK – 12
Enrollment: total, 1,102
Nationalities of student body: U.S., 36; host, 1,057; other, 9
Capacity: preK, 100; K, 100; 1 – 6, 660; 7 – 9, 300; 10 – 12, 150; total, 1,310

Teacher/student ratio: 1/13
Tuition (annual): preK, $1,241; K, $1,419; 1 – 6, $2,157; 7 – 9,
$2,622; 10 – 12, $3,016
Other fees (annual): registration, $1,000 (new student), $330 (return-
ing student); busing, $150; insurance, $25
School year: August to June

Year founded: 1950. **Type of school:** day, private nonprofit. **Governed
by:** elected board of directors. **Accredited by:** Southern.

Curriculum/physical plant

Type: U.S., Mexican. **Languages of instruction:** English, Spanish. **Staff
specialists:** counselor, psychologist, doctor. **Special programs:** ESL. **Special
curricular:** art, chorus, physical education, computer instruction. **Extracurricular:** drama, gymnastics, dance. **Sports:** basketball, soccer, tennis, volleyball. **Tests:** PSAT, SAT, ACT, Stanford, CTBS. **Graduates attending college:**
98%. **Graduates have attended:** U. of Utah, U. of Washington, U. of Arizona,
U. of Illinois, Rice. **Location:** in city. **Campus:** 5 acres. **Library:** 10,000
volumes. **Facilities:** auditorium, cafeteria, infirmary, 2 tennis courts, gymnasium, playing field, 2 science labs, 2 computer labs, swimming pool, air
conditioning.

MOROCCO _____

Region: Northwest Africa
Size: 172,413 square miles
Population: 26,181,000
Capital: Rabat

Telephone code: 212
Currency: dirham
Languages: Arabic, Berber

CASABLANCA

CASABLANCA AMERICAN SCHOOL

Street address: Route de La Mecque, Lot. Ougoug, Qtr. Californie,
   21400 Casablanca, Morocco
Phone: (212)(2)212488/214115/211416   **Facsimile:** (212)(2)260259
   Telex: 93345941 CAS M
U.S. mail: Casablanca American School, PSC 74 Box 024, APO AE 09718
Director: John J. Randolph
Deputy director/IB coordinator: Anne Osman
Lower school principal: Kim Aba
Business manager: Saad Guessous
Staff: full-time, 41; part-time, 11
Nationalities of staff: U.S., 32; U.K., 2; host, 12; other, 6
Grade levels: N – 12
Enrollment: N – 20; K, 41; pre-1, 44; 1 – 6, 192; 7 – 9, 51; 10 – 12,
   33; total, 381
Nationalities of student body: U.S., 62; U.K., 10; host, 166; other,
   143
Capacity: total, 500
Teacher/student ratio: 1/8
Tuition (annual): N – K, $1,719; pre-1, $3,850; 1 – 5, $4,525; 6 – 8,
   $4,812; 9 – 12, $6,187
Other fees (annual): registration, $63; admission*, $575; application*,
   $63; sports, $81; building, $625
School year: September to June

   Year founded: 1973. **Type of school:** coed, day, private nonprofit, college
prep. **Governed by:** elected board, one member appointed by U.S. consul
general.

Curriculum/physical plant
   Type: U.S., IB. **Languages taught:** French, Arabic, other languages
available at extra cost. **Staff specialists:** computer, nurse, art, librarian,
music, physical education, special education. **Special programs:** ESL, Advanced Placement. **Special curricular:** art, physical education, music, computer science. **Extracurricular:** drama, choral music, computers, yearbook.
Sports: basketball, soccer, softball, swimming, track, volleyball. **Tests:** PSAT,
SAT, TOEFL, IB, AP, CTB III. **Graduates have attended:** Princeton, College of
William and Mary, Harvard, Duke, Boston College. **Location:** 12 kilometers
from downtown Casablanca. **Libraries:** 8,500 volumes. **Facilities:** new N –

12 suburban campus with art studio, cafeteria, infirmary, gymnasium, 3 science labs, 2 computer labs, dark room, music room, dance room, lower and upper school libraries.

*Once only fee

RABAT

Rabat American School

Phone: (212)(7)671476   **Facsimile:** (212)(7)670963
Mail: c/o U.S. Embassy, BP 120, Rabat, Morocco
U.S. mail: (no personal name) Rabat American School, American
  Embassy Rabat, PSC 74 Box 010, APO AE 09718
Director: Robert Sills
Staff: full-time, 33; part-time, 11
Nationalities of staff: U.S., 29; U.K., 2; host, 2; other, 11
Grade levels: N – 12
Enrollment: N – preK, 28; K, 33; 1 – 5, 158; 6 – 8, 70; 9 – 12, 63; total, 352
Nationalities of student body: U.S., 113; U.K., 5; host, 81; other, 153
Capacity: total, 352
Teacher/student ratio: 1/9
Tuition (annual, 1992–93 rates): N, $2,000 (half-day); K, $5,250; 1 –
  5, $6,800; 6 – 8, $7,700; 9 – 12, $7,850
Other fees (annual): registration*, $1,250; busing, $250 – 350
School year: September to June

Year founded: 1962. **Type of school:** coed, day, private nonprofit.
Governed by: elected board of governors. **Accredited by:** Middle States.

Curriculum/physical plant
Type: U.S. **Languages taught:** French, Arabic. **Staff specialists:** reading, computer, counselor, psychologist, learning disabilities, nurse, optimal match. **Special programs:** ESL, advanced placement, honors sections, independent study, remedial, IB. **Special curricular:** art, chorus, physical education, computer instruction, Moroccan studies, photography, newspaper, psychology, cold war debates. **Extracurricular:** drama, gymnastics, yearbook, excursions/expeditions, field trips. **Sports:** basketball, soccer, softball, volleyball, kickball. **Clubs:** Boy Scouts, Girl Scouts, Brownies, Cub Scouts, science, chess, Explorers. **Tests:** SSAT, PSAT, SAT, ACT, AP, ITBS, NEDT. **Graduates attending college:** 90%. **Graduates have attended:** Baylor, McGill, Cornell, Princeton, Harvard. **Location:** 5 minutes from downtown Rabat. **Campus:** 6 acres. **Library:** 15,000 volumes. **Facilities:** 10 buildings, 33 classrooms, auditorium, infirmary, covered play area, 3 playing fields, 2 science labs, computer lab, sports complex/swimming pool.

*Once only fee

TANGIER

THE AMERICAN SCHOOL OF TANGIER
Street address: Rue Christophe Colomb, Tangier, Morocco
Phone: (212)(9)939827 – 8   **Facsimile:** (212)(9)947535
Academic head: Joseph A. McPhillips III
Staff: full-time, 38; part-time, 5
Nationalities of staff: U.S., 7; U.K., 9; host, 17; other, 10
Grade levels: preK – 12
Enrollment: total, 362
Nationalities of student body: U.S., 27; host, 207; other, 128
Capacity: total, 400
Teacher/student ratio: 1/9
Boarders: boys, 20; girls, 6   **Grades:** 2 – 12   **Program:** planned 7-day
Tuition (annual): K, $2,278; 1 – 6, $8,094; 7 – 8, $8,360; 9 – 12, $9,460
Other fees (annual): registration, $100; room and board, $4,200
School year: September to June

Year founded: 1950. **Type of school:** coed, day, boarding, private nonprofit. **Governed by:** elected board of trustees.

Curriculum/physical plant
Type: U.S. **Languages taught:** French, Arabic. **Staff specialists:** math. **Special curricular:** physical education. **Extracurricular:** drama, dance, literary magazine, music, karate. **Sports:** basketball, soccer, softball, track, volleyball. **Tests:** SSAT, PSAT, SAT, TOEFL. **Graduates have attended:** Bryn Mawr, U. of Pennsylvania, Harvard, Sarah Lawrence, Stanford. **Location:** on wooded site near city. **Campus:** 6 acres. **Library:** 10,000 volumes. **Facilities:** 4 buildings, 22 classrooms, cafeteria, playing fields, science lab, 2 dormitories.

MYANMAR

Region: South Asia
Size: 261,789 square miles
Population: 42,112,000
Capital: Yangon

Telephone code: 95
Currency: kyat
Languages: Burmese, Karen, Shan

YANGON

INTERNATIONAL SCHOOL YANGON
Street address: 20 Shwe Taung Gyar, Yangon, Myanmar
Phone: (95)(1)33154/30678   **Facsimile:** (95)(1)80409
      Telex: 08321230 AMBYGN BM
U.S. mail: c/o American Embassy Myanmar, U.S. Department of State, Washington, D.C. 20521-4250

Director: David J. Shawver, Ph.D.
Business manager: Wai Wai Myaing
Staff: full-time, 25; part-time, 5
Nationalities of staff: U.S., 12; host, 15; other, 3
Grade levels: preK – 12
Enrollment: preK, 28; K, 20; 1 – 6, 103; 7 – 8, 16; 9 – 12, 50; total, 217
Nationalities of student body: U.S., 35; host, 32; other, 150
Capacity: preK, 30; K, 20; 1 – 6, 110; 7 – 8, 40; 9 – 12, 60; total, 260
Teacher/student ratio: 1/8
Tuition (annual): preK, $1,450; K, $3,800; 1 – 12, $5,800
Other fees: registration*, $500
School year: August to June

Year founded: 1955. **Type of school:** day, private nonprofit. **Governed by:** elected board of management. **Accredited by:** Western.

Curriculum/physical plant

Type: U.S. **Languages taught:** French, Spanish. **Staff specialists:** computer. **Special programs:** ESL, advanced placement. **Special curricular:** art, physical education, computer instruction, music. **Extracurricular:** drama, dance, computers, yearbook, newspaper, literary magazine, excursions/expeditions, field trips. **Sports:** basketball, soccer, softball, swimming, volleyball, martial arts. **Tests:** PSAT, SAT, TOEFL, AP, Iowa, ACH. **Location:** in suburban Yangon. **Campus:** 3 acres. **Library:** 10,000 volumes. **Facilities:** 5 buildings, 26 classrooms, covered play area, playing field, science lab, computer lab, air conditioning.

*Once only fee

NAMIBIA ───────────────────────────

Region: Southern Africa
Size: 317,818 square miles
Population: 1,520,000
Capital: Windhoek

Telephone code: 264
Currency: South African rand
Languages: Afrikaans, English,
        several others

WINDHOEK

Windhoek International School

Street address: Van Rhyn Street, Windhoek, Namibia
Phone: (264)(61)32248   **Facsimile:** (264)(61)32281
Mail: PO Box 9611, Windhoek, Namibia
Director/business manager: Mrs. B. Reske-Nielsen
Department director: M. A. Rainey
Staff: full-time, 12; part-time, 2
Nationalities of staff: U.S., 2; host, 6; other, 6
Enrollment: preK, 10; K, 12; 1 – 6, 110; 7 – 9, 28; 10, 10; total, 170

Nationalities of student body: U.S., 15; U.K., 4; host, 57; other, 94
Capacity: K, 20; 1 – 6, 120; 7 – 9, 60; 10, 20; total, 220
Teacher/student ratio: 1/13
Tuition (annual): K, 8,480**; 1 – 6, 10,000; 7 – 9, 12,000; 10, 14,000
Other fees (annual): registration*, 1,500**; ESL, 2,000
School year: August to June

Year founded: 1991. **Type of school:** coed, day, private nonprofit.
Governed by: appointed and elected board of trustees.

Curriculum/physical plant

Type: U.S., U.K., IGCSE after grade 10. **Languages taught:** French,
German. **Special programs:** ESL. **Special curricular:** art, physical education, computer instruction, music. **Extracurricular:** drama, gymnastics,
instrumental music, newspaper, pottery, stamp club. **Sports:** baseball,
soccer, swimming, tennis. **Tests:** GCSE. **Location:** sharing with a government school while in process of building own facilities. **Library:** 3,000
volumes. **Facilities:** 10 classrooms, 4 tennis courts, gymnasium, playing
field, science lab, computer lab.

*Once only fee   **South African rand

NEPAL _____

Region: Asia
Size: 56,136 square miles
Population: 19,611,000
Capital: Kathmandu

Telephone code: 977
Currency: rupee
Languages: Nepali, others

KATHMANDU

LINCOLN SCHOOL

Street address: Rabi Bhawan, Kathmandu, Nepal
Phone: (977)(1)270482   **Facsimile:** (977)(1)272685
    Cable: c/o U.S. Embassy
U.S. mail: c/o Kathmandu (LS), Department of State, Washington,
    D.C. 20521-6190
Director: Phillip Joslin
Middle/high school principal: Paul Poore
Staff: full-time, 30; part-time, 3
Nationalities of staff: U.S., 21; U.K., 4; host, 1; other, 7
Grade levels: K – 12
Enrollment: K, 18; 1 – 6, 134; 7 – 9, 54; 10 – 12, 40; total, 246
Nationalities of student body: U.S., 68; U.K., 7; host, 38; other, 133
Capacity: K, 42; 1 – 6, 200; 7 – 9, 69; 10 – 12, 69; total, 380
Teacher/student ratio: 1/8
Tuition (annual): K – 5, $7,240; 6 – 8, $7,790; 9 – 12, $8,740

Other fees (annual): busing, $500; capital development*, $2,000; admission*, $450
School year: August to June

Year founded: 1954. **Type of school:** coed, day, private nonprofit. **Governed by:** elected board of directors. **Sponsored by:** parents.

Curriculum/physical plant
Type: U.S. **Languages taught:** French, Spanish. **Staff specialists:** counselor, learning disabilities, nurse. **Special programs:** ESL. **Special curricular:** art, chorus, band, physical education, computer instruction, peer counseling, community service. **Extracurricular:** drama, gymnastics, dance, choral music, instrumental music, computers, yearbook, newspaper, photography, excursions/expeditions, field trips, annual 2-week trek for grades 5 – 12. **Sports:** baseball, basketball, soccer, swimming, tennis, track, volleyball, etc. **Clubs:** Brownies, Girl Scouts, etc. **Tests:** SSAT, PSAT, SAT, Iowa. **Location:** 10 minutes from downtown Kathmandu. **Campus:** 2.5 acres. **Library:** 12,000 volumes. **Facilities:** auditorium, infirmary, tennis court, 2 playing fields, science lab, computer lab, AV equipment, air conditioning.

*Once only fee

THE NETHERLANDS _____

Region: Europe
Size: 15,770 square miles
Population: 15,022,000
Capital: Amsterdam

Telephone code: 31
Currency: guilder
Language: Dutch

AMSTERDAM

INTERNATIONAL SCHOOL OF AMSTERDAM
Street address: A.J. Ernststraat 875, Amsterdam, The Netherlands
Phone: (31)(20)6422227   **Facsimile:** (31)(20)6428928
Mail: PO Box 7983, 1008 AD Amsterdam, The Netherlands
Director: Margaret Armstrong-Law
Upper school head: Dr. Livingston Merchant
Lower school head: Paul Lieblich
Business manager: Stuart Gilman
Staff: full-time, 54; part-time, 13
Nationalities of staff: U.S., 29; U.K., 20; host, 7; other, 11
Grade levels: N – 12
Enrollment: N, 28; preK, 43; K, 47; 1 – 6, 218; 7 – 8, 101; 9 – 12, 123; total, 560
Nationalities of student body: U.S., 136; U.K., 49; other, 375
Capacity: N , 25; preK, 30; K, 30; 1 – 6, 250; 7 – 8, 100; 9 – 12, 145; total, 580

Teacher/student ratio: 1/9
Tuition (annual): N, 14, 500**; preK – K, 16,600; 1 – 6, 18,400; 7 – 8,
  21,100; 9 – 12, 22,100
Other fees (annual): enrollment*, 2,110**; registration, 225; non-
  refundable deposit, 550; ESL, 1,025; Japanese language course,
  1,500; IB (full diploma), 1,025; IB courses, 175; PTA, 40
School year: August to June

Year founded: 1964. **Type of school:** coed, day, private nonprofit.
Governed by: elected board of governors. **Accredited by:** New England, ECIS.

Curriculum/physical plant

Type: IB, Anglo-American. **Languages taught:** French, German, Dutch,
Japanese. **Staff specialists:** reading, math, computer, counselor, learning
disabilities, art, music, design and technology, drama, Dutch. **Special
programs:** ESL. **Special curricular:** art, chorus, band, physical education,
computer instruction, instrumental lessons. **Extracurricular:** drama, gymnastics, choral music, computers, yearbook, photography, excursions/expe-
ditions, field trips, International Youth Award. **Sports:** basketball, field
hockey, soccer, softball, swimming, tennis, track, volleyball. **Clubs:** speech
and debate, photography, computer, chess, drama, forensics, Model UN.
Tests: PSAT, SAT, TOEFL, IB, IGCSE. **Graduates attending college:** more
than 90%. **Location:** in southwest suburb of Amsterdam next to Free
University. **Campus:** 3.5 acres. **Library:** 12,000 volumes. **Facilities:** 2
buildings, 40 classrooms, auditorium, gymnasium, 3 science labs, 4 computer labs.

*Once only fee   **Dutch guilder

BRUNSSUM

AFCENT International School

Street address: Ferd Bolstraat 1, 6445 EE Brunssum,
  The Netherlands
Phone: (31)(45)278220   **Facsimile:** (31)(45)278233
U.S. mail: (no personal name) AFCENT International School, APO New
  York 09011
Director: L. M. Gurtmann
Assistant director: Mr. L. Hortin
Principal, U.S. high school: Ms. K. Galloway
Principal, U.S. elementary school: Ms. P. Lopes
Principal, Canadian section: Mr. P. Avery
Head, U.K. section: Mr. G. W. C. Procter
Head, German section: Dr. R. Gehles
Staff: full-time, 119; part-time, 11
Nationalities of staff: U.S., 63; U.K., 20; other, 47

Grade levels: preK – 13
Enrollment: preK, 81; K, 124; 1 – 6, 623; 7 – 9, 317; 10 – 12, 226; 13, 10; total, 1,381
Nationalities of student body: U.S., 832; U.K., 174; other, 375
Teacher/student ratio: 1/12
School year: August to June

Year founded: 1967. **Type of school:** coed, day, limited to NATO personnel. **Governed and sponsored by:** governments/defense departments of U.S., U.K., Canada, Germany.

Curriculum
Staff specialists: reading, math, computer, speech/hearing, counselor, learning disabilities, nurse. **Special programs:** ESL, advanced placement, honors sections, GSL/FSL Extended German/French. **Special curricular:** art, chorus, band, physical education, computer instruction. **Extracurricular:** drama, gymnastics, dance, choral music, instrumental music, computers, yearbook, newspaper, photography, excursions/expeditions, field trips, sports. **Tests:** SSAT, PSAT, SAT, ACT, AP, Stanford, Iowa, SRA, Abitur (German). **Graduates attending college:** Americans, 70%; Germans 90%. **Graduates have attended:** U. of Washington, U. of California, Florida State U., McGill U., U. of Bonn.

Physical plant
Location: in suburban area, 1 mile from Brunssum. **Campus:** 12 acres. **Libraries:** 27,000 volumes. **Facilities:** 1 building, 102 classrooms, auditorium, cafeteria, infirmary, 3 gymnasiums, playing field, 10 science labs, 3 computer labs, AV equipment, track.

EINDHOVEN

INTERNATIONAL SECONDARY SCHOOL EINDHOVEN
Street address: Jerusalemlaan 1, 5625 PP Eindhoven, The Netherlands
Phone: (31)(40)413600   **Facsimile:** (31)(40)424973
Headmaster: J. M. Westerhout
Deputy headmaster: Peter J. H. Goosens
Head of year: Mr. S. Zeytountsian
Staff: full-time, 16; part-time, 14
Nationalities of staff: U.K., 8; host, 13; other, 9
Grade levels: 1 – 5 (English stream); 1 – 2 (International Baccalaureate); ESL
Enrollment: total, 253
Nationalities of student body: U.S., 23; U.K., 60; host, 63; other, 107
Capacity: total, 275
Teacher/student ratio: 1/11
Tuition (annual): 6,000** (including books)

Other fees (annual): company fee, 1,500**; insurance (voluntary); out-of-school activities; exams; education tax for students age 16 and over, 1,163
School year: September to July

Year founded: 1974. **Type of school:** coed, day, 50% company-sponsored. **Governed by:** Eindhoven Municipality. **Sponsored by:** government and companies. **Accredited by:** British Council Amsterdam, IBO Geneva, Netherlands Ministry of Education and Sciences, ECIS.

Curriculum/physical plant

Type: IB, IGCSE. **Languages taught:** English, French, Spanish, Dutch. **Staff specialists:** math, computer, counselor, ESL, librarian, form mentors. **Special programs:** ESL. **Special curricular:** art, physical education, computer instruction. **Extracurricular:** drama, computers, yearbook, photography, excursions/expeditions, field trips, magazine, Benelun Award. **Sports:** basketball, soccer, volleyball. **Tests:** IB, IGCSE, Cambridge Preliminary English Test (ESL). **Graduates have attended:** Dutch, U.K., Canadian, Swedish, and Japanese universities and colleges. **Location:** in quiet neighborhood, 10 minutes' drive from center of Eindhoven. **Library:** approximately 4,000 volumes, with computer facilities. **Facilities:** 2 buildings, 17 classrooms, auditorium, cafeteria, gymnasium, 2 playing fields, 3 science labs, computer lab, language lab, darkroom, arts and crafts shop, covered bike shed, parking lot.

**Dutch guilder

REGIONALE INTERNATIONALE SCHOOL

Street address: Humperdincklaan 4, 5654 PA Eindhoven,
    The Netherlands
Phone: (31)(40)519437   **Facsimile:** (31)(40)527675
Headmaster: H. A. Schol
Deputy headmasters: F. W. van der Schaaf, J. B. Bright
Staff: full-time, 24; part-time, 6
Grade levels: K – 6
Enrollment: total, 340
Nationalities of student body: U.S., 20; U.K., 50; host, 146;
    other, 124
Teacher/student ratio: 1/13
Tuition (annual): K – 6, 4,000**
School year: August to June

Year founded: 1965. **Type of school:** coed, day.

Curriculum

Type: U.K., French, Dutch. **Languages of instruction:** English, French, Dutch.

**Dutch guilder

GRONINGEN

MAARTENS COLLEGE INTERNATIONAL SCHOOL

Street address: Rijusstraatweg 24, Haren, Groningen, The Netherlands

Phone: (31)(50)340084   **Facsimile:** (31)(50)340056

Mail: Postbus 6105, 9702 HC Groningen, The Netherlands

Head: Wim H. M. Koopman

Middle school coordinator: Debbie Lindenberg

IGCSE coordinator: Andrew Williams

IB coordinator: Ton Heuvelmans

Staff: full-time, 3; part-time, 29

Nationalities of staff: U.S., 2; U.K., 4; host, 25; other, 1

Grade levels: 6 – 12

Enrollment: 6, 14; 7 – 9, 40; 10 – 12, 44; total, 98

Nationalities of student body: U.S., 10; U.K., 12; host, 19; other, 57

Capacity: 6, 20; 7 – 9, 60; 10 – 12, 60; total, 140

Teacher/student ratio: 1/6

Tuition (annual): 6 – 12, 12,000**

Other fees: excursions

School year: September to July

Year founded: 1984. **Type of school:** coed, day, company-sponsored, church-related. **Governed by:** appointed board. **Sponsored by:** Dutch government.

Curriculum/physical plant

Type: Dutch, IB, IGCSE. **Languages taught:** English, French, German, Dutch, all IB languages. **Staff specialists:** reading, math, computer, counselor, learning disabilities. **Special programs:** ESL, remedial. **Special curricular:** art, physical education, computer instruction. **Extracurricular:** drama, yearbook, excursions/expeditions, field trips. **Tests:** IB, IGCSE, Dutch state exams. **Graduates attending college:** 95%. **Graduates have attended:** University College London, U. of Leiden, Cambridge, U. of Edinburgh, U. of Groningen. **Location:** wooded suburban area, 3 miles from Groningen. **Facilities:** 2 campuses, 3 buildings, 3 auditoriums, 3 gymnasiums, 3 playing fields, 6 science labs, 3 computer labs.

**Dutch guilder

THE HAGUE

THE AMERICAN SCHOOL OF THE HAGUE

Street address: Rijksstraatweg 200, 2241 BX Wassenaar, The Netherlands

Phone: (31)(1751)40113   **Facsimile:** (31)(1751)12400

Superintendent: William H. Greenham, Ed.D.
High school principal: Ellen Y. Moceri
Middle school principal: Bert Boonstra
Elementary school principal: Roger Beilman
Staff: full-time, 77; part-time, 17
Nationalities of staff: U.S., 83; U.K., 2; host, 4; other, 5
Grade levels: preK – 12
Enrollment: preK, 43; K – 4, 309; 5 – 8, 247; 9 – 12, 271; total, 870
Teacher/student ratio: 1/10
Tuition (annual): preK, 6,300**; K – 4, 16,200; 5 – 8, 18,500;
   9 – 12, 19,600
Other fees (annual): capital levy, 3,000**; busing, 2,300 – 2,940;
   enrollment*, 1,000
School year: August to June

Year founded: 1953. **Type of school:** coed, day. **Governed by:** elected
executive committee. **Accredited by:** Middle States, ECIS.

Curriculum/physical plant

Type: U.S. **Languages taught:** French, Spanish, German, Dutch. **Staff
specialists:** speech/hearing, counselor, learning disabilities, nurse. **Special
programs:** ESL, advanced placement, learning skills center. **Special curricular:** art, choir, band, physical education, computer instruction, photography,
speech and debate. **Extracurricular:** drama, choral music, instrumental
music, computers, yearbook, newspaper, field trips, student council, Close-
Up. **Sports:** baseball, basketball, soccer, softball, swimming, track, volleyball,
cross-country, tennis. **Organizations**: International Political Association,
Alumni Association, International Model UN held in the Hague every January.
Tests: PSAT, SAT, ACT, TOEFL, AP, Iowa. **Graduates attending college:**
92%. **Graduates have attended:** Tufts, Brown, Harvard, Duke, Yale. **Location:** 15 minutes from downtown Den Haag by car. **Library:** 31,000 volumes.
Facilities: 78 classrooms, cafeteria, library, arts center, 360-seat theater,
sports complex, sports field.

*Once only fee   **Dutch guilder

OEGSTGEEST

HET RIJNLANDS LYCEUM OEGSTGEEST

Street address: Apollolaan 1, 2341 BA, Oegstgeest, Z. H.,
   The Netherlands
Phone: (31)(71)155640   **Facsimile:** (31)(71)153872
Headmaster: A. J. M. Vaessen
Head, international section: L. E. Timmermans
Staff: full-time, 40; part-time, 60
Nationalities of staff: U.S., 1; U.K., 2; host, 97
Grade levels: 7 – 12

Enrollment: 7 – 9, 610; 10 – 12, 700; total, 1,310
Nationalities of student body: U.S., 10; U.K., 5; host, 1,192;
   other, 103
Capacity: total, 1,500
Teacher/student ratio: 1/19
Tuition (annual): 7 – 9, 100 – 500**; 10 – 12, 500 – 3,900
Other fees (annual): book fund, 250**
School year: August to July

Year founded: 1958. **Type of school:** coed, day, private nonprofit.
Governed by: appointed foundation board. **Sponsored by:** Dutch government.

Curriculum/physical plant

Type: Dutch, IB, IB middle years program (grades 7 – 10). **Languages of instruction:** English, Dutch. **Languages taught:** English, French, Spanish, German, Dutch, others. **Special curricular:** art, band, physical education, computer instruction, vocational. **Extracurricular:** drama, gymnastics, dance, instrumental music, computers, yearbook, photography, excursions/expeditions, field trips. **Sports:** baseball, basketball, rugby, soccer, tennis, athletics. **Tests:** PSAT, SAT, TOEFL, IB, ISCO, HAVO, VWO. **Graduates attending college:** 90%. **Graduates have attended:** Yale, MIT, Cambridge, Oxford, all Dutch universities. **Location:** in suburb, 12 kilometers from The Hague. **Campus:** 200 acres. **Library:** 60,000 volumes. **Facilities:** 1 building, 65 classrooms, auditorium, tennis court, 2 gymnasiums, playing field, 5 science labs, 2 computer labs, large sports hall, 6 language labs, technology classroom, AV equipment, boarding accommodations nearby.

**Dutch guilder

ROTTERDAM

AMERICAN INTERNATIONAL SCHOOL
OF ROTTERDAM

Street address: Hillegondastraat 21, 3051 PA Rotterdam, The Netherlands
Phone: (31)(10)4225351/4225137   **Facsimile:** (31)(10)4224075
Director: Robert Werner
Staff: full-time, 12; part-time, 9
Nationalities of staff: U.S., 15; U.K., 3; host, 1; other, 2
Grade levels: preK – 8
Enrollment: preK, 10; K, 15; 1 – 6, 120; 7 – 8, 20; total, 165
Capacity: preK, 10; K, 20; 1 – 6, 120; 7 – 8, 30; total, 180
Teacher/student ratio: 1/10
Tuition (annual): preK, $2,500; K – 4, $7,000; 5 – 8, $7,500
Other fees (annual): registration*, $1,000; busing, $2,000
School year: August to June

Year founded: 1959. **Type of school:** coed, day, private nonprofit. **Governed by:** appointed and elected board of directors. **Accredited by:** New England, ECIS.

Curriculum/physical plant

Type: U.S. **Languages taught:** French, Dutch. **Staff specialists:** reading, counselor, learning disabilities, resource. **Special programs:** ESL, remedial. **Special curricular:** art, band, physical education, computer instruction. **Extracurricular:** drama, computers, yearbook. **Sports:** basketball, soccer, swimming, track, volleyball, gymnastics. **Tests:** Iowa. **Location:** on north side of city. **Library:** 12,000 volumes. **Facilities:** 2 buildings, 15 classrooms, gymnasium, science lab, computer lab, AV equipment, rented swimming pool. Moving to a new purpose-built school in September 1994. The International Education Center will be shared with the Japanese School of Rotterdam.

*Once only fee

VOORSCHOTEN

THE BRITISH SCHOOL IN THE NETHERLANDS

Street address: Jan van Hooflaan 3, 2252 BG Voorschoten, The
    Netherlands
Phone: (31)(71)616958   **Facsimile:** (31)(71)617144
Principal: M. J. Cooper
Head of secondary school: Mrs. P. C. V. Driel
Head of junior school: Mrs. M. Jonker-Carroll
Head of infant school: Mrs. A. Shaw
Staff: full-time, 115; part-time, 6
Nationalities of staff: U.K.,115; host, 2; other, 4
Grade levels: N – 13
Enrollment: total, 1,320
Nationalities of student body: U.S., 28; U.K., 750; host, 30; other, 512
Capacity: total, 1,400
Teacher/student ratio: 1/11
Tuition (annual): N – preK, 5,400**; 1 – 6, 12,600; 7 – 9, 13,080; 10 –
    13, 17,820
Other fees (annual): registration*, $1,000**; busing, 1,820
School year: September to July

Year founded: 1935. **Type of school:** coed, day, private nonprofit. **Governed by:** appointed association. **Accredited by:** ECIS, COBISEC.

Curriculum/physical plant

Type: U.K. **Languages taught:** French, Dutch, German, Spanish. **Staff specialists:** reading, math, computer, psychologist, learning disabilities. **Special programs:** ESL, remedial. **Special curricular:** art, chorus, band, physical education, computer instruction. **Extracurricular:** drama, gymnastics, dance, choral music, instrumental music, computers, newspaper, literary magazine, photography, excursions/expeditions, field trips. **Sports:** fencing, horseback riding, trampoline, others. **Clubs:** judo, photography, chess. **Tests:** A-level GCE, GCSE, MAT (ESL), ASS Board of Royal School of Music, Cambridge. **Graduates attending college:** 90%. **Graduates have attended:** universities in U.K., Japan, Switzerland and Sweden. **Campuses (3):** 2 urban, 1 rural. **Facilities:** auditorium, tennis court, gymnasium, playing field, 7 science labs, 2 computer labs, 2 music rooms, 3 art rooms.

*Once only fee   **Dutch guilder

WERKHOVEN

INTERNATIONAL SCHOOL BEVERWEERD

Street address: Beverweerdseweg 60, 3985 RE Werkhoven, The Netherlands
Phone: (31)(3437)1341   **Facsimile:** (31)(3437)2079
Headmaster: Dr. A. J. Vermet
Director of studies: Dr. D. M. Bleyberg
Housemaster/head of computer services: C.J. Davies
Staff†: full-time, 10; part-time, 9
Nationalities of staff: U.S., 1; U.K., 7; host, 6; other, 5
Grade levels: 7 – 12
Enrollment†: 7 – 8, 10; 9 – 12, 65; total, 75
Nationalities of student body: U.S., 6; host, 55; other, 14
Capacity†: 7 – 8, 10; 9 – 12, 70; total, 80
Teacher/student ratio: 1/5
Boarders†: boys, 42; girls, 30   **Grades:** 7 – 12
    Program: planned 7-day
Tuition and boarding (annual): 35,000**
Other fees (annual): registration*, 500**; books and other expenses, 500
School year: September to June

Year founded: 1934. **Type of school:** coed, day, boarding, private nonprofit. **Governed by:** appointed board of governors. **Regional organizations:** ECIS.

Curriculum
Type: U.K., IB. **Languages taught:** French, Spanish, German, Dutch, Japanese. **Staff specialists:** math, computer, minority languages, business studies, ESL, careers and higher education counselor, study guidance. **Special curricular:** art, physical education, computer instruction. **Extracurricular:** dance, instrumental music, newspaper, excursions/expeditions, creative art, conservation, debate, drama, photography, singing, woodwork, social service. **Sports:** basketball, soccer, softball, tennis, volleyball, badmin-

ton, athletics, fitness, horseback riding, karate, squash. **Tests:** PSAT, SAT, TOEFL, IB, IGCSE. **Graduates attending college:** 80%. **Graduates have attended:** U. of Utrecht, U. of Amsterdam, Imperial College London, Georgetown, U. of Heidelberg.

Physical plant
Location: large park in rural setting, 10 kilometers from Utrecht. **Campus:** 45 acres. **Library:** 2,500 volumes. **Facilities:** Castle housing 10 classrooms, computer room, library, administrative offices, faculty room, dining facilities, and students' common room; another building with science laboratories and art room (equipped for painting, drawing, sculpture, and textiles); modern boarding house opened in 1991; gymnasium, auditorium, playing field, all-weather tennis courts.

*Once only fee   **Dutch guilder   †International Section

OMMEN
International School Eerde
Address: Kasteellaan 1, 7731 PJ Ommen, The Netherlands
Phone: (31)(5291)51452/56502/56529
Facsimile: (31)(5291)56377

NICARAGUA _____

Region: Central America
Size: 50,193 square miles
Population: 3,751,000
Capital: Managua

Telephone code: 505
Currency: cordoba
Languages: Spanish, English

MANAGUA

AMERICAN-NICARAGUAN SCHOOL

Street address: UNAN Highway, Managua, Nicaragua
Phone: (505)(2)782565/780029   **Facsimile:** (505)(2)673088
Mail: PO Box 2670, Managua, Nicaragua
U.S. mail: American-Nicaraguan School, c/o American Embassy Managua, Unit No. 2710, Box 7, APO AA 34021
Director: Marvin Happel, Ph.D.
High school principal: Antonio Rios
Middle school principal: John Boswell
Primary school principal: Mary Ellen Normandin
Business manager: Roberto Cardenal
Staff: full-time, 80
Nationalities of staff: U.S., 36; host, 38; other, 6
Grade levels: preK – 12
Enrollment: preK, 73; K, 87; 1 – 4, 341; 5 – 8, 326; 9 – 12, 266; total, 1,093
Teacher/student ratio: 1/14
Tuition (annual): preK – K, $2,060; 1 – 4, $2,280; 5 – 12, $2,360
Other fees (annual): registration, $120; busing (optional), $675; entrance*, $1,000; construction*, $500
School year: August to June

Year founded: 1944. **Type of school:** coed, day, private nonprofit. **Governed by:** board of directors. **Accredited by:** Southern.

Curriculum/physical plant
Type: U.S., Nicaraguan. **Languages taught:** French, Spanish. **Staff specialists:** computer, counselor, nurse. **Special programs:** ESL. **Special curricular:** art, physical education, computer instruction, music. **Extracurricular:** drama, yearbook, newspaper, excursions/expeditions, field trips, student council. **Sports:** baseball, basketball, soccer, volleyball. **Tests:** SSAT, PSAT, SAT, ACT, TOEFL, Iowa. **Graduates attending college:** 98%. **Graduates have attended:** Purdue, Boston U., U. of Florida, Tufts, Wellesley. **Facilities:** tennis court, playing field, science lab, computer lab.

*Once only fee

NIGER _____

Region: Africa
Size: 489,189 square miles
Population: 8,154,000
Capital: Niamey

Telephone code: 227
Currency: CFA franc
Languages: French, Hausa,
 Fulani

NIAMEY

AMERICAN SCHOOL OF NIAMEY

Phone: (227)723942   **Facsimile:** (227)723918/723457
 Cable: c/o U.S. Embassy, Niamey
Mail: c/o U.S. Embassy, BP 11.201, Niamey, Niger, West Africa
U.S. mail: (for urgent business) JAO Director (ASN), Department of State,
 Niamey, Washington, D.C. 20521-2420.
Director: Ralph A. Reed
Business manager: Linda L. Okiror
Staff: full-time, 8; part-time, 8
Nationalities of staff: U.S., 12; other, 4
Grade levels: K – 9
Enrollment: K, 9; 1 – 5, 46; 6 – 9, 29; total, 84
Nationalities of student body: U.S., 35; other, 49
Capacity: preK, 20; K, 20; 1 – 5, 100; 6 – 8, 40; total, 180
Teacher/student ratio: 1/7
Tuition (annual): K, $5,200; 1 – 5, $6,900; 6 – 9, $7,900
Other fees (annual): registration*, $1,200; busing, $1,200; ESL assess-
 ment*, $1,200
School year: August to June

Year founded: 1982. **Type of school:** coed, day, private nonprofit.
Governed by: elected and appointed board of directors. **Accredited by:**
Middle States.

Curriculum/physical plant

Type: U.S. **Languages taught:** French. **Staff specialists:** computer,
librarian. **Special programs:** ESL, tutorial. **Special curricular:** art, physical
education, computer instruction, health, music, Nigerian studies, library.
Extracurricular: drama, field trips, sports/social exchanges/competition,
scouts, student council, Math Counts. **Sports:** basketball, soccer, softball,
swimming, track, volleyball. **Tests:** Iowa. **Location:** on U.S. Embassy grounds
at west edge of city. **Campus:** 8 acres. **Library:** 6,000 volumes. **Facilities:** 4
buildings, 12 classrooms, science lab, computer lab, swimming pool, air
conditioning.

*Once only fee

NIGERIA

Region: Africa
Size: 356,667 square miles
Population: 88,500,000
Capital: Lagos

Telephone code: 234
Currency: naira
Languages: English, Hausa,
Yoruba, Ibo

JOS

HILLCREST SCHOOL

Street address: 13 Bukuru Road, Jos, Nigeria
Phone: (234)(72)55410
Mail: Box 652, Jos, Nigeria
Principal: Ward Nicholsen
High school supervisor: John Sawyer
Middle school supervisor: Dick Seinen
Primary supervisor: Woodrow Arp
Business manager: Andy Horlings
Staff: full-time, 41; part-time, 2
Nationalities of staff: U.S., 38; U.K., 3; host, 1; other, 1
Grade levels: 1 – 12
Enrollment: 1 – 5, 168; 6 – 8, 104; 9 – 12, 119; total, 391
Nationalities of student body: U.S., 84; U.K., 14; host, 194; other, 99
Teacher/student ratio: 1/9
Boarders: boys, 53; girls, 51   **Grades:** 1 – 12   **Program:** planned 7-day
Tuition (annual): 1 – 5, 9,000** (plus $280); 6 – 8, 16,000 (plus $280);
9 – 12, 18,000 (plus $280)
Other fees (annual): boarding, 20,000**
School year: August through May

Year founded: 1942. **Type of school:** coed, day, boarding, church-
related. **Governed by:** appointed representatives from each of the 12 sponsoring churches. **Sponsored by:** 12 churches. **Accredited by:** Middle States.

Curriculum/physical plant

Type: U.S. **Languages taught:** French, Spanish. **Staff specialists:**
counselor, nurse. **Special programs:** advanced placement, remedial. **Special
curricular:** art, chorus, band, physical education, computer instruction.
Extracurricular: drama, yearbook, newspaper, field trips. **Sports:** basketball, soccer, track, volleyball. **Organizations:** honors society, student council.
Tests: PSAT, SAT, ACT, TOEFL, AP, Iowa. **Graduates attending college:**
95%. **Graduates have attended:** Valparaiso, Calvin College, Carleton College,
U. of Kansas, U. of Montana. **Location:** in suburb of Jos. **Campus:** 25 acres.
Library: 12,000 volumes. **Facilities:** 7 buildings, 25 classrooms, auditorium,
infirmary, 4 tennis courts, gymnasium, 2 playing fields, 3 science labs, 2
computer labs, swimming pool, 8 hostels.

1992–93 listing   **Nigerian naira

KADUNA

AISHA MOHAMMED INTERNATIONAL SCHOOL

Street address: 3 Gwanja Road, Kaduna, Nigeria
Phone: (234)(62)214563   **Facsimile:** (234)(62)231335 (Box 221)
Mail: PO Box 2947, Kaduna, Nigeria
U.S. mail: (letters only) c/o Administrative Officer, Department of
    State—Kaduna, Washington, D.C. 20521-2260
Headmaster: Daryl Barker
Head of juniors: Mrs. A. Barker
Head of infants: Mrs. V. Dodo
Staff: full-time, 10; part-time, 1
Nationalities of staff: U.S., 1; U.K., 3; host, 4; other, 3
Grade levels: preK – 6
Enrollment: preK, 11; K, 6; 1– 6, 39; total, 56
Nationalities of student body: U.S., 3; U.K., 13; host, 19; other, 21
Capacity: preK, 15; K, 15; 1 – 6, 75; total, 105
Teacher/student ratio: 1/5
Tuition (annual): preK, $1,460; K – 6, $1,850
Other fees (annual): registration, $80; initial fee*, $900
School year: September to June

Year founded: 1985. **Type of school:** coed, day, private nonprofit.
Governed by: appointed board of trustees.

Curriculum/physical plant
Type: U.K. **Languages taught:** French (elementary conversational).
Special programs: ESL. **Special curricular:** art, physical education, computer instruction, music. **Extracurricular:** drama, dance, instrumental music, computers, excursions/expeditions, field trips. **Sports:** football, kickball, netball, rounders. **Clubs:** stamp, wildlife. **Location:** spacious compound, 10 minutes from Kaduna City. **Campus:** 6,000 square meters. **Library:** 6,000 volumes. **Facilities:** 4 buildings, 7 classrooms, playing field, science lab, computer lab, air conditioning.

*Once only fee

SACRED HEART INTERNATIONAL PRIMARY SCHOOL

Street address: Independence Way, Kaduna, Nigeria
Phone: (234)(62)212929
Mail: PO Box 620, Kaduna, Nigeria
Headmistress: Dorothy Ajijola
Staff: full-time, 32; part-time, 1
Nationalities of staff: U.K., 1; host, 29; other, 3
Grade levels: 1 – 6
Enrollment: total, 330

Nationalities of student body: U.S., 1; host, 299; other, 20
Capacity: total, 330
Teacher/student ratio: 1/10
Tuition (annual): 1 – 6, 6,000**
Other fees (annual): registration, 750**
School year: September to July

Year founded: 1965. **Type of school:** coed, day, private nonprofit. **Governed by:** appointed board of governors. **Accredited by:** Nigerian government.

Curriculum/physical plant

Type: U.S., Nigerian. **Languages taught:** French, Hausa. **Staff specialists:** reading, computer, nurse, art, physical education. **Special curricular:** art, chorus, physical education, computer instruction. **Extracurricular:** drama, computers, literary magazine, excursions/expeditions. **Sports:** basketball, football, volleyball, judo, table-tennis. **Clubs:** Brownies, Cub Scouts, sewing, knitting. **Tests:** arranged individually. **Location:** in suburban Kaduna. **Facilities:** auditorium, infirmary, playing field, computer lab.

1992–93 listing

**Nigerian naira

LAGOS

AMERICAN INTERNATIONAL SCHOOL OF LAGOS

Street address: 1004 Federal Estates, Victoria Island, Lagos, Nigeria
Phone: (234)(1)617793 – 4   **Facsimile:** (234)(1)617794
Mail: PO Box 2803, Lagos, Nigeria
U.S. mail: A.I.S. c/o Dan Barkley, PO Box 1357, Tacoma, WA 98401-1357, U.S.A.
Superintendent: Pauline Yamashita
Assistant superintendent: Thomas Shearer
Staff: full-time, 50; part-time, 2
Nationalities of staff: U.S., 27; host, 7; other, 18
Grade levels: preK – 9
Enrollment: preK, 25; K, 54; 1 – 6, 342; 7 – 9, 104; total, 525
Nationalities of student body: U.S., 140; U.K., 41; host, 82; other, 262
Capacity: preK, 24; K, 60; 1 – 6, 360; 7 – 9, 132; total, 576
Teacher/student ratio: 1/10
Tuition (annual): preK, $1,500; K – 6, $4,900; 7 – 9, $6,400
Other fees: registration, $25; building assessment*: preK, $250; K – 9, $4,000
School year: August to June

Year founded: 1964. **Type of school:** coed, day, private nonprofit. **Governed by:** elected board of directors. **Accredited by:** Middle States.

Curriculum/physical plant

Type: U.S. **Languages taught:** French, English. **Staff specialists:** reading, computer, counselor, nurse, learning center, African studies. **Special curricular:** art, physical education, swimming, music, math (grades 7 – 9), health education (grades 7 – 9). **Extracurricular:** drama, gymnastics, computers, yearbook, newspaper, photography, excursions/expeditions, field trips, tennis, karate, Tae Kwon Do, table tennis. **Sports:** basketball, soccer, swimming, volleyball. **Clubs:** student council (grades 3 – 6), student senate (grades 7 – 9), Nigerian Conservation Club, Boy Scouts, Girl Scouts. **Tests:** SSAT, Iowa. **Graduates attending college:** 90%. **Location:** within Federal Estates housing complex. **Campus:** 8 acres. **Library:** 9,000 volumes. **Facilities:** 3 buildings, 2 tennis courts, auditorium/gymnasium, 2 playing fields, science lab, computer lab, swimming pool, air conditioning.

*Once only fee

WARRI

JOHN F. KENNEDY INTERNATIONAL SCHOOL NIGERIA

Location: Effurun, Warri, Delta State, Nigeria
Phone: (234)(58)231286   **Cable:** JFK SCHOOL, WARRI
Mail: PO Box 232, Warri, Delta State, Nigeria
Administrator: V. O. M. Omonuwa
Acting head, science: Mrs. A. L. Omokaro
Acting head, English: C. Dara
Head, hostel: Ms. Bose Osarieme
Business manager: Dr. Johnson Efeotor
Staff: full-time, 40; part-time, 5
Nationalities of staff: U.K., 1; host, 44
Grade levels: N – 13
Enrollment: total, 740
Nationalities of student body: U.S., 48; U.K., 15; host, 602; other, 70
Capacity: total, 1,500
Teacher/student ratio: 1/17
Boarders: boys, 105; girls, 52   **Grades:** K – 13   **Program:** planned 7-day
Tuition: N – preK, 2,000**; K – 6, 2,250; 7 – 13, 5,000
Other fees (annual): registration, 500**; boarding, 6,000; lunch, 500; books, 550
School year: September to July

Year founded: 1986. **Type of school:** coed, day, boarding, proprietary, private nonprofit. **Governed by:** elected 12-member governing council. **Accredited by:** Nigerian Ministry of Education.

Curriculum

Type: U.S., Nigerian. **Languages taught:** English, French. **Staff specialists:** reading, math, computer, speech/hearing, counselor, psychologist, nurse. **Special curricular:** art, chorus, band, physical education, computer instruction. **Extracurricular:** drama, gymnastics, dance, choral music, instrumental music, computers, yearbook, newspaper, literary magazine, photography, excursions/expeditions, field trips. **Sports:** basketball, football, hockey, swimming, volleyball, table tennis, lawn tennis. **Clubs:** science, press, debating society, dramatic society, current affairs. **Tests:** SAT, A-level GCE, GCSE, Primary School Examination, Junior and Senior Secondary School Examination.

Physical plant

Location: about 1 kilometer from airport in Effurun – Warri. **Campus:** 10 acres. **Library:** 5,000 volumes. **Facilities:** 15 buildings, 30 classrooms, auditorium, cafeteria, infirmary, covered play area, 2 tennis courts, gymnasium, 2 playing fields, 3 science labs, computer lab, swimming pool.

**Nigerian naira

IBADAN

International School

Address: University of Ibadan, Ibadan (Oyo State), Nigeria
Phone: (234)(22)400550/400579 ext. 1302

NORWAY_____

Region: Europe
Size: 125,181 square miles
Population: 4,273,000
Capital: Oslo

Telephone code: 47
Currency: kroner
Language: Norwegian

BERGEN

INTERNATIONAL SCHOOL OF BERGEN

Street address: Vilhelm Bjerknesvei 15, 5030 Landas, Bergen, Norway
Phone: (47)(5)287716   **Facsimile:** (47)(5)271488
Mail: PO Box 3268, Slettebakken, 5022 Bergen, Norway
Director: Brenda M. R. Eide
Staff: full-time, 16; part-time, 5

Nationalities of staff: U.S., 6; U.K., 7; other, 8
Grade levels: preK – 10
Enrollment: preK, 24; K, 18; 1 – 6, 64; 7 – 9, 19; total, 125
Nationalities of student body: U.S., 7; U.K., 20; host, 38; other, 60
Teacher/student ratio: 1/7
Tuition (annual): company-sponsored: preK, 27,000**; K – 10, 92,500;
noncompany-sponsored: K – 10, 32,000
School year: August to June

Year founded: 1975. **Type of school:** coed, day, private nonprofit.
Governed by: appointed board of trustees. **Accredited by:** New England, ECIS.

Curriculum/physical plant

Type: U.S., U.K. **Languages taught:** French, Norwegian. **Staff special-ists:** computer, music, physical education. **Special programs:** ESL, IGCSE.
Special curricular: art, physical education, computer instruction, music.
Extracurricular: drama, computers, yearbook, field trips. **Sports:** skiing, swimming, ice skating. **Tests:** Iowa. **Location:** on a lake surrounded by mountains, 10 kilometers from Bergen. **Campus:** 5 acres. **Library:** 4,500 volumes. **Facilities:** 3 buildings, 9 classrooms, infirmary, covered play area, 2 gymnasiums, 2 playing fields, science lab, computer lab.

**Norwegian kroner

STAVANGER

INTERNATIONAL SCHOOL OF STAVANGER

Street address: Treskeveien 3, 4042 Hafrsfjord, Norway
Phone: (47)(51)559100   **Facsimile:** (47)(51)552962
Director: Raymond L. Marshall, Ed.D.
Assistant director/elementary principal: Linda M. Duevel
Secondary principal: Adrian Allan
Staff: full-time, 48; part-time, 2
Nationalities of staff: U.S., 33; U.K., 11; host, 3; other, 3
Grade levels: preK (3 years) – 18 years
Enrollment: preK, 45; K, 35; 1 – 6, 240; 7 – 9, 100; 10 – 12, 80; total, 500
Nationalities of student body: U.S., 230; U.K., 60; host, 60; other, 150
Capacity: preK, 40; K, 50; 1 – 6, 300; 7 – 9, 120; 10 – 12, 120; total, 630
Teacher/student ratio: 1/10
Tuition (annual): private students: preK, 16,000**; K – 12, 33,000;
company-sponsored students: K – 12, 80,000
School year: August to June

Year founded: 1966. **Type of school:** coed, day, private nonprofit.
Governed by: board of trustees. **Accredited by:** New England, ECIS.

Curriculum

Type: U.S., U.K. **Languages taught:** English, French, Spanish, Norwegian. **Staff specialists:** reading, math, computer, counselor, learning disabilities, nurse. **Special programs:** ESL, advanced placement, independent study, A-level, GCSE. **Special curricular:** art, chorus, band, physical education, computer instruction. **Extracurricular:** drama, choral music, instrumental music, computers, yearbook, literary magazine, photography, excursions/expeditions, field trips. **Sports:** basketball, soccer, track, volleyball. **Clubs:** science, fine arts, golf, photo. **Tests:** SSAT, PSAT, SAT, ACT, TOEFL, AP, A-level GCE, GCSE, Iowa. **Graduates attending college:** 90%. **Graduates have attended:** Baylor, Purdue, Southern Methodist U., St. Andrews (Scotland), U. of Exeter.

Physical plant

Location: in suburb of Stavanger, a city on a fjord on the southwest coast of Norway. **Campus:** 15 acres. **Library:** 14,000 volumes. **Facilities:** 1 building, 36 classrooms, auditorium, cafeteria, infirmary, 2 covered play areas, 3 gymnasiums, 3 playing fields, 3 science labs, 3 computer labs, AV equipment.

**Norwegian kroner

OSLO

British International School

   Address: PO Box 7531, Skillebekk, 0205 Oslo 2, Norway
   Phone: (47)(22)444916   **Facsimile:** (47)(22)551135
   Headmistress: Margaret G. Stark

OMAN ⎯⎯⎯⎯⎯⎯⎯⎯⎯⎯⎯⎯⎯⎯⎯⎯⎯

Region: Middle East
Size: 82,030 square miles
Population: 1,534,000
Capital: Muscat

Telephone code: 968
Currency: rial omani
Language: Arabic

MUSCAT

AMERICAN-BRITISH ACADEMY

   Phone: (968)603646   **Facsimile** (968)603544
   Mail: PO Box 372, Medinat Qaboos-115, Sultanate of Oman
   Superintendent: Brian Wilks, Ed.D.
   Principals: Richard E. Hayles, Wayne Morton
   Staff: full-time, 64

Nationalities of staff: U.S., 23; U.K., 34; other, 7
Grade levels: preK – 12
Enrollment: preK, 20; K, 59; 1 – 6, 286; 7 – 9, 166; 10 – 12, 127; total, 658
Nationalities of student body: U.S., 102; U.K., 172; other, 384
Capacity: preK, 20; K, 60; 1 – 6, 300; 7 – 9, 180; 10 – 12, 130; total, 690
Teacher/student ratio: 1/10
Tuition (annual): preK – K, $3,173; 1 – 3, $4,025; 4 – 5, $4,102;
    6 – 7, $5,379; 8 – 10, $6,192; 11 – 12, $7,314
Other fees: registration*
School year: September to June

Year founded: 1987. **Type of school:** coed, day, private nonprofit.
Accredited by: Middle States.

Curriculum/physical plant
Type: U.S., U.K., IB. **Languages taught:** French, Spanish, German. **Staff specialists:** reading, nurse. **Special programs:** ESL, remedial. **Special curricular:** art, music, physical education, computer instruction. **Extracurricular:** drama, dance, computers, yearbook, photography, typewriting, music, Boy Scouts. **Sports:** basketball, rugby, soccer, softball, netball, rounders, karate, cricket, ice skating. **Tests:** SAT, IB, GCSE, ERB, Royal Society of Arts. **Location:** 2 kilometers from Medinat Qaboos. **Facilities:** 40 instructional areas, covered play area, use of playing field, 4 science labs, 2 computer labs, air conditioning, shaded drama court, multi-purpose hall (gymnasium, theater).

*Once only fee

PAKISTAN ⸻

Region: South Asia
Size: 310,403 square miles
Population: 117,490,000
Capital: Islamabad

Telephone code: 92
Currency: rupee
Languages: Urdu, Punjabi,
    Sindhi, Pushtu,
    Baluchi, Brahvi

ISLAMABAD

INTERNATIONAL SCHOOL OF ISLAMABAD
Street address: Sector H-9/1, Islamabad, Pakistan
Phone: (92)(51)252454   **Facsimile:** (92)(51)282257
    Telex: 95254238 ISISB PK
Mail: Sector H-9/1, PO Box 1124, Islamabad, Pakistan
U.S. mail (official business only): Superintendent's Office, International

School of Islamabad, Unit 62202, APO AE 09812-2202
Superintendent: Emmanuel J. Pavlos
High school principal: John Gates
Elementary school principal: John K. Ligon
Business manager: Sue Mills
Staff: full-time, 61; part-time, 3
Nationalities of staff: U.S., 45; U.K., 3; host, 7; other, 9
Grade levels: N – 12
Enrollment: N – preK, 10; K, 36; 1 – 5, 240; 6 – 8, 152; 9 – 12, 185; total, 623
Nationalities of student body: U.S., 250; U.K., 28; host, 130; other, 215
Capacity: N – preK, 18; K, 40; 1 – 5, 280; 6 – 8, 162; 9 – 12, 200; total, 700
Teacher/student ratio: 1/10
Tuition (annual): N, $2,850; K – 12, $7,000
Other fees (annual): registration*, $1,000
School year: August through May

Year founded: 1965. **Type of school:** coed, day, private nonprofit. **Governed by:** appointed and elected board of directors. **Accredited by:** Middle States.

Curriculum

Type: U.S. **Languages taught:** French, Spanish, Urdu. **Staff specialists:** reading, math, counselor, learning disabilities, nurse. **Special programs:** ESL, advanced placement, honors sections, independent study, correspondence, remedial. **Special curricular:** art, chorus, band, physical education, computer instruction, vocational. **Extracurricular:** drama, gymnastics, choral music, instrumental music, computers, yearbook, newspaper, literary magazine, photography, excursions/expeditions, field trips. **Sports:** basketball, field hockey, soccer, swimming, tennis, volleyball, athletics, table tennis, track, squash, racquetball, badminton. **Clubs:** National Honor Society, student council, National Junior Honor Society, Community Education Center, outdoor, debate and college bowl teams, French, Spanish. **Tests:** SSAT, PSAT, SAT, ACT, TOEFL, ERB. **Graduates attending college:** 90%. **Graduates have attended:** Cal Tech, MIT, Michigan, Virginia, Georgetown.

Physical plant

Location: equidistant (8 kilometers) from Islamabad and Rawalpindi, in a suburban-rural setting with several Pakistani schools. **Campus:** 23 acres. **Library:** 24,000 volumes. **Facilities:** 14 buildings, 54 classrooms, auditorium, infirmary, covered play area, 2 tennis courts, gymnasium, 3 playing fields, 4 science labs, 2 computer labs, new cafeteria, snack bar, AV room, weight room, squash court, air conditioning.

*Once only fee

KARACHI

KARACHI AMERICAN SOCIETY SCHOOL

Street address: Amir Khusro Road, KDA Scheme No. I, Karachi 75350, Pakistan

Phone: (92)(21)433557/433559/438339/437332

    Facsimile: (92)(21)4547305   **Telex:** 95224655 KAS PK

U.S. mail: Admin/1, AmConGen, Unit 62400 Box 131, APO AE 09814-2400

Superintendent: Ralph Jahr, Ph.D.

Secondary principal: Philip Sylla

Elementary principal: Gary Winning

Business manager: Erna Faruqui

Staff: full-time, 38; part-time, 2

Nationalities of staff: U.S., 28; U.K., 1; host, 6; other, 5

Grade levels: N – 12

Enrollment: N – preK, 15; K, 21; 1 – 6, 148; 7 – 9, 93; 10 – 12, 86; total, 363

Nationalities of student body: U.S., 126; U.K., 21; host, 117; other, 99

Capacity: N – preK, 20; K, 25; 1 – 6, 150; 7 – 9, 100; 10 – 12, 105; total, 400

Teacher/student ratio: 1/9

Tuition (annual): N, $3,270; K, $6,540; 1 – 6, $6,555; 7 – 12, $6,565

Other fees: registration*, $1,800

School year: August through May

Year founded: 1953. **Type of school:** coed, day. **Governed by:** elected board of directors. **Sponsored by:** U.S. Embassy. **Accredited by:** Middle States.

Curriculum

Type: U.S. (AP). **Languages taught:** French, Spanish, Urdu. **Staff specialists:** computer, counselor, nurse, art, physical education, vocal music, instrumental music, drama, elementary science, ESL. **Special co-curricular:** art, chorus, band, physical education, computer instruction, drama, yearbook, journalism. **Extracurricular:** drama, computers, literary magazine, jazz band, chorus, student government, arts and crafts, Great Books. **Sports:** basketball, field hockey, soccer, softball, swimming, tennis, volleyball, track & field, squash, T-ball, middle school cooperative games. **Clubs:** chess, art, International Club, Key Club, National Honor Society, National Junior Honor Society. **Tests:** SSAT, PSAT, ACT, AP, Iowa, COGAT. **Graduates attending college:** 90%. **Graduates have attended:** Brown, MIT, U. of Pennsylvania, U. of California, Rice.

Physical plant

Location: in a well-developed residential area 20 minutes from city center. **Campus:** 10 acres. **Facilities:** 11 buildings, 38 classrooms, auditorium, cafeteria, 2 tennis courts, gymnasium, 3 science labs, swimming pool, 2 libraries, performing arts center, clinic, 2 squash courts, athletic field, completely air conditioned.

*Once only fee

LAHORE

LAHORE AMERICAN SOCIETY SCHOOL

Street address: Al-Riaz, Canal Bank, Lahore, Pakistan
Phone: (92)(42)870895   **Facsimile:** (92)(42)5711901
    Cable: AMCONSUL LAHORE
U.S. mail: c/o U.S. Consulate General Lahore, Agency, Unit 62216, APO
    AE 09812-2216
Superintendent: John J. Higgs
High school principal: Shanaz Ali
Middle school principal: Michael Kent
Elementary coordinator: Dennis Kramer
Staff: full-time, 37; part-time, 3; aides, 8
Nationalities of staff: U.S., 21; host, 20; other, 7
Grade levels: preK – 12
Enrollment: preK, 17; K, 22; 1 – 5, 151; 6 – 9, 119; 10 – 12, 93; total, 402
Nationalities of student body: U.S., 64; host, 231; other, 107
Capacity: preK, 25; K, 50; 1 – 6, 175; 7 – 9, 75; 10 – 12, 75; total, 400
Teacher/student ratio: 1/10
Tuition (annual): preK – K, $2,900; 1 – 5, $3,625; 6 – 12, $4,350
Other fees: registration*, $2,000
School year: August to May

Year founded: 1956. **Type of school:** coed, day, proprietary. **Governed
by:** elected board of directors. **Accredited by:** Middle States.

Curriculum/physical plant

Type: U.S. **Languages taught:** French, Urdu. **Staff specialists:** reading,
counselor. **Special programs:** ESL, advanced placement. **Special curricular:**
art, physical education, computer instruction, music. **Extracurricular:** computers, yearbook, excursions/expeditions, field trips, chorus. **Sports:** basketball, field hockey, soccer, tennis, volleyball. **Tests:** PSAT, SAT, ACT, TOEFL,
AP, Iowa. **Graduates attending college:** 95%. **Graduates have attended:**
Cornell, Stanford, Smith, Princeton, Harvard. **Location:** in suburban area,
2 – 3 miles from city center. **Campus:** 4 acres. **Library:** 26,000 volumes.
Facilities: 6 buildings, infirmary, science lab, computer lab, swimming pool,
soccer field, air conditioning.

*Once only fee

MURREE HILLS

MURREE CHRISTIAN SCHOOL

Phone: (92)(593)2321/2328
Mail: PO Jhika Gali, Murree Hills, 47180 Pakistan
Principal: Phil Billing
Staff: full-time, 23
Nationalities of staff: U.S., 4; U.K., 12; host, 2; other, 5
Grade levels: K – 12
Enrollment: K, 14; 1 – 6, 71; 7 – 9, 29; 10 – 12, 20; total, 134
Nationalities of student body: U.S., 31; U.K., 18; host, 6; other, 79
Capacity: total, 200
Teacher/student ratio: 1/6
Boarding capacity: boys, 75; girls, 75   **Grades:** 1 – 12
    Program: planned 7-day
Tuition (annual): 1 – 12, $1,400 (mission), $4,600 (non-mission)
Other fees (annual): boarding, $980; security deposit, $1,538 for non-mission only
School year: August to July

Year founded: 1956. **Type of school:** coed, day, boarding, church-related, private nonprofit. **Governed by:** elected board of directors. **Sponsored by:** more than 20 mission groups.

Curriculum
Type: U.S., U.K. **Languages taught:** French, Urdu; German and Finnish as mother tongue. **Staff specialists:** computer, counselor, nurse. **Special curricular:** art, chorus, physical education, computer instruction. **Extracurricular:** drama, gymnastics, instrumental music, computers, yearbook, photography, excursions/expeditions, field trips. **Sports:** basketball, football, hockey, volleyball, table tennis. **Clubs:** photography, gymnastics, computer, chess. **Tests:** PSAT, SAT, Iowa, IGCSE, Scottish Highers. **Graduates have attended:** Southern Illinois U., Trinity Western U., Sterling College, Houghton College, Heriot Watt U. (Edinburgh).

Physical plant
Location: in wooded setting in Himalayan foothills, 3 miles from Murree, 31 miles from Islamabad. **Campuses (2):** 4 acres. **Library:** 8,000 volumes. **Facilities:** 7 buildings, 17 classrooms, auditorium, 2 cafeterias, infirmary, 2 tennis courts, gymnasium, playing field, science lab, computer lab, AV equipment, 2 boarding hostels.

PESHAWAR

THE INTERNATIONAL SCHOOL OF PESHAWAR

Street address: 17 Park Avenue Road, University Town, Peshawar, NWFP
Pakistan
Phone: (92)(521)40481
Mail: c/o American Consulate, 11 Hospital Road, Peshawar, Pakistan
Head: Rebecca N. Qarghah
Staff: full-time, 7; part-time, 1
Nationalities of staff: U.S., 4; other, 4
Grade levels: K – 6
Enrollment: K, 8; 1 – 6, 35; total, 43
Nationalities of student body: U.S., 7; other, 36
Capacity: K, 10; 1 – 6, 40; total, 50
Teacher/student ratio: 1/6
Tuition (annual): K, $4,000; 1 – 6, $4,500
Other fees: registration*, $500
School year: September to June

Year founded: 1987. **Type of school:** coed, day, private nonprofit.
Governed by: elected school board. **Sponsored by:** U.S. government.

Curriculum/physical plant

Type: U.S. **Languages taught:** English. **Staff specialists:** reading, ESL.
Special programs: ESL. **Special curricular:** art, physical education, music.
Location: in suburban area, 6 kilometers from Peshawar. **Library:** 1,500
volumes. **Facilities:** 2 buildings, 7 classrooms, playing field, computer lab, air
conditioning.

*Once only fee

PANAMA

Region: Central America
Size: 29,208 square miles
Population: 2,426,000
Capital: Panama

Telephone code: 507
Currency: balboa
Languages: Spanish, English

PANAMA CITY

THE INTERNATIONAL SCHOOL OF PANAMA

Street address: Carretera al Nuevo Club de Golf, Cerro Viento, Panama City, Republic of Panama
Phone: (507)667037/669532   **Facsimile:** (507)667808
Mail: PO Box 6-7589, El Dorado, Panama, Republic of Panama
U.S. mail: (no personal name) Director, The International School of Panama, Unit 0945, APO AA 34002-0008
Director: Gary F. Kenny
Secondary school principal: Jutta Patterson
Elementary school principal: Diane Guevara
Business manager: Laurie M. Lewter
Staff: full-time, 26; part-time, 7
Nationalities of staff: U.S., 6; U.K., 1; host, 23; other, 3
Grade levels: JK – 12
Enrollment: JK, 20; K, 35; 1 – 6, 181; 7 – 9, 80; 10 – 12, 47; total, 363
Nationalities of student body: U.S., 87; U.K., 11; host, 97; other, 168
Teacher/student ratio: 1/11
Tuition (annual): JK, $2,550; K, $4,050; 1 – 6, $4,225; 7 – 12, $4,700
Other fees (annual): registration, $100; capital levy*, $3,000 (first child), $2,000 (siblings); testing: JK, $25; K – 12, $50
School year: August to June

Year founded: 1982. **Type of school:** coed, day, private nonprofit. **Governed by:** elected board of directors. **Accredited by:** Southern.

Curriculum/physical plant

Type: international. **Languages of instruction:** English, Spanish. **Languages taught:** French, Spanish. **Staff specialists:** computer, counselor, art, ESL, music, physical education. **Special programs:** ESL, Spanish as a Second Language. **Special curricular:** art, physical education, computer instruction. **Extracurricular:** drama, computers, yearbook, newspaper, music, folk dancing, team sports. **Organizations:** student council, CAS program, science club. **Tests:** PSAT, SAT, TOEFL, Iowa, TAP. **Diplomas offered:** Panamanian, U.S., IB. **Graduates attending college:** 98%. **Graduates have attended:** U. of Panama, Harvard, MIT, Notre Dame, McGill. **Location:** outer city limits. **Campus:** 16+ acres. **Library:** 7,500 volumes. **Facilities:** 2 building complexes, 27 classrooms, covered play area, 2 playing fields, prep and science labs, computer lab, art room, air conditioning.

*Once only fee

PUERTO ARMUELLES

Escuela Las Palmas
Mail: Apartado 6-2637, Panama, Panama
Phone: (507)707283
Director: Aleida Molina

PAPUA NEW GUINEA _____

Region: Southeast Asia
Size: 178,260 square miles
Population: 3,913,000
Capital: Port Moresby

Telephone code: 675
Currency: kina
Languages: English, Melanesian
languages, Papuan
languages

GOROKA

GOROKA INTERNATIONAL SCHOOL

Phone: (675)721466/721452   **Facsimile:** (675)722146
Mail: PO Box 845, Goroka, E.H.P., Papua New Guinea
Principal: Mr. A. A. Armstrong
Staff: full-time, 9; part-time, 5
Grade levels: preK – 10
Enrollment: preK, 50; K – 6, 165; 7 – 10, 14; total, 229
Capacity: preK, 60; K – 6, 200; 7 – 10, 30; total, 290
Teacher/student ratio: 1/19
Tuition (annual): preK, 1,570**; K – 6, 3,140; 7 – 10, 4,950
School year: February to December

Year founded: 1953. **Type of school:** coed, day. **Governed by:** elected
board of governors. **Accredited by:** International Education Agency (PNG) Ltd.

Curriculum/physical plant

Type: international, U.K., Australia, New Zealand. **Special curricular:**
computer instruction. **Extracurricular:** instrumental music, computers.
Sports: soccer, softball, swimming, volleyball, Aussie sports, cross-country,
athletics, netball, cricket. **Clubs:** squash, swimming, golf, tennis. **Location:**
on two separate sites, both within town boundary. **Facilities:** playing fields,
outdoor education areas, libraries, computer labs.

**Papua New Guinea kina

LAE

The International School of Lae
Phone: (675)423588   **Facsimile:** (675)422394
Mail: PO Box 2130, Lae, Papua New Guinea
Principal: Bruce Gamwell
Staff: full-time, 30
Grade levels: preK – 12
Enrollment: K, 30; 1 – 6, 400; 7 – 9, 110; 10 – 12, 60; total, 600
Nationalities of student body: U.S., 20; U.K., 30; host, 150; other, 400
Teacher/student ratio: 1/20
Boarders: boys, 12; girls, 6
    Grades: 5 – 12   **Program:** planned 7-day
Tuition (annual): K – 6, 3,700**; 7 – 12, 6,155
Other fees (annual): boarding, 5,000**
School year: January to December

Type of school: coed, day, boarding, private nonprofit. **Governed by:** International Education Agency. **Accredited by:** Papua New Guinea Department of Education.

Curriculum/physical plant
Type: U.K., IGCSE (grade 10); Australian Capital Territories (grade 12, university entrance). **Languages taught:** French. **Staff specialists:** math, computer. **Special programs:** correspondence. **Special curricular:** art, physical education, computer instruction. **Extracurricular:** drama, gymnastics, instrumental music, computers, yearbook, literary magazine, field trips. **Sports:** hockey, rugby, soccer, softball, tennis, squash, golf. **Tests:** SAT, IGCSE, Australian Capital Territories Grade 12 Certificate. **Graduates attending college:** 80%. **Facilities:** 2 campuses, 2 cafeterias, covered play area, 3 tennis courts, 2 playing fields, 4 science labs, 2 computer labs, swimming pool, partial air conditioning.

**Papua New Guinea kina

PORT MORESBY

Port Moresby International High School
Street address: Bava Street, Boroko, Port Moresby, Papua New Guinea
Phone: (675)253166   **Facsimile:** (675)254439   **Cable:** POMHI
Mail: PO Box 276, Boroko, Papua New Guinea
Principal: Colin Brown
Administrative staff: Mrs. D. Korare, Ms. J. Conway
Staff: full-time, 54; part-time, 4

Nationalities of staff: U.S., 3; U.K., 13; host, 3; other, 39
Grade levels: 7 – 12
Enrollment: 7 – 9, 470; 10 – 12, 260; total, 730
Nationalities of student body: U.S., 7; U.K., 32; host, 266; other, 425
Capacity: 7 – 9, 630; 10 – 12, 300; total, 930
Teacher/student ratio: 1/13
Tuition (annual): 7 – 12, $6,000
Other fees (annual): registration*, $250; books, approximately $200
School year: February to December

Year founded: 1959. **Type of school:** coed, day, private nonprofit.
Governed by: elected board of governors. **Accredited by:** International
Education Agency of Papua New Guinea; Australian Capital Territory Education Department; ECIS.

Curriculum

Type: IB. **Languages taught:** French, German, Indonesian. **Staff specialists:** reading, math, counselor. **Special programs:** ESL, advanced placement, remedial. **Special curricular:** art, physical education, computer instruction, home economics, technics. **Extracurricular:** drama, gymnastics, dance, choral music, instrumental music, computers, yearbook, newspaper, literary magazine, photography, excursions/expeditions, field trips, wide range of clubs covering most interests. **Sports:** basketball, soccer, softball, tennis, volleyball, cricket, rugby union, cross-country, netball, athletics, etc. **Tests:** SAT, TOEFL, IB, IGCSE. **Graduates have attended:** U. of Sydney, U. of Auckland, U. of Papua New Guinea, U. of London, U. of Cambridge.

Physical plant

Location: in suburb of Port Moresby. **Campus:** 25 acres. **Library:** 16,000 volumes. **Facilities:** 17 buildings, 50 classrooms, 2 tennis courts, 2 playing fields, 6 science labs, 2 computer labs, auditorium/gymnasium, 2 home science rooms, 3 art rooms, 3 technical rooms, darkroom.

*Once only fee

UKARUMPA

AIYURA INTERNATIONAL PRIMARY SCHOOL

Phone: (675)773550   **Facsimile:** (675)773507
    Telex: 79577611 LING NG NE
Mail: PO Box 407, Ukarumpa via Lae, Papua New Guinea
Principal: Perry Bradford
Vice-principal: Nate Kruger
Staff: full-time, 20; part-time, 3
Nationalities of staff: U.S., 17; other, 6
Grade levels: K – 6
Enrollment: total, 310

Nationalities of student body: U.S., 154; host, 80; other, 76
Capacity: K, 50; 1 – 6, 300; total, 350
Teacher/student ratio: 1/14
Tuition (annual): K – 6, $2,800
Other fees (annual): busing, $80
School year: February to December

Year founded: 1975. **Type of school:** coed, day, church-related. **Governed by:** elected committee of sponsoring organization. **Sponsored by:** Summer Institute of Linguistics. **Accredited by:** Western.

Curriculum/physical plant
Type: multinational curriculum. **Languages taught:** French, German, Korean. **Staff specialists:** learning disabilities. **Special programs:** correspondence, remedial. **Special curricular:** art, band, physical education, computer instruction, music. **Extracurricular:** choral music, instrumental music, computers, field trips, outdoor education. **Sports:** baseball, basketball, hockey, soccer. **Tests:** SAT, OLSAT, diagnostic. **Location:** in rural area. **Campus:** 10 acres. **Library:** 10,000 volumes. **Facilities:** 16 buildings, 14 classrooms, auditorium, covered play area, playing field, computer lab, AV room, basketball court.

Ukarumpa High School
Phone: (675)774575   **Facsimile:** (675)774111
  E-mail: 62006899
  Cable: LINGUISTA KAINANTU (PAPUA NEW GUINEA)
Mail: PO Box 406, Ukarumpa via Lae, Papua New Guinea
Principal: Steve Walker
Assistant principals: Randell Foxworth, Peter Belcher
Staff: full-time, 27; part-time, 15
Nationalities of staff: U.S., 27; U.K., 3; other, 12
Grade levels: 7 – 12
Enrollment: 7 – 9, 106; 10 – 12, 100; total, 206
Nationalities of student body: U.S., 104; host, 12; other, 90
Capacity: 7 – 9, 120; 10 – 12, 120; total, 240
Teacher/student ratio: 1/6
Tuition (annual): 7 – 12, $4,000
School year: February to December

Year founded: 1962. **Type of school:** coed, day, church-related. **Governed by:** appointed and elected education committee of sponsoring body. **Sponsored by:** Summer Institute of Linguistics. **Accredited by:** Western.

Curriculum/physical plant
Type: U.S., U.K., Australian. **Languages taught:** French, Spanish, German. **Staff specialists:** reading, math, computer, counselor. **Special programs:** advanced placement, honors sections, independent study, correspondence. **Special curricular:** art, chorus, band, physical education, com-

puter instruction, vocational. **Extracurricular:** drama, choral music, instrumental music, yearbook, newspaper, photography, excursions/expeditions, field trips. **Sports:** basketball, soccer, softball, volleyball, track and field (athletics). **Tests:** PSAT, SAT, ACT, AP, GCSE, MAT, Higher School Certificate (New South Wales, Australia). **Graduates attending college:** 70%. **Graduates have attended:** Wheaton, Baylor, U. of Sydney, California Polytech, Azusa Pacific. **Location:** in rural area, 10 kilometers from Kainantu. **Campus:** 5 acres. **Library:** 13,000 volumes. **Facilities:** 8 buildings, auditorium, 7 tennis courts, playing field, 3 science labs, computer lab, reading lab, AV theater.

PORT MORESBY
Murray International School
   Address: PO Box 1137, Boroko, NCD, Paupa New Guinea
   Phone: (675)252833   **Facsimile:** (675)257925
   Headmistress: Maureen Stubberfield

RABAUL
Rabaul International School
   Address: PO Box 571, Rabaul, ENBP, Papua New Guinea
   Phone: (675)921485   **Facsimile:** (675)921498
   Principal: Ian Smith

PARAGUAY
Region: South America
Size: 157,047 square miles
Population: 4,798,000
Capital: Asuncion
Telephone code: 595
Currency: guarani
Languages: Spanish, Guarani

ASUNCIÓN

THE AMERICAN SCHOOL OF ASUNCIÓN
   Street address: General Genes 1172-75, Asunción, Paraguay
   Phone: (595)(21)600479   **Facsimile:** (595)(21)603518
   Mail: c/o U.S. Embassy, Asunción, Paraguay
   U.S. mail: Director, The American School (ASA), American Embassy – Asunción, Unit 4750, APO AA 34036
   Director: Ralph A. Davia, Ph.D.
   Assistant director: Nelson Aguilera
   Secondary principal: Alan Everest, Ed.D.
   Elementary principal: Wayne McCullar, Ph.D.
   Staff: full-time, 52; part-time, 4
   Nationalities of staff: U.S., 40; host, 13; other, 3

Grade levels: preK – 12
Enrollment: preK, 42; K, 42; 1 – 6, 231; 7 – 9, 135; 10 – 12, 90; total, 540
Nationalities of student body: U.S., 120; host, 270; other, 150
Capacity: preK, 44; K, 44; 1 – 6, 231; 7 – 9, 135; 10 – 12, 90; total, 544
Teacher/student ratio: 1/10
Tuition (annual): preK – K, $1,800; 1 – 7, $2,700; 8 – 12, $3,200
Other fees (annual): registration, $100; entrance*, $2,500
School year: August to December / February to July

Year founded: 1956. **Type of school:** coed, day, private nonprofit.
Governed by: elected board of directors. **Accredited by:** Southern, Paraguayan Ministry of Education.

Curriculum

Type: U.S., Paraguayan. **Languages of instruction:** English, Spanish for national program. **Languages taught:** French, German, Portuguese, Guarani (Indian). **Staff specialist:** counselor. **Special programs:** ESL, SSL, learning disabilities. **Special curricular:** art, physical education, computer instruction. **Extracurricular:** drama, computers, yearbook, photography, excursions/expeditions, field trips, cheerleading, student council. **Sports:** soccer, girls' volleyball, boys' basketball, futbol de salon. **Tests:** SSAT, PSAT, SAT, ACT, ERB. **Graduates attending college:** 98%. **Graduates have attended:** Boston College, U.S. Naval Academy, U. of Pennsylvania, Cornell, Texas A&M.

Physical plant

Location: within city limits of Asunción. **Campus:** 14 acres. **Library:** 13,000 volumes. **Facilities:** 11 buildings, 40 classrooms, cafeteria, infirmary, tennis court, gymnasium, 3 playing fields, 2 science labs, computer lab, art/photography labs, air conditioning.

*Once only fee

ASUNCIÓN CHRISTIAN ACADEMY

Street address: 1181 Avenida Santisimo Sacramento, Asunción, Paraguay
Phone: (595)(21)607378   **Facsimile:** (595)(21)604907
Mail: Casilla 1562, Asunción, Paraguay
U.S. mail: Director, American Embassy, ACA; Unit 4751; APO AA 34036
Director: Bethany Abreu
Staff: full-time, 25; part-time, 2
Nationalities of staff: U.S., 23; host, 4
Grade levels: preK – 12
Enrollment: preK, 13; K, 15; 1 – 6, 83; 7 – 9, 36; 10 – 12, 19; total, 166
Nationalities of student body: U.S., 73; U.K., 2; host, 46; other, 45
Capacity: preK, 13; K, 13; 1 – 6, 78; 7 – 9, 39; 10 – 12, 39; total, 182
Teacher/student ratio: 1/6
Tuition (annual): preK, $1,140; K – 6, $1,795; 7 – 12, $2,075
Other fees (annual): registration, $250; entrance fee, $800/family

School year: August to December / February to June

Year founded: 1958. **Type of school:** coed, day, private nonprofit, Christian. **Governed by:** elected board of directors from evangelical missions in Paraguay.

Curriculum/physical plant

Type: U.S. **Languages taught:** English. **Staff specialists:** reading resource, counselor, learning disabilities. **Special curricular:** art, chorus, physical education, computer instruction. **Extracurricular:** drama, choral music, computers, yearbook, newspaper, photography, excursions/expeditions, field trips. **Sports:** basketball, soccer, volleyball, American football. **Tests:** PSAT, SAT, ACT, MAT. **Graduates attending college:** 90%. **Graduates have attended:** U. of Pennsylvania, Georgia Tech., Evangel College, U. of California at LaJolla, Northeastern. **Location:** in suburban area. **Campus:** 5 acres. **Library:** 7,500 volumes. **Facilities:** 11 buildings, 21 classrooms, auditorium, covered play area, playing field, science lab, computer lab, AV room.

PERU ⎯⎯⎯⎯⎯⎯⎯⎯⎯⎯⎯⎯⎯⎯⎯⎯⎯

Region: South America
Size: 496,222 square miles
Population: 22,361,000
Capital: Lima

Telephone code: 51
Currency: sole
Languages: Spanish, Quechua, Aymara

ILO

SOUTHERN PERU COPPER CORPORATION

STAFF SCHOOLS

Street address: Casilla 303, Tacna, Toquepala, Peru, S.A.
Phone: (51)(54)726296   **Facsimile:** (51)(54)726344
    Telex: 39453777 PE SMELTILO
U.S. mail: 180 Maiden Lane, New York, NY 10038, U.S.A.
Director: (to be announced)
Principals: Ron Bromert, John Dennis, Terry Weakley
Staff: full-time, 28
Nationalities of staff: U.S., 25; host, 3
Grade levels: K – 9
Enrollment: K, 25; 1 – 6, 120; 7 – 9, 10; total, 155
Nationalities of student body: U.S., 30; host, 110; other, 15
Capacity: K, 15; 1 – 6, 120; 7 – 9, 45; total, 180
Teacher/student ratio: 1/5
School year: September to June

Year founded: 1956. **Type of school:** coed, day, company sponsored. **Governed and sponsored by:** Southern Peru Copper Corporation. **Accredited by:** Southern.

Curriculum/physical plant

Type: U.S. **Languages taught:** Spanish. **Staff specialists:** reading, learning disabilities. **Special curricular:** physical education, computer instruction. **Extracurricular:** yearbook, newspaper, photography, field trips. **Tests:** SSAT, TOEFL, Iowa. **Location:** company-owned campsites. **Campuses (3):** 5 acres. **Library:** 6,000 volumes. **Facilities:** 8 buildings, 24 classrooms, 3 infirmaries, 3 tennis courts, 3 playing fields, 3 science labs, 3 swimming pools.

LIMA

COLEGIO FRANKLIN D. ROOSEVELT

Street address: Avda. Las Palmeras 325, Urb. Camacho, La Molina, Lima, Peru
Phone: (51)(14)350890   **Facsimile:** (51)(14)360927
Cable: AMERSCHOOL
Mail: Apartado 18-0977, Lima 18, Peru, S.A.
U.S. mail: (official use only) Superintendent, Colegio Franklin D. Roosevelt, Unit 3804, APO AA 34031
Superintendent: Anthony C. Horton, Ph.D.
Assistant superintendent/secondary principal: Brian Atkins
Middle school principal: Timothy Boyer
Elementary principal: Susan Young
Elementary assistant principal: Doris de las Casas
Peruvian director: Jose Jordan
Finance and business manager: Edwing Suni
Staff: full-time, 87; part-time, 7
Nationalities of staff: U.S., 39; U.K., 1; host, 47; other, 7
Grade levels: preK – 12
Enrollment: preK, 118; K, 77; 1 – 6, 399; 7 – 9, 209; 10 – 12, 168; total, 971
Nationalities of student body: U.S., 148; U.K., 21; host, 708; other, 94
Capacity: N – preK, 86; K, 84; 1 – 6, 520; 7– 9, 240; 10 – 12, 250; total, 1,180
Teacher/student ratio: 1/11
Tuition (annual): preK (half day), $2,700; K, $6,255; 1 – 12, $6,950
Other fees (annual): busing, $600; entrance*, $5,500
School year: August to July

Year founded: 1946. **Type of school:** coed, day, private nonprofit. **Governed by:** appointed board of directors. **Sponsored by:** American companies/Embassy. **Accredited by:** Southern. **Regional organizations:** AASSA.

Curriculum

Type: U.S., Peruvian, IB. **Languages of instruction:** English, Spanish (limited). **Languages taught:** English, French, Spanish. **Staff specialists:** reading, math, computer, counselor, psychologist, learning disabilities, nurse, gifted & talented, elementary science, resource. **Special programs:** ESL, Advanced Placement, independent study, remedial. **Special curricular:** art, chorus, band, physical education, computer instruction. **Extracurricular:** drama, gymnastics, dance, choral music, instrumental music, computers, yearbook, newspaper, literary magazine, photography, field trips. **Sports:** baseball, softball, basketball, field hockey, soccer, volleyball. **Clubs:** community service, varsity, computer, National Honor Society, Tri-M, chess, debate. **Tests:** SSAT, PSAT, SAT, ACT, TOEFL, IB, AP, Iowa. **Graduates attending college:** 69%. **Graduates have attended:** Cornell, Babson, Stanford, MIT, U. of Pennsylvania.

Physical plant

Location: in La Molina, a suburb of Lima. **Campus:** 24 acres. **Library:** 40,000 volumes. **Facilities:** 5 buildings, 90 classrooms, 2 auditoriums, infirmary, covered play area, 4 tennis courts, gymnasium, 6 playing fields, 6 science labs, 5 computer labs.

*Once only fee

AREQUIPA

Prescott Anglo-American School

Address: Av. Alfonso Ugarte No. 565 (Tingo) Arequipa, Peru
Mail: PO Box 1036, Arequipa, Peru
Phone: (51)(54)232507   **Headmaster:** Augusto Gonzales Torres

LIMA

Abraham Lincoln School

Address: Ave. Jose Antonio S/N, Urb. Parque de Monterrico, La Molina, Lima, Peru   **Mail:** PO Box 6167, Lima 100, Peru

PHILIPPINES —————————————————

Region: Southeast Asia
Size: 115,831 square miles
Population: 65,758,000
Capital: Quezon City,

Manila (de facto)
Telephone code: 63
Currency: peso
Languages: Pilipino, English, others

BAGUIO

BRENT SCHOOL

Street address: Brent Road, Baguio City, Philippines
Phone: (63)(74)4424050/4422260/4423628
    Facsimile: (63)(74)4423638   **Telex:** 73240115 BRENT PM
Mail: PO Box 35, Baguio City 2600, Philippines
Headmaster: Paul Gysin
Deputy head, upper/lower school coordinator: Ursula B. Daoey
Business manager: Marcial Esquejo
Staff: full-time, 32; part-time, 1; part-time volunteers, 6
Grade levels: preK – 12
Enrollment: preK, 9; K, 21; 1 – 6, 116; 7 – 9, 80; 10 – 12, 75; total, 301
Nationalities of student body: U.S., 60; host, 71; other, 170
Capacity: preK, 20; K, 20; 1 – 6, 240; 7 – 9, 120; 10 – 12, 120; total, 520
Teacher/student ratio: 1/9
Boarders: boys, 36; girls, 37   **Grades:** 4 – 12   **Program:** planned 7-day
Tuition (annual): preK, $1,100; K, $1,483; 1 – 3, $2,051; 4 – 6, $2,379;
    7 – 8, $3,368; 9 – 12, $4,596
Other fees (annual): registration, $45; boarding, $5,092; capital levy,
    $156; lunch, $138; books, $96 – 120; miscellaneous, $168 – 280,
    matriculation*, $281
School year: September to June

Year founded: 1909. **Type of school:** coed, day, boarding, church-related, private nonprofit. **Governed by:** appointed board of trustees. **Accredited by:** Western, PAASCU (Philippine Accrediting Association of Schools, Colleges and Universities).

Curriculum

Type: International, IB. **Languages taught:** French, Spanish, Pilipino. **Staff specialists:** computer, counselor, nurse. **Special programs:** ESL, remedial, ability groupings in math. **Special curricular:** art, chorus, physical education, computer instruction. **Extracurricular:** drama, dance, choral music, yearbook, newspaper, photography, field trips. **Sports:** basketball, football, soccer, volleyball. **Clubs:** science, Pilipino, drama. **Tests:** PSAT, SAT, ACT, IB. **Graduates attending college:** 86%. **Graduates have attended:** Mount Holyoke, U. of Texas, Chaminade U., Oberlin College, Young Harris College.

Physical plant
Location: in Baguio City, nestled in mountains on island of Luzon. **Campus:** 13 hectares. **Library:** 21,000 volumes. **Facilities:** 21 buildings, 34 classrooms, 2 auditoriums, 2 cafeterias, infirmary, gymnasium, playing field, 4 science labs, computer lab, 4 dormitories plus housing/apartments for resident staff.

*Once only fee

CAINTA

FAITH ACADEMY

Street address: Victoria Valley Subdivision, Valley Golf Road, Cainta, Rizal, Philippines
Phone: (63)(2)6580047 – 8/6650644   **Facsimile:** (63)(2)6580026
    Cable: FAITHCADMY, Manila
Mail: PO Box 2016, Makati Central Post Office, 0706 Makati, Metro Manila, Philippines
Superintendent: Dennis Vogan, Ed.D.
Secondary school principal: Philip Parsons
Middle school principal: David Venable
Elementary school principal: Judy Severns
Staff: full-time, 51; part-time, 6
Nationalities of staff: U.S., 42; U.K., 8; other, 7
Grade levels: K – 12
Enrollment: K, 28; 1 – 6, 260; 7 – 9, 194; 10 – 12, 178; total, 660
Nationalities of student body: U.S., 447; U.K., 29; host, 4; other, 180
Capacity: K, 36; 1 – 6, 292; 7 – 9, 210; 10 – 12, 210; total, 748
Teacher/student ratio: 1/12
Boarders: boys and girls, 74   **Grades:** 4 – 12   **Program:** planned 7-day
Tuition (annual): preK, $20 (4 – 5 weeks); K – 5, $805; 6 – 8, $893; 9 – 12, $911; nonmissionary, $2,306 – 2,412
Other fees (annual): registration, $30; boarding, $2,328 – 2,521; busing, $190 – 660; facilities/equipment/scholarship, $335; campus development, $500
School year: August to June

Year founded: 1957. **Type of school:** coed, day, boarding, church-related, private nonprofit. **Governed by:** appointed board of trustees. **Sponsored by:** evangelical mission boards. **Accredited by:** Western, Association of Christian Schools International.

Curriculum
Type: U.S., U.K. **Languages taught:** French, Spanish, German, Tagalog. **Staff specialists:** reading, computer, speech/hearing, learning disabilities, nurse, family counselor, gifted elementary, counselors, chaplain. **Special programs:** advanced placement. **Special curricular:** art, chorus, band,

physical education, computer instruction, vocational, homemaking, industrial arts. **Extracurricular:** drama, choral music, instrumental music, yearbook, newspaper, photography, field trips. **Sports:** basketball, soccer, softball, tennis, volleyball, cross-country, wrestling. **Clubs:** French, forensics, chess, Boy Scouts. **Tests:** PSAT, SAT, ACT, TOEFL, GCSE, Iowa, MAT, TAP, Otis-Lennon. **Graduates attending college:** 85%. **Graduates have attended:** Biola, Wheaton, Le Tourneau, Westmont, West Point.

Physical plant
Location: 13 kilometers east of Manila. **Campuses (2):** 12 acres. **Library:** 16,000 volumes. **Facilities:** 11 buildings, 56 classrooms, auditorium, 2 covered play areas, 2 tennis courts, gymnasium, 2 playing fields, 3 science labs, 3 computer labs, 3 boarding homes on campus, 2 off campus, air conditioning.

CEBU CITY

CEBU INTERNATIONAL SCHOOL
Phone: (63)(32)97268/70193   **Facsimile:** (63)(32)311556
Mail: Banilad, PO Box 735, Cebu City, Philippines 6000
Superintendent/high school principal: Carolina Q. San Luis, Ed.D.
Elementary principal: Lolita S. Dormitorio, Ed.D.
Registrar: Menezquieta P. Geverola
Guidance counselor: Liberty B. Vicentillo
Chief, educational media: Geogenes J. Biongcog
Administrative and finance officer: Teresa D. Pareja
Staff: full-time, 23; part-time, 13
Nationalities of staff: U.S., 3; host, 29; other, 4
Grade levels: K – 12
Enrollment: K, 37; 1 – 8, 218; 9 – 12, 91; total, 346
Nationalities of student body: U.S., 79; host, 153; other, 114
Capacity: K, 50; 1 – 8, 300; 9 – 12, 100; total, 450
Teacher/student ratio: 1/12
Tuition (annual): K, $528; 1 – 5, $640; 6 – 8, $700; 9 – 12, $1,200
Other fees (annual): registration, $24; insurance, $2; books: K, $20;
    1 – 2, $60; 3 – 6, $65; 7 – 12, $80; miscellaneous, $302
School year: July to April

Year founded: 1924. **Type of school:** coed, day, private nonprofit, nonsectarian. **Governed by:** elected board of trustees. **Accredited by:** Western (in process).

Curriculum
Type: U.S., Philippine. **Languages taught:** French, Spanish, German, Filipino. **Staff specialists:** reading, math, computer, counselor, nurse, science, pre-school, Filipino, performing arts, art education. **Special pro-**

grams: ESL, remedial, guidance counseling. **Special curricular:** art, drama, performance choir, photojournalism. **Extracurricular:** yearbook, field trips, scouting, journalism. **Sports:** basketball, soccer, swimming, tennis, volleyball, track and field, kickball, golf. **Organizations:** supreme student council, school newspaper. **Clubs:** math, science, sports, drama, photo-journalism. **Tests:** SAT, National College Entrance Examination (NCEE), placement test, intelligence, career. **Graduates attending college:** 100%. **Graduates have attended:** Ateneo de Manila U., U. of the Philippines, Cebu Doctor's College, various American universities.

Physical plant

Location: in suburban area. **Campus:** 2.2 hectares. **Library:** 12,000 volumes. **Facilities:** 4 buildings, 16 classrooms, cafeteria, playing field, science lab, computer lab, 2 offices, music room, AV room, covered court, clinic, guidance office, faculty room, CAT/PE office.

MANILA

BRENT INTERNATIONAL SCHOOL MANILA

Street address: University of Life Complex, Meralco Avenue, Pasig, Metro Manila, Philippines
Phone: (63)(2)6311265 – 68/6338016 – 17   **Facsimile:** (63)(2)6338420
Mail: PO Box 12201, Ortigas Center Post Office, 1600 Pasig, Metro Manila, Philippines
Headmaster: Rev. Canon Gabriel Dimanche
Deputy headmaster/director for student services: Michael F. Caldwell, Ph.D.
Upper school master: Jeremy Carter
Middle school master: Brian Marquand
Lower school master: Dick Robbins
Head media center/textbook coordinator: Aida Albarracin
Director for administrative services: Maria Elena Samson
Finance officer: Edna Ballesteros
Staff: full-time, 72
Nationalities of staff: U.S., 10; U.K., 4; host, 38; other, 20
Grade levels: N – 12
Enrollment: N – preK, 19; K, 27; 1 – 6, 287; 7 – 9, 153; 10 – 12, 168; ESL, 48; total, 702
Nationalities of student body: U.S., 105; U.K., 24; host, 241; other, 332
Capacity: N – preK, 15; K, 30; 1 – 6, 360; 7 – 9, 160; 10 – 12, 160; ESL, 60; total, 785
Teacher/student ratio: 1/10
Tuition (annual): N – K, $1,584; 1 – 3, $2,172; 4 – 6, $2,640; 7 – 8, $3,230; 9 – 12, $4,107
Other fees (annual): capital levy, $1,270; books, $118 – 158; matricula-

tion*, $2,308; application/testing*, $76; registration and miscellaneous: N – K, $239; 1 – 3, $272; 4 – 6, $291; 7 – 8, $319; 9 – 10, $352; 11 – 12, $433

School year: August to June

Year founded: 1984. **Type of school:** coed, day, church-related, private nonprofit. **Governed by:** elected board of trustees. **Accredited by:** Western, PAASCU. **Regional organizations:** EARCOS, NAIS.

Curriculum

Type: U.S., IB. **Languages taught:** English, French, Spanish, Filipino, Chinese. **Staff specialists:** nurse, ESL, guidance counselor, physician. **Special programs:** ESL, remedial, computer-assisted instructor. **Special curricular:** art, chorus, band, physical education, computer instruction, musical presentation. **Extracurricular:** choral music, instrumental music, computers, yearbook, newspaper, field trips, academic bowl, student council. **Sports:** basketball, soccer, softball, swimming, tennis, volleyball, track and field. **Clubs:** community service, crafts, debating, glee, scouting, drama, literary, environmental, photography, computer, math, science. **Tests:** PSAT, SAT, ACET, TOEFL, IB, MAT, ITBS, OLMAT, DAT, CII, SLEP, CAPT. **Graduates attending college:** 100%. **Graduates have attended:** Cambridge, London School of Economics, Boston U., New York U., U. of the Philippines.

Physical plant

Location: on University of Life campus, 3 minutes to new Asian Development Bank, 10 minutes to Quezon City, 15 minutes to Makati. **Facilities:** 6 buildings, cafeteria, infirmary, covered play area, tennis court, 3 science labs, 2 computer labs, swimming pool, 2 libraries, chapel, amphitheater, soccer field, covered gymnasium, band room, music room, 3 AV rooms, air conditioning.

*Once only fee

INTERNATIONAL SCHOOL, MANILA

Street address: Gen. Luna Street and Kalayaan Avenue, Bel Air, Makati, Metro Manila, Philippines
Phone: (63)(2)889891 – 95   **Facsimile:** (63)(2)8186127
Telex: 71214867 ISMNL PS   **Cable:** ISMANILA
Mail: PO Box 323, MCPO, 1299 Makati, Metro Manila, Philippines
Superintendent: Rodney C. Hermes, Ed.D.
Director of instructional services: Timothy Hansen, Ed.D.
Director of administrative services: LiliaTantoco
High school principal: Arthur Aaronson, Ed.D.
Middle school principal: Jeffrey W. Hammett
Elementary school principal: Dennis Larkin
Administrative finance officer: Samuel J. Yap

Staff: full-time, 188; part-time, 9
Nationalities of staff: U.S., 69; U.K., 4; host, 102; other, 22
Grade levels: K – 12
Enrollment: K, 75; 1 – 5, 678; 6 – 8, 484; 9 – 12, 693; total, 1,930
Nationalities of student body: U.S., 453; U.K., 35; host, 393; other, 1,049
Capacity: K – 5, 1,000; 6 – 8, 700; 9 – 12, 800; total, 2,500
Teacher/student ratio: 1/10
Tuition (annual): K, $3,300; 1 – 5, $4,500; 6 – 8, $5,600; 9 – 12, $6,000
Other fees (annual): matriculation*, $1,400; capital projects, $450; assorted fees for special courses
School year: August to June

Year founded: 1920. **Type of school:** coed, day, private nonprofit. **Governed by:** elected board of trustees. **Accredited by:** Western.

Curriculum

Type: U.S., IB. **Languages taught:** French, Spanish, German, Japanese, Chinese, Filipino. **Staff specialists:** counselor, nurse, dentist, doctor. **Special programs:** ESL, advanced placement, independent study, optimal learning. **Extracurricular:** drama, gymnastics, dance, choral music, instrumental music, computers, yearbook, newspaper, literary magazine, photography, excursions/expeditions, field trips. **Sports:** baseball, basketball, cheerleading, rugby, soccer, softball, swimming, tennis, volleyball, cricket, cross-country, golf, handball, track and field, water polo, wrestling. **Organizations:** student government, councils and committees, Cum Laude, Quill and Scroll, Scholia. **Clubs:** chess, Chinese, debate, Mabuhay, math, Model UN, pep, Philippine culture, photography, Psi, science, social studies. **Tests:** SSAT, PSAT, SAT, ACT, TOEFL, IB, AP, Iowa. **Graduates attending college:** 90%. **Graduates have attended:** Bryn Mawr, Harvard-Radcliffe, Haverford, MIT, Stanford.

Physical plant

Location: in the suburb of Makati. **Campus:** 11 acres. **Libraries:** 56,000 volumes. **Facilities:** 16 buildings, 171 classrooms, auditorium, 3 cafeterias, infirmary, 2 covered play areas, 2 tennis courts, 3 gymnasiums, playing field, 16 science labs, 7 computer labs, 2 swimming pools, fine arts center, 2 theaters, 2 media centers, air conditioning.

*Once only fee

POLAND

Region: Europe
Size: 120,727 square miles
Population: 37,799,000
Capital: Warsaw

Telephone code: 48
Currency: zloty
Language: Polish

WARSAW

THE AMERICAN SCHOOL OF WARSAW

Street address: Ul. Konstancinska 13, Warsaw, Poland
Phone: (48)(22)423952   **Facsimile:** (48)(22)6429392
    Cable: AMEMBASSY WARSAW
Mail: c/o American Consulate General, Frankfurt am Main,
    Siessmeierstrasse 19/21, Federal Republic of Germany
U.S. mail: American School of Warsaw, Warsaw (DOS), Washington, D.C.
    20520-5010
Director: Gail Schoppert, Ed.D.
Upper school principal: Michael Saffarewich
Lower school principal: Frank Rowland
Business manager: Jolanta Wilmanska
Staff: full-time, 42; part-time, 9
Nationalities of staff: U.S., 35; U.K., 3; host, 3; other, 10
Grade levels: preK – 12
Enrollment: preK, 12; K, 46; 1 – 6, 251; 7 – 9, 80; 10 – 11, 27; 12, 12;
    total, 428
Nationalities of student body: U.S., 135; U.K., 20; host, 53; other, 220
Teacher/student ratio: 1/9
Tuition (annual): preK, $2,400; K – 6, $7,400; 7 – 12, $7,700
Other fees: building fund: new student*, $1,000; returning student
    (annual), $500
School year: late August to June

Year founded: 1953. **Type of school:** coed, day, private nonprofit.
Governed by: elected board of directors. **Sponsored by:** parents' association.
Accredited by: New England, ECIS.

Curriculum/physical plant
Type: U.S. **Languages taught:** French, Polish. **Staff specialists:** reading,
math, computer, learning disabilities, nurse. **Special programs:** ESL, remedial. **Special curricular:** art, chorus, physical education, computer instruction, photography. **Extracurricular:** drama, dance, instrumental music,
computers, yearbook, newspaper, field trips, sports, student council. **Organizations:** ballet, Boy Scouts, Cub Scouts, Girl Guides, Brownies. **Tests:** SSAT,
SAT, Iowa. **Location:** in city. **Library:** 10,000 volumes. **Facilities:** 3 buildings
on 2 sites, 33 classrooms, gymnasium, 2 playing fields, 2 science labs, 2
computer labs.

*Once only fee

PORTUGAL _____

Region: Europe
Size: 36,390 square miles
Population: 10,387,000
Capital: Lisbon

Telephone code: 351
Currency: escudo
Language: Portuguese

LISBON

AMERICAN CHRISTIAN INTERNATIONAL ACADEMY

Street address: Avenida de Sintra, Lote 1, 2750 Cascais, Portugal
Phone: (351)(1)4842279/4861860
Director: Rev. Gary G. Siefers
Business manager: John Ellis
Staff: full-time, 9; part-time, 5
Nationalities of staff: U.S., 11; host, 3
Grade levels: K – 10
Enrollment: K, 10; 1 – 8, 55; 9 – 10, 10; total, 75
Nationalities of student body: U.S., 40; other, 35
Capacity: K, 10; 1 – 10, 80; total, 90
Teacher/student ratio: 1/6
Boarders: grades 7 – 10
Tuition (annual): K, 600,000**; 1 – 3, 1,000,000; 4 – 6, 1,100,000; 7 – 10, 1,200,000
Other fees (annual): boarding, 900,000**; capital levy, 100,000; application, 20,000; busing, 153,000
School year: September to June

Year founded: 1983. **Type of school:** coed, day, boarding, church-related. **Governed by:** appointed independent board. **Accredited by:** accreditation in process with Association of Christian Schools International, Middle States, and ECIS. **Regional organization:** ECIS.

Curriculum/physical plant

Type: U.S. **Languages taught:** English. **Special programs:** ESL, independent study, remedial. **Special curricular:** art, chorus, physical education, computer instruction. **Extracurricular:** yearbook, newspaper, excursions/expeditions, field trips. **Tests:** Stanford, OLSAT. **Location:** 20 kilometers from Lisbon, in quaint oceanside city on Portugal's Costa del Sol. **Campus:** 1 acre. **Library:** 4,000 volumes. **Facilities:** 2 buildings, 6 classrooms, auditorium, playground, outdoor basketball court, rented soccer field.

**Portuguese escudo

AMERICAN INTERNATIONAL SCHOOL – LISBON

Street address: Quinta da Casa Branca, Carnaxide, 2795 Linda-a-Velha,
Portugal
Phone: (351)(1)4171819   **Facsimile:** (351)(1)4187649
Mail: Apartado 10, Carnaxide, 2795 Linda-a-Velha, Portugal
Director: Robert Romano
Upper school principal: Roger Frost
Lower school principal: Roxie Demirjian
Early childhood assistant principal: Barbara Carvalho
Staff: full-time, 54; part-time, 5
Nationalities of staff: U.S., 38; U.K., 2; host, 18; other, 1
Grade levels: early childhood – 12
Enrollment: early childhood – K, 40; 1 – 6, 128; 7 – 9, 71; 10 – 12, 81;
total, 320
Nationalities of student body: U.S., 82; host, 75; other, 163
Capacity: early childhood – K, 50; 1 – 6, 200; 7 – 9, 120; 10 – 12, 120;
total, 490
Teacher/student ratio: 1/6
Tuition (annual): early childhood, 400,000**; K, 780,000; 1–4, 1,361,200;
5 – 6, 1,440,000; 7 – 12, 1,582,000
Other fees (annual): registration, 31,000**; capital levy*, 124,200;
busing, 173,880; lunch: (daily) 550 each, (monthly) 500 each
School year: September through June

Year founded: 1956. **Type of school:** coed, day, proprietary. **Governed
by:** board of directors. **Accredited by:** New England, ECIS, Portuguese
Ministry of Education.

Curriculum
Type: U.S. **Languages taught:** French, Portuguese. **Staff specialists:**
reading, computer, counselor, nurse, art, music, resource room. **Special
programs:** ESL, physical education, computer instruction. **Extracurricular:**
drama, computers, yearbook, field trips, choir, chess club, French club,
student exchanges. **Sports:** basketball, soccer, swimming, tennis, volleyball,
track and field. **Organizations:** National Honor Society, National Junior
Honor Society, Model UN. **Tests:** PSAT, SAT, TOEFL, AP. **Graduates attending college:** 85%. **Graduates have attended:** Vanderbilt, Pennsylvania State
U., Boston U., Lafayette, Bennington.

Physical plant
Location: Carnaxide campus (grades 5 – 12) on main auto route from
Lisbon to Estoril; Monte Estoril campus (grades 2 – 4) in area next to Estoril;
Sao Joao campus (early childhood center) in Estoril area. **Campuses (3):** 6
acres. **Library:** 15,000 volumes. **Facilities:** 14 buildings, 40 classrooms,
cafeteria, infirmary, 3 playing fields, 3 science labs, 2 computer labs, AV
equipment; rented tennis court, gymnasium, and swimming pool.

*Once only fee   **Portuguese escudo

St. Julian's School (English Section)

Street address: Quinta Nova, Carcavelos, Portugal
Phone: (351)(1)4570140   **Facsimile:** (351)(1)4566817
Mail: Quinta Nova, Carcavelos, 2777 Parede Codex, Portugal
Headmaster: Mr. T. A. Bull
Deputy head of senior school: Mr. T. Hamilton
Head of junior school: Mr. R. Bienkowski
Head of first school: Mrs. A. Costa Gomes
Staff: full-time, 64; part-time, 4
Nationalities of staff: U.S., 2; U.K., 47; host, 13; other, 6
Grade levels: N – 12
Enrollment: N – preK, 66; K, 37; 1 – 6, 257; 7 – 9, 157; 10 – 12, 115;
    total, 632
Nationalities of student body: U.S., 10; U.K., 216; host, 266; other, 140
Capacity: N – preK, 66; K, 36; 1 – 6, 260; 7 – 9, 180; 10 – 12, 140;
    total, 682
Teacher/student ratio: 1/10
Tuition (annual): N – preK, $4,608; K, $5,157; 1 – 6, $6,252; 7 – 9, $7,798;
    10 – 12, $10,440
Other fees: registration*, $196; capital levy*, $490; insurance, $7; lunch,
    $4.60 each
School year: September to July

Year founded: 1932. **Type of school:** coed, day, private nonprofit.
Governed by: elected St. Julian's School Association.

Curriculum/physical plant

Type: U.K., IB. **Languages taught:** French, Portuguese. **Staff specialists:** reading, math, learning disabilities, nurse. **Special programs:** ESL. **Special curricular:** art, physical education, computer instruction, choir. **Extracurricular:** drama, gymnastics, dance, choral music, computers, literary magazine, photography, excursions/expeditions, field trips, Guides, Brownies. **Sports:** basketball, football, hockey, soccer, tennis, volleyball, badminton, weight training, cricket. **Tests:** IB, GCSE. **Location:** in suburban area, 40 minutes from center of Lisbon. **Campus:** 19 acres. **Libraries:** 9,000 volumes. **Facilities:** 5 buildings, 40 classrooms, auditorium, infirmary, 4 tennis courts, 3 gymnasiums, 3 playing fields, 6 science labs, computer lab, 3 dining rooms.

*Once only fee

PUERTO RICO ————————————

Region: Caribbean
Size: 3,435 square miles
Population: 3,566,000
Capital: San Juan

Telephone code: 809
Currency: U.S. dollar
Languages: Spanish, English

BAYAMON

BALDWIN SCHOOL OF PUERTO RICO

Street address: RD 833, KM 13.1, Guaynabo, Puerto Rico 00970
Phone: (1)(809)7202421   **Facsimile:** (1)(809)7900619
Mail: PO Box 1827, Bayamon, Puerto Rico, 00960-1827
Head of school: Dr. Ted N. Okey
Middle/high school principal: Sylvia Ruiz
Elementary school principal: Carmen Gil
Controller: Nancy Wallace
Staff: full-time, 65; part-time, 4
Nationalities of staff: U.S., 9; U.K., 55; other, 5
Grade levels: preK – 12
Enrollment: preK, 24; K, 55; 1 – 6, 341; 7 – 9, 110; 10 – 12, 110; total, 640
Nationalities of student body: U.S., 226; U.K., 10; host, 320; other, 84
Capacity: preK, 24; K, 55; 1 – 6, 330; 7 – 9, 130; 10 – 12, 120; total, 659
Teacher/student ratio: 1/10
Tuition (annual): preK – K, $4,000; 1 – 6, $4,200 – $4,500; 7 – 10, $4,800; 11 – 12, $4,900
Other fees (annual): busing, $233 – 388; initial enrollment*, $1,500; building fee, $600
School year: August to June

Year founded: 1968. **Type of school:** coed, day, private nonprofit. **Governed by:** appointed board of directors. **Accredited by:** Middle States, Department of Instruction of Puerto Rico.

Curriculum/physical plant

Type: U.S. **Languages taught:** English, French, Spanish. **Special programs:** ESL, advanced placement, honors sections, independent study. **Special curricular:** art, physical education, computer instruction. **Extracurricular:** computers, yearbook, newspaper, photography, field trips, band. **Sports:** baseball, basketball, soccer, softball, swimming, tennis, volleyball, cross-country. **Clubs:** student council, National Honor Society, National Junior Honor Society, math, computer, science, French, Young Astronauts, Interact, Close-Up, board games, drama, poise & charm, photography, calligraphy, forensics, logic puzzles. **Tests:** PSAT, SAT, TOEFL, AP, Stanford,

ERB. **Graduates attending college:** 100%. **Graduates have attended:** Cornell, Yale, Notre Dame, Purdue, U. of Michigan. **Location:** in suburban area of San Juan. **Facilities:** cafeteria, infirmary, covered play area, 2 tennis courts, 3 playing fields, 2 science labs, 2 computer labs, swimming pool.

*Once only fee

PONCE

CARIBBEAN SCHOOL

Street address: Calle 9, La Rambla, Ponce, Puerto Rico 00731
Phone: (1)(809)8432048   **Facsimile:** (1)(809)8431174
Head: Elena Martinez
Principal, upper school: Elizabeth Lago
Principal, lower school: Clarissa Moscosco
Business manager: Irma Ruiz
Staff: full-time, 47; part-time, 2
Nationalities of staff: U.S., 5; host, 44
Grade levels: preK – 12
Enrollment: preK, 25; K, 51; 1 – 5, 262; 6 – 8, 136; 9 – 12, 153; total, 627
Nationalities of student body: host, 557; other, 70
Teacher/student ratio: 1/13
Tuition (annual): preK, $1,245; K – 2, $2,350; 3 – 5, $2,510; 6 – 8, $2,720; 9 – 12, $2,860
Other fees (annual): registration*, $100; capital levy, $300; new family fee*, $400
School year: August through June

Year founded: 1954. **Type of school:** coed, day. **Governed by:** elected board of directors. **Sponsored by:** Caribbean corporation. **Accredited by:** Middle States.

Curriculum/physical plant
Type: U.S., AP. **Languages taught:** French, Spanish. **Staff specialists:** computer. **Special programs:** ESL, independent study. **Special curricular:** art, physical education, computer instruction, music. **Extracurricular:** drama, computers, yearbook, newspaper, field trips, Close-Up, band. **Sports:** basketball, soccer, softball, tennis, volleyball, track and field. **Tests:** PSAT, SAT, ACT, Iowa. **Graduates attending college:** 100%. **Graduates have attended:** Stanford, Yale, Princeton, U. of Virginia, Harvard. **Location:** 2 miles from Ponce. **Campus:** 6 acres. **Libraries:** 19,000 volumes. **Facilities:** 3 buildings, 42 classrooms, auditorium, cafeteria, infirmary, covered play area, 2 tennis courts, 3 playing fields, 4 science labs, computer lab.

*Once only fee

SAN JUAN

ACADEMIA DEL PERPETUO SOCORRO

Street address: Jose Marti and Central Streets, Miramar, Santurce, Puerto Rico 00907
Phone: (1)(809)7214540   **Facsimile:** (1)(809)7234550
Principal: Sr. Armand Marie, SSND
Vice-principal (10 – 12): Jose M. Leavitt
Vice-principal (7 – 9): Elizabeth Cintrón
Business manager: Julia Roake
Staff: full-time, 48; part-time, 9
Nationalities of staff: U.S., 57
Grade levels: 7 – 12
Enrollment: 7 – 9, 298; 10 – 12, 284; total, 582
Capacity: 7 – 9, 300; 10 – 12, 300; total, 600
Teacher/student ratio: 1/11
Tuition (annual): 7 – 8, $1,863; 9 – 12, $2,160
Other fees (annual): registration, $300; insurance, $3; books, $250 – 300; entrance*, $800; building fund, $200; other fees, $300
School year: September to June

Year founded: 1921. **Type of school:** coed, day, church-related, private nonprofit. **Accredited by:** Middle States, Puerto Rican Department of Education.

Curriculum/physical plant

Type: U.S. **Languages of instruction:** English, Spanish. **Languages taught:** French, German, Italian. **Staff specialists:** computer, counselor. **Special programs:** advanced placement, honors sections. **Special curricular:** art, physical education, computer instruction. **Extracurricular:** drama, computers, yearbook, newspaper, photography, excursions/expeditions, field trips, home arts. **Sports:** baseball, basketball, softball, swimming, volleyball, track and field. **Clubs:** French, Model UN, student council, computer, science, Sign Post, camera, math, honor academy, art, honor society, tennis, aerobics, needlecraft, yearbook, history, geophysical science, English and Spanish forensics. **Tests:** PSAT, SAT, ACT, AP. **Graduates attending college:** 100%. **Graduates have attended:** Harvard, Princeton, Georgetown, Brown, Boston U. **Location:** in city. **Facilities:** auditorium, cafeteria, 2 infirmaries, covered play area, gymnasium, playing field, 2 science labs, computer lab, air conditioning.

*Once only fee

CARIBBEAN PREPARATORY SCHOOL

Phone: (1)(809)7654411   **Facsimile:** (1)(809)7643809
Mail: Box 70177, San Juan, Puerto Rico 00936-8177
Headmaster: F. Richard Marracino

Principals: Miguel Arzola (Commonwealth Campus), Linda Fernández (Parkville Campus)
Admissions and development directors: Angie Casañas, Ivette Collazo
Head of library: Maritza Irizarry
Head of computer services: Gamaliel Figueroa
Business manager: David Lugo
Staff: full-time, 76; part-time, 4
Nationalities of staff: U.S., 80
Grade levels: preK – 12
Enrollment: preK, 23; K, 50; 1 – 6, 336; 7 – 9, 106; 10 – 12, 123; total, 638
Nationalities of student body: U.S., 597; other, 41
Capacity: preK, 25; K, 50; 1 – 6, 400; 7 – 9, 145; 10 – 12, 135; total, 755
Teacher/student ratio: 1/8
Tuition (annual): preK, $2,800; K, $3,160; 1 – 6, $3,740; 7 – 9, $4,090; 10 – 12, $4,320
Other fees (annual): registration*, $800; capital levy, $600; books, $260; graduation*, $80
School year: August to June

Year founded: 1952. **Type of school:** coed, day, private nonprofit. **Governed by:** appointed and elected board of directors. **Accredited by:** Middle States, Puerto Rican Department of Education.

Curriculum/physical plant

Type: U.S. **Languages taught:** English, French, Spanish. **Staff specialists:** computer, counselor, learning disabilities. **Special programs:** ESL, advanced placement, honors sections. **Special curricular:** art, physical education, computer instruction, music, poetry, dance. **Extracurricular:** drama, dance, computers, yearbook, newspaper, literary magazine, photography, field trips, forensics. **Sports:** baseball, football, soccer, softball, volleyball, indoor soccer, track and field. **Organizations**: National Honor Society, National Junior Honor Society, varsity, student council, photography, radio, science, drama. **Tests:** PSAT, SAT, Stanford. **Graduates attending college:** 96%. **Graduates have attended:** West Point, Harvard, Georgetown, Penn State, Loyola. **Location:** 6 miles from San Juan metro area, in business district at Hato Rey. **Campuses (2):** 3 acres. **Libraries:** 20,000 volumes. **Facilities:** 3 buildings, 43 classrooms, auditorium, 2 cafeterias, 2 playing fields, 4 science labs, 2 computer labs, air conditioning.

*Once only fee

EPISCOPAL CATHEDRAL SCHOOL

Street address: 309 Canals Street, Santurce, Puerto Rico 00908
Phone: (1)(809)7215478/7214958   **Facsimile:** (1)(809)7246668
Mail: PO Box 13305, Santurce Station, San Juan, Puerto Rico 00908
Director: Rev. Canon Gary J. DeHope
Assistant headmaster: Fr. Roberto Kringel
Staff: full-time, 20

Nationalities of staff: U.S., 20
Grade levels: K – 12
Enrollment: K, 35; 1 – 6, 165; 7 – 9, 66; 10 – 12, 63; total, 329
Nationalities of student body: U.S., 309; other, 20
Capacity: K, 35; 1 – 6, 175; 7 – 9, 75; 10 – 12, 75; total, 360
Teacher/student ratio: 1/16
Tuition (annual): K – 6, $1,750; 7 – 12, $1,850
Other fees (annual): registration, $400; books, $100 – 175; graduation/
    yearbook
School year: August to May

Year founded: 1946. **Type of school:** coed, day, church-related, private nonprofit. **Governed by:** Iglesia Episcopal Puertorriquena. **Accredited by:** Middle States.

Curriculum/physical plant

Type: college preparatory. **Staff specialists:** computer, counselor. **Special curricular:** computer instruction. **Extracurricular:** drama, yearbook, newspaper, excursions/expeditions, field trips. **Clubs:** computer, National Honor Society, performing arts, science, library, Club Cultural. **Tests:** PSAT, SAT, ACT, TOEFL, Iowa, Kulmann-Anderson-K. **Graduates attending college:** 100%. **Graduates have attended:** U. of Puerto Rico, George Washington U., Xavier, Harvard, MIT. **Location:** in city. **Facilities:** 1 building, 18 classrooms, auditorium, cafeteria, science lab, computer lab, library, air conditioning.

ROBINSON SCHOOL

Street address: 5 Nairn Street, Condado, Puerto Rico 00907
Phone: (1)(809)7286767   **Facsimile:** (1)(809)7262833
Executive director: Daniel W. Sheehan
Secondary school principal: Gilberto Quintana
Elementary school principal: Carmen Morales
Business manager: Ileana Pizarro
Staff: full-time, 39
Grade levels: preK – 12
Enrollment: pre-preK, newly added; preK, 9; K, 24; 1 – 6, 145; 7 – 9, 58;
    10 – 12, 62; learning resource center, 34; total, 332
Nationalities of student body: U.S., 288; U.K., 4; other, 40
Capacity: pre-preK, 25; preK, 25; K, 40; 1 – 6, 200; 7 – 9, 100; 10 – 12,
    100; learning resource center, 50; total, 540
Teacher/student ratio: 1/9
Tuition (annual): pre-preK, $1,500; preK, $3,090; K, $3,405; 1 – 6,
    $4,140; 7 – 8, $4,298; 9 – 12, $4,560; learning resource center,
    $5,166
Other fees: application, $150; books (7 – 12); testing, $75; restoration
    fund, $350/5 years
School year: August to June

Year founded: 1902. **Type of school:** coed, day, private nonprofit. **Governed by:** appointed and elected board of directors. **Accredited by:** Middle States, Puerto Rican Department of Instruction. **Affiliated with:** United Methodist Church.

Curriculum

Type: U.S. **Languages taught:** French, Spanish. **Staff specialists:** reading, math, computer, counselor, learning disabilities, speech pathologist. **Special programs:** advanced placement, honors sections, Spanish for continentals, English for native speakers of Spanish. **Special curricular:** art, physical education, computer instruction, music. **Extracurricular:** yearbook, newspaper, field trips. **Sports:** basketball, soccer, softball, volleyball, indoor soccer. **Clubs:** French, Spanish, science, math, student council, National and Junior Honor Societies. **Tests:** PSAT, SAT, ACT, TOEFL, AP, NEDT, Puerto Rican College Board, Strong-Campbell. **Graduates attending college:** 100%. **Graduates have attended:** Columbia, Cornell, Tufts, Georgia Tech, U. of Pennsylvania.

Physical plant

Location: Condado resort section near San Juan. **Campus:** 4 acres. **Secondary library:** 14,000 volumes. **Elementary library:** 11,000. **Political science library:** 1,200 volumes. **Facilities:** 3 buildings, 28 classrooms, auditorium, cafeteria, gymnasium, playing field, 3 science labs, computer lab, large playing field, outdoor basketball court, air conditioning.

SAINT JOHN'S SCHOOL

Street address: 1454-66 Ashford Avenue, San Juan,
    Puerto Rico 00907-1560
Phone: (1)(809)7285343   **Facsimile:** (1)(809)2681454
Headmaster: Russell Beecher, Ed.D.
Secondary school principal: Dana M. Nigaglioni
Elementary school principal: Marguerite P. Kocher
Director of admissions: Evangeline Segarra
Business manager: Ivan Ortiz
Staff: full-time, 76; part-time, 5
Grade levels: preK – 12
Enrollment: preK, 26; K, 48; 1 – 5, 273; 6 – 8, 167; 9 – 12, 216; total, 730
Nationalities of student body: U.S., 682; U.K., 8; other, 40
Capacity: preK, 26; K, 54; 1 – 5, 275; 6 – 8, 168; 9 – 12, 224; total, 747
Teacher/student ratio: 1/9
Tuition (annual): preK, $4,450; K, $4,700; 1 – 5, $5,070; 6 – 12, $5,450
Other fees (annual): registration, $500 (included in tuition);
    building fund, $500 per family; entrance*, $500 per family; special
    tuition assessment*, $1,000 per family
School year: August to June

Year founded: 1915. **Type of school:** coed, day, private nonprofit. **Governed by:** appointed and elected board of trustees. **Sponsored by:** parents. **Accredited by:** Middle States, Puerto Rican Department of Instruction.

Curriculum

Type: U.S., college preparatory. **Languages taught:** French, Spanish. **Staff specialists:** reading, computer, counselor, psychologist, art, music, math remediation. **Special programs:** advanced placement, independent study, remedial. **Special curricular:** art, physical education, computer instruction, music, humanities. **Extracurricular:** drama, choral music, instrumental music, computers, yearbook, newspaper, field trips, literary magazines. **Sports:** basketball, soccer, softball, tennis, volleyball, indoor soccer, golf, track and field. **Clubs:** French, OAS, English forensics, Spanish and French oratory, fine arts, science, varsity, Natural Resources Society, science fair, Kids Care, National and Junior Honor Societies, National Art Honor Society, Interact, Cum Laude Society, International Thespian Society. **Tests:** PSAT, SAT, AP, Iowa. **Graduates attending college:** 100%. **Graduates have attended:** MIT, Harvard, U. of Pennsylvania, Yale, Princeton.

Physical plant

Location: in heart of San Juan. **Campus:** 2.05 acres. **Library:** 25,000 volumes. **Facilities:** 5 buildings, 49 classrooms, auditorium, cafeteria, covered play area, gymnasium, 5 science labs, 3 computer labs, 2 outdoor courts, photo lab, air conditioning.

*Once only fee

QATAR _____

Region: Middle East
Size: 4,247 square miles
Population: 518,000
Capital: Doha

Telephone code: 974
Currency: riyal
Languages: Arabic, English

DOHA

AMERICAN INTERNATIONAL SCHOOL

Phone: (974)806770   **Facsimile:** (974)806311
Mail: PO Box 22090, Doha, Qatar
Director: Robert B. Conlan
Administrative assistant: Susan J. Peters
Head of library: Gloriana Amarsingham
Head of computer services: Jean Said
Staff: full-time, 28; part-time, 3
Nationalities of staff: U.S., 15; U.K., 6; other, 10
Grade levels: N (age 3) – 10
Enrollment: N – preK, 41; K, 27; 1 – 5, 128; 6 – 8, 55; 9 – 10, 12;
    total, 263
Nationalities of student body: U.S., 50; U.K., 4; host, 64; other, 145
Capacity: N – preK, 44; K, 25; 1 – 5, 150; 6 – 8, 69; 9 – 10, 30; total, 318
Teacher/student ratio: 1/9
Tuition (annual): N – K, 8,100**; 1 – 5, 11,300; 6 – 8, 15,600; 9 – 10,
    16,500
Other fees (annual): registration*, 1,500**; busing, 2,100
School year: September to June

Year founded: 1988. **Type of school:** coed, day. **Governed by:** board of
trustees, board of directors. **Sponsored by:** U.S. Embassy. **Accredited by:**
New England (in process). **Regional organizations:** NE/SA.

Curriculum/physical plant

Type: U.S. **Languages taught:** French, Arabic. **Staff specialists:** computer, nurse. **Special programs:** ESL, special education (limited program).
Special curricular: art, chorus, physical education, computer applications,
field trips. **Extracurricular:** drama, choral music, computers, yearbook,
newspaper. **Sports:** intramural volleyball, basketball, and soccer; interscholastic volleyball and basketball. **Clubs:** student leadership. **Tests:** Iowa.
Location: in suburban Doha. **Campus:** 3 acres. **Library:** 5,000 volumes.
Facilities: 22 (air-conditioned) classrooms, infirmary, science lab, 2 computer labs, early childhood center, art room, 2 playgrounds, surfaced sports
area, access to a soccer field and to nearby swimming pools during warmer
months.

*Once only fee   **Qatari riyal

ROMANIA

Region: Europe
Size: 91,699 square miles
Population: 23,397,000
Capital: Bucharest

Telephone code: 40
Currency: lei
Languages: Romanian, German, Hungarian, English

BUCHAREST

AMERICAN SCHOOL OF BUCHAREST

Phone: (40)(1)3127718 – 9 /(40)(1)3126386 (U.S. Embassy)
   Facsimile: (40)(1)3127719/(40)(1)3120395 (U.S. Embassy)
   Telex: 86411416 AMEMB R
Mail: Amer Con Gen-BUCHAREST, 21 Seissmaier Street, 6000 Frankfurt Am Main, Germany
U.S. mail: c/o U.S. Embassy - Bucharest, Department of State, Washington, D.C. 20521-5260
Director: Larry N. Crouch
Assistant director: Andrew Garbely
Staff: full-time, 16; part-time, 5
Nationalities of staff: U.S., 15; host, 2; other, 4
Grade levels: N4 – 9
Enrollment: N – preK, 16; K, 20; 1 – 6, 108; 7 – 9, 31; total, 175
Nationalities of student body: U.S., 49; U.K., 17; host, 10; other, 99
Capacity: N – preK, 16; K, 30; 1 – 6, 114; 7 – 9, 40; total, 200
Teacher/student ratio: 1/9
Tuition (annual): N – preK, $2,200; K – 8, $6,400
Other fees: application*, $100
School year: August to June

Year founded: 1962. Type of school: coed, day. Governed by: 7-member appointed board of directors. Sponsored by: U.S. Embassy. Accredited by: New England, ECIS.

Curriculum/physical plant

Type: U.S. Languages taught: French. Staff specialists: computer, art, ESL, music. Special programs: ESL, after-school activities. Special curricular: art, physical education, computer instruction, music. Extracurricular: drama, computers, yearbook, newspaper, excursions/expeditions, field trips. Sports: basketball, soccer, volleyball. Clubs: arts and crafts, cooking, drama, chess, board games, jogging. Tests: Iowa. Location: in Bucharest. Library: 5,000 volumes. Facilities: 2 campuses, 30 classrooms, computer lab, P.E. room.

*Once only fee

RUSSIAN FEDERATION ⎯⎯⎯⎯⎯

Region: Europe and Asia
Size: 6,592,800 square miles
Population: 148,542,000
Capital: Moscow

Telephone code: 7
Currency: ruble
Language: Russian

MOSCOW

ANGLO-AMERICAN SCHOOL OF MOSCOW

Street address: 78 Leninsky Prospekt, Moscow, Russia
Phone: (7)(95)1318700   **Facsimile:** (7)(95)1318756 **Telex:**
871413160 USGSOSU   **Cable:** AMEMBASSY, Moscow, Russia
U.S. mail: (no personal name) Anglo-American School of Moscow,
U.S. Embassy – Moscow, PSC 77 (AAS), APO AE New York 09721
Director: Kenneth Wrye, Ed.D.
Principal, 7 – 10: Steve Bannell
Principal, K – 6: Stephen O'Donnell
Business manager: Ted Burgon
Staff: full-time, 43; part-time, 11
Nationalities of staff: U.S., 27; U.K., 12; other, 15
Grade levels: K – 11
Enrollment: K, 36; 1 – 6, 293; 7 – 11, 150; total, 479
Capacity: K, 36; 1 – 6, 293; 7 – 11, 150; total, 479
Teacher/student ratio: 1/10
Tuition (annual): K – 4, $7,600; 5 – 9, $7,900; 10 – 11, $8,200
Other fees (annual): application*, $50; seat fee, $2,500
School year: September to June

Year founded: 1949. **Type of school:** coed, day. **Governed by:** appointed
and elected school board. **Sponsored by:** U.S., U.K., Canada. **Accredited by:**
New England, ECIS.

Curriculum/physical plant
Type: U.S., U.K. **Languages taught:** French, Russian. **Staff specialists:**
counselor, nurse. **Special programs:** ESL, honors sections (occasional),
independent study, remedial. **Special curricular:** art, physical education,
computer instruction, music. **Extracurricular:** drama, dance, instrumental,
music, computers, newspaper, photography, excursions/expeditions, field
trips. **Sports:** basketball, hockey, soccer, swimming, ice skating. **Location:** K
– 6 school in residential area of Moscow; 7 – 9 school on grounds of U.S.
Embassy. **Campuses (2):** 3 acres. **Facilities:** 2 buildings, 25 classrooms,
auditorium, infirmary, 2 gymnasiums, playing field, science lab, 2 computer
labs, library, art room, music room, ice rink, AV equipment, swimming pool
(U.S. Embassy).

*Once only fee

ST. PETERSBURG
Leningrad Branch School
Address: c/o American Consulate General St. Petersburg, Department of State, Washington, D.C. 20521-5440

RWANDA

Region: Central Africa
Size: 10,169 square miles
Population: 7,902,000
Capital: Kigali

Telephone code: 250
Currency: franc
Languages: French, Rwanda

KIGALI

KIGALI INTERNATIONAL SCHOOL
Phone: (250)83504 **Facsimile:** (250)72128
Mail: B.P. 1375, Kigali, Rwanda, Central Africa
U.S. mail: U.S. Embassy Kigali, Department of State, Washington, D.C. 20521-2210
Administrator: Paul Olson
Staff: full-time, 5; part-time, 4
Nationalities of staff: U.S., 4; host, 1; other, 4
Grade levels: preK – 8
Enrollment: preK, 4; K, 10; 1 – 8, 48; total, 62
Nationalities of student body: U.S., 15; host, 7; other, 40
Capacity: preK, 10; K, 10; 1 – 8, 60; total, 80
Teacher/student ratio: 1/9
Tuition (annual): preK, $3,000; K – 8, $5,500
Other fees: enrollment*, $1,000
School year: September to June

Year founded: 1988. **Type of school:** coed, day, private nonprofit. **Governed by:** elected board of directors. **Sponsored by:** school association. **Accredited by:** New England (in process). **Regional organization**: AAIE.

Curriculum/physical plant
Type: U.S. **Languages taught:** French. **Staff specialists:** art, ESL, library, music, physical education. **Location:** in suburban area, 5 kilometers from Kigali. **Library:** 2,800 volumes. **Facilities:** 2 large buildings.

*Once only fee

SAUDI ARABIA _____

Region: Middle East
Size: 839,996 square miles
Population: 17,869,000
Capital: Riyadh

Telephone code: 966
Currency: riyal
Language: Arabic

DHAHRAN

SAUDI ARABIAN INTERNATIONAL SCHOOL, DHAHRAN DISTRICT†

Phone: (966)(3)8913842   **Facsimile:** (966)(3)8912450
   Telex: 928801937 YES SJ
Mail: PO Box 677, Dhahran International Airport, Dhahran 31932,
   Saudi Arabia
U.S. mail: (no personal name) Dhahran Academy, Unit 66804, APO
   AE 09858-6804
Superintendent: Leo A. Ruberto, Ph.D.
Deputy superintendent: Dixie McKay
Personnel director: Cornelius Rieske
Finance director: Walter Lanz
Staff (all SAIS schools): full-time, 277
Nationalities of staff: U.S., 218; other, 59
Grade levels: JuniorK (4 years) – 9 (15 years)
Enrollment (all SAIS schools): K, 610; 1 – 6, 2,440; 7 – 9, 707;
   total, 3,757
Nationalities of student body: U.S., 1,062; U.K., 689; other, 2,006
Capacity: K, 690; 1 – 6, 2,522; 7 – 9, 788; total, 4,000
Teacher/student ratio: 1/14
Tuition (annual, Dhahran Academy only): JuniorK, $2,597;
   K – 9, $5,140
Other fees: registration*, $533
School year: late August to mid-June

Year founded: 1963 (Dhahran Academy). **Type of school:** coed, day, private nonprofit. **Governed by:** appointed and elected board of directors. **Sponsored by:** Saudi Arabian Ministry of Education. **Accredited by:** Middle States.

Curriculum/physical plant

Type: U.S., U.K. **Languages taught:** French, Arabic. **Staff specialists:** reading, computer, counselor, psychologist, nurse. **Special programs:** ESL. **Special curricular:** art, chorus, band, physical education, computer instruction, vocational. **Extracurricular:** drama, gymnastics, choral music, instrumental music, computers, photography, excursions/expeditions, field trips. **Sports:** basketball, soccer, softball, volleyball. **Clubs:** student council, computer, drama, photography. **Tests:** SSAT, Stanford. **Location:** (Dhahran Academy) close to Arabian Gulf. **Campus:** 40 acres. **Library:** 50,000 volumes. **Facilities:** infirmary, 3 covered play areas, gymnasium, 2 playing fields, 3 science labs, 4 computer labs, tennis courts, air conditioning.

*Once only fee   †11 schools within Saudi Arabia

SAUDI ARABIAN OIL COMPANY
SAUDI ARAMCO SCHOOLS

Phone: (966)(3)8771675   **Facsimile:** (966)(3)8771638
    Telex: 928601220 ASAO SJ
Mail: Box 73, Dhahran 31311, Saudi Arabia
U.S. mail: c/o Pat Halliburton, MS 1098, R 10007, Aramco Services
    Company, Box 4534, Houston, TX 77210-4534, U.S.A.
Superintendent: Owen Harrison, Ed.D.
Staff: full-time, 222
Nationalities of staff: U.S., 216; host, 1; other, 5
Grade levels: K – 9
Enrollment: total, 2,434
Nationalities of student body: U.S., 1,718; host, 27; other, 689
Capacity: total, 3,200
Teacher/student ratio: 1/11
School year: September through July (year round)

Year founded: 1941. **Type of school:** coed, day, company sponsored. **Governed by:** appointed and elected (advisory) school board. **Owned and operated by:** Saudi Arabian Oil Company.

Curriculum

Type: U.S. **Languages taught:** French, Spanish, Arabic for native speakers. **Staff specialists:** reading, speech/hearing, counselor, psychologist, nurse, transition/remedial. **Special programs:** ESL, independent study, remedial. **Special curricular:** art, chorus, band, physical education, computer instruction, industrial arts, home economics. **Extracurricular:** drama, gymnastics, choral music, instrumental music, yearbook, newspaper, photography, field trips. **Sports:** basketball, bowling, softball, tennis, track, volleyball. **Clubs:** knowledge bowl, library/media, classroom newspaper, computer, student congress, National Junior Honor Society. **Tests:** SSAT, Iowa.

Physical plant

Location: 5 schools in 4 communities within Eastern Province. **Facilities:** 5 covered play areas, 6 gymnasiums, 8 science labs, 5 computer labs, swimming pools, tennis courts, bowling alleys, squash and racquetball courts, playing fields and tracks shared with the local community, air conditioning.

JEDDAH

THE CONTINENTAL SCHOOL
S.A.I.S. BRITISH SECTION

Phone: (966)(2)6542354   **Facsimile:** (966)(2)6542354 ext. 164
   Telex: 601043 BRTAIN SJ
Mail: PO Box 6453, Jeddah 21442, Saudi Arabia
Director: Russ Law
Headteacher, upper school: Campbell Millar
Headteacher, middle school: Tony Laverick
Headteacher, lower school: Paul Guy-Byrne
Staff: full-time, 102; part-time, 14
Nationalities of staff: U.S., 7; U.K., 79; other, 30
Grade levels: preK – 11
Enrollment: preK, 60; K, 100; 1 – 6, 758; 7 – 9, 281; 10 – 11, 167;
   total, 1,366
Capacity: preK, 60; K, 110; 1 – 6, 758; 7 – 9, 300; 10 – 11, 200;
   total, 1,428
Teacher/student ratio: 1/12
Tuition (annual): preK, $3,679; K – 2, $5,359; 3 – 6, $5,479;
   7 – 11, $7,038
Other fees: registration*, $53; entrance*, $800
School year: September to July

Year founded: 1977. **Type of school:** coed, day, private nonprofit.
Governed by: elected board of governors. **Sponsored by:** British Embassy.
Accredited by: ECIS, Cambridge. **Regional Organizations:** British Schools
of Middle East Heads' Conference; Heads of British-style Schools in Saudi
Arabia Conference.

Curriculum
   Type: U.K. **Languages taught:** French, Spanish, German, Arabic. **Staff
specialists:** math, computer, counselor, nurse, art, physical education,
English, biology, geography, history, home economics, Arabic, business
studies, outdoor education, music, information technology, natural economy,
physics, chemistry, modern languages. **Special programs:** ESL. **Special
curricular:** art, physical education, computer instruction, instrumental
music. **Extracurricular:** drama, gymnastics, dance, choral music, computers, photography, excursions/expeditions, field trips. **Sports:** basketball,
hockey, badminton, soccer, swimming, tennis, volleyball, squash, kayaking,
boardsailing, dinghysailing. **Clubs:** many different clubs, outdoor education
program. **Tests:** IGCSE (PSAT, SAT, and TOEFL arranged). **Graduates have
attended:** Arizona State, Texas State, North Dakota.

Physical plant
   Location: 20 kilometers north of downtown Jeddah, 10 minutes from Red
Sea. **Campus:** 40,000 square meters. **Libraries:** more than 18,000 volumes.

Facilities: 10 buildings, 50 classrooms, cafeteria, infirmary, 2 covered play areas, 3 tennis courts, gymnasium, 2 hard playing fields, 5 science labs, 5 computer labs, 2 swimming pools, sports hall/theater, staff residences, air conditioning.

*Once only fee

Saudia – S.A.I.S.

Phone: (966)(2)6674566   **Facsimile:** (966)(2)6674536
   Telex: 928600184 PCSSCH SJ
Mail: c/o Saudi Arabian Airlines, CC 100, PO Box 167, Jeddah 21231, Saudi Arabia
Superintendent: John K. Hazelton
Middle school principal: Paul E. Frank
Elementary school principal: Richard E. Lehman
Business manager: Ahmed Taweeli
Staff: full-time, 108 (teaching); 69 (other)
Nationalities of staff: U.S., 134; U.K., 15; other, 28
Grade levels: K-I – 9
Enrollment: K-I, 25; K-II, 120; 1 – 4, 642; 5 – 9, 674; total, 1,461
Nationalities of student body: U.S., 662; U.K., 255; other, 544
Capacity: K-1 – II, 154; 1 – 4, 680; 5 – 9, 770; total, 1,604
Teacher/student ratio: 1/13
Tuition (annual): KI – II (full day), $4,480; K-II (half day), $3,280; 1 – 9, $6,400
Other fees: registration*, $267
School year: August to June

Year founded: 1952. **Type of school:** coed, day, company sponsored. **Governed and sponsored by:** Saudi Arabian Airlines. **Accredited by:** Middle States, Saudi Arabian Ministry of Education.

Curriculum/physical plant

Type: U.S. **Languages taught:** French, Spanish, Arabic. **Staff specialists:** counselor, psychologist, learning disabilities, nurse, more abled student, staff development. **Special programs:** ESL, honors sections, remedial. **Special curricular:** art, chorus, band, physical education, computer instruction, Islamic studies, industrial arts. **Extracurricular:** drama, gymnastics, choral music, instrumental music, computers, yearbook, excursions/expeditions, field trips. **Sports:** baseball, basketball, soccer, softball, gymnastics. **Clubs:** science, gymnastics, computer. **Tests:** SSAT, SAT, Stanford. **Location:** in northwest Jeddah. **Campuses (2):** 14 acres. **Library:** 40,000 volumes. **Facilities:** 5 buildings, 85 classrooms, 2 infirmaries, 4 covered play areas, 2 gymnasiums, 3 playing fields, 4 science labs, 3 computer labs, AV room, closed-circuit TV, 4-channel video network, air conditioning.

*Once only fee

RIYADH

SAUDI ARABIAN INTERNATIONAL SCHOOL – RIYADH (AMERICAN SECTION)

Phone: (966)(1)4914270   **Facsimile:** (966)(1)4917101
Mail: PO Box 990, Riyadh 11421, Saudi Arabia
U.S. mail: (no personal name) SAIS – R (American Section), Unit 61320, APO AE 09803-1320
Superintendent: John C. Davis, Ph.D.
Junior high school principal: Monti Hallberg
Elementary school principal: Don Shoemaker
Director of administrative services: Duane Root
Director of personnel services: John Rehman
Director of financial services: Charles Mast
Staff: full-time, 181
Nationalities of staff: U.S., 163; other, 18
Grade levels: preK – 9
Enrollment: preK, 75; K, 185; 1 – 6, 1,200; 7 – 9, 540; total, 2,000
Nationalities of student body: U.S., 920; U.K., 100; other, 980
Capacity: preK, 85; K, 180; 1 – 6, 1,435; 7 – 9, 600; total, 2,300
Teacher/student ratio: 1/11
Tuition (annual): preK, $3,520; K – 9, $5,680
Other fees (annual): registration, $1,333; ESL, $533
School year: September to June

Year founded: 1963. **Type of school:** coed, day. **Governed by:** elected parent board. **Sponsored by:** Parents Association. **Accredited by:** Middle States.

Curriculum/physical plant

Type: U.S. **Languages taught:** French, Arabic. **Staff specialists:** reading, computer, counselors, nurse. **Special programs:** ESL. **Special curricular:** art, chorus, band, physical education, orchestra, computer education, drafting. **Extracurricular:** drama, gymnastics, dance, choral music, instrumental music, computers, yearbook, field trips. **Sports:** basketball, soccer, softball, volleyball, extensive after-school activities program. **Organizations**: National Junior Honor Society, student council. **Tests:** SSAT, SAT. **Location:** northeast section of the capital city. **Campus:** 20 acres. **Library:** 40,000+ volumes. **Facilities:** 9 buildings, 170 classrooms, auditorium, 2 infirmaries, covered play area, gymnasium, 6 playing fields, 6 science labs, 7 computer labs, air conditioning.

JEDDAH
Dar Al Fikr Schools
>**Address:** Prince Majed Street, Jeddah, Hejaz, Saudi Arabia
>**Mail:** PO Box 14279, Jeddah 21424, Saudi Arabia
>**Phone:** (966)(2)6800005   **Facsimile:** (966)(2)6800808
>**Principal:** Mohammed Khodary

SENEGAL

Region: Africa
Size: 75,750 square miles
Population: 7,952,000
Capital: Dakar

Telephone code: 221
Currency: CFA franc
Languages: French, tribal languages

DAKAR

DAKAR ACADEMY

>**Street address:** Rue des Peres Maristes, 69, Hann, Dakar, Senegal
>**Phone:** (221)320682   **Facsimile:** (221)321721
>**Mail:** Attention Director, B.P. 3189, Dakar, Senegal, West Africa
>**Director:** Fred Zobrist
>**Staff:** full-time, 25; part-time, 5
>**Nationalities of staff:** U.S., 28; host, 2
>**Grade levels:** K – 12
>**Enrollment:** K, 8; 1 – 6, 52; 7 – 9, 34; 10 – 12, 39; total, 133
>**Nationalities of student body:** U.S., 55; other, 78
>**Capacity:** K, 15; 1 – 6, 90; 7 – 9, 66; 10 – 12, 66; total, 237
>**Teacher/student ratio:** 1/5
>**Boarders:** boys, 9; girls, 8   **Grades:** 1 – 12
>>**Program:** planned 7-day
>**Tuition (annual):** K – 4, $5,500; 5 –12, $6,100
>**Other fees:** registration*, $170; building fund, $1,000/family
>**School year:** August to June

Year founded: 1961. **Type of school:** coed, day, boarding, church-related. **Governed by:** Assemblies of God, Conservative Baptist Foreign Mission Society, United World Mission, Southern Baptist Convention. **Accredited by:** Middle States, Association of Christian Schools, Association of Christian Schools International.

Curriculum/physical plant
Type: U.S. **Languages taught:** English, French. **Staff specialists:** computer, nurse, guidance counselor. **Special programs:** ESL, special education. **Special curricular:** art, chorus, physical education, computer instruction,

business education. **Extracurricular:** drama, yearbook, field trips. **Sports:** soccer, track, volleyball. **Tests:** SSAT, SAT, Stanford. **Location:** in suburban area, 8 kilometers north of Dakar. **Campus:** 2.44 hectares. **Library:** 8,000 volumes. **Facilities:** 7 buildings, 12 classrooms, auditorium, tennis court, playing field, science lab, computer lab, darkroom, fully equipped dormitory.

*Once only fee

THE INTERNATIONAL SCHOOL OF DAKAR

Street address: Fenetre Mermoz, Dakar, Senegal
Phone: (221)230871   **Facsimile:** (221)222991
Mail: PO Box 5136, Dakar, Senegal
U.S. mail: c/o Administrative Officer, Dakar, Department of State, Washington, D.C. 20521-2130
Director: Peter Todd
Staff: full-time, 14; part-time, 5
Nationalities of staff: U.S., 8; U.K., 2; other, 9
Grade levels: K – 8
Enrollment: K, 20; 1 – 6, 80; 7 – 8, 25; total, 125
Capacity: K, 20; 1 – 6, 120; 7 – 9, 60; total, 200
Teacher/student ratio: 1/7
Tuition (annual): $7,700
Other fees: registration: $50 (new students), $25 (returning students); capital development*, $2,000; ESL, $500; native French instruction, $500
School year: September to June

Year founded: 1983. **Type of school:** coed, day, private nonprofit. **Governed by:** elected board of directors. **Accredited by:** Middle States.

Curriculum/physical plant

Type: U.S. **Languages taught:** French. **Staff specialists:** learning disabilities. **Special programs:** ESL. **Special curricular:** art, physical education, computer instruction, music. **Extracurricular:** dance, computers, field trips, computer club, student council. **Sports:** soccer, swimming. **Location:** in residential suburb. **Library:** 8,000 volumes. **Facilities:** 3 buildings, science lab, computer lab, swimming pool, multi-purpose auditorium/gymnasium, air conditioning.

*Once only fee

SEYCHELLES

Region: Africa
Size: 171 square miles
Population: 68,000
Capital: Victoria

Telephone code: 248
Currency: rupee
Languages: English, French

VICTORIA

INTERNATIONAL SCHOOL (SEYCHELLES)

Street address: Mont Fleuri, Victoria, Seychelles
Phone: (248)22641
Mail: PO Box 315, Victoria, Seychelles
Headmaster: Tony Irons
Staff: full-time, 16; part-time, 2
Grade levels: N – 11
Enrollment: N – preK, 22; K, 30; 1 – 5, 133; 6 – 11, 75; total, 260
Nationalities of student body: U.S., 19; U.K., 26; other, 215
Capacity: N – K, 52; 1 – 5, 140; 6 – 11, 75; total, 267
Teacher/student ratio: 1/15
Tuition (annual): N – K, 3,000**; 1 – 5, 4,500; 6 – 11, 6,000
Other fees (annual): registration, 210**; enrollment deposit*, 5,000
    (refundable); subscription, 75; ESL classes, 25/half hour
School year: September to July

Year founded: 1969. **Type of school:** coed, day, private nonprofit.
Governed by: elected board of governors. **Accredited by:** Seychelles and
British governments, Middle States (in process).

Curriculum/physical plant

Type: U.K., international. **Languages taught:** English, French. **Special
curricular:** physical education, computer instruction, ESL. **Extracurricular:**
drama, gymnastics, photography, excursions/expeditions, field trips, ballet,
craft, Brownies. **Sports:** basketball, soccer, swimming, volleyball, squash,
sailing, canoeing, windsurfing, scuba diving. **Tests:** Common Entrance
Examinations, IGCSE. **Location:** in suburban area, 2 kilometers from city
center. **Campus:** 2 acres. **Facilities:** 3 buildings, 12 classrooms, auditorium,
covered canteen area; new secondary block, with labs and other facilities, due
for construction.

*Once only fee   **Seychelles rupee

SIERRA LEONE

Region: West Africa
Size: 27,925 square miles
Population: 4,274,000
Capital: Freetown

Telephone code: 232
Currency: leone
Languages: English, tribal
languages

FREETOWN

THE AMERICAN INTERNATIONAL SCHOOL OF FREETOWN

Street address: 24 Hillcott Brow, Hill Station, Freetown, Sierra Leone
Phone: (232)(22)232480   **Telex:** 9893509 USEMB SL
Mail: c/o U.S. Embassy, Walpole Street, Freetown, Sierra Leone
U.S. mail: c/o U.S. Embassy – Freetown, Sierra Leone, Department of
State, Washington, D.C. 20521-2160
Principal: Allan V. Young
Assistant principal: Edna Thomas
Staff: full-time, 8
Nationalities of staff: U.S., 5; host, 1; other, 2
Grade levels: preschool – 8
Enrollment: preschool, 14; K, 7; 1 – 8, 33; total, 54
Nationalities of student body: U.S., 12; U.K., 4; other, 38
Capacity: preschool, 24; K, 15; 1 – 8, 90; total, 129
Teacher/student ratio: 1/7
Tuition (annual): preschool, $2,000; K – 8, $5,800
Other fees (annual): registration, $100; capital levy: preschool, $100;
K – 8, $200
School year: September to June

Year founded: 1986. **Type of school:** coed, day. **Governed by:** elected
board of directors.

Curriculum/physical plant

Type: U.S. **Staff specialists:** computer, ESL, music, physical education.
Extracurricular: gymnastics, newspaper, field trips, karate, ballet, swimming. **Tests:** Iowa. **Location:** in suburban area. **Library:** 6,000 volumes.
Facilities: 2 buildings, 12 classrooms, playing field, preschool I and II annex,
air conditioning.

KABALA

Kabala Rupp Memorial School

Address: Box 28 Kabala, Sierra Leone, West Africa
U.S. mail: c/o Missionary Church, 3901 South Wayne, Fort Wayne, IN
46807, U.S.A.

SINGAPORE, Republic of _____

Region: Southeast Asia
Size: 224 square miles
Population: 2,756,000
Capital: Singapore

Telephone code: 65
Currency: Singapore dollar
Languages: Chinese, Malay,
Tamil, English

SINGAPORE

OVERSEAS FAMILY SCHOOL

Street address: 25 F Paterson Road, Singapore 0923, Republic of
Singapore
Phone: (65)7380211   **Facsimile:** (65)7338825
Principal: Jenny Gay
Business manager: Irene Chee
Staff: full-time, 70; part-time, 5
Nationalities of staff: U.S., 18; U.K., 27; host, 10; other, 20
Grade levels: preK – 12
Enrollment: preK, 20; K, 118; 1 – 5, 388; 6 – 8, 231; 9 – 12, 177; total, 934
Nationalities of student body: U.S., 60; U.K., 120; host, 10; other, 744
Capacity: preK, 20; K, 160; 1 – 5, 450; 6 – 8, 350; 9 – 12, 320; total, 1,300
Teacher/student ratio: 1/13
Tuition (annual): preK – 5, 10,000**; 6 – 8, $13,000; 9 – 12, 14,000
Other fees: refundable deposit*, one semester's tuition
School year: September to June

Year founded: 1991. **Type of school:** coed, day, proprietary. **Governed
by:** elected board of governors.

Curriculum/physical plant
Type: U.S./U.K. **Languages taught:** French, Spanish, Japanese. **Staff
specialists:** computer, counselor, nurse. **Special programs:** ESL. **Extracurricular:** drama, computers, yearbook, excursions/expeditions, field trips.
Sports: basketball, rugby, soccer, tennis, badminton, table tennis. **Clubs:**
Brownies, Guides, Scouts. **Tests:** SAT, TOEFL, A-level GCE, GCSE. **Location:**
inner city at previous teachers' college site. **Library:** 10,000 volumes. **Facilities:** 5 buildings, 80 classrooms, auditorium, cafeteria, infirmary, covered
play area, tennis court, gymnasium, playing field, 5 science labs, 2 computer
labs, swimming pool, air conditioning.

*Once only fee   **Singapore dollar

SINGAPORE AMERICAN SCHOOL

Street address: (high school) 60 King's Road, Singapore 1026, Repub-
lic of Singapore; (elementary and middle schools) 201 Ulu Pandan
Road, Singapore 2159, Republic of Singapore
Phone: (65)4665611   **Facsimile:** (65)4695957   **Cable:** SASCHOOL
Mail: 60 King's Road, Singapore 1026, Republic of Singapore

Superintendent: Don Bergman, Ed.D.
Assistant superintendent for business: Bill Pearson
High school principal: Jim Doran
Middle school principal: Joan Adams
Elementary school principal: Peter Larson
Director of curriculum: Mary Frances Greer
Staff: full-time, 165; part-time, 14
Nationalities of staff: U.S., 137; U.K., 10; host, 14; other, 18
Grade levels: pre-school (age 3), preK (age 4), K – 12
Enrollment: preS – K, 268; 1 – 5, 770; 6 – 8, 429; 9 – 12, 695; total, 2,162
Nationalities of student body: U.S., 1,533; host, 20; other, 609
Teacher/student ratio: 1/13
Tuition (annual): preS – preK, 5,350**; K – 5, 11,350; 6 – 8, 14,200; 9 – 12, 16,050
Other fees (annual): registration*, 3,000**; capital levy, 6,000 (new student), 3,000 (returning student); ESL, 2,000
School year: September to June

Year founded: 1956. **Type of school:** coed, day, private nonprofit. **Governed by:** elected board of governors. **Accredited by:** Western.

Curriculum

Type: U.S. **Languages taught:** French, Spanish, Mandarin. **Staff specialists:** reading, math, computer, speech/hearing, counselor, learning disabilities, nurse, ESL, school psychologist. **Special programs:** ESL, advanced placement, honors sections, independent study, remedial, technical education, learning disabilities, resource room. **Special curricular:** art, chorus, band, physical education, computer instruction, vocational, technical education. **Extracurricular:** drama, gymnastics, dance, choral music, instrumental music, computers, yearbook, newspaper, literary magazine, photography, excursions/expeditions, field trips. **Sports:** basketball, hockey, rugby, soccer, softball, swimming, tennis, volleyball, badminton, track and field. **Clubs:** computer, dance, humanities, Model UN, social services, stamp, student newspaper, Tri-M (music). **Tests:** SSAT, PSAT, SAT, ACT, TOEFL, AP, Iowa, PACT, TAP, COGAT. **Graduates attending college:** 94%. **Graduates have attended:** Duke, Brown, Harvard, U. of California (Berkeley),Wake Forest.

Physical plant

Location: 3 campuses, each in private, prime residential area, about a 10-minute drive from city. **Libraries:** 40,000 volumes. **Facilities:** 97 classrooms, 2 auditoriums, 2 cafeterias, 2 infirmaries, 3 gymnasiums, 3 playing fields, 8 science labs, 3 computer labs, swimming pool, 2 media centers, fine arts center, technical education lab, language lab, drafting labs, practical arts workshop, air conditioning.

*Once only fee   **Singapore dollar

TANGLIN TRUST SCHOOLS

Street address: Portsdown Road, Singapore 0513, Republic of
  Singapore
Phone: (65)7780771   **Facsimile:** (65)7775862
Headteacher (infant/junior schools): Mrs. V. E. Goodban
Headteacher (Winchester school): Mrs. B. Emblem
Staff: full-time, 68; part-time, 6
Grade levels: ages 3 – 11
Enrollment: ages 3 – 5, 212; ages 4 1/2 – 7, 574; ages 7 – 11, 644;
  total, 1,430
Capacity: ages 3 – 5, 212; ages 4 1/2 – 7, 574; ages 7 – 11, 644;
  total, 1,430
Teacher/student ratio: 1/20
Tuition (annual): ages 3 – 5, 5,400**; ages 4 1/2 – 7, 7,500;
  ages 7 – 10, 7,950; ages 10 – 11, 8,250
Other fees: registration*: ages 3 – 5, 400**; ages 4 1/2 – 11, 1,750
School year: September to August

Year founded: 1961. **Type of school:** coed, day, nonprofit trust. **Governed by:** appointed board of governors. **Administered by:** The Tanglin Trust
Ltd.

Curriculum/physical plant

Type: U.K. **Languages taught:** English. **Staff specialists:** reading, math,
computer, psychologist, nurse. **Special programs:** remedial. **Special curricular:** art, physical education, computer instruction, music. **Extracurricular:** drama, gymnastics, computers, yearbook, field trips, recorder, arts and
crafts, needlework. **Sports:** rugby, soccer, netball, athletics, cricket, rounders, badminton. **Graduates have attended:** United World College of South
East Asia; schools in England and Australia. **Location:** 6 miles from center
city, in parklike surroundings near National University of Singapore. **Campus:** 4.715 hectares. **Facilities:** 3 buildings, 52 classrooms, 3 auditoriums,
infirmary, 2 covered play areas, 3 gymnasiums, 2 playing fields, computer lab,
7 libraries, partial air conditioning.

*Once only fee   **Singapore dollar

UNITED WORLD COLLEGE OF SOUTH EAST ASIA

Street address: Dover Road, Singapore 0513, Republic of Singapore
Phone: (65)7755344   **Facsimile**: (65)7785846
Mail: Pasir Panjang PO Box 15, Singapore 9111, Republic of Singapore
Headmaster: Mr. M. D. Watson
Deputy headmaster: Mr. A.W. Bennett
Business manager: Mr. L. H. da Silva
Staff: full-time, 104; part-time, 13
Nationalities of staff: U.S., 3; U.K., 81; host, 9; other, 24
Grade levels: 6 – 12
Enrollment: 6 – 8, 644; 9 – 12, 751; total, 1,395

Nationalities of student body: U.S., 49; U.K., 425; host, 29;
other, 892
Teacher/student ratio: 1/13
Boarders: boys, 137; girls, 116   **Grades:** 6 – 12
   Program: planned 7-day
Tuition (annual): 13,800**
Other fees (annual): registration*, 1,500**; boarding, 13,500; capital
levy*, 450; busing, varies with distance
School year: September to July

Year founded: 1971. **Type of school:** coed, day, boarding, private
nonprofit. **Governed by:** board of governors. **Member:** United World College
Movement.

Curriculum

Type: U.K., IB. **Languages taught:** French, Spanish, German, Dutch,
Japanese, Indonesian, Malay, Chinese. **Staff specialists:** reading, math,
computer, nurse. **Special programs:** ESL. **Special curricular:** art, chorus,
physical education, drama. **Extracurricular:** drama, gymnastics, dance,
choral music, instrumental music, computers, yearbook, newspaper, literary
magazine, photography, excursions/expeditions, field trips, more than 100
different clubs and activities. **Sports:** aerobics, basketball, fencing, hockey,
rugby, soccer, swimming, tennis, volleyball, athletics, sailing, windsurfing,
canoeing, netball, waterskiing, squash, badminton, cricket, scuba, karate,
gymnastics. **Tests:** PSAT, SAT, ACT, TOEFL, IB, GCSE, Oxford and Cambridge entrance, London U. scholarship exams. **Graduates attending college:** 90%. **Graduates have attended:** U. of Sydney, Australia; Oxford;
Cambridge; Harvard; Utrecht, Netherlands.

Physical plant

Location: in suburb of Singapore, next to National U. of Singapore and
Singapore Polytechnic. **Campus:** 43.5 acres. **Libraries:** 40,000 volumes.
Facilities: 12 buildings, 80 classrooms, 2 auditoriums, cafeteria, infirmary,
8 tennis courts, gymnasium, 3 playing fields, 15 science labs, 3 computer
labs, swimming pool, 4 boarding houses, sports hall, air conditioning.

*Once only fee   **Singapore dollar

SOUTH AFRICA, Republic of _____

Region: Africa
Size: 472,359 square miles
Population: 40,600,000
Capitals: Cape Town, Pretoria, Bloemfontein

Telephone code: 27
Currency: rand
Languages: Afrikaans,
English, Sotho
languages, Nguni

JOHANNESBURG

THE AMERICAN INTERNATIONAL SCHOOL OF JOHANNESBURG

Street address: Portion of Plot 160, Diepsloot, Midrand, Transvaal, Republic of South Africa
Phone: (27)(11)4641505 – 8   **Facsimile:** (27)(11)4641327
Mail: Private Bag X4, Bryanston 2021, Republic of South Africa
Director: Everett G. Gould
Staff: full-time, 20
Nationalities of staff: U.S., 15; host, 4; other, 1
Grade levels: K – 12
Enrollment: K, 14; 1 – 4, 55; 5 – 8, 51; 9 – 12, 62; total, 182
Nationalities of student body: U.S., 91; host, 36; other, 55
Teacher/student ratio: 1/9
Boarders: total, 15   **Grades:** 6 – 12   **Program:** planned 5- and 7-day
Tuition (annual): K, $7,440; 1 – 4, $9,910; 5 – 8, $11,076; 9 – 12, $12,820
Other fees (annual): placement/registration*, 50**; boarding, 21,000; capital levy*, $3,000/family; busing, 4,610 (Sandton/Bryanston), 7,526 (Pretoria)
School year: August through June

Year founded: 1982. **Type of school:** coed, day, boarding, private nonprofit. **Governed by:** elected school board. **Accredited by:** Middle States.

Curriculum/physical plant
Type: U.S. **Languages taught:** French, Spanish. **Staff specialists:** counselor. **Special programs:** ESL. **Special curricular:** art, physical education, computer instruction, drama. **Extracurricular:** yearbook, newspaper, excursions/expeditions, field trips. **Sports:** basketball, swimming, tennis, volleyball. **Tests:** PSAT, SAT, TOEFL, AP, Iowa, diagnostic testing. **Graduates attending college:** 90%. **Graduates have attended:** U. of Southern California, MIT, U. of Cape Town, U. of Western Ontario, U.S. Naval College. **Location:** midway between Johannesburg and Pretoria. **Campus:** 60 acres. **Library:** 10,000 volumes. **Facilities:** 3 buildings, 19 classrooms, auditorium, cafeteria, covered play area, 2 tennis courts, 2 playing fields, 2 science labs, computer lab, swimming pool, AV equipment, boarding facilities approximately 4 kilometers from school.

*Once only fee   **South African rand

SPAIN

Region: Europe
Size: 194,896 square miles
Population: 39,384,000
Capital: Madrid

Telephone code: 34
Currency: peseta
Languages: Spanish, Catalan,
Galician, Basque

BARCELONA

AMERICAN SCHOOL OF BARCELONA

Street address: Balmes 7, Esplugas (Barcelona), Spain
Phone: (34)(3)3714016/3715012   **Facsimile:** (34)(3)4734787
Director: Elsa Lamb
Assistant director: Anna Prieto
High school principal: Raymond Kern
Staff: full-time, 44; part-time, 1
Nationalities of staff: U.S., 23; U.K., 6; host, 12; other, 4
Grade levels: N – 12
Enrollment: preK, 40; K, 40; 1 – 6, 205; 7 – 9, 80; 10 – 12, 75; total, 440
Capacity: preK, 40; K, 40; 1 – 6, 225; 7 – 9, 100; 10 – 12, 95; total, 500
Teacher/student ratio: 1/10
Tuition (annual): preK – K, $4,000; 1 – 4, $5,250; 5 – 8, $6,000;
9 – 12, $7,000
Other fees (annual): registration, $570; capital levy*, $1,350;
busing, $1,200; lunch, $1,200
School year: September to June

Year founded: 1962. **Type of school:** coed, day, proprietary. **Governed by:** elected board of governors. **Sponsored by:** parents' association. **Accredited by:** Middle States, Spanish Ministry of Education.

Curriculum/physical plant

Type: U.S., Spanish. **Languages taught:** Spanish, Catalan. **Special programs:** ESL, advanced placement. **Special curricular:** art, physical education, computer instruction. **Extracurricular:** computers, yearbook, newspaper, literary magazine, excursions/expeditions, field trips. **Sports:** basketball, soccer, swimming, volleyball. **Clubs:** Model UN, Close-Up, student council, chess. **Tests:** PSAT, SAT, ACT, Iowa. **Graduates attending college:** 90%. **Graduates have attended:** Northwestern, Marymount, Texas A&M, U. of South Carolina, Minnesota. **Location:** pleasant residential area in suburb of Barcelona. **Library:** 7,000 volumes. **Facilities:** 3 science labs, large playground, sports court and dressing rooms, soccer field, computer room, art room, music room, dining room.

*Once only fee

THE BENJAMIN FRANKLIN INTERNATIONAL SCHOOL

Street address: Matorell i Peña 9, 08017 Barcelona, Spain
Phone: (34)(3)4186545   **Facsimile:** (34)(3)4173633
Superintendent/director: Stan Key
Assistant director: Cindy Moyer
Spanish program director: Pilar Hernando
Staff: full-time, 24; part-time, 3
Nationalities of staff: U.S., 18; host, 7; other, 2
Grade levels: preK – 12
Enrollment: preK, 15; K, 11; 1 – 5, 88; 6 – 8, 45; 9 – 12, 66; total, 225
Nationalities of student body: U.S., 43; host, 116; other, 66
Capacity: preK, 15; K, 15; 1 – 5, 100; 6 – 8, 60; 9 – 12, 100; total, 290
Teacher/student ratio: 1/9
Tuition (annual): preK – K, 438,000**; 1 – 5, 625,000; 6 – 8, 690,000;
    9 – 12, 915,000
Other fees (annual): matriculation, 69,000** (first child), 64,000 (other
    children); capital levy*, 145,000; busing, 132,000 – 160,000 (op-
    tional); lunch, 122,000 (optional); graduation*, 7,000
School year: September through June

Year founded: 1986. **Type of school:** coed, day, private nonprofit.
Governed by: appointed school board commission of the Benjamin Franklin
Foundation. **Accredited by:** Middle States, Spanish Ministry of Education.

Curriculum/physical plant

Type: U.S. **Languages taught:** Spanish, Catalan. **Staff specialists:**
computer, art, ESL, music, physical education, Spanish as a Second Language. **Special programs:** ESL, advanced placement, independent study,
Spanish as a Second Language, Catalan. **Special curricular:** art, computer
instruction, drama, sports, yearbook, Model European Parliament, Model UN.
Extracurricular: excursions/expeditions, field trips, softball, volleyball, ultimate frisbee, soccer, basketball, track & field, swimming, hockey. **Tests:**
PSAT, SAT, ACT, TOEFL, AP, Iowa, TAP. **Graduates attending college:** 90%.
Graduates have attended: U. of Pennsylvania, Bryn Mawr, Rutgers, Carnegie
Mellon, U. of California (Irvine). **Location:** Bonanova/Sarriá residential area
of Barcelona. **Library:** 5,000 volumes. **Facilities:** elementary school in large,
converted, private residence; pre-school and high school housed in separate
building; computer lab, music room, playing court, art room, cafeteria,
science labs in separate building.

*Once only fee   **Spanish peseta

BILBAO

AMERICAN SCHOOL OF BILBAO

Street address: Soparda Bidea s/n, 48990 Berango (Vizcaya) Spain
Phone: (34)(4)6680860 – 1   **Facsimile:** (34)(4)6680452
Director: George Selby
Assistant director: Terry Orueta
Business manager: Begona Loizaga
Staff: full-time, 29; part-time, 3
Nationalities of staff: U.S., 16; U.K., 6; host, 10
Grade levels: N – 10
Enrollment: N, 18; preK – K, 48; 1 – 6, 142; 7 – 10, 75; total, 283
Nationalities of student body: U.S., 23; U.K., 14; host, 220; other, 26
Capacity: N, 18; preK – K, 48; 1 – 6, 150; 7 – 10, 88; total, 304
Teacher/student ratio: 1/9
Tuition (annual): N – K, 339,000**; 1 – 6, 440,000; 7 – 10, 500,000
Other fees (annual): capital levy, 250,000**; busing, 48,000; insurance*
School year: September to June

Year founded: 1967. **Type of school:** coed, day, private nonprofit.
Governed by: appointed and elected board of directors. **Accredited by:** New
England, ECIS.

Curriculum/physical plant
Type: U.S. **Languages of instruction:** English, Spanish for Spanish
citizens. **Languages taught:** French, Spanish, Latin, Basque. **Staff specialists:** computer, psychologist, art, music, physical education. **Extracurricular:** excursions/expeditions, field trips. **Sports:** basketball, soccer, volleyball.
Tests: Iowa. **Location:** 20 kilometers from Bilbao, on hill surrounded by
farms. **Campus:** 14 acres. **Library:** 7,000 volumes. **Facilities:** 8 buildings, 17
classrooms, covered play area, 2 playing fields, science lab, computer lab, art
studio.

*Once only fee   **Spanish peseta

CARTAGENA

ISS INTERNATIONAL SCHOOL OF CARTAGENA

Street address: La Manga Club, Los Belones, CP 30385, Cartagena
(Murcia) Spain
Phone/Facsimile: (34)(68)564511 ext. 2238
Principal: Kristin Russell
Staff: full-time, 4; part-time, 1
Nationalities of staff: U.S., 3; host, 1; other, 1

Grade levels: preK – 7
Enrollment: preK – K, 6; 1 – 7, 22; total, 28
Nationalities of student body: U.S., 4; U.K., 5; host, 8; other, 11
Capacity: preK – K, 10; 1 – 7, 45; total, 55
Teacher/student ratio: 1/6
Tuition: $5,300 – 5,600
Other fees: registration*, 10,000**
School year: September to June

Year founded: 1989. **Type of school:** coed, day, company sponsored, private nonprofit. **Governed by:** appointed board. **Sponsored by:** General Electric Plastics de España. **Operated by:** International Schools Services, Princeton, New Jersey. **Accredited by:** New England (in process). **Regional organizations:** MAIS, ECIS.

Curriculum/physical plant
Type: U.S. **Languages taught:** Spanish. **Special curricular:** art, physical education, computer instruction, cooking. **Extracurricular:** newspaper, excursions/expeditions, field trips. **Sports:** soccer, swimming, tennis, volleyball, golf. **Location:** country-club setting, in suburban area near Murcia and Cartagena. **Campus:** 1 acre. **Library:** 1,000 volumes. **Facilities:** science lab, computer lab, playing fields, air conditioning.

*Once only fee   **Spanish peseta

LAS PALMAS

AMERICAN SCHOOL OF LAS PALMAS
Street address: Ctra. de Los Hoyos Km.5, Tafira Alta, 35017 Las Palmas, Gran Canaria, Spain
Phone: (34)(28)350400   **Facsimile:** (34)(28)355258
Mail: Apartado 15, Tafira Alta, 35017 Las Palmas, Gran Canaria, Spain
Director: Cynthia Gause
Assistant director: Celine Hammond
Business manager: Eduardo Medina
Staff: full-time, 39
Nationalities of staff: U.S., 19; U.K., 6; host, 9; other, 5
Grade levels: N – 12
Enrollment: N – preK, 50; K, 25; 1 – 5, 175; 6 – 8, 75; 9 – 12, 90; total, 415
Nationalities of student body: U.S., 19; U.K., 3; host, 238; other, 155
Capacity: N – preK, 50; K, 25; 1 – 6, 175; 7 – 9, 75; 10 – 12, 75; total, 400
Teacher/student ratio: 1/11
Tuition (annual): N – 5, 323,670**; 6 – 8, 458,700; 9 – 12, 501,220
Other fees (annual): registration, 25,000**; capital levy*, 300,000; busing, at cost; lunch, at cost
School year: September to June

Year founded: 1967. **Type of school:** coed, day, private nonprofit. **Governed by:** elected board of directors. **Accredited by:** New England, ECIS, Spanish Ministry of Education.

Curriculum/physical plant

Type: U.S. **Languages of instruction:** English, Spanish for national program. **Languages taught:** French, German. **Staff specialists:** computer, counselor. **Special programs:** ESL. **Special curricular:** art, physical education, computer instruction, music. **Extracurricular:** drama, computers, yearbook, newspaper, excursions/expeditions, horseback riding, team sports. **Sports:** basketball, soccer, volleyball. **Tests:** SSAT, PSAT, SAT, TOEFL, ERB. **Graduates attending college:** 95%. **Graduates have attended:** Boston Conservatory of Music, Smith, Brown, U. of Boston. **Location:** in country setting, 20 minutes from Las Palmas. **Campus:** 10 acres. **Library:** 8,000 volumes. **Facilities:** 8 buildings, 26 classrooms, cafeteria, infirmary, 2 playing fields, science lab, computer lab, basketball courts, multiple-use room.

*Once only fee   **Spanish peseta

MADRID

AMERICAN SCHOOL OF MADRID

Street address: Carretera de Aravaca-Humera, Km. 2, 28023 Madrid, Spain
Phone: (34)(1)3572154   **Facsimile:** (34)(1)3572678
Mail: Apartado 80, 28080 Madrid, Spain
Superintendent: William O'Hale
Director, upper school: B. J. Nelson
Director, lower school: Cindy C. Stabile, Ph.D.
Director of admissions: Anne Albritton
Business manager: Jesus L. Hortal
Staff: full-time, 63; part-time, 6
Nationalities of staff: U.S., 38; U.K., 5; host, 18; other, 8
Grade levels: N – 12
Enrollment: N – preK, 63; K, 37; 1 – 6, 254; 7 – 9, 123; 10 – 12, 131; total, 608
Nationalities of student body: U.S., 313; host, 152; other, 143
Capacity: preK, 72; K, 50; 1 – 6, 288; 7 – 9, 144; 10 – 12, 158; total, 712
Teacher/student ratio: 1/9
Tuition (annual): preK, $3,878; K, $5,348; 1 – 3, $7,870; 4 – 6, $8,843; 7 – 9, $10,461; 10 – 12, $10,687
Other fees (annual): registration, $250; busing (optional), $1,322; development fund*, $1,739; yearbook (optional), $65
School year: September to June

Year founded: 1961. **Type of school:** coed, day, private nonprofit. **Governed by:** appointed board of directors. **Accredited by:** Middle States, ECIS, Spanish Ministry of Education.

Curriculum

Type: U.S., Spanish EGB, BUP, and COU. **Languages taught:** French, Spanish. **Staff specialists:** reading, computer, counselor, learning disabilities, nurse. **Special programs:** ESL, advanced placement, remedial. **Special curricular:** art, chorus, physical education, computer instruction, field trips, Young Authors' Festival. **Extracurricular:** drama, gymnastics, dance, computers, yearbook, literary magazine. **Sports:** baseball, basketball, soccer, softball, tennis, volleyball, gymnastics, T-ball, track-and-field meets. **Clubs:** arts and crafts, creative dramatics, judo, scouting, bookmaking, cheerleaders. **Tests:** PSAT, SAT, TOEFL, AP, ERB, achievement tests. **Graduates attending college:** 95%. **Graduates have attended:** Boston College, Lehigh, Princeton, Clarkson, U. of California at Berkeley.

Physical plant

Location: 5 miles from Madrid, near suburb of Aravaca. **Campus:** 10 acres. **Library:** 40,000 volumes. **Facilities:** 3 buildings, 42 classrooms, cafeteria, infirmary, 2 tennis courts, 2 playing fields, 2 science labs, computer lab, gymnasium/auditorium, AV room, music room, track, partial air conditioning.

*Once only fee

EVANGELICAL CHRISTIAN ACADEMY

Street address: Calle Talia 26, 28022 Madrid, Spain
Phone: (34)(1)7412900   **Facsimile:** (34)(1)3208606
Headmaster: Paul Wrobbel
Staff: full-time, 10; part-time, 4
Nationalities of staff: U.S., 14
Grade levels: K – 12
Enrollment: 1 – 6, 35; 7 – 9, 23; 10 – 12, 23; total, 81
Nationalities of student body: U.S., 72; other, 9
Capacity: K, 6; 1 – 6, 36; 7 – 9, 30; 10 – 12, 30; total, 102
Teacher/student ratio: 1/7
Tuition (annual): K, $1,560; 1 – 12, $2,600
Other fees (annual): registration, $50; activity, $75
School year: September through May

Year founded: 1973. **Type of school:** coed, day, church-related. **Governed by:** appointed board.

Curriculum/physical plant

Type: U.S. **Languages taught:** Spanish. **Staff specialists:** computer, learning disabilities, music. **Special programs:** advanced placement, independent study, correspondence, remedial. **Special curricular:** chorus, band, physical education, computer instruction. **Extracurricular:** choral music, instrumental music, yearbook, newspaper, National Honor Society, student council. **Tests:** PSAT, SAT, AP, Iowa. **Graduates attending college:** 92%. **Graduates have attended:** Wheaton College, Masters College, Cedarville College, Biola College, North Carolina State U. **Location:** residential area of Madrid. **Library:** 10,000 volumes. **Facilities:** 2 buildings, 11 classrooms, science lab, computer lab.

INTERNATIONAL COLLEGE SPAIN

Street address: Calle Vereda Norte, 3, 28109 La Moraleja, Madrid, Spain
Phone: (34)(1)6502398   **Facsimile:** (34)(1)6501035
Mail: Apartado 271, Alcobendas, Madrid, Spain
Director: John V. Hutchinson
Deputy director: Peter J. Samaranayake
Head of primary: Tony Damore
Staff: full-time, 46; part-time, 7
Nationalities of staff: U.S., 10; U.K., 19; host, 7; other, 17
Grade levels: preK – 12
Enrollment: K, 78; 1 – 6, 222; 7 – 9, 101; 10 – 12, 112; total, 513
Nationalities of student body: U.S., 85; U.K., 60; host, 145; other, 223
Capacity: total, 550
Teacher/student ratio: 1/10
Boarders: boys, 7; girls, 1   **Grades:** 7 – 12   **Program:** planned 5-day
Tuition (annual): K, 360,000 – 588,000**; 1 – 6, 660,000 – 879,000;
       7 – 9, 945,000 – 1,137,000; 10 – 12, 1,161,000 – 1,266,000
Other fees (annual): registration*, 15,000**; busing, 135,000; lunch,
       145,000; books, 13,250 – 37,250; refundable deposit, 80,000
Boarding fees (annual): 771,000**; insurance*, 55,000; deposit, 50,000
School year: September through June

Year founded: 1980. **Type of school:** coed, day, boarding, private. **Governed by:** appointed independent board of trustees with advisory group.

Curriculum

Type: U.S., U.K., IB. **Languages taught:** French, Spanish, Dutch, Swedish, others by arrangement. **Staff specialists:** reading, math, computer, counselor, learning disabilities, nurse. **Special programs:** ESL, remedial. **Special curricular:** art, physical education, computer instruction, drama, music. **Extracurricular:** drama, gymnastics, dance, choral music, instrumental music, computers, yearbook, newspaper, excursions/expeditions, field trips, ski trips. **Sports:** aerobics, basketball, football, tennis, volleyball, athletics, judo, karate. **Clubs:** Brownies, community service, ecology, chess, service credit program, guitar, ballet. **Tests:** SSAT, PSAT, SAT, ACT, TOEFL, IB, AP, Iowa, IGCSE. **Graduates attending college:** 95%. **Graduates have attended:** Georgetown (USA), Sussex (UK), Erasmus (Holland), Grenoble (France), Pamplona (Spain).

Physical plant
    Location: in residential area, 9 kilometers north of Madrid. **Campus:** 7.5 acres. **Library:** 11,000 volumes. **Facilities:** 2 buildings, 39 classrooms, auditorium, cafeteria, infirmary, tennis court, gymnasium, playing field, track, science labs, 2 computer labs, small boarding facility.

*Once only fee   **Spanish peseta

MALLORCA

AMERICAN INTERNATIONAL SCHOOL OF MALLORCA

    Street address: Calle Oratorio 4, 07015 Portals Nous, Mallorca, Spain
    Phone: (34)(71)675850 – 1   **Facsimile:** (34)(71)676820
        Telex: 83169651 AMSC E
    Headmaster: James Berry
    Lower school coordinator: Hilary Walliker
    Staff: full-time, 21; part-time, 2
    Nationalities of staff: U.S., 10; U.K., 8; host, 5
    Grade levels: N – 12
    Enrollment: N – K, 21; 1 – 6, 75; 7 – 9, 31; 10 – 12, 68; total, 195
    Nationalities of student body: U.S., 30; U.K., 30; host, 83; other, 52
    Capacity: N – K, 15; 1 – 6, 80; 7 – 9, 30; 10 – 12, 85; total, 210
    Teacher/student ratio: 1/9
    Boarders: boys, 10; girls, 8   **Grades:** 7 – 12
    Tuition (annual): K, 284,000**; 1 – 6, 315,000 – 413,000;
        7 – 9, 481,000 – 609,000; 10 – 12, 689,000 – 799,000
    Other fees (annual): registration, 33,000**; boarding, $8,300;
        insurance, $385; books, $500; trips, $1,350
    School year: September to June

    Year founded: 1969. **Type of school:** coed, day, boarding. **Governed by:** Sociedad Anonima. **Accredited by:** Middle States.

Curriculum
    Type: U.S.; Spanish EGB, BUP, COU; IGCSE (Cambridge Syndicate), A-level U. of London. **Languages taught:** French, Spanish, German. **Staff specialists:** reading, learning disabilities. **Special programs:** ESL, advanced placement, honors sections, independent study, remedial, dyslexia. **Special curricular:** art, physical education, computer instruction. **Extracurricular:** drama, computers, excursions/expeditions, field trips. **Sports:** basketball, soccer, tennis, track, volleyball, golf, horseback riding. **Clubs:** National Honor Society, student government, dorm council, chess, computer, community service projects. **Tests:** PSAT, SAT, ACT, TOEFL, AP, Stanford, IGCSE, A-level U. of London. **Graduates attending college:** 95%. **Graduates have attended:** Baylor, Wellesley College, U. of Virginia (U.S.); St. Louis U. (Spain); Richmond College/University (England).

Physical plant

Location: in residential village, 9 kilometers from Palma de Mallorca. **Campus:** 8,000 square meters. **Library:** 16,000 volumes. **Facilities:** 6 buildings, 18 classrooms, cafeteria, playing field, 2 science labs, computer lab, student lounge, video lounge, boarding in double and triple rooms with private baths.

**Spanish peseta

THE BALEARES INTERNATIONAL SCHOOL

Street address: C/Cabo Mateu Coch 17, San Agustin, 07015 Palma de Mallorca, Baleares, Spain
Phone: (34)(71)403161/401812   **Facsimile:** (34)(71)700319
Headmaster: J. Barrie Wiggins
Business manager: Zanetta Kennedy
Staff: full-time, 17; part-time, 6
Nationalities of staff: U.S., 1; U.K., 13; host, 4; other, 5
Grade levels: K – 13
Enrollment: total, 220
Nationalities of student body: U.S., 8; U.K., 94; host, 4; other, 114
Capacity: K, 20; 1 – 6, 120; 7 – 9, 60; 10 – 12, 60; 13, 10; total, 270
Teacher/student ratio: 1/11
Boarders: boys, 7; girls, 5   **Grades:** 7 – 13   **Program:** planned 5- and 7-day
Tuition (annual): K, 240,000**; 1 – 6, 300,000 – 405,000;
  7 – 9, 469,000 – 615,000; 10 – 13, 663,000 – 699,000
Other fees (annual): registration, 20,000 – 40,000**; boarding: 5-day, 1,512,000; 7-day, 1,572,000; deposit, 10,000
School year: September to June

Year founded: 1957. **Type of school:** coed, day, boarding, proprietary.
Accredited by: Her Majesty's Inspectors of Schools.

Curriculum

Type: U.S., U.K. **Languages taught:** French, Spanish, German. **Staff specialists:** reading, math, computer, counselor. **Special programs:** ESL, advanced placement, honors sections, independent study, German language for native speakers. **Special curricular:** art, physical education, computer instruction, vocational. **Extracurricular:** drama, gymnastics, choral music, instrumental music, computers, yearbook, newspaper, photography, excursions/expeditions, field trips. **Sports:** basketball, soccer, swimming, tennis, volleyball, judo, sailing, athletics. **Clubs:** mountain hiking, body building, Boy Scouts, Girl Scouts, Cub Scouts, Brownies. **Tests:** PSAT, SAT, TOEFL, AP, A-level GCE, IGCSE. **Graduates attending college:** 80%. **Graduates have attended:** Harvard, Yale, London, Berlin, McGill.

Physical plant

Location: 3 miles from Palma de Mallorca. **Campus:** 3 acres. **Library:** 10,000 volumes. **Facilities:** 3 buildings, 18 classrooms, cafeteria, covered play area, playing field, 2 science labs, 2 computer labs, senior lounge, shared 2- and 3-bedrooms, boarders' lounge.

**Spanish peseta

BELLVER INTERNATIONAL COLLEGE

Street address: 5, Jose Costa Ferrer, Palma de Mallorca, Baleares 07015, Spain
Phone: (34)(71)401679/404263   **Facsimile:** (34)(71)401762
Administrator: Mark Muirhead
Principals: Daphne Martin, Barbara Bauza
Registrar: Stephanie Muirhead
Staff: full-time, 20; part-time, 2
Nationalities of staff: U.K., 20; host, 2
Grade levels: N – 13
Enrollment: N – preK, 12; K, 20; 1 – 6, 142; 7 – 9, 62; 10 – 13, 28; total, 264
Nationalities of student body: U.S., 12; U.K., 98; host, 144; other, 10
Capacity: N – preK, 22; K, 24; 1 – 6, 144; 7 – 9, 72; 10 – 13, 72; total, 334
Teacher/student ratio: 1/13
Tuition (annual): N – K, 270,000**; 1 – 6, 372,000; 7 – 9, 446,000; 10 – 13, 555,000
Other fees (annual): registration*, 75,000**; insurance, 1,500; busing, 61,000; books, 41,000
School year: September to June

Year founded: 1950. **Type of school:** coed, day, proprietary. **Governed by:** appointed administrator and shareholders. **Accredited by:** Spanish Ministry of Education, British HMI's.

Curriculum

Type: U.K., part Spanish. **Languages taught:** French, Spanish, German, Catalan. **Staff specialists:** English, math, history, geography, languages, computer, sciences. **Special programs:** ESL. **Special curricular:** art, physical education, computer instruction, typing. **Extracurricular:** drama, dance, instrumental music, yearbook, newspaper, excursions/expeditions, field trips. **Sports:** basketball, soccer, swimming, sailing, karate. **Clubs:** Girl Guides, Boy Scouts, 4 internal houses. **Tests:** A-level GCE, GCSE, EGB, BUP. **Graduates attending college:** 80%. **Graduates have attended:** Cambridge, Imperial College London, Michigan State, Newcastle, Kent.

Physical plant

Location: 3 kilometers west of Palma center, opposite king's summer palace, on cul-de-sac street in residential area. **Campus:** .5 acre. **Library:** 5,000 volumes. **Facilities:** 2 buildings, 20 classrooms, covered play area, science lab, computer lab, local playing field, AV equipment, 450 square-meter hall/gymnasium.

*Once only fee   **Spanish peseta

VALENCIA

AMERICAN SCHOOL OF VALENCIA

Street address: Sierra Calderona 25, 46530, Puzol (Valencia), Spain
Phone: (34)(6)1421412   **Facsimile:** (34)(6)1464639
Mail: Apartado de Correos no. 9, 46530 Puzol (Valencia), Spain
Director: Gillian Flaxman
Administrator: Rafael Boscá Canet
Staff: full-time, 58; part-time, 6
Grade levels: N – 12
Enrollment: N – preK, 100; K, 75; 1 – 6, 300; 7 – 12, 200; total, 675
Capacity: N – preK, 100; K, 50; 1 – 6, 300; 7 – 9, 150; 10 – 12, 150; total, 750
Teacher/student ratio: 1/11
Tuition: 600,000**
Other fees (annual): registration, (refundable)*, 600,000**; insurance,
    2,876 – 13,419; busing, 11,900; lunch, 53,000; materials, 21,000
School year: September to June

Year founded: 1979. **Type of school:** coed, day, private nonprofit.
Governed by: board of directors and parents' association. **Accredited by:**
Middle States, Spanish Ministry of Education.

Curriculum/physical plant

Type: U.S., Spanish. **Languages taught:** French, Spanish, German.
Staff specialists: computer, art, ESL, music, physical education. **Special
curricular:** art, physical education, computer instruction, music. **Extracurricular:** drama, computers, excursions/expeditions, field trips, foreign languages. **Sports:** basketball, soccer, volleyball. **Location:** on residential estate
overlooking orange groves and Mediterranean Sea, 25 kilometers from Valencia.
Campus: 30,000 square meters. **Library:** 5,000 volumes. **Facilities:** 2
buildings, 2 cafeterias, science labs, computer lab, art room, music room,
technical drawing room, new sports hall, outside sports facilities.

*Once only fee   **Spanish peseta

BARCELONA

The Anglo-American School

Address: Paseo de Garbi 152, Castelldefels, Barcelona, Spain
Principal: Anne McEwan de Farré

SRI LANKA

Region: South Asia (Indian Ocean)
Size: 25,332 square miles
Population: 17,423,000
Capital: Colombo

Telephone code: 94
Currency: rupee
Languages: Sinhalese, Tamil

COLOMBO

COLOMBO INTERNATIONAL SCHOOL

Street address: 28, Gregory's Road, Colombo 7, Sri Lanka
Phone: (94)(1)697587   **Facsimile:** (94)(1)699592
Principal: Elizabeth Moir
Staff: full-time, 80; part-time, 20
Nationalities of staff: U.S., 1; U.K., 22; host, 74; other, 3
Grade levels: N – 13
Enrollment: N – preK, 43; K, 95; 1 – 6, 306; 7 – 9, 181;
    10 – 12, 140; 13, 65; total, 830
Nationalities of student body: U.S., 9; U.K., 35; host, 577; other, 209
Capacity: N – preK, 60; K, 120; 1 – 6, 360; 7 – 9, 180;
    10 – 12, 200; 13, 80; total, 1,000
Teacher/student ratio: 1/9
Tuition (annual): N – preK, $775; K – 1, $1,060; 2 – 6, $1,350; 7 – 9,
    $1,575; 10 – 13, $1,725
Other fees (annual): registration*, $310; capital levy*, $1,500; books, $80 – 100
School year: September to July

Year founded: 1982. **Type of school:** coed, day, private nonprofit.

Curriculum/physical plant
Type: U.K. **Languages taught:** French, Sinhala, Tamil. **Staff specialists:** reading, math, computer. **Special programs:** ESL, advanced placement. **Special curricular:** art, chorus, band, physical education, computer instruction, vocational. **Extracurricular:** drama, dance, choral music, instrumental music, computers, literary magazine, excursions/expeditions, field trips. **Sports:** basketball, rugby, soccer, swimming, tennis, cricket, athletics, netball, badminton, table tennis. **Clubs:** social work, drama. **Tests:** SAT, TOEFL, A-level GCE, O-level GCE. **Graduates attending college:** 95%. **Graduates have attended:** Oxford, Cambridge, Harvard, Yale, MIT. **Location:** in prime residential area. **Campuses (2):** 3 acres. **Libraries:** 20,000 volumes. **Facilities:** 7 buildings, 28 classrooms, 2 tennis courts, 4 science labs, computer lab, satellite dish, 4 video rooms.

*Once only fee

Overseas Children's School

Phone: (94)(1)564920 – 22   **Facsimile:** (94)(1)564999
Telex: 95421305 AMEMB CE
Mail: Pelawatte, PO Box 9, Battaramulla, Sri Lanka
Headmaster: Phillipa Legatte
Senior school principal: Sean O'Maonaigh
Primary school principal: Dr. Donald Wetmore
Staff: full-time, 69
Nationalities of staff: U.S., 13; U.K., 11; host, 41; other, 4
Grade levels: N – 12
Enrollment: N – preK, 23; K, 21; 1 – 6, 186; 7 – 9, 99; 10 – 12, 116; total, 445
Nationalities of student body: U.S., 63; U.K., 33; host, 81; other, 268
Capacity: N – preK, 55; K, 40; 1 – 6, 390; 7 – 9, 200; 10 – 12, 150; total, 835
Teacher/student ratio: 1/6
Tuition (annual): N – K, $2,700; 1 – 2, $4,560; 3 – 5, $4,800; 6 – 8, $5,475;
   9 – 10, $6,960; 11 – 12, $7,740
Other fees (annual): registration*, $1,800; capital levy, $250 per child;
   activities: 1 – 5, $50, 6 – 12, $100; refundable deposits, N – 6,
   15,000**, 7 – 12, 30,000
School year: September to June

Year founded: 1957 – 58. **Type of school:** coed, day, private nonprofit.
Governed by: elected board of directors. **Accredited by:** Middle States, ECIS.

Curriculum

Type: U.S., U.K., IB. **Languages taught:** French, Spanish, Sinhala. **Staff specialists:** computer, counselor, learning disabilities, nurse, resource. **Special programs:** ESL, remedial. **Special curricular:** art, chorus, physical education, computer instruction, vocational, literary magazine, social service program, yearbook. **Extracurricular:** drama, dance, choral music, instrumental music, computers, yearbook, newspaper, literary magazine, photography, excursions/expeditions, field trips. **Sports:** baseball, basketball, field hockey, rugby, soccer, softball, swimming, tennis, volleyball, squash, track and field, weight training. **Clubs:** student council, drama, aerobic dancing, Kandyan dancing, home economics, woodshop, pottery/sculpture, karate. **Tests:** PSAT, SAT, TOEFL, IB, Iowa, IGCSE. **Graduates attending college:** 95%. **Graduates have attended:** MIT, U. of Pennsylvania, FIT, Lafayette, Vassar.

Physical plant

Location: 8 kilometers from center of Colombo. **Campus:** 5 acres. **Libraries:** 15,000 volumes. **Facilities:** 5 buildings, 42 classrooms, cafeteria, infirmary, 2 playing fields, 6 science labs, 3 computer labs, new gymnasium/ auditorium, 2 AV rooms, art room, resource rooms, ESL labs, language rooms, partial air conditioning.

*Once only fee   **Sri Lankan rupee

SUDAN

Region: Africa
Size: 966,757 square miles
Population: 27,220,000
Capital: Khartoum

Telephone code: no direct dial
Currency: dinar
Languages: Arabic, tribal
languages

KHARTOUM

KHARTOUM AMERICAN SCHOOL

Street address: Street 69 and Cemetery Road, Khartoum, Sudan
Phone: (no direct dial)222916/221386   **Telex:** 97022619 AMEMB SD
Mail: PO Box 699, Khartoum, Sudan
U.S. mail: c/o American Embassy Khartoum, Department of State, Washington, D.C. 20521-2200
Superintendent: Sally A. Hadden
Staff: full-time, 20
Nationalities of staff: U.S., 16; other, 4
Grade levels: preK – 10
Enrollment: preK, 15; K, 15; 1 – 6, 100; 7 – 10, 45; total, 175
Nationalities of student body: U.S., 30; U.K., 8; host, 30; other, 107
Teacher/student ratio: 1/9
Tuition (annual): preK, $3,200; K – 8, $6,700; 9 – 10, $8,100
Other fees: capital levy*, $1,500
School year: August to May

Year founded: 1956. **Type of school:** coed, day. **Governed by:** elected school board. **Accredited by:** Middle States.

Curriculum/physical plant
Type: U.S. **Languages taught:** French, Arabic. **Staff specialists:** ESL, resource. **Special programs:** ESL, resource. **Special curricular:** art, physical education, computer instruction, music. **Extracurricular:** drama, computers, yearbook, intramural sports. **Tests:** SSAT, SAT, Iowa. **Location:** in new section of city near airport. **Campus:** 7 acres. **Library:** 10,000 volumes. **Facilities:** 8 buildings, 17 classrooms, covered play area, playing field, science lab, computer lab, music room, air conditioning.

*Once only fee

KHARTOUM

Khartoum International High School
Address: PO Box 805, Khartoum, Sudan

SURINAME ─────────────────

Region: South America
Size: 63,037 square miles
Population: 402,000
Capital: Paramaribo

Telephone code: 597
Currency: guilder
Language: Dutch, Sranantonga,
 English

PARAMARIBO

AMERICAN COOPERATIVE SCHOOL

Street address: Lawtonlaan 20, Paramaribo, Suriname, S.A.
Phone: (597)499806/499461   **Facsimile:** (597)498853
U.S. mail: A.C.S.-Suriname, 8073 N.W. 67th Street, Miami, FL 33166, U.S.A.
Principal: Leo Limoges
Staff: full-time, 10; part-time, 6
Nationalities of staff: U.S., 15; host, 1
Grade levels: 1 – 12
Enrollment: 1 – 6, 50; 7 – 8, 16; 9 – 12, 16; total, 82
Nationalities of student body: U.S., 43; other, 39
Capacity: 1 – 6, 52; 7 – 8, 16; 9 – 12, 12; total, 80
Teacher/student ratio: 1/7
Tuition (annual): 1 – 12, $4,994
Other fees: registration*, 50**
School year: August to May

Year founded: 1966. **Type of school:** coed, day, Christian. **Governed by:** appointed cooperative mission board. **Sponsored by:** 5 mission groups.

Curriculum/physical plant

Type: U.S. **Special programs:** independent study, high school by correspondence. **Special curricular:** art, chorus, band, physical education. **Extracurricular:** choral music, instrumental music, field trips. **Sports:** basketball, soccer, softball, volleyball, ping-pong. **Tests:** SAT, CAT. **Graduates attending college:** 95%. **Location:** in city. **Campus:** 1 acre. **Library:** 6,000 volumes. **Facilities:** 8 classrooms, tennis/basketball court, AV equipment, air conditioning.

*Once only fee   **Suriname guilder

SWAZILAND

Region: Africa
Size: 6,704 square miles
Population: 859,000
Capital: Mbabane

Telephone code: 268
Currency: lilangeni
Languages: Swazi, English

MBABANE

SIFUNDZANI SCHOOL

Mail: Principal, Sifundzani School, PO Box A286, Swazi Plaza, Mbabane, Swaziland
Phone: (268)42465
Principal: Mary C. L. Fraser
Staff: full-time, 17; part-time, 4
Nationalities of staff: U.S., 3; U.K., 4; host, 4; other, 10
Grade levels: 1 – 7
Enrollment: total, 390
Capacity: 1 – 6, 360; 7, 60; total, 420
Teacher/student ratio: 1/21
Tuition (annual): 1 – 7: nationals, 840**; expatriates, 2,820
Other fees (annual): registration*, 10**; building fund, 180; government levy, 60
School year: January to December

Year founded: 1981. **Type of school:** coed, day. **Governed by:** Ministry of Education.

Curriculum/physical plant

Type: U.K. **Languages taught:** French, SiSwati. **Extracurricular:** drama, choral music, instrumental music, excursions/expeditions, sports. **Tests:** Swaziland Primary Certificate. **Location:** in hillside suburban setting, 10 minutes' drive from town center. **Campus:** 5 acres. **Library:** 5,500 volumes. **Facilities:** 6 buildings, 14 classrooms, auditorium, playing field, swimming pool.

*Once only fee   **Swazi emalangeni

WATERFORD KAMHLABA
UNITED WORLD COLLEGE OF SOUTHERN AFRICA

Street address: Waterford Park Estate, Mbabane, Swaziland
Phone: (268)42966 – 8   **Facsimile:** (268)46792
Mail: PO Box 52, Mbabane, Swaziland
Headmaster: Richard G. Eyeington
Deputy head: Felicity Townsend

Bursar: Michel Mathis
Staff: full-time, 32; part-time, 12
Nationalities of staff: U.S., 1; U.K., 20; host, 1; other, 22
Grade levels: 7 – 13
Enrollment: 7 – 9, 193; 10 – 12, 215; 13, 59; total, 467
Nationalities of student body: U.S., 25; U.K., 49; host, 99; other, 294
Capacity: total, 467
Teacher/student ratio: 1/12
Boarders: boys, 167; girls, 160   **Grades:** 7 – 13
    Program: planned 7-day
Tuition (annual): 7 – 11, 9,360**; 12 – 13, 12,240
Other fees (annual): registration*, 600**; boarding, 6,768; busing, 864; lunch, 648; O-level exam, approximately 550; IB exam, approximately 1,200; IB textbooks, approximately 1,200
School year: January to December

    Year founded: 1963. **Type of school:** coed, day, boarding, private nonprofit. **Governed by:** governing council. **Accredited by:** Swaziland Ministry of Education.

Curriculum

    Type: U.K., IB. **Languages taught:** English, French, Spanish, German, Portuguese, siSwati, Afrikaans. **Staff specialists:** math, computer, counselor, nurse. **Special curricular:** art, chorus, physical education, computer instruction, vocational. **Extracurricular:** drama, gymnastics, dance, choral music, instrumental music, computers, yearbook, newspaper, literary magazine, photography, excursions/expeditions, field trips. **Sports:** basketball, soccer, swimming, tennis, volleyball, squash, badminton, netball, athletics. **Clubs:** debating, chess, current Southern African affairs, Amnesty International, astronomy, drama. **Tests:** SAT, IB, GCSE. **Graduates attending college:** 90%. **Graduates have attended:** Harvard, Princeton, Drew, Pennsylvania, Maryland.

Physical plant

    Location: on hillside, 8 kilometers from Mbabane, at elevation of 4,000 feet. **Campus:** several hundred acres. **Library:** 20,000 volumes. **Facilities:** 20 buildings, 21 classrooms, auditorium, cafeteria, infirmary, 4 tennis courts/squash court, gymnasium, 3 playing fields, 7 science labs, computer center, swimming pool, music/languages wing, 4 residences with recreation rooms and TV.

*Once only fee   **Swazi emalangeni

SWEDEN

Region: Europe
Size: 173,731 square miles
Population: 8,564,000
Capital: Stockholm

Telephone code: 46
Currency: krona
Language: Swedish

GÖTEBORG

HVITFELDTSKA GYMNASIET

Street address: Rektorsgatan 2, S-411 33 Göteborg, Sweden
Phone: (46)(31)7786454/7786452   **Facsimile:** (46)(31)811797
Principal: Olof Johnard
Assistant principal: Carl-Eric Blomqvist
IB coordinator: Agneta Santesson
Staff: full-time, 6; part-time, 20
Nationalities of staff: U.S., 2; U.K., 2; other, 22
Grade levels: 9 – 12
Enrollment: total, 85
Capacity: total, 90
Teacher/student ratio: 1/5
Tuition (annual): 9 – 12, 13,600**
Other fees (annual): exam, 3,000**
School year: August to June

Year founded: 1647. **Type of school:** coed, day.

Curriculum/physical plant
Type: IB. **Languages taught:** English, French, Swedish, Portuguese.
Staff specialists: math, computer, counselor, nurse. **Special curricular:** art, chorus, physical education. **Tests:** IB. **Location:** in city. **Facilities:** 3 buildings, auditorium, cafeteria, gymnasium, science lab, computer lab, library.

**Swedish krona

SIGTUNA

SIGTUNASKOLAN HUMANISTISKA LAROVERKET

Street address: Manfred Bjorkquists Alle 6-8, S-193 28 Sigtuna, Sweden
Phone: (46)(8)59250135   **Facsimile:** (46)(8)59251525
Superintendent: Leif Berntsen
Headmaster: Folke Bergman
Director of studies: Ake Sorman
Business manager: Jan Peter Grundstrom

Staff: full-time, 42; part-time, 18
Nationalities of staff: U.S., 2; U.K., 5; host, 48; other, 5
Grade levels: 7 – 12
Enrollment: 7 – 9, 80; 10 – 12, 470; total, 550
Nationalities of student body: U.S., 15; U.K., 5; host, 485; other, 45
Capacity: total, 550
Teacher/student ratio: 1/11
Boarders: boys, 180; girls, 185   **Grades:** 7 – 12
     Program: planned 7-day
Tuition (annual): 7 – 12, 19,000**
Other fees (annual): registration*, 2,500**; boarding 69,000 – 93,000
School year: August to June

Year founded: 1924. **Type of school:** coed, day, boarding. **Governed by:** Foundation of Sigtuna School. **Accredited by:** Swedish Ministry of Education.

Curriculum/physical plant

Type: Swedish, IB. **Languages of instruction:** English, Swedish. **Languages taught:** English, French, Spanish, German, Latin, Swedish, Greek. **Staff specialists:** reading, computer, counselor, psychologist, nurse, doctor. **Special curricular:** art, chorus, computer instruction. **Extracurricular:** drama, gymnastics, dance, choral music, instrumental music, computers, yearbook, newspaper, photography, excursions/expeditions, field trips, sports. **Tests:** IB. **Location:** on the banks of Lake Malaren, 45 kilometers from Stockholm. **Facilities:** 25 buildings, 40 classrooms, auditorium, cafeteria, tennis court, gymnasium, science lab, computer lab, swimming pool, playing fields, 12 boarding houses.

*Once only fee   **Swedish krona

STOCKHOLM

THE INTERNATIONAL SCHOOL OF STOCKHOLM

Street address: Johannesgatan 18, 111 38 Stockholm, Sweden
Phone: (46)(8)249715   **Facsimile:** (46)(8)105289
Principal: Claes-Göran Widlund
Business manager: Christina McLaughlin
Staff: full-time, 22; part-time, 2
Nationalities of staff: U.S., 8; U.K., 7; host, 4; other, 5
Grade levels: K – 9
Enrollment: K, 27; 1 – 5, 112; 6 – 8, 98; 9, 39; total, 276
Nationalities of student body: U.S., 40; U.K., 14; host, 35; other, 187
Capacity: K, 30; 1 – 5, 125; 6 – 8, 120; 9 40; total, 315
Teacher/student ratio: 1/12
Tuition (annual): K, 34,500**; 1 – 5, 44,100; 6 – 8, 50,100; 9, 53,700
Other fees (annual): registration*, 6,000**; lunch, 5,100
School year: August to June

Year founded: 1951. **Type of school:** coed, day. **Governed by:** appointed and elected board of directors. **Accredited by:** School Board of Stockholm, Swedish Ministry of Education, ECIS, Middle States.

Curriculum/physical plant
Type: U.S., U.K. **Languages taught:** French. **Staff specialists:** nurse. **Special programs:** ESL. **Special curricular:** art, physical education, computer instruction. **Extracurricular:** drama, dance, photography, excursions/expeditions, field trips. **Sports:** basketball, volleyball. **Tests:** SSAT, Iowa. **Location:** in park, near downtown area. **Library:** 15,500 volumes. **Facilities:** 25 classrooms, auditorium, cafeteria, gymnasium, 2 science labs, computer lab, AV room.

*Once only fee   **Swedish krona

KUNGSHOLMEN'S GYMNASIUM – INTERNATIONAL SECTION†
Street address: Bergslagsvägen 80, S-161 54 Stockholm-Bromma, Sweden
Phone: (46)(8)870092   **Facsimile:** (46)(8)870016
Principal: Olov Eriksson
Head, International Section: Anthony Chamberlin
Staff: full-time, 15; part-time, 18
Nationalities of staff: U.S., 7; U.K., 4; host, 13; other, 9
Grade levels: 10 – 12
Enrollment: total, 270
Teacher/student ratio: 1/11
Tuition (annual): 35,000** (IB course only)
School year: August to June

Year founded: 1672. **Type of school:** coed, day, state.

Curriculum/physical plant
Type: IB, Swedish Social Sciences and Natural Sciences programs. **Languages taught:** French, Spanish, German, Swedish. **Staff specialists:** counselor, nurse, career adviser. **Special curricular:** physical education. **Tests:** SAT, IB. **Location:** temporarily in Bromma, a suburb west of Stockholm. **Facilities:** auditorium, cafeteria, gymnasium, science labs, computer labs.

**Swedish krona   †temporarily located in Bromma until facilities in Stockholm are rebuilt (1995 completion projected)

SWITZERLAND

Region: Europe
Size: 15,941 square miles
Population: 6,783,000
Capital: Bern

Telephone code: 41
Currency: franc
Languages: German, French,
Italian

BASEL

INTERNATIONAL SCHOOL OF BASEL

Street address: Schulstrasse 5, Bottmingen, Switzerland
Phone: (41)(61)4218483   **Facsimile:** (41)(61)4217635
Mail: PO Box 319, CH – 4103 Bottmingen, Switzerland
Headmaster: Geoffrey Tomlinson
Staff: full-time, 20; part-time, 10
Nationalities of staff: U.S., 7; U.K., 12; host, 3; other, 8
Grade levels: preK – 12
Enrollment: preK, 48; K, 34; 1 – 6, 135; 7 – 12, 63; total, 280
Nationalities of student body: U.S., 60; U.K., 65; host, 20; other, 135
Capacity: preK, 48; K, 36; 1 – 6, 135; 7 – 12, 108; total, 327
Teacher/student ratio: 1/11
Tuition (annual): preK, 5,250**; K, 9,600; 1 – 6, 10,400; 7 – 8, 12,550;
9 – 12, 14,850
Other fees: registration*, 500**; building fee*, 500
School year: September to June

Year founded: 1979. **Type of school:** coed, day, private nonprofit.
Governed by: elected school board. **Regional organizations:** ECIS.

Curriculum/physical plant

Type: U.S., U.K. **Languages taught:** French, German. **Staff specialists:**
reading, math, physical education, science, English, art. **Special programs:**
ESL. **Special curricular:** art, physical education, science. **Extracurricular:**
choral music, instrumental music, computers, yearbook, field trips. **Tests:**
ERB, IGCSE. **Location:** 5 mintues by car from center city. **Library:** 12,500
volumes. **Facilities:** 2 buildings, 14 classrooms, covered play area, 2 gymnasiums, playing field, science lab, swimming pool.

*Once only fee   **Swiss franc

BERNE

INTERNATIONAL SCHOOL OF BERNE

Street address: Mattenstrasse 3, 3073 Gümligen, Switzerland
Phone: (41)(31)9512358   **Facsimile:** (41)(31)9511710
Director: David Gatley

Assistant director: Anne Ponisch
High school coordinator: Rosemary McGuigan
Upper school coordinator: Chris Warren
Middle school coordinator: Roberta Siegfried
Lower school coordinator: Priscilla Schneider
Administrative assistants to the director: Rosmarie Buehler, Ellen Beaudry
Staff: full-time, 19; part-time, 16
Nationalities of staff: U.S., 10; U.K., 15; other, 10
Grade levels: K – 12
Enrollment: K, 12; 1 – 6, 87; 7 – 9, 50; 10 – 12, 33; total, 182
Nationalities of student body: U.S., 46; U.K., 18; other, 118
Capacity: K, 15; 1 – 6, 100; 7 – 9, 50; 10 – 12, 50; total, 215
Teacher/student ratio: 1/7
Tuition (annual): K, 5,400** (half day), 12,195 (full day); 1 – 2, 13,245; 3 – 5, 13,725; 6 – 8, 14,610; 9 – 12, 16,500
Other fees (annual): registration*, 700**; busing, 1,620 – 2,250; capital assessment*, 1,800; skiing, 350 – 420
School year: September to June

Year founded: 1960. **Type of school:** coed, day, private nonprofit. **Governed by:** parent-teacher association and elected board. **Accredited by:** New England, ECIS.

Curriculum/physical plant

Type: U.S., U.K. **Languages taught:** French, German, ESL. **Staff specialists:** computer, counselor, psychologist, disabilities. **Special programs:** ESL, advanced placement, independent study, correspondence, remedial, gifted. **Special curricular:** art, physical education, computer instruction. **Extracurricular:** drama, dance, instrumental music, computers, yearbook, newspaper, photography, excursions/expeditions, field trips, rock climbing. **Sports:** soccer, swimming, volleyball, track and field, orienteering, skiing, skating. **Tests:** PSAT, SAT, ACT, AP, IGCSE, ERB, ACH. **Graduates attending college:** 95%. **Graduates have attended:** Smith, Dartmouth, Tufts, Notre Dame, William and Mary. **Location:** in suburb, 5 miles from Bern. **Campus:** 4,800 square meters. **Library:** 8,000 volumes. **Facilities:** 3 buildings, 17 classrooms, gymnasium, playing field, 2 science labs, computer lab.

*Once only fee   **Swiss franc

CHESIÈRES

AIGLON COLLEGE

Phone: (41)(25)352721   **Facsimile:** (41)(25)352811
Telex: 845456211 ACOL CH
Mail: 1885 Chesières, Switzerland
Headmaster: Philip Parsons

Deputy headmaster: Neil McWilliam
Director of studies: Richard Lunn
Staff: full-time, 44; part-time, 13
Nationalities of staff: U.S., 2; U.K., 43; host, 1; other, 11
Grade levels: 6 – 13
Enrollment: 6 – 7, 45; 8 – 10, 125; 11 – 13, 110; total, 280
Nationalities of student body: U.S., 37; U.K., 53; host, 13; other, 177
Teacher/student ratio: 1/6
Boarders: boys, 150; girls, 130   **Grades:** 6 – 13
    Program: planned 7-day
Tuition and board (annual): 6 – 9, 40,900**; 10 – 13, 46,885
Other fees: registration*, 2,000**
School year: September to July

Year founded: 1949. **Type of school:** coed, boarding, private nonprofit.
Governed by: appointed board of governors. **Accredited by:** Swiss cantonal
authorities.

Curriculum

Type: U.K., IB (on limited basis). **Languages taught:** French, Spanish,
German, Italian. **Special programs:** ESL, advanced placement. **Special
curricular:** art, band, church, adventure training. **Extracurricular:** drama,
gymnastics, choral music, instrumental music, computers, yearbook, newspaper, literary magazine, photography, excursions/expeditions, field trips.
Sports: basketball, skiing, soccer, swimming, tennis, athletics, squash,
cross-country. **Clubs:** cooking, debating, yearbook, theater, choir, photography, band, astronomy, karate, crafts, science. **Tests:** SSAT, PSAT, SAT, ACT,
TOEFL, IB, AP, A-level GCE. **Graduates attending college:** 95%. **Graduates
have attended:** Harvard, Brown, Princeton, Cambridge, McGill.

Physical plant

Location: in rural area, 60 kilometers from Lausanne, 30 minutes from
Montreux, and 1.5 hours from Geneva. **Library:** 20,000 volumes. **Facilities:**
10 buildings, 29 classrooms, auditorium, 2 covered play areas, 5 tennis
courts, gymnasium, 2 playing fields, 4 science labs, computer lab, 2 swimming pools, 7 dining rooms, AV equipment, 8 boarding houses including 2 for
junior boys and girls.

*Once only fee   **Swiss franc

CRANS-SUR-SIERRE

INTERNATIONAL SCHOOL LE CHAPERON ROUGE

Phone: (41)(27)412500   **Facsimile:** (41)(27)412502
Mail: 3963 Crans-sur-Sierre, Switzerland
Directors: Mr. and Mrs. Prosper Bagnoud
Vice-director: Miss Gabrielle Bagnoud

Staff: full-time, 6; part-time, 2
Nationalities of staff: U.S., 2; other, 6
Grade levels: 1 – 10
Enrollment: total, 60
Teacher/student ratio: 1/9
Boarders: boys, 30; girls, 30   **Program:** planned 7-day
Tuition (annual): 21,600**
Other fees: registration, 500**; miscellaneous,
     approximately 1,600/term
School year: September through June

Year founded: 1955. **Type of school:** coed, day, boarding, private nonprofit.

Curriculum/physical plant
Type: U.S., U.K., Swiss, French, German, Italian. **Languages of instruction:** English, French, German, Italian (4 different sections). **Languages taught:** English, French, German, Italian. **Special programs:** ESL, remedial, full curriculum in four languages for children aged 5 to 16. **Special curricular:** physical education. **Extracurricular:** gymnastics, dance, instrumental music, excursions/expeditions, field trips, picnics. **Sports:** basketball, football, skiing, soccer, swimming, tennis, volleyball, ice-skating, golf, hiking, excursions, horseback-riding, minigolf, hockey. **Location:** in Crans-sur-Sierre, the sunniest resort in Switzerland.

**Swiss franc

GATTIKON

THE RIVERSIDE SCHOOL
Street address: Gattikonerstrasse 130, 8136 Gattikon/Thalwil,
     Switzerland
Phone: (41)(1)7208066   **Facsimile:** (41)(1)7209094
Director: August L. Zemo
Staff: full-time, 6; part-time, 4
Nationalities of staff: U.S., 4; U.K., 3; host, 3
Grade levels: 7 – 13 (nongraded system)
Enrollment: total, 52
Nationalities of student body: U.S., 12; U.K., 4; host, 10; other, 26
Capacity: total, 80
Teacher/student ratio: 1/7
Tuition (annual): 7 – 13, 20,000**
Other fees (annual): capital levy*, 1,000**; books, 600
School year: August to June

Year founded: 1990. **Type of school:** coed, private nonprofit.

Curriculum
Type: U.S. **Languages taught:** French, German. **Staff specialists:** reading, counselor, learning disabilities. **Special programs:** advanced placement, independent study. **Special curricular:** art, computer instruction. **Extracurricular:** drama, dance, yearbook, newspaper, excursions/expeditions. **Sports:** basketball, skiing, swimming, tennis, volleyball, track and field. **Tests:** PSAT, SAT, ACT, TOEFL, AP. **Graduates attending college:** 95%. **Graduates have attended:** U. of Durham (England), McGill, Cornell, Lehigh, Goucher.

Physical plant
Location: 1 1/2 floors of an office building overlooking a river, 10 kilometers from Zurich. **Library:** 3,000 volumes. **Facilities:** 7 classrooms, computer lab, music recording studio; other facilities rented from local community as needed.

*Once only fee   **Swiss franc

GENEVA

COLLÈGE DU LÉMAN INTERNATIONAL SCHOOL

Street address: 74, route de Sauverny, 1290 Versoix/Geneva, Switzerland
Phone: (41)(22)7552555   **Facsimile:** (41)(22)7551993
　　Telex: 845419211 CDL CH
Director general: Francis A. Clivaz
Director of studies: Cyril A. Boschert
Principal: Terence B. Gale
Doyen: Pierre-Marie Salamin
Staff: full-time, 88; part-time, 14
Nationalities of staff: U.S., 10; U.K., 27; host, 33; other, 32
Grade levels: K – 13
Enrollment: K, 90; 1 – 6, 324; 7 – 9, 214; 10 – 12, 278; 13, 9; total, 915
Nationalities of student body: U.S., 119; U.K., 66; host, 117; other, 613
Capacity: K, 85; 1 – 6, 355; 7 – 9, 220; 10 – 12, 300; 13, 10; total, 970
Teacher/student ratio: 1/10
Boarders: boys, 60; girls, 75   **Grades:** 3 – 13   **Program:** planned 7-day
Tuition (annual): K, 4,000 – 7,000**; 1 – 6, 10,300 – 11,100;
　　7 – 11, 12,600 – 13,700; 12 – 13, 14,700
Other fees (annual): registration*, 200**; boarding, 19,300 – 21,700;
　　busing, 2,150 – 2,600; lunch, 2,200; books, 1,100;
　　insurance, 120 – 150; lab, 300; computer, 300; refundable deposit*:
　　400 (day), 5,000 (boarding)
School year: September to June

Year founded: 1960. **Type of school:** coed, day, boarding, proprietary.
Accredited by: Middle States, ECIS.

Curriculum

Type: U.S., U.K., Swiss Maturité, French Baccalaureate. **Languages of instruction:** English, French. **Languages taught:** English, Spanish, German, Italian, Latin, Arabic. **Staff specialists:** reading, counselor, psychologist, nurse. **Special programs:** ESL, advanced placement, GCE A-level. **Special curricular:** computer instruction. **Extracurricular:** drama, gymnastics, dance, instrumental music, computers, yearbook, newspaper, literary magazine, photography, excursions/expeditions, field trips. **Sports:** basketball, bowling, rugby, skiing, soccer, softball, tennis, volleyball, track and field, weight-training, judo, cross-country, horseback riding, karate. **Clubs:** chess, debate, math, alpine, art, aerobics, student council, Student UN, Model UN, National Honor Society, SIMEX simulated political games. **Tests:** PSAT, SAT, TOEFL, AP, A-level GCE, IGCSE. **Graduates attending college:** 90%. **Graduates have attended:** Harvard, MIT, U. of Geneva, Wellesley, Smith.

Physical plant

Location: in suburban area about 5 miles from Geneva. **Campus:** 19 acres. **Library:** 19,000 volumes. **Facilities:** 17 buildings, 65 classrooms, auditorium, 2 cafeterias, 2 infirmaries, 2 covered play areas, 3 tennis courts, gymnasium, 2 playing fields, 4 science labs, 2 computer labs, swimming pool, language labs, AV room, 2 music rooms, 7 residences with snack bar/lounge, dining room and 3 TV rooms.

*Once only fee   **Swiss franc

THE INTERNATIONAL SCHOOL OF GENEVA

Street address: 62, route de Chêne, 1208 Geneva, Switzerland
Phone: (41)(22)7367130   **Facsimile:** (41)(22)7367702
Director general: George Walker
Financial manager: Charles Grimardias
Assistant to director general: Graziella Rossoni
Staff: full-time, 179; part-time, 67
Nationalities of staff: U.S., 22; U.K., 102; host, 50; other, 72
Grade levels: early childhood – 13
Enrollment: early childhood, 27; K, 191; 1 – 6, 1,030; 7 – 9, 674; 10 – 12, 668; 13, 178; total, 2,768
Nationalities of student body: U.S., 396; U.K., 509; host, 405; other, 1,458
Capacity: early childhood, 30; K, 90; 1 – 6, 1,040; 7 – 9, 650; 10 – 12, 850; 13, 150; total, 2,810
Teacher/student ratio: 1/13
Boarders: boys, 25; girls, 28   **Program:** planned 5- and 7-day
Tuition (annual): early childhood, 3,410 – 5,000**; pre-reception, 9,810; reception, 11,920; 1 – 4, 12,890; 5 – 6, 13,500; 7 – 9, 15,920; 10 – 11, 16,780; 12 – 13, 17,260
Other fees (annual): registration*, 400**; boarding, 21,190 – 23,215; insurance, 110; capital development*, 700; boarding deposit*, 8,000 (refundable); busing, lunch, books (classes 7 – 13), external exams, field trips

School year: September through June

Year founded: 1924. **Type of school:** coed, day, boarding, private nonprofit. **Governed by:** elected board. **Accredited by:** Middle States.

Curriculum
Type: U.S., U.K., Swiss, IB. **Languages of instruction:** English, French. **Languages taught:** Spanish, German, Italian, Latin. **Staff specialists:** reading, math, counselor, psychologist, learning disabilities, nurse. **Special programs:** ESL, advanced placement, remedial. **Special curricular:** computer instruction. **Extracurricular:** drama, gymnastics, dance, choral music, instrumental music, computers, yearbook, newspaper, literary magazine, photography, excursions/expeditions, field trips. **Sports:** basketball, rugby, skiing, soccer, volleyball, athletics, badminton, canoeing, hockey, table tennis, trampoline. **Organizations:** alpine, chess, student councils, Student Day Fair, Simex (political simulation exercises), ECIS, math competition, student UN. **Tests:** PSAT, SAT, TOEFL, IB, AP, A-level GCE, GCSE, Stanford, Iowa, SRA, GAP, Gapadol, Otis-Lennon, Raven, Salford sentence, Schonell reading and spelling. **Graduates attending college:** 90%. **Graduates have attended:** Major U.S., U.K., and world universities.

Physical plant
Campuses (3): 2 suburban, 1 in rural area. **Libraries:** approximately 100,000 volumes. **Facilities:** 160 classrooms, 2 cafeterias, infirmary, 2 tennis courts, 3 gymnasiums, 3 playing fields, 18 science labs, 6 computer labs, swimming pool, AV department, 3 boarding villas. Extensive new buildings on rural campus (1992 – 94).

*Once only fee   **Swiss franc

GSTAAD

GSTAAD INTERNATIONAL SCHOOL
Phone: (41)(30)42373   **Facsimile:** (41)(30)43578
Mail: 3780 Gstaad, Switzerland
Director: Alain Souperbiet
Staff: full-time, 4; part-time, 1
Nationalities of staff: U.S., 2; U.K., 2; host, 1
Grade levels: 8 – 12
Enrollment: 8 – 9, 6; 10 – 12, 8; total, 14
Nationalities of student body: U.S., 3; U.K., 2; host, 9
Capacity: total, 15
Teacher/student ratio: 1/3
Boarders: boys and girls, 15   **Grades:** 8 – 12   **Program:** planned 7-day
Tuition and board (annual): 8 – 12, 53,400**
School year: September through June†

Year founded: 1962. **Type of school:** coed, boarding. **Accredited by:** Swiss Board of Education, ECIS.

Curriculum/physical plant

Type: U.S., U.K. **Languages taught:** French, German. **Staff specialists:** reading, math, counselor, learning disabilities. **Special curricular:** physical education. **Extracurricular:** computers, excursions/expeditions. **Sports:** basketball, skiing, swimming, tennis, squash, golf, hiking, rock climbing, ice skating. **Tests:** PSAT, SAT, ACT, TOEFL, AP, ACH, IGCSE, First Certificate in English (Cambridge). **Graduates have attended:** Sarah Lawrence, Colorado State U., Webster Geneva, Pepperdine U., Clark. **Location:** in Gstaad in the Swiss Alps. **Facilities:** 1 building, 4 classrooms, library, off-campus gymnasium, Olympic swimming pool, tennis courts, squash courts.

**Swiss franc   †summer camps in July and August

HASLIBERG/GOLDERN

ECOLE D'HUMANITÉ

Phone: (41)(36)711515
Mail: 6085 Hasliberg/Goldern, Switzerland
Directors: A. and N. Luethi-Peterson
Business manager: Hans Willi
Staff: full-time, 33; part-time, 2
Nationalities of staff: U.S., 5; U.K., 2; host, 20; other, 8
Grade levels: 1 – 13
Enrollment: 1 – 6, 16; 7 – 9, 59; 10 – 12, 73; 13, 2; total, 150
Nationalities of student body: U.S., 11; U.K., 1; host, 75; other, 63
Capacity: total, 150
Teacher/student ratio: 1/4
Boarders: boys, 70; girls, 70   **Grades:** 1 – 13   **Program:** planned 7-day
Tuition and board (annual): 1 – 13, 24,600**
Other fees (annual): registration*, 80**; insurance, 1,620; incidentals, 1,000
School year: September to July

Year founded: 1934. **Type of school:** coed, day, boarding, private nonprofit. **Governed by:** Genossenschaft der Ecole d'Humanité. **Accredited by:** Departments of Youth and Education of the Canton of Bern.

Curriculum

Type: U.S., Swiss. **Languages of instruction:** English, German. **Languages taught:** English, French, German, Italian, Latin, Greek. **Staff specialists:** counselor, psychologist, nurse, art, music, drama coaches. **Special programs:** ESL, independent study, remedial. **Special curricular:** art, chorus, band, physical education, computer instruction. **Extracurricular:** drama, gymnastics, dance, choral music, instrumental music, computers, newspaper, photography, excursions/expeditions, field trips. **Sports:** basketball, skiing, soccer, swimming, volleyball, hiking, kayaking, judo, folk dancing, jazz dance, badminton, ping-pong. **Clubs:** sports, student council, library, social action, current events, entertainment, drama, maintenance, gardening, film, music, student committee on discipline, etc. **Tests:** SAT, ACT, TOEFL. **Graduates attending college:** 100%. **Graduates have attended:** Brown, American U., Wellesley, George Washington U., Middlebury.

Physical plant

Location: small alpine farming village in skiing area, an hour's drive from Lucerne and Interlaken. **Campus:** 3 acres. **Library:** 20,000 volumes. **Facilities:** 20 buildings, 32 classrooms, auditorium, cafeteria, gymnasium, 3 playing fields, 2 science labs, swimming pool in Meiringen, 16 "family groups" in 12 buildings.

*Once only fee   **Swiss franc

LAUSANNE

COMMONWEALTH–AMERICAN SCHOOL

Street address: 73 Avenue C.F. Ramuz, 1009 Pully/Lausane, Switzerland
Phone: (41)(21)7281733   **Facsimile:** (41)(21)7287868
Headmaster: Robert Landau
Staff: full-time, 17; part-time, 8
Nationalities of staff: U.S., 4; U.K., 10; host, 7; other, 4
Grade levels: preK – 8
Enrollment: preK, 12; K, 16; 1 – 6, 115; 7 – 8, 29; total, 172
Nationalities of student body: U.S., 38; U.K., 36; host, 25; other, 73
Capacity: preK, 12; K, 16; 1 – 6, 115; 7 – 8, 29; total, 172
Teacher/student ratio: 1/9
Tuition (annual): preK, 6,750**; K, 10,700; 1 – 4, 12,560; 5 – 8, 14,930
Other fees: registration*, 600**
School year: September to June

Year founded: 1962. **Type of school:** coed, day, private nonprofit. **Governed by:** appointed school council. **Accredited by:** New England, ECIS.

Curriculum/physical plant

Type: U.S., U.K. **Language taught:** French. **Special programs:** ESL, remedial, special needs. **Special curricular:** art, chorus, physical education, computer instruction. **Extracurricular:** computers, yearbook, newspaper, excursions/expeditions, field trips, French club, Cub Scouts. **Sports:** skiing, soccer, swimming, athletics, skating. **Tests:** ERB, Slingerland. **Location:** in suburb adjoining Lausanne. **Campus:** 1 acre. **Library:** 6,500 volumes. **Facilities:** 3 buildings, 17 classrooms, science room, computer room.

*Once only fee   **Swiss franc

INSTITUTION CHÂTEAU MONT-CHOISI

Street address: Bd. de la Forêt/Ch. des Ramiers 16, 1009 Pully/
Lausanne, Switzerland
Phone: (41)(21)7288777   **Facsimile:** (41)(21)7288864
General director: Jeno Pusztaszeri
Academic director: Dr. B. Hourcade
Director of American program: Mr. B. Glick
Staff: full-time, 20; part-time, 10
Nationalities of staff: U.S., 4; U.K., 5; host, 13; other, 8
Grade levels: 9 – 12, postgraduate
Enrollment (American section): 9, 6; 10 – 12, 27; 13, 8; total, 41
Nationalities of student body: U.S., 10; U.K., 5; host, 5; other, 21
Boarders: girls, 120 (American section and other divisions)
    Program: planned 7-day
Tuition and board (annual): 42,500**
Other fees: registration, 5,000** (refundable)
School year: September to June

   Year founded: 1885. **Type of school:** coed, day, girls' boarding, proprietary. **Accredited by:** New England, ECIS.

Curriculum

   Type: U.S., intensive language and secretarial courses. **Languages of
instruction:** English, French. **Languages taught:** English, French, Spanish,
German, Italian. **Staff specialists:** reading, math, computer, counselor,
psychologist, nurse, resource. **Special programs:** ESL, advanced placement,
independent study, tutoring. **Special curricular:** art, physical education,
computer instruction, commercial courses. **Extracurricular:** computers,
yearbook, photography, excursions/expeditions, design, music. **Sports:**
aerobics, basketball, skiing, swimming, tennis, volleyball, jazz, riding, squash.
Clubs: drama, photography. **Tests:** PSAT, SAT, TOEFL, AP, ACH, First
Certificate in English, Certificate of Proficiency in English, Certificate of the
London Pitman Institute, Diplomas of Alliance Francaise, Diploma in Commerce. **Graduates attending college:** 90%. **Graduates have attended:**
Georgetown, Boston U., Wheaton College, Miami U., Pepperdine.

Physical plant

   Location: in suburban area, 3 kilometers from center of Lausanne.
Library: 3,000 volumes. **Facilities:** 6 buildings, 16 classrooms, auditorium,
cafeteria, infirmary, tennis court, gymnasium, playing field, science lab,
computer lab, swimming pool, photography lab, AV equipment.

**Swiss franc

LENK

THE WINTER TERM

>**Street address:** Chalet Hohliebi, 3775 Lenk, Switzerland
>**Phone:** (41)(30)31403/31223   **Facsimile:** (41)(30)31426
>**Director:** John N. Curtis, Jr.
>**Staff:** full-time, 5
>**Nationalities of staff:** U.S., 5
>**Grade levels:** 7 – 8
>**Enrollment:** total, 28
>**Teacher/student ratio:** 1/6
>**Boarders:** boys, 15; girls, 13   **Grades:** 7 – 8   **Program:** planned 7-day
>**Tuition (annual):** 11,800**
>**Other fees:** registration, 500**
>**School year:** January to April

>**Year founded:** 1988. **Type of school:** coed, boarding, proprietary.

Curriculum/physical plant

>**Type:** U.S. **Special curricular:** physical education, computer instruction. **Extracurricular:** drama, newspaper, excursions/expeditions. **Sports:** skiing, swimming. **Location:** chalet on ski slope in Swiss Alps, overlooking village of Lenk. **Campus:** 1 acre. **Library:** 600 volumes. **Facilities:** 2 buildings, 3 classrooms.

**Swiss franc

LEYSIN

KUMON LEYSIN ACADEMY OF SWITZERLAND†

>**Street address:** Case Postale 108, 1854 Leysin, Switzerland
>**Phone:** (41)(25)342021   **Facsimile:** (41)(25)342580
>   **Telex:** 845456312 LASCH
>**U.S. mail:** PO Box 4016, Portsmouth, NH 03802-4016, U.S.A.
>**U.S. phone:** (1)(603)4317654   **U.S. facsimile:** (1)(603)4311280
>   **U.S. telex:** 953133 LASUS
>**Headmaster:** K. Steven Ott, Ph.D.
>**Academic dean:** Alan Locke, Ph.D.
>**Staff:** full-time, 15; part-time, 5
>**Nationalities of staff:** U.S., 6; U.K., 2; Japan, 7; other, 5
>**Grade levels:** 10 – 12
>**Enrollment:** total, 112
>**Nationalities of student body:** Japan, 112
>**Teacher/student ratio:** 1/6
>**Boarders:** boys, 38; girls, 72   **Grades:** 10 – 12

Tuition and board (annual): 33,000**
Other fees (annual): registration, $500
School year: year-round

Year founded: 1990. **Type of school:** coed, boarding, bilingual. **Accredited by:** Department of Education, Canton of Vaud.

Curriculum
Type: U.S., IB, Japanese. **Languages of instruction:** English, Japanese. **Programs:** ESL; 3-year course requirements for U.S. diploma, including Advanced Placement and college preparatory courses; complete curriculum requirements for Japanese university admission. **Special curricular:** band, physical education, drama, studio and performing arts, computer sciences. **Extracurricular:** gymnastics, choral music, instrumental music, yearbook, photography, field trips, band, excursions in European and Eastern Bloc countries, Alpine activities. **Sports:** basketball, rugby, soccer, tennis, volleyball, Alpine and Nordic skiing, parachute gliding, ice skating, horseback riding, fitness, weight-lifting. **Organizations**: National Honor Society, Model UN, faculty family, photo and video club, chess club. **Test:** IB.

Physical plant
Location: in sunny, southern Swiss Alps above Lake Geneva. **Campuses (2):** 6 and 10 acres. **Library:** 20,000 volumes. **Facilities:** 3 buildings, 10 classrooms, cafeteria, computer lab, music practice rooms, AV equipment, theater stages, 2 dormitories. Joint facilities with Leysin American School: gymnasium, playing field, infirmary, auditorium, science labs, library.

**Swiss franc   †sister school to the Leysin American School in Switzerland

LEYSIN AMERICAN SCHOOL IN SWITZERLAND
Street address: The Savoy, 1854 Leysin, Switzerland
Phone: (41)(25)341361   **Facsimile:** (41)(25)341585
    Telex: 845456312 LAS CH   **Cable:** LASSA
U.S. mail: PO Box 4016, Portsmouth, NH 03802-4016, U.S.A.
U.S. phone: (1)(603)4317654   **U.S. facsimile:** (1)(603)4311280
Executive director: K. Steven Ott, Ph.D.
Headmaster: Grant Fiedler
Staff: full-time, 36; part-time, 9
Nationalities of staff: U.S., 32; U.K., 4; host, 3; other, 6
Grade levels: 9 – 13
Enrollment: 9 – 12, 220; 13, 20; total, 240
Capacity: 250
Teacher/student ratio: 1/6
Boarders: boys, 113; girls, 127   **Grades:** 9 – 13
    Program: planned 7-day
Tuition and board (annual): 9 – 13, $18,500; corporate plan, $15,400
Other fees (annual): registration, $1,100
School year: September to June

Year founded: 1961. **Type of school:** coed, boarding. **Accredited by:** Middle States, ECIS.

Curriculum

Type: U.S., AP, IB. **Languages taught:** French, German. **Staff specialists:** counselor, nurse, resource. **Special programs:** ESL, advanced placement, honors sections, independent study. **Special curricular:** chorus, band, physical education, computer instruction, drama, yearbook, studio and performing arts. **Extracurricular:** choral music, instrumental music, literary magazine, photography, excursions/expeditions, field trips, ice skating, parachute gliding, horseback riding, weight lifting, aerobics. **Sports:** basketball, rugby, skiing, soccer, tennis, volleyball. **Organizations:** National Honor Society, Model UN, student council, Quill and Scroll, faculty families, Amnesty International, OXFAM. **Tests:** PSAT, SAT, ACT, TOEFL, IB, AP. **Graduates attending college:** 99%. **Graduates have attended:** Cornell, Duke, Princeton, Baylor, Brown.

Physical plant

Location: in the sunny, southern Swiss Alps above Lake Geneva. **Campus:** 10 acres. **Library:** 11,000 volumes and SIRS. **Facilities:** 6 buildings, 20 classrooms, auditorium, cafeteria, gymnasium, playing field, 3 science labs, computer lab, theatrical stage, AV equipment, 3 girls' residences, 2 boys' residences, health center.

MONTAGNOLA/LUGANO

THE AMERICAN SCHOOL IN SWITZERLAND (TASIS)

Phone: (41)(91)546471   **Facsimile:** (41)(91)542364
Mail: CH-6926 Montagnola/Lugano, Switzerland
U.S. mail: 326 East 69th Street, New York, NY 10021, U.S.A.
Headmaster: John Engstrom, Ed.D.
Staff: full-time, 35; part-time, 5
Nationalities of staff: U.S., 28; U.K., 6; host, 4; other, 2
Grade levels: 7 – 12, postgraduate
Enrollment: 7 – 8, 17; 9 – 12, 211; PG, 17; total, 245
Nationalities of student body: U.S., 110; U.K., 3; host, 3; other, 129
Capacity: total, 250
Teacher/student ratio: 1/6
Boarders: boys, 110; girls, 135   **Grades:** 7 – PG
    Program: planned 7-day
Tuition (annual): 7 – PG, $18,500
Other fees (annual): boarding, $16,750; travel and activities, $1,100; books, laundry, lab, insurance, $650
School year: September to June

Type of school: coed, day, boarding, proprietary. **Accredited by:** New England, ECIS.

Curriculum

Type: U.S. **Languages taught:** French, Spanish, German, Italian. **Staff specialists:** counselor, nurse, resource. **Special programs:** ESL, advanced placement, honors sections, postgraduate year. **Special curricular:** art, chorus, physical education, computer instruction. **Extracurricular:** drama, dance, choral music, instrumental music, computers, yearbook, newspaper, photography, excursions/expeditions, field trips, 2-week mini-term in St. Moritz. **Sports:** aerobics, basketball, rugby, skiing, soccer, swimming, tennis, volleyball, track, cross-country, hiking, bicycling, water polo. **Tests:** PSAT, SAT, ACT, TOEFL, AP. **Graduates attending college:** 99%. **Graduates have attended:** Yale, Dartmouth, MIT, Stanford, Wellesley.

Physical plant

Location: south of the Alps, on hillside overlooking beautiful Lake Lugano, 5 kilometers from town center. **Campus:** 6 acres. **Library:** 13,000 volumes. **Facilities:** 12 buildings, 22 classrooms, infirmary, tennis court, gymnasium, 3 science labs, computer lab, swimming pool, dining room, AV equipment.

MONTREUX

INSTITUT CHÂTEAU BEAU-CÈDRE

Street address: Rue du lac 59, 1815 Clarens/Montreux,
    Vaud, Switzerland
Phone: (41)(21)9643831   **Facsimile:** (41)(21)9643834
Mail: CH-1815 Clarens, Switzerland
Principal: Pierre Gay
Staff: full-time, 9; part-time, 10
Nationalities of staff: U.S., 1; U.K., 3; other, 15
Grade levels: 9 – 12
Enrollment (American section): 9, 4; 10 – 12, 5; total, 9
Capacity: 9, 8; 10 – 12, 8; total, 16
Teacher/student ratio: 1/4
Boarders: girls, 40 (American and General Culture sections)
    Program: planned 5-day
Tuition and board (annual): 9 – 12, 43,000**
Other fees (annual): inscription and guarantee deposit, 3,000**
School year: September to June

Year founded: 1955. **Type of school:** girls, day, boarding, proprietary. **Governed by:** Pierre Gay, proprietor.

Curriculum/physical plant

Type: U.S., languages and finishing course. **Languages of instruction:** English, French. **Languages taught:** English, French, Spanish, German, Italian. **Staff specialists:** reading, math, computer, speech/hearing. **Special**

curricular: physical education, computer instruction. **Extracurricular:** gymnastics, computers, yearbook. **Sports:** aerobics, skiing, tennis, riding. **Tests:** SAT, TOEFL, London University levels 1 – 6, Alliance Française. **Graduates attending college:** 80%. **Location:** little castle on banks of lake of Geneva, 2 miles from Montreux. **Facilities:** 2 buildings, cafeteria, computer lab, full board and lodging for a limited number of girls, aged 14 to 22.

**Swiss franc

St. George's School in Switzerland

Phone: (41)(21)9643411   **Facsimile:** (41)(21)9644932
Telex: 845453131 GEOR CH
Mail: 1815 Clarens/Montreux, Switzerland
Principal: Mrs. L. G. Zund
Staff: full-time, 19; part-time, 11
Nationalities of staff: U.K., 23; host, 4; other, 3
Grade levels: 7 – 13
Enrollment: 7 – 9, 36; 10 – 12, 63; 13, 15; total, 114
Nationalities of student body: U.S., 6; U.K., 17; host, 10; other, 81
Capacity: 7 – 9, 45; 10 – 12, 75; 13, 20; total, 140
Teacher/student ratio: 1/5
Boarders: girls, 82   **Grades:** 7 – 13   **Program:** planned 7-day
Tuition and boarding (annual): 7 – 8, 39,710**; 9 – 13, 41,270
Other fees (annual): registration, 850**
School year: September to July†

Year founded: 1927. **Type of school:** girls, day, boarding, proprietary, nondenominational. **Governed by:** board of Swiss and British governors. **Accredited by:** Educational Department of the Canton of Vaud. **Regional organization:** ECIS.

Curriculum

Type: U.S., U.K. **Languages taught:** French, Spanish, German, Italian, Latin, Arabic. **Staff specialists:** reading, math, computer, speech/hearing, counselor, music, sciences, drama. **Special programs:** ESL. **Special curricular:** art, chorus, physical education, computer instruction. **Extracurricular:** drama, gymnastics, dance, choral music, instrumental music, computers, yearbook, photography, excursions/expeditions, field trips. **Sports:** basketball, skiing, swimming, tennis, volleyball, ice skating, squash, rounders, windsurfing, horseback-riding, judo, etc. **Clubs:** chess, bridge, play reading, cooking, computers, photography, soft toys. **Tests:** PSAT, SAT, TOEFL, AP, A-level GCE, IGCSE, ICE (International Certificate of Education–Cambridge University Board). **Graduates attending college:** 95%. **Graduates have attended:** universities worldwide.

Physical plant

Location: on edge of Lake Geneva, outside the town of Montreux. **Campus:** 160,000 square meters. **Library:** 15,000 volumes. **Facilities:** 2

buildings, 18 classrooms, auditorium, infirmary, 5 tennis courts, gymnasium, playing field, 2 science labs, computer lab, swimming pool, basketball court, indoor sports hall, dormitories, lounges, TV rooms, chalet for grades 12 and 13.

**Swiss franc   †coed summer camp in July and August, ages 10 – 16

ROLLE

Institut Le Rosey

Phone: (41)(21)8254721   **Facsimile:** (41)(21)8252056
Cable: ROSEY ROLLE
Mail: 1180 Rolle, Switzerland/(January – March) 3780 Gstaad, Switzerland
Director: Philippe Gudin
Staff: total, 60
Grade levels: 3 – 12
Enrollment: total, 300
Capacity: total, 300
Teacher/student ratio: 1/5
Boarders: boys, 180; girls, 120   **Grades:** 3 – 12   **Program:** planned 7-day
Tuition (annual): 3 – 12, 45,600**
Other fees: 2,500** per term
School year: September through June

Year founded: 1880. **Type of school:** coed, boarding, proprietary. **Accredited by:** New England.

Curriculum
Type: U.S., U.K., Swiss, French. **Languages of instruction:** English, French. **Languages taught:** French, Spanish, German, Dutch, Italian, Arabic, Swedish, Portuguese, Persian, Greek, Turkish, others on demand. **Staff specialists:** psychologist, music. **Special programs:** ESL, intensive English and French. **Special curricular:** art, computer instruction, choral, instrumental music, field trips. **Extracurricular:** yearbook, school music group, drama (English and French), excursions. **Sports:** basketball, football, rugby, swimming, tennis, volleyball, gymnastics, squash, rowing, horseback riding, wind-surfing, sailing, bicycling, table-tennis, skiing, judo, pistol-shooting. **Clubs:** debating, English, French Academy, photography, gun, squash, charity committee. **Tests:** SSAT, PSAT, SAT, TOEFL, AP, GCSE, ACH, IGCSE, French Baccalaureat, Swiss Maturité, GCE A- and O-levels. **Graduates attending college:** 100%. **Graduates have attended:** Harvard, Brown, Princeton, Oxbridge, London.

Physical plant

Location: winter campus in Gstaad (Bernese Oberland); spring/fall campus in the village of Rolle (Lake of Geneva). **Library:** 16,000 volumes. **Facilities:** 10 tennis courts, science lab, computer lab, swimming pool, science and computer labs, basketball, rugby, and soccer fields, sailing marina, art and drama.

**Swiss franc

SAANEN

JOHN F. KENNEDY INTERNATIONAL SCHOOL

Phone: (41)(30)41372   **Facsimile:** (41)(30)48982
Mail: 3792 Saanen, Switzerland
Director: William M. Lovell
Staff: full-time, 15; part-time, 3
Nationalities of staff: U.S., 3; host, 1; other, 14
Grade levels: K – 8
Enrollment: K – 6, 40; 7 – 8, 10; total, 50
Capacity: K – 6, 40; 7 – 8, 10; total, 50
Teacher/student ratio: 1/3
Boarders: boys, 13; girls, 12   **Grades:** K – 8   **Program:** planned 7-day
Tuition (annual): day student, 17,400**; boarder, 30,000
Other fees (annual): ski school, 1,300**; excursions, 1,000
School year: September to June

Year founded: 1949. **Type of school:** coed, day, boarding, proprietary. **Accredited by:** Canton of Bern Department of Education.

Curriculum

Type: U.S., Canadian. **Languages taught:** French. **Staff specialists:** reading, psychologist. **Special programs:** ESL. **Special curricular:** art, physical education, computer instruction, drama, skiing in winter. **Extracurricular:** drama, dance, computers, yearbook, excursions/expeditions, field trips. **Sports:** skiing, swimming, tennis, track and field, hiking, ice-skating, ball sports, horseback riding. **Tests:** ERB. **Graduates have attended:** Le Rosey, Aiglon College, St. George's School (Switzerland), Deerfield Academy, Choate.

Physical plant

Location: at mountain skiing resort, 2 miles from Gstaad, 2 hours from Geneva, 2.5 hours from Zurich. **Library:** 6,500 volumes. **Facilities:** 3 buildings, 5 classrooms, cafeteria, playing field, tennis courts, ski lifts; easy access to gymnasium, swimming pool, auditorium; large boarding chalet with bedrooms, classrooms, library, video room, computer room, staff accommodations.

**Swiss franc

ZUG

INSTITUT MONTANA, AMERICAN SCHOOL

Street address: 6316 Zugerberg, 6300 Zug, Switzerland
Phone: (41)(42)211722 **Facsimile:** (41)(42)215465
Director: Karl Storchenegger, Ph.D.
Headmaster, American School: John C. L. M. Mather
Academic dean: V. Kevin O'Brien
Staff: full-time, 12; part-time, 5
Nationalities of staff: U.S., 9; U.K., 1; host, 2; other, 5
Grade levels: 5 – 13
Enrollment: total, 55
Nationalities of student body: U.S., 8; other, 46
Capacity: 5 – 6, 8; 7 – 9, 24; 10 – 12, 32; 13, 5; total, 69
Teacher/student ratio: 1/4
Boarders: boys, 27; girls, 10 **Grades:** 5 – 13 **Program:** planned 7-day
Tuition (annual): 5 – 13, 20,100**
Other fees (annual): boarding, 33,600 – 43,800**
School year: September to June

Year founded: 1926. **Type of school:** coed, day, boarding, private nonprofit. **Governed by:** appointed board of trustees. **Accredited by:** Swiss Federation of Private Schools. **Regional organizations:** NAIS, ECIS

Curriculum

Type: U.S., IB. **Languages taught:** French, German, Dutch. **Special programs:** ESL, advanced placement. **Special curricular:** physical education, computer instruction, drawing, calligraphy. **Extracurricular:** drama, gymnastics, choral music, computers, yearbook, literary magazine, excursions/expeditions, field trips. **Sports:** basketball, skiing, soccer, tennis, volleyball. **Clubs:** stamp, video, chess, outings. **Tests:** SSAT, PSAT, SAT, ACT, TOEFL, IB, AP. **Graduates attending college:** 100%. **Graduates have attended:** Carnegie-Mellon U., Cornell, New York U., Rhode Island School of Design, U. of Pennsylvania.

Physical plant

Location: in foothills of Alps, 15 minutes from Zug by public transportation. **Campus:** 65 acres. **Library:** 8,000 volumes. **Facilities:** 12 buildings, 9 classrooms, auditorium, infirmary, 4 tennis courts, gymnasium, 3 playing fields, 3 science labs, computer lab, dining room, 3 dormitories.

**Swiss franc

International School of Zug

Street address: Altesteinhauserstrasse 15, 6330 Cham, Switzerland
Phone: (41)(42)417874   **Facsimile:** (41)(42)420209
Headmaster: Martin Latter
Staff: full-time, 13; part-time, 9
Nationalities of staff: U.S., 4; U.K., 10; host, 3; other, 5
Grade levels: preK – 8
Enrollment: preK, 15; K, 16; 1 – 6, 111; 7 – 8, 12; total, 154
Nationalities of student body: U.S., 11; U.K., 40; host, 15; other, 88
Teacher/student ratio: 1/9
Tuition (annual): preK, 10,750**; K – 5, 11,750; 6 – 8, 13,000
Other fees: registration*, 300**; extra English, 1,000
School year: September to June

Year founded: 1961. **Type of school:** coed, day, proprietary.

Curriculum/physical plant

Type: U.S., U.K. **Languages taught:** French, German. **Special programs:** ESL, remedial. **Special curricular:** art, physical education, computer instruction. **Extracurricular:** drama, yearbook, excursions/expeditions, field trips. **Clubs:** arts and crafts, cooking, drama, football, basketball, volleyball, science, chess. **Tests:** Iowa. **Location:** in rural area, 5 kilometers from town of Zug. **Library:** 8,000 volumes. **Facilities:** 1 building, 12 classrooms, gymnasium, playing field, swimming pool, skating rink.

*Once only fee   **Swiss franc

ZURICH

The American International School

of Zurich

Street address: Nidelbadstrasse 49, 8802 Kilchberg, Switzerland
Phone: (41)(1)7152795   **Facsimile:** (41)(1)7152694
Headmaster: Peter C. Mott
Staff: full-time, 26; part-time, 9
Nationalities of staff: U.S., 16; U.K., 7; host, 7; other, 5
Grade levels: 7 – 13
Enrollment: 7 – 9, 103; 10 – 12, 127; total, 230
Nationalities of student body: U.S., 55; U.K., 23; host, 16; other, 136
Capacity: 7 – 9, 110; 10 – 12, 145; 13, 5; total, 260
Teacher/student ratio: 1/7
Tuition (annual): 7, 18,200**; 8 – 12, 19,800
Other fees: registration*, 1,000**(900 credited toward capital levy); capital
    levy*, 2,500; other, approximately 600
School year: late August to mid-June

Year founded: 1963. **Type of school:** coed, day, private nonprofit. **Governed by:** elected board of trustees. **Accredited by:** New England, ECIS.

Curriculum/physical plant

Type: U.S. **Languages taught:** French, German. **Staff specialists:** computer, counselor, psychologist. **Special programs:** advanced placement, honors sections, independent study, EFL. **Special curricular:** art, computer instruction, theater, music. **Extracurricular:** drama, computers, yearbook, newspaper, photography, excursions/expeditions, field trips, Model UN, video, community service. **Sports:** basketball, rugby, skiing, swimming, tennis, track, volleyball. **Tests:** PSAT, SAT, TOEFL, AP, ACH. **Graduates attending college:** 90%. **Graduates have attended:** U. of Michigan, Cornell, Princeton, Brown, Cambridge. **Location:** in residential suburb, 8 kilometers from center Zurich, on ridge overlooking Lake Zurich and Alps. **Campus:** 3 acres. **Library:** 8,000 volumes. **Facilities:** 3 buildings, 18 classrooms, 2 tennis courts, playing field, 3 science labs, computer lab (over 40 computers), theater, AV equipment.

*Once only fee   **Swiss franc

THE INTER-COMMUNITY SCHOOL

Street address: Strubenacher 3, 8126 Zumikon, Switzerland
Phone: (41)(1)9181656   **Facsimile:** (41)(1)9190026
Headmaster: Robert J. Lilburn
Head of upper school: Nick Darlington
Head of lower school: Clive Greaves
Staff: full-time, 41; part-time, 12
Nationalities of staff: U.S., 10; U.K., 24; host, 6; other, 13
Grade levels: preK – 10 (grades 11 and 12 in 1994)
Enrollment: preK, 61; K, 45; 1 – 6, 297; 7 – 8, 65; 9 – 12, 26; total, 494
Nationalities of student body: U.S., 106; U.K., 68; host, 64; other, 256
Capacity: preK, 65; K, 50; 1 – 6, 325; 7 – 8, 60; 9 – 10, 40; total, 540
Teacher/student ratio: 1/11
Tuition (annual): preK, 7,200**; K, 9,000; 1 – 6, 12,300; 7 – 10, 16,800
Other fees (annual): registration*, 200**; capital levy*, 1,000;
    busing, 2,100
School year: September through June

Year founded: 1960. **Type of school:** coed, day, private nonprofit. **Governed by:** board of trustees.

Curriculum/physical plant

Type: U.S., U.K. (IGCSE, grades 9 and 10; IB, grades 11 and 12 in 1994). **Languages of instruction:** English, German. **Languages taught:** English, French, German. **Staff specialists:** computer, speech/hearing, learning disabilities, librarian, music, science, pottery, languages, physical education, swimming. **Special programs:** ESL, remedial. **Special curricular:** art, chorus, band, physical education, computer instruction. **Extracurricular:** drama, dance, choral music, instrumental music, computers, yearbook, literary magazine, photography, excursions/expeditions, field trips. **Sports:** basketball, skiing, soccer, softball, tennis, swimming, volleyball. **Clubs:** Girl/Boy Scouts of America. **Location:** 5 miles from city center. **Campus:** 20 acres. **Library:** 17,000 volumes. **Facilities:** 5 buildings, 40 classrooms, auditorium, gymnasium, playing field, science lab, all-weather pitch, video room.

*Once only fee   **Swiss franc

INTERNATIONAL PRIMARY SCHOOL OF ZURICH

Street address: Seestrasse 169, 8802 Kilchberg, Switzerland
Phone: (41)(1)7153547   **Facsimile:** (41)(1)7153745
Director: David R. Winter
Staff: full-time, 12; part-time, 8
Nationalities of staff: U.S., 4; U.K., 7; host, 7; other, 2
Grade levels: playgroup – grade 6
Enrollment: total, 155
Nationalities of student body: U.S., 38; U.K., 45; host, 8; other, 64
Capacity: preK, 27; K, 17; 1 – 6, 102; 7, 17; total, 163
Teacher/student ratio: 1/10
Tuition (annual): playgroup, 6,300**; preK, 11,900; K – 6, 15,100
Other fees (annual): registration, 500**; busing; ESL
School year: September to June

Year founded: 1970. **Type of school:** coed, day, private nonprofit. **Governed by:** elected board of trustees.

Curriculum/physical plant

Type: Anglo-American. **Languages taught:** German. **Special programs:** ESL, remedial. **Special curricular:** physical education, computer instruction. **Extracurricular:** instrumental music, excursions/expeditions, field trips. **Sports:** skiing, soccer, swimming. **Clubs:** art, cooking, music, science. **Location:** 2.5 miles from center city, in private villa beside Zurichsee. **Library:** 10,000 volumes. **Facilities:** 1 building, 14 classrooms, auditorium, playing field.

**Swiss franc

LAUSANNE

Brillantmont International School

Address: Avenue Secretan 16, 1005 Lausanne, Switzerland
Phone: (41)(21)3124741   **Facsimile:** (41)(21)3208417

SYRIA
Region: Middle East
Size: 71,498 square miles
Population: 12,965,000
Capital: Damascus

Telephone code: 963
Currency: pound (lira)
Languages: Arabic, Kurdish,
Armenian, French,
English

ALEPPO

INTERNATIONAL SCHOOL OF ALEPPO
Street address: Damascus Road, Aleppo, Syria
Phone: (963)(21)551280   **Facsimile:** (963)(21)225105/213490
    Telex: 924331206 ICARDA SY   **Cable:** ICARDA, ALEPPO
Mail: PO Box 5466, Aleppo, Syria
Principal: Valyn Anderson
Staff: full-time, 36; part-time, 13
Nationalities of staff: U.S., 10; U.K., 5; host, 27; other, 7
Grade levels: K – 12,
Enrollment: K, 45; 1 – 6, 130; 7 – 9, 60; 10 – 12, 45; total, 280
Nationalities of student body: U.S., 24; U.K., 9; host, 143; other, 104
Capacity: K, 40; 1 – 6, 130; 7 – 9, 60; 10 – 12, 60; total, 290
Teacher/student ratio: 1/7
Tuition (annual): K – 12, $4,000
Other fees (annual): testing, supplies, registration, transportation,
    $400
School year: September to June

Year founded: 1976. **Type of school:** coed, day, company sponsored, private nonprofit. **Governed by:** appointed committee. **Sponsored by:** International Center for Agricultural Research in the Dry Areas. **Accredited by:** Middle States.

Curriculum/physical plant
Type: international. **Languages taught:** French, Arabic. **Special programs:** ESL, IB, IGCSE. **Extracurricular:** drama, dance, choral music, computers, newspaper, excursions/expeditions, field trips, Girl Scouts, athletics, music. **Sports:** basketball, soccer, swimming, volleyball, gymnastics, running. **Tests:** IB, IGCSE. **Location:** a walled campus with gardens, play and sports areas, 1 kilometer from Aleppo. **Campus:** 4 hectares. **Library:** 10,000 volumes. **Facilities:** 3 buildings, 22 classrooms, infirmary, 2 tennis courts, playing field, 3 science labs, 2 computer labs, basketball court, sports club, snack bar.

DAMASCUS

DAMASCUS COMMUNITY SCHOOL

Street address: Al-Mahdi Ben Baraka Street, Damascus, Syria
Phone: (963)(11)337737   **Telex:** 924411919 USDAMA
Mail: c/o American Embassy, Damascus, Syria
U.S. mail: c/o U.S. Embassy, Damascus, Syria, Department of State, Washington, D.C. 20521-6110
Director: Charles Barder, Ph.D.
Principal: Jan Thomas
Staff: full-time, 38; part-time, 7
Nationalities of staff: U.S., 30; U.K., 1; host, 12; other, 2
Grade levels: N – 12
Enrollment: N, 12; K, 25; 1 – 5, 125; 6 – 8, 70; 9 – 12, 70; total, 302
Nationalities of student body: U.S., 32; U.K., 4; host, 130; other, 136
Capacity: N, 18; K, 36; 1 – 5, 180; 6 – 8, 108; 9 – 12, 144; total, 486
Teacher/student ratio: 1/7
Tuition (annual): N, $4,850; K – 5, $8,050; 6 – 8, $8,900; 9 – 12, $9,300
Other fees (annual, included in tuition): registration, $250; building surcharge, $1,300; testing, $100; entrance fee, $500
School year: late August to June

Year founded: 1950. **Type of school:** coed, day, private nonprofit. **Governed by:** appointed and elected board of directors. **Accredited by:** Middle States.

Curriculum/physical plant

Type: U.S. **Languages taught:** French, Arabic. **Staff specialists:** computer. **Special programs:** ESL. **Special curricular:** art, physical education, music, computer education. **Extracurricular:** drama, yearbook, excursions/expeditions, field trips. **Sports:** basketball, soccer, tennis, volleyball. **Tests:** PSAT, SAT, Iowa. **Location:** in center of residential district, surrounded by high wall. **Campus:** 3 acres. **Library:** 10,000 volumes. **Facilities:** 10 buildings, tennis court, 2 science labs, 2 computer labs, physical education building, cafeteria/theater, secondary and administration building, running track, soccer field, basketball court, baseball field, play equipment.

TAIWAN

Region: Asia
Size: 13,885 square miles
Population: 20,658,000
Capital: Taipei

Telephone code: 886
Currency: New Taiwan dollar
Languages: Mandarin Chinese, Taiwan, Hakka dialects

KAOHSIUNG

KAOHSIUNG AMERICAN SCHOOL

Phone: (886)(7)7315565/7313712   **Facsimile:** (886)(7)7315565
Mail: No. 123-7, Ta Pei Road, Niao-Sung Hsiang, Kaohsiung County (83305), Taiwan, Republic of China
Principal: Rupert Bale, Ph.D.
Staff: full-time, 9; part-time, 2
Nationalities of staff: U.S., 5; U.K., 2; other, 4
Grade levels: preK – 12 (correspondence 9 – 12)
Enrollment: K, 20; 1 – 8, 50; 9 – 12, 10; total, 80
Nationalities of student body: U.S., 40; U.K., 6; other, 34
Capacity: total, 160
Teacher/student ratio: 1/8
Tuition (annual): preK, (3 mornings), 35,000**; preK (5 mornings), 55,000; K, 170,000; 1 – 3, 204,000; 4 – 8, 214,000
Other fees (annual): registration, 30,000**; preK, registration 5,000; capital levy, 22,000; busing, 30,000; activity, 4,000; ESL: (elementary) 40,000, (middle) 70,000
School year: August to June

Year founded: 1989. **Type of school:** coed, day, private nonprofit. **Governed by:** elected board of directors. **Operated by:** International Schools Services, Princeton, New Jersey. **Accredited by:** Western.

Curriculum/physical plant
Type: U.S. **Languages taught:** Chinese. **Staff specialists:** reading, math, computer, ESL. **Special programs:** ESL. **Special curricular:** computer instruction. **Extracurricular:** computers, yearbook, newspaper, excursions/expeditions, field trips, sports. **Tests:** Iowa. **Location:** suburb of Kaohsiung. **Facilities:** located on hospital grounds while new campus is being built.

**New Taiwan dollar

TAICHUNG/KAOHSIUNG/TAIPEI/YANG MEI

MORRISON ACADEMY

Phone: (886)(4)2921171   **Facsimile:** (886)(4)2956140
Mail: PO Box 27-24, Taichung 406, Taiwan, ROC
Acting superintendent: Greg Meeks, Ed.D.
High school principal: Donald Petersen (Taichung)
Elementary/middle school principals: Fred Wentz (Taichung),
    James Hull (Kaohsiung), Ralph Bressler (Taipei)
Dormitory supervisor: Mark Winslow
Business manager: Gordon Helsby
Staff: full-time, 95; part-time, 29
Nationalities of staff: U.S., 94; host, 19; other, 11
Grade levels: K – 12
Enrollment: K, 51; 1 – 6, 394; 7 – 9, 175; 10 – 12, 98; total, 718
Teacher/student ratio: 1/7
Boarders: boys, 13; girls, 12   **Grades:** 9 – 12   **Program:** planned 7-day
Tuition (semester)†: K (half day), 60,000**; K (full day), 80,000; 1 – 8,
    106,000 – 111,000;   9 – 12, 121,000
Other fees (semester): registration, 5,000** per year; boarding:
    missionary, 47,500, nonmissionary, 95,000; insurance, 1,000 per
    year; meals, 13,500; ESL, 12,000 – 18,000; music lessons, 2,250;
    instrument rental, 1,000; piano practice rental, 1,500; high school
    activity fee, 2,000 – 3,000
School year: August through May

Year founded: 1952. **Type of school:** coed, day, boarding, church-related, private nonprofit. **Governed by:** appointed board of trustees. **Sponsored by:** Morrison Christian Association. **Accredited by:** Western.

Curriculum
Type: U.S. **Languages taught:** French, Spanish, Chinese. **Staff specialists:** counselor, psychologist, nurse, resource. **Special programs:** ESL, independent study, remedial. **Special curricular:** art, chorus, band, physical education, computer instruction, vocational. **Extracurricular:** drama, choral music, instrumental music, computers, yearbook, newspaper, photography, field trips, King's Players. **Sports:** basketball, soccer, tennis, track, volleyball. **Tests:** PSAT, SAT, ACT, AP, Stanford, Iowa, DAT. **Graduates attending college:** 95%. **Graduates have attended:** Wheaton, Goshen, Biola, Colgate, Purdue.

Physical plant
Campuses (4): Taichung, 18 acres; Taipei, .25 acre; Kaohsiung, 3 acres; Yang Mei, .1 acre. **Libraries:** 29,500 volumes. **Facilities:** auditoriums, cafeteria, infirmary, covered play area, tennis courts, gymnasiums, playing fields, science labs, computer labs, swimming pool, 2 boys' dormitories, 2 girls' dormitories.

**New Taiwan dollar   †Missionary discount available upon application

TAIPEI

DOMINICAN SCHOOL

Street address: 76 Tah Chih Street, Taipei, Taiwan, ROC
Phone: (886)(2)5028451   **Facsimile:** (886)(2)5042914
Principal: Sr. Francisca Rogando, O.P.
Assistant principal: Sr. Leticia Estero, O.P.
Staff: full-time, 30
Nationalities of staff: U.S., 3; host, 8; other, 19
Grade levels: preK – 8
Enrollment: total, 440
Capacity: preK, 21; K, 38; 1 – 6, 304; 7 – 8, 77; total, 440
Teacher/student ratio: 1/15
Tuition (annual): preK – K, 68,000**; 1 – 4, 102,000; 5 – 8, 110,000
Other fees (annual): registration*, 5,000**; busing, 12,000/semester;
    lunch, 65; capital development: preK – 4, 1,500; 5 – 8, 2,500;
    guidance, 800
School year: August to May

Year founded: 1957. **Type of school:** coed, day, church-related, private
nonprofit. **Governed by:** Dominican Sisters.

Curriculum/physical plant
Type: U.S. **Languages taught:** French, Spanish, Chinese. **Staff special-ists:** reading, math, counselor, nurse. **Special curricular:** art, chorus, band, physical education, computer instruction. **Extracurricular:** drama, gymnas-tics, dance, choral music, instrumental music, computers, yearbook, news-paper, excursions/expeditions, field trips, sports, student council, choir membership. **Tests:** Iowa, SRA, intelligence tests. **Location:** in suburb. **Library:** 13,500 volumes. **Facilities:** 3 buildings, 24 classrooms, cafeteria, infirmary, covered play area, playing field, science lab, computer lab, AV room, gymnasium/auditorium, air conditioning.

1992–93 listing

*Once only fee   **New Taiwan dollar

TAIPEI AMERICAN SCHOOL

Street address: 800 Chung Shan N. Road, Sec. 6, Shihlin District,
    Taipei 111, Taiwan, Republic of China
Phone: (886)(2)8739900   **Facsimile:** (886)(2)8731641
Superintendent: John Stander
Assistant superintendent: Ira B. Weislow
Upper school principal: (to be announced)
Middle school principal: Catherine Funk
Lower school principal: Mark Ulfers

Staff: full-time, 179; part-time, 12
Nationalities of staff: U.S., 162; host, 13; other, 16
Grade levels: K – 12
Enrollment: K, 94; 1 – 5, 746; 6 – 8, 555; 9 – 12, 721; total, 2,116
Nationalities of student body: U.S., 1,310; U.K., 43; other, 763
Capacity: K, 126; 1 – 6, 1,033; 7 – 9, 570; 10 – 12, 575; total, 2,304
Teacher/student ratio: 1/11
Tuition (annual): K, 141,400**; lower school, 202,900; middle/upper
  schools, 256,700
Other fees (annual): registration, 25,000**; insurance, 900; busing,
  21,000; application, 1,500; ESL: elementary, 74,000, secondary,
  89,000; activity, 2,400; Mandarin class, 5,500;
  lunch: K, 9,000; 1 – 12, 13,500
School year: August to June

Year founded: 1949. **Type of school:** coed, day, private nonprofit.
Governed by: elected board of directors. **Accredited by:** Western.

Curriculum

Type: U.S., IB. **Languages taught:** French, Spanish, Chinese; for native
speakers: Dutch, German, Japanese. **Staff specialists:** computer, counselor,
psychologist, learning disabilities, nurse, resource. **Special programs:** ESL,
advanced placement, honors sections. **Special curricular:** art, chorus, band,
physical education, computer instruction. **Extracurricular:** drama, choral
music, instrumental music, computers, yearbook, newspaper, literary magazine, photography, excursions/expeditions, field trips. **Sports:** basketball,
soccer, softball, swimming, tennis, track, volleyball, diving, badminton.
Clubs: cheerleaders, computer, creative writing, drama, film, key, orphanage,
Model UN, publicity, National Honor Society, National Junior Honor Society,
Spanish Honor Society, Chinese Honor Society, Société Honoraire de Français.
Tests: SSAT, PSAT, SAT, ACT, IB, AP, Iowa, ACH. **Graduates attending
college:** 89%. **Graduates have attended:** Brown, Harvard, Stanford, Cornell,
Princeton.

Physical plant

Location: in suburban area, 11 kilometers from Taipei City. **Campus:** 22
acres. **Libraries:** 75,000 volumes. **Facilities:** 142 classrooms, 2 auditoriums,
cafeteria, 4 tennis courts, 3 gymnasiums, 3 playing fields, 12 science labs, 6
computer labs, swimming pool, nurse's office, air conditioning.

**New Taiwan dollar

TANZANIA

Region: East Africa
Size: 364,886 square miles
Population: 26,869,000
Capital: Dar es Salaam

Telephone code: 255
Currency: shilling
Languages: Swahili, English

DAR ES SALAAM

INTERNATIONAL SCHOOL OF TANGANYIKA LTD.

Street address: United Nations Road, Dar es Salaam, Tanzania
Phone: (255)(51)30076 – 7   **Facsimile:** (255)(51)46754/66756/
    67869   **Telex:** 97541487 COVMAT IST
Mail: PO Box 2651, Dar es Salaam, Tanzania
Chief executive officer: William Powell
Secondary school headmaster: Nick Bowley
High school principal: John Roberts
Junior high school principal: Areta Williams
Middle school principal: Sally Gordon
Lower school principal: Janet Gould
Elementary school headmaster: Ian Rysdale
Business manager: Frans Cadee
Staff: full-time, 126; part-time, 8
Nationalities of staff: U.S., 35; U.K., 50; host, 12; other, 37
Grade levels: preK – 13
Enrollment: preK, 40; K, 79; 1 – 6, 601; 7 – 9, 301; 10 – 12, 257; 13,
    45; total, 1,323
Nationalities of student body: U.S., 52; U.K., 181; host, 75;
    other, 1,015
Capacity: preK, 40; K, 80; 1 – 6, 650; 7 – 9, 300; 10 – 12, 230; 13, 45;
    total, 1,345
Teacher/student ratio: 1/10
Tuition (annual): preK, $3,685; K – 3, $3,895; 4 – 6, $4,615; 7 – 11,
    $5,775; 12 – 13, $8,170
Other fees: capital levy*, $3,285; family deposit*, $432
School year: August to June

Year founded: 1963. **Type of school:** coed, day, private nonprofit.
Governed by: elected board of directors. **Accredited by:** Middle States, ECIS.

Curriculum

Type: U.S., U.K., IB. **Languages taught:** French, German, Kiswahili.
Staff specialists: computer, counselor, learning disabilities, nurse. **Special programs:** ESL, honors sections, remedial, learning disabilities. **Special curricular:** art, physical education, computer instruction. **Extracurricular:** drama, gymnastics, choral music, instrumental music, computers, yearbook, photography, excursions/expeditions, field trips. **Sports:** field hockey, soc-

cer, softball, swimming, volleyball, netball, badminton, sailing, squash, cricket, canoeing. **Clubs:** Interact, Model UN, chess, arts and crafts, student government, house sports competition, Duke of Edinburgh Awards Scheme; all students participate in social service education. **Tests:** PSAT, SAT, TOEFL, IB, GCSE, Stanford. **Graduates attending college:** 85 – 90%. **Graduates have attended:** MIT, London School of Economics, Harvard, Cornell, Bryn Mawr.

Physical plant
Location: preK/kindergarten in city; elementary campus on edge of city; secondary campus in suburbs. **Campuses (3):** 40 acres. **Libraries:** 10,000 volumes. **Facilities:** 91 buildings, 70 classrooms, 2 auditoriums, 2 infirmaries, covered play area, 2 tennis courts, 2 gymnasiums, 2 playing fields, 7 science labs, 4 computer labs, 2 swimming pools, AV theater, photography darkroom, 2 music rooms, purpose-built studio theater.

*Once only fee

MOROGORO

INTERNATIONAL SCHOOL OF MOROGORO
Phone: (255)(56)4864
Mail: PO Box 1015, University Campus, Morogoro, Tanzania
Headteacher: Ms. S. Huxtabel
Staff: full-time, 8
Nationalities of staff: host, 3; other, 5
Grade levels: N – 6
Enrollment: N – preK, 20; K, 7; 1 – 6, 53; total, 80
Nationalities of student body: host, 16; other, 64
Capacity: N – preK, 20; K, 12; 1 – 6, 72; total, 104
Teacher/student ratio: 1/10
Tuition (annual): N – 6, 3,000**
School year: September to July

Year founded: 1976. **Type of school:** coed, day, private nonprofit. **Governed by:** parent representatives.

Curriculum/physical plant
Type: U.K. **Languages taught:** English, Swahili. **Special curricular:** art, chorus, band, physical education. **Extracurricular:** instrumental music, newspaper, excursions/expeditions, volleyball. **Location:** pleasant grounds on university campus in suburban area of Morogoro. **Campus:** 2 acres. **Library:** 5,000 volumes. **Facilities:** 2 buildings, 9 classrooms, playing field.

**Pound sterling

MOSHI

INTERNATIONAL SCHOOL MOSHI

Street address: Lema Road, Moshi, Tanzania
Phone: (255)(55)55003 – 4   **Facsimile:** (255)(55)50236
   Telex: 97543162
Mail: PO Box 733, Moshi, Tanzania
Headmaster: Mike Linden
Deputy head: Keiron White
Headteacher, Arusha campus: Jan Hughes
Business manager: Ashak Taki
Staff: full-time, 48; part-time, 3
Nationalities of staff: U.S., 3; U.K., 21; host, 5; other, 22
Grade levels: K – IB
Enrollment: K, 12; 1 – 6 (Moshi), 128; 1 – 6 (Arusha), 116; 7 – 10,
   153; 11 – 12, 62; total, 471
Nationalities of student body: U.S., 31; U.K., 57; host, 146;
   other, 237
Teacher/student ratio: 1/10
Boarders: boys, 53; girls, 48   **Program:** planned 7-day
Tuition (annual): K, 1,980**; 1, 2,150; 2, 2,500; 3 – 4, 2,650; 5 – 7,
   2,900; 8 – 9, 3,350; 9 – 10, 3,750; IB, 4,250
Other fees (annual): registration*, 1,100**; boarding, 3,350
School year: August to June

Year founded: 1969. **Type of school:** coed, day, boarding, private
nonprofit. **Governed by:** board of directors. **Accredited by:** Middle States,
ECIS.

Curriculum/physical plant

Type: IB, International, IGCSE. **Languages taught:** French, German,
Kiswahili. **Staff specialists:** computer, special needs, EFL. **Special curricular:** art, physical education, computer instruction. **Extracurricular:** drama,
dance, choral music, literary magazine, excursions/expeditions, field
trips, sports. **Tests:** PSAT, SAT, TOEFL, IB, IGCSE. **Location:** in suburban
area.

*Once only fee   **Pound sterling

MWANZA

VICTORIA PRIMARY SCHOOL

Mail: Box 1414, Mwanza, Tanzania, East Africa
Principal: Norman Dilworth
Business manager: Virginia Tanner

Staff: full-time, 3; part-time, 2
Nationalities of staff: U.S., 2; other, 3
Grade levels: K – 5
Enrollment: total, 12
Nationalities of student body: U.S., 4; host, 2; other, 6
Capacity: total, 18
Teacher/student ratio: 1/4
Boarders: boys, 4; girls, 7
Tuition (annual): $2,000 – 2,500
School year: September to July

Year founded: 1953. **Type of school:** coed, day, boarding, church-related. **Governed by:** school board. **Sponsored by:** Africa Inland Mission.

Curriculum/physical plant

Type: U.S. **Languages taught:** English, Kiswahili. **Staff specialists:** reading, counselor, nurse. **Special curricular:** art, chorus, physical education. **Extracurricular:** choral music, instrumental music, field trips. **Sports:** soccer, softball, camping trips in Serengeti National Park, fishing in Lake Victoria, hill climbing. **Location:** on hill overlooking Lake Victoria, 60 miles from Mwanza, 700 miles from Dar es Salaam. **Campus:** 2 acres. **Facilities:** 4 buildings, 2 classrooms, cafeteria, covered play area, 2 playing fields, library, full boarding facilities.

THAILAND ─────────────────────────

Region: South Asia
Size: 198,456 square miles
Population: 54,814,000
Capital: Bangkok

Telephone code: 66
Currency: baht
Languages: Tahi, regional dialects, Chinese, Malay

BANGKOK

INTERNATIONAL COMMUNITY SCHOOL

Street address: 72 Sriphumpen Road, Soi Prong Jai, Thangmahamak, Sathorn, Bangkok 10120, Thailand
Phone/facsimile: (66)(2)2874530
U.S. mail: c/o Network of International Christian Schools, PO Box 18151, Memphis, TN 38181, U.S.A.
Superintendent: Dr. Lee Bruckner
Principal: Dr. Lila Bruckner
Staff: full-time, 20; part-time, 6
Nationalities of staff: U.S., 21; host, 5
Grade levels: K – 9, (adding one grade each year)
Enrollment (projected): K, 30; 1 – 5, 175; 6 – 8, 75; 9, 25; ESL, 15; total, 320

Nationalities of student body (projected): U.S., 180; other, 140
Capacity: total, 320
Teacher/student ratio: 1/14
Tuition (annual): K – 5, 87,000**; 6 – 9, 95,000
Other fees: registration*, 50,000**
School year: August to June

Year founded: 1993. **Type of school:** coed, day, church-related, private nonprofit. **Governed by:** elected school board. **Sponsored by:** Nework of International Christian Schools.

Curriculum/physical plant
Type: U.S. **Languages taught:** Spanish, German, Thai. **Staff specialists:** early childhood development. **Special programs:** ESL. **Special curricular:** art, physical education, computer instruction, music. **Extracurricular:** drama, yearbook, newspaper, excursions/expeditions, field trips, band, choral music. **Clubs:** science, drama, computer, YouthQuest. **Tests:** SAT, ACT, TOEFL, Stanford. **Location:** central Bangkok (Sathorn area), easily accessible from all mid-city locations. **Facilities:** 2 buildings, 16 classrooms, cafeteria, science lab, computer lab, counseling room, chapel, nurse's station.

*Once only fee   **Thai baht

INTERNATIONAL SCHOOL BANGKOK
Street address: 39/7 Soi Nichada Thani, Samakee Road, Amphur Pakkret, Nonthaburi 11120, Thailand
Phone: (66)(2)5835401   **Facsimile:** (66)(2)5835431
Cable: ISBAN, BANGKOK
Mail: PO Box 20-1015, Ha Yaek Pakkret, Nonthaburi 11120, Thailand
Superintendent: Robert W. Brewitt
Assistant superintendent: David Randall
Secondary school principal: Bruce Kramer
Middle school principal: Marilyn Holladay
Elementary school principal: Terrence Factor
Manager/headmaster: Punya Somboonsilp, Ph.D.
Staff: full-time, 168; part-time, 10
Nationalities of staff: U.S., 140; U.K., 9; host, 6; other, 23
Grade levels: K – 12
Enrollment: K – 5, 640; 6 – 8, 500; 9 – 12, 690; total, 1,830
Nationalities of student body: U.S., 680; U.K., 110; host, 160; other, 880
Capacity: K – 5, 775; 6 – 8, 525; 9 – 12, 750; total, 2,050
Teacher/student ratio: 1/11
Tuition (annual): K – 5, 180,000**; 6 – 8, 195,000; 9 – 12, 198,000
Other fees (annual): registration*, 71,000**; busing, 18,360 – 29,160; assessment*, 280,000; ESL, 38,000 – 53,500
School year: August to June

Year founded: 1951. **Type of school:** coed, day, private nonprofit. **Governed by:** elected board of directors. **Accredited by:** Western.

Curriculum

Type: U.S., IB. **Languages taught:** French, Spanish, German, Japanese, Thai. **Staff specialists:** reading, computer, speech/hearing, counselor, psychologist, learning disabilities, nurse. **Special programs:** ESL. **Special curricular:** art, chorus, band, physical education, computer instruction. **Extracurricular:** drama, choral music, instrumental music, computers, yearbook, newspaper, literary magazine, photography, excursions/expeditions, field trips. **Sports:** basketball, soccer, softball, swimming, tennis, track, volleyball. **Clubs:** Thai history and culture, Cosmopolitan, Keyettes, computer, chess, stagecraft, Model UN, Close-Up, science, windsurfing, skateboard, National Honor Society. **Tests:** SSAT, PSAT, SAT, ACT, IB, AP, Iowa, DAT. **Graduates attending college:** 90%. **Graduates have attended:** Harvard, Bucknell, Australian National U., Johns Hopkins, International Christian U. (Japan).

Physical plant

Location: 26 kilometers from central Bangkok in the residential area of Nonthaburi Province. **Campus:** 36 acres. **Libraries:** over 66,000 volumes. **Facilities:** over 120 classrooms, 2 cafeterias, 4 gymnasiums, 3 playing fields, 7 science labs, 5 computer labs, swimming pool, 750-seat theater, instructional media center and administration building, 400-meter track, full air conditioning.

*Once only fee   **Thai baht

THE NEW INTERNATIONAL SCHOOL OF THAILAND†

Street address: 36 Soi 15 (Ruamchai) Sukhumvit Road, Bangkok
  10110, Thailand
Phone: (66)(2)2530109/2538600   **Facsimile:** (66)(2)2533800
Principal: (to be announced)
Headmistress: Dr. Pusadee Tamthai
Head of elementary school: Richard W. Ryden
Staff: full-time, 72; part-time, 12
Nationalities of staff: U.S., 13; U.K., 21; host, 8; other, 42
Grade levels: K – 11 (grade 12 in 1994)
Enrollment: K, 120; 1 – 6, 500; 7 – 11, 200; total, 820
Nationalities of student body: U.S., 123; U.K., 25; host, 164;
  other, 508
Capacity: K, 120; 1 – 6, 500; 7 – 12, 450; total, 1,070
Teacher/student ratio: 1/11
Tuition (annual): K, 80,000**; 1 – 6, 120,000; 7 – 9, 140,000; 10 – 11,
  160,000
Other fees: registration*, 60,000**; ESL, 10,000 – 30,000 per trimester; transportation; uniform
School year: late August through June

Year founded: 1992. **Type of school:** coed, day, private nonprofit. **Governed by:** Foundation for International Education and elected school board. **Approved by:** IBO (accreditation in process). **Affiliated with:** United Nations.

Curriculum/physical plant

Type: international. **Languages taught:** French, Spanish, German, Dutch, Italian, Japanese, Swedish, Finnish, Thai, Hindi, Korean, Mandarin, Russian (others offered by request). **Staff specialists:** computer, counselor, learning disabilities, nurse, ESL (approximately 8). **Special curricular:** native language and culture, art, physical education, drama, music, design and technology, home economics, Thai culture/traditions. **Extracurricular:** various programs and clubs (including sports) determined by faculty abilities and student interests. **Location:** in heart of Bangkok's major residential district. **Campus:** 7 acres. **Facilities:** 4 buildings, 45 classrooms, libraries, cafeteria, 3 gymnasiums, 2 playing fields, 5 science labs, 2 computer labs, dispensary, playground, air conditioning.

*Once only fee   **Thai baht
†Not associated with International School Bangkok, which formerly
    occupied the same campus

RUAMRUDEE INTERNATIONAL SCHOOL

Street address: 42 Moo 4, Ramkhamhaeng (Sukapibal 3) Road,
    Minburi, Bangkok 10510, Thailand
Phone: (66)(2)5180320 – 9   **Facsimile:** (66)(2)5180334
Director: Rev. Fr. Tom Griffith
Manager: Rev. Fr. John Phairot
Principal: Mrs. Thavida Bijayendrayodhin
Acting high school supervisor: Mr. Jim Souza
Middle school supervisor: Mr. Samuel Phillips
Elementary school supervisor: Dr. Shirl Spelgatti
Head of library: Mrs. Jan Blank
Head of computer services: Mrs. Leovy Sahaphong
Staff: full-time, 132; part-time, 10
Grade levels: K – 12, ESL 1 – 10
Enrollment: total, 1,700
Capacity: total, 2,500
Teacher/student ratio: 1/12
Tuition (annual): K – 5, $3,177; 6 – 8, $3,451; 9 – 12, $3,765;
    ESL 1 – 4, $3,765; ESL 5 – 8, $4,118; ESL 9 – 10, $4,510
Other fees: registration*, $1,177; book deposit*, $196
School year: August to June

Year founded: 1957. **Type of school:** day, church-affiliated, international. **Operated by:** Redemptorist Fathers of Thailand. **Sponsored by:** Thai Ministry of Foreign Affairs. **Accredited by:** Western, Thai Ministry of Education, Association of Indian University.

Curriculum/physical plant

Type: U.S. **Languages taught:** English, French, Spanish, German, Thai. **Staff specialists:** counselors, psychologist, art, music, physical education, school health officer. **Special programs:** ESL, special education classes. **Special curricular:** speech, debate, Model UN, forensics. **Extracurricular:** sports program, chorus, newspaper, yearbook. **Sports:** basketball, soccer, swimming, volleyball, tennis, badminton, table tennis. **Clubs:** drama, computer, Keyette (community service), health, math/AHSME, chess, weight lifting, speakers' debate, Model UN, cheerleaders, Thai traditional dance, photography, French, Spanish, stamp, cosmopolitan, modern dance, ecology, knowledge bowl. **Tests:** PSAT, SAT, TOEFL, Iowa, COGAT, TAP. **Graduates attending college:** 95%. **Graduates have attended:** Pepperdine U., Tufts, U. of Michigan, U. of Rochester, Oberlin. **Location:** in residential area of Bangkok. **Campus:** 20 acres. **Library:** 18,000 volumes. **Facilities:** 5 buildings, auditorium/gymnasium, 2 cafeterias, canteen, 6 science labs, high school library and arts building, teachers' flat, swimming pool, playing fields, outside gymnasium.

*Once only fee

CHIANG MAI

CHIANG MAI INTERNATIONAL SCHOOL

> **Street address:** 13 Chetupon Road, Chiang Mai, Thailand
> **Phone:** (66)(53)242027   **Facsimile:** (66)(53)242455
> **Mail:** PO Box 38, Chiang Mai, Thailand 50000
> **Director/principal:** Kamol Boonprohm
> **Vice-principal:** John Ault
> **Staff:** full-time, 20; part-time, 1
> **Nationalities of staff:** U.S., 11; host, 4; other, 6
> **Grade levels:** K – 10
> **Enrollment:** K, 20; 1 – 6, 150; 7 – 8, 50; 9 – 10, 30; total, 250
> **Nationalities of student body:** U.S., 60; U.K., 12; host, 25; other, 153
> **Capacity:** K, 20; 1 – 6, 215; 7 – 9, 60; 9 – 10, 60; total, 355
> **Teacher/student ratio:** 1/12
> **Tuition (annual):** K, $1,400; 1 – 6, $2,400; 7 – 8, $2,600;
>   9 – 10, $3,000
> **Other fees:** application, $40
> **School year:** September to June

Year founded: 1954. **Type of school:** coed, day, church-affiliated, private nonprofit. **Governed by:** appointed administrative advisory board. **Sponsored by:** Foundation of the Church of Christ in Thailand. **Accredited by:** Western (K – 8); Thai Ministry of Education.

Curriculum/physical plant

Type: U.S. **Special programs:** ESL, Thai language and culture. **Special curricular:** art, chorus, physical education, computer instruction. **Extracurricular:** drama, computers, yearbook, newspaper, photography, field trips, sports. **Tests:** MAT. **Location:** in city. **Library:** 10,000 volumes. **Facilities:** 5 buildings, 15 classrooms, auditorium, 3 covered play areas, playing field, science lab, computer lab, AV equipment, multi-use court area.

PHUKET

PHUKET INTERNATIONAL PREPARATORY SCHOOL

Phone: (66)(76)381337　**Facsimile:** (66)(76)381337
Mail: PO Box 432, Phuket 83000, Thailand
Director/curriculum coordinator: Mrs. Agnes Hebler
Headmaster: Miss Sunanta Tamsoonthornkul
Business manager: Mrs. Panthip Boonsoong
Staff: full-time, 10; part-time, 4
Nationalities of staff: U.S., 4; host, 4; other, 6
Grade levels: preK – 8
Enrollment: preK, 25; K, 10; 1 – 6, 70; 7, 10; total, 115
Nationalities of student body: U.S., 10; host, 40; other, 65
Capacity: preK, 25; K – 8, 90; total, 115
Teacher/student ratio: 1/10
Tuition (annual): preK, 27,000**; K – 6, 50,000; 7, 70,000;
　ESL, 58,000
Other fees: registration*, 10,000**
School year: September to June

Year founded: 1989. **Type of school:** coed, day, private nonprofit. **Accredited by:** Thai government, Western (in process).

Curriculum/physical plant

Type: U.S. **Languages taught:** English, French, German, Thai. **Staff specialists:** reading, computer. **Special curricular:** computer instruction. **Extracurricular:** swimming. **Tests:** SAT, CAT. **Location:** in tropical rural area, 1 mile from center of town. **Campus:** 2 acres. **Library:** 450 volumes. **Facilities:** two-story building with 14 classrooms and an all-purpose room.

*Once only fee　**Thai bhat

TOGO ─────────────────────────

Region: West Africa
Size: 21,622 square miles
Population: 3,810,000
Capital: Lomé

Telephone code: 228
Currency: CFA franc
Languages: French, Gur, Kwa

LOMÉ

AMERICAN INTERNATIONAL SCHOOL OF LOMÉ

Street address: 35 Kayigan Lawson, Lomé, Togo
Phone: (228)213000   **Facsimile:** (228)217952
   Cable: U.S. Embassy, Lomé
U.S. mail: c/o U.S. Embassy – Lomé, Department of State, Washington, D.C. 20521-2300
Director: Mary Jo Gabiam
Staff: full-time, 5; part-time, 6
Nationalities of staff: U.S., 4; host, 4; other, 3
Grade levels: preK – 8
Enrollment: preK, 13; K – 8, 35; total, 48
Nationalities of student body: U.S., 16; other, 32
Capacity: preK, 15; K, 10; 1 – 6, 60; 7 – 8, 20; total, 105
Teacher/student ratio: 1/6
Tuition (annual): preK, $1,500; K – 8, $4,500
Other fees: registration*, $300
School year: September to June

Year founded: 1967. **Type of school:** coed, day, private nonprofit.
Governed by: elected board of directors.

Curriculum/physical plant

Type: U.S. **Languages taught:** French (required daily). **Staff specialists:** computer, art, ESL, music, physical education. **Special programs:** ESL. **Special curricular:** art, physical education, French, music, computer. **Extracurricular:** yearbook, field trips, basketball, swimming, ceramics. **Tests:** Iowa. **Location:** in city. **Campus:** 1 acre. **Library:** 4,000 volumes. **Facilities:** 1 building, 11 classrooms, lunchroom, partly covered play area, playing field, computer lab, air conditioning.

*Once only fee

TRINIDAD AND TOBAGO ─────────

Region: Caribbean
Size: 1,980 square miles
Population: 1,285,000
Capital: Port of Spain

Telephone code: 809
Currency: Trinidad dollar
Language: English

MAYARO

Amoco Galeota School

Street address: 4-1/2 Mile Guayaguayare Road, Mayaro, Trinidad and
   Tobago
Phone: (1)(809)6308361   **Telex:** 38722287 AMOCO WG
   Cable: AMOCO TRI PORT-OF-SPAIN
Mail: PO Box 714, Port of Spain, Trinidad and Tobago, West Indies
U.S. mail: Amoco Galeota School, Expatriate–Trinidad and Tobago,
   PO Box 4381, Houston, TX 77210, U.S.A.
Principal: Barbara Punch
Staff: full-time, 7
Nationalities of staff: U.S., 2; host, 5
Grade levels: preK – 7
Enrollment: preK, 2; K, 12; 1 – 7, 44; total, 58
Nationalities of student body: U.S., 17; host, 41
Capacity: preK, 5; K, 10; 1 – 6, 55; 7 – 8, 5; total, 75
Teacher/student ratio: 1/10
School year: September to June

Year founded: 1972. **Type of school:** coed, day, company sponsored.
Sponsored by: Amoco Trinidad Oil Company. **Operated by:** International
Schools Services, Princeton, New Jersey.

Curriculum/physical plant
Type: U.S., Trinidadian. **Languages taught:** Spanish. **Staff specialists:**
reading, computer, learning disabilities, music. **Special programs:** indepen-
dent study, remedial, Spanish conversation. **Special curricular:** art, physical
education, computer instruction. **Extracurricular:** drama, dance, choral
music, instrumental music, computers, yearbook, field trips, crafts, karate.
Sports: baseball, basketball, football, tennis, cricket. **Tests:** Iowa, Common
Entrance Examination (national examination). **Graduates have attended:**
Presentation College, St. Augustine Girls' High School, St. Stephen's College,
Naparima Girls' High School. **Location:** on seacoast, in the southeastern
corner of the island. **Library:** 8,000 volumes. **Facilities:** 2 buildings, 6
classrooms, auditorium, covered play area, 2 tennis courts, playing field,
computer lab, swimming pool, air conditioning.

TUNISIA ———————————————————

Region: North Africa
Size: 63,170 square miles
Population: 8,276,000
Capital: Tunis

Telephone code: 216
Currency: dinar
Languages: Arabic, French

SFAX

INTERNATIONAL SCHOOL OF SFAX

Street address: 2.5 km Route de Gremda, Sfax, Tunisia
Phone: (216)(4)67718   **Facsimile:** (216)(4)67718
U.S. mail: c/o British Gas Exploration and Production,
1100 Louisiana, Suite 2500, Houston, TX 77002, U.S.A.
Director: John C. Mitchell
Staff: full-time, 6; part-time, 2
Nationalities of staff: U.S., 3; U.K., 2; Canadian, 1; host, 2
Grade levels: K – 8
Enrollment: K, 3; 1 – 8, 23; total, 26
Nationalities of student body: U.S., 8; U.K., 9; other, 9
Capacity: K, 15; 1 – 8, 50; total, 65
Teacher/student ratio: 1/3

Year founded: 1992. **Type of school:** coed, day. **Sponsored by:** British Gas. **Operated by:** International Schools Services, Princeton, New Jersey.

Curriculum/physical plant
Type: U.S., U.K. **Languages taught:** French. **Special curricular:** physical education, yearbook. **Extracurricular:** drama, computers, literary magazine, excursions/expeditions, field trips. **Tests:** Stanford. **Library:** 3,000 volumes. **Facilities:** covered play area, playing field, science lab, computer lab.

TUNIS

AMERICAN COOPERATIVE SCHOOL OF TUNIS

Street address: Km. 10 Route de la Marsa – El Aouina, Tunis, Tunisia
Phone: (216)(1)760517/760905   **Facsimile:** (216)(1)761412
Telex: 93418379 AMB TUN
Mail: c/o American Embassy, 144 Avenue de la Liberté, Tunis, Tunisia
U.S. mail: TUNIS – A.C.S.T., Department of State, Washington, D.C.
20521-6360
Director: Richard L. Spradling, Ph.D.
Business manager: Faouzi Ben Sedrine

Accountant: Margaret Duggan
Staff: full-time, 14; part-time, 5
Nationalities of staff: U.S., 15; U.K., 2; other, 2
Grade levels: preK – 10
Enrollment: preK, 15; K, 20; 1 – 5, 80; 6 – 10, 40; total, 155
Nationalities of student body: U.S., 69; U.K., 6; host, 10; other, 70
Capacity: preK, 15; K, 20; 1 – 5, 110; 6 – 10, 90; total, 235
Teacher/student ratio: 1/9
Tuition (annual): preK (half day), $2,500 (other fees do not apply); K – 8,
     $6,800; 9 – 10, $7,800
Other fees: registration*, $500; capital levy, $400; busing, $700
School year: September to June

Year founded: 1958. **Type of school:** coed, day, private nonprofit.
Governed by: elected board of governors. **Accredited by:** Middle States.

Curriculum/physical plant

Type: U.S. **Languages taught:** French, Arabic. **Special programs:** ESL.
Special curricular: art, physical education, computer instruction, music.
Extracurricular: choral music, instrumental music, computers, yearbook,
excursions/expeditions, field trips, Girl Scouts, Boy Scouts. **Sports:** soccer,
softball, tennis. **Tests:** SSAT, Iowa. **Location:** in suburban area, 10 kilometers from Tunis city. **Library:** 8,000 volumes. **Facilities:** 4 buildings, 18
classrooms, playing field, science lab, computer lab, multipurpose room.

*Once only fee

TURKEY _____

Region: Middle East
Size: 301,381 square miles
Population: 58,580,000
Capital: Ankara

Telephone code: 90
Currency: lira
Languages: Turkish, Kurdish, Arabic

ISTANBUL

Istanbul International Community School

Street address: Meydan Mahallesi, Eski, Sokak, Rumeli Hisar, Istanbul,
     Turkey
Phone: (90)(1)2651591   **Facsimile:** (90)(1)2650580
Mail: P. K. 29, Bebek 80810, Istanbul, Turkey
Headmaster: Kenneth Hillmann
Staff: full-time, 27; part-time, 12
Nationalities of staff: U.S., 17; U.K., 7; host, 5; other, 10
Grade levels: K – 10
Enrollment: K, 36; 1 – 6, 202; 7 – 10, 82; total, 320

Nationalities of student body: U.S., 65; U.K., 50; other, 205
Teacher/student ratio: 1/10
Tuition (annual): K – 5, $7,500; 6 – 8, $7,700; 9 – 10, $8,500
Other fees (annual): capital levy, $1,700
School year: September to June

Year founded: 1911. **Type of school:** coed, day, private nonprofit.
Governed by: appointed board of governors. **Accredited by:** New England.

Curriculum/physical plant

Type: U.S. **Languages taught:** French, Latin, Turkish. **Staff specialists:**
reading, math, counselor, learning disabilities. **Special programs:** ESL.
Special curricular: art, chorus, physical education, computer instruction.
Extracurricular: drama, gymnastics, computers, yearbook, newspaper, ex-
cursions/expeditions, field trips. **Sports:** basketball, soccer, softball, volleyball. **Clubs:** Brownies, Cub Scouts, Girl Scouts, Boy Scouts. **Tests:** SSAT,
ERB. **Graduates have attended:** Exeter, Williston, Northampton, Northfield
Mount Hermon, Avon Old Farm. **Location:** in small village overlooking the
Bosphorus, 5 miles from old city. **Library:** 7,000 volumes. **Facilities:** 13
buildings, 20 classrooms, playing field, science lab, computer lab, AV room,
physical education bubble, playground.

THE KOÇ SCHOOL

Phone: (90)(1)3041003 – 14   **Facsimile:** (90)(1)3041048
  Telex: 82130896 KOC TR (Koç Holding Co.)
  Cable: KOC-Istanbul (via Koç Holding Co.)
Mail: PO Box 38, Pendik-Istanbul, Turkey
Headmaster: Gerald Shields
Assistant headmaster: Atakan Demirseren
Academic dean: Zühal Altayli
Business manager: Gurkan Key
Staff: full-time, 69; part-time, 3
Nationalities of staff: U.S., 24; U.K., 8; host, 37; other, 3
Grade levels: 6 – 12
Enrollment: 6, 124; 7 – 9, 332; 10 – 12, 302; total, 758
Nationalities of student body: host, 755; other 3
Teacher/student ratio: 1/11
Boarders: boys, 215; girls, 135   **Grades:** 6 – 12   **Program:** planned
  5-day
Tuition (annual): 25,000,000**
Other fees (annual): boarding, 24,500,000**; busing, 540 – 980,000;
  lunch, 300,000/month; books, 1,800,000; uniform, 1,180,000
School year: September to June

Year founded: 1988. **Type of school:** coed, day, boarding, private nonprofit. **Governed by:** appointed school committee of Vehbi Koç Foundation board. **Sponsored by:** Koç Foundation. **Accredited by:** Turkish Ministry of Education.

Curriculum

Type: U.S., Turkish. **Languages of instruction:** English, Turkish. **Languages taught:** English, French, German, Turkish. **Staff specialists:** computer, counselor, nurse, ESL, drama. **Special programs:** ESL, advanced placement, honors sections. **Special curricular:** art, chorus, physical education, computer instruction, debating, ensemble music, English conversation and music. **Extracurricular:** drama, dance, choral music, instrumental music, computers, yearbook, newspaper, literary magazine, photography, excursions/expeditions, field trips. **Sports:** basketball, soccer, tennis, track, volleyball, handball, ping-pong, cross-country, mini-football, badminton. **Clubs:** hiking, chess, student council, Turkish culture, aerobics. **Tests:** PSAT, SAT, TOEFL, AP, Cambridge Language Proficiency, Turkish university entrance exams. **Graduates attending college:** 98%.

Physical plant

Location: rural setting, in rolling hills of active farm area, 5 kilometers from Kurtköy ("Wolf Village") and 35 kilometers to the east of Istanbul. **Campus:** 200 acres. **Library:** 6,000 volumes. **Facilities:** 10 buildings, 40 classrooms, 2 auditoriums, 2 cafeterias, infirmary, covered play area, 2 tennis courts, gymnasium, 2 playing fields, 4 science labs, 2 computer labs, canteen, music room, bookstore, art room. **Boarding facilities:** 2 four-story buildings with dormitory, study, recreational areas/facilities, and supervisors' apartments.

**Turkish lira

ROBERT COLLEGE OF ISTANBUL

Phone: (90)(1)2653430   **Facsimile:** (90)(1)2575443/2572146
     Cable: ROBCOLL, ISTANBUL
Mail: P.K. 1, Arnavutkoy 80820, Istanbul, Turkey
U.S. mail: 850 Third Avenue, New York, NY 10022, U.S.A.
Headmaster: Christopher Wadsworth
Turkish assistant head: Mehmet Camoglu
Upper school principal: Ayfer Yenicag
Middle school principal: George Damon
Business manager: Umran Uras
Staff: full-time, 85; part-time, 4
Nationalities of staff: U.S., 33; U.K., 11; host, 36; other, 9
Grade levels: 7 – 12

Enrollment: 7 – 9, 515; 10 – 12, 419; total, 934
Nationalities of student body: U.S., 5; host, 922; other, 7
Capacity: 7 – 9, 515; 10 – 12, 419; total, 934
Teacher/student ratio: 1/11
Boarders (host students only): boys, 109; girls, 82   **Grades:** 7 – 12
   Program: planned 5-day
Tuition (annual): 34,000,000 – 44,200,000**
Other fees (annual): boarding, 17,850,000 – 34,000,000**; lunch, 30,000/
   meal; books, 2,500,000
School year: September to June

Year founded: 1863. **Type of school:** coed, day, boarding, private
nonprofit. **Governed by:** Turkish Ministry of Education. **Sponsored by:** board
of trustees. **Accredited by:** NYSAIS.

Curriculum
Type: U.S., Turkish. **Languages of instruction:** English, Turkish.
Languages taught: French, German. **Staff specialists:** counselor, nurse,
part-time physician. **Special programs:** ESL, advanced placement. **Special
curricular:** art, physical education, computer instruction. **Extracurricular:**
drama, instrumental music, computers, yearbook, newspaper, literary magazine, photography, excursions/expeditions, field trips. **Sports:** basketball,
soccer, tennis, track, volleyball. **Clubs:** braille, social service, folklore. **Tests:**
PSAT, SAT, ACT, TOEFL, AP. **Graduates attending college:** 100%. **Graduates have attended:** Bryn Mawr, MIT, Harvard, Stanford, Cornell.

Physical plant
Location: 5 miles up the Bosphorus on wooded, hilly site near residential
area, Arnavutkoy. **Campus:** 60 acres. **Library:** more than 30,000 volumes.
Facilities: 10 buildings, 55 classrooms, auditorium, cafeteria, infirmary,
covered play area, tennis courts, gymnasium, playing field, science lab,
computer lab, 2 dormitories.

**Turkish lira

ÜSKÜDAR AMERICAN ACADEMY
Street address: Vakif Sok. 16 Baglarbasi, Istanbul, Turkey
Phone: (90)(1)3106823   **Facsimile:** (90)(1)3331818
Mail: 81130 Baglarbasi, Üsküdar, Istanbul, Turkey
Principal: John Heard
Turkish director: Esin Hoyi
Business manager: Ali Sirin
Staff: full-time, 38; part-time, 16
Nationalities of staff: U.S., 22; U.K., 5; host, 26; other, 3
Grade levels: 6 – 12
Enrollment: total, 670
Teacher/student ratio: 1/14

Tuition (annual, for Turkish students): 6 – 12, $2,900
Other fees (annual): tuition includes English textbooks and student fees; lunch, uniforms, and daily buses are extra
School year: September to June

Year founded: 1876. **Type of school:** coed, day. **Governed by:** American and Turkish board. **Sponsored by:** American Mission Board (ABH). **Accredited by:** Turkish Ministry of Education.

Curriculum/physical plant
Type: U.S., Turkish. **Languages of instruction:** English, Turkish. **Languages taught:** English, French, German. **Staff specialists:** computer, counselor, nurse, librarian. **Special programs:** ESL. **Special curricular:** art, chorus, physical education, computer instruction, math contests. **Extracurricular:** drama, computers, yearbook, literary magazine, excursions/expeditions, speech/debate, social service. **Sports:** basketball, track, volleyball, table tennis, gymnastics, handball. **Clubs:** art, folklore, Model UN. **Tests:** PSAT, SAT, TOEFL. **Graduates attending college:** 99%. **Graduates have attended:** Istanbul U., Marmara U., Cornell, MIT, Bosphorus U. **Location:** in Istanbul, on Asian side of Bosphorus. **Library:** 18,000 volumes. **Facilities:** 9 buildings, 27 classrooms, auditorium, cafeteria, infirmary, gymnasium, playing field, 4 science labs, 2 computer labs, canteen, faculty housing.

IZMIR

Izmir American Collegiate Institute
Phone: (90)(51)153401   **Facsimile:** (90)(51)461674
   Telex: 82152590 IG TX TR 235   **Cable:** AMERICOL
Mail: Inonu Caddesi 476, 35290 Goztepe, Izmir, Turkey
U.S. mail: Friends of American Board Schools in Turkey, 850 Third Avenue, 18th Floor, New York, NY 10022, U.S.A.
U.S. phone and facsimile: (1)(617)2321617
Principal: (to be announced)
Turkish first vice-principal: Alpaslan Ozbay
Upper school vice-principal: Bercis Togulga
Middle school vice-principal: Betsy Cakir
Prep school vice-principal: Elizabeth Orbasli
Foreign faculty coordinator: Linda Aytan
Business manager: Sadan Tutüncü
Staff: full-time, 95; part-time, 6
Nationalities of staff: U.S., 34; U.K., 9; host, 57; other, 1
Grade levels: preparatory, 7 – 12
Enrollment: prep, 144; 7 – 9, 444; 10 – 12, 630; total, 1,218
Nationalities of student body: U.S., 7; host, 1,210; other, 1

Teacher/student ratio: 1/12
Tuition (annual): $4,000 (paid in Turkish lira)
School year: September to June

Year founded: 1878. **Type of school:** coed, day, private nonprofit. **Governed by:** Turkish Ministry of Education. **Sponsored by:** United Church Board for World Ministries of the United Church of Christ. **Accredited by:** Turkish Ministry of Education; New England (in process); ECIS (in process).

Curriculum/physical plant

Type: U.S., Turkish. **Languages of instruction:** English, Turkish. **Languages taught:** French, German. **Staff specialists:** counselor, nurse, doctor. **Special programs:** advanced placement. **Special curricular:** art, chorus, physical education, computer instruction. **Extracurricular:** drama, dance, computers, yearbook, newspaper, photography, social service, 96 various clubs and committees. **Sports:** basketball, soccer, tennis, track, volleyball. **Tests:** PSAT, SAT, ACT, TOEFL, AP. **Graduates attending college:** 100%. **Graduates have attended:** MIT, Wellesley, Cornell, Yale, Middle East Technical U. **Location:** in urban area called Goztepe, overlooking Izmir Bay. **Campus:** 11 acres. **Library:** 22,000 volumes. **Facilities:** 10 buildings, 45 classrooms, auditorium, cafeteria, infirmary, tennis court, gymnasium, playing field, 5 science labs, computer lab, library, amphitheater, vollyball/basketball courts, typing room, video room, 2 art rooms, music room, lounges.

TARSUS

TARSUS AMERICAN SCHOOL

Street address: 64 Cengiz Topel Caddesi, Tarsus 33401, Turkey
Phone: (90)(761)41198/42674/44140/31661 – 2
   Facsimile: (90)(761)46347
Mail: P.K. 6, Tarsus 33401, Turkey
Director: Richard C. Conrath
Turkish vice-principal: Jale Sever
Foreign vice-principal: Marjorie Osier
Academic dean: Mina Moatazedi
Deans: prep, Feyyaz Yardim; middle school, Beverly Agler, Ed.D.; high school, Ali Karamik
Business manager: Kemal Tarim
Staff: full-time, 55; part-time, 5
Nationalities of staff: U.S., 25; host, 29; other, 6
Grade levels: preparatory, 7 – 12

Enrollment: prep, 120; 7 – 9, 360; 10 – 12, 360; total, 840
Nationalities of student body: host, 835; other, 5
Teacher/student ratio: 1/15
Tuition (annual): 30,000,000**
Other fees (annual): lunch, 2,000,000**; book rental, 350,000 – 450,000; other, 300,000
School year: September to June

Year founded: 1888. **Type of school:** coed, day, private nonprofit. **Governed by:** appointed board of governors. **Sponsored by:** United Church Board for World Ministries. **Accredited by:** Turkish Ministry of Education.

Curriculum

Type: U.S., Turkish. **Languages of instruction:** English, Turkish for Turkish cultural subjects. **Languages taught:** French, German. **Staff specialists:** psychologist, counselors, doctor. **Special curricular:** art, physical education, computer instruction, music. **Extracurricular:** drama, computers, yearbook, newspaper, photography, excursions/expeditions, speech, Model UN, social service club, sports, folk dance, library club, various other clubs. **Sports:** basketball, soccer, tennis, track, volleyball. **Tests:** SAT, AFS. **Graduates attending college:** 95%. **Graduates have attended:** major Turkish, U.S., and European universities.

Physical plant

Location: in central Tarsus. **Campus:** 4 acres. **Library:** 18,000 volumes. **Facilities:** 11 buildings, 26 classrooms, auditorium, infirmary, 4 science labs, 2 computer labs, dining room, art room, music room, counseling center, sports fields, volleyball/basketball/tennis courts, canteen, lounges, faculty living quarters.

**Turkish lira

UGANDA

Region: Africa
Size: 93,354 square miles
Population: 18,690,000
Capital: Kampala

Telephone code: 256
Currency: shilling
Languages: English, Luganda, Swahili

KAMPALA

LINCOLN INTERNATIONAL SCHOOL

Street address: 41 Kira Road Close, Kampala, Uganda
Phone: (256)(41)254900   **Facsimile:** (256)(41)243328
    Telex: 97362119 USEMBY
Mail: PO Box 4200, Kampala, Uganda
U.S. mail: c/o U.S. Embassy Kampala, Department of State, Washington, D.C. 20521-2190
Principal: Margaret Bell
Administrative assistant: Marjorie Moray
Staff: full-time, 29; part-time, 7
Nationalities of staff: U.S., 8; U.K., 18; host, 5; other, 5
Grade levels: preK – 10
Enrollment: preK, 60; K, 24; 1 – 6, 177; 7 – 10, 61; total, 322
Nationalities of student body: U.S., 63; U.K., 67; host, 32; other, 160
Capacity: preK, 65; K, 40; 1 – 5, 150; 6 – 10, 125; total, 380
Teacher/student ratio: 1/10
Tuition (annual): preK, $2,163; K, $5,115; 1 – 5, $5,843; 6 – 10, $6,789
Other fees: capital levy: preK, $1,000; K – 10, $2,500
School year: September to June

Year founded: 1966. **Type of school:** coed, day, private nonprofit. **Governed by:** elected board of management. **Accredited by:** Middle States, ECIS.

Curriculum/physical plant

Type: U.S., U.K. **Languages taught:** French. **Staff specialists:** reading, math, computer, art, music, physical education, history, geography, science, personal development, tutoring, drama, local cultural studies. **Special curricular:** art, chorus, physical education, computer instruction, lifeskills, community service, class meetings. **Extracurricular:** drama, choral music, yearbook, field trips. **Sports:** basketball, soccer, softball, swimming, volleyball, table tennis, martial arts. **Clubs:** student council, wildlife, camping, archery, guitar, weaving, pottery, sailing on nearby Lake Victoria, silk-screen, dance, leather work. **Tests:** Iowa (on request), IGCSE (optional). **Location:** in quiet, pleasant rural setting, 1 kilometer from Kampala city center. **Campus:** 4 acres. **Library:** 9,000 volumes. **Facilities:** 5 connected buildings, 14 classrooms, 2 playing fields, science lab, computer lab, covered play area and multi-purpose hall, tarmac basketball pitch, use of swimming pool.

UNITED ARAB EMIRATES _____

Region: Middle East
Size: 32,000 square miles
Population: 2,389,000
Capital: Abu Dhabi

Telephone code: 971
Currency: dirham
Languages: Arabic, several others

ABU DHABI

AL AIN ENGLISH SPEAKING SCHOOL

Phone: (971)(3)678636   **Facsimile:** (971)(3)671973
Mail: PO Box 1419, Al Ain, Abu Dhabi, United Arab Emirates
Principal: James G. Crawford
Assistant principal: Gillian Didcott
Staff: full-time, 22
Nationalities of staff: U.K., 18; other, 4
Grade levels: N – 7
Enrollment: N, 27; reception – 2, 79; 3 – 7, 90; total, 196
Nationalities of student body: U.S., 25; U.K., 54; other, 117
Capacity: K, 70; 1 – 7, 130; total, 200
Teacher/student ratio: 1/9
Tuition: N, 7,870**; reception – 2, 12,190; 3 – 7, 12,620 – 14,440
School year: September to June

Year founded: 1978. **Type of school:** coed, day, company sponsored.
Governed by: board of governors. **Sponsored by:** D. Balfour & Sons.
Accredited by: U.A.E. Ministry of Education.

Curriculum/physical plant
Type: U.S., U.K. **Languages taught:** French, Arabic. **Special programs:**
ESL, remedial. **Extracurricular:** gymnastics, choral music, instrumental
music, computers, newspaper. **Sports:** football, rugby, rounders, netball,
athletics. **Clubs:** doll making, pinatas, board games. **Tests:** various standard-
ized tests. **Location:** in suburban Al Ain at edge of desert. **Campus:** 80,000
square meters. **Library:** 2,000 volumes. **Facilities:** 8 buildings, 10 classrooms, auditorium, 2 covered play areas, playing fields, air conditioning.

**U.A.E. dirham

AMERICAN COMMUNITY SCHOOL OF ABU DHABI

Phone: (971)(2)661461/666385/660938   **Facsimile:** (971)(2)653234
Mail: PO Box 4005, Abu Dhabi, United Arab Emirates
Superintendent: James M. Ambrose
High school principal: John Hackworth
Elementary principal: Dixie Stanton
Staff: full-time, 42; part-time, 12
Nationalities of staff: U.S., 36; U.K., 6; other, 12
Grade levels: preK – 12
Enrollment: preK, 27; K, 30; 1 – 6, 244; 7 – 8, 86; 9 – 12, 116; total, 503
Nationalities of student body: U.S., 221; U.K., 30; host, 18; other, 234
Capacity: preK, 32; K, 32; 1 – 6, 268; 7 – 12, 242; total, 574
Teacher/student ratio: 1/10
Tuition (annual): K, $2,861 – 3,406; 1 – 6, $5,858; 7 – 8, $6,294;
    9 – 12, $8,038
Other fees (annual): admission, $681
School year: September to June

Year founded: 1971. **Type of school:** coed, day, private nonprofit.
Governed by: elected board of trustees. **Sponsored by:** Ministry of Education.
Accredited by: Middle States.

Curriculum/physical plant
Type: U.S. **Languages taught:** French, Arabic. **Staff specialists:** computer, counselor, art, ESL, music, physical education. **Special programs:** ESL. **Special curricular:** art, chorus, physical education, computer instruction, Model UN. **Extracurricular:** drama, choral music, computers, yearbook, newspaper, photography, excursions/expeditions, field trips, math league, fine arts festival, academic games. **Sports:** basketball, soccer, softball, swimming, tennis, volleyball, badminton. **Clubs:** art, Arabic, service, Girl Scouts, Boy Scouts, computers. **Tests:** SSAT, PSAT, SAT, Iowa, COGAT. **Location:** within city. **Library:** 13,000 volumes. **Facilities:** 1 building (6 sections), 39 classrooms, cafeteria, covered play area, gymnasium, playing field, swimming pool, tennis courts, science labs, computer rooms, media center, air conditioning.

DUBAI

THE AMERICAN SCHOOL OF DUBAI†

Phone: (971)(4)440824   **Facsimile:** (971)(4)441510
Telex: 95845423 DPC EM   **Cable:** DUPETCO – Dubai
Mail: PO Box 2222, Dubai, United Arab Emirates
Headmaster: Roger G. Hove
Principal, 7 – 12: Greg L. Von Spreecken
Principal, K – 6: Bruce W. McWilliams
Staff: full-time, 73; part-time, 5
Nationalities of staff: U.S., 65; other, 13
Grade levels: preK – 12
Enrollment: preK, 52; K, 56; 1 – 6, 361; 7 – 9, 137; 10 – 12, 57; total, 663
Nationalities of student body: U.S., 408; U.K., 27; host, 2; other, 226
Capacity: preK, 52; K, 60; 1 – 6, 420; 7 – 9, 150; 10 – 12, 150; total, 832
Teacher/student ratio: 1/9
Tuition (annual): preK, $1,945; K, $5,497; 1 – 12, $8,300
Other fees (annual): registration*, $68; books, $27 (deposit); seat rental, $1,525 – 3,050
School year: August to June

Year founded: 1966. **Type of school:** coed, day, private nonprofit. **Governed by:** board of trustees. **Accredited by:** Middle States.

Curriculum
Type: U.S. **Languages taught:** French, Spanish, Arabic. **Staff specialists:** reading, math, computer, counselor, learning disabilities. **Special programs:** ESL, advanced placement, remedial. **Special curricular:** art, chorus, physical education, computer instruction, instrumental music. **Extracurricular:** drama, gymnastics, choral music, computers, yearbook, literary magazine, excursions/expeditions, field trips, band, Model UN. **Sports:** baseball, basketball, soccer, softball, swimming, tennis, volleyball, T-ball, roller skating. **Organizations**: National Junior Honor Society, National Honor Society, parents' organization. **Tests:** SSAT, PSAT, SAT, ACT, TOEFL, ACH.

Physical plant
Location: in suburban area, 15 minutes from Dubai. **Campus:** 8 acres. **Library:** 22,500 volumes. **Facilities:** 3 buildings, 55 classrooms, small auditorium, 2 tennis courts, 2 gymnasiums, 2 playing fields, 4 science labs, 3 computer labs, swimming pool, cafeteria, first-aid station, drama room, 2 art rooms, journalism room, video production room, fitness center, air conditioning.

*Once only fee   †formerly The Jumairah American School

EMIRATES INTERNATIONAL SCHOOL

Street address: Al Wasl Road, Dubai, United Arab Emirates
Phone: (971)(4)489804/487650   **Facsimile:** (971)(4)482586/482813
Mail: PO Box 6446, Dubai, United Arab Emirates
Headmaster: Trevor A. Williams
Principal/senior school: John Woodcock
Principal/junior school: Mary Hopkin
Staff: full-time, 60
Nationalities of staff: U.S., 15; U.K., 25; host, 10; other, 10
Grade levels: K – 12
Enrollment: total, 850
Capacity: K, 90; 1 – 12, 1,500; total, 1,590
Teacher/student ratio: 1/14
Tuition (annual): K, 7,500**; 1 – 12, 8,500 – 25,000
School year: September through June

Year founded: 1991. **Type of school:** coed, day, private nonprofit.

Curriculum/physical plant

Type: U.S., U.K. **Languages taught:** French, Spanish, Arabic. **Staff specialists:** nurse, ESL, special needs. **Special curricular:** art, physical education, computer instruction. **Extracurricular:** drama, gymnastics, dance, choral music, instrumental music, yearbook, excursions/expeditions, field trips, sports. **Location:** in suburban area, 20 kilometers from center of Dubai, 5 kilometers from Jumairah. **Campus:** 10 acres. **Facilities:** 5 buildings, 65 classrooms, 2 auditoriums, infirmary, covered/open play area, theater, 7 science labs, library/media center, sports hall, dining hall, specialist art/craft/CDT workshops, music rooms, air conditioning.

**U.A.E. dirham

JUMEIRAH ENGLISH SPEAKING SCHOOL†

Phone: (971)(4)381515   **Facsimile:** (971)(4)381531
Mail: PO Box 24942, Dubai, United Arab Emirates
Headmistress: R. Biro (Lane)
Staff: full-time, 31; part-time, 8
Nationalities of staff: U.K., 34; other, 5
Grade levels: K – 6
Enrollment: K, 75; 1 – 6, 450; total, 525
Nationalities of student body: U.S., 10; U.K., 405; host, 5; other, 105
Teacher/student ratio: 1/15
Tuition (annual): K – 6, 14,400**
Other fees: entrance/registration/capital levy*, 10,350**
School year: September to June

Year founded: 1976. **Type of school:** coed, day, private nonprofit. **Governed by:** board of governors. **Accredited by:** HMI (U.K.).

Curriculum/physical plant
Type: U.K. **Languages taught:** French, Arabic. **Staff specialists:** learning disabilities, nurse. **Special programs:** remedial. **Special curricular:** chorus, band, physical education, computer instruction. **Extracurricular:** drama, gymnastics, dance, choral music, instrumental music, computers, literary magazine, excursions/expeditions, field trips. **Sports:** football, swimming, tennis, netball, gymnastics, cricket, athletics. **Location:** 10 kilometers from Dubai City. **Library:** 3,000 volumes. **Facilities:** 25 classrooms, tennis court, gymnasium, 2 playing fields, swimming pool, air conditioning.

*Once only fee   **U.A.E. dirham
†Member of Incorporated Association of Preparatory Schools

SHARJAH

INTERNATIONAL SCHOOL OF CHOUEIFAT
Phone: (971)(6)582211   **Facsimile:** (971)(6)582865
  Telex: 95868050 EM SCHOOL
Mail: PO Box 2077, Sharjah, United Arab Emirates
Director: Dorothy Miles, MBE
Deputy director: Mr. J. Hazbun
Business director: Mr. E. Sawaya
Staff: full-time, 84
Nationalities of staff: U.S., 6; U.K., 46; other, 32
Grade levels: N – 13, EFL department
Enrollment: N – preK, 55; K, 90; 1 – 6, 708; 7 – 9, 420; 10 – 12, 288;
  13, 23; EFL, 56; total, 1,640
Nationalities of student body: U.S., 36; U.K., 80; host, 203; other, 1,321
Capacity: N – preK, 60; K, 100; 1 – 6, 780; 7 – 9, 450; 10 – 12, 365;
  13, 70; EFL, 105; total, 1,930
Teacher/student ratio: 1/19
Tuition (annual): N – K, 11,400**; 1 – 6, 11,400 – 13,600; 7 – 9,
  14,500 – 16,200; 10 – 12, 17,000 – 18,000; 13, 18,900
Other fees (annual): busing, 2,000 – 3,000**; lunch, 4,200; books,
  200 – 600
School year: September to June†

Year founded: 1886. **Type of school:** coed, day. **Governed by:** Choueifat Schools. **Accredited by:** London University/IBO/Cambridge.

Curriculum
Type: U.K., IB. **Languages taught:** English, French, Arabic. **Staff specialists:** reading, math, computer, counselor, nurse. **Special programs:** ESL. **Special curricular:** art, band, physical education, computer instruction, vocational, choirs. **Extracurricular:** gymnastics, dance, choral music, instrumental music, computers, photography, excursions/expeditions, field trips,

pottery. **Sports:** basketball, hockey, soccer, swimming, squash, badminton, cricket, netball, table tennis. **Clubs:** video, chess, astronomy, computer, aerobics, gymnastics, trampolining, photography, music, art, student council. **Tests:** SAT, TOEFL, IB, AP, GCSE, ACH, A-, AS- and O-levels, IGCSE, STEP. **Graduates attending college:** 99%. **Graduates have attended:** MIT, U. of Pennsylvania, Tufts, London School of Economics, McGill.

Physical plant
    Location: in suburbs, 3 miles from center of Sharjah. **Campus:** 76 acres. **Library:** 12,000 volumes. **Facilities:** 21 buildings, 60 classrooms, auditorium, cafeteria, infirmary, tennis court, gymnasium, 3 science labs, 2 computer labs, swimming pool, covered play areas, AV equipment, squash court, cricket pitch, air conditioning.

**U.A.E. dirham   †Summer school: mid-June to August

ABU DHABI
Al Sanawbar School
    Address: PO Box 1781, Al Ain, United Arab Emirates
    Phone: (971)(3)679889   **Facsimile:** (971)(3)679885
    Telex: 94934006 HEKMA EM
International School of Choueifat
    Address: PO Box 7212, Abu Dhabi, United Arab Emirates
    Phone: (971)(2)461444   **Facsimile:** (971)(2)461048

RAS AL KHAIMAH
Ras Al Khaimah English Speaking School
    Address: PO Box 975, Ras Al Khaimah, United Arab Emirates
    Phone: (971)(7)352441
    Head teacher: Deryck Michael Wilson

UNITED KINGDOM ───────────────

Region: Europe
Size: 94,226 square miles
Population: 55,486,800
Capital: London

Telephone code: 44
Currency: pound
Languages: English, Welsh, Gaelic

ENGLAND/LONDON

THE AMERICAN SCHOOL IN LONDON

Street address: 2-8 Loudoun Road, London NW8 0NP, England
Phone: (44)(71)7220101   **Facsimile:** (44)(71)5866885
  Cable: AMSCHOOL LONDON NW 8
Head of school: Judith R. Glickman, Ph.D.
High school principal: Clayton W. Lewis
Middle school principal: Jim Slemp
Lower school principal: (to be announced)
Head of library: Joan Dyer-Westacott
Head of computers: John Servente
Business manager: Alan D. Walker
Staff: full-time, 138; part-time, 12
Nationalities of staff: U.S., 123; U.K., 21; other, 6
Grade levels: preK – 12 (grade 13 available)
Enrollment: preK, 34; K, 57; 1 – 5, 379; 6 – 8, 334; 9 – 12, 452;
  total, 1,256
Nationalities of student body: U.S., 924; U.K., 37; other, 295
Capacity: preK, 40; K, 60; 1 – 5, 420; 6 – 8, 360; 9 – 12, 520; total, 1,400
Teacher/student ratio: 1/9
Tuition (annual): preK – 5, 7,000**; 6 – 8, 7,700; 9 – 13, 8,000
Other fees (annual): registration*, 75**; busing, at cost; lunch, at cost;
  tuition deposit, 400
School year: September to June

Year founded: 1951. **Type of school:** coed, day, private nonprofit.
Governed by: The American School in London Educational Trust Ltd.
Accredited by: Middle States, ECIS.

Curriculum
Type: U.S. **Languages taught:** French, Spanish, German. **Staff specialists:** reading, math, computer, speech/hearing, counselor, psychologist, learning disabilities, nurse, language pathologist. **Special programs:** advanced placement, independent study, lower and middle school ESL, learning disabilities, senior apprenticeships. **Special curricular:** art, chorus, band, strings, physical education, computer instruction, drama, photography, yearbook, newspaper, excursions/expeditions. **Extracurricular:** drama, literary magazine, gymnastics, dance, choral music, instrumental music, computers, Model UN, student council. **Sports:** baseball, basketball, field hockey, rugby, soccer, softball, swimming, tennis, track, volleyball, cross-

country, wrestling, gymnastics. **Clubs:** computer, juggling, Amnesty International, task force, film, theater, debate, fencing, weight training, table tennis, hiking. **Tests:** PSAT, SAT, ACT, AP, Stanford, Iowa. **Graduates attending college:** 95%. **Graduates have attended:** Boston U., Brown, Georgetown, Tufts, Duke.

Physical plant

Location: in pleasant residential area of central London. **Campus:** 3.5 acres. **Library:** 50,000 volumes. **Facilities:** 1 building, 75 classrooms, auditorium, cafeteria, infirmary, 3 tennis courts, 2 gymnasiums, 8 science labs, 3 computer labs, 5 music rooms, 5 art studios, AV equipment, air conditioning.

*Once only fee   **Pound sterling

SOUTHBANK INTERNATIONAL SCHOOL

Street address: 36/38 Kensington Park Road, London W11 3BU,
   England
Phone: (44)(71)2298230   **Facsimile:** (44)(71)2293784
Headmaster: Milton E. Toubkin
High school coordinator: Nigel Hughes
Middle/lower school principal: Jane Treftz
Staff: full-time, 30; part-time, 23
Nationalities of staff: U.S., 14; U.K., 19; other, 20
Grade levels: K – 13
Enrollment: K – 6, 48; 7 – 9, 64; 10 – 12, 128; 13, 20; total, 260
Nationalities of student body: U.S., 30; U.K., 55; other, 175
Teacher/student ratio: 1/6
Tuition (annual): K – 5, 6,930**; 6 – 8, 7,560; 9 – 11, 7,920; 12 – 13, 8,550
Other fees: registration*, 50**; capital levy*, 500
School year: September to June

Year founded: 1979. **Type of school:** coed, day, private nonprofit. **Governed by:** board of directors. **Accredited by:** Independent Schools Joint Council.

Curriculum/physical plant

Type: U.S., U.K., IB. **Languages taught:** French, Spanish, German, Italian, Japanese, Swedish, plus 10 others by demand. **Special programs:** ESL. **Special curricular:** art, physical education, computer instruction, drama, music. **Extracurricular:** drama, dance, instrumental music, computers, yearbook, newspaper, photography, excursions/expeditions, field trips, Model UN, ISTA. **Sports:** basketball, soccer, swimming, tennis, volleyball, badminton, ice skating. **Tests:** PSAT, SAT, ACT, TOEFL, IB, GCSE. **Graduates attending college:** 97%. **Graduates have attended:** London, Oxford, Harvard, Princeton. **Location:** in central London, near Notting Hill Gate. **Facilities:** 3 buildings, 16 classrooms, auditorium, cafeteria, 4 science labs, computer center, music and art rooms.

*Once only fee   **Pound sterling

HILLINGDON, MIDDLESEX

AMERICAN COMMUNITY SCHOOL

Street address: 108 Vine Lane, Hillingdon, Uxbridge,
Middlesex UB10 OBE, England
Phone: (44)(895)259771   **Facsimile:** (44)(895)256974
Telex: 851886645 ACS G
Superintendent: Peter Hlozek
Headmaster: Brian Duncan
High school principal: Susan Masters
Middle school principal: Paul Berg
Lower school principal: Tony Pearson
Academic dean: Barbara Prechek
Staff: full-time, 67; part-time, 9
Nationalities of staff: U.S., 38; U.K., 29; other, 9
Grade levels: preK – 12 (grade 13 available)
Enrollment: preK – 4, 198; 5 – 8, 157; 9 – 13, 192; total, 547
Nationalities of student body: U.S., 234; U.K., 28; other, 285
Capacity: preK – 4, 212; 5 – 8, 160; 9 – 13, 227; total, 599
Teacher/student ratio: 1/8
Tuition (annual): preK, 3,200** (half day), 4,580 (full day); K – 4, 6,530;
5 – 8, 7,140; 9 – 13, 7,500
Other fees (annual): registration*, 75**; busing, 1,130; debenture sub-
scription*, 500
School year: August to June

Year founded: 1967. **Type of school:** coed, day. **Governed by:** board of
directors. **Accredited by:** New England.

Curriculum

Type: U.S., IB. **Languages taught:** French, Spanish, German. **Staff
specialists:** nurse, speech therapist (lower school), study skills (middle
school), counselors (high school). **Special programs:** ESL. **Special curricular:** art, band, physical education, computer instruction, choir. **Extracurricular:** drama, gymnastics, instrumental music, computers, yearbook, newspaper, photography, excursions/expeditions, field trips, cheerleading. **Sports:**

basketball, rugby, soccer, softball, swimming, tennis, volleyball, track and field, cross-country. **Clubs:** Model UN, National Honor Society, student council, Boy Scouts, Girl Scouts, art. **Tests:** PSAT, SAT, ACT, TOEFL, IB, ACH. **Graduates attending college:** 95%. **Graduates have attended:** Georgetown, Duke, Purdue, Harvard, Princeton.

Physical plant
Location: in suburbs, 15 miles northwest of London. **Campus:** 11 acres. **Libraries:** 22,600 volumes. **Facilities:** 8 buildings, 55 classrooms, cafeteria, infirmary, 2 tennis courts, 3 science labs, auditorium/gymnasium, playing fields, computer labs, art and music rooms.

*Once only fee   **Pound sterling

COBHAM, SURREY

AMERICAN COMMUNITY SCHOOL

Street address: "Heywood," Portsmouth Road, Cobham,
   Surrey KT11 1BL, England
Phone: (44)(932)867251   **Facsimile:** (44)(932)866694
   Telex: 851886645 ACS G
Superintendent: Peter Hlozek
Headmaster: Thomas Lehman
High school principal: Malcolm Kay
Middle school principal: Ann Haynes
Academic dean: Craig Worthington
Staff: full-time, 120; part-time, 11
Nationalities of staff: U.S., 89; U.K., 30; other, 12
Grade levels: preK – 12 (grade 13 available)
Enrollment: preK, 70; K, 80; 1 – 6, 481; 7 – 9, 235; 10 – 13, 267; total, 1,133
Nationalities of student body: U.S., 691; other, 442
Capacity: preK, 80; K, 80; 1 – 6, 527; 7 – 9, 270; 10 – 13, 277; total, 1,234
Teacher/student ratio: 1/9
Boarders: boys, 51; girls, 52   **Grades:** 7 – 13   **Program:** planned 5- and 7-day
Tuition (annual): preK, 3,200** (half day), 4,580 (full day); K – 4, 6,530;
   5 – 8, 7,140; 9 – 13, 7,500
Other fees (annual): registration*, 75**; boarding, (includes tuition),
   10,830 (5-day), 12,130 (7-day); busing, 1,130; debenture*, 500
School year: August to June

Year founded: 1967. **Type of school:** coed, day, boarding, proprietary. **Governed by:** appointed board of directors. **Accredited by:** New England, Independent Schools Joint Council.

Curriculum

Type: U.S., IB. **Languages taught:** French, Spanish, German, (IB only: Danish, Japanese, Swedish, Norwegian, and others by demand). **Special curricular:** art, chorus, physical education, computer instruction. **Extracurricular:** drama, instrumental music, computers, yearbook, newspaper, photography, excursions/expeditions, field trips, community service. **Sports:** baseball, basketball, rugby, soccer, softball, tennis, volleyball, track and field, cross-country. **Clubs:** public speaking, Boy Scouts, Girl Scouts, student council, National Honor Society, Model UN, math competition teams. **Tests:** PSAT, SAT, IB, AP, ACH, ERB. **Graduates attending college:** 95%. **Graduates have attended:** U. of Pennsylvania, Duke, U. of California, Boston College.

Physical plant

Location: 25 miles southwest of London. **Campus:** 128 acres. **Libraries:** 21,094 volumes. **Facilities:** 35 buildings, 83 classrooms, 2 auditoriums, cafeteria, infirmary, 7 tennis courts, gymnasium, 6 playing fields, 8 science labs, 4 computer labs, AV equipment, outdoor Olympic-standard track, 7-hole golf course, art and music rooms, purpose-built boarding facility, new purpose-built high school.

*Once only fee　**Pound sterling

KINGSTON UPON THAMES, SURREY

MARYMOUNT INTERNATIONAL SCHOOL

Street address: George Road, Kingston upon Thames, Surrey KT2 7PE, England

Phone: (44)(81)9490571　**Facsimile:** (44)(81)3362485

Principal: Sr. Rosaleen Sheridan, RSHM

Business manager: Mr. W. D. B. Lord

Staff: full-time, 24; part-time, 4

Nationalities of staff: U.S., 5; U.K., 9; other, 14

Grade levels: 6 – 12

Enrollment: total, 205

Nationalities of student body: U.S., 23; U.K., 30; other, 152

Capacity: 6 – 9, 80; 10 – 12, 150; total, 230

Teacher/student ratio: 1/8

Boarding capacity: girls, 100　**Grades:** 6 – 12　**Program:** planned 5- and 7-day

Tuition (annual): 6 – 8, 6,450**; 9 – 12, 7,100

Other fees (annual): registration*, 100**; boarding: 5-day, 5,100; 7-day, 5,300; busing, variable; lunch, 350; books, 100; initial enrollment*, 500

School year: September to June

Year founded: 1955. **Type of school:** girls, day, boarding, church-related. **Governed by:** appointed board of trustees and board of regents. **Accredited by:** Middle States, ECIS.

Curriculum/physical plant

Type: U.S., IB. **Staff specialists:** computer, counselor, psychologist, nurse. **Special programs:** ESL. **Special curricular:** art, chorus, physical education, computer instruction. **Extracurricular:** drama, gymnastics, dance, instrumental music, yearbook, photography, excursions/expeditions, field trips, National Honor Society. **Tests:** PSAT, SAT, ACT, IB, AP. **Graduates attending college:** 98%. **Graduates have attended:** Pembroke College Oxford, Bryn Mawr, London School of Economics, Cornell, Sophia U. in Japan. **Location:** in suburban location, 12 miles from central London. **Campus:** 7 acres. **Library:** 7,000 volumes. **Facilities:** 8 buildings, 23 classrooms, auditorium, cafeteria, infirmary, 2 tennis courts, gymnasium, playing field, 3 science labs, computer lab, AV equipment, art studio, language lab, bedrooms, lounges, TV rooms, kitchenette.

*Once only fee   **Pound sterling

THORPE, SURREY

TASIS ENGLAND AMERICAN SCHOOL

Street address: Coldharbour Lane, Thorpe, Surrey TW20 8TE, England
Phone: (44)(932)565252   **Facsimile:** (44)(932)564644
U.S. mail: 326 East 69 Street, New York, NY 10021, U.S.A.
Headmaster: Lyle D. Rigg
Upper school head: Diana E. Dearth
Middle school head: Michael Popinchalk
Lower school head: Deborah Cross
Academic dean: Karl Christiansen
Staff: full-time, 72; part-time, 21
Nationalities of staff: U.S., 64; U.K., 23; other, 6
Grade levels: preK – 12
Enrollment: preK, 15; K, 30; 1 – 6, 205; 7 – 9, 160; 10 – 12, 250; total, 660
Nationalities of student body: U.S., 450; U.K., 30; other, 180
Capacity: preK, 15; K, 30; 1 – 6, 205; 7 – 9, 160; 10 – 12, 250; total, 660
Teacher/student ratio: 1/8
Boarders: boys, 75; girls, 70   **Grades:** 7 – 12   **Program:** planned 7-day
Tuition (annual): preK, 3,360**; K – 3, 6,350; 4 – 8, 6,910; 9 – 12, 7,250
Other fees (annual): registration, 30**; boarding, 4,475; capital levy*, 500; busing, 1,000; lunch, 255; books, 225; in-program travel, 900
School year: September to June

Year founded: 1976. **Type of school:** coed, day, boarding, proprietary. **Governed by:** appointed governing board. **Accredited by:** New England, ECIS.

Curriculum

Type: U.S. **Languages taught:** French, Spanish, German, Latin. **Special programs:** ESL, advanced placement, honors sections, independent study, summer school. **Special curricular:** art, chorus, physical education, computer instruction, drama. **Extracurricular:** drama, dance, choral music, instrumental music, computers, yearbook, newspaper, photography, excursions/expeditions, field trips, film, theater, community service, in-program European travel. **Sports:** aerobics, baseball, basketball, rugby, soccer, softball, tennis, volleyball, horseback riding, squash, cross-country. **Clubs:** Brownies, computer, Cub Scouts, Model UN, student council, Webelos, Junior Girl Scouts, Cum Laude Society, International Club, parents' council, chess. **Tests:** PSAT, SAT, ACT, TOEFL, AP, Stanford, ERB. **Graduates attending college:** 98%. **Graduates have attended:** Boston U., Brown, Harvard, U. of Virginia, U. of Pennsylvania.

Physical plant

Location: a Georgian country estate set in the Surrey countryside near Windsor, 18 miles southwest of London. **Campus:** 35 acres. **Library:** 15,000 volumes. **Facilities:** 10 buildings, 50 classrooms, infirmary, 6 tennis courts, gymnasium, 4 playing fields, 5 science labs, 2 computer labs, 2 dining rooms, AV equipment, study hall, art and music rooms, theater, snack bar, lounge, 12 supervised residential boarding cottages/dormitories.

*Once only fee   **Pound sterling

SCOTLAND/ABERDEEN

AMERICAN SCHOOL IN ABERDEEN

EDUCATIONAL TRUST LTD.

Street address: Secondary School: Craigton Road, Cults, Aberdeen AB1 9QD, Scotland; Elementary School: Fairgirth, North Deeside Road, Milltimber, Aberdeen AB1 0AB, Scotland

Phone: Secondary School: (44)(224)868927/867964; Elementary School: (44)(224)732267/734879   **Facsimile:** (44)(224)869753

Mail: Craigton Road, Cults, Aberdeen AB1 9QD, Scotland

Superintendent: John C. Thomas

Secondary school principal: Stephen Sibley

Elementary school principal: Eric F. Klauda

Business manager: Cyria Scott

Staff: full-time, 32; part-time, 9

Nationalities of staff: U.S., 24; U.K., 8; other, 9

Grade levels: preK – 12
Enrollment: preK, 29; K, 25; 1 – 6, 175; 7 – 9, 91; 10 – 12, 65; total, 385
Nationalities of student body: U.S., 327; other, 58
Teacher/student ratio: 1/10
Tuition (annual): 7,300**
School year: August to June

Year founded: 1972. **Type of school:** coed, day, company sponsored. **Governed by:** elected and appointed board of directors. **Sponsored by:** oil/service companies. **Accredited by:** Middle States, ECIS.

Curriculum/physical plant

Type: U.S. **Staff specialists:** reading, math, counselor, resource. **Special programs:** advanced placement, honors sections, independent study. **Special curricular:** art, physical education, computer instruction, drama, school musical. **Extracurricular:** drama, gymnastics, instrumental music, computers, yearbook, newspaper, photography, excursions/expeditions, field trips. **Sports:** basketball, soccer, volleyball. **Clubs:** AV/disco, Helping Hands, Model UN. **Graduates attending college:** 85%. **Graduates have attended:** Texas A&M, U. of Texas, Rice, Oklahoma State, U. of Washington. **Location:** in rural setting, 5 miles west of Aberdeen. **Campuses (2):** 10 acres. **Library:** 25,000 volumes. **Facilities:** 5 buildings, 30 classrooms, 2 gymnasiums, 2 playing fields, 3 science labs, 3 computer labs.

**Pound sterling

EDINBURGH

Edinburgh Tutorial College & American School

Street address: 29 Chester Street, Edinburgh EH3 7EN, Scotland
Phone: (44)(31)2259888   **Facsimile:** (44)(31)2252133
Principal: Mr. A. W. Morris
Director of studies: Mr. H. R. Chell
Staff: full-time, 5; part-time, 15
Nationalities of staff: U.K., 20
Grade levels: 9 – 12
Enrollment: 9, 5; 10, 10; 11, 10; 12, 10; total, 35
Nationalities of student body: U.S., 5; U.K., 25; other, 5
Capacity: 9, 10; 10, 10; 11, 15; 12, 15; total, 50
Teacher/student ratio: 1/3
Boarders: boys, 5; girls, 5   **Grades:** 9 – 12   **Program:** planned 5- and 7-day
Tuition (annual): 9 – 12, 5,287.50**

Other fees (annual): boarding, 3,112.50**; books, 100
School year: September to June

Year founded: 1976. **Type of school:** coed, day, boarding. **Accredited by:** Scottish Education Department.

Curriculum/physical plant

Type: U.S., U.K. **Languages taught:** French, Spanish, Italian. **Staff specialists:** reading, math, counselor. **Special programs:** ESL, advanced placement. **Special curricular:** art, computer instruction. **Extracurricular:** drama, computers, photography, field trips. **Tests:** PSAT, SAT, ACT, TOEFL, A-level GCE, GCSE, Scottish Examination Board. **Graduates attending college:** 70%. **Graduates have attended:** Edinburgh U., St. Andrews U. **Location:** in city. **Library:** 6,000 volumes. **Facilities:** 1 building, 11 classrooms, cafeteria, science lab, computer lab, AV equipment, boarding at Douglas House (2 minutes' walk from school).

**Pound sterling

WALES/GLAMORGAN

UNITED WORLD COLLEGE OF THE ATLANTIC

Street address: St. Donat's Castle, Llantwit Major, South Glamorgan, Wales
Phone: (44)(446)792530   **Facsimile:** (44)(446)794163
Principal: C. D. O. Jenkins
Director of studies: J. R. Fletcher
Staff: full-time, 40; part-time, 4
Grade levels: Form 6
Enrollment: total, 360
Nationalities of student body: U.S., 11; U.K., 90; other, 259
Capacity: total, 360
Teacher/student ratio: 1/9
Boarders: boys, 180; girls, 180   **Grades:** Form 6   **Program:** planned 7-day
Tuition and board (annual): 10,000** (most students on scholarships through National Committees)
School year: September through May

Year founded: 1962. **Type of school:** coed, boarding. **Governed by:** appointed governing body. **Sponsored by:** United World Colleges. **Accredited by:** British Department of Education and Science.

Curriculum/physical plant

Type: IB. **Languages taught:** English, French, Spanish, German, Dutch, Italian, Russian, Chinese, Norwegian. **Services:** (at least one is compulsory) life boat, coast guard, environmental monitoring, beach rescue, social service, arts center service, extramural service, estate service, construction service. **Activities:** sports, wide range of activities. **Tests:** SAT, ACT, IB. **Graduates have attended:** Cambridge, Oxford, Harvard, Princeton, Sorbonne. **Location:** 2 miles from small town, 20 miles from Cardiff. **Campus:** 200 acres. **Library:** 30,000 volumes. **Facilities:** auditorium, cafeteria, gymnasium, swimming pool, AV room, playing fields, science labs, tennis courts, social center, gardens.

**Pound sterling

LONDON

International Community School

Address: 4 York Terrace East, Regent's Park, London NW1 4PT,
England
Phone: (44)(71)9351206   **Facsimile:** (44)(71)9357915 (ref: ICS)
Telex: 851295271 SKOLA G

UNITED STATES OF AMERICA ___

Region: North America
Size: 3,618,770 square miles
Population: 248,709,873
Capital: Washington, D.C.

Telephone code: 1
Currency: U.S. dollar
Language: English

SAN FRANCISCO, CALIFORNIA

FRENCH-AMERICAN INTERNATIONAL SCHOOL

Street address: 220 Buchanan Street, San Francisco, CA, 94102-6124, U.S.A.
Phone: (1)(415)6268564   **Facsimile:** (1)(415)6268551
Headmaster: Alain Weber
Middle and high school principal: Jane Camblin
Lower school principal: Claude Farrugia
Business manager: Marcelle Urruty
Staff: full-time, 54; part-time, 10
Nationalities of staff: U.S., 25; U.K., 2; other, 37
Grade levels: preK – 12
Enrollment: preK, 23; K, 61; 1 – 6, 231; 7 – 9, 76; 10 – 12, 69; total, 460
Nationalities of student body: U.S., 277; U.K., 10; other, 173
Capacity: preK, 24; K, 54; 1 – 6, 248; 7 – 9, 105; 10 – 12, 120; total, 551
Teacher/student ratio: 1/8
Tuition (annual): preK – K, $6,875; 1 – 5, $7,300 (average); 6 – 7, $7,800 (average); 8, $8,565; 9, $8,785; 10 – 11, $9,200 (average); 12, $9,410
Other fees: enrollment*, $250; deposit, $150
School year: September to June

Year founded: 1962. **Type of school:** coed, day, nondenominational. **Governed by:** elected board of directors. **Accredited by:** Western, French Ministry of National Education, California Association of Independent Schools.

Curriculum

Type: U.S., French Baccalaureate, IB. **Languages of instruction:** English, French. **Languages taught:** Spanish, German, Mandarin. **Staff specialists:** math, computer, counselor, art, music, drama, physical education. **Special programs:** ESL, advanced placement, remedial, FSL. **Special curricular:** art, physical education, computer instruction, drama, music. **Extracurricular:** drama, gymnastics, dance, instrumental music, computers, yearbook, photography, field trips, film. **Sports:** basketball, soccer, swimming, volleyball, aikido. **Clubs:** drama, photography, student government. **Tests:** PSAT, SAT, IB, AP, ERB, CTBS, French Baccalaureate. **Graduates attending college:** 100%. **Graduates have attended:** Yale, Stanford, Oxford, U. of California campuses, Georgetown.

Physical plant
 Location: central San Francisco. **Campus:** 50,000 square feet. **Library:** 14,000 volumes. **Facilities:** 2 buildings, 30 classrooms, auditorium, gymnasium, 3 recreational areas, 2 science labs, computer lab, play area, art room, music/theater room.

*Once only fee

WASHINGTON, D.C.

WASHINGTON INTERNATIONAL SCHOOL
 Street address: 3100 Macomb Street, NW, Washington, DC 20008, U.S.A.
 Phone: (1)(202)3641815   **Facsimile:** (1)(202)3644940
 Head of school: Anne-Marie Pierce
 Upper school principal: David Merkel
 Intermediate school principal: Sonja Cowie
 Lower school principal: Tina Thuermer
 Staff: full-time, 91; part-time, 29
 Grade levels: N – 12
 Enrollment: N – preK, 52; K, 45; 1 – 6, 282; 7 – 9, 145; 10 – 12, 131; total, 655
 Nationalities of student body: U.S., 270; U.K., 48; other, 337
 Capacity: N – preK, 47; K, 48; 1 – 6, 280; 7 – 9, 145; 10 – 12, 135; total, 655
 Teacher/student ratio: 1/6
 Tuition (annual): N – preK, $5,000 (half-day), $7,500 (full-day); K – 5, $9,050; 6 – 12, $10,500
 Other fees (annual): busing, $415 – 830; books, $200 – 500; science, $50 – 100; activity, $65 – 80; application*, $40; IB*, $700 (average)
 School year: September to June

 Year founded: 1966. **Type of school:** coed, day, private nonprofit. **Governed by:** appointed board of trustees. **Accredited by:** Middle States, ECIS.

Curriculum/physical plant
 Type: IB, international. **Languages of instruction:** English, French, Spanish. **Languages taught:** French, Spanish, Latin (3 years), Dutch (4 – 12). **Special programs:** ESL, advanced placement (languages). **Special curricular:** art, chorus, physical education, computer instruction, debating, music, public speaking. **Extracurricular:** drama, choral music, instrumental music, yearbook, newspaper, literary magazine, excursions/expeditions, field trips, Model UN, mock trial competitions, Model OAS. **Sports:** basketball, soccer, softball, tennis, track, volleyball. **Tests:** PSAT, SAT, TOEFL, IB, AP (languages), ERB. **Graduates attending college:** 99%. **Graduates have attended:** Stanford, Cornell, McGill, London School of Economics, universities

in Netherlands, Norway, Australia, and France. **Campuses (2):** Cleveland Park, 6 acres; Georgetown, 1.5 acres. **Libraries:** 17,000 volumes. **Facilities:** 8 buildings, 80 classrooms, playing field, 6 science labs, 3 computer labs, basketball court, assembly hall, partial air conditioning.

*Once only fee

ATLANTA, GEORGIA

ATLANTA INTERNATIONAL SCHOOL

Street address: 4820 Long Island Drive, Atlanta, GA 30342, U.S.A.
Phone: (1)(404)8433380   **Facsimile:** (1)(404)2520584
Director: Alex Horsley
Head, middle/upper school: Eugene Stevelberg
Head, lower school: Andrew Hill
Business manager: Richard Gillen
Staff: full-time, 50; part-time, 8
Nationalities of staff: U.S., 25; U.K., 8; other, 25
Grade levels: preK – 12
Enrollment: preK, 35; K, 45; 1 – 6, 215; 7 – 12, 195; total, 490
Nationalities of student body: U.S., 210; U.K., 40; other, 240
Capacity: preK, 35; K, 45; 1 – 6, 215; 7 – 12, 220; total, 515
Teacher/student ratio: 1/9
Tuition (annual): preK – K, $6,350; 1 – 5, $6,675; 6 – 8, $7,350; 9 – 10, $7,800; 11 – 12, $8,200
Other fees (annual): registration*, $100; books, $300 (middle/upper school)
School year: September to June

Year founded: 1984. **Type of school:** coed, day. **Governed by:** elected board of trustees. **Accredited by:** Southern, ECIS, French Ministry of Education, International Baccalaureate Organization.

Curriculum/physical plant
Type: U.S., IB, French, German. **Languages of instruction:** English, French, Spanish, German. **Languages taught:** Latin. **Special programs:** ESL. **Special curricular:** art, chorus, band, physical education, computer instruction. **Extracurricular:** drama, instrumental music, yearbook, newspaper, field trips. **Sports:** basketball, soccer, track, volleyball. **Tests:** PSAT, SAT, IB, ERB. **Graduates have attended:** Bryn Mawr, Harvard, Georgia Tech, U. of London, U. of Wales. **Location:** in residential area, 6 miles from downtown Atlanta. **Campus:** 8 acres. **Library:** 8,000 volumes. **Facilities:** 35 classrooms, auditorium, playing field, 2 science labs, air conditioning.

*Once only fee

MONTEZUMA, NEW MEXICO

THE ARMAND HAMMER UNITED WORLD COLLEGE OF THE AMERICAN WEST

Phone: (1)(505)4544200 **Facsimile:** (1)(505)4544274
  Telex: 660841 AHUWC MEZA†
Mail: PO Box 248, Montezuma, NM 87731, U.S.A.
President: Philip O. Geier, Ph.D.
Vice-president: Barbara Johnson
Staff: full-time, 24; part-time, 4
Nationalities of staff: U.S., 16; other, 12
Grade levels: 12 – 13
Enrollment: total, 200
Nationalities of student body: U.S., 50; other, 150
Capacity: total, 200
Teacher/student ratio: 1/8
Boarding capacity: boys, 100; girls, 100
Tuition and board (annual): $15,000
School year: September to June

Year founded: 1981. **Type of school:** coed, boarding, private nonprofit. **Governed by:** board of directors. **Accredited by:** North Central.

Curriculum/physical plant

Type: IB. **Languages taught:** French, Spanish, German. **Special programs:** ESL. **Special curricular:** art, computer instruction. **Extracurricular:** drama, choral music, instrumental music, computers, yearbook, newspaper, photography, excursions/expeditions, field trips. **Sports:** basketball, skiing, soccer, softball, swimming, tennis, volleyball, skating. **Tests:** SSAT, PSAT, SAT, ACT, TOEFL, IB. **Graduates attending college:** 98%. **Graduates have attended:** Oxford, Harvard, Yale, MIT, Brown. **Location:** 5 miles from Las Vegas, New Mexico; 60 miles east of Santa Fe; 60 miles southeast of Taos. **Campus:** 110 acres. **Facilities:** 11 buildings, 20 classrooms, cafeteria, infirmary, covered play area, 3 tennis courts, 3 playing fields, 9 science labs, computer lab, 4 dormitories.

†from outside U.S., use telex number 230660841

NEW YORK, NEW YORK

THE DWIGHT SCHOOL†

Street address: 291 West 89th Street, New York, NY 10024, U.S.A.
Phone: (1)(212)7246360   **Facsimile:** (1)(212)8744232
Chancellor: Stephen Spahn
Headmaster: William Goodin
Academic dean: Anthony Foster
Dean of admissions: Elizabeth Callaway
Director of admissions: Kathleen Brigham
Staff: full-time, 45; part-time, 5
Nationalities of staff: U.S., 30; U.K., 3; other, 17
Grade levels: 1 – 13 (postgraduate year)
Enrollment: 1 – 4, 30; 5 – 8, 90; 9 – 12, 230; total, 350
Nationalities of student body: U.S., 200; other, 150
Teacher/student ratio: 1/7
Tuition (annual): 1 – 5, $10,250; 6 – 8, $11,800; 9 – 12, $12,900
Other fees (annual): application, $35; registration*, $500; books/activities, $840 – 1,300
School year: September to June

Year founded: 1880. **Type of school:** coed, day, private, international.
Governed by: elected board of trustees. **Accredited by:** Middle States, New
York State.

Curriculum/physical plant

Type: U.S., U.K., IB. **Languages taught:** French, Spanish, Italian, Latin,
Japanese. **Special services:** reading, math, computer, ESL, learning specialist, remedial reading. **Special curricular:** art, computer instruction, music,
theater, student exchange, sports teams. **Extracurricular:** drama, computers, yearbook, newspaper, literary magazine, photography, excursions/expe-
ditions, field trips, chess. **Sports:** basketball, soccer, softball, tennis, volleyball, wrestling, weight training. **Clubs:** Model UN, National Honor Society.
Tests: PSAT, SAT, TOEFL, IB, GCSE, Stanford, AP Achievement. **Graduates
attending college:** 100%. **Graduates have attended:** Harvard, U. of Pennsylvania, Columbia, Exeter (U.K.), London School of Economics. **Location:** on
Upper West Side of Manhattan. **Library:** 35,000 volumes. **Facilities:** 28
classrooms, infirmary, 2 gymnasiums, 4 science labs, computer lab, lunch
room, music room, 2 art rooms, language lab.

*Once only fee   †Anglo-American International School has merged with The
Dwight School and is in the process of expanding facilities and programs.

UNITED NATIONS INTERNATIONAL SCHOOL

Street addresses: 24-50 Franklin D. Roosevelt Drive, New York, NY 10010-4046, U.S.A.; 173-53 Croydon Road, Jamaica Estates, New York, NY 11432, U.S.A.

Phones: (1)(212)6847400; (1)(718)6586166
Facsimiles: (1)(212)8898959; (1)(718)6585742

Director: Joseph J. Blaney, Ed.D.

Comptroller: Robert Carey

Personnel officer: George Dymond

Principal, Tutorial House: Raymond Taylor

Principal, Middle House: Radha Rajan, Ph.D.

Principal, Junior House: Lea Rangel-Ribeiro

Principal, Jamaica, Queens, campus: Mary Blake

Staff: full-time, 143; part-time, 19

Nationalities of staff: U.S., 64; U.K., 14; other, 84

Grade levels: K – 12

Enrollment: K, 106; 1 – 6, 705; 7 – 9, 323; 10 – 12, 304; total, 1,438

Nationalities of student body: U.S., 710; other, 728

Teacher/student ratio: 1/9

Tuition (annual): K – 4, $8,100; 5, $8,400; 6, $8,650; 7, $9,350; 8, $9,800; 9, $9,900; 10, $10,050; 11, $10,650; 12, $10,900

Other fees (annual): registration*, $125; insurance, $20; books, $60; endowment fund*, $1,000; yearbook, $25; camps, $150; graduation*, $75; UNIS Society, $20; IB dues, $15; ISA, $10

School year: September to June

Year founded: 1947. **Type of school:** coed, day, independent nonprofit. **Governed by:** appointed and elected board of trustees. **Sponsored by:** United Nations. **Accredited by:** New York State Board of Regents, Middle States.

Curriculum/physical plant

Type: IB. **Languages taught:** French, Spanish, German, Dutch, Italian, Russian, Latin, Arabic, Japanese, Swedish, Chinese. **Staff specialists:** psychologist, nurse, counselors, technologist. **Special programs:** ESL. **Special curricular:** art, chorus, band, drama, sports teams, computer, UNIS/UN conference, nuclear issues. **Extracurricular:** drama, gymnastics, dance, choral music, instrumental music, computers, yearbook, newspaper, literary magazine, photography, excursions/expeditions, field trips, drivers' education, extended-day program. **Sports:** basketball, skiing, soccer, softball, tennis, volleyball, track and field, judo. **Clubs:** French, chess, German, Spanish, Amnesty International. **Tests:** IB, ACH. **Graduates attending college:** 98%. **Graduates have attended:** Cambridge, MIT, Yale, Princeton, Williams. **Campuses (2):** Manhattan, 3 acres; Jamaica, Queens, 1.5 acres. **Library:** 48,000 volumes. **Facilities:** 2 buildings, 112 classrooms, 3 auditoriums, 2 cafeterias, infirmary, covered play area, tennis court, 2 gymnasiums, playing field, 9 science labs, 4 computer labs, AV equipment, garden, 3 art studios, 8 music rooms, air conditioning.

*Once only fee

HOUSTON, TEXAS

THE AWTY INTERNATIONAL SCHOOL

Street address: 7455 Awty School Lane, Houston, TX 77055-7222, U.S.A.
Phone: (1)(713)6864850   **Facsimile:** (1)(713)6864956
Headmaster: William L. Moon, Jr.
Dean of students: Samuel Waugh
Lower school principal: Chantal Vessali
Business manager: Kearney Morgan
Staff: full-time, 61; part-time, 10
Nationalities of staff: U.S., 30; other, 41
Grade levels: preK – 12
Enrollment: preK, 38; K, 42; 1 – 5, 201; 6 – 8, 129; 9 – 12, 140; total, 550
Capacity: preK, 45; K, 45; 1 – 5, 210; 6 – 8, 130; 9 – 12, 160; total, 590
Teacher/student ratio: 1/8
Tuition (annual): preK, $3,670 (half-day), $5,000 (full-day); K, $5,400; 1 – 5, $5,900; 6 – 8, $6,700; 9 – 12, $7,300
Other fees (annual): registration, $150; advance tuition payment, $200/child; new-family fee*, $500; testing*, $40; senior*, $250
School year: August to June

Year founded: 1956. **Type of school:** coed, day, private nonprofit. **Governed by:** board of trustees (self-perpetuating). **Accredited by:** ISAS, ECIS.

Curriculum

Type: U.S., IB, French Baccalaureate. **Languages taught:** French, Spanish, German, ESL, Italian, Arabic. **Staff specialists:** computer, nurse. **Special programs:** ESL, advanced placement, independent study. **Special curricular:** art, physical education, computer instruction. **Extracurricular:** drama, dance, computers, yearbook, newspaper, literary magazine, photography, excursions/expeditions, field trips. **Sports:** basketball, soccer, swimming, tennis, volleyball, track and field. **Clubs:** French, Model UN, Spanish. **Tests:** PSAT, SAT, ACT, TOEFL, IB, AP, ERB. **Graduates attending college:** 99%. **Graduates have attended:** Rice, U. of Texas, Columbia, Johns Hopkins, Harvard.

Physical plant

Location: in Houston, with easy access to downtown and residential areas. **Campus:** 12.5 acres. **Library:** 17,000 volumes. **Facilities:** 4 buildings, 32 classrooms, cafeteria, 3 covered play areas, 2 playing fields, 3 science labs, 2 computer labs, air conditioning.

*Once only fee

U.S. VIRGIN ISLANDS _____

Region: Caribbean
Size: 133 square miles
Population: 101,809
Capital: Charlotte Amalie, St. Thomas

Telephone code: 809
Currency: U.S. dollar
Languages: English, Spanish, Creole

ST. CROIX

THE GOOD HOPE SCHOOL

Phone: (1)(809)7720022   **Facsimile:** (1)(809)7724626
Mail: Frederiksted, St. Croix, U.S. Virgin Islands 00840
Head of school: Tanya L. Nichols
Director, upper school: Mary Jane Provost
Director, middle school: Luther Renee
Director, lower school: Sarah Otis
Business manager: Brian Romine
Staff: full-time, 42
Nationalities of staff: U.S., 41; other, 1
Grade levels: preK – 12
Enrollment: preK, 27; K, 18; 1 – 6, 233; 7 – 9, 114; 10 – 12, 88; total, 480
   (East Campus: preK, 10; K, 14; total, 24)
Capacity: total, 500
Teacher/student ratio: 1/11
Tuition (annual): preK, $2,800 (half-day); K, $3,700; 1, $3,850; 2 – 3,
   $4,160; 4 – 6, $4,485; 7 – 12, $4,795
Other fees (annual): registration, $100; books, $75 – 150
School year: September to June

Year founded: 1967. **Type of school:** coed, day, private nonprofit.
Governed by: elected board of trustees. **Accredited by:** Middle States.

Curriculum
Type: U.S. **Languages taught:** French, Spanish. **Staff specialists:**
computer, nurse. **Special programs:** advanced placement, honors sections.
Special curricular: art, chorus, band, physical education, computer instruction, Spanish (K – 12). **Extracurricular:** drama, gymnastics, computers,
yearbook, literary magazine, photography, field trips, sports. **Tests:** PSAT,
SAT, ACT, AP, Stanford, NEDT. **Graduates attending college:** 98%. **Graduates have attended:** Tulane, Columbia, Harvard, U. of Pennsylvania, American U.

Physical plant
Location: in small town near the Caribbean Sea, amidst a grove of
mahogany trees. East campus located east of Christiansted, St. Croix.
Campuses (2): 34 acres. **Library:** 17,000 volumes. **Facilities:** 11 buildings,
23 classrooms, covered play area, gymnasium, 3 playing fields, 3 science labs,
computer lab, swimming pool, library media center, amphitheater, weight
training room.

St. Croix Country Day School

Phone: (1)(809)7781974
Mail: Rt. 1, Box 6199, Kingshill, St. Croix, U.S. Virgin Islands 00850
Head: Margery Boulanger
Dean, upper school: John Kimbrough
Dean, lower and middle schools: Charles S. Adams
Business manager: Anita Turbyfill
Staff: full-time, 65
Nationalities of staff: U.S., 62; other, 3
Grade levels: N – 12
Enrollment: N – 8, 392; 9 – 12, 120; total, 512
Capacity: N – 8, 392; 9 – 12, 150; total, 542
Teacher/student ratio: 1/8
Tuition (annual): $3,400 – 4,500
Other fees (annual): registration, $150; testing (admission)*, $25
School year: September to June

Year founded: 1964. **Type of school:** coed, day, private nonprofit. **Governed by:** appointed board of trustees. **Accredited by:** Middle States.

Curriculum/physical plant

Type: U.S. **Languages taught:** French, Spanish. **Staff specialists:** counselor, nurse, technology coordinator. **Special programs:** advanced placement. **Special curricular:** art, chorus, physical education, computer instruction. **Extracurricular:** drama, gymnastics, dance, choral music, instrumental music, computers, yearbook, newspaper, literary magazine, photography, excursions/expeditions. **Sports:** baseball, basketball, football, hockey, soccer, softball, swimming, volleyball. **Tests:** PSAT, SAT, ACT, Stanford. **Graduates attending college:** 100%. **Graduates have attended:** Fairleigh Dickinson, Georgetown, Tulane, Ohio State U., U.S. Naval Academy. **Location:** on outskirts of Christiansted. **Campus:** 25 acres. **Library:** 15,000 volumes. **Facilities:** gymnasium, 2 playing fields, 2 science labs, Olympic swimming pool, fine arts center.

*Once only fee

ST. THOMAS

Antilles School

Phone: (1)(809)7741966   **Facsimile:** (1)(809)7742119
Mail: PO Box 7280, St. Thomas, U.S. Virgin Islands 00801
Headmaster: Mark C. Marin
Head, upper and middle schools: Kaye Knoepfel
Head, lower school: Polly Watts
Academic dean: Alan Eberhart
Dean of faculty: Bruce Wray

Business manager: Joycelyn Kirwan
Staff: full-time, 38; part-time, 10
Nationalities of staff: U.S., 37; other, 11
Grade levels: preK – 12
Enrollment: K, 53; 1 – 5, 145; 6 – 8, 110; 9 – 12, 120; total, 428
Capacity: K, 73; 1 – 5, 157; 6 – 8, 120; 9 – 12, 160; total, 510
Teacher/student ratio: 1/10
Tuition (annual): preK – 5, $5,900; 6 – 8, $6,050; 9 – 11, $6,350;
    12, $6,500
Other fees (annual): registration, $40; refundable deposit*, $350
School year: September to June

Year founded: 1950. **Type of school:** coed, day, private nonprofit.
Governed by: elected board of trustees. **Accredited by:** Middle States.

Curriculum/physical plant

Type: U.S. **Staff specialists:** reading, computer, counselor, learning disabilities, gifted & talented, 2 fine arts, choral music, 2 librarians, 2 physical education. **Special programs:** advanced placement, honors sections. **Special curricular:** art, chorus, physical education, computer instruction, elementary Spanish. **Extracurricular:** drama, choral music, computers, yearbook, newspaper, literary magazine, photography, excursions/expeditions, field trips. **Sports:** girls: volleyball, softball, soccer, tennis; boys: flag football, basketball, soccer, tennis, softball. **Clubs:** ecology, French, National Honor Society, scouting, student council, science, SADD, intramural sports. **Tests:** PSAT, SAT, Stanford, MAT. **Graduates attending college:** 100%. **Graduates have attended:** Georgetown, Amherst, Swarthmore, California Tech, Johns Hopkins. **Location:** 2.5 miles from Charlotte Amalie. **Campus:** 27 acres. **Library:** 13,000 volumes, 100 periodicals. **Facilities:** 6 buildings, 32 classrooms, auditorium, covered play area, tennis court, 2 playing fields, 3 science labs, computer lab, 2 art studios.

*Once only fee

URUGUAY _____

Region: South America
Size: 68,037 square miles
Population: 3,121,000
Capital: Montevideo

Telephone code: 598
Currency: new peso
Language: Spanish

MONTEVIDEO

Uruguayan American School

Street address: Dublin 1785, CP 11500, Montevideo, Uruguay
Phone: (598)(2)607681   Facsimile: (598)(2)606316
U.S. mail: Administrative Officer (UAS), U.S. Embassy – Montevideo,
U.S. Department of State, Washington, D.C. 20520-3360
Director: Larry Snyder
Business manager: Juan Carlos Nikodem
Staff: full-time, 26; part-time, 10
Nationalities of staff: U.S., 8; U.K., 2; host, 24; other, 2
Grade levels: N – 12
Enrollment: N – preK, 29; K, 14; 1 – 6, 95; 7 – 9, 46; 10 – 12, 36;
total, 220
Nationalities of student body: U.S., 101; U.K., 1; host, 31; other, 87
Capacity: N – preK, 36; K, 20; 1 – 6, 108; 7 – 9, 54; 10 – 12, 54; total, 272
Teacher/student ratio: 1/7
Tuition (annual): N – preK, $1,700; K – 6, $5,060; 7 – 12, $7,800
Other fees: registration*, $2,000
School year: August to June

Year founded: 1959. **Type of school:** coed, day, private nonprofit.
Governed by: elected board of directors. **Accredited by:** Southern.

Curriculum/physical plant
Type: U.S. **Languages taught:** French, Spanish. **Staff specialists:**
reading, math, computer, speech/hearing, counselor, learning disabilities.
Special programs: ESL, advanced placement, independent study, full-day
kindergarten. **Special curricular:** art, chorus, band, physical education,
computer instruction. **Extracurricular:** drama, gymnastics, choral music,
instrumental music, computers, yearbook, photography, excursions/expedi-
tions, field trips. **Sports:** basketball, soccer, volleyball, team handball. **Tests:**
SSAT, PSAT, SAT, ACT, AP, Stanford. **Graduates attending college:** 90 –
100%. **Graduates have attended:** Texas A&M, George Washington U.,
Virginia Tech, Yale, Amherst. **Location:** in suburban area, Carrasco, 20
kilometers east of Montevideo. **Campus:** 2.5 acres. **Library:** 10,000 volumes.
Facilities: 3 buildings, 27 classrooms, auditorium, cafeteria, gymnasium, 2
science labs, computer lab, play area, art room, photo lab, AV equipment.

*Once only fee

VENEZUELA ─────────────────────

Region: South America
Size: 352,143 square miles
Population: 20,189,000
Capital: Caracas

Telephone code: 58
Currency: bolivar
Language: Spanish

CARACAS

COLEGIO INTERNACIONAL DE CARACAS

Street address: Calle Colegio, Las Minas de Baruta, Caracas, Venezuela
Phone: (58)(2)930444/930508   **Facsimile:** (58)(2)930533/9414161
Mail: POBA International #233, PO Box 02-5255, Miami, FL 33102-5255, U.S.A.
Superintendent: Brian McCauley, Ph.D.
High school principal: Winthrop Sargent
Elementary school principal: Billie Allio
Registrar: Teresa Smith
Head of library: Diane Austin
Staff: full-time, 70; part-time, 5
Nationalities of staff: U.S., 45; U.K., 1; host, 25; other, 4
Grade levels: N – 12
Enrollment: preK, 26; K, 19; 1 – 6, 195; 7 – 9, 151; 10 – 12, 235; total, 626
Nationalities of student body: U.S., 200; U.K., 6; host, 130; other, 290
Capacity: preK, 30; K, 15; 1 – 6, 150; 7 – 9, 150; 10 – 12, 370; total, 715
Teacher/student ratio: 1/9
Tuition (annual): N – preK, $2,717; K – 6, $5,608; 7 – 12, $7,197
Other fees (annual): registration, $500; busing, $400; share per student*, $44 (refundable); capital assessment*, $1,500
School year: August to June

Year founded: 1971. **Type of school:** coed, day, private nonprofit. **Governed by:** elected board of directors. **Sponsored by:** parents. **Accredited by:** Southern. **Regional organization:** AASSA.

Curriculum/physical plant
Type: U.S., IB, AP. **Languages taught:** French, Spanish, German, Italian, Japanese. **Staff specialists:** computer, counselor, psychologist, learning disabilities, nurse, gifted & talented, resource. **Special programs:** ESL, honors sections, independent study, correspondence, remedial, IB, Advanced Placement. **Special curricular:** art, chorus, physical education, computer instruction. **Extracurricular:** drama, yearbook, newspaper, photography, excursions/expeditions, field trips. **Sports:** basketball, soccer, softball, volleyball, futbolito. **Clubs:** chess, scuba, photography, French, Ayuda y Amistad,

student council, adventure, debate, Italian. **Tests:** PSAT, SAT, ACT, TOEFL, IB, AP, Iowa. **Graduates attending college:** 98%. **Graduates have attended:** Brown, Yale, U. of Pennsylvania, MIT, Georgetown. **Location:** on hilltop overlooking Caracas. **Campus:** 15 acres. **Library:** 30,000 volumes. **Facilities:** 6 buildings, 51 classrooms, auditorium, cafeteria, infirmary, gymnasium, playing field, science lab, computer lab, air conditioning.

*Once only fee

Escuela Campo Alegre

Street address: Final Calle La Cinta, Las Mercedes, Caracas D.F., Venezuela
Phone: (58)(2)7528402/7527389/7523790
Facsimile: (58)(2)7515146   **Cable:** ESCAAL
Mail: Apartado del Este 60382, Caracas 1060-A, Venezuela
U.S. mail: Escuela Campo Alegre M – 314, Jet International Cargo, PO Box 020010, Miami, FL 33102-0010, U.S.A.
Superintendent: Forrest A. Broman, JDL
Deputy superintendent, curriculum/instruction: William Gerritz, Ed.D.
Principal, upper school: Gary Crippin, Ph.D.
Principal, middle school: Bambi Betts
Co-principal, lower school: Susan O'Brien
Business manager: Virginia Abascal
Staff: full-time, 124; part-time, 4
Grade levels: preK – 12
Enrollment: preK, 33; K, 56; 1 – 5, 480; 6 – 8, 230; 9 – 12, 240; total, 1,039
Nationalities of student body: U.S., 305; U.K., 25; host, 170; other, 539
Teacher/student ratio: 1/8
Tuition (annual): preK, $3,556; K – 6, $5,670; 7 – 12, $7,015
Other fees (annual): matriculation, $388; prepaid semester carries 5% discount; capital fund*, $2,500
School year: August to June

Year founded: 1937. **Type of school:** coed, day, company sponsored, private nonprofit. **Governed by:** appointed board of directors. **Sponsored by:** multinational companies, parents. **Accredited by:** Southern, NAIS.

Curriculum/physical plant
Type: U.S., IB. **Languages taught:** French, Spanish. **Staff specialists:** math, computer, speech/hearing, psychologist, learning disabilities, nurse, ESL, language arts, science, counselors. **Special programs:** advanced placement, honors sections, remedial, IB, child study team. **Special curricular:** art, physical education, computer instruction, drama, music. **Extracurricular:** gymnastics, dance, choral music, computers, yearbook, newspaper,

literary magazine, field trips, community service, after school program (bus transportation). **Sports:** basketball, soccer, softball, volleyball, kicking ball. **Organizations**: National Honor Society, National Junior Honor Society, student council, Boy Scouts, Cub Scouts, Girl Scouts, Brownies. **Tests:** SSAT, PSAT, SAT, AP, IB, CTP, Otis-Lennon. **Location:** in city. **Campus:** 11 acres. **Library:** 30,000 volumes. **Facilities:** 9 buildings, 77 classrooms, theater-auditorium, infirmary, covered play area, 2 gymnasiums, playing field, 5 science labs, 2 computer labs, AV equipment.

*Once only fee

MARACAIBO

Escuela Bella Vista

Street address: Calle 67 entre Ave. 3D y 3E, Maracaibo, Venezuela
Phone: (58)(61)911674/911696   **Facsimile:** (58)(61)919417
    Cable: BELVIS
Mail: Apartado 290, Maracaibo, Venezuela 4002
U.S. mail: (letter mail only) BUZOOM C-MAR-P 1815,
    PO Box 02-8537, Miami, FL 33102-8537, U.S.A.
Superintendent: Bert Webb, Ed.D.
Staff: full-time, 32
Nationalities of staff: U.S., 18; host, 11; other, 3
Grade levels: N – 12
Enrollment: N – preK, 35; K, 27; 1 – 6, 138; 7 – 9, 53; 10 – 12, 39;
    total, 292
Nationalities of student body: U.S., 81; host, 166; other, 45
Capacity: N – preK, 40; K, 40; 1 – 6, 240; 7 – 9, 75; 10 – 12, 75; total, 470
Teacher/student ratio: 1/9
Tuition (annual): N – preK, $1,100; K, $2,000; 1 – 6, $4,000; 7 – 9,
    $5,100; 10 – 12, $5,700
Other fees (annual): registration, $200; capital levy*, $300; insurance, $10
School year: August to June

Year founded: 1948. **Type of school:** coed, day, private nonprofit. **Governed by:** elected board of directors. **Sponsored by:** shareholders. **Accredited by:** Southern.

Curriculum/physical plant
    Type: U.S. **Languages taught:** Spanish. **Staff specialists:** reading, computer, counselor, special education. **Special programs:** ESL, SSL. **Special curricular:** art, chorus, band, physical education, computer instruction, advanced placement, Model UN. **Extracurricular:** drama, gymnastics, choral music, instrumental music, computers, yearbook, newspaper, excursions/expeditions, field trips. **Sports:** basketball, soccer, softball, tennis, volleyball, track and field. **Organizations**: National Honor Society, National Junior Honor Society, student council, Model UN. **Tests:** PSAT, SAT, ACT, Iowa.

Graduates attending college: 95%. **Graduates have attended:** Boston U., Florida International U., U. of Pennsylvania, Northeastern U., Baylor. **Location:** in city, within walking distance of cultural complex, shopping center, recreational facilities, bus routes. **Campus:** 8 acres. **Library:** 16,000 volumes. **Facilities:** 5 buildings, 36 classrooms, cafeteria, covered play area, 2 tennis courts, 2 gymnasiums, playing field, science lab, computer lab, partial air conditioning, 2 large playgrounds, darkroom.

*Once only fee

VALENCIA

COLEGIO INTERNACIONAL DE CARABOBO

Street address: Calle Zuloaga Cruce Con Calle El Colegio, El Trigal Centro, Valencia, Venezuela
Phone: (58)(41)421807/426551   **Facsimile:** (58)(41)426510
Mail: BAMCO-VLN 001200, PO Box 522237, Miami, FL 33152-2237, U.S.A.
Superintendent: Frank Anderson
High school principal: Joseph Walker
Elementary school principal: Judith Tostenrud
Business manager: Virginia Campi
Staff: full-time, 24; part-time, 12
Nationalities of staff: U.S., 24; U.K., 1; host, 7; other, 4
Grade levels: JK – 12
Enrollment: JK, 13; K, 23; 1 – 6, 129; 7 – 9, 40; 10 – 12, 56; total, 261
Nationalities of student body: U.S., 80; host, 78; other, 103
Capacity: total, 400
Teacher/student ratio: 1/9
Tuition (annual): JK – K, $5,200; 1 – 8, $6,700; 9 – 12, $7,100
Other fees (annual): registration, $300 (new student), $150 (returning student); capital levy, $1,500; busing, $500; entrance*, $1,200
School year: August to June

Year founded: 1955. **Type of school:** coed, day, corporate sponsored. **Governed by:** elected board of education. **Sponsored by:** corporate/private sectors. **Accredited by:** Southern.

Curriculum/physical plant
Type: U.S. **Languages taught:** French, Spanish. **Staff specialists:** math, computer, counselor, nurse. **Special programs:** ESL. **Special curricular:** art, chorus, physical education, computer instruction. **Extracurricular:** drama, dance, choral music, computers, yearbook, literary magazine, field trips. **Sports:** basketball, soccer, softball, volleyball, frequent student-parent/ faculty sports competition. **Clubs:** high school and elementary activities programs, intramurals, mothers' service club. **Tests:** PSAT, SAT, TOEFL,

Iowa. **Graduates attending college:** more than 95%. **Graduates have attended:** prestigious U.S. and other international universities. **Location:** on picturesque, sprawling campus in suburb of El Trigal, 5 minutes from central Valencia, 90 miles from Caracas. **Campuses (2):** 12 acres. **Library:** 14,780 volumes. **Facilities:** 7 buildings, 27 classrooms, auditorium, cafeteria, 2 computer labs, covered recreational area, athletic field, science labs.

*Once only fee

YEMEN _____

Region: Middle East
Size: 205,356 square miles
Population: 10,062,000
Capital: Sanaa

Telephone code: 967
Currency: rial
Language: Arabic

SANAA

SANAA INTERNATIONAL SCHOOL

Phone: (967)(1)234437   **Facsimile:** (967)(1)234436
　　Telex: 9482697 EMBSAN YE   **Cable:** SANINTSCHOOL
Mail: Box 2002, Sanaa, Yemen
Director: James E. Gilson
Director of instruction: H. Duane Root
Staff: full-time, 27; part-time, 11
Nationalities of staff: U.S., 23; U.K., 1; other, 14
Grade levels: K – 12
Enrollment: K, 20; 1 – 6, 140; 7 – 9, 35; 10 – 12, 30; total, 225
Capacity: K, 20; 1 – 6, 150; 7 – 9, 75; 10 – 12, 75; total, 320
Teacher/student ratio: 1/7
Tuition (annual): K, $6,000; 1 – 12, $8,000
Other fees (annual): registration*, $50 deposit; capital levy, $1000 or
　　$2,500 deposit; busing, $600
School year: September to June

Year founded: 1971. **Type of school:** coed, day, private nonprofit. **Governed by:** appointed board of directors. **Accredited by:** Middle States.

Curriculum/physical plant
　　Type: U.S. **Languages taught:** French, Spanish, and Arabic as foreign languages; Arabic, Dutch, and Hindi as native languages. **Staff specialists:** nurse, resource. **Special programs:** ESL, independent study. **Special curricular:** art, band, physical education, computer instruction. **Extracurricular:** drama, excursions/expeditions, field trips. **Sports:** basketball, soccer, track, volleyball. **Tests:** IGCSE, WRAT-R. **Graduates have attended:** U. of

California at Santa Barbara, Michigan State U., Seattle Pacific U. **Location:** agricultural area in hills, 5 kilometers from Sanaa. **Campus:** 34 acres. **Library:** 9,000 volumes. **Facilities:** 3 buildings, 21 classrooms, 3 playing fields, 2 science labs, computer lab, auditorium/multi-purpose room.

*Once only fee

TAIZ
Mohammed Ali Othman School
Address: PO Box 5713, Taiz, Yemen
Phone: (967)(4)2112247 – 9
Principal: Saleh A. Zokari

YUGOSLAVIA

Region: Europe
Size: 39,000 square miles
Population: 10,337,000
Capital: Belgrade

Telephone code: 38
Currency: dinar
Language: Serbian

BELGRADE

INTERNATIONAL SCHOOL OF BELGRADE
Street address: Temisvarska 19, Belgrade, Serbia 11040, Yugoslavia
Phone: (38)(11)651832   **Facsimile:** (38)(11)652619
U.S. mail: Department of State, Washington, D.C. 20520-5070
Interim director/business manager: Dr. Nikola Kodzas
Staff: full-time, 15
Nationalities of staff: U.S., 7; U.K., 4; other, 4
Grade levels: K – 9
Enrollment: K, 9; 1 – 6, 65; 7 – 9, 11; total, 85
Nationalities of student body: U.S., 17; U.K., 1; host, 10; other, 57
Capacity: K, 36; 1 – 6, 124; 7 – 9, 36; total, 196
Teacher/student ratio: 1/6
Tuition (annual): K – 9, $9,500
School year: August to June

Year founded: 1947. **Type of school:** coed, day. **Governed by:** international school board. **Accredited by:** New England, ECIS.

Curriculum/physical plant
Type: U.S. **Languages taught:** French. **Staff specialists:** nurse, librarian. **Special programs:** ESL. **Special curricular:** chorus, physical education,

swimming, computer instruction. **Extracurricular:** computers, newspaper, field trips, afterschool enrichment/activity program. **Tests:** Iowa, CAT, DAT. **Graduates attending college:** 90%. **Location:** in suburban area. **Campus:** 1.5 acres. **Library:** 8,000 volumes. **Facilities:** 5 buildings, 15 classrooms, playing field, science lab, computer lab, nearby gymnasium, AV room.

ZAIRE ⸻

Region: Central Africa
Size: 905,563 square miles
Population: 37,832,000
Capital: Kinshasa

Telephone code: 243
Currency: zaire
Languages: French, Bantu
    dialects

KINSHASA

THE AMERICAN SCHOOL OF KINSHASA (TASOK)

Street address: Route de Matadi, Ngaliema, Kinshasa, Zaire
Phone: (243)(12)50001; MCI from U.S. (243)(88)44878
    Telex: 96821405 USEMB ZR   **Cable:** c/o USEMBASSY
    KINSHASA
Mail: BP 4702, Kinshasa II, Zaire
U.S. mail: Superintendent, The American School of Kinshasa (TASOK),
    c/o U.S. Embassy – Kinshasa, Unit 31550, APO AE 09828
Superintendent: Ralph Hollis
Staff: full-time, 9; part-time, 2
Grade levels: preK – 10
Enrollment: total, 100
Nationalities of student body: U.S., 20; Canada, 20; host, 2; other, 58
Capacity: preK, 20; K, 40; 1 – 6, 300; 7 – 9, 135; 10, 190; total, 685
Teacher/student ratio: 1/10
Tuition (annual): preK, $3,500; K, $5,600; 1 – 6, $8,400; 7 – 10,
    $8,950
Other fees: registration*, $1,500; ESL*, $1,200
School year: August to June

    Year founded: 1961. **Type of school:** coed, day. **Governed by:** school board elected by parent assembly. **Accredited by:** Middle States.

Curriculum/physical plant
    Type: U.S. **Languages taught:** French. **Staff specialists:** reading, computer, counselor, ESL. **Special programs:** ESL. **Special curricular:** art, physical education, computer instruction. **Extracurricular:** drama, choral music, instrumental music, computers, yearbook, excursions/expeditions, field trips. **Sports:** basketball, soccer, softball, swimming, track, volleyball. **Clubs:** cheerleaders, National Honor Society, photography, student government. **Tests:** PSAT, SAT, ACT, TOEFL, AP, Iowa. **Graduates attending**

college: 90%. **Graduates have attended:** Yale, Grinnell, Seattle Pacific, Wheaton, Michigan State. **Location:** 10 kilometers from the center of Kinshasa. **Campus:** 42 acres. **Library:** 20,000 volumes. **Facilities:** 22 buildings, 40 classrooms, tennis court, 2 playing fields, 3 science labs, 2 computer labs, swimming pool, multipurpose room, air conditioning.

*Once only fee

ZAMBIA ⸻

Region: Southern Africa
Size: 290,586 square miles
Population: 8,445,000
Capital: Lusaka

Telephone code: 260
Currency: kwacha
Languages: English, Bantu dialects

LUSAKA

AMERICAN EMBASSY SCHOOL OF LUSAKA

Street address: 242B Kakola Road, Lusaka, Zambia
Phone: (260)(1)291998   **Facsimile:** (260)(1)261538
    Telex: 96541970 AMEMB ZA
Mail: PO Box 31617, Lusaka, Zambia
U.S. mail: c/o Department of State – Lusaka, Washington, D.C.
    20521-2310
Director: John Ritter
Staff: full-time, 13; part-time, 4
Nationalities of staff: U.S., 11; U.K., 2; other, 4
Grade levels: K – 8
Enrollment: K, 15; 1 – 6, 93; 7 – 8, 22; total, 130
Nationalities of student body: U.S., 58; U.K., 10; other, 62
Capacity: K, 15; 1 – 6, 90; 7 – 8, 30; total, 135
Teacher/student ratio: 1/9
Tuition (annual): K – 6, $7,000; 7 – 8, $7,500
Other fees (annual): admission*, $3,000; busing, $1,000; ESL, $1,350
School year: August to June

Year founded: 1986. **Type of school:** coed, day. **Governed by:** American Embassy and elected board of directors. **Sponsored by:** American Embassy. **Accredited by:** Middle States.

Curriculum/physical plant
Type: U.S. **Languages taught:** French. **Special programs:** ESL. **Special curricular:** art, physical education, drama, computers, music. **Extracurricular:** drama, computers, field trips, music, conservation club. **Sports:** basket-

ball, field hockey, soccer, softball, swimming, tennis, volleyball. **Tests:** Iowa. **Location:** in suburban area of Lusaka. **Campus:** 3 acres. **Library:** more than 5,000 volumes. **Facilities:** 3 buildings, 9 classrooms, infirmary, covered play area, playing field, computer lab, swimming pool, ball court, video room, art studio, ESL room.

*Once only fee

INTERNATIONAL SCHOOL OF LUSAKA

Street address: Nangwenya Road, Lusaka, Zambia
Phone: (260)(1)252291/253959   **Facsimile:** (260)(1)261538
Mail: PO Box 50121, Ridgeway, Lusaka, Zambia
Superintendent: (to be announced)
Staff: full-time, 79; part-time, 4
Nationalities of staff: U.S., 4; U.K., 17; host, 22; other, 40
Grade levels: K – 13
Enrollment: 1 – 6, 485; 7 – 13, 473; total, 958
Teacher/student ratio: 1/12
Tuition (per term): K, $750; 1 – 6, $990; 7 – 9, $1,560; 10 – 11, $1,600; A-level, $2,400
Other fees: registration*
School year: August to June

Year founded: 1963. **Type of school:** coed, day, private nonprofit. **Governed by:** board of governors. **Accredited by:** Middle States.

Curriculum/physical plant

Type: U.K., IGCSE. **Languages taught:** English, French, Spanish. **Staff specialists:** reading, nurse, resource, diagnostician. **Special programs:** ESL, remedial. **Special curricular:** art, physical education, computer instruction, drama, music, field trips. **Extracurricular:** gymnastics, dance, computers, yearbook, newspaper. **Sports:** basketball, rugby, soccer, swimming, tennis, volleyball, karate, badminton. **Clubs:** Boy Scouts, Lechwe guides, Chongololo club, photography. **Tests:** SSAT, PSAT, SAT, ACT, TOEFL, A-level GCE, GCSE, Iowa. **Graduates attending college:** 60%. **Location:** in suburb, 5 kilometers from city center. **Campus:** 33 acres. **Library:** 20,313 volumes. **Facilities:** 8 buildings, 54 classrooms, auditorium, infirmary, covered play area, computer lab, tennis courts, playing fields, science labs, use of Olympic-size swimming pool nearby.

*Once only fee

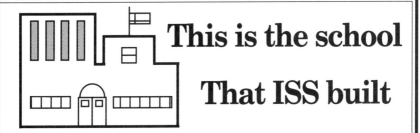

This is the school
That ISS built

- 🚶 This is the administrator who ISS hired to run the school that ISS built.
- 👫 These are the teachers who ISS recruited to staff the school that ISS built.
- 💻 This is the computer that ISS bought to send to the school that ISS built.
- 📚 These are the books that ISS ordered to ship to the school that ISS built.
- 🏢 This is the gym that ISS designed and equipped to enhance the school that ISS built.
- 🌍🌍 These are the children who play in the gym, read the books, use the computers, and learn from the teachers in the school that ISS built.

ISS does all these things
for a good reason.
The world's children.

International Schools Services
PO Box 5910, Princeton, NJ 08543
Phone: 609-452-0990; Fax: 609-452-2690

MAPS

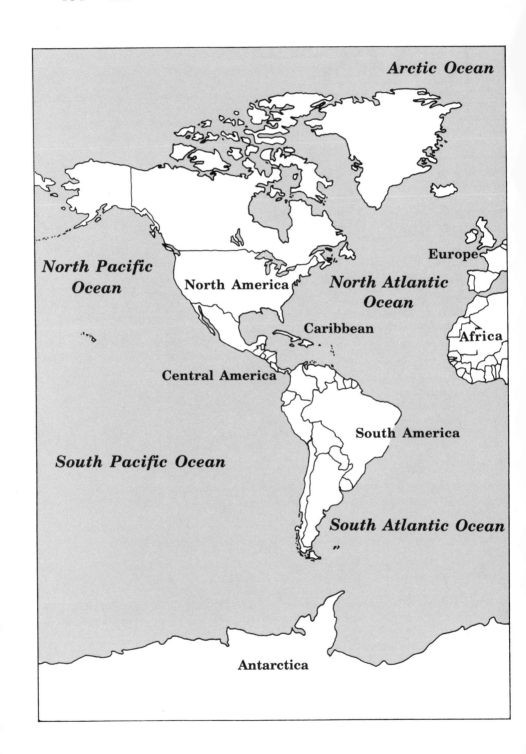

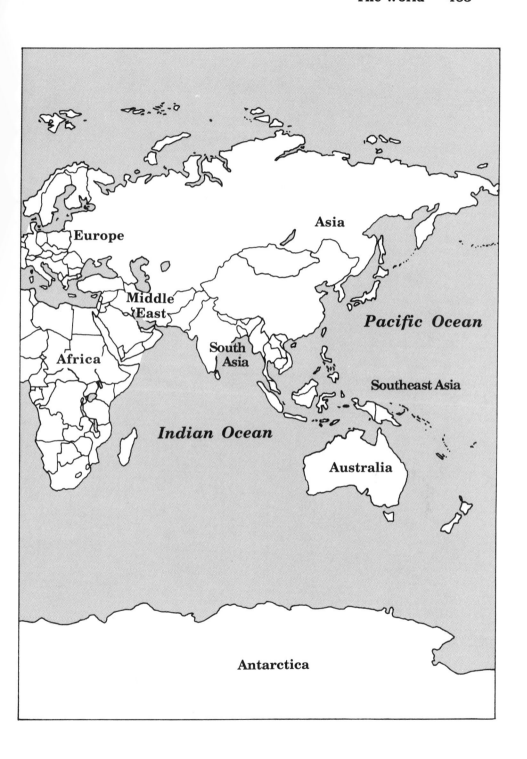

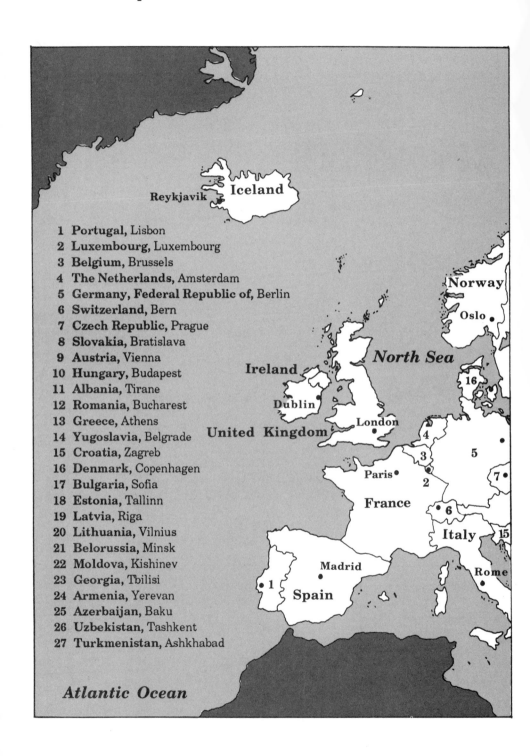

1 Portugal, Lisbon
2 Luxembourg, Luxembourg
3 Belgium, Brussels
4 The Netherlands, Amsterdam
5 Germany, Federal Republic of, Berlin
6 Switzerland, Bern
7 Czech Republic, Prague
8 Slovakia, Bratislava
9 Austria, Vienna
10 Hungary, Budapest
11 Albania, Tirane
12 Romania, Bucharest
13 Greece, Athens
14 Yugoslavia, Belgrade
15 Croatia, Zagreb
16 Denmark, Copenhagen
17 Bulgaria, Sofia
18 Estonia, Tallinn
19 Latvia, Riga
20 Lithuania, Vilnius
21 Belorussia, Minsk
22 Moldova, Kishinev
23 Georgia, Tbilisi
24 Armenia, Yerevan
25 Azerbaijan, Baku
26 Uzbekistan, Tashkent
27 Turkmenistan, Ashkhabad

Reykjavik   Iceland

Norway
Oslo

North Sea

Ireland

Dublin

London

United Kingdom

Paris

France

Madrid

Spain

Italy

Rome

Atlantic Ocean

Arctic Ocean

Sweden

Finland

Helsinki

Stockholm

Russian Federation

18

Baltic
Sea

19

20

Moscow

21

Poland

Warsaw

Kiev

Ukraine

Kazakhstan

9

10

22

Alma-Ata

14

12

Black Sea

Caspian
Sea

26

17

11

23

13

24

25

27

Mediterranean
Sea

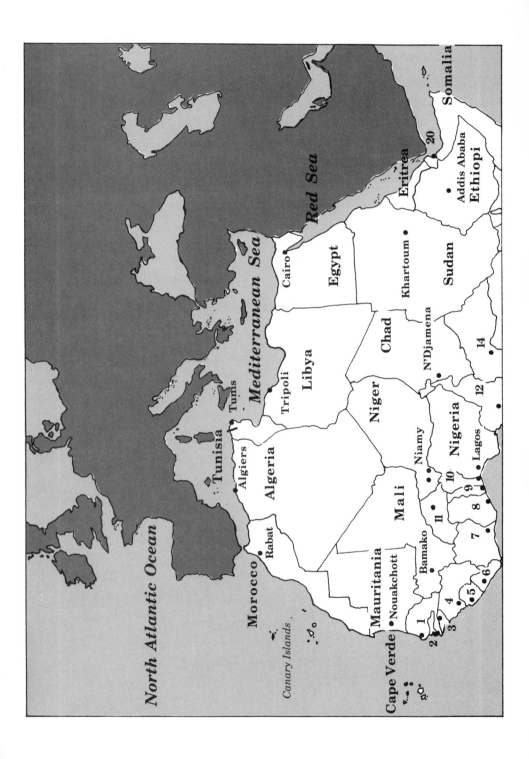

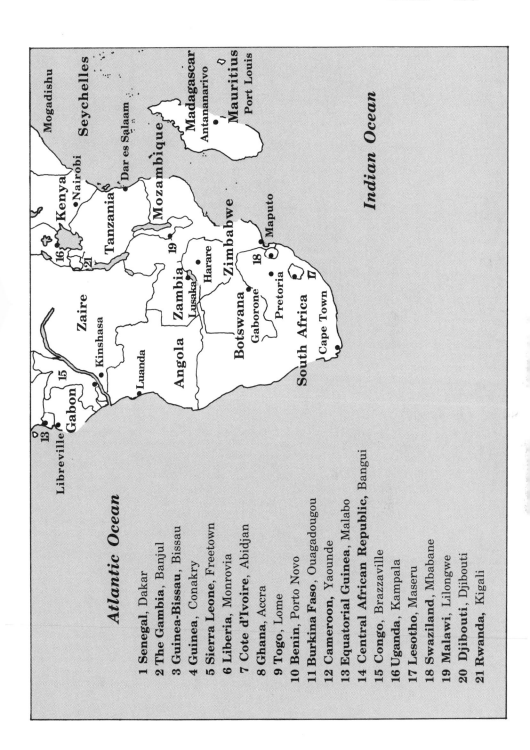

Atlantic Ocean

Indian Ocean

Mogadishu

Seychelles

Madagascar

Antananarivo

Mauritius

Port Louis

Kenya

Nairobi

Dar es Salaam

Tanzania

Mozambique

Zimbabwe

Maputo

Harare

Zambia

Lusaka

16

21

Zaire

Kinshasa

Angola

Botswana

Gaborone

Pretoria

18

17

Luanda

South Africa

Cape Town

15

Gabon

Libreville

13

1 Senegal, Dakar
2 The Gambia, Banjul
3 Guinea-Bissau, Bissau
4 Guinea, Conakry
5 Sierra Leone, Freetown
6 Liberia, Monrovia
7 Cote d'Ivoire, Abidjan
8 Ghana, Accra
9 Togo, Lome
10 Benin, Porto Novo
11 Burkina Faso, Ouagadougou
12 Cameroon, Yaounde
13 Equatorial Guinea, Malabo
14 Central African Republic, Bangui
15 Congo, Brazzaville
16 Uganda, Kampala
17 Lesotho, Maseru
18 Swaziland, Mbabane
19 Malawi, Lilongwe
20 Djibouti, Djibouti
21 Rwanda, Kigali

19

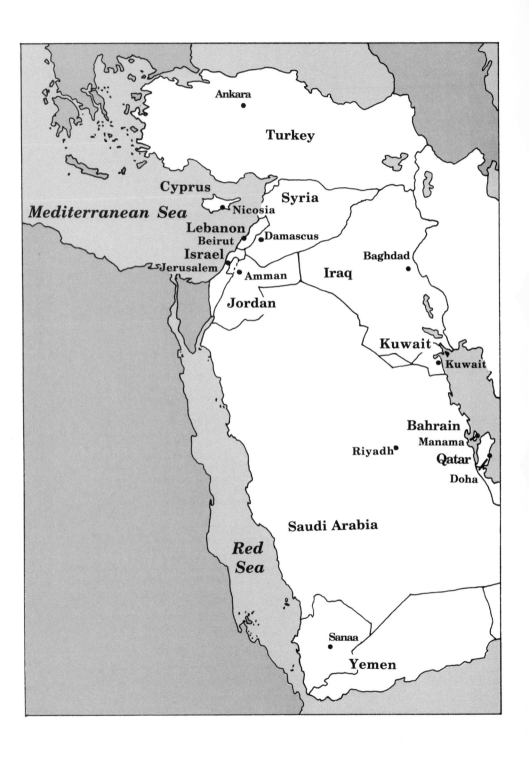

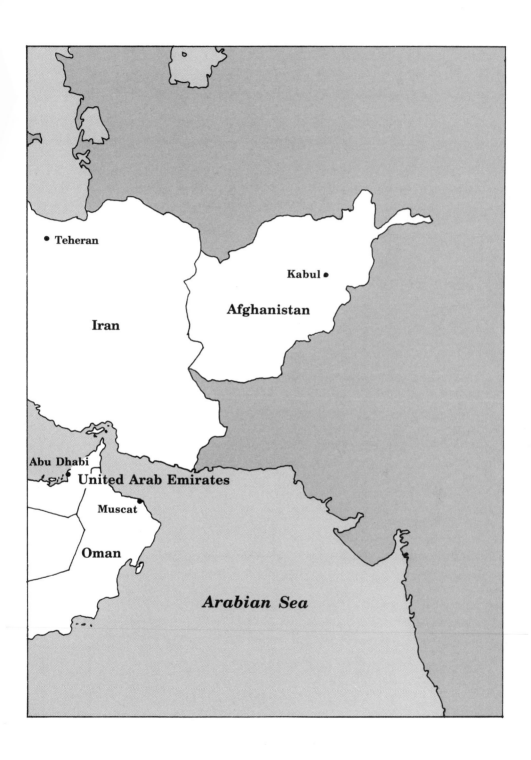

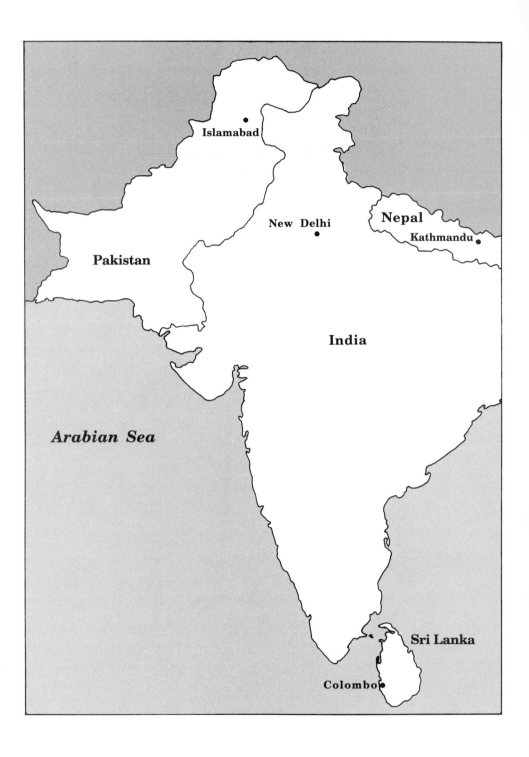

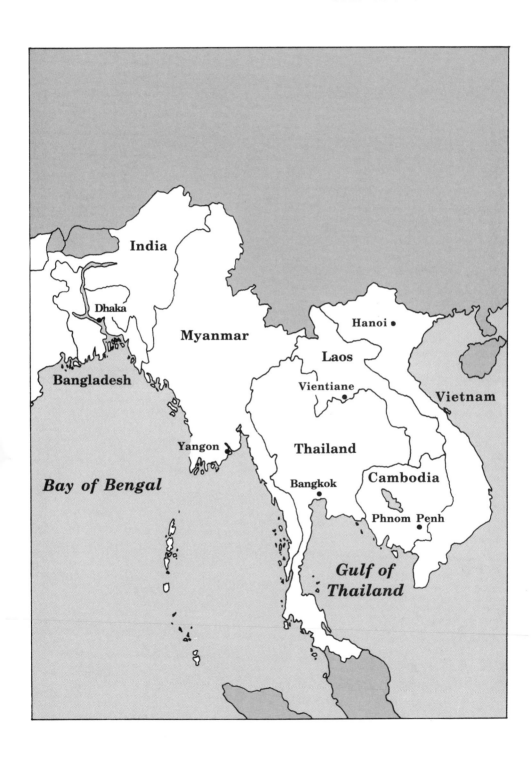

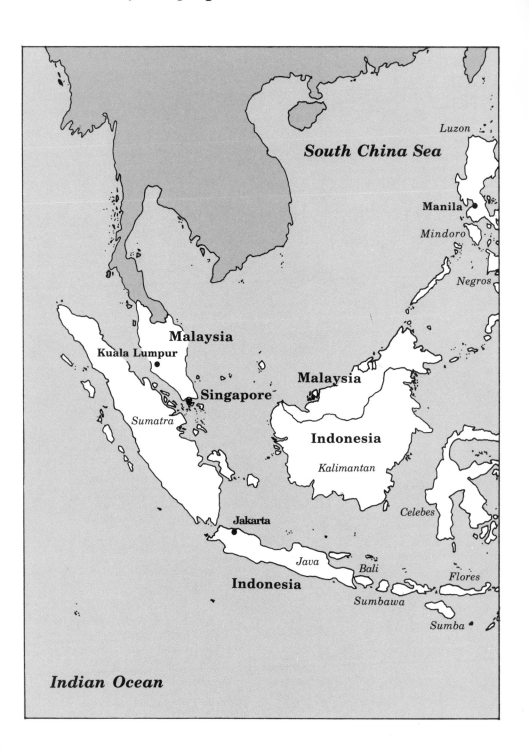

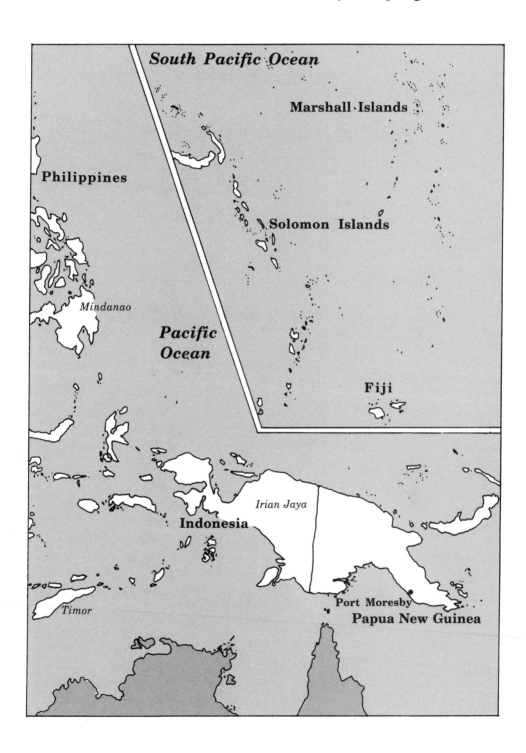

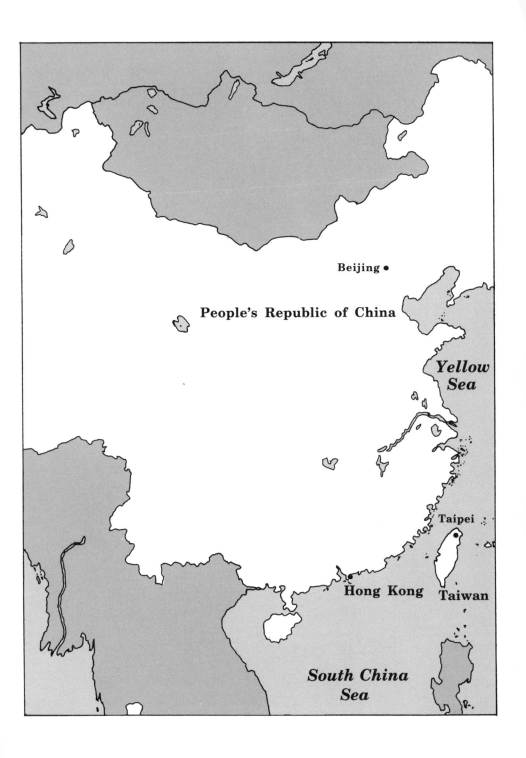

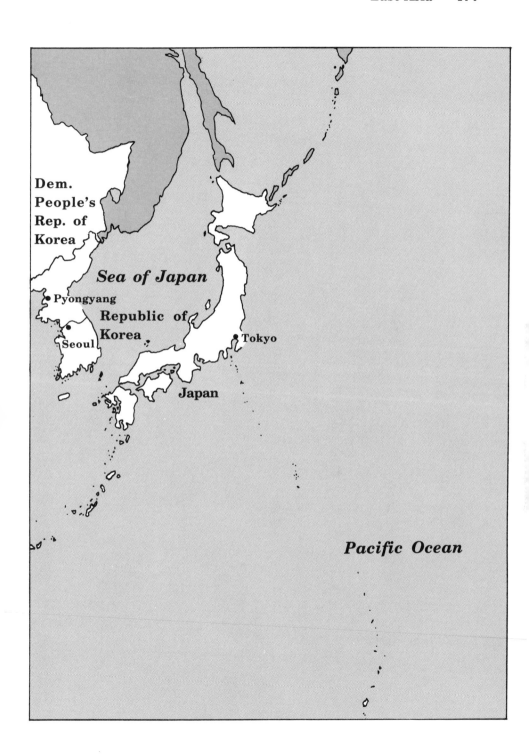

Dem.
People's
Rep. of
Korea

Sea of Japan

• Pyongyang

**Republic of
Korea**

Seoul

• Tokyo

Japan

Pacific Ocean

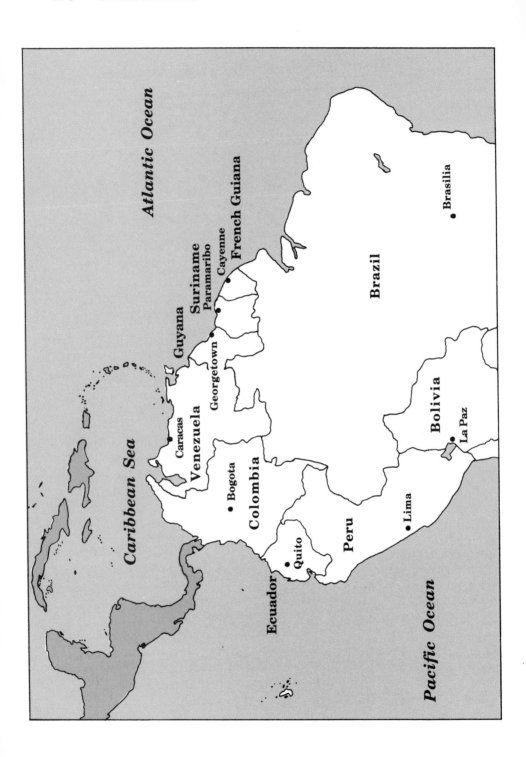

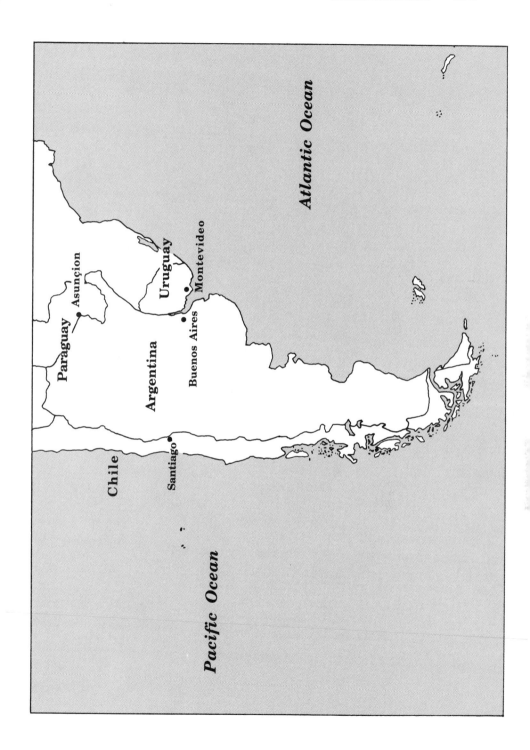

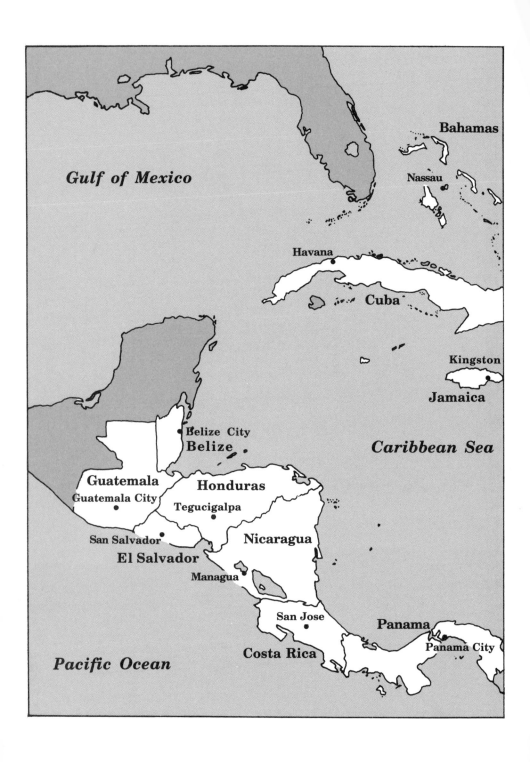

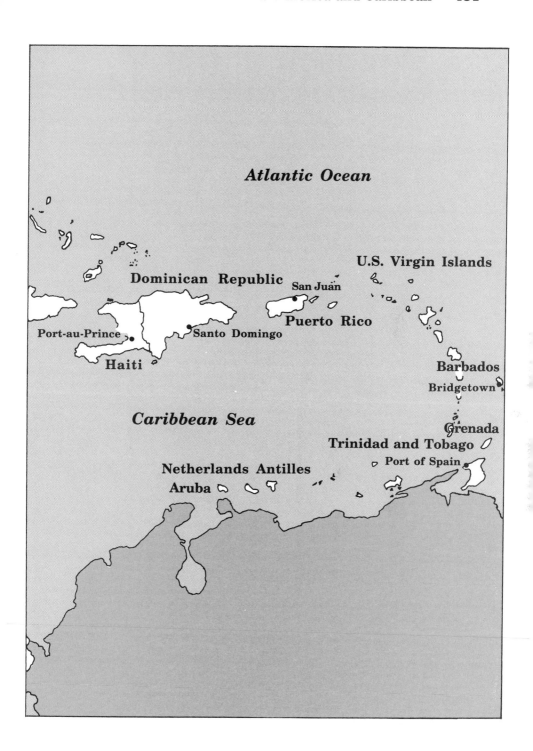

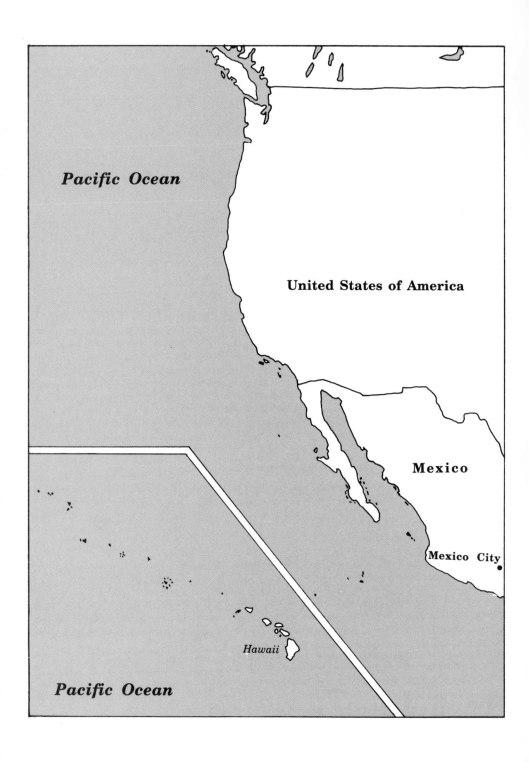

Schools Offering the International Baccalaureate Program

Schools which list the International Baccalaureate offer specialized intensive curriculum during the final two years of high school. The program culminates with the IB Examination, which is comparable to the British GCE A-level, the French Baccalaureate, and other national examinations. The IB Diploma is recognized by most universities throughout the world and enables students to gain advanced placement in university courses.

Argentina
St. Catherine's School, *Buenos Aires*
St. George's College, *Buenos Aires*
St. John's School, *Buenos Aires*

Austria
Salzburg International Preparatory School, *Salzburg*
American International School, *Vienna*
Vienna International School, *Vienna*

Bahrain
Ibn Khuldoon National School, *Manama*
Bahrain School, *Manama*

Belgium
Antwerp International School, *Antwerp*
The International School of Brussels, *Brussels*
Scandinavian School of Brussels, *Brussels*
St. John's International School, *Waterloo*

Brazil
Associacao Internacional de Educacao, *Belo Horizonte*
Escola Americana de Campinas, *Campinas*
Escola Americana do Rio de Janeiro, *Rio de Janeiro*
Associacao Escola Graduada de Sao Paulo, *Sao Paulo*
Escola Maria Imaculada, *Sao Paulo*
St. Paul's School (Escola Britanica de Sao Paulo), *Sao Paulo*

Canada
Lester B. Pearson College of the Pacific, *Victoria, British Columbia*

Chile
St. John's School, *Concepcion*
The Grange School S.A., *Santiago*
The International School Nido de Aguilas, *Santiago*
Santiago College, *Santiago*

China, People's Republic of
The International School of Beijing, *Beijing*

Denmark
Copenhagen International School, *Copenhagen*

Ecuador
Colegio Americano de Guayaquil, *Guayaquil*
Inter-American Academy, *Guayaquil*
American School of Quito, *Quito*
Cotopaxi Academy, American International School, *Quito*

Egypt
The American International School in Egypt, *Cairo*
British International School Cairo, *Cairo*
Cairo American College, *Cairo*

El Salvador
Academia Britanica Cuscatleca, *Santa Tecla*

Ethiopia
International Community School/Addis Ababa, *Addis Ababa*

Fiji
International School, Suva, *Suva*

Finland
International School of Helsinki, *Helsinki*

France
College Lycee Cevenol International, *Le Chambon-sur-Lignon*
Ecole Internationale de Lille Metropole, *Lille*
American International School on the Cote d'Azur, *Nice*
American School of Paris, *Paris*
Ecole Active Bilingue Jeannine Manuel, *Paris*
International School of Paris, *Paris*
Centre International de Valbonne: International School of Sophia
    Antipolis, *Valbonne*

Germany, Federal Republic of
Bonn American High School, *Bonn*
International School of Dusseldorf e.V., *Dusseldorf*
The Frankfurt International School e.V., *Frankfurt*
International School Hamburg, *Hamburg*
Munich International School, *Munich*
International Schule Berlin/Potsdam, *Potsdam*

Greece
American Community Schools of Athens, *Athens*

Guam
St. John's School, *Tumon Bay*

Hong Kong
Chinese International School, *Hong Kong*
Li Po Chun United World College of Hong Kong, *Hong Kong*

India
Kodaikanal International School, *Kodaikanal*
American Embassy School, *New Delhi*

Indonesia
Jakarta International School, *Jakarta*

Ireland
St. Andrew's College, *Dublin*

Italy
American International School of Florence, *Florence*
American School of Milan, *Milan*
International School of Milan, *Milan*
American Overseas School of Rome, *Rome*
Marymount International School, *Rome*
St. Stephen's School, Rome, *Rome*
United World College of the Adriatic, *Trieste*
International School of Turin (ACAT), *Turin*
Vicenza International School, *Vicenza*

Japan
Canadian Academy, *Kobe*
International School of the Sacred Heart, *Tokyo*
Osaka International School, *Osaka*
St. Mary's International School, *Tokyo*

Seisen International School, *Tokyo*
Saint Maur International School, *Yokohama*
Yokohama International School, *Yokohama*

Jordan
Amman Baccalaureate School, *Amman*

Kenya
International School of Kenya, Ltd., *Nairobi*
St. Mary's School, *Nairobi*

Korea, Republic of
Seoul Foreign School, *Seoul*

Lebanon
American Community School at Beirut, *Beirut*

Lesotho
Machabeng High School, *Maseru*

Macau
School of the Nations, *Macau*

Malaysia
The International School of Kuala Lumpur, *Kuala Lumpur*

Mexico
Greengates School, *Mexico City*

Morocco
Casablanca American School, *Casablanca*
Rabat American School, *Rabat*

The Netherlands
International School of Amsterdam, *Amsterdam*
International Secondary School Eindhoven, *Eindhoven*
Maartens College International School, *Groningen*
Het Rijnlands Lyceum Oegstgeest, *Oegstgeest*
International School Eerde, *Ommen*
International School Beverweerd, *Werkhoven*

Nigeria
International School, *Ibadan*

Norway
British International School, *Oslo*

Oman
American-British Academy, *Muscat*

Papaua New Guinea
Port Moresby International High School, *Port Moresby*

Peru
Colegio Franklin D. Roosevelt, *Lima*

Philippines
Brent School, *Baguio*
Brent School – Manila, *Manila*
International School, Manila, *Manila*

Portugal
St. Julian's School (English Section), *Lisbon*

Singapore, Republic of
United World College of South East Asia, *Singapore*

Spain
International College Spain, *Madrid*

Sri Lanka
Overseas Children's School, *Colombo*

Swaziland
Waterford Kamhlaba United World College of Southern Africa,
    Mbabane

Sweden
Hvitfeldtska Gymnasiet, *Goteborg*
Sigtunaskolan Humanistiska Laroverket, *Sigtuna*
Kungsholmen's Gymnasium – International Section, *Stockholm*

Switzerland
Aiglon College, *Chesieres* (limited basis)
The International School of Geneva, *Geneva*
Kumon Leysin Academy of Switzerland, *Leysin*
Leysin American School in Switzerland, *Leysin*

Institut Montana, American School, *Zug*

Syria
International School of Aleppo, *Aleppo*

Taiwan
Taipei American School, *Taipei*

Tanzania
International School of Tanganyika Ltd., *Dar es Salaam*
International School Moshi, *Moshi*

Thailand
International School Bangkok, *Bangkok*

United Arab Emirates
International School of Choueifat, *Abu Dhabi*
International School of Choueifat, *Sharjah*

United Kingdom
Southbank–The American International School, *London*
American Community School, *Middlesex*
American Community School, *Surrey*
Marymount International School, *Surrey*
United World College of the Atlantic, *Glamorgan, Wales*

United States
French American International School, *San Francisco, California*
Washington International School, *Washington, D.C.*
Atlanta International School, *Atlanta, Georgia*
The Armand Hammer United World College of the American West,
    Montezuma, New Mexico
Anglo-American International School, *New York, New York*
United Nations International School, *New York, New York*
The Awty International School, *Houston, Texas*

Uruguay
The British Schools, *Montevideo*

Venezuela
Colegio Internacional de Caracas, *Caracas*
Escuela Campo Alegre, *Caracas*

Yemen
Mohammed Ali Othman School, *Taiz*

SCHOOLS OFFERING BOARDING FACILITIES _____

Argentina
St. George's College, *Buenos Aires*

Austria
Innsbruck International High School, *Innsbruck*
Salzburg International Preparatory School, *Salzburg*

Bahrain
Bahrain School, *Manama*

Belgium
EEC International School, *Antwerp*
The British School of Brussels, *Brussels*

Botswana
Maru a Pula School, *Gaborone*

Canada
Lester B. Pearson College of the Pacific, *Victoria, British Columbia*

Cyprus
Logos School of English Education, *Limassol*
American International School of Cyprus, *Nicosia*
The International School of Paphos, *Paphos*

Dominican Republic
Escuela Caribe, Caribe – Vista School, *Jarabacoa*

Ecuador
Alliance Academy, *Quito*

Ethiopia
Bingham Academy, *Addis Ababa*

France
Bordeaux International School, *Bordeaux*
College Lycee Cevenol International, *Le Chambon-sur-Lignon*
Ecole Internationale de Lille Metropole, *Lille*
American School of Paris, *Paris*
Centre International de Valbonne: International School of Sophia
    Antipolis, *Valbonne*

Greece
American Community Schools of Athens, *Athens*
Green Hill International School, *Athens*
TASIS HELLENIC International School in Athens, *Athens*
Anatolia College, *Thessaloniki*
Pinewood Schools of Thessaloniki, Greece, *Thessaloniki*

Hong Kong
California International (U.S.A.) School, *Hong Kong*
Li Po Chun United World College of Hong Kong, *Hong Kong*

India
Kodaikanal International School, *Kodaikanal*
Woodstock School, *Mussoorie*

Indonesia
Bandung Alliance School, *Bandung*
Central Java Intermission School, *Salatiga*
Sentani International School, *Sentani*
Bamboo River International School, *Serukam*

Ireland
St. Andrew's College, *Dublin* (boys only)

Italy
Avezzano International School, *Avezzano*
The International Academy, *Rome*
Marymount International School, *Rome* (girls only)
St. Stephen's School, Rome, *Rome*

Jamaica
Belair School, *Mandeville*

Japan
Canadian Academy, *Kobe*

Kenya
Rift Valley Academy, *Kijabe*
Kenton College, *Nairobi*

Korea, Republic of
Taejon Christian International School, *Taejon*

Lesotho
Machabeng High School, *Maseru*

Malaysia
Dalat School, *Penang*

Malta
Verdala International School, *St. Andrews*

Morocco
The American School of Tangier, *Tangier*

The Netherlands
International School Beverweerd, *Werkhoven*

Nigeria
Hillcrest School, *Jos*
John F. Kennedy International School, *Warri*

Pakistan
Murree Christian School, *Murree Hills*

Papua New Guinea
The International School of Lae, *Lae*

Philippines
Brent School, *Baguio*
Faith Academy, *Cainta*

Senegal
Dakar Academy, *Dakar*

Singapore, Republic of
United World College of South East Asia, *Singapore*

South Africa
The American International School of Johannesburg,
   Johannesburg

Spain
International College Spain, *Madrid*
American International School of Mallorca, *Mallorca*
The Baleares International School, *Mallorca*

Swaziland
Waterford Kamhlaba United World College of Southern Africa,
   Mbabane

Sweden
Sigtunaskolan Humanistiska Laroverket, *Sigtuna*

Switzerland
International School Le Chaperon Rouge, *Crans-sur-Sierre*
Aiglon College, *Chesieres*
College du Leman International School, *Geneva*
The International School of Geneva, *Geneva*
Gstaad International School, *Gstaad*
Ecole d'Humanite, *Hasliberg/Goldern*
Institution Chateau Mont-Choisi, *Lausanne* (girls only)
The Winter Term, *Lenk*
Kumon Leysin Academy of Switzerland, *Leysin*
Leysin Academy of Switzerland, *Leysin*
The American School in Switzerland (TASIS), *Montagnola/Lugano*
Institut Château Beau-Cèdre, *Montreux*
St. George's School in Switzerland, *Montreux* (girls only)
Institut Le Rosey, *Rolle*
John F. Kennedy International School, *Saanen*
Institut Montana, American School, *Zug*

Taiwan
Morrison Academy, *Taichung*

Tanzania
International School Moshi, *Moshi*
Victoria Primary School, *Mwanza*

Turkey
The Koç School, *Istanbul*
Robert College of Istanbul, *Istanbul* (host students only)

United Kingdom
American Community School *Surrey*
Marymount International School, *Surrey* (girls only)
TASIS England American School, *Surrey*
Edinburgh Tutorial College & American School, *Edinburgh, Scotland*
United World College of the Atlantic, *Glamorgan, Wales*

United States
The Armand Hammer United World College of the American West, *Montezuma, New Mexico*

Accrediting Associations

ECIS: European Council of International Schools
Director of Accreditation Services: Carol Esposito
Address: 21b Lavant Street, Petersfield, Hampshire, GU32 3EL, U.K.
Telephone: (44)(730)268244
Facsimile: (44)(730)267914
Telex: 9312102171 ECG

Middle States: Middle States Association of Colleges and Schools
Executive Directors: Dr. John Michalcewiz, Commission on Secondary
    Schools; Dr. John Stoops, Commission on Elementary Schools
Address: 3624 Market Street, Philadelphia, PA 19104, U.S.A.
Telephone: (215)6625600
Facsimile: (215)6625950

New England: New England Association of Schools and Colleges
Executive Director: Dr. Richard J. Bradley
Address: The Sanborn House, 15 High Street, Winchester, MA 01890, U.S.A.
Telephone: (617)7296762
Facsimile: (617)7290924

North Central: North Central Association of Colleges and Schools
Executive Director: Dr. Kenneth F. Gose
Address: Commission on Schools, Arizona State University, Box 873011,
    Tempe, AZ 85287-3011, U.S.A.
Telephone: (602)9658700, (800)5259517
Facsimile: (602)9659423

Southern: Southern Association of Colleges and Schools
Chief Administrative Officer: Dr. John M. Davis
Address: 1866 Southern Lane, Decatur, GA 30033-4097, U.S.A.
Telephone: (404)6794500
Facsimile: (404)6794556

Texas Education Agency
Commissioner of Education: Dr. Lionel R. Meno
Address: 1701 North Congress Avenue, Austin, TX 78701-1494, U.S.A.
Telephone: (512)4638985
Facsimile: (512)4639838

Western: Western Association of Schools and Colleges
Accrediting Commission for Schools Executive Director: Dr. Donald Haught
Address: 1606 Rollins Road, Burlingame, CA 94010
Telephone: (415)6977711
Facsimile: (415)6977715

REGIONAL AND INTERNATIONAL ORGANIZATIONS___

AAIE: Association for the Advancement of International Education
Executive Director: Dr. Lewis A. Grell
Address: Thompson House, Westminster College,
New Wilmington, PA 16172, U.S.A.
Telephone: (412)9467192   **Facsimile:** (412)9467194

AASCA: Association of American Schools in Central America
President: Dr. James M. Shepherd
Address: The American School of Tegucigalpa c/o U.S. Embassy,
Tegucigalpa, Honduras
Telephone: (504)324696/324697   **Facsimile:** (504)322380

AASSA: Association of American Schools in South America
Executive Director: James Morris
Address: 6972 NW 50 Street, Miami, FL 33166, U.S.A.
Telephone: (305)5943936   **Facsimile:** (305)5946945

ACCAS: Association of Colombian-Caribbean American Schools
President: Dr. John Schober
Address: The Columbus School, AA 5225, Medellin, Colombia
Telephone: (57)(4)4415151   **Facsimile:** (57)(4)2577531

AISA: Association of International Schools in Africa
Executive Director: Dr. Constance Buford
Address: c/o International School of Kenya, PO Box 14103,
Nairobi, Kenya
Telephone: (254)(2)582578/582421/582422
Facsimile: (254)(2)580596/582451
Telex: (963)22370 CALWANG

A/OS: Office of Overseas Schools
Director: Dr. Ernest N. Mannino
Address: Room 245, SA-29, U.S. Department of State,
Washington, D.C. 20522-2902 U.S.A.
Telephone: (703)8757800   **Facsimile:** (703)8757979

ASOMEX: Association of American Schools in Mexico
Vice President: Dr. Donald Wise
Address: c/o American School Foundation of Monterrey A.C.,
Apartado Postal 1762, Monterrey, NL 64000, Mexico
Telephone: (52)(83)353181/354850
Facsimile: (52)(83)782535

American Schools Association of Central America, Colombia-Caribbean and Mexico

Executive Secretary: Mary Virginia Sanchez
Address: (no personal name) c/o U.S. Embassy Quito,
Unit 5372 Box 004, APO AA 34039-3420
Telephone: (593)(2)472974/447534/472075
Facsimile: (593)(2)434985/472972

CAIS: Canadian Association of Independent Schools
President: Robert P. Bedard
Address: c/o St. Andrew's College, 15800 Yonge St., Aurora,
Ontario L4G 3H7, Canada
Telephone: (416)7273178   **Facsimile:** (416)8416911

CEESA: Central and Eastern European Schools Association
Executive Director: David M. Cobb
Address: Dept. of State–Warsaw, Washington, D.C. 20521-5010
Tel/Fax: (48)(22)424061

EARCOS: East Asia Regional Council of Overseas Schools
Executive Secretary: Dr. Fred Brieve
Address: 2990 Telestar Court, Room 314, Falls Church, VA
22042, U.S.A.
Telephone: (703)2804690   **Facsimile:** (703)2804890

ECIS: European Council of International Schools
Executive Secretary: T. Michael Maybury
Address: 21B Lavant Street, Petersfield, Hampshire, GU32 3EL, U.K.
Telephone: (44)(730)268244   **Facsimile:** (44)(730)267914
Telex: 265871 MONREF G (ref 87: ECL001)

ECIS: European Council of International Schools (Madrid Office)
Regional Representative: Bernard Briquet
Address: c/Barquillo 15B, 1-C, 28004 Madrid, Spain
Telephone: (34)(1)5322381
Facsimile: (34)(1)5325289/5218179

IBNA: International Baccalaureate North America
Regional Director: Nancy Weller
Address: 200 Madison Avenue. Suite 2007, New York, NY 10016,
   U.S.A.
Telephone: (212)6964464   **Facsimile:** (212)8899242

IBO: International Baccalaureate Organization
Director General: Roger Peel
Address: Route des Morillons 15, 1218 Le Grand-Saconnex,
   Geneva, Switzerland
Telephone: (41)(22)7910274   **Facsimile:** (41)(22)7910277

IRC: Inter-Regional Center for Curriculum and Materials
   Development
Director: Dr. Burton Fox
Address: Apartado Aereo 3250, Barranquilla, Colombia
Telephone: (57)(58)568589

ISA: International Schools Association
Address: CIC Case 20, CH-1211 Geneva 20, Switzerland
Telephone: (41)(22)7336717

ISS: International Schools Services
President: William P. Davison
Address: 15 Roszel Road, PO Box 5910, Princeton, NJ 08543, U.S.A.
Telephone: (609)4520990
Facsimile: (609)4522690
Telex: 843 308 SCHOLSERV PRIN

MAIS: Mediterranean Association of International Schools
Executive Director: Reina O'Hale
Address: c/o American School of Madrid, Apartado 80, 28080
    Madrid, Spain
Telephone: (34)(1)3572154/3527795
Facsimile: (34)(1)3572678

NAIS: National Association of Independent Schools
President: Peter D. Relic
Address: 1620 L Street, N.W., 11th Floor, Washington, D.C.
    20036, U.S.A.

NE/SA: Near East/South Asia Council of Overseas Schools
Executive Director: Dr. Stanley Haas
Address: c/o The American College of Greece, PO Box 60018,
GR153 42 Aghia Paraskevi, Attikis, Greece
Telephone: (30)(1)6009821
Facsimile: (30)(1)6009928
Telex: 219817 DPC GR

KEY TO EXAMINATIONS

A-level GCE: Advanced-level General Certificate of Education
ACER: Australian Council for Educational Research Tests
ACH: National Achievement Tests
ACT: American College Testing
AP: Advanced Placement
AS-level GCE: Advanced Supplementary-level General Certificate of Education
BAT: Bristol Achievement Test
Botel: Reading Inventory
Brigance: Test of Basic Skills
Cambridge: First Certificate
CAT: California Achievement Test
CEEB: College Entrance Examination Board
CELT: Comprehensive English Language Test for Speakers of English as a Second Language; Listening
CLEP: College-Level Examination Program
COGAT: Cognitive Abilities Test
CSA: Career Skills Assessment
CSE: Certification of Secondary Education
CTBS: California Test of Basic Skills
CTP: Comprehensive Testing Program
DAT: Differential Aptitude Test
DTA: Diagnostic Achievement Test for Adolescents
Durrell: Reading Test
ERB: Education Records Bureau Comprehensive Testing Program
GAP: Reading Comprehension Test
Gates-MacGinitie: Reading Test
GCSE: General Certificate of Secondary Education
GMAT: General Mental Ability Test
Gray Oral and Comprehension: Reading Test
GRE: Graduate Record Examinations
Holborn: Reading Scale
IB: International Baccalaureate
IGCSE: International General Certificate of Secondary Education
Iowa: Iowa Tests of Basic Skills
ITBS: Iowa Tests of Basic Skills
Kuder: Vocational Preference Test
LAB: Language Assessment Battery
MAT: Metropolitan Achievement Test
McGraw-Hill: Basic Skills Systems
Michigan: Tests for Emotional Adjustment
Monroe: Diagnostic Reading Test

MTBS: Metropolitan Test of Basic Skills
NCEE: National Council of Engineering Examiners; Principles and Practice of Engineering
NEDT: National Educational Development Test
Nelson-Denny: Reading Test
NFER: Neale Analysis of Reading Ability
NMSQT: National Merit Scholarship Qualifying Test
NZCER: New Zealand Council for Educational Research Tests
O-level GCE: Ordinary-level General Certificate of Education
OLMAT: Otis-Lennon Mental Ability Test
Otis-Lennon: Mental Ability Test
PIAT: Peabody Individual Achievement Test
PSAT: Preliminary Scholastic Aptitude Test
Purdue: Multipurpose Vocational Test
Richmond: Test of Basic Skills
SAT: Scholastic Aptitude Test
SCAT: School and College Ability Test
SLEP: Secondary-Level English Proficiency Test
SRA: Science Research Associates, Primary Mental Abilities
SSAT: Secondary School Admission Test
Stanford: Achievement Test
STEP: Sequential Test of Educational Progress
Strong-Campbell: Interest Inventory
TAP: Tests of Achievement and Proficiency
TASK: Stanford Test of Academic Skills
TOEFL: Test of English as a Foreign Language
TSE: Test of Spoken English
Wechsler: Intelligence Scale for Children
WRAT: Wide Range Achievement Test

INDEX